I0815059

ROMANS

WISDOM COMMENTARY

Volume 46

Romans

Christian A. Eberhart

Mary Ann Beavis
Volume Editor

Barbara E. Reid, OP
General Editor

A Michael Glazier Book

LITURGICAL PRESS
Collegeville, Minnesota

litpress.org

A Michael Glazier Book published by Liturgical Press

Library of Congress Cataloging-in-Publication Data

Names: Eberhart, Christian, author. | Beavis, Mary Ann, editor. | Reid, Barbara E., editor.

Title: Romans / Christian A. Eberhart ; Mary Ann Beavis, volume editor ; Barbara E. Reid, OP, general editor.

Description: Collegeville, Minnesota : Liturgical Press, [2025] | Series: Wisdom commentary ; volume 46 | "A Michael Glazier book." | Includes bibliographical references and index. | Summary: "Can a feminist interpretation of Romans discover anything new? In this volume, Christian Eberhart pays special attention to the fact that Paul entrusted Phoebe, a gentile woman, with the task of delivering the letter to Rome. This multi-faceted engagement of a woman gives new meaning to the vision of human society in Romans that celebrates the full participation of women and men, Jews and gentiles, weak and strong, and free and slave"—Provided by publisher.

Identifiers: LCCN 2024041649 (print) | LCCN 2024041650 (ebook) | ISBN 9780814681701 (hardcover) | ISBN 9780814681954 (epub) | ISBN 9780814669778 (pdf)

Subjects: LCSH: Bible. Romans—Commentaries.

Classification: LCC BS2665.53 .E24 2025 (print) | LCC BS2665.53 (ebook) | DDC 227/.107—dc23/eng/20240925

LC record available at https://lccn.loc.gov/2024041649

LC ebook record available at https://lccn.loc.gov/2024041650

Detail of the beginning of Florus, *Expositio*, commentary on Romans.
Paris, Bibliothèque nationale de France, Lat. 11575, fol. 1r.
Source: gallica.bnf.fr / Bibliothèque nationale de France.
This historiated initial "P" features from left to right the production and delivery of Romans. It depicts Paul, with his hand raised to speak, while a scroll representing the letter to the Romans emanates from him and is being received by Phoebe (identified by name), who also raises her hand to speak. To her right is a group of people (identified as "Romans") outside their city (identified as "Rome").

O the depth of the riches and wisdom and knowledge of God!

Romans 11:33

I want you to be wise.

Romans 16:19

Holy God, holy and Only Wise,
Wisdom of great price, You choose the way of folly:
God the crucified,
Yet we behold your wisdom.

Stanza 4 of the hymn "Holy God, holy and glorious,"
Lyrics by Susan R. Briehl, © 2002 GIA Publications, Inc.

Contents

Abbreviations

AAR	American Academy of Religion
AB	Anchor Bible
ABD	*Anchor Bible Dictionary*. Edited by D. N. Freedman. 6 vols. New York, 1992
AHB	*Ancient History Bulletin*
ANRW	*Aufstieg und Niedergang der römischen Welt: Geschichte und Kultur Roms im Spiegel der neueren Forschung. Part 2, Principat.* Edited by Hildegard Temporini and Wolfgang Haase. Berlin: de Gruyter, 1972–
AThANT	Abhandlungen zur Theologie des Alten und Neuen Testaments
ATSAT	Arbeiten zu Text und Sprache im Alten Testament
AW	*Antike Welt*
AYBRL	Anchor Yale Bible Reference Library
BAR	*Biblical Archaeology Review*
BBR	*Bulletin for Biblical Research*
BECNT	Baker Exegetical Commentary on the New Testament
BETL	Bibliotheca Ephemeridum Theologicarum Lovaniensium
Bib	*Biblica*
BibInt	*Biblical Interpretation*
BibInt	Biblical Interpretation Series
BJS	Brown Judaic Studies
BRP	Brill Research Perspectives in Biblical Interpretation

BTB	*Biblical Theology Bulletin*
BW	Bible and Women
BWANT	Beiträge zur Wissenschaft vom Alten und Neuen Testament
BZ	*Biblische Zeitschrift*
BZAW	Beihefte zur Zeitschrift für die alttestamentliche Wissenschaft
BZNW	Beihefte zur Zeitschrift für die neutestamentliche Wissenschaft
CBQ	*Catholic Biblical Quarterly*
CBQMS	Catholic Biblical Quarterly Monograph Series
ColSB	Coll. Sciences bibliques
ConBNT	Coniectanea Biblica: New Testament Series
CP	*Classical Philology*
CurTM	*Currents in Theology and Mission*
CWS	Classics of Western Spirituality
DCLS	Deuterocanonical and Cognate Literature Studies
EBR	*Encyclopedia of the Bible and Its Reception*
EBTC	Evangelical Biblical Theology Commentary
EKKNT	Evangelisch-katholischer Kommentar zum Neuen Testament
EPRO	Etudes préliminaires aux religions orientales dans l'empire romain
ET	English Translation
ETS	Erfurter theologisch Studien
EvTh	*Evangelische Theologie*
ExpTim	*Expository Times*
FAT	Forschungen zum Alten Testament
FCB	Feminist Companion to the Bible
FCNTECW	Feminist Companion to the New Testament and Early Christian Writings
FilN	*Filologia Neotestamentaria*
FKDG	Forschungen zur Kirchen- und Dogmengeschichte

FRLANT	Forschungen zur Religion und Literatur des Alten und Neuen Testaments
GBS	Guides to Biblical Scholarship
GNS	Good News Studies
GR	*Greece and Rome*
GTR	Gender, Theory, and Religion
HNT	Handbuch zum Neuen Testament
HThKAT	Herders theologischer Kommentar zum Alten Testament
HTKNT	Herders theologischer Kommentar zum Neuen Testament
HTR	*Harvard Theological Review*
ICC	International Critical Commentary
IFT	Introductions in Feminist Theology
Int	*Interpretation*
JAC	*Jahrbuch für Antike und Christentum*
JAOS	*Journal of the American Oriental Society*
JBL	*Journal of Biblical Literature*
JES	*Journal of Ecumenical Studies*
JFSR	*Journal of Feminist Studies in Religion*
JQR	*Jewish Quarterly Review*
JRS	*Journal of Roman Studies*
JSJ	*Journal for the Study of Judaism in the Persian, Hellenistic, and Roman Periods*
JSJSup	Supplements to the Journal for the Study of Judaism
JSNT	*Journal for the Study of the New Testament*
JSNTSup	Journal for the Study of the New Testament Supplement Series
JSOT	*Journal for the Study of the Old Testament*
JSOTSup	Journal for the Study of the Old Testament Supplement series
JSPSup	Journal for the Study of the Pseudepigrapha: Supplement Series
KJV	King James Version

LD	Lectio Divina
LHBOTS	The Library of Hebrew Bible/Old Testament Studies
LNTS	Library of New Testament Studies
LXX	Septuagint
MAAR	*Memoirs of the American Academy in Rome*
MNTC	Moffatt New Testament Commentary
MT	Masoretic Text
MThZ	*Münchener theologische Zeitschrift*
NAB	New American Bible
NASB	New American Standard Bible
Neot	*Neotestamentica*
NICNT	New International Commentary on the New Testament
NIGTC	New International Greek Testament Commentary
NIV	New International Version
NKJV	New King James Version
NovT	*Novum Testamentum*
NovTSup	Novum Testamentum Supplements
NRSV	New Revised Standard Version
NRSVue	New Revised Standard Version Updated Edition
NTOA	Novum Testamentum et Orbis Antiquus
NTS	*New Testament Studies*
OBT	Overtures to Biblical Theology
PL	Patrologia Latina
PNTC	Pelican New Testament Commentaries
QD	Quaestiones disputatae
RB	*Revue Biblique*
RGG	*Religion in Geschichte und Gegenwart*
RNT	Regensburger Neues Testament
RSV	Revised Standard Version
SBL	Society of Biblical Literature
SBLDS	Society of Biblical Literature Dissertation Series
SBLWAW	Society of Biblical Literature Writings from the Ancient World

SBS	Stuttgarter Bibelstudien
SBT	Studies in Biblical Theology
SD	Studies and Documents
SemeiaSt	Semeia Studies
SJT	*Scottish Journal of Theology*
SKKNT	Stuttgarter kleiner Kommentar, Neues Testament
SNT	Studien zum Neuen Testament
SNTSMS	Society for New Testament Studies Monograph Series
SNTW	Studies of the New Testament and Its World
SOTSMS	Society for Old Testament Studies Monograph Series
SP	Sacra Pagina
SR	*Studies in Religion*
StBibLit	Studies in Biblical Literature
StPB	Studia post-biblica
SymS	Symposium Series
TB	Theologische Bücherei
TDNT	*Theological Dictionary of the New Testament*
TDOT	*Theological Dictionary of the Old Testament*
ThHK	Theologischer Kommentar zum Neuen Testament
THKNT	Theologischer Handkommentar zum Neuen Testament
ThZ	*Theologische Zeitschrift*
TOBITH	Topoi Biblischer Theologie / Themes of Biblical Theology
TRE	*Theologische Realenzyklopädie*. Edited by G. Krause and G. Müller. Berlin: de Gruyter, 1977–
TSAJ	Texts and Studies in Ancient Judaism
UTB	Uni-Taschenbücher
VCSup	Supplement to *Vigiliae Christianae*
WBC	Word Biblical Commentary
WCS	Wisdom Commentary Series
WGRW	Writings from the Greco-Roman World
WMANT	Wissenschaftliche Monographien zum Alten und Neuen Testament
WuD	*Wort und Dienst*

WUNT	Wissenschaftliche Untersuchungen zum Neuen Testament
WW	*Word and World*
ZNW	*Zeitschrift für die Neutestamentliche Wissenschaft*

Contributors

Marianne Bjelland Kartzow is professor of New Testament studies at the University of Oslo, Norway. Her recent book, *The Slave Metaphor and Gendered Enslavement in Early Christian Discourse: Double Trouble Embodied* (New York: Routledge, 2018), employs intersectionality and metaphor theory to explore texts on enslavement. She is also the editor of the interdisciplinary volume *The Ambiguous Figure of the Neighbor in Jewish, Christian and Islamic Texts and Receptions* (New York: Routledge, 2022).

Dr. Yuria Celidwen is an Indigenous scholar of Nahua and Maya descent from Chiapas, Mexico. Her research focuses on the experience of self-transcendence and the cultivation of prosocial behaviors such as compassion, kindness, awe, reverence, and a sense of sacredness and love in Indigenous contemplative traditions of the world.

Laura Marshall Clark is a member of the Mvskoke Nation and an interdisciplinary scholar, writer, and curator. Her work centers on North America's numerous and distinct tribal histories, cultures, and transnational narratives through education and the arts. She is a lecturer in the Department of Comparative Cultural Studies at the University of Houston, Texas.

Florence Draguet is a researcher at the Institut de Recherche Religions Spiritualités Cultures Sociétés (Religions, Spiritualities, Cultures, and Societies) and a PhD student at the Université Catholique of Louvain, Belgium. She is the author of several articles and papers in the subject areas of biblical studies (New Testament), spiritualities, and feminist mysticism.

Dr. Yii-Jan Lin is professor of New Testament at Yale Divinity School, New Haven, Connecticut. She is the author of *The Erotic Life of Manuscripts* (Oxford, 2016), focusing on the history of textual criticism, and *Immigration and Apocalypse: The Revelation of John in the History of American Immigration* (Yale, forthcoming), which explores the use of Revelation in American immigration discourse.

Sr. Dr. MarySylvia Nwachukwu is professor of biblical theology in the Department of Philosophy and Religious Studies, Faculty of Arts of Godfrey Okoye University, Enugu, Nigeria. Her academic work focuses on references to the Pentateuch in Pauline letters. She is the author of *Creation-Covenant Scheme and Justification by Faith: A Canonical Study of the God-Human Drama in the Pentateuch and the Letter to the Romans* (Rome: Gregoriana, 2002).

Bernard Philippe is a member of the European Union, Service Européen d'Action Extérieure, in Jerusalem, Israel.

Véronique A. Pioch-Eberhart is a success coach in Houston, Texas. She is the CEO of the coaching company *Joyous Living* and a doctoral student at the University of Strasbourg, France.

Eloise M. Rosenblatt, PhD, is a state-licensed civil attorney in private practice in family law in San Jose, California. A Sister of Mercy of the Americas, she is a theologian with a background in university and seminary teaching in biblical studies as well as administration. She authored the volume on *2 Peter* in the Wisdom Commentary series.

Khiok-khng Yeo is the Harry R. Kendall Professor of New Testament at Garrett-Evangelical Seminary. He works on cross-cultural hermeneutics and global theologies.

Foreword

"Come Eat of My Bread . . . and Walk in the Ways of Wisdom"

Elisabeth Schüssler Fiorenza

Harvard University Divinity School

Jewish feminist writer Asphodel Long has likened the Bible to

> a magnificent garden of brilliant plants, some flowering, some fruiting, some in seed, some in bud, shaded by trees of age old, luxurious growth. Yet in the very soil which gives it life the poison has been inserted. . . . This poison is that of misogyny, the hatred of women, half the human race.[1]

To see Scripture as such a beautiful garden containing poisonous ivy requires that one identify and name this poison and place on all biblical texts the label "Caution! Could be dangerous to your health and survival!" As critical feminist interpretation for well-being this Wisdom Commentary seeks to elaborate the beauty and fecundity of this

1. Asphodel Long, *In a Chariot Drawn by Lions: The Search for the Female in the Deity* (London: Women's Press, 1992), 195.

Scripture-garden and at the same time points to the harm it can do when one submits to its world of vision. Thus, feminist biblical interpretation engages two seemingly contradictory insights: The Bible is written in kyriocentric (i.e., lord/master/father/husband-elite male) language, originated in the patri-kyriarchal cultures of antiquity, and has functioned to inculcate misogynist mind-sets and oppressive values. At the same time it also asserts that the Bible as Sacred Scripture has functioned to inspire and authorize wo/men[2] in our struggles against dehumanizing oppression. The hermeneutical lens of wisdom/Wisdom empowers the commentary writers to do so.

In biblical as well as in contemporary religious discourse the word *wisdom* has a double meaning: It can either refer to the quality of life and of people and/or it can refer to a figuration of the Divine. Wisdom in both senses of the word is not a prerogative of the biblical traditions but is found in the imagination and writings of all known religions. Wisdom is transcultural, international, and interreligious. Wisdom is practical knowledge gained through experience and daily living as well as through the study of creation and human nature. Both word meanings, that of capability (wisdom) and that of female personification (Wisdom), are crucial for this Wisdom Commentary series that seeks to enable biblical readers to become critical subjects of interpretation.

Wisdom is a state of the human mind and spirit characterized by deep understanding and profound insight. It is elaborated as a quality possessed by the sages but also treasured as folk wisdom and wit. Wisdom is the power of discernment, deeper understanding, and creativity; it is the ability to move and to dance, to make the connections, to savor life, and to learn from experience. Wisdom is intelligence shaped by experience and sharpened by critical analysis. It is the ability to make sound choices and incisive decisions. Its root meaning comes to the fore in its Latin form *sapientia*, which is derived from the verb *sapere*, to taste and to savor something. Hence, this series of commentaries invites readers to taste, to evaluate, and to imagine. In the figure of *Chokhmah-Sophia-Sapientia-Wisdom*, ancient Jewish Scriptures seek to hold together belief in the "one" G*d[3] of Israel with both masculine and feminine language and metaphors of the Divine.

2. I use wo/man, s/he, fe/male and not the grammatical standard "man" as inclusive terms and make this visible by adding /.

3. I use the * asterisk in order to alert readers to a problem to explore and think about.

In distinction to traditional Scripture reading, which is often individualistic and privatized, the practice and space of Wisdom commentary is public. Wisdom's spiraling presence (*Shekhinah*) is global, embracing all creation. Her voice is a public, radical democratic voice rather than a "feminine," privatized one. To become one of Her justice-seeking friends, one needs to imagine the work of this feminist commentary series as the spiraling circle dance of wisdom/Wisdom,[4] as a Spirit/spiritual intellectual movement in the open space of wisdom/Wisdom who calls readers to critically analyze, debate, and reimagine biblical texts and their commentaries as wisdom/Wisdom texts inspired by visions of justice and well-being for everyone and everything. Wisdom-Sophia-imagination engenders a different understanding of Jesus and the movement around him. It understands him as the child and prophet of Divine Wisdom and as Wisdom herself instead of imagining him as ruling King and Lord who has only subalterns but not friends. To approach the N*T[5] and the whole Bible as Wisdom's invitation of cosmic dimensions means to acknowledge its multivalence and its openness to change. As bread—not stone.

In short, this commentary series is inspired by the feminist vision of the open cosmic house of Divine Wisdom-Sophia as it is found in biblical Wisdom literatures, which include the N*T:

> Wisdom has built Her house
> She has set up Her seven pillars . . .
> She has mixed Her wine,
> She also has set Her table.
> She has sent out Her wo/men ministers
> to call from the highest places in the town . . .
> "Come eat of my bread
> and drink of the wine I have mixed.
> Leave immaturity, and live,
> And walk in the way of Wisdom." (Prov 9:1-3, 5-6)

4. I have elaborated such a Wisdom dance in terms of biblical hermeneutics in my book *Wisdom Ways: Introducing Feminist Biblical Interpretation* (Maryknoll, NY: Orbis Books, 2001). Its seven steps are a hermeneutics of experience, of domination, of suspicion, of evaluation, of remembering or historical reconstruction, of imagination, and of transformation. However, such Wisdom strategies of meaning making are not restricted to the Bible. Rather, I have used them in workshops in Brazil and Ecuador to explore the workings of power, Condomblé, Christology, imagining a the*logical wo/men's center, or engaging the national icon of Mary.

5. See the discussion about nomenclature of the two testaments in the introduction, pages xxxvii–xxxviii.

Editor's Introduction to Wisdom Commentary

"She Is a Breath of the Power of God" (Wis 7:25)

Barbara E. Reid, OP

General Editor

Wisdom Commentary is the first series to offer detailed feminist interpretation of every book of the Bible. The fruit of collaborative work by an ecumenical and interreligious team of scholars, the volumes provide serious, scholarly engagement with the whole biblical text, not only those texts that explicitly mention women. The series is intended for clergy, teachers, ministers, and all serious students of the Bible. Designed to be both accessible and informed by the various approaches of biblical scholarship, it pays particular attention to the world in front of the text, that is, how the text is heard and appropriated. At the same time, this series aims to be faithful to the ancient text and its earliest audiences; thus the volumes also explicate the worlds behind the text and within it. While issues of gender are primary in this project, the volumes also address the intersecting issues of power, authority, ethnicity, race, class, and religious belief and practice. The fifty-eight volumes include the books regarded as canonical by Jews (i.e., the Tanakh); Protestants (the "Hebrew Bible" and the New Testament); and Roman Catholic, Anglican, and Eastern

Orthodox Communions (i.e., Tobit, Judith, 1 and 2 Maccabees, Wisdom of Solomon, Sirach/Ecclesiasticus, Baruch, including the Letter of Jeremiah, the additions to Esther, and Susanna and Bel and the Dragon in Daniel).

A Symphony of Diverse Voices

Included in the Wisdom Commentary series are voices from scholars of many different religious traditions, of diverse ages, differing sexual identities, and varying cultural, racial, ethnic, and social contexts. Some have been pioneers in feminist biblical interpretation; others are newer contributors from a younger generation. A further distinctive feature of this series is that each volume incorporates voices other than that of the lead author(s). These voices appear alongside the commentary of the lead author(s), in the grayscale inserts. At times, a contributor may offer an alternative interpretation or a critique of the position taken by the lead author(s). At other times, they may offer a complementary interpretation from a different cultural context or subject position. Occasionally, portions of previously published material bring in other views. The diverse voices are not intended to be contestants in a debate or a cacophony of discordant notes. The multiple voices reflect that there is no single definitive feminist interpretation of a text. In addition, they show the importance of subject position in the process of interpretation. In this regard, the Wisdom Commentary series takes inspiration from the Talmud and from *The Torah: A Women's Commentary* (ed. Tamara Cohn Eskenazi and Andrea L. Weiss; New York: URJ Press and Women of Reform Judaism, The Federation of Temple Sisterhoods, 2008), in which many voices, even conflicting ones, are included and not harmonized.

Contributors include biblical scholars, theologians, and readers of Scripture from outside the scholarly and religious guilds. At times, their comments pertain to a particular text. In some instances they address a theme or topic that arises from the text.

Another feature that highlights the collaborative nature of feminist biblical interpretation is that a number of the volumes have two lead authors who have worked in tandem from the inception of the project and whose voices interweave throughout the commentary.

Woman Wisdom

The title, Wisdom Commentary, reflects both the importance to feminists of the figure of Woman Wisdom in the Scriptures and the distinct wisdom that feminist women and men bring to the interpretive process. In the Scriptures, Woman Wisdom appears as "a breath of the power of God, and a pure emanation of the glory of the Almighty" (Wis 7:25), who was present and active in fashioning all that exists (Prov 8:22-31; Wis 8:6). She is a spirit who pervades and penetrates all things (Wis 7:22-23), and she provides guidance and nourishment at her all-inclusive table (Prov 9:1-5). In both postexilic biblical and nonbiblical Jewish sources, Woman Wisdom is often equated with Torah, e.g., Sirach 24:23-34; Baruch 3:9–4:4; 2 Baruch 38:2; 46:4-5; 48:33, 36; 4 Ezra 5:9-10; 13:55; 14:40; 1 Enoch 42.

The New Testament frequently portrays Jesus as Wisdom incarnate. He invites his followers, "take my yoke upon you, and learn from me" (Matt 11:29), just as Ben Sira advises, "put your neck under her [Wisdom's] yoke, and let your souls receive instruction" (Sir 51:26). Just as Wisdom experiences rejection (Prov 1:23-25; Sir 15:7-8; Wis 10:3; Bar 3:12), so too does Jesus (Mark 8:31; John 1:10-11). Only some accept his invitation to his all-inclusive banquet (Matt 22:1-14; Luke 14:15-24; compare Prov 1:20-21; 9:3-5). Yet, "wisdom is vindicated by her deeds" (Matt 11:19, speaking of Jesus and John the Baptist; in the Lukan parallel at 7:35 they are called "her [wisdom's] children"). There are numerous parallels between what is said of Wisdom and of the *Logos* in the Prologue of the Fourth Gospel (John 1:1-18). These are only a few of many examples. This female embodiment of divine presence and power is an apt image to guide the work of this series.

Feminism

There are many different understandings of the term "feminism." The various meanings, aims, and methods have developed exponentially in recent decades. Feminism is a perspective and a movement that springs from a recognition of inequities toward women, and it advocates for changes in whatever structures prevent full flourishing of human beings and all creation. Three waves of feminism in the United States are commonly recognized. The first, arising in the mid-nineteenth century and lasting into the early twentieth, was sparked by women's efforts to be involved in the public sphere and to win the right to vote. In the 1960s and 1970s, the second wave focused on civil rights and equality for women. With the third wave, from the 1980s forward, came global feminism and the emphasis on the contextual nature of interpretation. Now a fourth wave is emerging, with a stronger emphasis on the intersectionality of women's concerns with those of other marginalized groups and the increased use of the internet as a platform for discussion and activism.[1] As feminism has matured, it has recognized that inequities based on gender are interwoven with power imbalances based on race, class, ethnicity, religion, sexual identity, physical ability, and a host of other social markers.

Feminist Women and Men

Men as well as nonbinary people who choose to identify with and partner with feminist women in the work of deconstructing systems of domination and building structures of equality are rightly regarded as feminists. Some men readily identify with experiences of women who are discriminated against on the basis of sex/gender, having themselves had comparable experiences; others who may not have faced direct discrimination or stereotyping recognize that inequity and problematic characterization still occur, and they seek correction. This series is pleased to include feminist men and nonbinary persons both as lead authors and as contributing voices.

Feminist Biblical Interpretation

Women interpreting the Bible from the lenses of their own experience is nothing new. Throughout the ages women have recounted the biblical stories, teaching them to their children and others, all the while interpreting them afresh for their time and circumstances.[2] Following is a very brief sketch of select foremothers who laid the groundwork for contemporary feminist biblical interpretation.

One of the earliest known Christian women who challenged patriarchal interpretations of Scripture was a consecrated virgin named Helie, who lived in the second century CE. When she refused to marry, her

1. See Martha Rampton, "Four Waves of Feminism" (October 25, 2015), at https://www.pacificu.edu/magazine/four-waves-feminism; and Ealasaid Munro, "Feminism: A Fourth Wave?," *Political Insight* (September 2013), https://journals.sagepub.com/doi/pdf/10.1111/2041-9066.12021.

2. For fuller treatments of this history, see chap. 7, "One Thousand Years of Feminist Bible Criticism," in Gerda Lerner, *The Creation of Feminist Consciousness: From the Middle Ages to Eighteen-Seventy*, Women and History 2 (New York: Oxford University Press, 1993), 138–66; Susanne Scholz, "From the 'Woman's Bible' to the 'Women's Bible,' The History of Feminist Approaches to the Hebrew Bible," in *Introducing the Women's Hebrew Bible*, IFT 13 (New York: T&T Clark, 2007), 12–32; Marion Ann Taylor and Agnes Choi, eds., *Handbook of Women Biblical Interpreters: A Historical and Biographical Guide* (Grand Rapids: Baker Academic, 2012).

parents brought her before a judge, who quoted to her Paul's admonition, "It is better to marry than to be aflame with passion" (1 Cor 7:9). In response, Helie first acknowledges that this is what Scripture says, but then she retorts, "but not for everyone, that is, not for holy virgins."[3] She is one of the first to question the notion that a text has one meaning that is applicable in all situations.

A Jewish woman who also lived in the second century CE, Beruriah, is said to have had "profound knowledge of biblical exegesis and outstanding intelligence."[4] One story preserved in the Talmud (b. Ber. 10a) tells of how she challenged her husband, Rabbi Meir, when he prayed for the destruction of a sinner. Proffering an alternate interpretation, she argued that Psalm 104:35 advocated praying for the destruction of sin, not the sinner.

In medieval times the first written commentaries on Scripture from a critical feminist point of view emerge. While others may have been produced and passed on orally, they are for the most part lost to us now. Among the earliest preserved feminist writings are those of Hildegard of Bingen (1098–1179), German writer, mystic, and abbess of a Benedictine monastery. She reinterpreted the Genesis narratives in a way that presented women and men as complementary and interdependent. She frequently wrote about the Divine as feminine.[5] Along with other women mystics of the time, such as Julian of Norwich (1342–ca. 1416), she spoke authoritatively from her personal experiences of God's revelation in prayer.

In this era, women were also among the scribes who copied biblical manuscripts. Notable among them is Paula Dei Mansi of Verona, from a distinguished family of Jewish scribes. In 1288, she translated from Hebrew into Italian a collection of Bible commentaries written by her father and added her own explanations.[6]

Another pioneer, Christine de Pizan (1365–ca. 1430), was a French court writer and prolific poet. She used allegory and common sense

3. Madrid, Escorial MS, a II 9, f. 90 v., as cited in Lerner, *Feminist Consciousness*, 140.

4. See Judith R. Baskin, "Women and Post-Biblical Commentary," in *The Torah: A Women's Commentary*, ed. Tamara Cohn Eskenazi and Andrea L. Weiss (New York: URJ Press and Women of Reform Judaism, The Federation of Temple Sisterhoods, 2008), xlix–lv, at lii.

5. Hildegard of Bingen, *De Operatione Dei*, 1.4.100; PL 197:885bc, as cited in Lerner, *Feminist Consciousness*, 142–43. See also Barbara Newman, *Sister of Wisdom: St. Hildegard's Theology of the Feminine* (Berkeley: University of California Press, 1987).

6. Emily Taitz, Sondra Henry, and Cheryl Tallan, *The JPS Guide to Jewish Women 600 B.C.E.–1900 C.E.* (Philadelphia: JPS, 2003), 110–11.

to subvert misogynist readings of Scripture and celebrated the accomplishments of female biblical figures to argue for women's active roles in building society.[7]

By the seventeenth century, there were women who asserted that the biblical text needs to be understood and interpreted in its historical context. For example, Rachel Speght (1597–ca. 1630), a Calvinist English poet, elaborates on the historical situation in first-century Corinth that prompted Paul to say, "It is good for a man not to touch a woman" (1 Cor 7:1). Her aim was to show that the biblical texts should not be applied in a literal fashion to all times and circumstances. Similarly, Margaret Fell (1614–1702), one of the founders of the Religious Society of Friends (Quakers) in Britain, addressed the Pauline prohibitions against women speaking in church by insisting that they do not have universal validity. Rather, they need to be understood in their historical context, as addressed to a local church in particular time-bound circumstances.[8]

Along with analyzing the historical context of the biblical writings, women in the eighteenth and nineteenth centuries began to attend to misogynistic interpretations based on faulty translations. One of the first to do so was British feminist Mary Astell (1666–1731).[9] In the United States, the Grimké sisters, Sarah (1792–1873) and Angelina (1805–1879), Quaker women from a slaveholding family in South Carolina, learned biblical Greek and Hebrew so that they could interpret the Bible for themselves. They were prompted to do so after men sought to silence them from speaking out against slavery and for women's rights by claiming that the Bible (e.g., 1 Cor 14:34) prevented women from speaking in public.[10] Another prominent abolitionist, Isabella Baumfree, was a former slave who adopted the name Sojourner Truth (ca. 1797–1883); she quoted the Bible liberally in her speeches[11] and in so doing challenged cultural assumptions and biblical interpretations that undergird gender inequities.

7. See further Taylor and Choi, *Handbook of Women Biblical Interpreters*, 127–32.

8. Her major work, *Women's Speaking Justified, Proved and Allowed by the Scriptures*, published in London in 1666, gave a systematic feminist reading of all biblical texts pertaining to women.

9. Mary Astell, *Some Reflections upon Marriage* (New York: Source Book Press, 1970, reprint of the 1730 edition; earliest edition of this work is 1700), 103–4.

10. See further Sarah Grimké, *Letters on the Equality of the Sexes and the Condition of Woman* (Boston: Isaac Knapp, 1838).

11. See, for example, her most famous speech, "Ain't I a Woman?," delivered in 1851 at the Ohio Women's Rights Convention in Akron; Modern History Sourcebook, https://sourcebooks.fordham.edu/mod/sojtruth-woman.asp.

Another monumental work that emerged in nineteenth-century England was that of Jewish theologian Grace Aguilar (1816–1847), *The Women of Israel*,[12] published in 1845. Aguilar's approach was to make connections between the biblical women and contemporary Jewish women's concerns. She aimed to counter the widespread antisemitic notion that women were degraded in Jewish law and that only in Christianity were women's dignity and value upheld. Her intent was to help Jewish women find strength and encouragement by seeing the evidence of God's compassionate love in the history of every woman in the Bible. While not a full commentary on the Bible, Aguilar's work stands out for its comprehensive treatment of every female biblical character, including even the most obscure references.[13]

The first person to produce a full-blown feminist commentary on the Bible was Elizabeth Cady Stanton (1815–1902). A leading proponent in the United States for women's right to vote, she found that whenever women tried to make inroads into politics, education, or the work world, the Bible was quoted against them. Along with a team of like-minded women, she produced her own commentary on every text of the Bible that concerned women. Her pioneering two-volume project, *The Woman's Bible*, published in 1895 and 1898, urges women to recognize that texts that degrade women come from the men who wrote the texts, not from God, and to use their common sense to rethink what has been presented to them as sacred.[14]

Nearly a century later, *The Women's Bible Commentary*, edited by Carol A. Newsom and Sharon H. Ringe (Louisville: Westminster John Knox, 1992), appeared. This one-volume commentary features North American feminist scholarship on each book of the Protestant canon. Like Cady Stanton's commentary, it does not contain comments on every section of the biblical text but only on those passages deemed relevant to women. It was revised and expanded in 1998 to include the Apocrypha/Deuterocanonical books, and the contributors to this new volume reflect the global face of contemporary feminist scholarship. The revisions made in the third edition, which appeared in 2012, represent the profound

12. The full title is *The Women of Israel or Characters and Sketches from the Holy Scriptures and Jewish History: Illustrative of the Past History, Present Duties, and Future Destiny of the Hebrew Females, as Based on the Word of God*.

13. See further Eskenazi and Weiss, *The Torah: A Women's Commentary*, xxxviii; Taylor and Choi, *Handbook of Women Biblical Interpreters*, 31–37.

14. While Cady Stanton's work was groundbreaking in its feminist approach, it nonetheless reflected racist and antisemitic attitudes she and the like-minded white Christian women who worked with her held.

advances in feminist biblical scholarship and include newer voices (with Jacqueline E. Lapsley as an additional editor). In both the second and third editions, *The* has been dropped from the title.

Also appearing at the centennial of Cady Stanton's *The Woman's Bible* were two volumes edited by Elisabeth Schüssler Fiorenza with the assistance of Shelly Matthews. The first, *Searching the Scriptures: A Feminist Introduction* (New York: Crossroad, 1993), charts a comprehensive approach to feminist interpretation from ecumenical, interreligious, and multicultural perspectives. The second volume, published in 1994, provides critical feminist commentary on each book of the New Testament as well as on three books of Jewish Pseudepigrapha and eleven other early Christian writings.

In Europe, similar endeavors have been undertaken, such as the one-volume *Kompendium Feministische Bibelauslegung*, edited by Luise Schottroff and Marie-Theres Wacker (Gütersloh: Gütersloher Verlagshaus, 2007), featuring German feminist biblical interpretation of each book of the Bible, along with Deuterocanonical apocryphal books, and several extrabiblical writings. This work, now in its third edition, was translated into English.[15] A multivolume project, The Bible and Women: An Encyclopaedia of Exegesis and Cultural History, edited by Charlotte Methuen, Irmtraud Fischer, Mercedes Navarro Puerto, and Adriana Valerio, is currently in production. This project presents a history of the reception of the Bible as embedded in Western cultural history and focuses particularly on gender-relevant biblical themes, biblical female characters, and women recipients of the Bible. The volumes are published in English, Spanish, Italian, and German.[16]

15. *Feminist Biblical Interpretation: A Compendium of Critical Commentary on the Books of the Bible and Related Literature*, trans. Lisa E. Dahill, Everett R. Kalin, Nancy Lukens, Linda M. Maloney, Barbara Rumscheidt, Martin Rumscheidt, and Tina Steiner (Grand Rapids: Eerdmans, 2012). Another notable collection is the three volumes edited by Susanne Scholz, *Feminist Interpretation of the Hebrew Bible in Retrospect*, Recent Research in Biblical Studies 5, 8, 9 (Sheffield: Sheffield Phoenix, 2013, 2014, 2016).

16. The first volume, on the Torah, appeared in Spanish in 2009, in German and Italian in 2010, and in English in 2011 (Atlanta: SBL). The other available volumes are as follows: *Feminist Biblical Studies in the Twentieth Century*, ed. Elisabeth Schüssler Fiorenza (2014); *The Writings and Later Wisdom Books*, ed. Christl M. Maier and Nuria Calduch-Benages (2014); *Gospels: Narrative and History*, ed. Mercedes Navarro Puerto and Marinella Perroni; Amy-Jill Levine, English ed. (2015); *The High Middle Ages*, ed. Kari Elisabeth Børresen and Adriana Valerio (2015); *Early Jewish Writings*, ed. Eileen Schuller and Marie-Theres Wacker (2017); *Faith and Feminism in Nineteenth-Century Religious Communities*, ed. Michaela Sohn-Kronthaler and Ruth Albrecht (2019); *The*

Another groundbreaking work is the collection The Feminist Companion to the Bible Series, edited by Athalya Brenner (Sheffield: Sheffield Academic, 1993–2015), which comprises twenty volumes of commentaries on the Old Testament. The parallel series, Feminist Companion to the New Testament and Early Christian Writings, edited by Amy-Jill Levine with Marianne Blickenstaff and Maria Mayo Robbins (Sheffield: Sheffield Academic, 2001–2010), contains thirteen volumes. These two series are not full commentaries on the biblical books but comprise collected essays on discrete biblical texts.

Works by individual feminist biblical scholars in all parts of the world abound, and they are now too numerous to list in this introduction. Feminist biblical interpretation has reached a level of maturity that now makes possible a commentary series on every book of the Bible. In recent decades, women have had greater access to formal theological education, have been able to learn critical analytical tools, have put their own interpretations into writing, and have developed new methods of biblical interpretation. Until recent decades the work of feminist biblical interpreters was largely unknown, both to other women and to their brothers in the synagogue, church, and academy. Feminists now have taken their place in the professional world of biblical scholars, where they build on the work of their foremothers and connect with one another across the globe in ways not previously possible. In a few short decades, feminist biblical criticism has become an integral part of the academy.

Methodologies

Feminist biblical scholars use a variety of methods and often employ a number of them together.[17] In the Wisdom Commentary series, the authors will explain their understanding of feminism and the feminist reading strategies used in their commentary. Each volume treats the biblical text in blocks of material, not an analysis verse by verse. The entire text

---

Early Middle Ages, ed. Franca Ela Consolino and Judith Herrin (2020); *Prophecy and Gender in the Hebrew Bible*, ed. L. Juliana Claassens and Irmtraud Fischer (2021); *Rabbinic Literature*, ed. Tal Ilan, Lorena Miralles-Maciá, and Ronit Nikolsky (2022); *Ancient Christian Apocrypha*, ed. Outi Lehtipuu and Silke Petersen (2022); *The Jewish Middle Ages*, ed. Carol Bakhos and Gerhard Langer (2023); and *Nineteenth-Century Women's Movements and the Bible*, ed. Angela Berlis and Christiana de Groot (2024). For further information, see https://www.bibleandwomen.org.

17. See the seventeen essays in Caroline Vander Stichele and Todd Penner, eds., *Her Master's Tools? Feminist and Postcolonial Engagements of Historical-Critical Discourse* (Atlanta: SBL, 2005), which show the complementarity of various approaches.

is considered, not only those passages that feature female characters or that speak specifically about women. When women are not apparent in the narrative, feminist lenses are used to analyze the dynamics in the text between male characters, the models of power, binary ways of thinking, and the dynamics of imperialism. Attention is given to how the whole text functions and how it was and is heard, both in its original context and today. Issues of particular concern to women—e.g., poverty, food, health, the environment, water—come to the fore.

One of the approaches used by early feminists and still popular today is to lift up the overlooked and forgotten stories of women in the Bible. Studies of women in each of the Testaments have been done, and there are also studies on women in particular biblical books.[18] Feminists recognize that the examples of biblical characters can be both empowering and problematic. The point of the feminist enterprise is not to serve as an apologetic for women; it is rather, in part, to recover women's history and literary roles in all their complexity and to learn from that recovery.

Retrieving the submerged history of biblical women is a crucial step for constructing the story of the past so as to lead to liberative possibilities for the present and future. There are, however, some pitfalls to this approach. Sometimes depictions of biblical women have been naïve and romantic. Some commentators exalt the virtues of both biblical and contemporary women and paint women as superior to men. Such reverse discrimination inhibits movement toward equality for all. In addition, some feminists challenge the idea that one can "pluck positive images out of an admittedly androcentric text, separating literary characterizations from the androcentric interests they were created to serve."[19] Still other feminists find these images to have enormous value.

18. See, e.g., Alice Bach, ed., *Women in the Hebrew Bible: A Reader* (New York: Routledge, 1999); Tikva Frymer-Kensky, *Reading the Women of the Bible* (New York: Schocken Books, 2002); Carol Meyers, Toni Craven, and Ross S. Kraemer, eds., *Women in Scripture* (Grand Rapids: Eerdmans, 2001); Irene Nowell, *Women in the Old Testament* (Collegeville, MN: Liturgical Press, 1997); Katharine Doob Sakenfeld, *Just Wives? Stories of Power and Survival in the Old Testament and Today* (Louisville: Westminster John Knox, 2003); Mary Ann Getty-Sullivan, *Women in the New Testament* (Collegeville, MN: Liturgical Press, 2001); Bonnie Thurston, *Women in the New Testament: Questions and Commentary*, Companions to the New Testament (New York: Crossroad, 1998).

19. J. Cheryl Exum, "Second Thoughts about Secondary Characters: Women in Exodus 1.8–2.10," in *A Feminist Companion to Exodus to Deuteronomy*, FCB 6, ed. Athalya Brenner (Sheffield: Sheffield Academic, 1994), 75–87, at 76.

One other danger with seeking the submerged history of women is the tendency for Christian feminists to paint Jesus and even Paul as liberators of women in a way that demonizes Judaism.[20] Wisdom Commentary aims to enhance understanding of Jesus as well as Paul as Jews of their day and to forge solidarity among Jewish and Christian feminists.

Feminist scholars who use historical-critical methods analyze the world behind the text; they seek to understand the historical context from which the text emerged and the circumstances of the communities to whom it was addressed. In bringing feminist lenses to this approach, the aim is not to impose modern expectations on ancient cultures but to unmask the ways that ideologically problematic mind-sets that produced the ancient texts are still promulgated through the text. Feminist biblical scholars aim not only to deconstruct but also to reclaim and reconstruct biblical history as women's history, in which women were central and active agents in creating religious heritage.[21] A further step is to construct meaning for contemporary women and men in a liberative movement toward transformation of social, political, economic, and religious structures.[22] In recent years, some feminists have embraced new historicism, which accents the creative role of the interpreter in any construction of history and exposes the power struggles to which the text witnesses.[23]

20. See Judith Plaskow, "Anti-Judaism in Feminist Christian Interpretation," in *Searching the Scriptures: A Feminist Introduction*, vol. 1, ed. Elisabeth Schüssler Fiorenza with Shelly Matthews (New York: Crossroad, 1993), 117–29; Amy-Jill Levine, "The New Testament and Anti-Judaism," in *The Misunderstood Jew: The Church and the Scandal of the Jewish Jesus* (San Francisco: HarperSanFrancisco, 2006), 87–117.

21. See, for example, Phyllis A. Bird, *Missing Persons and Mistaken Identities: Women and Gender in Ancient Israel* (Minneapolis: Fortress, 1997); Elisabeth Schüssler Fiorenza, *In Memory of Her: A Feminist Theological Reconstruction of Christian Origins* (New York: Crossroad, 1994); Ross Shepard Kraemer and Mary Rose D'Angelo, eds., *Women and Christian Origins* (New York: Oxford University Press, 1999).

22. See, e.g., Sandra M. Schneiders, *The Revelatory Text: Interpreting the New Testament as Sacred Scripture*, rev. ed. (Collegeville, MN: Liturgical Press, 1999), whose aim is to engage in biblical interpretation not only for intellectual enlightenment but, even more important, for personal and communal transformation. Elisabeth Schüssler Fiorenza (*Wisdom Ways: Introducing Feminist Biblical Interpretation* [Maryknoll, NY: Orbis Books, 2001]) envisions the work of feminist biblical interpretation as a dance of Wisdom that consists of seven steps that interweave in spiral movements toward liberation, the final one being transformative action for change.

23. See Gina Hens-Piazza, *The New Historicism*, GBS, Old Testament Series (Minneapolis: Fortress, 2002).

Literary critics analyze the world of the text: its form, language patterns, and rhetorical function.[24] They do not attempt to separate layers of tradition and redaction but focus on the text holistically, as it is in its present form. They examine how meaning is created in the interaction between the text and its reader in multiple contexts. Within the arena of literary approaches are reader-oriented approaches, narrative, rhetorical, structuralist, poststructuralist, deconstructive, ideological, autobiographical, and performance criticism.[25] Narrative critics study the interrelation among author, text, and audience through investigation of settings, both spatial and temporal; characters; plot; and narrative techniques (e.g., irony, parody, intertextual allusions). Reader-response critics attend to the impact that the text has on the reader or hearer. They recognize that when a text is detrimental toward women there is the choice either to affirm the text or to read against the grain toward a liberative end. Rhetorical criticism analyzes the style of argumentation and attends to how the author is attempting to shape the thinking or actions of the hearer. Structuralist critics analyze the complex patterns of binary oppositions in the text to derive its meaning.[26] Post-structuralist approaches challenge the notion that there are fixed meanings to any biblical text or that there is one universal truth. They engage in close readings of the text and often engage in intertextual analysis.[27] Within this approach is

24. Phyllis Trible was among the first to employ this method with texts from Genesis and Ruth in her groundbreaking book *God and the Rhetoric of Sexuality*, OBT (Philadelphia: Fortress, 1978). Another pioneer in feminist literary criticism is Mieke Bal (*Lethal Love: Feminist Literary Readings of Biblical Love Stories* [Bloomington: Indiana University Press, 1987]). For surveys of recent developments in literary methods, see Terry Eagleton, *Literary Theory: An Introduction*, anniversary ed. (Minneapolis: University of Minnesota Press, 2008); Janice Capel Anderson and Stephen D. Moore, eds., *Mark and Method: New Approaches in Biblical Studies*, 2nd ed. (Minneapolis: Fortress, 2008); Michal Beth Dinkler, *Literary Theory and the New Testament*, AYBRL (New Haven: Yale University Press, 2019).

25. See, e.g., J. Cheryl Exum and David J. A. Clines, eds., *The New Literary Criticism and the Hebrew Bible* (Valley Forge, PA: Trinity Press International, 1993); Elizabeth Struthers Malbon and Edgar V. McKnight, eds., *The New Literary Criticism and the New Testament*, JSNTSup 109 (Sheffield: JSOT Press, 1994).

26. See, e.g., David Jobling, *The Sense of Biblical Narrative: Three Structural Analyses in the Old Testament*, JSOTSup 7 (Sheffield: University of Sheffield Press, 1978).

27. See, e.g., Stephen D. Moore, *Poststructuralism and the New Testament: Derrida and Foucault at the Foot of the Cross* (Minneapolis: Fortress, 1994); *The Bible in Theory: Critical and Postcritical Essays* (Atlanta: SBL, 2010); Yvonne Sherwood, *A Biblical Text and Its Afterlives: The Survival of Jonah in Western Culture* (Cambridge: Cambridge University Press, 2000).

deconstructionist criticism, which views the text as a site of conflict, with competing narratives. The interpreter aims to expose the fault lines and overturn and reconfigure binaries by elevating the underling of a pair and foregrounding it.[28] Feminists also use other postmodern approaches, such as ideological and autobiographical criticism. The former analyzes the system of ideas that underlies the power and values concealed in the text as well as that of the interpreter.[29] The latter involves deliberate self-disclosure while reading the text as a critical exegete.[30] Performance criticism attends to how the text was passed on orally, usually in communal settings, and to the verbal and nonverbal interactions between the performer and the audience.[31]

From the beginning, feminists have understood that interpreting the Bible is an act of power. In recent decades, feminist biblical scholars have developed hermeneutical theories of the ethics and politics of biblical interpretation to challenge the claims to value neutrality of most academic biblical scholarship. Feminist biblical scholars have also turned their attention to how some biblical writings were shaped by the power of empire and how this still shapes readers' self-understandings today. They have developed hermeneutical approaches that reveal, critique, and evaluate the interactions depicted in the text against the context of empire, and they consider implications for contemporary contexts.[32] Feminists also analyze

28. David Penchansky, "Deconstruction," in *The Oxford Encyclopedia of Biblical Interpretation*, ed. Steven McKenzie (New York: Oxford University Press, 2013), 196–205. See, for example, Danna Nolan Fewell and David M. Gunn, *Gender, Power, and Promise: The Subject of the Bible's First Story* (Nashville: Abingdon, 1993); David Rutledge, *Reading Marginally: Feminism, Deconstruction and the Bible*, BibInt 21 (Leiden: Brill, 1996).

29. See David Jobling and Tina Pippin, eds., *Ideological Criticism of Biblical Texts*, SemeiaSt 59 (Atlanta: Scholars Press, 1992); Terry Eagleton, *Ideology: An Introduction* (London: Verso, 2007).

30. See, e.g., Ingrid Rosa Kitzberger, ed., *Autobiographical Biblical Criticism: Between Text and Self* (Leiden: Deo, 2002); P. J. W. Schutte, "When *They*, *We*, and the *Passive* Become *I*—Introducing Autobiographical Biblical Criticism," *HTS Teologiese Studies / Theological Studies* 61 (2005): 401–16.

31. See, e.g., Holly E. Hearon and Philip Ruge-Jones, eds., *The Bible in Ancient and Modern Media: Story and Performance* (Eugene, OR: Cascade Books, 2009).

32. E.g., Gale Yee, ed., *Judges and Method: New Approaches in Biblical Studies* (Minneapolis: Fortress, 1995); Warren Carter, "Matthaean Christology in Roman Imperial Key: Matthew 1.1," in *The Gospel of Matthew in Its Roman Imperial Context*, ed. John Riches and David C. Sim (London: T&T Clark, 2005); Warren Carter, *The Roman Empire and the New Testament: An Essential Guide* (Nashville: Abingdon, 2006); Elisabeth Schüssler Fiorenza, *The Power of the Word: Scripture and the Rhetoric of Empire* (Minneapolis:

the dynamics of colonization and the mentalities of colonized peoples in the exercise of biblical interpretation. As Kwok Pui-lan explains, "A postcolonial feminist interpretation of the Bible needs to investigate the deployment of gender in the narration of identity, the negotiation of power differentials between the colonizers and the colonized, and the reinforcement of patriarchal control over spheres where these elites could exercise control."[33] Methods and models from sociology and cultural anthropology are used by feminists to investigate women's everyday lives, their experiences of marriage, childrearing, labor, money, illness, and so forth.[34]

As feminists have examined the construction of gender from varying cultural perspectives, they have become ever more cognizant that the way gender roles are defined within differing cultures varies radically. As Mary Ann Tolbert observes, "Attempts to isolate some universal role that cross-culturally defines 'woman' have run into contradictory evidence at every turn."[35] Some women have coined new terms to highlight the particularities of their socio-cultural context. Many African American feminists, for example, call themselves *womanists* to draw attention to the double oppression of racism and sexism they experience.[36] Similarly, many US Hispanic feminists speak of themselves as *mujeristas* (*mujer* is

---

Fortress, 2007); Judith E. McKinlay, *Reframing Her: Biblical Women in Postcolonial Focus* (Sheffield: Sheffield Phoenix, 2004).

33. Kwok Pui-lan, *Postcolonial Imagination and Feminist Theology* (Louisville: Westminster John Knox, 2005), 9. See also Musa W. Dube, ed., *Postcolonial Feminist Interpretation of the Bible* (St. Louis: Chalice, 2000); Christl M. Maier and Carolyn J. Sharp, eds., *Prophecy and Power: Jeremiah in Feminist and Postcolonial Perspective*, LHBOTS 577 (London: Bloomsbury T&T Clark, 2013); L. Juliana Claassens and Carolyn J. Sharp, eds., *Feminist Frameworks and the Bible: Power, Ambiguity, and Intersectionality*, LHBOTS 630 (London: Bloomsbury T&T Clark, 2017).

34. See, for example, Carol Meyers, *Rediscovering Eve: Ancient Israelite Women in Context* (New York: Oxford University Press, 2013); Luise Schottroff, *Lydia's Impatient Sisters: A Feminist Social History of Early Christianity*, trans. Barbara and Martin Rumscheidt (Louisville: Westminster John Knox, 1995); Susan Niditch, *"My Brother Esau Is a Hairy Man": Hair and Identity in Ancient Israel* (New York: Oxford University Press, 2008).

35. Mary Ann Tolbert, "Social, Sociological, and Anthropological Methods," in *Searching the Scriptures*, 1:255–71, at 265.

36. Alice Walker coined the term (*In Search of Our Mothers' Gardens: Womanist Prose* [New York: Harcourt Brace Jovanovich, 1967, 1983]). See also Katie Geneva Cannon, "The Emergence of Black Feminist Consciousness," in *Feminist Interpretation of the Bible*, ed. Letty M. Russell (Philadelphia: Westminster, 1985), 30–40; Renita J. Weems, *Just a Sister Away: A Womanist Vision of Women's Relationships in the Bible* (San Diego: Lura Media, 1988); Nyasha Junior, *An Introduction to Womanist Biblical Interpretation* (Louisville: Westminster John Knox, 2015).

Spanish for "woman").[37] Others prefer to be called "Latina feminists."[38] As a gender-neutral or nonbinary alternative, many today use Latinx or Latine. *Mujeristas*, Latina and Latine feminists emphasize that the context for their theologizing is *mestizaje* and *mulatez* (racial and cultural mixture), done *en conjunto* (in community), with *lo cotidiano* (everyday lived experience) of Latina women as starting points for theological reflection and the encounter with the divine. Intercultural analysis has become an indispensable tool for working toward justice for women at the global level.[39]

Some feminists are among those who have developed interpretations from the perspectives of lesbian, gay, bisexual, transgender, queer and/or questioning, intersex, asexual, and other ways people choose to identify (LGBTQIA+). These approaches focus on issues of sexual identity and use various reading strategies. Some point out the ways in which categories that emerged in recent centuries are applied anachronistically to biblical texts to make modern-day judgments. Others show how the Bible is silent on contemporary issues about sexual identity. Still others examine same-sex relationships in the Bible by figures such as Ruth and Naomi or David and Jonathan. In recent years, queer theory has emerged; it emphasizes the blurriness of boundaries not just of sexual identity but also of gender roles. Queer critics often focus on texts in which figures transgress what is traditionally considered proper gender behavior.[40]

37. Ada María Isasi-Díaz (*Mujerista Theology: A Theology for the Twenty-First Century* [Maryknoll, NY: Orbis Books, 1996]) is credited with coining the term.

38. E.g., María Pilar Aquino, Daisy L. Machado, and Jeanette Rodríguez, eds., *A Reader in Latina Feminist Theology* (Austin: University of Texas Press, 2002).

39. See, e.g., María Pilar Aquino and María José Rosado-Nunes, eds., *Feminist Intercultural Theology: Latina Explorations for a Just World*, Studies in Latino/a Catholicism (Maryknoll, NY: Orbis Books, 2007). See also Michelle A. Gonzalez, "Latina Feminist Theology: Past, Present, and Future," *JFSR* 25 (2009): 150–55. See also Elisabeth Schüssler Fiorenza, ed., *Feminist Biblical Studies in the Twentieth Century: Scholarship and Movement*, BW 9.1 (Atlanta: SBL Press, 2014), who charts feminist studies around the globe as well as emerging feminist methodologies.

40. See, e.g., Bernadette J. Brooten, *Love Between Women: Early Christian Responses to Female Homoeroticism* (Chicago: University of Chicago Press, 1996); Mary Rose D'Angelo, "Women Partners in the New Testament," *JFSR* 6 (1990): 65–86; Deirdre J. Good, "Reading Strategies for Biblical Passages on Same-Sex Relations," *Theology and Sexuality* 7 (1997): 70–82; Deryn Guest, *When Deborah Met Jael: Lesbian Biblical Hermeneutics* (London: SCM, 2005); Teresa J. Hornsby and Ken Stone, eds., *Bible Trouble: Queer Reading at the Boundaries of Biblical Scholarship*, SemeiaSt 67 (Atlanta: SBL, 2011); Joseph A. Marchal, "Queer Studies and Critical Masculinity Studies in Feminist Biblical Studies," in *Feminist Biblical Studies in the Twentieth Century*, ed. Schüssler Fiorenza, 261–80.

Feminists have also been engaged in studying the reception history of the text[41] and have engaged in studies in the emerging fields of disability theory and of children in the Bible.

Feminists also recognize that the struggle for women's equality and dignity is intimately connected with the struggle for respect for Earth and for the whole of the cosmos. Ecofeminists interpret Scripture in ways that highlight the link between human domination of nature and male subjugation of women. They show how anthropocentric ways of interpreting the Bible have overlooked or dismissed Earth and Earth community. They invite readers to identify not only with human characters in the biblical narrative but also with other Earth creatures and domains of nature, especially those that are the object of injustice. Some use creative imagination to retrieve the interests of Earth implicit in the narrative and enable Earth to speak.[42]

Biblical Authority

By the late nineteenth century, some feminists, such as Elizabeth Cady Stanton, began to question openly whether the Bible could continue to be regarded as authoritative for women. They viewed the Bible itself as the source of women's oppression, and some rejected its sacred origin and saving claims. Some decided that the Bible and the religious traditions that enshrine it are too thoroughly saturated with androcentrism and patriarchy to be redeemable.[43]

In the Wisdom Commentary series, questions such as these may be raised, but the aim of this series is not to lead readers to reject the authority of the biblical text. Rather, the aim is to promote better understanding of the contexts from which the text arose and of the rhetorical effects it has on people in contemporary contexts. Such understanding can lead to a deepening of faith, with the Bible serving as an aid to bring flourishing of life.

41. See Sharon H. Ringe, "When Women Interpret the Bible," in *Women's Bible Commentary*, ed. Carol A. Newsom, Sharon H. Ringe, and Jacqueline E. Lapsley, 3rd ed. (Louisville: Westminster John Knox, 2012), 5; Taylor and Choi, *Handbook of Women Biblical Interpreters*; Yvonne Sherwood, "Introduction," in *The Bible and Feminism: Remapping the Field*, ed. Yvonne Sherwood with Anna Fisk (New York: Oxford University Press, 2017).

42. E.g., Norman C. Habel and Peter Trudinger, *Exploring Ecological Hermeneutics*, SymS 46 (Atlanta: SBL, 2008); Mary Judith Ress, *Ecofeminism in Latin America*, Women from the Margins (Maryknoll, NY: Orbis Books, 2006).

43. E.g., Mary Daly, *Beyond God the Father: A Philosophy of Women's Liberation* (Boston: Beacon, 1985).

Language for God

Because of the ways in which the term "God" has been used to symbolize the divine in predominantly male, patriarchal, and monarchical modes, feminists have designed new ways of speaking of the divine. Some have called attention to the inadequacy of the term *God* by trying to visually destabilize our ways of thinking and speaking of the divine. Rosemary Radford Ruether proposed *God/ess*, as an unpronounceable term pointing to the unnameable understanding of the divine that transcends patriarchal limitations.[44] Some have followed traditional Jewish practice, writing *G-d*. Elisabeth Schüssler Fiorenza has adopted *G*d*.[45] Others draw on the biblical tradition to mine female and non-gender-specific metaphors and symbols.[46] In Wisdom Commentary, there is not one standard way of expressing the divine; each author will use her or his preferred ways. The one exception is that when the tetragrammaton, YHWH, the name revealed to Moses in Exodus 3:14, is used, it will be without vowels, respecting the Jewish custom of avoiding pronouncing the divine name out of reverence.

Nomenclature for the Two Testaments

In recent decades, some biblical scholars have begun to call the two Testaments of the Bible by names other than the traditional nomenclature: Old and New Testament. Some regard "Old" as derogatory, implying that it is no longer relevant or that it has been superseded. Consequently, terms like Hebrew Bible, First Testament, and Jewish Scriptures and, correspondingly, Christian Scriptures or Second Testament have come into use. There are a number of difficulties with these designations. The term "Hebrew Bible" does not take into account that parts of the Old Testament are written not in Hebrew but in Aramaic.[47] Moreover, for Roman Catholics and Eastern Orthodox believers, the Old

44. Rosemary Radford Ruether, *Sexism and God-Talk: Toward a Feminist Theology* (Boston: Beacon, 1993).

45. Elisabeth Schüssler Fiorenza, *Jesus: Miriam's Child, Sophia's Prophet; Critical Issues in Feminist Christology* (New York: Continuum, 1994), 191n3.

46. E.g., Sallie McFague, *Models of God: Theology for an Ecological, Nuclear Age* (Philadelphia: Fortress, 1987); Catherine Mowry LaCugna, *God for Us: The Trinity and Christian Life* (San Francisco: HarperCollins, 1991); Elizabeth A. Johnson, *She Who Is: The Mystery of God in Feminist Theological Discourse* (New York: Crossroad, 1992). See further Elizabeth A. Johnson, "God," in *Dictionary of Feminist Theologies*, ed. Letty M. Russell and J. Shannon Clarkson (Louisville: Westminster John Knox, 1996), 128–30.

47. Gen 31:47; Jer 10:11; Ezra 4:7–6:18; 7:12-26; Dan 2:4–7:28.

Testament includes books written in Greek—the Deuterocanonical books, considered Apocrypha by Protestants.[48] The term "Jewish Scriptures" is inadequate because these books are also sacred to Christians. Conversely, "Christian Scriptures" is not an accurate designation for the New Testament, since the Old Testament is also part of the Christian Scriptures. Using "First and Second Testament" also has difficulties, in that it can imply a hierarchy and a value judgment.[49] Jews generally use the term Tanakh, an acronym for Torah (Pentateuch), Nevi'im (Prophets), and Ketuvim (Writings).

In Wisdom Commentary, if authors choose to use a designation other than Tanakh, Old Testament, and New Testament, they will explain how they mean the term.

Translation

Modern feminist scholars recognize the complexities connected with biblical translation, as they have delved into questions about philosophy of language, how meanings are produced, and how they are culturally situated. Today it is evident that simply translating into gender-neutral formulations cannot address all the challenges presented by androcentric texts. Efforts at feminist translation must also deal with issues around authority and canonicity.[50]

Because of these complexities, the editors of the Wisdom Commentary series have chosen to use an existing translation, the New Revised Standard Version Updated Edition (NRSVue),[51] which is provided for easy reference at the top of each page of commentary. The NRSVue was produced by a team of ecumenical and interreligious scholars, is a fairly literal translation, and uses inclusive language for human beings. Brief discussions about problematic translations appear in the inserts labeled "Translation Matters." When more detailed discussions are available, these will be indicated in footnotes. In the commentary, wherever

48. Representing the *via media* between Catholic and reformed, Anglicans generally consider the Apocrypha to be profitable, if not canonical, and utilize select Wisdom texts liturgically.

49. See Levine, *The Misunderstood Jew*, 193–99.

50. Elizabeth Castelli, "*Les Belles Infidèles*/Fidelity or Feminism? The Meanings of Feminist Biblical Translation," in *Searching the Scriptures*, 1:189–204, here 190.

51. The volumes of Wisdom Commentary produced through 2023 use the edition of NRSV published in 1989; subsequent volumes use the updated edition, NRSVue, released in 2021.

Hebrew or Greek words are used, English translation is provided. In cases where a wordplay is involved, transliteration is provided to enable understanding.

Art and Poetry

Artistic expression in poetry, music, sculpture, painting, and various other modes is very important to feminist interpretation. Where possible, art and poetry are included in the print volumes of the series. In a number of instances, these are original works created for this project. Regrettably, copyright and production costs prohibit the inclusion of color photographs and other artistic work.

Glossary

Because there are a number of excellent readily available resources that provide definitions and concise explanations of terms used in feminist theological and biblical studies, this series will not include a glossary. We refer you to works such as *Dictionary of Feminist Theologies*, edited by Letty M. Russell and J. Shannon Clarkson, and volume 1 of *Searching the Scriptures*, edited by Elisabeth Schüssler Fiorenza with the assistance of Shelly Matthews. Individual authors in the Wisdom Commentary series will define the way they are using terms that may be unfamiliar.

A Concluding Word

In just a few short decades, feminist biblical studies has grown exponentially, both in the methods that have been developed and in the number of scholars who have embraced it. We realize that this series is limited and will soon need to be revised and updated. It is our hope that Wisdom Commentary, by making the best of current feminist biblical scholarship available in an accessible format to ministers, preachers, rabbis, teachers, scholars, and students, will aid all readers in their advancement toward God's vision of dignity, equality, and justice for all.

Acknowledgments

There are a great many people who have made this series possible: first, Peter Dwyer, retired director of Liturgical Press, and Hans Christoffersen, editorial director of Liturgical Press, who have believed in this project and have shepherded it since it was conceived in 2008. I am grateful to Therese L. Ratliff, the Press's director and CEO, who is now championing this project.

Editorial consultants Athalya Brenner-Idan and Elisabeth Schüssler Fiorenza have not only been an inspiration with their pioneering work but have encouraged us all along the way with their personal involvement. Volume editors Mary Ann Beavis, Mahri Leonard-Fleckman, Amy-Jill Levine, Linda M. Maloney, Song-Mi Suzie Park, Ahida Pilarski, Sarah J. Tanzer, and Lauress Wilkins Lawrence have lent their extraordinary wisdom to the shaping of the series, have used their extensive networks of relationships to secure authors and contributors, and have worked tirelessly to guide their work to completion. Others who have contributed greatly to the shaping of the project are Linda M. Day, Carol J. Dempsey, Gina Hens-Piazza, Mignon Jacobs, Seung Ai Yang, and Barbara E. Bowe of blessed memory (d. 2010). Editorial and research assistant Susan M. Hickman provided invaluable support with administrative details and arrangements at the outset of the project. I am grateful to Brian Eisenschenk and Christine Henderson who assisted Susan Hickman with the Wiki. I am especially thankful to Lauren L. Murphy and Justin Howell for their work in copyediting; and to the staff at Liturgical Press, especially Colleen Stiller, retired production manager; Angie Steffens, production manager; Elizabeth Elin, production coordinator; Stephanie Lancour, production editor; Julie Surma, desktop publisher; and Tara Durheim, marketing director.

Author's Introduction

Romans and Sophia

The author of the letter to the Romans states a simple wish for audiences or readers: "I want you to be wise" (Rom 16:19). The letter also acknowledges the complexity and inconceivability of the divine mystery in a powerful theological statement: "O the depth of the riches and wisdom and knowledge of God!" (11:33). Is Romans, therefore, an important New Testament text source for the exploration of wisdom? It seems that, at first glance, the response is negative. With the one occurrence of the noun "wisdom" (σοφία) in 11:33 and one of the adjective "wise" (σοφός) in 16:19 (plus another one in a textual variant in 16:27), the term "wisdom" is rare in this letter of Paul. It is specifically absent from the large christological sections of Romans over which biblical scholars have spilled much ink in past centuries. By contrast, these terms are, for example, attested no fewer than twelve times in the Greek text of 1 Corinthians 1:18-31.[1] The observation that wisdom terminology is rare in Romans corresponds to, and is corroborated by, the fact that indices in many commentaries and other major scholarly works on the letter even lack an entry on the subject of "wisdom."[2] Nevertheless, Robert Jewett

1. These twelve occurrences compare to thirteen attestations of English equivalents in the NRSVue.

2. Robert Jewett, *Romans: A Commentary*, Hermeneia (Minneapolis: Fortress, 2007); Alain Gignac, *L'épître aux Romains*, Commentaire biblique: Nouveau Testament 6 (Paris: Cerf, 2014); Thomas Schreiner, *Romans*, 2nd ed., BECNT 6 (Grand Rapids: Baker Academic, 2018); see also, for example, the comprehensive handbook by J. Paul Sampley, ed., *Paul in the Greco-Roman World: A Handbook*, 2 vols., 2nd ed. (London: Bloomsbury, 2016). An exception is Joseph A. Fitzmyer, *Romans: A New Translation with Introduction and Commentary*, AB 33 (New York: Doubleday, 1993).

concludes: "If Paul's gospel is accepted by the Roman believers, that God's mercy is wide enough to cover habitual antagonisms between Jews and Gentiles, Greco-Romans and barbarians, educated and uneducated, they will be able to join him in praising God for this 'depth of wisdom' that offers an end to lethal human conflict."[3]

In traditional Jewish literature, the figure of *Chokmah-Sophia-Sapientia-Wisdom* is indeed more than just what emerges from lexical occurrences. Drawing on and partially incorporating wisdom traditions from the broad spectrum of the ancient Near East,[4] it is a flexible image or concept of the ever-changing figuration of the divine. At the same time, it represents a state of the human mind and its capacity to reflect on the universe. It is also fluid regarding its gender characteristics, with dominantly female and occasionally male features. In the Hebrew Bible/Septuagint, the personification of *Chokmah-Sophia-Sapientia-Wisdom* shifts from a body that is desired and grasped (Prov 3:13, 15, 18) to one that seeks out (Wis 6:13), pervades, and penetrates all things (Wis 7:24). Wisdom is also depicted as inebriating men by lavishing them with her fruits (Sir 1:16, 26). The shifts in imagery from submissive to dominant may be due to a gradual process of male gendering, although ultimately Wisdom remains elusive and ambiguous.[5] In such a broader sense, the letter to the Romans is indeed about wisdom, as this commentary will show. But what kind of wisdom does Romans convey about God and beyond?

The letter to the Romans has had an unparalleled formative influence on the history of Christianity. In fact, throughout history, Romans has often been considered the quintessential letter of the *Corpus Paulinum*;

3. Jewett, *Romans*, 717.

4. Ancient Israel and Second Temple Judaism were acquainted with sapiential traditions of the Babylonians (Jer 50:35; 51:57; cf. Isa 44:25; 47:10) and the Egyptians (1 Kgs 4:30; cf. Gen 41:8; Exod 7:11), the Canaanites and Phoenicians (Ezek 27:8; 28:3, 17; Zech 9:2), etc. Wisdom literature has a universal appeal as it is based on shared human experience. In general, the topic of wisdom was focused on reciprocal justice and the most prudent ways to live in light of the unpredictability of the human predicament. With such parameters, wisdom can still easily be communicated today, even in social contexts outside of religious communities. Cf. Ulrich Wilckens and Georg Fohrer, "σοφία, σοφός, σοφίζω," *TDNT* 7 (1971): 465–528; Alice M. Sinnott, *The Personification of Wisdom*, SOTSMS (Aldershot: Ashgate, 2005), 10–52. See also Starhawk, "Witchcraft and Women's Culture," in *WomanSpirit Rising: A Feminist Reader in Religion*, ed. Carol P. Christ and Judith Plaskow (New York: HarperOne, 1992), 260–61.

5. Mary Ann Beavis and HyeRan Kim-Cragg, *Hebrews*, WCS 54 (Collegeville, MN: Liturgical Press, 2015), 5–6.

it has rightly been called "a monument."[6] Origen wrote the first commentary on Romans; it featured his arguments against the teachings of Marcion, who opposed Judaism and disavowed the Hebrew Scriptures. Augustine of Hippo was converted to Christianity after reading a section of Romans. In the wake of the Reformation, Martin Luther developed his doctrine of justification primarily based on his interpretation of Romans and wrote an important preface to it; born with the last name "Luder," he even decided to undergo a name change upon being struck by the implications of reading the eighth chapter of Romans.[7] Soon thereafter, Philipp Melanchthon published several books and commentaries on Romans (and other Pauline epistles). John Wesley experienced his own conversion by reading Luther's preface to Romans. Two editions of Karl Barth's commentary on Romans had a lasting impact on the theology of the twentieth century and brought its author fame and recognition. The list could be continued.

Due to its importance, there is no shortage of commentaries on Romans, many of which have become classics in the field of biblical studies or modern religious studies.[8] Furthermore, an impressive number of commentaries in various languages have arrived on the shelves of academic libraries in the past years alone.[9] So what is the point of setting out to write yet another commentary on Romans? Can anything new be brought to light?

6. Laura S. Nasrallah, *Archaeology and the Letters of Paul* (Oxford: Oxford University Press, 2019), 182; on the description of the impact and interpretive strategies, see 182–87, 219–23.

7. For further details, see below on Romans 8:2 (p. 181).

8. See the impressive list of commentaries on Romans in Fitzmyer, *Romans*, 173–214.

9. See, for example, in chronological order: Fitzmyer, *Romans*; Douglas J. Moo, *The Epistle to the Romans*, NICNT (Grand Rapids: Eerdmans, 1996); Brendan Byrne, *Romans*, SP 6 (Collegeville, MN: Liturgical Press, 1996); Klaus Haacker, *Der Brief des Paulus an die Römer*, THKNT 6 (Leipzig: Evangelische Verlagsanstalt, 1999); Jewett, *Romans*; Frank J. Matera, *Romans*, Paideia: Commentaries on the New Testament (Grand Rapids: Baker Academic, 2010); Gignac, *L'épître*; Michael Wolter, *Der Brief an die Römer*, vol. 1: *Röm 1–8*, EKKNT 6/1 (Neukirchen-Vluyn: Neukirchener Verlag; Ostfildern: Patmos, 2014); Michael Wolter, *Der Brief an die Römer*, vol. 2: *Röm 9–16*, EKKNT 6/2 (Göttingen: Vandenhoeck & Ruprecht; Ostfildern: Patmos, 2019); Richard N. Longenecker, *The Epistle to the Romans: A Commentary on the Greek Text*, NIGTC (Grand Rapids: Eerdmans, 2016); Schreiner, *Romans*; Aaron Sherwood, *Romans: A Structural, Thematic, and Exegetical Commentary* (Bellingham, WA: Lexham Press, 2020); David G. Peterson, *Romans*, EBTC (Bellingham, WA: Lexham Press, 2020).

Moreover, Romans is a long document (acknowledged as such already in the *Canon Muratori*/Muratorian fragment).[10] It is indeed the longest letter in the *Corpus Paulinum*. Its arguments are complex and complicated. More broadly, Paul's letters were already known among later peers for a certain level of difficulty, as the remark in 2 Peter 3:15-16 evinces. If Romans is rather a dogmatic treatise or summary of Paul's theology, why not read the other shorter letters of the apostle that tackle actual community problems?

A Commentary from a Feminist Perspective

What is new about the current commentary is its perspective of feminist biblical interpretation. Such a task requires some initial reflections on the goals of this scholarly endeavor. After all, the question of what exegesis in the context of the "feminist enterprise"[11] should or needs to accomplish is itself contested ground. Three main positions and goals have been outlined in the recent past: Feminist biblical interpretation seeks to attain a comprehensive study of the complete Bible (i.e., all of its books in their entirety); it is motivated by an egalitarian ethos to challenge androcentric textual traditions of the Bible and their patriarchal interpretive communities; finally, it aims at ending oppression and marginalization of women (in cooperation with intersectionality and postcolonial hermeneutics).[12] These three main goals shall now be described in more detail.

First, there is a lot of new ground to cover for feminist biblical interpretation in matters related to Romans. No full-sized commentary has ever been written on this book from a feminist perspective. Is Paul perhaps the reason for this? Feminist biblical scholarship has, until recently, not evinced much interest in the apostle, other than to dismiss him as a misogynist. As Sheila E. McGinn observes, "Paul and feminists . . . have

10. Already *Canon Muratori* notes about Romans, which is number seven in its listing of Paul's letters: "And then to the Romans, explaining that Christ is both the measure of the writings and also their principle—he wrote *here* at length." See also Harry Y. Gamble Jr., "The Formation of the Pauline Corpus," in *The Oxford Handbook of Pauline Studies*, ed. Matthew V. Novenson and R. Barry Matlock (Oxford: Oxford University Press, 2022), 338–54.

11. This term has been used by Amy-Jill Levine, "The Disease of Postcolonial New Testament Studies and the Hermeneutics of Healing," *JFSR* 20 (2004): 91–99, at 97.

12. It is nevertheless acknowledged that the construction of gender varies relative to different cultural perspectives, social status, etc.

not always been seen as the most amicable of 'bedfellows.'"[13] Olivette Genest provocatively asks if it might not be preferable to omit Paul from any discussion about women in Christianity and within humanity.[14] There may be good reasons why the famous apostle to the gentiles should stop preaching, considering that for many centuries, women's efforts to develop their own interpretive stance and to shed patriarchal oppression were curbed through a specific selection of biblical resources poetically summarized as "Genesis, the Fall, and St. Paul."[15]

But while Pauline and Deutero-Pauline literature may be criticized for its treatment of women, other texts paint a different picture. Thecla is the female protagonist in the *Acts of Paul and Thecla*, a text that circulated widely in the Eastern Church in Greek, Syriac, and Armenian translation. Thecla is portrayed as being mesmerized by Paul's ascetic teachings, disappointing her betrothed, and following the apostle instead. As a disciple of Paul, she may be considered the personification of women's resistance in the early centuries of Christianity. So, can the historical character of Paul and his texts be the stuff of a positive engagement from a feminist perspective?

The situation is ambiguous, and there is much history to recover. The reason is that, in the patriarchal world of antiquity, history has far too often been *his story* (the story of *men*). Its textual products are androcentric; women were customarily omitted, although they were often dynamic agents of history. Particularly with regard to the development of the churches of early Christ believers, women must be considered as the "unsung heroes." Their roles ranged from active participants to leaders, but their stories as *her* stories were not mentioned or recorded in subsequent patriarchal traditions, which are now also labeled as "malestream." Remedying this situation has been an explicit goal of feminist exegesis for a long time.[16] One may say that correcting the problem of

13. Sheila E. McGinn, "Feminist Approaches to Paul's Letter to the Romans," in *Celebrating Romans: Template for Pauline Theology; Essays in Honor of Robert Jewett*, ed. Sheila E. McGinn (Grand Rapids: Eerdmans, 2004), 165.

14. Olivette Genest, "Faut-il que Paul se taise dans la discussion sur la situation des femmes en christianisme?," *Lumen Vitae* 52 (1997): 297–314, at 312. Cf. also Pamela Eisenbaum, "Is Paul the Father of Misogyny and Antisemitism?," *CrossCurrents* 50 (2000): 506–24, at 506.

15. Gerda Lerner, *The Creation of Feminist Consciousness: From the Middle Ages to Eighteen-Seventy*, Women and History 2 (New York: Oxford University Press, 1993), 138.

16. Elisabeth Schüssler Fiorenza, *In Memory of Her: A Feminist Theological Reconstruction of Christian Origins* (New York: Crossroad, 1983), 52.

the studies of *his*-story toward retrieving *her* stories requires feminist *her*-meneutics, so that women are finally granted their rightful place in the history of interpretation. Women have too long and too often been neglected and their important contributions too long silenced.

One such strategy has been to "use women to think with"; it adopts their perspective in the process of interpreting biblical texts.[17] While this has been a valuable method, it has also led to a certain dilemma. As long as the goal and purpose was to retrieve information about women in texts from the Bible that explicitly mentioned them, often large sections of the texts remained out of reach. Specifically for the task of interpreting Romans, the first goal of feminist interpretation is to present a study of the entire book from a feminist perspective.[18] In the present volume, this has, among other things, been accomplished through special attention to Phoebe's role during the letter's production and recitation.

Second, the principal concern of feminist exegesis may be seen in a vision of equality between women and men, which generally implies that the inferior status traditionally accorded to women requires being questioned and improved. In the words of Mary Ann Beavis and HyeRan Kim-Cragg:

> Feminist biblical interpretation can be defined very simply as a method of interpretation of biblical texts that *presupposes* women's full humanity and equality (the equality of all human beings), *recognizes and celebrates* biblical traditions and interpretations that support these values, and *critiques* biblical traditions and interpretations that imply that women and other marginalized people are inferior socially, intellectually, morally, or spiritually.[19]

With this program, feminist exegesis confronts the twofold problem that biblical texts have originated in ancient patriarchal societies, such as the ancient Near East (including ancient Egypt) and the Greco-Roman world. These texts (somewhat naturally) reflect their norms and values; therefore, they are mostly androcentric. They have, furthermore, been interpreted for centuries in societies and within privileged scholarly

17. McGinn, "Feminist Approaches," 169–70, with reference to both Elisabeth Schüssler Fiorenza, *But She Said: Feminist Practices of Biblical Interpretation* (Boston: Beacon, 1992), 20–50; and Elizabeth A. Castelli, "Romans," in *Searching the Scriptures*, vol. 2: *A Feminist Commentary*, ed. Elisabeth Schüssler Fiorenza (New York: Crossroad, 1994), 272–300.

18. McGinn, "Feminist Approaches," 170.

19. Beavis and Kim-Cragg, *Hebrews*, xlv (italics original).

circles that were or still are predominantly patriarchal/malestream.[20] As the centuries have passed, many religious/denominational groups in both Judaism and Christianity have further regressed into patriarchy, for instance, by exclusively restricting leadership positions to men and relegating women to secondary roles of servitude.[21] Against those socio-political trends, scholars have pointed to the egalitarianism of Pauline assemblies that was similar to those of ancient utopian movements.[22] That egalitarianism was a challenge to patriarchal structures and the androcentric texts they helped to generate. It has been honored in the present volume through attention to Phoebe's involvement during the letter's production and recitation, all of which are a testimony to the egalitarian ethos of Pauline assemblies. This explains a certain focus on reader-response criticisms (attention to the impact of the text on the audiences and readers) in this volume.

The aim of achieving equality between women and men requires more broadly a process of social, political, economic, and religious transformation of society. Thus, the third goal of feminist biblical interpretation is "a critique of culture and faith in light of misogyny"[23] to end the oppression of women, which includes sexism and sexual exploitation as its corollary.[24] Elisabeth Schüssler Fiorenza rightly insists that feminism cannot simply be an academic discipline focused on historical-critical methods without any practical relevance outside of the ivory tower or further social consequence. Instead, the outcome of such scholarly endeavor needs to be liberation from oppression, marginalization, and subjugation. She takes as a reference point the experience of Sojourner Truth,

20. Castelli, "Romans," 273–74; Elisabeth Schüssler Fiorenza, *Wisdom Ways: Introducing Feminist Biblical Interpretation* (Maryknoll, NY: Orbis Books, 2001), 37.

21. A few selected publications describe facets of the problem: Stuart Charmé, "The Political Transformation of Gender Traditions at the Western Wall in Jerusalem," *JFSR* 21 (2005): 5–34; Marian Ronan, "Ethical Challenges Confronting the Roman Catholic Women's Ordination Movement in the Twenty-First Century," *JFSR* 23 (2007): 149–69; Ronit Irshai, "Toward a Gender Critical Approach to the Philosophy of Jewish Law (Halakhah)," *JFSR* 26 (2010): 55–77.

22. Mary Ann Beavis, "Christian Origins, Egalitarianism, and Utopia," *JFSR* 23 (2007): 27–49.

23. Phyllis Trible, *Texts of Terror: Literary-Feminist Readings of Biblical Narratives*, OBT 13 (Philadelphia: Fortress, 1984), 3.

24. bell hooks, *Feminism Is for Everybody: Passionate Politics* (Cambridge: South End, 2000), 1.

an American enslaved woman, "to formulate a different christology for change, or . . . for turning the world rightside up again."[25] In other words, feminist biblical interpretation should make a positive difference in the face of ongoing suffering. In recent decades, much opposition from scholars marginalized by ethnicity, race, or continental location has been voiced against historical criticism as the only adequate methodology for biblical exegesis. Specifically, this method has been recognized as being indebted to the European cultural-philosophical context but not having universal validity. Through its focus on the past, it tends to evade crucial contemporary problems.[26]

Schüssler Fiorenza has coined the neologism *kyriarchy* (which literally describes the "rule" of the "Lord") to describe intersecting systems of gender/sexuality and colonialism in the ancient and modern world. She demands "that feminist christological reflection first must critically scrutinize its academic and doctrinal frames of reference to determine whether its own christological articulations break through the kyriarchal sex/gender system and hence inspire transformation and change rather than legitimate kyriarchal relations of domination."[27] Therefore, the *outcome* of the interpretive endeavor needs to be taken into consideration. "Only a feminist christological approach concerned with justice and well-being for all can overcome the dualistic either-or alternative of feminist Christian or post-Christian theology."[28] Both the historical reality and the human experience of oppression require that liberation is the ultimate goal of feminist biblical interpretation.[29] More than the

25. Elisabeth Schüssler Fiorenza, *Jesus: Miriam's Child, Sophia's Prophet; Critical Issues in Feminist Christology*, 2nd ed., Cornerstones (London: Bloomsbury T&T Clark, 2015), 65.

26. William H. Myers, "The Hermeneutical Dilemma of the African American Biblical Student," in *Stony the Road We Trod: African American Biblical Interpretation*, ed. Cain Hope Felder (Minneapolis: Fortress, 1991), 41; Susanne Scholz, " 'Tandoori Reindeer' and the Limitations of Historical Criticism," in *Her Master's Tools? Feminist and Postcolonial Engagements of Historical-Critical Discourse*, ed. Caroline Vander Stichele and Todd Penner, Global Perspectives on Biblical Scholarship 9 (Atlanta: SBL, 2005), 52, 68.

27. Schüssler Fiorenza, *Jesus*, 65–66. See also Schüssler Fiorenza, *Wisdom Ways*, 118–24.

28. Schüssler Fiorenza, *Jesus*, 66.

29. Elisabeth Schüssler Fiorenza, *Bread Not Stone: The Challenge of Feminist Biblical Interpretation*, ann. ed. (Boston: Beacon, 1995), 47, with reference to James H. Cone, *God of the Oppressed* (New York: Seabury, 1975), 51–52. See, furthermore, Élisabeth Parmentier, *Les filles prodigues: Défis des théologies féminists*, Lieux théologiques 32 (Geneva: Labor et Fides, 1998), 103–5; Stephanie Y. Mitchem, "Womanists and (Unfinished) Constructions of Salvation," *JFSR* 17 (2001): 85–100, at 98–99.

other two, this third aspect of feminist biblical interpretation constitutes a real paradigm change in scholarship. Positively speaking, the goal is the formation of a radically democratic "*ekklēsia* of wo/men."[30]

Given such an ethos of egalitarianism and openness, two questions must be raised. First, are soteriological systems or ecclesiological models that employ hierarchical structures legitimate, or are they inherently "oppressive"? For example, should the christological claim of the subordination of Jesus, the "Son," to God, the "Father," or the ecclesiological image of subordinate humans vis-à-vis Jesus as "Lord" be tolerated? Can any form of binary epistemological categories be overcome—or deconstructed—to allow for a more wholesome vision of the text and its theology? To allow for wisdom that is truly acceptable to all, including women? Second, what may be done to conscientize academia about the still pervasive anti-Jewish biases in some feminist biblical interpretation?[31] Kwok Pui-lan rightly suggests that meetings with real dialogue have been brought up time and again as an important element to overcome the problem.[32] And in order for dialogue to take place, empathetic listening to the concerns of one's dialogue partners is required to take their views seriously. While it is "messy" to work against marginalization and create a better future, the common hope is that an open dialogue among all participants will help to alleviate different experiences of oppression in different cultures and thus improve the world for all.[33]

To attain a more holistic perception of the full range of oppressive factors, the term "intersectionality" has been coined by American lawyer and civil rights advocate Kimberlé Williams Crenshaw. The term describes an analytical framework and refers to interwoven power systems

30. See, for instance, Schüssler Fiorenza, *Wisdom Ways*, 130: "Feminist biblical discourses, then, are best understood in the classical sense of deliberative rhetoric that seeks to persuade the democratic assembly and to adjudicate arguments in order to make decisions for the sake of the welfare of everyone."

31. See, for instance, the criticism in Katharina von Kellenbach, *Anti-Judaism in Feminist Religious Writings*, AAR Cultural Criticism 1 (Atlanta: Scholars Press, 1994).

32. Kwok Pui-lan, "Roundtable Discussion: Anti-Judaism and Postcolonial Biblical Interpretation; Response," *JFSR* 20 (2004): 99–106, at 100.

33. See, for example, the complaint of Hisako Kinukawa, "Roundtable Discussion: Anti-Judaism and Postcolonial Biblical Interpretation; Response," *JFSR* 20 (2004): 115–18, at 118, where she voices concerns that sharing her personal experience of oppression was not always appreciated by academic conversation partners.

composed of a variety of ideologies of marginalization.[34] In other words, intersectionality is about the experience of "double trouble"[35] (or even "triple trouble"?) of many. It has become a new analytic tool to analyze the complex situation of oppression for marginalized groups.[36] Confronting the Bible with intersectionality, Renita J. Weems declares that "it is my responsibility as a woman and an African American to make certain that the scholarship I engage in as a biblical scholar does its part to work toward the larger project of critical, yet creative wrestling with biblical God-talk."[37] These words make clear that Weems still considers the Bible—and with it also Judaism and Christianity per se—"redeemable" while for many other feminist/womanist scholars it is no longer so.

The most recent development of feminism or feminist biblical interpretation has to do with the recognition of its internal diversity. "There is no one and the same female identity everywhere and at all times," states Kathy Ehrensperger.[38] This insight is specifically connected to the global reach of feminist biblical interpretation, necessitating its adaptability and polymorphy. "Scholars emerged with new contextual allegiances as Womanists, Mujeristas, African, African-American, Asian, Caribbean, European, and Jewish feminists. Womanists and Mujeristas developed their particular agendas according to their United States and Latina identities. Emergent global feminist scholars addressed their own interpretive agendas, while redefining and recontextualizing feminist NT hermeneutics."[39]

34. Kimberlé Williams Crenshaw, "Demarginalizing the Intersection of Race and Sex: A Black Feminist Critique of Antidiscrimination Doctrine, Feminist Theory and Antiracist Politics," *University of Chicago Legal Forum* 1989 (1989): 139–67.

35. For this term, see Marianne Bjelland Kartzow, *The Slave Metaphor and Gendered Enslavement in Early Christian Discourse: Double Trouble Embodied*, Routledge Studies in the Early Christian World (London: Routledge, 2018), 3, 145.

36. Jennifer C. Nash, "Re-Thinking Intersectionality," *Feminist Review* 89 (2008): 1–15; Elisabeth Schüssler Fiorenza, "Introduction: Exploring the Intersection of Race, Gender, Status, and Ethnicity in Early Christian Studies," in *Prejudice and Christian Beginnings: Investigating Race, Gender, and Ethnicity in Early Christian Studies*, ed. Laura Nasrallah and Elisabeth Schüssler Fiorenza (Minneapolis: Fortress, 2009), 1–23.

37. Renita J. Weems, *Battered Love: Marriage, Sex, and Violence in the Hebrew Prophets*, OBT (Minneapolis: Fortress, 1995), 11.

38. Kathy Ehrensperger, *That We May Be Mutually Encouraged: Feminism and the New Perspective in Pauline Studies* (New York: T&T Clark, 2004), 192.

39. Althea Spencer Miller, "Feminism, Feminist Hermeneutics: II. New Testament," *EBR* 8 (2014): 1128–30, at 1128–29. See also Clarice J. Martin, "Womanist Interpretations of the New Testament: The Quest for Holistic and Inclusive Translation and Inter-

Since patriarchy is a global problem, feminist and postcolonial studies have sometimes been considered as "disciplinary siblings."[40] Both share the goal of alleviating oppression by exposing sources of illegitimate authority. Feminism is naturally of particular relevance in geographic areas that have suffered from colonialism. In Asia, for example, women wonder whether Christianity may be intrinsically associated with Western imperialism and claims of the cultural superiority of the Western world. Integrating, therefore, feminist-liberationist approaches to the Bible with intersectionality leads inexorably to postcolonial hermeneutics, a critical stance examining the interconnection of gender, race, class, and sexuality by challenging any notion of scholarly objectivity.[41] Biblical texts of both testaments have been recognized as useful resources in this struggle because many of them have emerged in marginalized and oppressed communities that were forced to renegotiate their identity vis-à-vis Babylonian, Persian, or Roman empires.[42] Since postcolonial hermeneutics can also be understood as a critique of all systems of binary hegemony and normativity that cause oppression, the recent development of critical gender studies and queer theory is a logical corollary as it challenges binary gender categories as such.[43] As these models of deconstruction gradually extend their reach, the next binary to overcome is potentially that between human culture and the planet/the universe.

By applying particularly postcolonial hermeneutics to the study of the *Corpus Paulinum*, Melanie Johnson-DeBaufre and Laura S. Nasrallah problematize the general focus of much of New Testament scholarship on "a heroic Paul and the magnification of his voice as *the* voice of the

---

pretation," *JFSR* 6 (1990): 41–61; bell hooks, "The Oppositional Gaze: Black Female Spectators," in *Feminist Postcolonial Theory: A Reader*, ed. Reina Lewis and Sara Mills (New York: Routledge, 2003), 207–21.

40. Leela Gandhi, *Postcolonial Theory: A Critical Introduction* (New York: Columbia University Press, 1998), 83.

41. Susan B. Abraham, "Critical Perspectives on Postcolonial Theory," in *The Colonized Apostle: Paul through Postcolonial Eyes*, ed. Christopher D. Stanley, Paul in Critical Contexts (Minneapolis: Fortress, 2011), 29; Pui-lan, "Discussion," 102.

42. Fernando Segovia, "Biblical Criticism and Postcolonial Studies: Toward a Postcolonial Optic," in *The Postcolonial Bible*, ed. R. S. Sugirtharajah (Sheffield: Sheffield Academic, 1998), 56–63.

43. Judith Butler, *Gender Trouble: Feminism and the Subversion of Identity*, Thinking Gender (New York: Routledge, 1990); Joseph A. Marchal, "Queer Studies and Critical Masculinity Studies in Feminist Biblical Studies," in *Feminist Biblical Studies in the Twentieth Century: Scholarship and Movement*, ed. Elisabeth Schüssler Fiorenza, BW 9.1 (Atlanta: SBL Press, 2014), 261–80.

Christ-assemblies."[44] On the one hand, they encourage interpreters of these texts to contextualize Paul within the social communities that he addressed and to acknowledge how much the apostle may have owed to them as generative sources of his theology and as foundational resources of his missionary success. In short, reflections on the audience of Paul's letters may be more crucial than those on the author. Data to be mined for this scholarly trajectory have been provided through recent sociological studies of ancient Mediterranean societies and of the city of Rome in particular.[45] Yet this trajectory may, on the other hand, initiate a process of questioning to what degree the widespread image of Paul as a "hero" is sustainable. With reference to Joseph A. Marchal and Elisabeth Schüssler Fiorenza, Johnson-DeBaufre and Nasrallah problematize that "the scholarly production of the singularly anti-imperial Paul births its opposite: a singularly imperial Paul."[46] And regarding his writings: "These epistles—produced, read, and debated by multiple voices and dialogical in their very nature, even if we lack half of the correspondence and all of the oral communications—inscribe a variety of communities that were engaged in negotiating, contesting, and colluding in the context of empire."[47] We will need to explore whether Romans, exposed to such a multifaceted critical program, yields an image of Paul that is chauvinist and/or misogynist or whether it is justified to call him, with Beverly Roberts Gaventa, "Our Mother Saint Paul."[48]

Authorship

This leads us now to the consideration of the authorship of Romans. Knock, knock, who's there? At first glance, the answer seems easy. In

44. Melanie Johnson-DeBaufre and Laura S. Nasrallah, "Beyond the Heroic Paul: Toward a Feminist and Decolonizing Approach to the Letters of Paul," in Stanley, *The Colonized Apostle*, 162 (italics original).

45. See, for instance, the voluminous *ANRW* project and Peter Lampe's detailed study of the assemblies of believers in Christ in Rome; Peter Lampe, *Die stadtrömischen Christen in den ersten beiden Jahrhunderten: Untersuchungen zur Sozialgeschichte*, 2nd ed., WUNT 2/18 (Tübingen: Mohr Siebeck, 1989).

46. Johnson-DeBaufre and Nasrallah, "Beyond," 167.

47. Johnson-DeBaufre and Nasrallah, "Beyond," 168.

48. See two publications with almost identical main titles: Beverly Roberts Gaventa, "Our Mother St. Paul: Toward the Recovery of a Neglected Theme," in *A Feminist Companion to Paul*, ed. Amy-Jill Levine with Marianne Blickenstaff, FCNTECW 6 (London: T&T International, 2004), 85–97; Beverly Roberts Gaventa, *Our Mother Saint Paul* (Louisville: Westminster John Knox, 2007).

antiquity, it was standard praxis for the author of a letter to mention his or her name right at the start. This is also the case with Romans, where Paul presents himself as the only sender (Rom 1:1). This is different from, for example, the introduction of 1 Thessalonians where "Paul, Silvanus, and Timothy" are collectively mentioned as senders (1:1). Sometimes Paul also introduces coworkers who accompanied him, for example, "our brother Sosthenes" in 1 Corinthians 1:1 or "Timothy our brother" in 2 Corinthians 1:1. In the latter, his collaborators and partners are also mentioned in the body of the letter: "the Son of God, Jesus Christ, whom we proclaimed among you, Silvanus and Timothy and I" (2 Cor 1:19). Paul likewise mentions Barnabas and Titus in Galatians 2:1, 9. Such a host of names around Paul correlates with grammatical aspects manifest, for example, in 2 Corinthians 1:13: "For we write you nothing other than what you can read and also understand." Here as in 1:19, the plural of the verbs indicates an authorial collective (it is no so-called literary plural for Paul himself). In fact, "we"-sections are frequent in other letters such as 1 Thessalonians.[49] Paul was clearly not a lone rider.

By contrast, the opening lines of Romans mention only Paul and confirm him as the author. Modern scholarship does not question the authenticity of this information. The information in Romans 1:1 may, however, support modern, romantic conceptions that envision authorship as the activity of an individualistic genius working in creative solitude. Traditional Christian art has often depicted the apostle to the Gentiles as a letter writer, pondering all by himself how to articulate complex christological concepts while holding a pen in hand. But even if Romans 1:1 mentions only Paul as the author, this does not mean that he was alone when writing it. According to another standard in antiquity, further assistants could be mentioned at the end of a letter. And the concluding chapter of Romans indeed mentions Timothy, Lucius, Jason, and Sosipater as Paul's coworkers (Rom 16:21). It then features the following sentence: "I Tertius, writing this letter in the Lord, greet you" (v. 22).[50] The phrase allows limited, but interesting insights into the historical circumstances of how Romans was written as it indicates that Paul apparently dictated the letter to a scribe. This was by no means unusual but was common practice in antiquity. We know that Cicero dictated more

49. Samuel Byrskog, "Co-Senders, Co-Authors and Paul's Use of the First Person Plural," *ZNW* 87 (1996): 230–50; Bernhard Oestreich, *Performanzkritik der Paulusbriefe*, WUNT 296 (Tübingen: Mohr Siebeck, 2012), 100.

50. This translation, which differs from that of NRSVue, will be discussed in more detail below in the comments on Romans 16:22.

letters than he wrote in his own hand (Cicero, *Ad Att.* 2.23.1; 10.3a.1). In antiquity, however, scribes usually remained invisible.[51] Therefore, the names of secretaries or scribes are not to be found in any other New Testament letter. Yet in the case of Romans we learn that a certain person by the name of Tertius was involved in the process of producing the letter. In other letters of Paul, occasional remarks that he is writing the final greeting with his own hand (1 Cor 16:21; Gal 6:11; Phlm 19) amount to the same; they imply that the remainder of the letter was actually penned by somebody else. There, however, the names of the scribal assistants are never mentioned. The sentence in Romans 16:22 remains the exception, which makes it remarkable despite its brevity.

What would have been specific aspects of the task of Tertius as Paul's scribe?[52] In antiquity, both literacy and the ability to write were the purview of few. Hence, secretaries who had learned the skill of a scribe assisted with the production of private and public correspondence. Whether or not such a scribe was a skilled worker who was being paid for the job or an enslaved person is a matter of conjecture for modern interpreters. Paul was clearly not illiterate, however. Already his education "at the feet" of the great Rabban Gamaliel (Acts 22:3) prevents such an assumption (if this information is deemed historically reliable).[53] The occasional notes in his own handwriting further confirm his literacy, but this does not mean that he would have been able to take down a letter the size of Romans. In addition, there was the problem that, in most provinces of the Roman Empire, several local dialects were spoken while the official language was Greek or Latin. Hence, literacy in one's native language or dialect was not the same as literacy in the official languages. In Paul's situation, the former education under Gamaliel happened in Aramaic and with Hebrew Scriptures. Writing letters in Greek may have been an additional challenge.

51. Sometimes, scribes added their name with a note that their services had been requested because the sender was illiterate; cf. Hans-Josef Klauck, *Die antike Briefliteratur und das Neue Testament: Ein Lehr- und Arbeitsbuch*, UTB 2022 (Paderborn: Schöningh, 1998), 62–63.

52. On further details about the identity of Tertius, see comments below on the subscriptions of Romans (p. lvii) and on Romans 16:22 (pp. 359–360).

53. There is some discussion regarding the reliability of this tradition of Acts, which has been called into question by some (Linda M. Maloney, *Acts of the Apostles*, WCS 45 [Collegeville, MN: Liturgical Press, 2022], 301–2) and confirmed by others (Michael Wolter, *Paulus: Ein Grundriss seiner Theologie*, 3rd ed. [Neukirchen-Vluyn: Neukirchener Verlag, 2021], 12–13).

Yet at a more basic level, already the provision of the materials to take down the text would have required an assistant. These tools were not generally available as they are in our modern societies saturated with print media and characterized by mass production of goods. The technicality of their actual production would have been part of the work of a scribe. As Jerome Murphy-O'Connor suggests, Tertius "would not have used pen and papyrus . . . , but a metal stylus and a wax tablet,"[54] or most likely several of the latter. Then, at the moment of dictation, scribes had to make themselves available. The time required to dictate/write such a long letter would have been about one week.[55] There were generally three different modes of dictation: *syllabatim* dictation ("syllable by syllable"), dictation recorded in shorthand by the secretary (to be completed later), or rough ideas given to the secretary to formulate at a later time.[56]

The assistance of a scribal secretary comprising these various tasks was thus common in antiquity. Other roles for participation in the creative process of writing are also known. Just a few years after Paul, Josephus worked with literary assistants "to improve his Greek style" when producing his *Jewish War*.[57] But more than that, it was customary to orally recite literary works during the stage of their production to solicit feedback and creative input from listeners before final versions were released. This was also the case with the books of Josephus, and given the sheer length of his literature, such a "recital phase" must have stretched for a considerable amount of time and required a lot of commitment or interest from the audience.[58] In sum, scribes rendered services out of technical necessity and assisted with editorial tasks. Their contributions

54. Jerome Murphy-O'Connor, "Review of *Paul and First-Century Letter Writing: Secretaries, Composition and Collection* by E. Randolph Richards," *RB* 112 (2005): 628–33, at 630.

55. Jerome Murphy-O'Connor estimates that the dictation of First Corinthians (6,831 words in Greek), which is slightly shorter than Romans (7,126 words), would have taken this long (Murphy-O'Connor, "Review," 630).

56. Gordon J. Bahr, "The Subscriptions in the Pauline Letters," *JBL* 87 (1968): 27–41, at 27; Christoph Heilig, *Paulus als Erzähler? Eine narratologische Perspektive auf die Paulusbriefe*, BZNW 237 (Berlin: de Gruyter, 2020), 154.

57. Kenneth Atkinson, *A History of the Hasmonean State: Josephus and Beyond*, Jewish and Christian Texts in Contexts and Related Studies 23 (New York: Bloomsbury, 2016), 16.

58. Steve Mason, *Josephus, Judea, and Christian Origins: Methods and Categories* (Peabody, MA: Hendrickson, 2009), 7–15, 45–46; Adrian Goldsworthy, *Caesar: Life of a Colossus* (New Haven: Yale University Press, 2006), 186–90.

have been described as recorders/transcribers, contributors, and composers.[59] Other preliminary audiences provided feedback to improve literary works. In light of this, it is not surprising that "the writer and his regular secretary frequently had a personal relationship despite their divergent social classes."[60]

One should pause here for a moment to acknowledge such important aspects of the communal nature of producing literature. Today, we must concede that almost all of the names of secretarial assistants, scribes, and patient listeners have perished from the collective memory without a trace. Such reflections on the process of producing literature in antiquity put into new perspective the fact that Paul mentions, and thus relates for posterity, the names of some of his companions who assisted him. Therefore, we still know Silvanus, Timothy, or Sosthenes, furthermore the scribe Tertius (Rom 16:22), then Paul's host Gaius (16:23), and Phoebe who carried his letter to Rome (16:1-2).[61] All things considered, therefore, "corporate authorship, inclusive of the co-workers, has a priority over individual authorship."[62]

At this point, the roles of Gaius and Phoebe deserve attention. Paul wrote the letter to Rome in Corinth, where he enjoyed the support of these two people. Gaius had an influential position in the Corinthian congregations (Rom 16:23). It is likely that Paul could stay at his house free of charge or for only modest pay. Phoebe is presented as a "benefactor" (Rom 16:2) to Paul and many others. Paul profited in some undisclosed manner from her patronage; it may be conjectured that she paid for the services of the scribal secretary Tertius. Yet another service needs to be mentioned as well. The recommendation that Paul includes on her behalf (16:1-2) is proof that she is the person who actually visited Rome. As will be mentioned below, these lines imply that she was designated to carry the letter to its recipients. This important aspect is also confirmed in the

59. E. Randolph Richards, *The Secretary in the Letters of Paul*, WUNT 2/42 (Tübingen: Mohr Siebeck, 1991), 23–53.

60. Richards, *The Secretary*, 63.

61. A comprehensive list of the names of Paul's coworkers is compiled in Esther Kobel, *Paulus als interkultureller Vermittler: Eine Studie zur kulturellen Positionierung des Apostels der Völker*, Studies in Cultural Contexts of the Bible 1 (Paderborn: Brill; Schöningh, 2019), 125–27.

62. Johannes A. Loubser, "Media Criticism and the Myth of Paul, the Creative Genius, and His Forgotten Co-workers," *Neot* 34 (2000): 329–45, at 330. See also Beverly Roberts Gaventa, *When in Romans: An Invitation to Linger with the Gospel According to Paul* (Grand Rapids: Baker Academic, 2016), 13.

subscriptions found in several biblical manuscripts of Romans. They add at the end of the letter any one of the six following lines:

A. "To the Romans";[63]

B. "To the Romans, written from Corinth";[64]

C. "Letter of the holy Paul to the Romans, written through Phoebe, minister [ἐγράφη διὰ Φοίβης διακόνου]";[65]

D. "Letter to the Romans, written through Phoebe, minister";[66]

E. "Letter to the Romans, written through Phoebe, minister of the church at Cenchreae";[67]

F. "Letter to the Romans, written through Tertius [ἐγράφη διὰ Τερτίου], but sent by Phoebe, minister [ἐπεμφθη δὲ διὰ Φοίβης διακόνου]."[68]

Most of these different versions of the subscription convey the active role Phoebe had for many important aspects of Romans. The first subscription (A) just serves the purpose of separating the text body of this letter from the next when they were collected into a Scripture canon, yet it does not add any further information. By contrast, all other subscription lines (B–F) add interesting aspects about the historical situation of its production and delivery, thus also honoring the two people who were particularly involved in its creation. In this regard, the note that the letter was "written through Phoebe, minister" is striking as it appears to be in contradiction to Romans 16:22 where Tertius self-identifies as the scribe of the letter. This remark can possibly be understood, however, as envisioning something other than the more technical aspect of recording/transcribing the dictation.

63. Attested in mss א (fourth century CE), A (fifth century CE), B (fourth century CE), C (fifth century CE), D (fifth century CE).

64. Mss B[1] (fourth century CE), D[2] (fifth century CE), P (ninth century CE).

65. Ms L (ninth century CE). On the translation of διάκονος as "minister," see below, pp. 321–322.

66. *Koinē* text-tradition.

67. Ms 424 (twelfth/thirteenth century CE).

68. Ms 337. See also Fitzmyer, *Romans*, 755. The different versions of subscriptions were included in older Nestle-Aland editions of the Greek New Testament text and in Jacobus Wettstein, *Novum Testamentum Graecum*, 2 vols. (Graz: Akademische Druck- und Verlagsanstalt, 1962) but have been omitted from the Nestle-Aland, twenty-eighth edition.

Paul affirms his authorship of Romans in the first sentence, and no modern scholar doubts the correctness of this statement. What is more, in the canonical order of New Testament books, the Epistle to the Romans follows the Acts of the Apostles, the narrative of which concludes with the travels of Paul, now accompanied by Roman soldiers to guard him, from the island of Malta to Rome (Acts 28:1-16). There he is said to have met local people and stayed for two years to preach the gospel (28:23-31). The canonical sequence thus not only provides a connection between Acts and Romans through the location of Rome but also invites the readers of the New Testament to envisage Paul in the capital of the Roman Empire. Yet—knock, knock, who's *really* there? The person who indeed traveled to the assemblies in Rome to deliver the letter was Phoebe. She would have recited the letter aloud in front of the recipients, provided further information, and preached the gospel to the believers in Christ.[69] Paul was, of course, fully aware of all of that and trusted her. In that sense, Phoebe may be considered Paul's "avatar."[70]

In consideration of this aspect, it is likely that Paul, during his extended stay in Corinth, discussed the letter's content with Phoebe in advance. He would have integrated arguments from *her* perspective, which explains a number of arguments in the letter from a female vantage point (Rom 7:1-6; 8:22-23; for more details, see below).[71] Thus, while Phoebe was not necessarily implicated in the more technical work of recording the text, she may have been active as a significant contributor to the letter. In addition, one may wonder about the origins of some of the diatribes in it. While the following remains speculative, it is possible that these dialogical sections go, at least in part, back to a discussion between Paul, the Jewish Christ believer, and Phoebe, the gentile Christ believer. For example, Paul's sudden change in attitude concerning who is to blame for human sin and ungodliness may have been due to a successful intervention of Phoebe

69. Elsa Tamez, "Der Brief an die Gemeinde in Rom: Eine feministische Lektüre," in *Kompendium feministische Bibelauslegung*, ed. Luise Schottroff and Marie-Theres Wacker, 2nd ed. (Gütersloh: Kaiser; Gütersloher Verlagshaus, 1999), 559.

70. Derived from Sanskrit, the term "avatar" refers to the phenomenon of embodiment or appearance. Vedic literature relates embodiments of deities like Indra or Vishnu on earth. About Phoebe as "avatar," see also below on Romans 16:1-2.

71. Beverly Roberts Gaventa, "Romans," in *Women's Bible Commentary*, ed. Carol A. Newsom, Sharon H. Ringe, and Jacqueline E. Lapsley, 3rd ed. (Louisville: Westminster John Knox, 2012), 555; Reta Halteman Finger, "Getting Along When We Don't Agree: Using Simulation and Controversy to Help Students and Lay Persons Interpret Romans," in McGinn, *Celebrating Romans*, 235.

who called the apostle out on his chauvinistic attitudes. Previously, Paul had put the blame for human sin and ungodliness on Eve (2 Cor 11:3), but in Romans, he assigns it to Adam (Rom 5:12-14). In the end, the consideration of corporate authorship means that it is not certain which passage in Romans was actually Paul's and which was that of Phoebe (or other coworkers in Paul's entourage, or his host Gaius). Whereas some passages evince a female vantage point, the entire text may have been the product of the cooperation between Paul and Phoebe (and others in Corinth). It is, therefore, problematic to refer to any given passage in Romans with the simple statement that "Paul wrote . . ." or "Paul says . . . ," as is so often done in much secondary literature and many commentaries, if this is intended as a reference to his sole authorship. Unless a passage has a parallel in a previous letter by Paul that allows a clear attribution to, or alignment with the apostle's former thought, or unless it features a direct reference to his personal identity or past, the modern interpreter should be cautious about reading Romans wholesale as his work. It simply is not, if the historical reality of corporate authorship is taken seriously. Three of the ancient subscription lines with variations of "Letter to the Romans, written through Phoebe, minister" demonstrate that a woman was definitely considered to have been part of the joint venture production of this letter. While recent studies of ancient faith communities advocate decentering Paul, it appears as if this is what Paul himself has done through his cooperation with Phoebe (and others) to share the gospel with those in Rome.

Moreover, it is even conceivable that the verb "written" in the subscription lines of Romans were meant more broadly, including all the above-mentioned steps and aspects of Phoebe's presence in the assemblies in Rome. After all, the ancient culture of the Mediterranean was fundamentally an oral culture. Literature was written in preparation of an anticipated act of oral communication.[72] It is possible, therefore, that the subscription lines refer to Phoebe being the "virtual face" or "avatar" of Paul in Rome. It would then be somewhat equivalent to the commentary on Romans in Florus's *Expositio*, created in 1164 CE, featuring an image of Phoebe in Rome, depicting her speaking to the assembly on behalf of Paul (see above, p. v). Hence, while it is historically no longer accurate to uncritically refer to some passages in Romans with statements such as "Paul wrote . . . ," it is historically uncontested to state that "Phoebe said . . ." or "Phoebe argued . . ." because she was

72. Oestreich, *Performanzkritik*, 249.

the one who presented the letter's content in Rome.[73] This new view of historical realities will be reflected throughout on the pages of this commentary—and sets it apart from much secondary literature written hitherto on the subject matter. Special attention will, therefore, be given to the situation of the letter's performance in correlation to the specific person whom Paul had chosen to carry out the task.

Place of Composition and Date

Paul had been staying in the city of Corinth in Achaia for approximately three months after his second trip through Macedonia (2 Cor 1:12-17; 7:5).[74] It was there that he wrote the letter to the Romans. This is also mentioned in the subscription of the biblical manuscripts B[1] and D[2]. What is known about Corinth? Interestingly, the Roman poet Horace (65–8 BCE) had coined the Latin proverb: "Not everyone is able to go to Corinth" (*Non cuivis homini contingit adire Corinthum, Ep.* 1.17.36).[75] It could not be a reference to geographic remoteness; Horace was from the south of Italy, which was relatively close to Corinth, just across the Ionian Sea. Moreover, Corinth was at a distance of less than six hundred miles from Rome. If anything, Corinth was close to Italy. Horace, however, had other aspects in mind. Three special aspects need to be considered.

First, already Homer spoke of the "wealthy Corinthian" (ἀφνειὸς κόρινθος, *Il.* 2.570), and Romans knew the "two sea Corinth" (*corinthus bimaris*, Horace, *Carm.* 1.7.2; Ovid, *Metam.* 407). These ancient references show that Corinth was an important economic center due to its unique topographical location and its two harbors: Lechaion on the Corinthian Gulf or western side of the isthmus and Cenchreae (or Kenchreia) on the Saronic Gulf or eastern side.[76] This second harbor is named after Kenchrias, son of Poseidon and Peirene; a bronze statue of Poseidon was displayed at the harbor.[77] The Greek geographer and historian Strabo

73. See, for example, Sigve K. Tonstad, *The Letter to the Romans: Paul among the Ecologists*, Earth Bible Commentary 7 (Sheffield: Sheffield Phoenix, 2016), 259–60, who presents a portion of Romans 8:31-37 as a responsive dialogue between Phoebe and the "congregation" in Rome.

74. Heinrich Schlier, *Der Römerbrief*, HTKNT 6 (Freiburg: Herder, 1977), 2; Arland J. Hultgren, *Paul's Letter to the Romans: A Commentary* (Grand Rapids: Eerdmans, 2011), 2.

75. Richard Fletcher, "Corinth: I. Archaeology," *EBR* 5 (2012): 769–70, at 770.

76. Joan C. Campbell, *Phoebe: Patron and Emissary*, Paul's Social Network: Brothers and Sisters in Faith (Collegeville, MN: Liturgical Press, 2009), 38.

77. Campbell, *Phoebe*, 43.

(64/63 BCE – ca. 24 CE) stated: "Corinth is called 'wealthy' because of its commerce, since it is situated on the Isthmus and is master of two harbors, of which the one leads straight to Asia, and the other to Italy; and it makes easy the exchange of merchandise from both countries that are so far distant from each other" (*Geogr.* 8).6.20). Corinth was, therefore, close to Italy, but it had been one of the wealthiest and most important cities in Greece. "Not everyone is able to go to Corinth" meant, among other things, that it was too expensive for most people to stay there. This changed in 146 BCE when the city was completely destroyed by the Roman army under Lucius Mummius (Pausanias 7.15.1–16.8).[78] Mostly deserted for more than a century, the city was refounded by Julius Caesar in 44 BCE as *Colonia Laus Iulia Corinthiensis* ("colony of Corinth in honor of Julius"). Before long, it had reclaimed its former status and importance, and when Paul visited the city, it was the capital of the Roman province of Achaia (Acts 18:12-26) as well as the second-largest city in Greece (behind Thessalonica). Even though there were also many who lived at or below poverty level,[79] the apostle probably met many a ἀφνειὸς κόρινθος—which explains why, in 1 Corinthians 1:5, he could not resist the joke that "in every way you have been enriched (ἐν παντὶ ἐπλουτίσθητε) in him [Christ Jesus]."

There were yet two further reasons why "not everyone is able to go to Corinth." Besides notorious wealth and luxury, another characteristic often associated with harbor cities of all times and places did apply here as well, namely, some elevated degree of immorality of its inhabitants specifically with regard to sexuality. The latter was the reason why Corinth actually had a rather undesirable reputation in the ancient Greco-Roman world. This is epitomized by, but not limited to, the temple of Aphrodite, the goddess of love and fertility. This sanctuary was located on the Acrocorinth that towers over the city; its "chief source of income was sacred prostitution, performed by female slaves, many of whom were gifts to the goddess from both men and women."[80] Still in the

78. Cicero would declare in *Agr*. 2.87: "*Corinthi vestigium vix relictum est*" ("There is scarcely a trace of Corinth left").

79. Steven J. Friesen, "Poverty in Pauline Studies: Beyond the So-Called New Consensus," *JSNT* 26 (2004): 323–61; Luise Schottroff, *Der erste Brief an die Gemeinde in Korinth*, ThHK 7 (Stuttgart: Kohlhammer, 2013), 42–43.

80. Peter Cohee, "Temple Slaves in Ancient Greece and Rome," in *Macmillan Encyclopedia of World Slavery*, vol. 2, ed. Paul Finkelman and Joseph C. Miller (New York: Macmillan, 1998), 888.

second century CE, Corinth could, therefore, be referenced as "the city of Aphrodite" (Aelius Aristides, *Orationes* 46.25). Strabo associates Corinth with commercialized pleasures and affirms that they were another source of its financial wealth (*Geogr.* 8.6.20). The Greek verb "to corinthianize" (κορινθιάζεσθαι) came to connote sexual depravities and a promiscuous lifestyle (Aristophanes, *Fragm.* 354); "a Corinthian maid" was a term for a harlot (Plato, *Resp.* 3.404d). It would, however, be historically inaccurate and a belittlement of the matter to assume that sexual depravity was restricted to the private or interpersonal realm. An ancient literary source describes circus games in Corinth where the public rape of an accused woman who was then to be killed by beasts was part of the mass entertainment (Apuleius, *Met.* 10.18-35). The debauchery in circus games drew strong criticism by, for example, Seneca, a contemporary of Paul, who relates his disgust when he accidentally happened to witness such events (Seneca, *ep.* 1.7.2-6).[81] Paul himself was, of course, well aware of problems related to sexual immorality; he mentions them—now without a joke—in his own correspondence to the congregation in Corinth (1 Cor 6:9-11a).

And third, the city was, upon its reestablishment in 44 BCE, settled by freedpersons, which means by former enslaved persons. They even occupied high positions in the city administration. But, as will be shown below, the social stigma of enslavement remained even after manumission; hence, the "sense of insecurity of the successful freedman became a favourite topic in literature."[82] In fact, freedpersons were a general target of mockery and satire.[83] As for Paul, these various aspects were clearly a concern. He could not, however, change the fact that people from this city often had to face prejudices and cope with them when traveling elsewhere. And so, there may have been yet another reason why "not everyone is able to go to Corinth." Due to the peculiar combination of notorious luxury, sexual immorality, and a population of freedpersons, prejudices against people from this city abounded. The citizens of Italy were disciplined and had a matter-of-fact attitude; the proverb of Horace

81. Jerome Murphy-O'Connor, *Paul: His Story* (Oxford: Oxford University Press, 2004), 78–85; Michel Quesnel, *La première épître aux Corinthiens*, Commentaire biblique, Nouveau Testament 7 (Paris: Cerf, 2018), 30–32; Schottroff, *Der erste Brief*, 72–74.

82. Murphy-O'Connor, *Paul*, 87.

83. Benjamin W. Millis, "The Social and Ethnic Origins of the Colonists in Early Roman Corinth," in *Corinth in Context: Comparative Studies on Religion and Society*, ed. Steven J. Friesen, Daniel N. Schowalter, and James C. Walters, NovTSup 134 (Leiden: Brill, 2010), 17–21; Nasrallah, *Archaeology*, 61–62. See also below, p. 62.

conveys in concise and memorable format the reason why an honorable and pious Roman would not and should not go there.

Paul, however, had gone to Corinth—not once, but repeatedly. According to Acts 18:11, his initial stay there in 51–52 CE lasted a year and a half.[84] His interactions with the church at Corinth cover a period of no less than seven years, until his final visit there en route to Jerusalem. At first, he was the church's founder; later he would be its apostolic leader operating from other locations, mainly Ephesus. Thanks to the extended list of concluding greetings in Romans 16, we are well informed about various circumstances of Paul's stay in Corinth. This is how we know that he dictated Romans in the house of Gaius (Rom 16:23) and that his local secretarial scribe was Tertius (16:22). We also know that the letter was to be delivered through Phoebe, the "[minister] of the church at Cenchreae" (16:1; on these details, see above and below). In consideration of these aspects, a comparison of some recurrent themes and phrases of earlier Pauline letters also found in Romans leads to an interesting observation. Scholars have listed many of these recurrent topics and themes but typically not drawn much of a conclusion regarding the circumstances of the composition of Romans.[85] The recurring themes show, however, that Paul's earlier letter to the Galatians and his two letters to the Corinthians were the "treasury" for writing Romans. Themes and phrases from these writings have, more than others, been "recycled" for his newest letter. It is interesting to consider the possibility that these previous ideas of Paul may have left their imprint specifically on the congregations in Corinth. There, Phoebe and the couple Prisca and Aquila would have been among the recipients of Paul's Corinthian correspondence. After listening to these letters in their midst, they—together with the rest of the congregations—would have acted on Paul's advice and implemented at least some of his ideas to address local problems. If these well-known phrases and themes reappear in Romans, this may be seen as Paul's theological handwriting that left its imprint on Corinth.

Paul dictated the letter to the Romans during a winter between 56 and 58 CE. Phoebe was then to deliver it in the subsequent spring when

84. James Wiseman, "Corinth and Rome I: 228 B.C.–A.D. 267," *ANRW* 2.7.1 (1979): 438–548; at 503–5.

85. Cf. Helmut Koester, *Introduction to the New Testament*, vol. 2: *History and Literature of Early Christianity*, Hermeneia (New York: de Gruyter, 1987), 140; Fitzmyer, *Romans*, 71–73. See also Peter Oakes, "Galatians and Romans," in *The New Cambridge Companion to St. Paul*, ed. Bruce W. Longenecker, Cambridge Companions to Religion (Cambridge: Cambridge University Press, 2020), 92–118.

improving weather conditions would allow ship travels.[86] This happened immediately before Paul would depart on his final trip to Jerusalem with the collection of the Gentile churches. At the same time, he mentions his plan to continue his missionary work in Spain afterward (Rom 15:24-28). Hence, Paul announces two upcoming travel plans that would span the entire width of the Mediterranean Sea and extend years into the future. Besides the immediate perils of being shipwrecked during such a long expedition, Paul had already experienced delays with the collection (2 Cor 9:1-5) and knew that relations with the congregations in Jerusalem had not always been most amicable (Rom 15:31; see below). Paul must, therefore, have been preparing for somewhat unpredictable times ahead and a journey that turned out to be not only unsuccessful but personally disastrous. Indeed, the historical fact is that Paul never visited Rome in the way he had anticipated or hoped for. The letter was eventually in the hands of Prisca and Aquila, the couple who had received it in Rome. There were also Phoebe and Tertius who had assisted Paul in the process of its writing for a few months; they were still intimately familiar with its contents. Thus, after Paul's imprisonment, the cities of Corinth and Rome would have been locations in which the theology of Romans would have continued to shape communities through two women and one man who was potentially an enslaved person.

The Style of Romans

The letter to the Romans is artfully crafted according to high standards of rhetoric in antiquity, thus shifting the exegetical focus to the situation of the letter's delivery and the audiences. As stated above, this situation was anticipated as a visit of Phoebe to the assemblies in Rome. The letter was supposed to leave an impression; the goal was to persuade. At the same time, some of the features also facilitated and critically enhanced the oral presentation by Phoebe.[87]

86. A scholarly consensus has been established that Romans was produced during winter months; cf. Murphy-O'Connor, *Paul*, 197–99; Wolter, *Römer*, 1:30. Regarding the date of composition, cf. Klauck, *Briefliteratur*, 228 (56–57); Jewett, *Romans*, 18–23 (57 CE); Oda Wischmeyer, "The Letter to the Romans," in *Paul: Life, Setting, Work, Letters*, ed. Oda Wischmeyer, trans. Helen S. Heron (London: T&T Clark, 2012), 245, 261 ("56"); Gaventa, "Romans," 549 ("sometime between 55 and 57 CE"). A helpful summary of pertinent scholarship is presented in Wolter, *Römer*, 1:30.

87. Josef Martin, *Antike Rhetorik: Technik und Methode* (Munich: Beck, 1974), 97–119; Jewett, *Romans*, 23–46.

Invention (Latin *inventio*; Greek εὕρεσις) is the term for the means of persuasion that are appropriate in particular rhetorical situations, such as the *exordium* (prologue) to introduce a speech or letter, the main narrative that provides the background of the case, the argumentation with various kinds of proof, and the *peroration* (epilogue). To persuade the audiences, Paul and Phoebe incorporated credal formulas (Rom 1:3-4; 4:24) that were well known among members with traditional Jewish roots. They also used common arguments about the oneness of God (3:30) and divine justification as the creative force to establish a human community (12:5) that were likely borrowed from the Stoic philosopher Lucius Annaeus Seneca ("the Younger," ca. 4 BCE–65 CE) to appeal to the gentiles in the audiences. Paul and Phoebe integrated, moreover, a variety of liturgical elements such as hymns, benedictions, and doxologies. They similarly modeled homiletic benedictions after wishes and blessings in the Septuagint; they may have been informed by Prisca and Aquila that these liturgical elements had been in use in Rome. These materials would, therefore, have resonated with diverse groups of the local audiences.

Already the opening lines of the letter announce that the gospel is affirmed "in the holy scriptures" (ἐν γραφαῖς ἁγίαις, Rom 1:2). Romans indeed features a lot of Scripture quotations with certain preferences among these books; most quotations are from Isaiah, the Psalms, Genesis, and Deuteronomy. Beyond the sheer number of such quotations, it is also remarkable that Romans strings together some of these citations in extended scriptural catenae (Rom 3:10-18; 9:25-29; 15:9-12). This is all the more interesting as Paul barely used Scripture quotations in 1 Thessalonians, his first letter authored several years earlier, and prefers quotations from the Torah in Galatians. These quotations show, first, that Paul had read and studied these Scriptures. That is certainly the result of his education as a Pharisee. Second, the text of these quotations shows that he refers to and cites the Septuagint, the Greek version of the sacred Jewish Scriptures.[88] While his studies in Jerusalem were probably focused on the text of the Hebrew Bible, Paul had taken in some of the

88. The Jewish diaspora in particular was aware of many different versions of its sacred Scriptures, some of which were produced by and in use in its own synagogue congregations. An interesting question is, therefore, what kind of Scripture canon Paul might have had available, even if we focus only on those in Hebrew and Greek. Neither of these canons had the shape of the modern editions of the Hebrew Bible/Old Testament or the Septuagint. This complex question cannot, however, be discussed here (for further study, see, e.g., Reinhart Ceulemans, "The Septuagint and Other Translations," in *The Oxford Handbook of Early Christian Biblical Interpretation*, ed. Paul M. Blowers and Peter W. Martens, 33–54 [Oxford: Oxford University Press,

theology of the Septuagint that was characteristic of the Jewish diaspora community of Lower Egypt, where much of the translation project had been accomplished.[89] Yet, either way, Paul was a person who had trust in the Jewish Scriptures and posited their continuous theological relevance.

Romans also features different artificial proofs as stylistic forms to present arguments in a convincing and accessible manner, such as the diatribe (from Greek διατριβή). Developed by ancient teachers such as Teles, Dio of Prusa, and Maximus of Tyre in the Cynic and Stoic schools of philosophy, the diatribe was a literary tool for the instruction of particular students or audiences. The classroom was the typical location of this rhetorical form. Its main characteristic was a dialogical form of argumentation in the shape of a lively debate, thus featuring a familiar conversational style with an interlocutor instead of long-winded theoretical discourse. It was, therefore, peppered with rhetorical questions and fictitious speeches, punctured with short exclamations ("By no means!" [Rom 3:4, 6, 31; 6:2, 15, etc.]), and featured apostrophes, proverbs and maxims, paradoxes, parodies, antitheses, and parallel phrases. Everything that made an argumentation accessible and entertaining for an audience was acceptable.[90] In a way, sentences and phrases occurring in a diatribe resemble a Q&A format today or even text messaging in social media.

Owing to his thorough education in Jewish traditions, it is not surprising that Paul was a master of midrash (מדרש), which consists of a main text that is explained and interpreted for the present situation by secondary texts. Such a main text may be a Scripture quotation. Romans at times also combines midrashim with elements of the diatribe (e.g., Rom 4:1-25; 9:19-29).[91] It contains, moreover, examples (Latin *exemplum*;

2019]). Suffice it to say that the translation project of the Septuagint lasted from ca. 250 BCE until 100 CE, thus in the days of Paul it was not yet completed.

89. This Greek Septuagint was the "Bible" of Jewish believers in Christ in the Greco-Roman world. It should be stressed, however, that the text of the Septuagint may vary significantly from the Hebrew text. It is usually no accurate word-by-word rendering from Hebrew. Some relevant differences between the MT and the Septuagint will occasionally be discussed in this commentary (e.g., Deut 32:43; Isa 1:9; 8:14; 53:10; Ps 69:23-24 [MT]/68:23-24 [= ET 69:22-23]). Modern Bible editions are, however, based on the MT, hence the English translation presented in the NRSVue (or in the NRSV or NIV, etc.) will frequently differ from the English rendering of the Septuagint.

90. Changwon Song, *Reading Romans as a Diatribe*, StBibLit 59 (New York: Lang, 2004), 15–53.

91. Gary G. Porton, "Defining Midrash," in *The Study of Ancient Israel: 1. Mishnah, Midrash, Siddur*, ed. Jacob Neusner (New York: KTAV, 1981), 55–92; Günter Mayer, "Midrasch/Midraschim," *TRE* 22 (1992): 734–44.

Greek παράδειγμα) to illustrate certain arguments; these work through contents or images that are basic enough to be widely understood and easily accessible. Such is the case with the image of groaning in labor pains (8:22-23) or the encouragement to behave in an altruistic fashion (15:2-3). An example can be extended to an elaborate segment called speech-in-character (Latin *confirmatio*; Greek προσωποποιΐα). For that, a character is being created that acts out an argument in her or his own voice. A speech-in-character, therefore, helps to render complex or abstract arguments accessible by illustrating or personalizing them (7:7-25; 11:17-21). Its more developed form is the syllogism (Latin *ratiocinatio*; Greek συλλογισμός); it presents an entire logical argument with a major premise, some minor premises, and a conclusion (e.g., Rom 7:1-6).[92]

Romans sometimes features a shorter syllogism that remains incomplete considering the structure of its logical premises. An artificial proof of this type is called an *enthymeme* (Greek ἐνθύμημα). Technically, it is also a formal argument in which a major premise is supported by a minor premise and followed by a conclusion (Rom 6:5-7). A final type of artificial proof is the *a minore ad maius* inference (Hebrew קל וחמר, "light and heavy"). Belonging to the category of enthymeme, it proposes a minor argument that is generally accepted by the audience and then proceeds to posit that a similar argument at a larger scale must also be true. Occasionally, it is also deployed in the reverse direction: if the greater argument is understood to be acceptable, how much more so is the lesser? The *a minore ad maius* inference is characteristic for rabbinic and Greco-Roman rhetoric; Paul and Phoebe must, therefore, have been certain that it had a wide appeal in the assemblies of Rome. Thus, it is not surprising that it is used repeatedly (5:9, 10, 15, 17; 11:12, 15, 24).[93]

While these rhetorical tools all served to construct artificial proofs and bolster an argumentation, Romans also evinces a variety of stylistic features aimed at enhancing the aesthetic experience during the act of "reading," or rather of the performance in front of the intended audiences in Rome. At the same time and no less important, these tools helped the person who recited the letter aloud to memorize it. Paul and Phoebe would have consciously employed them as mnemotechnical devices. They can be detected at the level of word sequences and sentences and in the organization of entire paragraphs but also in the repeated sound

92. Jewett, *Romans*, 28. See also below.

93. Jörg Frey, "Paulus als Pharisäer und Antiochener: Biographische Grundlagen seiner Schriftrezeption," in *Von Jesus zur neutestamentlichen Theologie: Kleine Schriften II*, ed. Benjamin Schliesser, WUNT 368 (Tübingen: Mohr Siebeck, 2016), 329–30.

of single letters and syllables, such as the -ια endings in πάσῃ ἀδικίᾳ πονηρίᾳ πλεονεξίᾳ κακίᾳ (Rom 1:29) or the repetition of initial syllables and additional assonance in ἀσυνέτους ἀσυνθέτους ἀστόργους ἀνελεήμονας (1:31)—these two examples are taken from a single sentence! The problem for Bible translators and interpreters of all times, however, is that these latter features are notorious to literally "get lost in translation." Naturally, their aesthetic appeal and creative sophistication can only be appreciated in the original Greek text of Romans.[94]

All of these stylistic features evince the level of skill that had been applied in the process of composing and writing this letter. Hence, they are a lasting testimony to the rhetorical capacities of Paul, the author; of Tertius, the scribe who spent about one week with him to produce the first draft version of the letter on a wax tablet and then penned the first clean copies on vellum or parchment; and of Phoebe, "[minister] of the church at Cenchreae" and benefactor of Paul who assisted him during his months in Corinth and who would have relied on this rich spectrum of rhetorical features to memorize and then recite (or "perform") the letter upon her arrival at the assemblies in Rome.

Finally, the specific combination of the rather poetic style of this letter (or any other letter or text for that matter) and the public performance of a text that has been committed to memory needs to be taken into account. Poetry in particular was written for oral performance, and "it is a truism that oral performance is inescapably the self-presentation of a performer."[95] This truism applies to a somewhat lesser degree to Romans as it is a letter that contains no poetry. But it nevertheless applies because Romans was to be delivered in the style of oral performance (see above). The performer of Paul's choice, Phoebe, could and would have presented passages and arguments of Romans—perhaps some more than others—as her own. Therefore, rather than treating the performer as a medium for the text, one should treat the text as a medium for the performer.[96] To the audiences in Rome, Phoebe was the person on the ground who conveyed and, in a way, embodied the theology of Romans.

94. See the detailed list of rhetorical features in Jewett, *Romans*, 30–39.

95. Eva Stehle, *Performance and Gender in Ancient Greece: Nondramatic Poetry in Its Setting* (Princeton: Princeton University Press, 1997), 7.

96. Stehle, *Performance and Gender*, 8.

The Recipients/Audience of Romans

Conforming to ancient epistolary standards, Romans mentions the recipients in its opening section: "To all God's beloved in Rome" (Rom 1:7). Who were these recipients? As it turns out, a lot of data from textual and other material sources can be gathered to reconstruct their communities. They allow deeper insights for the task of a feminist interpretation of Romans, which benefits from a close examination of the social, cultural, and religious matrix of Mediterranean antiquity.

In the first century CE, the ancient societies of the Mediterranean world witnessed an impressive development of urban centers. The largest and most important cities were located in its East: Alexandria (Egypt), Corinth (Greece), and Antioch on the Orontes (Syria). Rome was the only important city on the Western half of the Mediterranean, but as the capital of the Roman Empire, it exceeded even Alexandria. Rome was, in a way, a microcosm of the larger Roman Empire.

Roman society was a multifaceted organism that had gradually developed over centuries and existed for more than a millennium. For much of this time, and certainly during the first century CE, it was characterized by a number of factors, among them its household/patronage structure, honor-shame system, and imperial (emperor) cult.[97] Of importance for the interpretation of Romans are also the housing situation in the capital and the position of women within the society.

The Housing Situation in Rome

The housing situation in the city of Rome is an important factor for understanding the living situations of the Jewish community in the city. It allows historically warranted insights into the spaces where the first assemblies of believers in Christ would have met, as separate church buildings for worship gatherings did not exist yet. Romans 16:3-5 features greetings to Prisca and Aquila and "the church in their house," suggesting that private households, perhaps with adjacent shop spaces, were the nucleus of early church assemblies and the "basic cells" of the believers in Christ. Familiarizing ourselves with the outline and architecture of a Roman house means, therefore, getting to know the space that Prisca and Aquila would have rented or acquired upon their return

97. See the sidebar paragraphs in chapter 1.

to Rome. After all, some customs were different between the Greek and Roman cultures; for instance, men invited to a dinner in Rome were allowed to be accompanied by their wives, men in Greece were not, and Roman women did not have to veil their heads. Thus, Greco-Roman culture was not monolithic. What did the houses in Rome look like, where was the space for men and women, and what does this mean for worship practices in these houses?

Typical for urban origins, Rome gradually grew at a location where a ford made it possible to cross the river Tiber. The city developed mostly on the right side of this river. In the middle of the first century CE, Rome boasted 1,100,000 inhabitants and was one of the leading cultural centers of the Mediterranean world. It was the city par excellence.[98] It was located somewhat at the center of Italy, which made it an ideal capital for the expanding state, and only about twenty kilometers (thirteen miles) from the coast of the Mediterranean Sea, thus allowing for easy commerce.

But with its size came associated problems. Due to the lack of proper city planning and sanitary equipment, trouble related to overpopulation affected many inhabitants. In the cities to which Paul traveled and where he stayed, people lived in small shanties, rented rooms, two-room apartments above shops, peristyled houses (*domus*), or elaborate villas.[99] In Rome, the nobility, the leadership, and the wealthy citizens, whether from traditional patrician family clans or the *nouveaux riches,* resided on the hills of the city—like the Palatine—and owned houses adorned with marble and columns.

Yet, the majority of the inhabitants of Rome lived in the upper levels of multistory tenement houses or in the rear of shops. Tenement houses were usually located in the lower areas of the city and occupied the space of an *insula*. The problem with such locations was that, during summer months, it was difficult to cope with the heat. Shops of small traders, artisans, and business folk were on the ground floor toward the street front. Behind and immediately above them were several spacious *cenacula* apartments for those who belonged to the small middle class. Yet, the upper levels of these tenement houses contained tiny rooms, only about ten square meters (less than 110 square feet) in size, many without windows (nor were there latrines or running water). An entire family

98. Christoff Neumeister, "Urban Culture in Ancient Rome," *Anthropological Journal on European Cultures* 2 (1993): 21–37, at 22.

99. Margaret Y. MacDonald, "Paul and Family Life," in Sampley, *Paul in the Greco-Roman World: A Handbook*, 1:255.

might have occupied such a quarter. "Vertical zoning" was, therefore, typical in Rome and in the ancient world. Most inhabitants knew living conditions that would be classified today as "overcrowding,"[100] with all the adverse consequences for personal health, safety, and so-called family values. It is in these kinds of domestic spaces and in such living situations that inhabitants of Rome believing in Christ would have met.

Nevertheless, Rome had its perks even for people from the middle and low classes. The male population spent most of the day in the houses of patrons and in public areas, equipped not only with public parks, squares, entertainment facilities such as the circus, and colonnades (*porticus*) but also with baths and public toilets.[101] Across the Mediterranean world, some Roman houses and other facilities such as baths built in the first centuries CE are still in use today.

From the perspective of intersectionality and postcolonialism, further information should be provided on the living quarters of women and those at the bottom of the social hierarchy due to poverty, ethnic origin, and/or their status as enslaved persons.[102] In fact, the housing situation was not only different for the rich and the poor or for men and women but also for those in Italy and those in other provinces like Greece. Only a few of the main aspects of this broad topic can be investigated here.

In the Etruscan period, men and women had been considered equal.[103] But that was the distant past. Their role and status had changed by the time of the early principate, with men occupying the place of pride. Women were subordinate to the *paterfamilias*, much like children, friends, employed servants, or enslaved persons. Thus remarks Gillian Clark: "A social system which restricted women to domestic life, and prevailing attitudes which assumed their inferiority, must seem to us oppressive. I know of no evidence that it seemed so at the time."[104] The fact that such restrictions were not necessarily regarded as oppressive back then may have had to do with the status of the *materfamilias* or *matrona* (that

100. Robert Jewett provides a helpful modern analogy by describing the population density as "almost two-and-a-half times higher than modern Calcutta and three times higher than Manhattan Island" (Jewett, *Romans*, 54).

101. David G. Horrell, "Domestic Space and Christian Meetings at Corinth: Imagining New Contexts and the Buildings East of the Theatre," *NTS* 50 (2004): 349–69.

102. Peter Oakes, "Constructing Poverty Scales for Graeco-Roman Society: A Response to Steven Friesen's 'Poverty in Pauline Studies,'" *JSNT* 26 (2004): 367–71.

103. Gilda Bartoloni, *La Cultura Villanoviana: All'inizio della storia etrusca* (Rome: Carocci Editore, 2002).

104. Gillian Clark, "Roman Women," *GR* 28 (1981): 193–212, at 209.

could, however, not be attained by all women). It was still relatively elevated in comparison to many others in the social hierarchy and also in comparison to, for example, neighboring cultures such as Greece or Palestine. The social status stipulated a specific set of behaviors for women who were more or less restricted to the private house (exceptions had usually to do with benefaction).[105]

Roman public and residential architecture showed some degree of equivalency between women and men. Bedrooms were located with no special division between women's and men's quarters. The kitchen was customarily the specific workspace of women, but also of—most likely female—servants and enslaved persons. In larger apartment and tenement buildings, shops at the street front were typically the space of male household members where they would have exercised their respective professions as artisans, small traders, and businesspeople. It is most likely in a shop like this in Corinth that Paul had encountered Prisca and Aquila. The narrative in Acts 18:2-3, however, suggests that both Prisca and Aquila were "tentmakers" and, thus, artisans. The New Testament occasionally mentions professions of women (e.g., Lydia, the "dealer in purple cloth," Acts 16:14); Roman legislation permitted it. The exact address of the shop or residence of Prisca and Aquila is no longer known. The sizes of their different houses, both in Corinth and later in Rome, are the subject of scholarly speculation. If they lived in apartments connected to their shop, perhaps even with an upstairs room, then it would have been possible to fit in approximately fifty people. Alternatively, it is possible that they owned a house, even if quite modest, equipped with a second section for general entertaining.[106] Whatever the historical truth, however, it was clear that circumstances did not allow for social distancing during worship meetings.

These early communities met as eucharistic groups. A shared meal was, thus, at the center of the event. At this point, it is important to highlight a difference between Greek and Roman domestic culture regarding dinner etiquette. Ancient literary sources evince that, among the Greeks, the exclusion of women from invitations to dinners was customary; among the Romans, however, women could join men without any

105. Zeba Crook, "Honor, Shame, and Social Status Revisited," *JBL* 128 (2009): 591–611.

106. Wendy Cotter, "Women's Authority Roles in Paul's Churches: Countercultural or Conventional?," *NovT* 36 (1994): 350–72, at 360.

shadow of indecency.[107] In the Circus Maximus in Rome, neither fixed seats nor any separation of men and women existed for a long time, permitting both genders to "enjoy" the shows together. The Isis cult was also on the rise in this city, allowing women to participate in various prominent roles. Moving from Rome to Corinth and ultimately back to Rome, Prisca and Aquila had to deal with and adjust to these cultural differences. Yet in Rome the encounter of women and men clearly might have been considered less problematic than in Corinth.

Meals have, in most human cultures, been points of establishing or maintaining social connections. In ancient Greece, a house community ate together; a visiting foreigner was first led to the hearth, the center of the house, to participate in a meal. This custom is institutionalized in the symposium, a lavish convivial banquet. The social standing and reputation of people or families broadly depended on who invited them to symposia. Given the importance of meals in ancient Mediterranean cultures, it is natural that women played a powerful role in the household. And it would only have been natural for them to assume important functions—including leadership positions—within the earliest house assemblies of Christ believers.[108]

Women in Rome

For a study that is committed to intersectionality, both the situation of women as such and that of enslaved persons in Rome and the Roman world deserve attention. The exploration in the preceding paragraphs has already been partially gendered to highlight customs and realities specific to women in the Roman world. A few aspects among them shall now be extrapolated or added for a more comprehensive picture.

Roman culture was a patriarchy/kyriarchy organized and structured through the patronage system, which the imperial cult in turn elevated to the status of an official state religion. Many of the grand narratives of Rome such as Caesar's *De Bello Gallico* or Augustus's *Res Gestae* were

107. Dacre Balsdon, "Der Alltag der Frau im antiken Rom," *AW* 10 (1979): 40–56, at 52.

108. For gendered studies on domestic architecture in the city of Rome and in the ancient Greco-Roman culture, see Neumeister, "Urban Culture," 27–31; Karen Torjesen, "The Early Controversies over Female Leadership," *Christian History* 17 (1988): 20–24; Richard S. Ascough, "What Kind of World Did Paul's Communities Live In?," in Longenecker, *The New Cambridge Companion to St. Paul*, 48–66.

not objective historiography but androcentric propaganda literature commissioned for the goal of relating *his*-stories to acquire honor in the competitive public court of reputation. Women were, at best, second in rank; there are by far fewer sources about them. Despite their androcentric perspectives, some information can be extracted from these texts as well as from additional legal documents and inscriptions.

A certain degree of variety existed relative to the roles and positions that women could and did assume between different countries and cultures. As Richard S. Ascough explains: "Women and children would have shared the social rank of their male guardian, usually either their father or their husband. That said, some of the rights accorded to those of particular ranks . . . would not have been extended to women."[109] Yet, an upper-class woman, such as a senator's wife, had a higher social status than a man of a lower rank.

Special rules and expectations governed the lives of women. For them, "shame" was positive and desirable. Their pertinent social norms were modesty, obedience, and piety, which had ramifications for their functions and roles in the house and regarding sexuality. The honorific title *materfamilias* refers to this context. Therefore, women would mainly stay in private spaces and associate with other women (Suetonius, *Aug.* 64.2, 73).[110] Rome also laid claim on women's reproductive capacities. The *lex Iulia de maritandis ordinibus* (18 BCE) and the *lex Papia Poppaea* (9 CE) had the goal of increasing the populace by encouraging marriage and bearing children. For that purpose, certain privileges were granted depending on the number of children a woman had (freeborn women: three children; freedwomen: four children). In rare gestures of female disagreement with the patriarchal bent of the Roman justice system, some women would choose the self-declaration to be prostitutes as a gesture of protest against restrictions imposed on "respectable" women by the Augustan law on adultery.[111]

The few occasions women had to leave the house were limited to going to a public bath, visiting temples, and joining their husbands at

109. Ascough, "What Kind of World," 52.

110. MacDonald, "Paul and Family Life," 259; David A. deSilva, "Paul, Honor, and Shame," in Sampley, *Paul in the Greco-Roman World: A Handbook*, 2:32–33.

111. Pilar Pavón, "La femme: Objet et sujet de la justice romaine," in *The Impact of Justice on the Roman Empire: Proceedings of the Thirteenth Workshop of the International Network Impact of Empire (Gent, June 21–24, 2017)*, ed. Olivier Hekster and Koenraad Verboven, Impact of Empire 34 (Leiden; Boston: Brill, 2019), 196–211.

banquets. The accompaniment of male relatives was generally required to leave the house. Women's fashion was modest and barely changed over several centuries. Bright colors were to be avoided as they would indicate prostitutes. It was, however, not rare for women to color their hair blond.[112]

Women were dependent on men. It was the *paterfamilias* who had the power of *patria potestas* that granted him the responsibility for the conduct, finances, and legal matters of his sons and daughters. Formerly extensive rights of women in terms of legal succession were gradually being restricted. In general, the parents arranged marriages for male and female children according to economic and social interests; the status of the future spouse was a key factor, and the expansion of family networks and upward mobility were important objectives. In the mid-50s of the first century CE when Romans was written, the difficult and ambiguous situation of women in the Roman Empire is somewhat epitomized in the fate of Julia Agrippina (15–59 CE, also known as Agrippina the Younger), sister of Emperor Caligula and mother of Nero. Agrippina was one of the most influential women in the Roman Empire at the time. She had not only been made a priestess of the imperial cult of the deified Claudius but also tried to be involved in ruling the empire through participation in senate meetings and some of her son's diplomatic meetings. If a woman could not rule officially, she at least attempted to do so vicariously through her influence on Nero. Yet, the young emperor was having affairs with Claudia Acte, an enslaved girl, and then with Poppaea Sabina, eventually Nero's second wife whom Agrippina opposed as she feared to lose control over her son. As the conflict escalated, Nero resorted to having both Britannicus, his foster brother whom his mother may have considered as replacement, and ultimately Agrippina herself murdered (Tacitus, *Ann.* 14.1-8).[113] These examples show that there was no real position of direct or immediate authority for women in the Roman Empire, neither in politics nor in society.

Few exceptions existed for ordinary women to leave this relatively restricted context of household and spousal duties to attain independence. Benefaction, for instance, was something women and men could engage in. Both could acquire honor for their support toward others outside of the

112. Balsdon, "Alltag," 42.

113. Helmut Koester, *Introduction to the New Testament*, vol. 1: *History, Culture, and Religion of the Hellenistic Age*, Hermeneia (New York: de Gruyter, 1987), 311–14; Richard A. Bauman, *Women and Politics in Ancient Rome* (London: Routledge, 1992), 190–203.

household, whether individuals or associations; recipients would reciprocate by publicly honoring the donors for their benevolence. Real independence did not exist for a woman; only the death of her husband combined with age could set her free. "A widow *sui iuris*, managing her own affairs with only token reference to her guardian and her agnates (or free from *tutela* altogether if she had borne enough children), and old enough (that is, fifty) to escape the obligation to remarry and have more children, was Rome's nearest approach to a legally independent woman."[114]

A last area of the social life of women in the Roman world to be explored is that of prostitution. Brothels (*lupanaria*) existed in all cities where prostitutes (*meretrices, scorta*) offered their services; alternatively, prostitutes could also have lived with a procuress (*lena*) or pimp (*leno*). Freedwomen (*libertinae*), former enslaved females working as *hetaerae* typically had an education, could sing or were knowledgeable in literature, but were more expensive. Christoff Neumeister remarks: "Their avarice is a leitmotiv in Roman love poetry."[115] Nevertheless, prostitution gave women a role outside of the nuclear family and, therefore, constituted an implicit threat to the patronage system. Female prostitutes were in peril of being branded "without reputation" (*infames*), a legal stigma attached to anyone considered not trustworthy within the expectations and definitions of the all-pervasive culture of patronage and its concomitant honor and shame attribution.[116] Women in the patriarchy of ancient Rome were, thus, easily victimized.

This exploration of two important aspects of the ancient Roman world is essential to our understanding of the letter to the Romans. Jewish believers in Christ in Rome lived amid the local Jewish communities that had been established there for at least a few centuries. Evidence for their presence is a note in 1 Maccabees 8:1-32 that a delegation led by Judas Maccabeus paid a visit to the Roman Senate in 161 BCE. They are mentioned in a few ancient sources by Cicero, Philo, and Josephus. The earliest of these dates to 59 BCE; in *Pro Flacco* 66, Cicero defends a *praetor* in a court case by polemicizing against the local Jewish population. Cicero mentions the size of the Jewish community, its unity, and its influence in popular assemblies. One century later, Philo was an eyewitness of the

114. Clark, "Roman Women," 206.

115. Neumeister, "Urban Culture," 27.

116. Rebecca Flemming, "*Quae Corpore Quaestum Facit*: The Sexual Economy of Female Prostitution in the Roman Empire," *JRS* 89 (1999): 38–61, at 43–44.

living conditions of Jews in Rome just before the time of Nero. In 39/40 CE, a delegation from the synagogues in Alexandria came to visit the city and was allowed to meet with the Roman emperor Caligula. Philo of Alexandria (20/13 BCE–ca. 45 CE) was a member of this delegation. He writes about the experience in his opus *Legatio ad Gaium*; there, his praise of Augustus includes a comment that the emperor knew of the historical origins of the Jewish presence in the capital (*Legat.* 155):

> How then did he look upon the great division of Rome which is on the other side of the river Tiber, which he was well aware was occupied and inhabited by the Jews? And they were mostly Roman citizens, having been emancipated; for, having been brought as captives into Italy, they were manumitted by those who had bought them for slaves.[117]

The urban district "on the other side of the river Tiber" is a reference to the ward of Trastevere. It is clear that Philo is well aware of the fact that the Jewish presence in Rome originated to some degree in the arrival of prisoners of war after the conquest of Palestine by Pompey in 63 BCE. Philo also explains that the Jews lived according to their customs and gathered on sabbaths in synagogues—he uses the term προσευχή—to be educated in the philosophy of their forefathers (*Legat.* 156). Today, the existence of fourteen synagogue congregations in Rome has been confirmed.[118] Roman law allowed Jews to organize as associations called *collegiae*; thus, they enjoyed the protection of the state. These associations also had integrative functions that bridged social barriers.[119] Hence, Rome had a growing Jewish diaspora community. While their number is estimated to have been between twenty thousand and sixty thousand for the middle of the first century CE, they had become the largest Jewish community outside of Palestine by the third century.[120]

117. ET according to Charles Duke Yonge, *The Works of Philo: Complete and Unabridged*, 3rd ed. (Peabody, MA: Hendrickson, 1995), all *ad loc.*; with moderate emendations.

118. Lampe, *Die stadtrömischen Christen*, 367–68; see also Harry J. Leon, *The Jews of Ancient Rome*, Morris Loeb (Philadelphia: Jewish Publication Society, 1960/5721), 135–66.

119. Peter Richardson, *Building Jewish in the Roman East*, JSJSup 92 (Waco, TX: Baylor University Press, 2004), 113–15; John S. Kloppenborg, "Associations, Christ Groups, and Their Place in the *Polis*," *ZNW* 108 (2017): 1–56, at 18.

120. Erich S. Gruen, *Diaspora: Jews amidst Greeks and Romans* (Cambridge, MA: Harvard University Press, 2002), 15.

What were the residential districts of Jews in the urban area of Rome? Since the first century BC, the traditional Jewish quarter has been Trastevere (i.e., the fourteenth Augustan region on the western bank of the Tiber where the important Jewish Monteverde cemetery is still located today). Furthermore, Jews settled in the areas between Porta Collina and Porta Esquilina and at Porta Capena.[121]

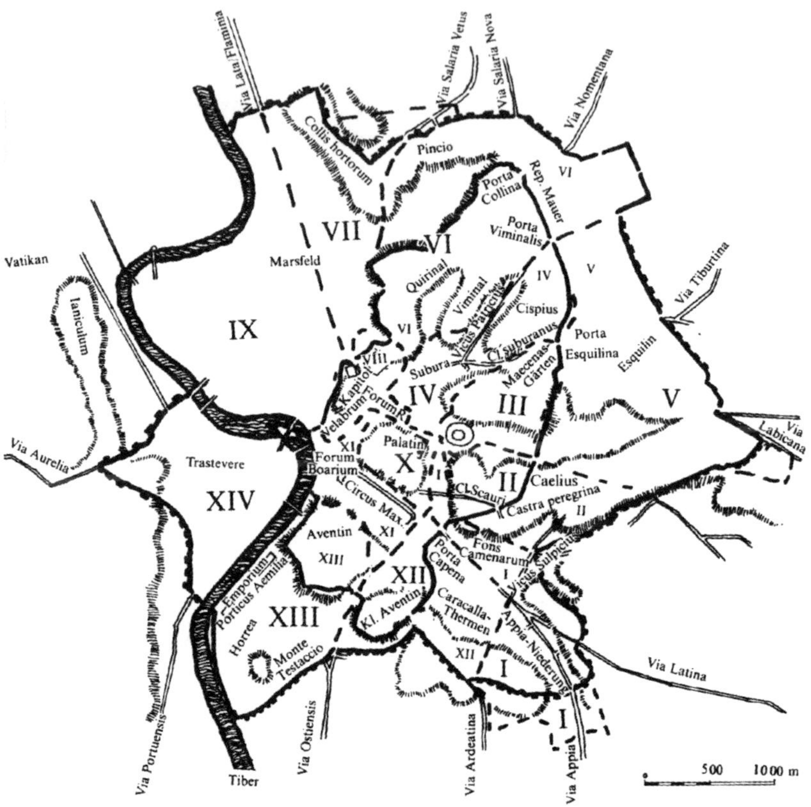

Map of the Ancient City of Rome. From Lampe, *Die stadtrömischen Christen*, Abb. 2 (Appendix). Roman numerals indicate the fourteen Augustan regions. Reproduced by permission of Mohr Siebeck, Tübingen.

All of these districts on either side of the Tiber were humid lowlands; residents lived in unhealthy conditions. These quarters were home to

121. Lampe, *Die stadtrömischen Christen*, 28.

the bottom social stratum of the city of Rome. Considering that a substantial portion of the Jewish population there was comprised of freedpeople, such insights are not surprising. In Trastevere, people inhabited overcrowded apartment buildings. They worked primarily at the port of the Tiber and the associated large warehouses to unload and carry ship cargo, to perform base manual labor, and as knackers and tanners. Already in antiquity, the notorious foul smell hanging over this district was mentioned with disgust.[122]

The situation of Jews in ancient Rome and, thus, also of the early Jewish synagogue communities was subject to change. One reality was the general support of the Jews by Augustus, as Philo mentioned; likewise, Josephus writes about respect and positive treatment under Julius Caesar (*Ant.* 14.185-216). The other reality, however, was that of rejection and exclusion, which led even to a ban on practicing religion. The Roman historiographer Suetonius, for instance, reports that Emperor Tiberius, whose principate (14–37 CE) immediately followed that of Augustus, issued regulations in 19 CE:

> He prohibited foreign religions, the Egyptian and Jewish cults, by forcing the adherents of such superstitions to burn the cult garments and all kinds of utensils. . . . He banished the other members of this people or those who pursued similar things from Rome. (*Tib.* 36)

This order was soon to be followed by direct expulsion, which was partly due to internal unrest. Years before, the Jewish community was known for its unity (*concordia*, see above). Yet, Emperor Claudius (principate: 41–54 CE) soon forbade their community meetings when implementing a conservative policy regarding foreign cults. And in 49 CE, he issued an edict requiring Jews to leave Rome due to internal disturbances over a certain "Chrestos" (*Claud.* 25.4; for further details, see below, pp. 338–339). This episode in the synagogue communities of Rome is both evidence of the existence of the faith in Jesus Christ in Rome and the gradual diversification within the Jewish mother community.[123] Some of those who were forced to leave were Prisca and Aquila. Romans, however, contains greetings to them (Rom 16:3-5), which means that, in ca. 56–58 CE, they had already returned to Rome and "set up camp" anew. The letter is addressed to the entire community of believers in Christ as "all God's beloved in Rome" (1:7). It mentions no synagogue assemblies, which may be seen in connection with the withdrawal of these groups from the established

122. Leon, *Jews*, 136–37.
123. Nasrallah, *Archaeology*, 188.

Jewish diaspora communities. This withdrawal, however, makes the groups of those who believed in Jesus no less Jewish than, for example, the sectarians who had settled in Qumran on the shores of the Dead Sea due to their opposition to the Second Temple authorities in Jerusalem. This group believed, after all, in a Jewish messiah. Judaism came to include, in the spectrum of its diverse customs and beliefs, another faction.

Just like the other Jews in Rome, these Jewish believers in Christ lived in the densely populated areas of Trastevere and the district around Porta Capena. This implies that the majority of its members also had a low socioeconomic status and typically inhabited upper levels of multistory tenement houses or the rears of shops. Thus, overcrowding was a persistent problem, the sanitary situation was bad, and privacy was impossible. They were harbor workers, knackers, tanners, and so forth, like the rest of the workforce in this ward and the other members of the Jewish community. Over the decades, their situation improved gradually until they reached higher social classes toward the end of the first century CE.[124]

What can be concluded about their meeting space for religious celebrations and worship around the time period when Paul dictated the letter? On the one hand, there were groups that enjoyed the patronage of upper- or middle-class members and gathered in their somewhat larger houses. On the other hand, groups consisting exclusively of the urban underclass, particularly enslaved people and poor freedmen and freedwomen, needed to meet in their crowded tenement apartments.[125] Among the twenty-six names in the list of greetings at the end of Romans, a large percentage indicates people who had once been enslaved.[126] Due to the secular orientation and parameters of these groups, it is likely that they met also in semiprivate settings such as shops, workshops, studios, and taverns, probably including marketplaces and watersides.[127] The latter would have allowed for assemblies of larger groups. It is important to mention, however, that typical assemblies were, nevertheless, relatively small, with some groups comprising perhaps forty to fifty members,

124. Kloppenborg, "Associations," 3–4.

125. Jewett, *Romans*, 64–66; Valeriy A. Alikin, *The Earliest History of the Christian Gathering: Origin, Development and Content of the Christian Gathering in the First to Third Centuries*, VCSup 102 (Leiden: Brill, 2010), 57.

126. Lampe, *Die stadtrömischen Christen*, 136–53.

127. Peter Oakes, *Reading Romans in Pompeii: Paul's Letter at Ground Level* (Minneapolis: Fortress; London: SPCK, 2009), 69–71; Edward Adams, *The Earliest Christian Meeting Places: Almost Exclusively Houses?*, LNTS 450 (London: T&T Clark, 2013).

other groups even fewer. "Thus, when we imagine an audience gathered to hear a reading of one of Paul's letters, there were not likely to be more than a small circle of extended family, friends, and acquaintances, the latter perhaps forged through network connections and, particularly, occupational or religious associations."[128] Compared to the traditional synagogue assemblies with their organizational structures and hierarchical positions, these small groups lacked all of that.

Finally, one other aspect needs to be considered: the ethnic origin and identity of members. The assemblies that are addressed in the letter to the Romans were not homogenous. Instead, the letter repeatedly mentions "Jews and Greeks," referring to those who were traditionally Jewish and those who were "gentiles" (Rom 3:9, see also 1:14, 16; 2:9-10, etc.). This ethnic diversity needs to be historically correlated with the expulsion under Claudius in 49 CE, which left the assemblies of Christ believers in Rome overwhelmingly gentile. In the period between the edict and the death of Claudius in 54 CE, gentile believers developed their own ways of worship and its manifestation in daily practice. When Jewish members returned to Rome after 54, among them Prisca and Aquila, it is obvious that the group of gentile members outnumbered that with traditional Jewish origins. For that and other reasons, problems developed.

> Conflict followed as Jewish Christians expected to resume leadership within the Christian community, while Gentile Christians saw no reason to yield to their returning sisters and brothers. According to this scenario, Paul's letter addresses a group of Christians whose conflict runs along ethnic lines (although some Jews may well have identified themselves with Gentile points of view and vice versa).[129]

Such internal tensions in the assemblies of Rome constituted a particular challenge. The letter stresses the christological topic of reconciliation because of this specific situation. Furthermore, what Phoebe recited was heard by the entire community, not just by those for whom a certain argument was intended. The "performance" of a letter "will have different meanings and impacts to different people in the same audience."[130] The purpose is, at the level of the performance of the letter, to achieve a resolution and reunion between the quarreling parties. Paul, together

128. Ascough, "What Kind of World," 57.

129. Gaventa, "Romans," 549.

130. David Rhoads, "Performance Criticism: An Emerging Methodology in Second Testament Studies," *BTB* 36 (2006): 118–33, 164–84, at 129.

with Phoebe, "wants each to overhear his communication to the other. The group letter is an ideal vehicle for encouraging reconciliation."[131] This is especially true if one reflects on the social function and consequence of the act of reading out a letter in front of an audience in antiquity. It was not just to educate others about religious traditions or history or even about the gospel as such, although listening to sixteen chapters of Romans must have been an edifying and informative event. It was specifically geared toward Phoebe's performative speech act by which the new social reality of the radically democratic *ekklēsia* of wo/men was constituted as the result of the gospel of Jesus Christ. "The resulting status-change is unlike anything that other political cosmopolitanisms have on offer."[132]

In line with this assessment, I assume that Romans was written to facilitate the reintegration of Jewish Christ believers into the assemblies in Rome. Yet, I combine this particular concern with another important one, namely, the fact that many Jewish Christ believers did not return from anywhere, but especially from the city of Corinth. As mentioned above, this city with its two harbors had, after its recent destruction, developed again into a thriving city of the *nouveaux riches*. In the process, it had either acquired or retained a particularly negative reputation. Aware of the problem, Paul had to face prejudices and cope with them when traveling; this would have been a specific problem for any journey to Rome. This is likewise the situation of three people mentioned by name in Romans: Phoebe (Rom 16:1-2) and the couple Prisca and Aquila (16:3-5) who were dear to him. In this commentary volume, I assume that Paul needed not just to promote his own theology, arguably in connection with his subsequent plans to engage in missionary activities to Spain. As the letter came *from Corinth*, Paul and Phoebe, the resident of that city, also needed to overcome potential prejudices among those gentiles who had not been targeted and affected by the edict of Claudius and, therefore, remained in Rome. Paul did so also on behalf of himself as he anticipated traveling to Rome within the foreseeable future and staying there for a while to establish his new support base.

131. Donald H. Liebert, "The 'Apostolic Form of Writing': Group Letters Before and After 1 Corinthians," in *The Corinthian Correspondence*, ed. Reimund Bieringer, BETL 125 (Leuven: University Press, 1996), 435.

132. James M. Scott, "Cosmopolitanism in Gal 3:28 and the Divine Performative Speech-Act of Paul's Gospel," *ZNW* 112 (2021): 180–200, at 199.

Remarks on Nomenclature

It has been customary to speak about "Judaism" or "early Judaism" and "Christians" or "early Christians" in studies of the life and literature of Paul as well as of other New Testament texts of the first century CE. This is, however, at least partially anachronistic.[133] In this commentary volume, I will be guided by the observation that the earliest occurrence of the term "Christians" is found in Acts 11:26, a book written by the author of the Gospel according to Luke, suggesting that this term was used first in the city of Antioch. The scholarly consensus is that Acts was written late in the first century CE, approximately between 80 and 90 (or even later).[134] Paul himself never deploys the term "Christian" in any of his letters. He therefore does not distinguish terminologically between "Jews" and "Christians." The edict of the Roman emperor Claudius issued in 49 CE does not distinguish between "Jews" and "Christians" either; instead, both groups are considered as "Jews." As the scholarly trend known as the "New Perspective on Paul" has shown, the so-called parting of the ways between Jews and Christians occurred toward the end of the first century CE or even later.[135] The authentic letters of Paul, however, were written decades before this time. Paul was a Jew. He considers himself an "Israelite" (Rom 11:1; see also Phil 3:5) and was educated as a Pharisee (Phil 3:5). He later adopted a calling as "an apostle to the gentiles" (Rom 11:13; see also Gal 1:15-16; Rom 1:5), not as a "Christian."

To denote or describe the specific faith perspective of Paul and those around him, I prefer to be guided by the terminology featured in Romans. Already at its outset, the letter contains a first succinct summary of the gospel message, which is "to bring about the obedience of faith among all the gentiles for the sake of his name, including you who are called to belong to Jesus Christ" (Rom 1:5-6). This concise statement focuses on

133. Caroline Johnson Hodge, *If Sons, Then Heirs: A Study of Kinship and Ethnicity in the Letters of Paul* (Oxford: Oxford University Press, 2007), 4.

134. Margaret Aymer, "Acts of the Apostles," in Newsom, Ringe, and Lapsley, *Women's Bible Commentary*, 537. See also Linda M. Maloney, *Acts of the Apostles*, WCS 45 (Collegeville, MN: Liturgical Press, 2022), lxvi.

135. For James Dunn, the "parting of the ways" between Judaism and Christianity happened only after the Bar Kokhba Revolt of 132–135 CE; cf. James D. G. Dunn, *The Partings of the Ways: Between Christianity and Judaism and their Significance for the Character of Christianity* (London: SCM Press, 1991). See also Robyn F. Walsh, *The Origins of Early Christian Literature: Contextualizing the New Testament within Greco-Roman Literary Culture* (Cambridge: Cambridge University Press, 2021), 31.

"faith" in connection with the importance of the "name" of Jesus, who is recognized as the Jewish Messiah. The assemblies are founded on the self-understanding of being "called to belong" to this Jewish Messiah, who is referred to by the Greek translation of his title, "Christ." In a similar way, Paul presents his own ministry—and that of Prisca and Aquila—as work "in Christ Jesus" (16:3); by contrast, he warns Phoebe's audiences of those who "do not serve our Lord Christ" (16:18). Hence, "Christ" is the crucial term in all of these references; the genitive of the term or various prepositions ("in," "for") frequently appear in connection with it.[136] That usage is, moreover, not limited to Romans. In Galatians, the most recent letter before Romans, Paul had employed the same terminology. Its origin was an early baptismal formula.[137]

Galatians 3:28	
There is no longer Jew or Greek;	οὐκ ἔνι Ἰουδαῖος οὐδὲ Ἕλλην,
there is no longer slave or free;	οὐκ ἔνι δοῦλος οὐδὲ ἐλεύθερος,
there is no longer male and female,	οὐκ ἔνι ἄρσεν καὶ θῆλυ·
for all of you are one in Christ Jesus.	πάντες γὰρ ὑμεῖς εἷς ἐστε ἐν Χριστῷ Ἰησοῦ.

It is interesting to note that these three binary pairs correspond to those in the daily prayer of thanksgiving according to the Talmud (b. Menaḥ. 43b):

> R. Judah says, "A person must recite three blessings every day: 'Praised are you, O Lord, who has not made me a gentile [גוי].' 'Praised are you, O Lord, who has not made me a slave [עבד].' And 'Praised are you, O Lord, who has not made me a woman [אשה].' "[138]

A similar tradition also exists in the Greco-Roman culture. Socrates supposedly said that he was grateful to the deity Fortuna for three blessings: "that, first, I was born a human [ἄνθρωπος] and not an animal, second, a man and not a woman [ὅτι ἀνὴρ καὶ οὐ γυνή], third, a Greek

136. Jens Herzer, *Petrus oder Paulus? Studien über das Verhältnis des Ersten Petrusbriefes zur paulinischen Tradition*, WUNT 103 (Tübingen: Mohr Siebeck, 1998), 90–99.

137. Sheila Briggs, "Galatians," in Schüssler Fiorenza, *Searching the Scriptures*, 2:218; Adela Yarbro Collins, "No Longer 'Male and Female' (Gal 3:28): Ethics and an Early Christian Baptismal Formula," *Journal of Ethics in Antiquity and Christianity* 1 (2019): 27–39.

138. Scott, "Cosmopolitanism," 195.

and not a barbarian [βάρβαρος]" (Diogenes Laertius, *Lives* 1.33).[139] Both of these traditions show a keen awareness of and pride in one's identity, defined along various sets of dialectic criteria, particularly gender and ethnicity/religion. The self is thus glorified. This happens at the expense of, and in fact directly leads to the creation of the "others" who the self is "not," thus shaming and denigrating them. In this way, these traditions celebrate sociopolitical hierarchies, to which patriarchy belongs as well, and sanction them through divine endorsement.

While these three binary pairs are similar to those in Galatians 3:28, the baptismal formula that Paul adopts envisions a different social reality. The participation in Christ is the core of "Paul's ever-generative eschatological framework."[140] It harks back to the priestly creation narrative with its classical sentence: "So God created humans in his image, in the image of God he created them; male and female he created them" (Gen 1:27).[141] This text depicts the creation of humans as "male and female," not hierarchically, but complementarily. The vision adopted in the baptismal formula and manifest also in Romans thus restores an older, egalitarian understanding of gender relations and reintroduces it as a new standard. According to Caroline Johnson Hodge, such an identity "in Christ" is not new or separate but falls within the boundaries of traditional Jewish identity. While it has a cosmopolitan outlook, it also does not erase ethnic differences:

> Paul suggests a radical unity among the different groups who belong to Christ, including Jews and Greeks. . . . In his own group-making project, Paul urges them to coalesce around the category of being "in Christ," which both Jews and gentiles would have understood as a Jewish position. But . . . he does so while insisting that gentiles remain gentiles. Paul is not asking for an ethnic transformation from non-Jew to Jew. Instead, he argues that gentiles adopt Jewish attributes but remain gentiles.[142]

139. Scott, "Cosmopolitanism," 195.

140. Matthew Croasmun, "'Real Participation': The Body of Christ and the Body of Sin in Evolutionary Perspective," in *"In Christ" in Paul: Explorations in Paul's Theology of Union and Participation*, ed. Kevin J. Vanhoozer, Constantine R. Campbell, and Michael J. Thate, WUNT 2/384 (Tübingen: Mohr Siebeck, 2014), 152.

141. Karin B. Neutel, *A Cosmopolitan Ideal: Paul's Declaration "Neither Jew Nor Greek, Neither Slave Nor Free, Nor Male and Female" in the Context of First-Century Thought*, LNTS 513 (London: T&T Clark, 2015), 187.

142. Caroline Johnson Hodge, "The Question of Identity: Gentiles as Gentiles—but also Not—in Pauline Communities," in *Paul within Judaism: Restoring the First-Century Context of the Apostle*, ed. Mark D. Nanos and Magnus Zetterholm, 153–73 (Minneapolis: Fortress, 2015), 172.

Whether or not the relationship between these ethnic identities is correctly described as hierarchical has been debated; Love L. Sechrest notes that such an interpretation would only invert "the old scourge of theological imperialism, rather than rooting it out."[143] Conceptually, however, the idea of a union "in Christ" forms the basics of an essentially "participationist," "personal," "relational," or "mystical" theology and Christology.[144]

Therefore, I will refer to Phoebe's audiences in Rome and the communities in Corinth and elsewhere as "Jewish believers in Christ" or, for short, as "Jewish Christ believers"; I call the topic itself "faith in Christ."[145] With such a messianic focus, these assemblies are part of the diverse matrix of Judaism during the middle of the first century CE. These groups may have been composed of members from both traditional Jewish and gentile backgrounds.

In light of this, we need to scrutinize the appropriate nomenclature for Paul's traditional religion. In Romans, Paul himself uses the Greek term Ἰουδαῖος repeatedly. Elsewhere, he calls his own religion Ἰουδαϊσμός (Gal 1:13-14). The NRSVue, NIV, and NKJV customarily render these terms as "Jew" and "Judaism," respectively.[146] Paul conceptualized Jewishness vis-à-vis "Greek" (Ἕλλην, Ἕλληνες) identity (Rom 1:16; 2:9-10, 17, 28-29; 3:1-2, 9, 29, etc.), sometimes also vis-à-vis "gentiles" (ἔθνος, Rom 9:24), but never in contrast to a Christian identity. Moreover, the appropriate meaning of "gentile" (ἔθνος) is itself subject to debate and has changed over time. Derived from the Latin noun *gens* ("clan, tribe"), the noun "gentile" usually means "nation" in ancient literature. In its modern

143. Love L. Sechrest, *A Former Jew: Paul and the Dialectics of Race*, LNTS 410 (London: T&T Clark, 2009), 222.

144. Wolfgang Kraus, *Das Volk Gottes: Zur Grundlegung der Ekklesiologie bei Paulus*, WUNT 85 (Tübingen: Mohr Siebeck, 1996), 178–84, 351.

145. It should be noted that the nomenclature in Contributing Voices to this volume has not been altered from their original submissions and may, therefore, reflect different standards.

146. On the question about the meaning and proper translation of the terms Ἰουδαῖος and Ἰουδαϊσμός, see Peter J. Tomson, *Studies on Jews and Christians in the First and Second Centuries*, WUNT 418 (Tübingen: Mohr Siebeck, 2019), 187–206; Daniel Boyarin, "Semantic Differences; or, 'Judaism'/'Christianity,'" in *The Ways That Never Parted: Jews and Christians in Late Antiquity and the Early Middle Ages*, ed. Adam H. Becker and Annette Yoshiko Reed, TSAJ 95 (Tübingen: Mohr Siebeck, 2003), 65–85, at 66–71; Johnson Hodge, *If Sons*, 11–15.

usage, however, it is typically understood as the antithesis of "Jew" or, less frequently, as a synonym for "heathen" or "pagan" (in the sense of "faithless"). The meaning of the term as the antithesis of "Jew" appears to have been established by the Septuagint where ἔθνη is systematically used to reference foreign nations while λαός is the term reserved for Israel. Therefore, ἔθνος may better be translated as "nations." As a term employed to establish a bipolar worldview that leads to "othering," its deployment sometimes indicates a certain degree of prejudice. Paul, who calls himself the "apostle to the gentiles" (Rom 1:1-5; Gal 1:16; 1 Thess 2:16), is willing to question such mindsets and take his mission to those under the stain of prejudice. As a Jew from Tarsus and a citizen of the Roman Empire, he knew and embodied hybrid identity: "Paul's multiple identities as Jew, believer in Christ, and apostle to the Gentiles coexisted, but were amplified and muted according to his audience. Emphasizing one does not mean jettisoning the other."[147] Such a multifaceted identity allowed him to be familiar with the attitudes of a typical Roman citizen who was generally disdainful of Jews. The goal was to overcome such prejudices and unite the factions in the audiences of Rome.[148]

In the end, Paul is a Jew. His religion is Second Temple Judaism. His reflections and comments on Judaism or on being a Jew are, therefore, rather emic (i.e., from *within* the social group) than etic (from *outside* the social group or from the *external* perspective of an observer).[149] Paul can at times, however, also distance himself from certain types of descriptions of Jewish identity. In an earlier letter, he wrote: "To the Jews I became as a Jew, in order to gain Jews. To those under the law I became as one under the law (though I myself am not under the law) so that I might gain those under the law" (1 Cor 9:20). There, Paul presents himself as someone who became a Jew and rejects the idea of being "under the law." This passage demonstrates that, from Paul's emic perspective, obedience to the Jewish law is essential for Jewish identity. Yet the latter has, over time, become questionable for him in his later reflections on Jewish identity.

147. Claudia Setzer, "Does Paul Need to Be Saved?," *BibInt* 13 (2005): 289–97, at 291.

148. Georg Bertram, "ἔθνος, ἐθνικός: People and Peoples in the LXX," *TDNT* 2 (1964): 364–69, at 368–69; Ishay Rosen-Zvi and Adi Ophir, "Paul and the Invention of the Gentiles," *JQR* 105 (2015): 1–41.

149. Caroline Johnson Hodge, "Apostle to the Gentiles: Construction of Paul's Identity," *BibInt* 13 (2005): 270–88, at 271.

Structure and Outline of Romans

The structure and outline of Romans are, by and large, not a matter of much scholarly dispute. Practically, all interpreters agree on its major divisions, which is manifest in most commentaries. The few matters of discussion are the extent of the letter opening (until 1:15 or 1:17?) and whether chapter 5 belongs to the section 1:18–4:25 or to 6:1–8:39. In this commentary, I have decided to regard 6:1–8:39 as a distinct literary unit, which appears to be justified in light of specific characteristics that have to do with the person who delivers the letter in Rome.[150]

Structure of Romans

1:1-17 Letter Opening

1:18–15:13 Letter Body: Five Proofs

- 1:18–11:36 *Theological Section*: Paul's Gospel in Four Sections
    - 1:18–3:31 Justification through Faith: No Distinction
    - 4:1–5:21 The Gift of Grace: Including Women
    - 6:1–8:39 Freedom through the Love of Christ
    - 9:1–11:36 The Election of Israel: The Depth of God's Wisdom
- 12:1–15:13 *Parenetic Section*: Living as God's Loving People

15:14–16:27 Letter Closing: About Phoebe and Other Important Women and Men

The letter body (1:18–15:13) contains a lengthy theological section (1:18–11:36) and a relatively shorter parenetic (or ethical) section (12:1–15:13). Other letters of Paul also feature this general structure, and parenetic sections can be identified in, for instance, Galatians 5:13–6:10 and Philippians 4:2-9 (see also 1 Thess 4:1–5:24).

150. See the corresponding comments below (table "Romans 6:1–8:30: Arguments and Imagery Based on Enslavement or the Situation of Women," pp. 213–214).

Romans 1:1-17

Letter Opening

Introduction (1:1-7)

In antiquity, letters were intended to convey authorial presence; they were, in the moment and situation of their recitation, stand-ins for their absent authors.[1] As texts, their purpose was also concise virtue instruction and promotion of cohesion, for example, the establishment of social cohesion ("networking") for greater communal trust (see Rom 16).

From a formal perspective, the letter to the Romans follows Greco-Roman epistolary customs. Its introduction (*exordium*) names the sender ("Paul," Rom 1:1), the recipients ("all God's beloved in Rome"), and conveys wishes (1:7).[2] With these elements, it serves the purpose of

1. Johan Christiaan Beker, *Paul the Apostle: The Triumph of God in Life and Thought* (Philadelphia: Fortress, 1980), 23; Kathy Ehrensperger, *That We May Be Mutually Encouraged: Feminism and the New Perspective in Pauline Studies* (New York: T&T Clark, 2004), 134; Robert L. Foster, "The Justice of the Gentiles: Revisiting the Purpose of Romans," *CBQ* 76 (2014): 684–703, at 688.

2. James D. G. Dunn, "Paul's Epistle to the Romans: An Analysis of Structure and Argument," *ANRW* 2.25.4 (1987): 2842–90, at 2845; Hans-Josef Klauck, *Die antike Briefliteratur und das Neue Testament: Ein Lehr- und Arbeitsbuch*, UTB 2022 (Paderborn: Schöningh, 1998), 36–37; John D. Harvey, *Listening to the Text: Oral Patterning in Paul's Letters*, ETS 1 (Grand Rapids: Baker Academic, 1998), 120–21; Peter Oakes, "Galatians and Romans," in *The New Cambridge Companion to St. Paul*, ed. Bruce W. Longenecker, Cambridge Companions to Religion (Cambridge: Cambridge University Press, 2020), 93–94.

Rom 1:1-7

[1:1]Paul, a servant of Christ Jesus, called to be an apostle, set apart for the gospel of God, [2]which he promised beforehand through his prophets in the holy scriptures, [3]the gospel concerning his Son, who was descended from David according to the flesh [4]and was declared to be Son of God with power according to the spirit of holiness by resurrection from the dead, Jesus Christ our Lord, [5]through whom we have received grace and apostleship to bring about the obedience of faith among all the gentiles for the sake of his name, [6]including you who are called to belong to Jesus Christ,

[7]To all God's beloved in Rome, who are called to be saints:

Grace to you and peace from God our Father and the Lord Jesus Christ.

establishing a relationship between the speaker/writer and the audience. Previous letters of Paul also feature these standard elements (1 Thess 1:1) but show that the introductory sections have been growing over time (1 Cor 1:1-3; 2 Cor 1:1-2; Gal 1:1-5). Romans starts with one complex sentence that extends over no fewer than the first seven verses.[3] Bible translations in various languages, therefore, often break this sentence down into various subsentences (NIV: four sentences; NKJV: two sentences; Revidierte Lutherübersetzung 2017: three sentences). The NRSVue renders it in a single but convoluted sentence.

The first word of Romans is simply "Paul" (Rom 1:1), affirming that he is the author of the letter. Modern scholars do not question the authenticity of that information. But it does not imply that Paul wrote the letter in solitude. On the one hand, a scribe by the name of Tertius was involved in the process of producing the letter (16:22). On the other hand, Phoebe from Cenchreae was designated to carry the letter to the recipients in Rome and recite it there (16:1-2). Despite the fact that she was a gentile woman and perhaps also formerly enslaved, Paul entrusted her with such an important task; she became his "avatar." As the leader of a Corinthian congregation, however, it is likely that she was also actively involved in the process of composing the letter.[4]

In Romans 1:1, the Greek term δοῦλος can be translated as "servant" or "slave/enslaved person." Bible editions tend to favor the former

3. The salutation has, therefore, been called "a grammatical monstrosity" (John C. O'Neill, *Paul's Letter to the Romans*, PNTC [Harmondsworth: Penguin, 1975], 26).

4. On the authorship of Romans, see the section above.

rendering,[5] recent scholarship the latter, which is preferable (see further comments on Rom 6:18, 20 below).[6] The self-introduction as a "slave/enslaved person" is rather shocking as it alludes to, and invokes, images of the lowest stratum of the society in Greco-Roman antiquity. Yet, Paul has used such terminology in his previous letters. To characterize the egalitarian ethos of the communities "in Christ," he writes that "there is no longer slave or free . . . for all of you are one in Christ Jesus" (Gal 3:28). In this statement, he contrasts being a "slave/enslaved person" with being "free" while implicitly hinting at the difference in social status and the exclusion of enslaved people, both of which are overcome in the assemblies of those believing in Christ.[7] Elsewhere, Paul also encouraged enslaved persons to seize the opportunity of manumission (1 Cor 7:20-21).[8] Why is the term "slave/enslaved person" employed in Romans and what does it mean? Two main interpretive options shall be explored.

5. Thus the RSV, NRSV, NRSVue, and NIV. The NKJV has: "bondservant," the NASB 1995: "bond-servant"; see also the Revidierte Lutherübersetzung 2017: "Knecht"; Traduction œcuménique de la Bible: "serviteur"; Reina Valera 1995: "siervo." See, furthermore, Alphonse Maillot, *L'épître aux Romains: Epître de l'œcuménisme et théologie de l'histoire* (Paris: Le Centurion; Geneva: Labor et Fides, 1984), 41–43; Brendan Byrne, *Romans*, SP 6 (Collegeville, MN: Liturgical Press, 1996), 37–38.

6. Robert Jewett, "Romans as an Ambassadorial Letter," *Int* 36 (1982): 5–20; Robert Jewett, *Romans: A Commentary*, Hermeneia (Minneapolis: Fortress, 2007), 95, 100–101; Clarice J. Martin, "Womanist Interpretations of the New Testament: The Quest for Holistic and Inclusive Translation and Interpretation," *JFSR* 6 (1990): 41–61; Elizabeth A. Castelli, "Romans," in *Searching the Scriptures*, vol. 2: *A Feminist Commentary*, ed. Elisabeth Schüssler Fiorenza (New York: Crossroad, 1994), 294; Michael Wolter, *Der Brief an die Römer*, vol. 1: *Röm 1–8*, EKKNT 6/1 (Neukirchen-Vluyn: Neukirchener Verlag; Ostfildern: Patmos, 2014), 75, 79–80.

7. Michael J. Brown, "Paul's Use of ΔΟΥΛΟΣ ΧΡΙΣΤΟΥ ΙΗΣΟΥ in Romans 1:1," *JBL* 120 (2001): 723–37, at 731, 734; Bruce Hansen, *'All of You Are One': The Social Vision of Galatians 3.28, 1 Corinthians 12.13 and Colossians 3.11*, LNTS 409 (London: T&T Clark, 2010), 103–6, 191–96; Esther Kobel, *Paulus als interkultureller Vermittler: Eine Studie zur kulturellen Positionierung des Apostels der Völker*, Studies in Cultural Contexts of the Bible 1 (Paderborn: Brill; Schöningh, 2019), 95.

8. Christian Wolff, *Der erste Brief des Paulus an die Korinther*, 3rd ed., THKNT 7 (Leipzig: Evangelische Verlagsanstalt, 2011), 149–50; Luise Schottroff, *Der erste Brief an die Gemeinde in Korinth*, ThHK 7 (Stuttgart: Kohlhammer, 2013), 135–36; J. Albert Harrill, "Paul and Slavery," in *Paul in the Greco-Roman World: A Handbook*, vol. 2, ed. J. Paul Sampley, 2nd ed. (London: Bloomsbury, 2016), 316; Bernadette J. Brooten, "Slavery," *Encyclopedia of Jewish-Christian Relations Online*, ed. Walter Homolka, Rainer Kampling, Amy-Jill Levine, Christoph Markschies, Peter Schäfer, and Martin Thurner (Berlin: de Gruyter, 2019), https://www.degruyter.com/database/EJCRO/entry/ejcro.12360416/html.

First, it has been suggested that the title "slave/enslaved person" may have been chosen because the recipients of the letter are in Rome, the capital of the Roman Empire. In this city, the title "slave of Caesar" was of special significance; it belonged to influential enslaved people of Caesar's household whose social and economic rank might have been higher than that of most of the free population of the empire.[9] In any case, the semantic profile is dominated by the notion of subjugation and obedience. Enslaved persons do what their masters command; this was especially the case of those enslaved in Caesar's household.[10] Paul, therefore, introduces himself as obedient to "Christ Jesus" and writes on his behalf. Caroline Johnson Hodge suggests, "Voluntarily lowering himself after the model of Christ is a condescension and a display of power that bolsters Paul's status as a teacher."[11] Such an understanding is reinforced through the choice of the terms "obedience of faith" in Romans 1:5 that still occurs in the same introductory sentence as 1:1 and designates the goal of Paul's apostolic work among gentiles. This very sense also emerges from another passage about Paul's ministry; in 15:16, Paul calls himself "a minister of Christ Jesus to the gentiles in the priestly service of the gospel of God." The terms "minister" (λειτουργός) and "[to carry out] priestly service" (ἱερουργέω) are equivalent; ultimately, both convey obedience to God. In his most recent letter before Romans, Paul includes similar ideas when self-referencing as "a slave/enslaved person of Christ" (Gal 1:10).[12] Here, Paul explains that he does not obey, or try to please, other humans; his allegiance is only to Jesus Christ. Thus, the term "slave/enslaved person" is intended to convey the authenticity of his message.

While it is correct that Paul has occasionally used the term "slave/enslaved person" in his previous letters, it should be noticed that he employs the word in a prominent location at the very beginning of Romans. Potential allusions to enslaved people in Caesar's household notwithstanding, the immediate deployment of the term remains shocking due to other distinct aspects of its semantic spectrum. Since Romans 15:16 shows that Paul could also have presented his mission in different,

9. Paul R. C. Weaver, "Social Mobility in the Early Roman Empire: The Evidence of the Imperial Freedmen and Slaves," *Past & Present* 37 (1967): 3–20; Brown, "Paul's Use," 723–37; Kobel, *Paulus als interkultureller Vermittler*, 94–96.

10. Orlando Patterson, *Slavery and Social Death: A Comparative Study* (Cambridge, MA: Harvard University Press, 1982), 300–308.

11. Caroline Johnson Hodge, "Apostle to the Gentiles: Construction of Paul's Identity," *BibInt* 13 (2005): 270–88, at 285.

12. The NRSVue, just like the NRSV and NIV, have "servant" in Gal 1:10. As noted above, this is not the preferable translation of Greek δοῦλος.

specifically more honorable imagery, one should be cautious to limit its meaning as conveying an influential position or powerful state (perhaps because it presents Paul as an envoy of Christ).

Second, therefore, the term "slave/enslaved person" may hint at the fact that Paul saw himself in a rather unenviable social position when dictating his letter. His desperation over the crisis of his missionary endeavors emerges in vivid colors from previous letters, such as 2 Corinthians, where Paul mentions problems experienced in Asia (2 Cor 1:8-11), and Galatians, which shows that he had lost his support base in Antioch. This is the reason why he was now in need of finding a new one; according to some modern interpreters, that was the purpose of writing Romans.[13] Did he achieve that purpose? As he mentions repeatedly throughout Romans, Paul was preparing a journey via Rome to Spain that was not only ultimately unsuccessful but also personally disastrous.[14] Even if, for the moment, he had a generous host and other well-meaning supporters in the city of Corinth where he dictated Romans, Paul was not sure if he could ultimately continue his mission. A more inauspicious setting for Romans could hardly be imagined. Such a personally distressing situation of Paul may be the reason for self-referencing as "slave/enslaved person" in Romans 1. He has, therefore, used this term (or for similar reasons the word "prisoner") in letters written before and after Romans (in the following passages, the translation of "servant/servants" in NRSVue has been corrected).

> Rom 1:1: "Paul, an enslaved person of Christ Jesus"
>
> Gal 1:1: "Paul an apostle—sent neither by human commission nor from human authorities"
> with Gal 1:10: "If I were still pleasing people, I would not be an enslaved person of Christ."
>
> Phil 1:1: "Paul and Timothy, enslaved persons of Christ Jesus"
>
> Phlm 1: "Paul, a prisoner of Christ Jesus, and Timothy our brother"

At the beginning of the letter to Philemon, Paul introduces himself as "a prisoner of Christ Jesus" while Timothy, his coworker, is "our brother." Here the term "prisoner" refers to the precarious predicament of Paul's imprisonment by Roman authorities, but he indicates that he understands it also as part of his mission. Similarly, Elsa Tamez notes on the usage of

13. Foster, "Justice," 684–85.

14. Jerome Murphy-O'Connor, *Paul: His Story* (Oxford: Oxford University Press, 2004), 199.

the term "enslaved persons" in Philippians 1:1: "To be in prison and to be a slave represents a double humiliation in the opinion of free persons."[15]

Fully consistent with these considerations is an additional reflection on the meaning of Paul's name and the fact that there is an alternate form. The book of Acts mentions his Jewish name as "Saul" (Σαούλ, Acts 9:4; 22:7; 26:14).[16] This was, of course, also the name of Israel's first king, Saul (Hebrew: שׁאול, Greek: Σαουλ), who was a member of the tribe of Benjamin just like Paul (Phil 3:5). Three aspects are of interest. First, the name "Paul" was not a result of his "conversion"; according to Acts, it is attested for the first time in 13:9, well after the time of the event on the Damascus road (9:1-22). Both names were used simultaneously and interchangeably ("Saul, also known as Paul," 13:9). Hence, it is more likely that "Paul" is the version of the traditional Jewish name that the apostle, a person with multiple citizenships, used when visiting his Greco-Roman audience and communicating with them thereafter. This cultural change was, therefore, also associated with a change in languages, namely from Hebrew/Aramaic to Greek.[17] In addition, it may be seen as an expression of his personal cosmopolitanism. Second, it should nevertheless be noted that, while "Saul" was the name of a king of Israel, Paul's Greek name, which was literally "*Paulos*" (Παῦλος), means "small, of little significance" in Latin. This denotation aligns well with the metaphor of "slave/ enslaved person" in Romans 1:1 if it is understood as an indication of personal modesty and compassion. And third, in light of the Roman naming practice of *tria nomina* (triple names)—*praenomen*, *nomen gentilicium*, and *cognomen* (see below)—"Paul" is neither the apostle's *praenomen* (first name) nor his *nomen gentilicium* (clan or family name), but his *cognomen*, the name for common usage in the Greco-Roman culture. As such, it was suitable to his various audiences regardless of their ethnicity or status. Insofar as the *nomen gentilicium* was a feature of ascribed honor, however, Paul relinquished a key aspect of honor within the honor-shame system. His name, therefore, already conveys his countercultural vision as a messenger of the gospel of Jesus Christ.[18]

15. Elsa Tamez, Cynthia Briggs Kittredge, Claire Miller Colombo, and Alicia J. Batten, *Philippians, Colossians, and Philemon*, WCS 51 (Collegeville, MN: Liturgical Press, 2016), 38.

16. It may be noted that Paul never mentions this name in his own writings.

17. On multiple citizenships, see below.

18. Giorgio Agamben, *The Time That Remains: A Commentary on the Letter to the Romans*, trans. Patricia Dailey, Meridian: Crossing Aesthetics (Stanford, CA: Stanford University Press, 2005), 9; Richard N. Longenecker, *The Epistle to the Romans: A Commentary on the Greek Text*, NIGTC (Grand Rapids: Eerdmans, 2016), 48–50.

The Slave Metaphor

New Testament texts present slaves as characters in a multitude of literary genres, for example, in the gospels, the letters, or the Acts of the Apostles. Slavery appears as a stock motif in the parables (e.g., Matt 18:23-35; 24:45-51). Early Christian texts mirror the social hierarchy of enslaved and free persons (e.g., Eph 6:6-9; Col 3:22-41). Several texts also employ slavery metaphors as a title: "Slave of Christ/God/the Lord" (e.g., Luke 1:38; Acts 16:17; Rom 1:1; Gal 1:10; Phil 1:1; Col 1:7; Titus 1:1). It may describe the relationship to sin or forces in the world (Gal 4:8-9) or the new relationship to God (Rom 6:15-23; 1 Thess 1:9-10).

Paul's usage of this metaphor has increasingly gained attention in modern research. It has proved to be a major task to find the "origin of Paul's slave metaphor." Conventionally, is it located within a Jewish or a Greco-Roman context—or both? Metaphorical slavery and slavery as a social institution are often treated as two separate themes. From an intersectional perspective, taking real slaves as marginalized and vulnerable people into account, this separation may be challenged.

A metaphor can mean more than one thing for the audience. For those who read or heard Romans, the slave metaphor probably had different associations. "Slave of God" or "slave of Jesus Christ" (see Rom 1:1) could be a title of honor, a way to express faith, loyalty, and belonging. But how was it for slaves or former slaves among the early Christian community, for example, in Rome, that the favorite metaphor describing their relationship to God was the term "slave," which belonged to the vocabulary of the juridical and economic institution in which some human beings owned other human beings? Slaves were owned bodies and property, available for their owners' needs, economically, physically, or sexually. A slave owner could sell, beat, violate, or humiliate a slave without being punished. A female slave could be valuable, since her reproductive capital also belonged to her owner. She could produce offspring, which meant more property for the owner.

In one way or another, the slave metaphor took its meaning from this practice of selling and buying bodies. Perhaps it was difficult for a slave with experiences of abuse and violence and forced labor to think of him- or herself as a slave of God. It might have added to the burden to be a slave not only of an earthly owner but also of God. Alternatively, to think of oneself as the slave of God may have helped to endure slavery: after all, God's love through Christ was at the core of the message as a way of comforting those who had to endure day after day in slavery.

As it were, all believers were slaves of God, but some were more slaves than others. All were potentially slaves of sin or death. To be a slave could both be a concrete status but also describe what power controlled the heart or soul. When reading Romans or other New Testament texts, it is important to pay attention to how slavery works on so many levels. In addition, with a critical intersectional perspective, we need to acknowledge that the slavery metaphor used as a way of describing the relationship to God could be nice and adequate for some while for others it could be problematic and offensive. How was it for a female slave, pregnant after being raped by her owner, to be called a slave of God? She would probably need other metaphors and images in order to describe her faith and belonging.

Marianne Bjelland Kartzow

Marianne Bjelland Kartzow identifies important problems about the usage of metaphors in general and the employment of the metaphor of "slave/enslaved person" in particular. Her contribution addresses the legitimacy of the practice of employing imagery from the realm of enslavement to illustrate or convey spiritual ideas or concepts. Is this imagery acceptable for those who suffer as enslaved people? Moreover, is it a way to critically engage the institution from which the imagery is taken? Can this practice be a tool of liberation, and can the God proclaimed in the context of such imagery be understood as a liberating God for the oppressed? It is true that, despite Paul's self-designation in Romans 1:1, his life in Corinth as a traveling artisan and missionary who found himself under the care of a somewhat wealthy patron had little to do with enslavement. These concerns need to be taken seriously.[19]

A final consideration regarding the term "slave/enslaved person" in Romans 1:1 is that reflections on its appropriateness should not neglect Phoebe. She is the benefactor of Paul who traveled to the assemblies in Rome to personally deliver the letter (16:1-2). And she would have recited the letter aloud to the recipients. It is often assumed, however, that Phoebe was a freedwoman, which means that formerly she was enslaved.[20] In that case, she would have experienced enslavement in her own life and with her own body. The question is how she would have

19. Sheila Briggs, "Can an Enslaved God Liberate? Hermeneutical Reflections on Philippians 2:6-11," *Semeia* 47 (1989): 137–53, at 139.

20. For more information, see comments on Romans 16:1-2 below.

reacted to the term "slave/enslaved person" early on in the letter (and also in later passages). Yet, if she had indeed been involved in consultations over the contents of the letter, and that appears to be plausible, then we should rather assume that she had endorsed the term. For both Paul, who knew enslavement from his context in the Greco-Roman world and from the congregations he founded, and Phoebe, who had perhaps been an enslaved person previously, the term "slave/enslaved person" with its multiple meanings was an appropriate self-introduction.

The next element of his self-introduction, "called to be an apostle," is familiar from Paul's previous letters (1 Cor 1:1; see also the shortened version "apostle": 2 Cor 1:1; Gal 1:1) and revisited later in Romans (11:13: "I am an apostle to the gentiles"; see also 1:5). According to 1 Corinthians 9:1 (and also Acts 1:21-22), a criterion for the title "apostle" is being an eyewitness of Jesus. According to 1 Corinthians 9:2 and 2 Corinthians 12:12, it has to do with the work of patiently establishing faith communities, and in Paul's case, this is specifically the mission to so-called gentiles (Rom 1:5). There have been attempts to deduce from this term that Paul saw himself as an ambassador.[21] But Paul no longer uses this title "apostle" after writing Romans; it is missing not only from the opening of Philippians but from that entire letter. This is an interesting observation. Elsa Tamez attributes the absence of the title to the absence of religious hierarchy; authority is construed to come from below in this letter.[22] I agree with Tamez, but I would add that it is accompanied by, and therefore may also reflect, the crisis that Paul experienced over the loss of his support base in Antioch. As the new base in Rome was not yet established, Paul was now reluctant to employ the term for himself.

The first chapter in Romans is still evidence of Paul's almost desperate attempt to convince those in Rome that he *was* such an apostle. This is corroborated by the simple fact that his self-presentation as apostle has grown exponentially from his earlier (1 Cor 1:1; 2 Cor 1:1) to his later letters (Gal 1:1). In Romans, Paul finally assigns no fewer than the first five verses to it. But at least the uniqueness of his claim to be the "apostle to the gentiles" (Rom 11:13; see also 1:5) must have become questionable since Paul writes to people in the city of Rome who are already believers in Christ; his fleeting comment in 15:23 indicates, moreover, that their assemblies had existed in Rome "for many years." This can only mean

21. Correspondingly, Paul's letter would be an "ambassadorial letter" (cf. Jewett, "Letter").

22. Tamez et al., *Philippians*, 39.

that there were or still are other people like him, and presumably before him, who must have proclaimed the gospel or "imported" it from Palestine. It is likely that this happened in Rome's Jewish synagogues. And despite some degree of initial turmoil and the expulsion of those who were perceived to be the leaders of the new Jewish sect in 49 CE, the movement was ultimately successful. We are fortunate to know the names of at least twelve of these leaders who were in charge of assemblies of believers in Christ by that time: Prisca and Aquila, Asyncritus, Phlegon, Hermes, Patrobas, Hermas, Philologus, Julia, Nereus and his sister, and Olympas (Rom 16:3-5, 14-15).

Paul states next that he is "set apart for the gospel of God" (Rom 1:1). Similar to the preceding "called to be an apostle," these words convey his sense of vocation, thus hinting at what had already been explicated in Galatians: Paul understands his identity as bestowed on him by God from birth (Gal 1:15). This gospel is not some new message or novel philosophy or innovative fancy life lesson. Instead, Paul's gospel was "promised beforehand through his prophets in the holy scriptures" (Rom 1:2). Thus, it is older than a bottle of good French red wine. Paul's statement shows that he had read and studied these Scriptures, owing to his education "at the feet" of Rabbi Gamaliel (Acts 22:3). His quotations also show that they are from the Greek Septuagint and reflect some of its theology. Paul had trust in these Jewish Scriptures and their soteriological significance.

Paul's gospel is about Jesus Christ, and Paul will explain (aspects of) it in the letter. The following is a short version: "the gospel concerning his Son, who was descended from David according to the flesh and was declared to be Son of God with power according to the spirit of holiness by resurrection from the dead, Jesus Christ our Lord" (Rom 1:3-4). According to a broad scholarly consensus, these phrases are adopted from an earlier confession or hymn. Its precise wording has been reconstructed in different ways.[23] These traditional manifestations of faith present Jesus with a "dual nature."[24] Such a depiction has later given rise to other, even

23. Klaus Wengst, *Christologische Formeln und Lieder des Urchristentums*, SNT 7 (Gütersloh: Gütersloher Verlagshaus, 1972), 112; Simon Légasse, *L'Épître de Paul aux Romains*, LD 10 (Paris: Cerf, 2002), 52; Bruce J. Malina and John J. Pilch, *Social-Science Commentary on the Letters of Paul* (Minneapolis: Fortress, 2006), 222. A survey of the arguments for the opinion that Romans 1:3-4 is an earlier confession or hymn is presented in Robert M. Calhoun, *Paul's Definitions of the Gospel in Romans 1*, WUNT 2/316 (Tübingen: Mohr Siebeck, 2011), 92–142.

24. Daniel Boyarin, "Paul and the Genealogy of Gender," in *A Feminist Companion to Paul*, ed. Amy-Jill Levine with Marianne Blickenstaff, FCNTECW 6 (London: T&T International, 2004), 21.

more fluid descriptions of Jesus, for example, as "gender queer, virgin born, intersex, transman."[25]

Most of the contents of this gospel message consist of relational imagery. The words "his Son" as well as the phrase "declared to be Son of God" place Jesus in relation to God and suggest that he also belongs to the divinity. In addition, the phrase "who was descended from David" (literally: "who was born of the seed/sperm of David") determines his identity as part of the royal genealogy of Israel.[26] Both aspects confer an elevated status on Jesus through legitimation. Paul has proclaimed Jesus Christ as God's Son in previous letters (e.g., 1 Cor 1:9; 2 Cor 1:19; Gal 2:20; 4:4).[27] In Romans, this concept of sonship is developed because gentiles are, in fulfillment of the prophecy in Hosea 1:10 (LXX), said to have been adopted into the kingdom of God (Rom 9:25-26).[28] The attribution of Jesus as "born of the seed/sperm of David," however, is unique within the corpus of authentic Pauline letters. Feminist biblical interpretation would note that this particular terminology firmly roots Jesus in a male ancestral lineage.

Such relational terminology is surprising. Previously, Paul had instead associated the divine sonship with the mother of Jesus, although he leaves her anonymous: "But when the fullness of time had come, God sent his Son, born of a woman" (Gal 4:4). This passage, which also features a reference to the Spirit (Gal 4:6), has been seen as corresponding to that of divine Wisdom and the Spirit in the book of Wisdom 9:10, 17.[29] Thus, one may note the exchange of a female character and a theological

25. Lewis Reay, "Towards a Transgender Theology: Que[e]rying the Eunuchs," in *Trans/Formations*, ed. Marcella Althaus-Reid and Lisa Isherwood (London: SCM Press, 2009), 154.

26. While the genealogy of Jesus in Matt 1:1-17, a so-called linear genealogical list (Ulrich Luz, *Matthew 1–7: A Commentary*, trans. James E. Crouch, Hermeneia, rev. ed. [Minneapolis: Fortress, 2007], 81), starts with Abraham and finishes with Joseph, that in Luke 3:23-38 starts with Jesus and finishes, via Abraham and Adam, with God. David is included in both of them (Matt 1:6; Luke 3:31); hence, according to both, Jesus is ultimately "of the seed/sperm of David."

27. Eduard Schweizer, "υἱός, υἱοθεσία: D. New Testament," *TDNT* 8 (1972): 363–92, at 383.

28. Caroline Johnson Hodge, *If Sons, Then Heirs: A Study of Kinship and Ethnicity in the Letters of Paul* (Oxford: Oxford University Press, 2007), 1, 43–66.

29. Schweizer, "υἱός," 375. The book of Wisdom probably originated in Alexandria between ca. 30 BCE and 41 CE; cf. Silvia Schroer, "Das Buch der Weisheit," in *Einleitung in das Alte Testament*, ed. Erich Zenger et al., 8th ed., Kohlhammer Studienbücher Theologie 1.1 (Stuttgart: Kohlhammer, 2012), 490–91.

concept associated with the female for male imagery in Romans.[30] Comparing these differences leads to the realization of an "ontological messiness of Jesus."[31] A few decades later, two of the New Testament Gospels restored their female quality by suggesting anew such a direct relation with Mary through birth (Matt 1:18-25; Luke 1:26-38; 2:1-7). While both Gospels introduce Joseph as Mary's fiancée (Matt 1:18; Luke 1:27), they explicitly exclude prior sexual relations between the couple and ascribe Mary's pregnancy to "the Holy Spirit" (Matt 1:18) or to the "Holy Spirit/the power of the Most High" (Luke 1:35). This potent conceptualization of the biological aspects of the birth of Jesus leaves no room for any σπέρμα. Thus, Jesus is biologically *disconnected* from Joseph's ancestral lineage, and with it likewise from the genealogy of David. He is, in fact, *no longer in any male lineage*. Rather, this God has chosen a young female, a vulnerable teenager without lineage—or at least not a lineage considered worthy of being mentioned by the male gospel redactor. But the meek virgin Mary is grateful that God "has looked with favor on the lowly state of his servant" and, therefore, hails God as "my Savior" and "the Mighty One" (Luke 1:47-49) in her song of praise that brims with excitement upon the realization that, in stark contrast to the power of the Roman Empire, the God of Judah cares for and protects the vulnerable.[32] Although severed from the male lineage of ancestral honors, the child will nevertheless be the Son of God through the generative agency of the "Holy Spirit/the power of the Most High." And as God's Son, the child will be divine. This is a functional equivalent to the identity of Jesus according to Romans 1:3, albeit here through a claim of a male ancestral lineage.

30. This is similar to later christological concepts, for example, those in Hebrews (e.g., Heb 1:3). That text also "submerges the origins of this christological language in the Wisdom tradition by never explicitly referring to Woman Wisdom/Sophia" (Mary Ann Beavis and HyeRan Kim-Cragg, *Hebrews*, WCS 54 [Collegeville, MN: Liturgical Press, 2015], 5; see also xlii–xliii).

31. Sheila Briggs, "What Is Feminist Theology?," in *The Oxford Handbook of Feminist Theology*, ed. Mary McClintock Fulkerson and Sheila Briggs, Oxford Handbooks (Oxford: Oxford University Press, 2012), 86.

32. The words "of his servant" convey the idea of "lowliness." Mary's response adopts a line from the prayer of the barren Hannah at the Shiloh sanctuary: "If only you will look on the lowliness of your servant" (1 Sam 1:11 [LXX] [1 Kgdms 1:11]). Cf. Barbara E. Reid and Shelly Matthews, *Luke 1–9*, WCS 43A (Collegeville, MN: Liturgical Press, 2021), 46, who argue that ταπείνωσις is more accurately translated "humiliation" rather than "lowliness."

Why does Paul reference the Davidic lineage of Jesus? Since genealogies were a very important aspect of one's pedigree in traditional Judaism, it appears to be part of Paul's strategy to confirm not only his own Jewishness but also that of Jesus, the Christ, in connection with royal overtones.

The earlier confession adopted here goes on to complement the statement about the Davidic sonship of Jesus with another one about sonship of God "by resurrection from the dead" (Rom 1:4). The first one asserted the sonship of Jesus "according to the flesh"; the second asserts it "according to the spirit." Yet according to both, the nature of Jesus is the same; he is the Son of God. Positing divine sonship of Jesus in connection to the resurrection is a typical aspect of Paul's gospel message. In Romans, Paul and Phoebe specifically proclaim the crucifixion and the resurrection as salvific events; they will return to this aspect in Romans 4:25 and elaborate on it in 6:5. Romans does not describe miraculous actions performed by Jesus or impressive parables or sermons, as the four New Testament Gospels will later do. Instead, "as of the resurrection he is the Son of God established in power and has become such for the vivifying of all human beings."[33] With this title, Jesus the Jewish Messiah is now also "our Lord" (κύριος ἡμῶν, 1:4).

While it appears that Romans, by means of referencing the traditional passage, affirms a "spiritual" sonship or divine adoption of Jesus through the resurrection, the question is how this statement fits with that in Galatians 4:4 affirming the sonship of Jesus at the moment of his earthly birth. Romans 1:4 is not, however, about adoption per se but rather about making Jesus "Son of God with power." With the resurrection, Jesus himself has achieved a new status of authority (hence the title "Lord"). Overall, however, this christological statement does presuppose the preexistence of Jesus, which is equivalent to the concept of *Chokmah-Sophia-Sapientia-Wisdom* in other Jewish traditions.[34] Traditional Jewish theology evinces no fixed or unchangeable image of the divine but a dynamic and flexible one. Therefore, Paul himself wrote previously that

33. Joseph A. Fitzmyer, *Romans: A New Translation with Introduction and Commentary*, AB 33 (New York: Doubleday, 1993), 235.

34. Ulrike Mittmann, *Die Weisheit und der Gottessohn: Studien zur hermeneutischen Grundlegung einer Theologie des Neuen Testaments*, WUNT 462 (Tübingen: Mohr Siebeck, 2021), 132–36, 390–91.

"Christ Jesus . . . became for us wisdom [σοφία] from God" (1 Cor 1:30).[35] Other New Testament authors have later continued this tradition. For instance, Hebrews 1:3 celebrates Jesus as the "reflection of God's glory and the exact imprint of God's very being [that] sustains all things by his powerful word." And the Alexandrian theologian and philosopher Clement (ca. 150–215 CE) states that "Christ is called Wisdom by all the prophets. This is he who is the teacher of all created beings, the fellow counselor of God who foreknew all things; and he from above, from the first foundation of the world" (*Strom.* 1.4).[36]

From the perspective of feminist biblical interpretation and its egalitarian ethos, christological concepts featuring such a construction of status and social power may be considered problematic. Would the hierarchical concepts not militate against the attempts of creating an affectionate society of equals? It may be helpful, however, to read such christological concepts against the backdrop of the larger political situation in the days of Paul and Phoebe, that is, in the mid-50s CE. The double attribution of Jesus as "Son of God" in Romans 1:3-4 was, like the christological titles of "Lord" and "Savior," by no means exclusively religious terminology or typical church jargon. Instead, these titles belonged to the spectrum of official references to the authority and divinity of the Roman emperors. In those days, it had been barely a century since Julius Caesar had been deified, which occurred in 42 BCE, two years after his assassination. Gaius Octavius/Octavian, his adopted son, then took the name "*divi Iuli(i) filius*" ("son of the divine Julius") or, for short, "*divi filius*" ("son of god"). The same applies to terminology such as "gospel" (εὐαγγέλιον), "presence" (παρουσία), or "faith" (πίστις, better rendered as "trust, loyalty"). Titles and vocabulary like these were, therefore, political and firmly rooted in the emperor cult.[37] It would have been impossible in the first century CE to hear titles like these any differently.

35. Susanne Scholz, "The Complexities of 'His' Liberation Talk: A Literary Feminist Reading of the Book of Exodus," in *A Feminist Companion to the Bible: Exodus to Deuteronomy*, ed. Athalya Brenner, FCB 5, 2nd ser. (Sheffield: Sheffield Academic, 2000), 29.

36. Beavis and Kim-Cragg, *Hebrews*, 5.

37. Davina Lopez, "Before Your Very Eyes: Roman Imperial Ideology, Gender Constructs, and Paul's Inter-Nationalism," in *Mapping Gender in Ancient Religious Discourses*, ed. Todd Penner and Caroline Vander Stichele, BibInt 84 (Leiden: Brill, 2006), 117–18; Nelson de Paiva Bondioli, "Roman Religion in the Time of Augustus," *Numen* 64 (2017): 49–63, at 57–59.

Rome and the Imperial Cult

Roman society was characterized by its imperial cult or emperor worship. "Deification at Rome . . . was a conferring of status; cult was a supreme form of honor."[38] The imperial cult thus focused on the continuous recognition, veneration, and celebration of the Roman emperor as the epitome of kyriarchal power at the top of the pyramid of honor and ensured its universal institutionalization. Assassinated in 44 BCE, Julius Caesar was being deified in 42 BCE. Therefore, his adopted son Gaius Octavius/Octavian or Augustus became known as "*divi filius*" ("son of God") and initiated the propaganda of the emperor cult in Rome. It developed progressively. In the days of Paul, Emperor Nero, who reigned from 54 to 68 CE, was already adorned with the title of "*ipse deus*" ("god himself"). The divinity of Roman emperors was being celebrated throughout the empire; temples, rituals, and festivities promoted their veneration. The allegiance of the Roman people to the emperor was called "faith"; the emperor himself was considered their "lord."[39] Occasionally, questions have been raised as to whether the imperial cult was genuinely religious and whether the Roman population actually believed that the emperors were gods. Yet, these kinds of concerns are rather the result of imposing modern viewpoints onto ancient socio-religious phenomena, assuming a distinction between politics and religion.[40]

Coins featuring the image of the emperor and monumental iconography were ubiquitous throughout the empire to convey this form of civic cult to the population.[41] Especially Herod the Great, the Roman client king of Judea, used the imperial

38. Everett Ferguson, *Backgrounds of Early Christianity*, 3rd ed. (Grand Rapids: Eerdmans, 2003), 197.

39. Donald L. Jones, "Christianity and the Roman Imperial Cult," *ANRW* 2.23.2 (1980): 1023–54; John Scheid, "Augustus and Roman Religion: Continuity, Conservatism, and Innovation," in *The Cambridge Companion to the Age of Augustus*, ed. Karl Galinsky, Cambridge Companion to the Classics (Cambridge: Cambridge University Press, 2005), 183–84, 187.

40. Philip A. Harland, "Imperial Cults within Local Cultural Life: Associations in Roman Asia," *AHB* 17 (2003): 85–107.

41. Henner von Hesberg, "Archäologische Denkmäler zum römischen Kaiserkult," *ANRW* 2.16.2 (1978): 911–95; Harry O. Maier, "Barbarians, Scythians and Imperial Iconography in the Epistle to the Colossians," in *Picturing the New Testament: Studies in Ancient Visual Images*, ed. Annette Weissenrieder, Friederike Wendt, and Petra von Gemünden, WUNT 2/193 (Tübingen: Mohr Siebeck, 2005); Zsuzsanna Várhelyi, "Statuary and Ritualization in Imperial Italy," *MAAR. Supplementary Volumes* 13 (2017): 87–98.

cult to demonstrate his political allegiance. According to L. Michael White, "His veneration of Augustus went far beyond what ordinary Romans would have experienced at Rome itself. . . . The growth of the imperial cult was much more typical in the eastern part of the empire than in Rome or the West, and Herod helped lead the way."[42]

Christological, soteriological, and ecclesiological terminology in Paul's letters is often considered to be specifically Christian, but it has its origins in the imperial cult of Rome. For example, the honorific title "*divi filius*" of Augustus is found, in its Greek translation υἱός τοῦ θεοῦ ("Son of God"), in Romans 1:4; 2 Corinthians 1:19; Galatians 2:20 (see also "his Son" with reference to God in Rom 1:3, 9; 5:10; 8:29; 1 Cor 1:9; Gal 4:4, 6).[43] One of the earliest creeds of believers in Jesus as the Christ contained the statement that he was the σωτήρ ("savior"). This was specifically a prominent title of Roman emperors. According to Josephus, during the Jewish Revolt the Roman general Vespasian was already hailed as "savior and benefactor" (σωτὴρ καὶ εὐεργέτης) upon his arrival in the city of Tiberias (*B.J.* 3.459) and, when returning to Rome as emperor, greeted "as benefactor [εὐεργέτης], savior [σωτήρ], and only worthy ruler of the city of Rome" (*B.J.* 7.71). The following imperial titles included the term σωτήρ:[44]

Julius Caesar, Claudius	σωτὴρ τῆς οἰκουμένης	Savior of the world
Augustus	σωτὴρ τῶν Ἑλλήνων τε καὶ τῆς οἰκουμένης πάσης	Savior of the Greeks and of the entire world
Augustus, Tiberius	εὐεργέτης καὶ σωτὴρ τοῦ σύμπαντος κόσμου	Benefactor and savior of the entire earth
Nero, Titus	σωτὴρ καὶ εὐεργέτης τῆς οἰκουμένης	Savior and benefactor of the world
Vespasian	σωτὴρ καὶ εὐεργέτης τοῦ κόσμου	Savior and benefactor of the earth

42. L. Michael White, "Herod and the Jewish Experience of Augustan Rule," in Galinsky, *The Cambridge Companion to the Age of Augustus*, 375.

43. Latin *divi filius* ("son of the divine") is not a literal translation of Greek υἱός (τοῦ) θεοῦ ("Son of God"). The former, however, is short for *divi Iuli(i) filius* ("son of the divine Julius"; see also below).

44. Craig R. Koester, "'The Savior of the World' (John 4:42)," *JBL* 109 (1990): 665–80, at 666–67. However, these titles were not invented by the Romans. See previously, for example, the following Seleucid Rulers Antiochus I Soter (280–261 BCE), Seleucus III Soter (225–223 BCE), or Demetrius I Soter (162–150 BCE).

The title "father" was also bestowed on the emperor. Mary Rose D'Angelo explains: "*Pater* reflects an understanding of the empire as *familia* in which the emperor functions as a *paterfamilias*, whose *auctoritas* is based on his ability to regard the whole Roman people as his clients."[45] The Romans had traditionally awarded the honorific title "*pater patriae*" ("Father of the Country") for great political achievements. Perfectly epitomizing the interconnection of imperial cult and ancient patronage system, this title connotes a position of supreme authority. It was given to Augustus in 2 BCE, decades after he had already been declared "*divi filius*" ("son of God"). The recognition of the problematic context and related semantic implications of the honorific title "father" has been important for feminist biblical interpretation. In the field of New Testament studies, the term had sometimes been singled out as conveying a high level of human trust and intimacy in God due to its alleged origins in babytalk.[46] This is not the case. Therefore, Paul avoids calling himself "father"; for him, this title is reserved for God (see also Matt 23:8-10). He envisions an alternative to the patronage of the Roman Empire and its imperial cult.

Paul employs, however, the term "savior" (σωτήρ) in Philippians 3:20 (with reference to Jesus Christ).[47] He also makes more frequent use of the noun σωτηρία ("salvation," Rom 1:16; 11:11; 13:11; 2 Cor 7:10; Phil 1:28) and the verb σῴζω ("to save," Rom 5:9, 10; 8:24; 10:1, 9-10; 1 Cor 5:5; 15:2; 1 Thess 2:16). These terms and others like παρουσία ("presence," referring to the triumphant arrivals of emperors into cities) and βασιλεία ("kingdom," or rather "empire") were familiar to residents of the Roman Empire who would have heard them as references to the authority

45. Mary Rose D'Angelo, "Abba and 'Father': Imperial Theology and the Jesus Traditions," *JBL* 111 (1992): 611–30, at 623.

46. See the exploration in D'Angelo, "Abba and 'Father,'" 612–16; and Mary Rose D'Angelo, "Theology in Mark and Q: Abba and 'Father' in Context," *HTR* 85 (1992): 149–74, at 151, in either case with reference to, e.g., Joachim Jeremias, *Abba: Studien zur neutestamentlichen Theologie und Zeitgeschichte* (Göttingen: Vandenhoeck & Ruprecht, 1966), 15–67; Robert Hamerton-Kelly, "God the Father in the Bible and in the Experience of Jesus: The State of the Question," in *God as Father?*, ed. Johann Baptist Metz and Edward Schillebeeckx, Eng. ed. Marcus Lefébure, Concilium 143 (Edinburgh: T&T Clark; New York: Seabury, 1981), 101.

47. The term σωτήρ occurs more regularly in the deutero-Pauline literature (Eph 5:23; 1 Tim 1:1; 2:3; 4:10; 2 Tim 1:10; Titus 1:3, 4; 2:10, 13; 3:4, 6) and other later New Testament writings.

and divinity of the emperors. In that matrix, the term εὐαγγέλιον ("gospel") referred to the good news that peace and security had been established through military victory. In response, the people were expected to have πίστις ("faith, trust, loyalty") in their leaders who were their saviors.[48]

What do these terminological observations mean for the interpretation of Paul's letters more broadly and of Romans in particular? The question is what the deployment of terminology and concepts from such patriarchal power systems means regarding the oppression of women and other marginalized groups. In the words of Stephanie Y. Mitchem: "Organized religions . . . do not escape the burden of empire but become partners in its maintenance."[49] Did Paul comply with Rome's imperial propaganda? A different understanding is proposed by scholars who depict Paul as someone who intended to wage war on the Roman Empire or to lead an ideological intifada against its imperial propaganda. Is he preparing a heroic stance on behalf of marginalized subcultures, countercultures, and liminal cultures by employing a rhetoric of resistance against the imperial domination of ancient Rome? Specifically, do the titles "Son of God" and "Lord" for Jesus in Romans 1:4 have a subversive undertone against the colonial power and pitch Jesus against the Roman emperor?[50] While these positions each may have some appeal, it has to be admitted that "Romans offers no direct critique of empire."[51] In fact, parenetical passages such as Romans 13:1-7 on being subject to political authorities rather appear to contradict any subversive intentions of Paul. There seems to be a difference between Paul's letters and other New Testament texts that evince an explicit critique of empire, such as the Gospel according

48. See also Neil Elliott, *The Arrogance of Nations: Reading Romans in the Shadow of Empire*, Paul in Critical Contexts (Minneapolis: Fortress, 2010); Brigitte Kahl, *Galatians Re-imagined: Reading with the Eyes of the Vanquished*, Paul in Critical Contexts (Minneapolis: Fortress, 2010).

49. Stephanie Y. Mitchem, "Thinking about Feminist Leadership," *JFSR* 25 (2009): 197–201, at 198–99.

50. James R. Harrison, *Reading Romans with Roman Eyes: Studies on the Social Perspective of Paul*, Paul in Critical Contexts (Lanham: Lexington; Fortress, 2020), 50–51.

51. Elliott, *Arrogance*, 61.

to Mark (e.g., 5:1-20) or the Revelation to John.[52] It would, however, not be appropriate to subject Paul's own letters to "false coherence" by inferring, from his alleged anti-imperialistic perspective, that the section in chapter 13 cannot be a commendation of the existing political authorities.

Such a political interpretation of Paul's terminology has been widely debated in the scholarship of recent decades. No consensus has yet been achieved. His christological-soteriological terminology may indeed be attested in the honor and shame culture of the Roman Empire and the imperial cult. But the noun σωτηρία ("salvation") that the apostle uses in, for example, 2 Corinthians 6:2 actually occurs in a quotation from the Septuagint (Isa 49:8 [LXX]). Any reference to the imperial cult of the Roman culture would, therefore, rather be coincidental. Of course, also the verb σῴζω is frequently attested across the Septuagint; it is a standard rendering of the verb ישׁע *hiph.* ("to keep, save"). Likewise, in the statement of the main thesis of the letter in Romans 1:16-17, the double usage of the noun πίστις ("faith, trust, loyalty") together with the verb πιστεύω ("to have faith, trust, to be loyal") is once more backed up by a quotation from Habakkuk 2:4 (LXX), and in the Masoretic practice, the title "Lord" was the translation of the *qᵉre perpetuum* אדני ("my Lord," based on the noun אדון "Lord" with suffix) for the *Tetragrammaton* and its Septuagint equivalent, the title κύριος ("Lord").[53] Finally, Paul can reference aspects of acquired and ascribed honor when he admonishes the congregation in Corinth that "not many of you were wise by human standards, not many were powerful, not many were of noble birth" (1 Cor 1:26). He is apparently conscious of where on the ladder of social achievements his people rank. Therefore, much of Paul's opposition to the Roman Empire consists first and foremost of traditional Jewish discourse. Indeed, Paul explicitly affirms that his own proclamation is based on the Jewish prophets and Scriptures (Rom 1:2). It is therefore corroborated by a host

52. Elisabeth Schüssler Fiorenza, *Revelation: Vision of a Just World*, Proclamation Commentaries (Minneapolis: Fortress, 1991); Christian A. Eberhart, "Beobachtungen zu Kommunikationsstrategien im frühen Christentum: Zu Insider-Informationen in Mk 5:1-20," in *Talking God in Society: Multidisciplinary (Re)constructions of Ancient (Con) texts; Festschrift for Peter Lampe*, vol. 1: *Theories and Applications*, ed. Ute E. Eisen and Heidrun E. Mader, NTOA 120 (Göttingen: Vandenhoeck & Ruprecht, 2020), 405–24.

53. Martin Rösel, *Adonaj—warum Gott 'Herr' genannt wird*, FAT 29 (Tübingen: Mohr Siebeck, 2000), 7–14; Mogens Müller, "Die Bedeutung der Septuaginta für die Entfaltung neutestamentlicher Theologie," in *Die Septuaginta—Geschichte, Wirkung, Relevanz: 6. Internationale Fachtagung veranstaltet von Septuaginta Deutsch (LXX.D), Wuppertal 21.–24. Juli 2016*, ed. Martin Meiser et al., 730–56, WUNT 405 (Tübingen: Mohr Siebeck, 2018), 747–48.

of Scripture quotations throughout his letter.[54] What, then, may be his stance toward the Roman Empire? Is he a revolutionary or not?[55]

Rome and the Honor-Shame System

A typical example of a patriarchal culture, Roman society, and with it the ancient Mediterranean world, operated on an honor-shame system. The quest for honor (or social esteem) was considered to be the supreme purpose in life. Shame (or dishonor, disgrace) was, by contrast, to be avoided at all cost.[56]

There were two sources of honor: *ascribed honor* and *acquired honor*. Ascribed honor was a rather static concept as it was usually due to birth into an honorific family. Key criteria were social class, ethnicity, family reputation, wealth, etc. (Livy, *Hist.* 34.7.8-9). One's social class was dependent on the *ordo*, a classification established in the official census and conducted regularly. Basic divisions were patricians (the elite, with ancestral lines purporting to go back to the foundation of the urbs), plebeians (or plebs, people with Roman citizenship), and noncitizens.[57] The *ordo* was exhibited in various ways. One of them was clothing, which was "restricted by law to certain status groups. . . . The regulation of clothing on the basis of status granted the elite a conspicuous and easily recognizable way to display aspects of their identity in public, and the assertion of identity through specific forms of attire was also therefore an assertion of power."[58] Similarly, Romans were eager to exhibit ancestral busts in the entrance halls of their private homes. Both clothing and

54. Beverly Roberts Gaventa, "Paul and the Roman Believers," in *The Blackwell Companion to Paul*, ed. Stephen Westerholm, Blackwell Companions to Religion (Malden: Wiley-Blackwell, 2011), 102.

55. Bruno Blumenfeld, *The Political Paul: Justice, Democracy and Kingship in a Hellenistic Framework*, JSNTSup 210 (Sheffield: T&T Clark International, 2003), 291: "I would call Paul a revolutionary if he were not so much of a reactionary."

56. David A. deSilva, "Paul, Honor, and Shame," in Sampley, *Paul in the Greco-Roman World: A Handbook*, 2:26.

57. Richard S. Ascough, "What Kind of World Did Paul's Communities Live In?," in Longenecker, *The New Cambridge Companion to St. Paul*, 49–50.

58. Michele George, "Slave Disguise in Ancient Rome," in *Representing the Body of the Slave*, ed. Thomas Wiedemann and Jane Gardner, Studies in Slave and Post-Slave Societies and Cultures (London: Frank Cass, 2002), 41–54, at 42–43.

ancestors were a representation of ascribed honor. This dominant aspect was also conveyed through the Roman naming practice of *tria nomina* (triple names)—a personal *praenomen* (first name), a *nomen gentilicium* (the clan or family name), and a *cognomen* (nickname) for common usage. Among these three, the *nomen gentilicium*, a hereditary surname that identified a person as a member of a distinct *gens* (clan or family), was the most important. For example, the original name of Augustus, the first Roman emperor (30 BCE–14 CE), was Gaius Octavius as he was born into a wealthy equestrian branch of the plebeian family Octavia. Hence his *praenomen* Gaius; Octavius was his *nomen gentilicium* evoking the estimable status of his ancestry. Early in his life, he had received, but later rejected, the *cognomen* Thurinus to celebrate a military victory at Thurii of his father. In 27 BCE, the senate decreed to bestow on him a title of religious authority, "Augustus" ("great/venerable"; after his reign, every emperor adopted the name "Caesar Augustus," which gradually became the imperial title). He also called himself "*princeps senatus*" ("leader of the senate"), hence the term "principate" for the Roman Empire. It had political ramifications and was equivalent to a regnal title. These titles all celebrated his acquired honor while simultaneously consolidating his reign as emperor. Almost thirty years later, in 2 BCE, universal acclaim gained him the further title "*pater patriae*" ("father of the country"; see also below). However, already in 42 BCE at only twenty-one years of age, Augustus had taken the name "*divi Iuli(i) filius*" ("son of the divine Julius") or, for short, "*divi filius*" ("son of God"; see above).[59]

In line with this practice, it was customary to mention the names of honored members of the society and to leave dishonorable ones unnamed. A gendered exploration of the topic will note that ascribed honor was available for both men and women. By contrast, acquired honor, which has to do with increasing one's social capital, was dynamic and primarily (but not exclusively) the endeavor of male Roman citizens. "Men competed among themselves to defend their masculinity."[60] Women had different role expectations. They rather needed to display modesty and were

59. Geraldine Herbert-Brown, "Caesar or Augustus? The Game of the Name in Ovid's 'Fasti,'" *Acta Classica* 54 (2011): 43–77.

60. Halvor Moxnes, "Honor and Shame," in *The Social Sciences and New Testament Interpretation*, ed. Richard L. Rohrbaugh (Peabody, MA: Hendrickson Publishers, 1996), 21.

restricted to the private house.[61] Enslaved persons were exempt from acquiring public honor in the Greco-Roman world.[62] For men, honor was closely related to economic capital but ultimately even more important. Honor could especially be acquired through successful political or military leadership that increased one's glory. Yet honor was usually a corporate concept. For example, the *paterfamilias* was also responsible for the behavior and well-being of women "embedded" in his household by protecting them and defending their chastity. Those who succeeded at these different levels were viewed as heroes and elevated above others; the sociological result was a highly stratified culture (aptly labeled "pyramid of honor"[63]).

Honor was ultimately distributed to individuals or family groups in the so-called public court of reputation/honor. It served for the reinforcement of the social good to which the members of the community had to contribute. The competition for esteem was all-pervasive and included all aspects of Roman society (from sponsoring private banquets to public games and celebrations to financing public buildings, etc.). Inscriptions, statues, and public monuments named and depicted those whose honor was being recognized by the public. Status could be conveyed through administrative positions within the government of the imperium, through attribution of military ranks, or at a lower level through employment in privately or regionally operating businesses. Praise of persons or specific honorific actions was conveyed in eloquent and elaborate speeches and poems and made public in songs and hymns.[64] Propagandistic literary works such as Julius Caesar's *De Bello Gallico* or the *Res Gestae* of Augustus were published to relate achievements to the public court of honor and ensure due honor attribution (while silencing critics).[65] In this

61. For more on the specific role of women, see "Women in Rome" in the introduction above, pp. lxxiii–lxxvi.

62. Orlando Patterson, "Paul, Slavery and Freedom: Personal and Socio-Historical Reflections," *Semeia* 83/84 (1998): 263–79. See also the excursus "Enslavement in Rome" below, pp. 152–154.

63. Jewett, *Romans*, 49–51.

64. Zeba Crook, "Honor, Shame, and Social Status Revisited," *JBL* 128 (2009): 591–611.

65. Consisting of eight books, *De Bello Gallico* (or *Commentarii de bello Gallico*) has received a lot of praise for its eloquent, clear Latin style (Hans Herzfeld, *Geschichte in Gestalten*, vol. 1, Das Fischer Lexikon [Frankfurt: Fischer, 1963], 214). Julius Caesar had most likely dictated the first seven books to a scribe in the years before 46 BCE;

variety of forms, exaggeration and boasting were not frowned upon but common.[66] The reason was that "reticence would only cause people to mistake modesty for a guilty conscience" (Sallust, *Bell.Jug.* 26). It is clear that these stories were by no means "objective" depictions of all aspects of Roman society; instead, they conveyed androcentric perspectives of a patriarchal culture. It was *his*-story, and to obtain a view of Roman society from the critical perspective of *her*-meneutics that is attentive to intersectionality, this *his*-story needs to be recognized as what it is and deconstructed.

The semantics of honor and shame are employed in Romans and other Pauline letters, for instance, "honor" (τιμή, Rom 2:7, 10; 9:21; 12:10; 1 Cor 12:23; 1 Thess 4:4), "to aspire to honor" (φιλοτιμέομαι, Rom 15:20; 2 Cor 5:9; 1 Thess 4:11), "glory" (δόξα, Rom 2:10; 8:17; 2 Cor 6:8), "to glorify" (δοξάζω, 1 Cor 12:26), "honored" (ἔνδοξος, 1 Cor 4:10), "honored/respected" (δόκιμος, Rom 14:18), "to receive great honor" (συνδοξάζω, Rom 8:17),

---

the last one was probably written in the year 43 after Caesar's violent death in 44. Many past *his*-storians used to consider this literary work an "infallible" account of Caesar's military campaign against the Celtic and Germanic peoples in Gaul. Already, however, Gaius Asinius Pollio, a Roman poet, literary critic, and historian who even served as a soldier under Caesar, criticized that the accounts were inaccurate and had been compiled without much care. Recently, David Henige critiqued *De Bello Gallico* as clever propaganda written for the purpose of self-aggrandizing Caesar. Their sober tone and accessible writing style were intended to help ancient audiences to accept not only outlandish exaggerations but also the portrayal of Caesar's aggression as a justified defense because of the barbarity of the Gauls (David Henige, "He Came, He Saw, We Counted: The Historiography and Demography of Caesar's Gallic Numbers," *Annales de Démographie Historique* 1 [1998]: 215–42). Augustus commissioned the *Res Gestae Divi Augusti* ("The Deeds of the Divine Augustus"), a monumental inscription composed mostly of thirty-five paragraphs, as a first-person record of his life and accomplishments. Inscribed on monuments or temples throughout the Roman Empire, the *Res Gestae* are a celebration of Augustus's political career, public benefactions, and military accomplishments but leave all of his enemies unnamed or anonymous. Augustus told *his* story to ensure his future veneration and deification (Helmut Koester, *Paul and His World: Interpreting the New Testament in Its Context* [Minneapolis: Fortress, 2007], 121; James R. Harrison, "Augustan Rome and the Body of Christ: A Comparison of the Social Vision of the *Res Gestae* and Paul's Letter to the Romans," *HTR* 106 [2013]: 1–36). In all colonial societies, the question of being celebrated as a hero (or acknowledged as a thief, slave trader, and murderer) is a matter of propaganda (Tink Tinker and Mark Freeland, "Thief, Slave Trader, Murderer: Christopher Columbus and Caribbean Population Decline," *Wicazo Sa Review* 23 [2008]: 25–50).

66. deSilva, "Paul," 31.

"to regard as exceptionally honored/to exalt" (ὑπερυψόω, Phil 2:9), and "wellborn" (εὐγενής, 1 Cor 1:26). In Romans 13:7, a certain type of behavior receives praise that is consistent with the attribution of deserved honor: "Pay to all what is due them: taxes to whom taxes are due, revenue to whom revenue is due, respect to whom respect is due, honor to whom honor is due [τῷ τὴν τιμὴν τὴν τιμήν]." Paul's writings also display vocabulary relating aspects of low status, such as "shame" (αἰσχύνη, 2 Cor 4:2), "to be ashamed" (ἐπαισχύνομαι, Rom 1:16; 6:21), "to put to shame/to disgrace" (καταισχύνω, Rom 5:5; 9:33; 10:11; 1 Cor 1:27 [bis]; 11:4, 5; 2 Cor 9:4), "to be put to shame/to be disgraced" (αἰσχύνω, 2 Cor 10:8), "dishonor" (ἀτιμία, Rom 1:26; 9:21), and "dishonored" (ἄτιμος, 1 Cor 4:10; 12:23). This terminology refers to both ethnic origin/identity ("Greek," "Jewish," "barbarians," Rom 1:14, 16; 2:9-10) and the difference between bondage (1:1; 6:16) or being "free" (6:18, 20-22; 8:2) as markers of ascribed honor. Above all, in Philippians 3:4-6, Paul refers to his proper socio-religious origin within Judaism as an example of ascribed honor and of his zealous execution of his mission to persecute "the church" for his acquired honor.[67]

But Paul's letters also show how he questions the honor-shame culture. In the illustration of the freedom from the law in Romans 7:3, the consequence of the woman being "called an adulteress" refers to the public court of honor, suggesting that she would be put to shame. Likewise, the attestation that "she is not an adulteress" implies that her behavior would be judged with approval without causing her dishonor. Yet, this passage also conveys a countercultural message about a status reversal and existential exchange: Just as the shameful cross turned into victory, so humiliation and shame become glory and fame, and death becomes life. Boasting, which is as frequent in the competitive arena of the honor-shame culture as it is characteristic for it, is now excluded (Rom 3:27). The political "body" metaphor (1 Cor 12:14-26; Rom 12:4-5) levels the kyriarchal "pyramid of honor" and uproots the Greco-Roman honor system by giving the perceived "lower" parts of the body greater honor.[68] The reversal of things and the ensuing attentiveness to those in need

67. Yara Matta, *À cause du Christ: Le retournement de Paul le Juif*, Lectio Divina 56 (Paris: Cerf, 2013), 128.

68. Elisabeth Schüssler Fiorenza, *Ephesians*, WCS 50 (Collegeville, MN: Liturgical Press, 2017), lxxx.

and suffering is clearly the main content of the message of Jesus who proclaimed salvation for the poor and disenfranchised. It even serves as an indication for others that Jesus is indeed the Messiah (Luke 7:18-23). This very message is manifest in Paul's paradoxical boasting about his weakness and suffering in 2 Corinthians. Paul used his own life story to convey in a personal and emotional way how God is partial toward the weak and how God's power is made perfect in weakness (see 2 Cor 12:9). He himself knew the meaning of existential exchange; he experienced how his own humiliation and shame became glory and fame.

Four historical reflections on Second Temple Judaism may further our understanding of Paul regarding this question and help to understand his struggle within the context of his Jewish contemporaries. They all have to do with the ambivalent dynamics of hegemonic powers such as the Roman Empire and show that no simplistic solution will do it justice. These reflections pertain to the stance of ancient Israelite and Jewish communities in face of the surrounding ancient Near Eastern hegemonic powers, alliances established by the Hasmonean state to ensure survival, the response of Judaism to the imperial cult, and finally glimpses at the early period of the reign of Emperor Nero.

1. The Israelite and Jewish communities themselves experienced oppression at the hands of other ancient Near Eastern hegemonic powers. Long before Paul, they negotiated their stance toward them in their own right; their scriptural traditions tell the story of that. The process of adaptation is manifest even in the temple worship of Israel and Judah. Many elements have been implemented from the cult practice of other ancient Near Eastern and Mediterranean cultures while some aspects have been deliberately rejected. Thus, the aniconism of Judaism can be interpreted as a response to the strong emphasis on visual aspect of the Egyptian cult; this process is called "normative inversion."[69] Moreover, the Jewish diaspora

69. Christian A. Eberhart, "Kult und die Begegnung mit dem einen Gott in der Septuaginta," in *Handbuch zur Septuaginta—Handbook of the Septuagint*, vol. 5: *Die Theologie der Septuaginta—The Theology of the Septuagint* (LXX.H 5), ed. Hans Ausloos and Bénédicte Lemmelijn (Gütersloh: Gütersloher Verlagshaus, 2020), 173.

community in Lower Egypt had to situate itself within the imperial cult of the Ptolemaic dynasty that later also adopted the veneration of the Roman emperors. In response to this situation, the book of Daniel contains, for example, a critique of the veneration of an emperor, historicized in the context of the Babylonian exile (Dan 3).[70] Nevertheless, relations of Jewish diaspora groups to their host societies were mostly positive.

2. Similar observations pertain to postexilic Judaism in Palestine. Late in the second and during the first century BCE, the Roman Empire became a significant ally and supporter of the Hasmonean state (152–63 BCE), the last politically autonomous embodiment of Judaism. According to Kenneth Atkinson, the Hasmonean dynasty enjoyed mostly good relations with the Romans and even owed them the survival of their state. Having to combat the Seleucid and Parthian Empires to the northeast and the Ptolemaic Kingdom to the southwest, several Hasmonean kings sought out and relied on political alliances with the Roman emperors who took them on as protégés. This is also attested in literary sources (1 Macc 15:16-24; see also Josephus, *Ant.* 14.145-147).[71] Quite understandably, matters became more ambiguous after Pompey's 63 BCE conquest of Jerusalem. But in general, Rome had been supportive of the Jews.

3. It has also been argued that the Jews were apparently content to disregard the Roman imperial cult, and the Romans were willing to grant the exception.[72] But depending on the specific political situation in Rome, the imperial cult at times ceased to be negligible or an abstract theological problem that could be ignored. For example, in the Jewish diaspora of the early first century CE, approximately 1 million Jews lived in Lower Egypt. Almost a quarter of them inhabited two of the five districts of Alexandria where they were organized in various synagogue congregations. Problems arose when the

70. The Hebrew version of the book of Daniel dates to ca. 164 BCE; its additions to ca. 155–145. The Greek translation of LXX was produced in ca. 145; the Greek revision by Theodotion in 115–95.

71. Kenneth Atkinson, *A History of the Hasmonean State: Josephus and Beyond*, Jewish and Christian Texts in Contexts and Related Studies 23 (New York: Bloomsbury, 2016), 166–77.

72. David Noy, "'A Sight Unfit to See': Jewish Reactions to the Roman Imperial Cult," *Classics Ireland* 8 (2001): 68–83.

Roman prefect Aulus Avilius Flaccus attempted to find favor with Gaius Caligula (38–41 CE). For that purpose, Flaccus had golden statues of the emperor placed in the synagogues and demanded his worship at altars and temples (Philo, *Flacc.* 6.43; Josephus, *Ant.* 18.8). The stern opposition to these measures led to the Alexandrian pogrom in 38 CE, during which Jews were either killed or driven out of their Alexandrian districts. Caligula himself criticized Flaccus's initiative, however; he recalled the Roman prefect from his position and had him executed in 39 CE. Nevertheless, in 40, the Jews in Alexandria felt compelled to send a delegation to Caligula; it was headed by Philo, the brother of the influential alabarch Alexander. This time, the contentious matter was the emperor's decision to have a colossal statue of himself erected in the temple of Jerusalem. Philo argued vehemently against the decree, as did Aristobulus, the brother of Herod Agrippa and the grandson of Herod the Great (possibly mentioned in Rom 16:10). But Caligula, whom many contemporary historiographers already described as insane, persisted. Fearing civil war, the governor of Syria delayed the implementation of the decree for a year. Eventually, the statue was being shipped to Jerusalem but never erected because, in the meantime, Caligula had been murdered by his entourage in Rome. The immediate reason for the assassination appears to have been Caligula's declaration to relocate to Alexandria to be worshiped as a living god.[73] Thus, while the imperial cult clearly constituted a theological challenge from the perspective of Jewish monotheism that would occasionally manifest itself in persecution, most of the time the situation of the Jewish communities in the Roman world was stable. Jews in the diaspora were typically granted an exemption from ruler worship.

4. Even though Emperor Nero is often portrayed as the quintessence of antagonism toward Christians,[74] his early reign was widely appreciated as perhaps the best of any emperor. Robert Jewett comments

73. Ray Barraclough, "Philo's Politics, Roman Rule, and Hellenistic Judaism," *ANRW* 2.21.1 (1984): 417–553; Miriam Pucci Ben Zeev, "New Perspectives on Jewish-Greek Hostilities in Alexandria during the Reign of Emperor Caligula," *JSJ* 21 (1990): 227–35; Erich S. Gruen, *The Construct of Identity in Hellenistic Judaism: Essays on Early Jewish Literature and History*, DCLS 29 (Berlin: de Gruyter, 2016), 73.

74. William B. Gwyn, "Cruel Nero: The Concept of the Tyrant and the Image of Nero in Western Political Thought," *History of Political Thought* 12 (1991): 421–55.

> that "the Nero administration was providing an exemplary form of government and law enforcement."[75] Ascending to the throne in 54 CE at only sixteen years of age (then under the tutelage of Seneca), Nero was initially "conscientious about legal decisions, tried to combat forgery, reformed the treasury, and improved public safety and order. The masses loved him."[76] Needless to say, Nero knew how to rally the masses behind himself. For instance, he granted freedom and immunity from taxation to the cities of Greece, a privilege that was soon revoked.[77] Writing Romans between 56 and 58 CE, not long after Nero's ascension, Paul most likely had a positive image of the teenaged emperor as well and was hopeful about his reign. It was only later in his reign that Nero came to be resented by the Roman aristocracy and others. The fire of Rome occurred in July 64, ten years after he was made emperor and some seven or eight years after the likely date of composition of Romans. The random and brutal executions of Christ believers as scapegoats for this incident soon became a notorious hallmark of his legislature.[78] Eventually seen as tyrannical and self-indulgent, Nero was overthrown by the Roman Senate and died by suicide at the age of thirty, in 68 CE.

These four historical episodes and aspects of Second Temple Judaism illustrate the variety of ways in which Jews in Palestine and in the diaspora related to the "big players" of global politics around them, including Rome. Even during its relatively short period of political autonomy, the Hasmonean state relied on political alliances with the Romans. In the diaspora, of course, the dependence on the dominant culture was even stronger, and such was the ambiguity over one's cultural and religious identity. And while most dominant cultures valued clearly defined identities based on traditional ancestral lines and membership within the nobility, a competing character was that of a person with two or even "multiple citizenships." According to Anna Heller, who studied that phenomenon in the culture of the Peloponnese during the imperial period, "multiple citizenships" (*citoyennetés multiples*) could be an

75. Jewett, *Romans*, 47–48.

76. Mark A. Phelps, "Nero, the Emperor," in *Dictionary of the Bible and Western Culture*, ed. Mary Ann Beavis and Michael J. Gilmour (Sheffield: Sheffield Phoenix, 2012), 363–64, at 364.

77. James Wiseman, "Corinth and Rome I: 228 B.C.–A.D. 267," *ANRW* 2.7.1 (1979): 438–548, at 505–6.

78. Hermann Lichtenberger, "Jews and Christians in Rome in the Time of Nero: Josephus and Paul in Rome," *ANRW* 2.26.3 (1996): 2142–76.

advantageous aspect for international careers and upward mobility: "Individuals capable of cumulating two effective citizenships . . . seem to belong preferably to powerful families integrated into a network of regional or even provincial relations, which gives them the means to leave the local framework to sometimes make a career in Rome."[79] Multiple citizenships could, therefore, be an advantage and help pave the way to a better future in Rome.

Paul, the Jew from Tarsus and citizen of the Roman Empire, had such multiple citizenships; he had a hybrid identity.[80] Attention to hybridity complexifies the concept of identity and allows a comparative assessment. Paul shares this dual self-understanding with other contemporaries; Josephus would be one of them. Although Josephus once fought against Rome in the Jewish War and later on was a spokesperson on behalf of Judaism and Jews in Rome, he nevertheless "socialized with those who still rejoiced at his nation's defeat. . . . It shows that he had become somewhat comfortable with the Romans."[81] Paul himself should be seen as a person who navigated three different cultural areas: Jewish, Greek (or rather "Hellenistic"), and Roman.[82] This is in line with the reflections above about the cultural divide between Rome and Corinth, as a result of which Paul (and Phoebe) would have needed to prepare against potential prejudices. Many in the audience of Rome also had such dual or even multiple identities. Therefore, Romans repeatedly mentions the topic of cultural differences (e.g., Rom 1:16). Like Josephus, Paul is later drawn to the world-renowned capital of the Roman Empire. Although occasionally feeling ambivalent about his dual identity, he had decided to take it as a factor of empowerment to lead him to destinies yet unknown. Throughout the endeavor, he could count on open reception among the Roman audiences because of their shared identities.

79. Anna Heller, "Stratégies de carrière et stratégies de distinction: La double citoyenneté dans le Péloponnèse d'époque impériale," in *Patrie d'origine et patries électives: Les citoyennetés multiples dans le monde grec d'époque romaine: Actes du colloque international de Tours, 6–7 novembre 2009*, ed. Anna Heller and Anne-Valérie Pont, Scripta Antiqua 40 (Paris: Ausonius Éditions, 2012), 149–50 (ET: CAE).

80. Hansen, *All of You Are One*, 191–96. For this reason, Tarcisius Mukuka calls Paul "a cultural mongrel" (Tarcisius Mukuka, "Reading/Hearing Romans 13:1-7 under an African Tree: Towards a *Lectio Postcolonica Contexta Africana*," *Neot* 46 [2012]: 105–38, at 112).

81. Atkinson, *History*, 169.

82. Marie-Françoise Baslez, "Paul et l'émergence d'un monde 'gréco-romain': Réflexions sur la romanité de l'apôtre," in *Paul's Graeco-Roman Context*, ed. Cilliers Breytenbach, BETL 277 (Leuven: Peeters, 2015), 29–46.

Marginalized or oppressed social groups develop their own attitudes toward colonizing powers. These groups will never be full members of the dominant society; hence, they acquire hybrid identities while developing ambivalent feelings (both adaptation and resistance) toward the colonial powers. As Homi K. Bhabha observes, members of the colonized culture often adopt aspects of the dominant culture in a process called "mimicry" that may itself be subversive and constitute a form of mockery.[83] For Paul, it would have been impossible to proclaim his message of Jesus, the Christ, without using well-known terminological and conceptual categories. To successfully communicate with audiences in Rome, he (and Phoebe) drew in part on the imperial cult as a means of efficaciously articulating his foreign gospel message. Yara Matta calls it Paul's way of "incarnating" his gospel.[84] Paul employed discourses of affiliation that colonial subjects have a tendency of generating. His terminology is a mélange of both resistant and affiliative responses. Like members of his Jewish communities before him, Paul engaged in "normative inversion" by adopting certain elements of the local reality while disavowing or reconfiguring some of them. Normative inversion thus contained a form of mimicry but could, at the same time, be a form of articulating protest and opposition.

It is more likely, then, that the deployment of political terminology and concepts from the Roman emperor cult, such as "Son of God" or "Lord," are a form of mimicry or normative inversion. It served in part to mock the Roman imperial cult and had subversive intentions due to its implicit challenge of the claim of Emperor Nero to be the son of the deified Claudius. That challenge is particularly manifest in the ethos of egalitarianism (Rom 12:1-8). But Paul's political terminology and concepts were, at the same time, characterized by some amount of ambivalence. Paul may have utilized them because he knew that the audiences were familiar with them and could apply them easily. Therefore, it is also appropriate to read Romans as an example of Paul's progressively Roman orientation.[85] It can be demonstrated that this letter shares a number of

83. Homi K. Bhabha, *The Location of Culture*, Routledge Classics (London: Routledge, 2004). See also the summary in Jennifer L. Koosed, *Reading the Bible as a Feminist*, BRP 2/2 (Leiden: Brill, 2017), 35.

84. Matta, *Christ*, 353.

85. J. Paul Sampley, "Living in an Evil Aeon: Paul's Ambiguous Relation to Culture (Toward a Taxonomy)," in Sampley, *Paul in the Greco-Roman World: A Handbook*, 2:392; Maren R. Niehoff, "A Roman Portrait of Abraham in Paul's and Philo's Later Exegesis," *NovT* 63 (2021): 452–76.

common features with speeches of Seneca.[86] The argumentative mélange of resistant and affiliative responses also does not disavow hierarchy as such. Paul and Phoebe know, acknowledge, and address different social statuses in the audiences in Rome, for example, the "weak" and the "strong" (Rom 14:1-12; 15:1), in order to reconcile the quarreling groups. For this goal, Romans proposes a theological vision that is likewise hierarchical: Jesus is the Son of God (1:3-4). Jesus is, thus, not God. But as Son, he is "our Lord." Such a christological concept has a certain similarity to traditional images of *Chokmah-Sophia-Sapientia-Wisdom*. This christological-theological hierarchy informs the status of both Jesus, the Christ, and the audience as those in relation with Jesus. Through this hierarchy, Jesus and the audience gain their status relative to the higher member within the hierarchy and are ultimately empowered.

All things considered, therefore, the topic of Paul versus the Roman Empire is not one in which Paul appears only as a hero. He does, however, provide an alternative. While the Roman Empire was based on faith in military victory to establish and maintain the *Pax Romana* (Roman peace), Paul sent Phoebe to Rome to proclaim an "empire" of justice and true peace based on nonviolence and selfless love. Freedom from the experience of a state of virtual death as enslaved people was, in the contemporary culture of the Roman world, only imaginable through manumission or redemption aiming at integration into the dominant society. This gospel message integrated the members of the assemblies into a network relationship with God. In this relationship, humans would always be subordinate. But subordinate status did not mean a loss of status. Instead, humans could still enjoy an elevated status because of the patron's position; they became a member of a privileged network. Thus were the logics of the patron-client culture.

Rome and Patronage

Many of the customs and social paradigms of the Roman society were shared with, and indeed had been taken over from, the Greek/Hellenistic culture. Since the time of Alexander the Great (356–323 BCE), the social structure of the ancient Mediterranean world was primarily based on the paradigm of the household

86. Stefan Krauter, "Mercy and Monarchy: Seneca's *De clementia* and Paul's Letter to the Romans," *NovT* 63 (2021): 477–88.

(οἰκουμένη, *domus*) centered on the patriarch or "father of the family" (*paterfamilias*). This was an extended rather than a nuclear family; the patriarch headed and managed a hierarchical structure with various levels below him—the wife or "mother of the family" (*materfamilias*),[87] their children, and various others, specifically clients/protégés, retainers, friends, employed servants, and enslaved people. Outsiders could be added lawfully to a family through the process of adoption. The household was also the template of the regional, national, and international social and political order. Not only international alliances but even some business relationships could have been established by patrons through arranging marriages of their children.

The patron (*patronus*) would be recognized in a leading position at the local and national level. Patrons used the authority and power (*potestas*) of their position to be protectors of, and benefactors to, those of lower social status, the protégés or clients (*cliens*). In return, the latter owed their patrons loyalty (*peitas*) and deference (*obsequium*). A third group of people in this system were mediators; they introduced clients to patrons and vice versa.[88] While this household paradigm with its clientele system was highly stratified, it was successful in allowing vertical social connections through the different strata. Thus, it was based on class stratification but nevertheless put people in touch through patron-client networks.[89] One's status may have been defined by descent, ethnicity, wealth, and/or other achievements but more important were, on the one hand, the status of one's patron for those of lower status and, on the other, the size of one's clientele for patrons.

Patron relations with clients were manifest in certain daily customs and rituals. In the morning, the patron would typically sit on a special chair in the atrium of his house, opposite to the main front door, to receive clients. Those would line up outside of the

87. It must be emphasized, however, that, in comparison to the *paterfamilias*, the role of the wife "was no equivalent legal concept for women, even though functional independence and personal authority to manage their own estates increased during the Principate" (L. Michael White, "Paul and *Pater Familias*," in Sampley, *Paul in the Greco-Roman World: A Handbook*, 2:171).

88. David A. deSilva, *Despising Shame: Honor Discourse and Community Maintenance in the Epistle to the Hebrews*, SBLDS 152 (Atlanta: Scholars Press, 1995), 226–39; White, "Paul," 172.

89. Richard P. Saller, "Poverty, Honor and Obligation in Imperial Rome," *Criterion* 37 (1998): 12–20; Peter Lampe, "Paul, Patrons, and Clients," in Sampley, *Paul in the Greco-Roman World: A Handbook*, 2:204.

house and be admitted by the chief household servant for the *salutatio*. After gestures of obeisance and devotion, they would vow their loyalty and ask for tasks to be accomplished in favor of the patron. In return for their services, clients were entitled to receive an allowance (*sportula*) in the form of either food or a fixed sum of money. The patron also hosted lavish dinners in the dining hall of his house, the *triclinium*. Both seating arrangement and food allotments were carefully chosen to respond to the status of guests and to maximize networking potential. The relation between patron and clients was officially based on the social tie of "friendship" (*amicitiae*).

Starting in Romans 1:5, Paul focuses on his apostolic mission in the larger world and particularly in Rome: "we have received grace and apostleship to bring about the obedience of faith among all the gentiles for the sake of his name." The specification that his apostolate is for "all the gentiles" is a reference to the territory outside of Palestine. This has been the turf of Paul's mission, and he has used similar language in previous letters (1 Thess 2:16; Gal 1:16).[90] Yet, Paul employs the term with different shades of meaning; its usage here does not mean that he imagines addressing exclusively gentiles in the sense of non-Jews in his letter. He rather writes to a mixed, ethnically diverse audience that includes believers in Christ with traditional Jewish adherence (e.g., Rom 3:1-8) and others without any (Paul reverts to a different usage in 1:13-14). It can be argued that certain passages in Romans are targeting specifically one of these two groups while other passages are more directed at the other. Only the believers in Christ with traditional Jewish adherence had been expelled from the city of Rome in 49 CE under the edict of Claudius; the other group was allowed to stay. The recent reintegration of the former is a special concern in this letter.

The members of the groups of believers in Christ are "God's beloved in Rome" (1:7). The adjective ἀγαπητοί, "beloved," is likewise attested in Romans 12:19 in a corporate sense (see also 1 Cor 4:14; 10:14; 15:58; 2 Cor 7:1; 12:19; Phil 2:12; 4:1). It reappears later in relation to Israel (Rom 11:28) and is then specifically applied to individuals (Rom 16:5-12;

90. Beverly Roberts Gaventa, *When in Romans: An Invitation to Linger with the Gospel According to Paul* (Grand Rapids: Baker Academic, 2016), 5.

1 Cor 4:17; Phlm 1, 16). It conveys the centrality and importance of the love ethos (or "love-mutualism") in the assemblies of believers in Christ (Rom 5:5; 8:31-39; 12:10; 13:8-10).[91] Paul and Phoebe, however, avoid the term "church" that they will employ only much later in the letter (16:5), and they mention no synagogue assemblies. This may be an indication that these groups had recently withdrawn from the established Jewish diaspora communities. Yet both communities, those of the traditional synagogues and those now associated with the groups who believed in Christ, belonged to the diverse spectrum of Second Temple Judaism.

Paul has always presented his calling as an experience of divine grace (χάρις, 1 Cor 3:10; Gal 2:9) and continues to do so in Romans (1:5, 7; see also 3:24; 12:3; 15:15).[92] The concept of grace will be explicated variously throughout Romans (see below, pp. 124, 137–140, 248). One of its key components is that God alone is the author of salvation and the sole agent of forgiveness, leaving no space for humans to boast of any achievements (3:21-31).[93] This levels the playing field sociologically. The vision of divine grace and of group adherence by being "in Christ" undermines the traditional competitive honor-shame culture of the Roman world, as is made clear later in the letter (12:1-8). Specifically, becoming or being a "saint" is no longer the goal of competitive acquired honor but a status imputed by God. *All* members of the groups of believers in Christ are "called to be saints" (1:7). Paul has used the standard term "saints," which designates the people of God, before (1 Cor 1:2; 2 Cor 1:1) and will use it again later (Phil 1:1).[94] His understanding of sainthood is a central element of the ethos of egalitarianism and openness that characterized Pauline communities.

This section of the letter concludes with his own form of epistolary greeting: "Grace to you and peace [χάρις ὑμῖν καὶ εἰρήνη] from God our Father and the Lord Jesus Christ" (Rom 1:7). Its poetic form with three lines of four words each and eight syllables in each line has been noted.[95] It is a standard phrase in Paul's letters (1 Cor 1:3; 2 Cor 1:2; Gal 1:3; Phil

91. Peter Oakes, *Reading Romans in Pompeii: Paul's Letter at Ground Level* (Minneapolis: Fortress; London: SPCK, 2009), 115–16; Arland J. Hultgren, *Paul's Letter to the Romans: A Commentary* (Grand Rapids: Eerdmans, 2011), 52.

92. Michael Wolter, *Paulus: Ein Grundriss seiner Theologie*, 3rd ed. (Neukirchen-Vluyn: Neukirchener Verlag, 2021), 24.

93. Beverly Roberts Gaventa, *Our Mother Saint Paul* (Louisville: Westminster John Knox, 2007), 138.

94. Wolfgang Kraus, *Das Volk Gottes: Zur Grundlegung der Ekklesiologie bei Paulus*, WUNT 85 (Tübingen: Mohr Siebeck, 1996), 160–64, 352.

95. Jewett, *Romans*, 115.

1:2; 1 Thess 1:1; Phlm 3). It can, however, be called intercultural as it modifies the traditional Greek greeting, "be joyful" (χαῖρε), and combines it with the conventional Jewish greeting, "peace" (εἰρήνη).[96] Both aspects are important for the assemblies in the city of Rome that had gone through rough times and were still experiencing internal tensions. These greetings were intentionally chosen.

The Prayer of Thanksgiving (1:8-15)

These verses feature, as an explicit prayer of thanksgiving to God (1:8-10), the announcement of Paul's anticipated visit to the assemblies in Rome and its reason. They are included here to provide the recipients/audiences with insights into the intimate sphere of the author's spiritual life so as to endear him to the recipients/audiences. They demonstrate the importance of the projected visit for Paul.

TRANSLATION MATTERS: Romans 1:13

The NRSV rendering "brothers and sisters" is based on the general decision of the NRSVue to present a Bible edition with bias-free language. Here, the specific aspect is gender-inclusive language. The Greek text of Romans 1:13 (and in Rom 7:1, 4; 8:12, 29; 10:1; 11:25; 12:1; 15:14, 30; 16:14, 17; 1 Cor 1:10-11; 2:1; 7:24; Gal 1:11; 3:15; 6:18, etc.) features the noun ἀδελφοί, which translates as "brothers" (or "brethren" in older Bible editions such as RSV; Traduction œcuménique de la Bible: "frères"; Reina Valera 1995: "hermanos"). In the NRSVue text, this term is being rendered as "brothers and sisters" while a footnote indicates that the Greek text has only "brothers." In NIV, an equivalent footnote provides: "The Greek word for *brothers and sisters* (*adelphoi*) refers here to believers, both men and women, as part of God's family." What can be said about the editorial decision of the NRSVue to issue a Bible edition with bias-free/gender-inclusive language? The noun ἀδελφοί in Romans 1:13 and elsewhere in Romans (as well as in other Pauline letters), a vocative plural, addresses the entire community. Yet the chapter in Romans 16 conveys greetings to several individual members of this community, thus mentioning their names. As will be pointed out below, already the first member of the assemblies in Rome to be greeted is a woman by the name of "Prisca"; the list then features an impressive number of other women and men. One should also take note of the following phrase in the list: "Greet Philologus, Julia, Nereus and his sister" (Rom 16:15). It features an actual occurrence of the term "sister," referring to a biological member of a nuclear

96. Tamez et al., *Philippians*, 41.

Rom 1:8-15

[8]First, I thank my God through Jesus Christ for all of you, because your faith is proclaimed throughout the world. [9]For God, whom I serve with my spirit by announcing the gospel of his Son, is my witness that without ceasing I remember you always in my prayers, [10]asking that by God's will I may somehow at last succeed in coming to you. [11]For I long to see you so that I may share with you some spiritual gift so that you may be strengthened—[12]or rather so that we may be mutually encouraged by each other's faith, both yours and mine. [13]I do not want you to be unaware, brothers and sisters, that I have often intended to come to you (but thus far have been prevented), in order that I may reap some harvest among you, as I have among the rest of the gentiles. [14]I am obligated both to Greeks and to barbarians, both to the wise and to the foolish, [15]hence my eagerness to proclaim the gospel to you also who are in Rome.

family. It is clear, then, that the Greek term ἀδελφοί in Romans 1:13, even though being a grammatical masculine plural, is used for groups of males and females while also being employed in a nonliteral meaning to designate members of the assembly. It can be translated according to its intended and figurative meaning as "brothers and sisters."[97] A feminist interpretation is committed to resisting the concealment of the presence of women in the audience through the terminological choice of "brothers/brethren"; it is committed to making their presence explicit.[98] With that in mind, one will nevertheless observe the tendency to leave the female member of the assembly anonymous while her biological brother Nereus is honored by having his name included (Rom 16:15).

The initial prayer of thanksgiving to God commends the "faith" (πίστις, Rom 1:8) that "is proclaimed throughout the world." This is an unusual choice of words; Paul typically mentions that the gospel is the object of proclamation (1 Cor 9:14; 11:26; Phil 1:18). Yet two aspects need to be clarified about this "faith": First, it is faith "in Christ [Jesus]" (Rom 16:3, 7, 9, 10, 16, etc.). As such, it is oriented toward the core of the gospel that Paul had been proclaiming in his letters and that is now explicated in,

97. Longenecker, *Romans*, 134–35; see also Peter Oakes, *Galatians*, Paideia: Commentaries on the New Testament (Grand Rapids: Baker Academic, 2015), 38–39.

98. Tamez et al., *Philippians*, 142.

for example, Romans 1:16-17; 3:21-31. Second, one may wonder whether Paul has been exaggerating. Why would the "faith" of a religious community be talked about elsewhere, and supposedly even in all of the world? Is this part of a *captatio benevolentiae* ("capture of goodwill"; see also later in 7:1; 15:14)? These words, however, gain historical credibility when considering that the faith of those in Rome, where Prisca and Aquila lived, was faith "in Christ." As such, it was the very cause of their expulsion from the city in 49 CE. As an imperial edict was a matter of political relevance that would have been known in most areas of the Roman Empire, the faith of these communities was indeed something that would, in the first century CE, have been broadcast throughout the Roman Empire—this is what "throughout the world" means.[99]

One may also ask if Paul does not likewise exaggerate when he mentions his ceaseless prayer in Romans 1:9-10. These words may just as well be interpreted as a *captatio benevolentiae* if we follow the traditional interpretation that Paul barely knows anyone in Rome. But the statement gains in plausibility under two assumptions. First, Paul has spent formative years in Corinth with Prisca and Aquila who were originally from Rome and are now back there. Paul's prayer includes his old friends whom he hopes to meet again in the future. He remembers his previous relationship with them and anticipates its continuation sometime soon. This is manifest at the rhetorical level as well; the section 1:8-12 is carefully structured along the interplay between "me, my" (verbs in first-person singular) and "you" (plural); it evinces a personal concern. Second, in Corinth, Prisca and Aquila would likely also have encountered Phoebe from the congregation in Cenchreae who was to carry the letter to Rome. Phoebe would have remembered her old friends and their faith in her own right and would have supported the statement about the prayer. She, too, had a previous relationship with them and anticipated more friendly encounters in the future. She would likely have endorsed these words as stand-in for the author, that is, as Paul's avatar. In the end, the prayer of Romans 1:9 is that of Paul and of Phoebe.

Paul then conveys his long-standing desire to visit Rome (Rom 1:10-15). All of Paul's letters had to do with personal contact and visits, but these have usually occurred in the past. While in this opening section of the letter, Paul conveys his plan to visit Rome, the later repetition of this aspect in Romans 15:22-33 contains the additional information that he ultimately intends to travel to Spain (15:24, 28). For the long term,

99. Jewett, *Romans*, 117–20.

he is oriented away from Jerusalem and Palestine, the homeland of the Jewish religion, even though he wants to visit this territory in the near future (15:25-26). Through his mission, he is implicitly challenging a prevailing negative definition of the concept of the Jewish diaspora. For Paul, this diaspora is his geographical, cultural, and spiritual home, and he anticipates to further diversify that existential experience.

How does Paul articulate the purpose of his expected visit to Rome? His words are: "For I long to see you so that I may share with you some spiritual gift so that you may be strengthened—or rather so that we may be mutually encouraged by each other's faith, both yours and mine" (Rom 1:11-12). These words are "carefully formulated so as to avoid giving offense to Roman believers."[100] Paul knows that the various assemblies of believers in the city of Rome had been established and sustained without his agency. He will not be the founder of anything. Using the disclosure formula "I do not want you to be unaware" in 1:13, therefore, he proposes "to travel to Rome to strengthen the Jesus communities there, to solidify their foundation, to set their faces firm in the midst of opposition."[101] He incorporates motifs from ancient friendship ethics into this passage, yet one should be careful not to push the idea too far that he has yet to meet members of these groups. To reiterate, Prisca and Aquila are some of his dearest friends, which means he knows at least a few of the recipients of the letter. Because of their spiritual maturity and previous success in leading an assembly in the city of Rome, Paul is careful to avoid any appearance of wanting to patronize them but instead proposes a collaborative process of mutual encouragement. In line with this approach is that he calls the intended outcome of his mission to reap some "harvest" (καρπός, literally "fruit," 1:13).

Phoebe gets to repeat from Romans 1:5 that Paul's mission is among the gentiles (1:13). She further specifies that he has a sense of obligation "both to Greeks and to barbarians" (Ἕλλησίν τε καὶ βαρβάροις) and toward the "wise" and the "foolish" (1:14). While "gentiles" is an umbrella term comprising the next two terms, "Greeks and barbarians" is a stereotypical formula of Greco-Roman antiquity (see, e.g., Isocrates, *Callim.* 27.5; *Phil.* 121.3; Demosthenes, *4 Philip.* 69.40; Strabo, *Geogr.* 1.4.9). "Greeks" is not equivalent to the modern usage where it designates citizens of the country of Greece. The first century CE knew of no country or nation

100. Jewett, *Romans*, 124.

101. Foster, "Justice," 687.

by that name; the territory of modern Greece was called "Macedonia" for its northern portion and "Achaia" for its southern part. What the NRSVue translates as "Greek" is the term Ἕλλην, which means what we call "Greco-Roman" in modern parlance. "Greek" is juxtaposed with "barbarians" (βάρβαροι), which refers to those who did not belong to the Greco-Roman culture and who had, for several centuries, been subjugated and colonized by the Roman Empire through its imperial quest. Moreover, "Greeks" is somewhat equivalent to "wise" and "barbarians" to "foolish." In fact, βάρβαροι is an ancient Greek onomatopoeic word (i.e., a word that sounds like what it means). It literally means something like "stammerers" or "stutterers," thus denigrated the other. "This concocted and highly pejorative term both mocked the way that foreign languages sounded to those who spoke Greek and denigrated the supposedly uncouth and inferior cultures of those who uttered such unintelligible sounds."[102] By contrast, the term Ἕλλην for the Greco-Roman world was defined by the use of language and through literacy. The term applied to someone who had adopted a Hellenistic lifestyle by undergoing a Hellenistic education.[103] This identity was a matter of both ascribed honor (for those born in Greco-Roman cultures) and of acquired honor (for those who had obtained the necessary education). Hellenistic identity was, therefore, a coveted asset in the competitive arena of the ancient honor-shame system.

The sentence in Romans 1:13 explains that Paul has been delayed on his way to the city of Rome: "I do not want you to be unaware, brothers and sisters, that I have often intended to come to you (but thus far have been prevented)." Revisited in 15:22, this is not just epistolary politeness. In his previous correspondence with the assemblies in Corinth, Paul had given a graphic list of the hardship that he needed to suffer (2 Cor 11:24-29). Little did he know that more of that trouble was ahead—or was he perhaps aware of it?

These binary terms, "Greeks and barbarians" in Romans 1:14, are notable because Paul's mission is to people who fall under both categories. This is not surprising considering Paul's own hybrid identity and multiple citizenships. As a Jew, he was not a full member of the "Greek"/ Hellenistic culture; Judaism had its own struggles with Hellenism. With

102. Longenecker, *Romans*, 138.

103. Malina and Pilch, *Social-Science Commentary*, 3–4; Joan C. Campbell, *Phoebe: Patron and Emissary*, Paul's Social Network: Brothers and Sisters in Faith (Collegeville, MN: Liturgical Press, 2009), 12.

that, he had a critical view of such binary stereotypes. On the other hand, based on an awareness of Jewish Scriptures, he ultimately had an inclusive vision of different cultures even if taking over inherent hierarchical concepts.[104] His intended travels were to bring him to Palestine at the eastern fringes of the Roman Empire, then to Rome at the center of Roman power, and from there to Spain at the utmost western periphery. The Romans considered Spaniards "as barbarians par excellence because so large a proportion continued to resist Roman rule, to rebel with frightening frequency, and to refuse to speak Latin or to use the Roman names for their cities"[105] (Livy, *Hist*. 25.33.2; 27.17.10; Caesar, *Bell. civ.* 1.38.3; 1.44.2; Pliny, *Ep*. 8.24.4). Paul nevertheless responded to the call to go there of all places.

The Power of the Gospel (Rom 1:16-17)

These two verses feature the thematic statement for the entire letter.[106] As such, they are the *propositio* ("main thesis") about the gospel, presented here as the powerful embodiment of the justification (NRSVue: "righteousness") of God. They also attest to the importance of "faith" for the gospel; the term occurs no fewer than four times in these two sentences.

TRANSLATION MATTERS: Romans 1:16

The translation of both the terms "Jews" and "Greek" needs to be clarified. In Romans, the Greek term Ἰουδαῖος appears repeatedly (1:16; 2:9-10, 17; 9:24; 10:12). Elsewhere, Paul calls his own religion Ἰουδαϊσμός (Gal 1:13-14). The NRSVue, NIV, and NKJV customarily render these terms as "Jew" and "Judaism," respectively. Paul conceptualizes Jewishness vis-à-vis "Greek" (Ἕλλην, Ἕλληνες) identity (Rom 1:16; 2:9-10, 17, 28-29; 3:1-2, 9, 29, etc.) and sometimes vis-à-vis "gentiles" (ἔθνος, Rom 9:24)[107] but never in contrast to Christian identity.

104. Kraus, *Volk*, 347–50.

105. Jewett, *Romans*, 131.

106. James D. G. Dunn, *Romans 1–8*, WBC 38a (Dallas: Word, 1988), 37; Morna D. Hooker, *From Adam to Christ: Essays on Paul* (Eugene, OR: Wipf & Stock, 2008), 83; François Vouga, "L'Épître aux Romains," in *Introduction au Nouveau Testament: Son histoire, son écriture, sa théologie*, ed. Daniel Marguerat (Geneva: Labor et Fides, 2000), 160.

107. Bernadette J. Brooten, *Love Between Women: Early Christian Responses to Female Homoeroticism*, Chicago Series on Sexuality, History, and Society (Chicago: University of Chicago Press, 1996), 220.

Rom 1:16-17

16For I am not ashamed of the gospel;
it is God's saving power for everyone
who believes, for the Jew first and also
for the Greek. 17For in it the righteousness of God is revealed through faith
for faith, as it is written, "The one who
is righteous will live by faith."

The question regarding the exact meaning and proper translation of the terms Ἰουδαῖος and Ἰουδαϊσμός has been hotly debated in recent scholarship. There are at least three aspects to consider, which have to do with semantics, the interpretive (abstract terminological) categories, and translation: First, the semantic problem is whether this terminology references the identity of a *socio-religious culture* with either specific rituals, celebrations, and practices or a common ancestry, or whether it functions as an *ethnic designation* for people from a specific geographic area, particularly the Persian administrative entity Judah/Yehud. A survey of ancient texts and inscriptions from different locations at different eras yields a variety of usages; in addition, there are, even for a specific ethnic or religious group, sometimes differences between emic (internal) and etic (external) nomenclatures. A single, unified terminology, however, has never existed; the term emerges as a dynamic and flexible terminological category and may also be used as a metaphor.[108]

Second, however, it has been questioned whether a distinct interpretive (or abstract terminological) category such as "religion" existed at all in antiquity, gradually favoring an ethnic meaning of the term.[109] There are, third, concerns about the proper translation and its ramifications. Current usage sometimes deploys "Jewish" for the ethnic designation and reserves "Judaean/Judean" (from the Greek translation of Hebrew: יהודי/יהודה/Aramaic: יהד), "Judaic," or "Judahite" for the religious movement (especially in the ancient period; another possible equivalent is "early Jewish"). The terms "Jew" or "Judaism" today should not, however, be construed as categorically distinguished from its own history in antiquity, which the employment of the distinct term suggests. The evident coherence or continuity between the Judaism of antiquity and its forms today should prevent such a construal of discontinuity.[110] In consideration of the ongoing debate of this terminological problem, some prefer to leave the

108. Oda Wischmeyer, "Paul's Religion: A Review of the Problem," in *Paul, Luke and the Graeco-Roman World: Essays in Honour of Alexander J.M. Wedderburn*, ed. Alf Christophersen et al., JSNTSup 217 (London: Sheffield Academic, 2002), 79–80; Ole Jakob Filtvedt, "A 'Non-Ethnic' People?," *Bib* 97 (2016): 101–20.

109. Daniel Boyarin, "Semantic Differences; or, 'Judaism'/'Christianity,'" in *The Ways That Never Parted: Jews and Christians in Late Antiquity and the Early Middle Ages*, ed. Adam H. Becker and Annette Yoshiko Reed, TSAJ 95 (Tübingen: Mohr Siebeck, 2003), 66–71.

110. Amy-Jill Levine, *The Misunderstood Jew: The Church and the Scandal of the Jewish Jesus* (San Francisco: HarperSanFrancisco, 2006), 160, 165; Johnson Hodge, *If Sons*, 11–15.

term untranslated.[111] David M. Miller concludes relative to this terminological dilemma: "Since *Ioudaios* is associated with geography, common ancestry and the distinctive religious beliefs and practices of the *Ioudaioi*, neither English term corresponds precisely to the ancient label."[112] Due to the ongoing debate, the terms Ἰουδαῖος and Ἰουδαϊσμός have been translated and used with a variety of meanings in recent scholarship; sometimes the same scholar has adopted different practices over time. In the present volume, this terminological dilemma cannot be resolved. As the recommendation of the series editors calls for the (critically reflected) usage of the NRSVue and its terminology, I shall, consistent with the NRSVue and continuing its practice, translate the term Ἰουδαῖος as "Jew" and Ἰουδαϊσμός as "Judaism."[113]

The gospel of Paul and Phoebe is a dynamic power that has "saving power for everyone who believes, for the Jew first and also for the Greek" (Rom 1:16). The "content" of his gospel message is Jesus, the Son of God (1:3-4), and this gospel is for both the Jews and the gentiles. It has universal reach.[114] All who think that Judaism is categorically about the law and Christianity, even at its earliest stage, only about faith may reconsider their opinion upon the realization that this passage features a quotation from the Jewish Scriptures (Hab 2:4 [LXX]). Paul did the same in his previous letter to the Galatians (3:11). A controversial discussion about the Jewish law occurred, therefore, at the very heart of Second Temple Judaism. This is also manifest, for example, in the so-called sectarian texts from Qumran. Later, the otherwise unknown Rabbi Hamnunah likewise commented on this passage in a reflection on how religious authorities had reduced the number of 613 Laws of Moses that every Jewish male was required to observe. Rabbi Hamnunah noted that David had reduced them to eleven in Psalm 15, Isaiah to six (Isa 33:15), Micah to three (Mic 6:8), Amos to two (Amos 5:4), and the prophet Habakkuk to one single sentence, namely, 2:4 (*Tab*. 43).[115]

111. Kobel, *Paulus als interkulturellerVermittler*, 2.

112. David M. Miller, "Ioudaios, Ioudaioi," *EBR* 13 (2016): 234–35, at 235.

113. Matthew Thiessen, *Paul and the Gentile Problem* (New York: Oxford University Press, 2016), 171.

114. Michael Theobald, "'Geboren aus dem Samen Davids . . .' (Röm 1,3): Wandlungen im paulinischen Christus-Bild?," *ZNW* 102 (2011): 235–60, at 240.

115. Thomas Staubli, "Alttestamentliche Konstellationen der Rechtfertigung des Menschen vor Gott," in *Biblische Anthropologie: Neue Einsichten aus dem Alten Testament*, ed. Christian Frevel, QD 237 (Freiburg: Herder, 2010), 88.

Romans mentions in quick succession "gentiles," then "Greeks and barbarians," "wise and foolish" (Rom 1:13-14), and finally "Jews" and "Greeks" (1:16). These were all fundamental categories that constructed people's identities in the competitive arena of the ancient honor-shame system. Paul's own calling for the foreseeable future was to gentiles and to barbarians; these are not necessarily honorable identities within the spectrum of this system. If the gospel calls him to go there, then that gospel itself may be shameful. In a similar way, Phoebe herself had been dispatched to travel to Rome, the center of the gentile world, speaking to assemblies of mostly gentile people. This pericope nevertheless asserts: "I am not ashamed of the gospel" (1:16). The choice of terminology reveals the countercultural dimension of their decisions. In a paradoxical way from the perspective of the prevalent mainstream culture, the gospel about the Son is God's saving power (literally "God's power for salvation," δύναμις . . . θεοῦ . . . εἰς σωτηρίαν). Paul and Phoebe choose a term from the propaganda of Rome's emperor cult to designate its outcome: It brings about "salvation" (σωτηρία). This is no distant, eschatological, or utopian hope but a present reality, manifest in social inclusion across and throughout the known world of antiquity while maintaining a positive recognition of difference and diversity.[116]

Ramifications for Paul through his calling to the gentiles and barbarians are not limited to visiting specific territories and living there. He had previously indicated that his success as a missionary was based on the adaptability and flexibility of his own identity. In 1 Corinthians 9:19-22 he described successively how he became an "enslaved person," "like a Jew," someone "under the law" or "outside of the law," or someone who was "weak"; he has ultimately "become all things to all people, that I might by all means save some" (see also the similar statement in 1 Cor 10:33). These descriptors relate to identities that are all characterized through dependency or lack thereof, which means the freedom of choice. His missionary or pedagogical strategy, therefore, required a high degree of identification with those among whom he was working. It is also "a theological imperative which is inextricably linked to his beliefs

116. Ehrensperger, *That We May Be Mutually Encouraged*, 191–92. See also Kenneth Mtata, "The 'Gospel' as the Hermeneutic of Emancipation in Paul's Letters: Contemporary Implications," in *Pauline Hermeneutics: Exploring the "Power of the Gospel,"* ed. Eve-Marie Becker and Kenneth Mtata, LWF Studies 2016/3 (Leipzig: Evangelische Verlagsanstalt, 2017), 19–20.

about Christ's life and death."[117] As such, it relates to a christological conviction about the importance of incarnation. It means that Paul shares the identities of those whom he visits, even if they are not considered honorable by dominant standards.

The gospel that is "God's saving power" is, according to the NRSVue, the "righteousness [δικαιοσύνη] of God" (Rom 1:17). This term, which has another nine occurrences in Pauline literature, has been at the focus of exegetical debates for a long time, in particular in scholarship related to the so-called New Perspective on Paul.[118] First, one needs to observe an inconsistency in how modern English Bible translations render the terminology derived from the Greek δικ- stem: The NRSVue renders the noun δικαιοσύνη as "righteousness" but the similar noun δικαίωσις as "justification" (4:25) and the related verb δικαιόω as "to justify" (3:24). To avoid this inconsistency and to indicate the semantic homogeneity of the different forms, I shall translate the noun δικαιοσύνη as "justification."[119] Likewise, the noun "justification" in 1:17 has to be understood in relation to the quotation from Habakkuk 2:4 (LXX) at the end of this sentence. The NRSVue translates Romans 1:17: "The one who is righteous will live by faith." The adjective is δίκαιος; it should then be rendered as "just" or "justified."

Second, the appropriate understanding of "justification of God" needs to be clarified. In Paul's usage as well as in Romans, the term is no ultimate divine attribute that is unattainable for humans, as an objective genitive would have it. Nor is it a punitive category that presents God as a judge bent on punishing humans (in the sense of distributive or retributive justice). Instead, the "justification of God" should be interpreted as a subjective genitive that articulates God's activity as global transformation and salvation of humans.[120] The translation of δικαιοσύνη as "justification," because of the Latin word component *facere* (to make, produce), conveys the semantic aspect of initiative and activity of divine salvation better than the rendering "righteousness of God," in which the final syllable "-ness"

117. Johnson Hodge, "Apostle," 285.

118. Calhoun, *Definitions*, 157.

119. This translation, which differs from that of NRSVue, will be discussed in more detail below in the comments under "Translation Matters" on Romans 3:21, 22.

120. Longenecker, *Romans*, 168–76, 393. The translation of δικαιοσύνη as "justification" is also found in Calhoun, *Definitions*, 157–68 (although Calhoun usually leaves the Greek term untranslated).

rather indicates a static quality.[121] Paul had previously indicated that this "justification" relies on God's activity and has its source in the state of being "in Christ": "For our sake he [God] made him [Jesus] to be sin who knew no sin, so that in him we might become the justification of God" (2 Cor 5:21).[122] One of the recipients of these words of Paul was Phoebe! The understanding that, in this passage, the "justification of God" would designate a descriptive quality of God is excluded as the subject is "we," humanity, who are to attain that status. In Romans, it is rhetorically linked to "God's saving power" (Rom 1:16) by two symmetrical statements.[123] It is, furthermore, intrinsically connected to, and explicated through, atonement concepts to convey God's mercy, explicated at length later in the letter (3:21-31). In Rome, Phoebe gets to proclaim a powerful message. She expresses the expectation that the audience will enact this status of justification through the agency of God's Spirit (6:12-23; 8:1-4). But the initiative and activity are that of God alone. This important aspect targets the honor-shame system of the patriarchal Roman society that required active competition for status. In this arena, justification was being attained by those seeking to acquire individual honor. But for many outside of the ancient malestream culture, justification was impossible due to the lack of ascribed honor. In Rome, Phoebe proclaimed a world in which these logics no longer have any place; the identity of the group relies not on competition but on God alone. Inclusive and restorative justification for every member in a diverse group of people is now the power to overcome divisions among the assemblies in Rome.[124] Tongue in cheek, one could say that, with these contents, Romans 1:16 about God's saving power is the John 3:16 passage of Paul and Phoebe for the audiences in Rome.

The fact that God justifies humans "is revealed through faith for faith" (Rom 1:17). This sentence alone features two of the four occurrences of the term "faith" (πίστις) in what is the main thesis statement (*propositio*) of Romans. Again, the question is how to best interpret these words. They are unclear due to ellipsis; some central words have been omitted and are to be inserted by the audience. For some modern interpreters, the first occurrence of "faith" refers to the faith or trust of Jesus Christ

121. See the comment that righteousness "has a peculiar ring in English, suggesting to many something like self-righteousness, which is the last thing that Paul would mean by it" (Fitzmyer, *Romans*, 258).

122. The NRSVue translates: "For our sake God made the one who knew no sin to be sin, so that in him we might become the righteousness of God."

123. Jewett, *Romans*, 136.

124. Jewett, *Romans*, 143.

that is thought to be the source of the faith of humanity.[125] The weakness of this proposal is that the missing information, namely, the "faith of Jesus" (if indeed understood as subjective genitive), is provided much later, in Romans 3:22. When drawing on the more immediate context, then first the various occurrences of the term "faith" in the preceding introduction (1:1-7) and thanksgiving (1:8-15) should be considered. There, Paul and Phoebe mention "the obedience of faith among all the gentiles" (1:5); they also praise the assemblies in Rome "because your faith is proclaimed throughout the world" (1:8) and desire that "we may be mutually encouraged by each other's faith" (1:12). This short survey of the way in which "faith" is employed in these introductory passages shows that it consistently refers to a religious expression among and by distinct human groups.

The proposal that the first occurrence of "faith" in Romans 1:17 could refer to the faith of Jesus Christ is rendered somewhat unlikely through Paul's quotation of Habakkuk 2:4 (LXX). In MT, the passage, which is part of an address by God, reads: "but the just lives by his faith" (in the sense of remaining alive in adverse circumstances). LXX changes it to: "but the just will live by my [God's] faith." Thus the attribution of faith is different in MT, where it is that of a human, while in LXX, it is that of God.[126] Interestingly, this passage is quoted in both Galatians 3:11 and Romans 1:17 without any pronoun. Paul and Phoebe were certainly aware of the difference between MT and LXX. But regardless, had they attempted to propose "through faith" as a reference to the faith of God or Jesus, then they could have included the pronoun μου ("my") from LXX; the result would have been unambiguous. By omitting the pronoun "my" from the quotation, the argument that "through faith" references faith as a human activity has become more likely.

Second, one needs to also consider the semantic range of the Greek noun πίστις, usually rendered as "faith," and the verb πιστεύω, usually rendered as "to have faith, to believe." As mentioned above, πίστις was, like the terms "gospel," "salvation," or the title "Son of God," an important term in the context of the Roman imperial cult. Conveying the proper expression of a person's piety, it associates several semantic aspects, such as belief, obedience, trust, hope, and faithfulness or loyalty. In Romans,

125. Stanley K. Stowers, *A Rereading of Romans: Justice, Jews, and Gentiles* (New Haven: Yale University Press, 1994), 202; Nijay K. Gupta, "Paul and *Pistis Christou*," in *The Oxford Handbook of Pauline Studies*, ed. Matthew V. Novenson and R. Barry Matlock (Oxford: Oxford University Press, 2022), 470–87.

126. Müller, "Bedeutung," 753.

such faith or trust in a crucified savior is an inclusive matter, indicated by the phrase "for everyone [πᾶς] who believes" (1:16). As such,

> it is part of the gospel *exposé* that the Roman imperial "savior" . . . does not deliver the life, salvation, and plenitude that are tirelessly and tiringly advertised in the imperial propaganda, whether in the person of Augustus as "the savior of the universe" or Nero as "the savior and benefactor of the universe." The imperial propaganda, its fallacies at times apparent to the Romans as an emperor without clothes apart from Paul's exposé, faces censure for being an idolatrous constellation and for failing the test of truth-in-advertising.[127]

Third, in the letter's *propositio* (Rom 1:16-17), the succession of "for the Jew first" and "also for the Greek" in 1:16 may likewise be considered a plausible reference. The two occurrences of "faith" in 1:17 directly connect to and further explicate the meaning of the preceding "everyone who believes," and these are, of course, "the Jew first" and "the Greek." This means that the faith of the Jew is the source of that of the "Greek," an interpretation that is consistent with Paul's self-understanding as a Jew who is an apostle to the gentiles and that of Phoebe as such a gentile. This line is about their own faith. Paul is proud about his Jewish identity, and he will soon demonstrate that it naturally includes faith (4:1-25).[128] Phoebe is proud about her identity as a gentile. The sentence in 1:17 designates a progression or movement and conveys the contagion of faith through missionary activities, such as Paul's—or those of Phoebe as his avatar. This progression of faith is the reason for the collection for Jerusalem (15:25-28).

In sum, "through faith for faith" in Romans 1:17 refers to a religious expression at the human level. While "faith of Jesus" in Romans 3:22 could theoretically be construed as referring to the faith *of* Jesus, the previous usages of "faith" (as well as those in chapter 4 about the faith of Abraham, etc.) render such an interpretation unlikely.

127. Sigve K. Tonstad, *The Letter to the Romans: Paul among the Ecologists*, Earth Bible Commentary 7 (Sheffield: Sheffield Phoenix, 2016), 73 (with reference to Jewett, *Romans*, 139). See also Paula Fredriksen, "Paul's Letter to the Romans, the Ten Commandments, and Pagan 'Justification by Faith,'" *JBL* 133 (2014): 801–8.

128. Gregory Tatum, "'To the Jew first' (Romans 1:16): Paul's Defense of Jewish Privilege in Romans," in *Celebrating Paul: Festschrift in Honor of Jerome Murphy-O'Connor, OP, and Joseph A. Fitzmyer, SJ*, ed. Peter Spitaler, CBQMS 48 (Washington, DC: Catholic Biblical Association of America, 2011), 275–86.

Romans 1:18–3:31

Justification through Faith: No Distinction

"The Guilt of Humankind" (1:18-32)

Regarding its overall rhetorical disposition, the corpus of the letter begins at Romans 1:18 and extends through 15:13.[1] The first section of the epistle, which I have divided into four large parts, is the theological section in 1:18–11:36. The first of these four parts deals with human sin and justification through faith (1:18–3:31).[2] The initial section is generally known as "the guilt of humankind" (NRSVue) or "God's Wrath against Sinful Humanity" (NIV).[3] The appropriateness of these headings remains to be discussed.

The passage in Romans 1:18-32 is an unexpected thesis and rationale for three reasons. First, the preceding *propositio* in 1:16-17 described God's initiative and activity on behalf of humanity. Therefore, the description of the fallen state of humanity is, to say the least, no continuation of this theme. Second, Paul has also never written anything like 1:18-32 in any of his previous letters. Therefore, anyone familiar with his letters

1. Michael Wolter, *Der Brief an die Römer*, vol. 1: *Röm 1–8*, EKKNT 6/1 (Neukirchen-Vluyn: Neukirchener Verlag; Ostfildern: Patmos, 2014), 69, 129.

2. See the exposition of the structure of Romans above.

3. Furthermore, the ESV and NKJV both have "God's Wrath on Unrighteousness."

Rom 1:18-32

[18]For the wrath of God is revealed from
heaven against all ungodliness and injustice of those who by their injustice
suppress the truth. [19]For what can be
known about God is plain to them, because God has made it plain to them.
[20]Ever since the creation of the world
God's eternal power and divine nature, invisible though they are, have
been seen and understood through
the things God has made. So they are
without excuse, [21]for though they knew
God, they did not honor him as God or
give thanks to him, but they became
futile in their thinking, and their senseless hearts were darkened. [22]Claiming
to be wise, they became fools, [23]and
they exchanged the glory of the immortal God for images resembling a
mortal human or birds or four-footed
animals or reptiles.

[24]Therefore God gave them over in
the desires of their hearts to impurity, to
the dishonoring of their bodies among
themselves. [25]They exchanged the
truth about God for a lie and worshiped
and served the creature rather than the
Creator, who is blessed forever! Amen.

must have been surprised about these poetic and dense sentences. A conclusion with words like "those who practice such things deserve to die" (1:32) is highly unusual for Paul. And third, none of the issues mentioned in this passage are picked up in the hortatory passage in Romans 12:1–15:13 that repeats important topics of ethical or practical relevance from previous sections. Therefore, already in 1975, John C. O'Neill was of the opinion that both vocabulary and style of 1:18-32 are unusual for Paul.[4] What exactly is so unusual?

No doubt, Romans 1:18-32 is "a rhetorical tour de force."[5] On the one hand, it is replete with different stylistic features aimed at enhancing the aesthetic experience during the performance in front of the intended audiences in Rome. To name but a few, there is a synonymous parallelism (two lines with identical meaning) in 1:21; there is a *paronomasia* (repetition of the same word or word stem in close proximity) in 1:23 (ἀφθάρτου θεοῦ . . . φθαρτοῦ ἀνθρώπου; "imperishable God . . . perishable human");[6] there is, also in 1:23, a *homoioptoton* (reiteration of the same case

4. John C. O'Neill, *Paul's Letter to the Romans*, PNTC (Harmondsworth: Penguin, 1975), 41. His arguments are supported by William O. Walker Jr., "Romans 1.18–2.29: A Non-Pauline Interpolation?," *NTS* 45 (1999): 533–52.

5. Robert Jewett, *Romans: A Commentary*, Hermeneia (Minneapolis: Fortress, 2007), 148.

6. In an attempt to reconstruct the *paronomasia* of the Greek, Robert Jewett proposes the following translation: "they changed the glory of the imperishable God into a likeness of an image of a perishable human" (Jewett, *Romans*, 31, 148).

26For this reason God gave them over to dishonorable passions. Their females exchanged natural intercourse for unnatural, 27and in the same way also the males, giving up natural intercourse with females, were consumed with their passionate desires for one another. Males committed shameless acts with males and received in their own persons the due penalty for their error.

28And since they did not see fit to acknowledge God, God gave them over to an unfit mind and to do things that should not be done. 29They were filled with every kind of injustice, evil, covetousness, malice. Full of envy, murder, strife, deceit, craftiness, they are gossips, 30slanderers, God-haters, insolent, haughty, boastful, inventors of evil, rebellious toward parents, 31foolish, faithless, heartless, ruthless. 32They know God's decree, that those who practice such things deserve to die, yet they not only do them but even applaud others who practice them.

ending in successive terminology), πετεινῶν καὶ τετραπόδων καὶ ἑρπετῶν, "birds or four-footed animals or reptiles"; there is a *homoioteleuton* (an occurrence of the same or similar endings) of the -ια endings in πάσῃ ἀδικίᾳ πονηρίᾳ πλεονεξίᾳ κακίᾳ, "every kind of injustice, evil, covetousness, malice" (1:29); and there is *anaphora* in ἀσυνέτους ἀσυνθέτους ἀστόργους ἀνελεήμονας, "foolish, faithless, heartless, ruthless" (1:31). Hence, these lines have been crafted very thoughtfully, evincing the level of expertise in the process of composing and writing the letter. These sentences were supposed to leave a deep impression!

On the other hand, there is a surprise element. Through its first word Ἀποκαλύπτεται ("it is revealed"), the section in Romans 1:18-32 connects well with the preceding *propositio* in 1:16-17. There, the main verb in the second sentence is exactly the same. Furthermore, both sentences of the *propositio* have "for" (γάρ) as their second word, just like 1:18. The new passage therefore appears to be a logical extrapolation, continuing previous ideas, themes, and terminology. But the exact opposite happens. The remainder of the passage in Romans 1:18-32 is decidedly different not only with regard to the *propositio* but also with regard to everything Paul has ever written in previous letters. These differences start with the next words, "the wrath of God" (ὀργὴ θεοῦ, 1:18). Elsewhere in the New Testament, they occur only twice in the Deutero-Pauline Epistles (Eph 5:6; Col 3:6) and once in Revelation (19:15).[7] The problem pertains also to the rest

7. Walker, "Romans," 536.

of the passage; a shorter summary of the findings is that approximately one-third of the words in this passage do not appear anywhere else in Pauline literature while almost half of them are not typical of Pauline vocabulary.[8] Such observations need to be taken seriously; they imply that Romans 1:18-32, in spite of the above-mentioned syntactic features, is no logical extrapolation of the letter opening in 1:1-17.

Therefore, proposals have been made that the passage may be an interpolation.[9] I will not follow this conjecture. Instead, I propose to read this section as an inherent part of the letter that follows a very specific rhetorical objective.

Romans 1:18-32 consists of two larger sections: a thesis and rationale of the exposure of human suppression of the truth about God (1:18-23), and a section on the human distortion as a current indication of wrath (1:24-32). Most sentences in 1:18-27 are presented as logical conclusions; they are connected with conjunctions such as γάρ ("for," 1:18, 20), διότι ("for," 1:19, 21), διό ("therefore," 1:24), and διὰ τοῦτο ("for this reason," 1:26). The exclamation ἀμήν ("amen") in the second section (1:25) signals the solicitation of an affirmation from the hearers.[10] The catalogue of evils (1:29-31) consists mostly of a lengthy enumeration of nouns. The consequence of wicked behavior, which is the perpetrator's death, is stated in 1:32.

The section about the truth that humans suppress sets out with an assertion that humans have the ability to obtain knowledge of God's eternal power and divine nature despite their invisibility. Such a statement is, to some degree, an "oxymoron."[11] It is in line with Stoic ideas and is a frequent reference text in many later scholarly discussions of the topic of natural theology.[12] This complex theme does not need to be explored here in detail. What is relevant is that such an argument is not to be found elsewhere in Paul's letters—in fact, he previously stated the opposite when writing that, "in the wisdom of God, the world did not know God through wisdom" (οὐκ ἔγνω ὁ κόσμος διὰ τῆς σοφίας τὸν θεόν,

8. Walker, "Romans," 535–56.

9. Walker, "Romans," 533–52.

10. Carl R. Holladay, *A Critical Introduction to the New Testament: Interpreting the Message and Meaning of Jesus Christ* (Nashville: Abingdon, 2005), 485.

11. Heinrich Schlier, *Der Römerbrief*, HTKNT 6 (Freiburg: Herder, 1977), 52. See also Sigve K. Tonstad, *The Letter to the Romans: Paul among the Ecologists*, Earth Bible Commentary 7 (Sheffield: Sheffield Phoenix, 2016), 386.

12. See the examples in Joseph A. Fitzmyer, *Romans: A New Translation with Introduction and Commentary*, AB 33 (New York: Doubleday, 1993), 273.

1 Cor 1:21).[13] The assertion in Romans 1:19-20 is all the more peculiar, therefore, considering that it goes on to construe a general human state of no excuse for the lack of appropriate acknowledgment of God. As a consequence, humans do not respond with suitable worship but turn to idolatry (1:21-23). The second section in 1:24-32 has an initial focus on same-sex practices. Because of the "desires of their hearts," God gave humanity up to "impurity." Here, idolatry is referenced once more as the reason for what follows (1:24-25) before same-sex practices between "their females" (θήλειαι αὐτῶν, 1:26b) and "the males" (οἱ ἄρσενες, 1:27) are singled out as examples of human depravity. In this sentence, human ontology is conceptualized in binary categories. In either case, the argument is that "natural intercourse" (φυσικὴ χρῆσις) was exchanged for "unnatural" (παρὰ φύσιν).[14] These are "shameless acts" and lead to "due penalty for their error" (1:27). The next pericope moves on to a broad catalogue of evils, including "murder" (1:29-31). It emulates "the Greek tradition of four cardinal vices that stand as the opposites of the cardinal virtues, paralleled by the four passions in Stoicism."[15]

The passage in Romans 1:18-32 has often been understood as a comprehensive description of human wickedness. Likewise, the one sentence about same-sex activities in 1:26-27 has frequently been presented as a full articulation of Paul's theological and moral stance.[16] Taken as such, it is the strongest statement against same-sex practices in the entire New Testament.[17] In past centuries and still today, it had and has a prominent

13. James D. G. Dunn, *Romans 1–8*, WBC 38a (Dallas: Word, 1988), 71; see also Antoinette Wire, "1 Corinthians," in *Searching the Scriptures*, vol. 2: *A Feminist Commentary*, ed. Elisabeth Schüssler Fiorenza (New York: Crossroad, 1994), 162.

14. Taking into consideration Romans 11:24, Daniel A. Helminiak suggests that "unnatural" is better rendered as "atypical"; cf. Daniel A. Helminiak, *What the Bible Really Says about Homosexuality*, millennium ed. (Tajique, NM: Alamo Square Press, 2000), 82.

15. Jewett, *Romans*, 183–84. See also Diana M. Swancutt, "Sexy Stoics and the Rereading of Romans 1.18–2.16," in *A Feminist Companion to Paul*, ed. Amy-Jill Levine with Marianne Blickenstaff, FCNTECW 6 (London: T&T International, 2004), 47–53; Matthew Thiessen, *Paul and the Gentile Problem* (New York: Oxford University Press, 2016), 53–54.

16. Cf. Beverly Roberts Gaventa, *Our Mother Saint Paul* (Louisville: Westminster John Knox, 2007), 113; Cynthia L. Westfall, *Paul and Gender: Reclaiming the Apostle's Vision for Men and Women in Christ* (Grand Rapids: Baker Academic, 2016), 200–201; Richard N. Longenecker, *The Epistle to the Romans: A Commentary on the Greek Text*, NIGTC (Grand Rapids: Eerdmans, 2016), 168–76, 217.

17. Longenecker, *Romans*, 168–76, 217; Alain Gignac, *L'épître aux Romains*, Commentaire biblique: Nouveau Testament 6 (Paris: Cerf, 2014), 117; Michael Theobald, "Paul and Same-Sex Sexuality: A Plea for a Sensible Approach to Scripture," in *"Who*

place in the establishment of heteronormativity and concomitant homophobia, which means the rejection and condemnation of homosexuality by Christian churches (and, informed by such disapproval, often also by secular society).[18] This stance has, in turn, solicited vehement and fervent pushback from LGBT (or LGBTQI+) groups.

Scholars have offered a variety of interpretive responses to the sentence in Romans 1:26-27. All of these arguments have been debated extensively and, to a lesser or larger degree, critiqued. The following five positions have emerged in this discourse:

1. Romans 1:26-27 has been understood as a statement against homosexuality as such.[19] Yet, an interpretation like that is anachronistic. The terminology and concepts of homo- and heterosexuality are relatively recent; they were coined in the nineteenth century CE. If these terms are understood as referring to committed relations embedded within a specific social environment and lifestyle, then it is clear that the ancient world did not know this phenomenon. It only knows of same-sex acts, which is what is mentioned in Romans 1:27 (and perhaps in 1:26). Therefore, it is preferable to speak about "same-sex practices" or "same-sex activities" instead of "homosexuality" or "homoeroticism" or "lesbian" or "gay" relations in exegetical discussions.[20]

Am I to Judge?" Homosexuality and the Catholic Church, ed. Stephan Goertz, trans. Alissa Jones Nelson (Berlin: de Gruyter, 2022), 44, 54.

18. Elizabeth A. Castelli, "Romans," in Schüssler Fiorenza, *Searching the Scriptures*, 2:282; Stephen D. Moore, *God's Beauty Parlor: And Other Queer Spaces in and around the Bible*, Contraversions (Stanford: Stanford University Press, 2001), 201–2; Stephan Goertz, "'Who Am I to Judge?' An Overview of the Context and the Themes of the Contributions," in Goertz, *"Who Am I to Judge?,"* 1–2.

19. See, e.g., Preston Sprinkle, "Paul and Homosexual Behavior: A Critical Evaluation of the Excessive-Lust Interpretation of Romans 1:26-27," *BBR* 25 (2015): 497–517, at 516; Robert M. Calhoun, "Same-Sex Relations," in *The Oxford Encyclopedia of the Bible and Law*, vol. 2, ed. Brent A. Strawn (Oxford: Oxford University Press, 2015), 2:265–71, at 270; Longenecker, *Romans*, 217.

20. For a discussion of the problem, see Eva Cantarella, *Bisexuality in the Ancient World*, trans. Cormac Ô Cuilleanâin (New Haven: Yale University Press, 1992), 211–22; Bernadette J. Brooten, *Love Between Women: Early Christian Responses to Female Homoeroticism*, Chicago Series on Sexuality, History, and Society (Chicago: University of Chicago Press, 1996), 17–26; Moore, *Beauty Parlor*, 135; Gerard Loughlin, "Pauline Conversations: Rereading Romans 1 in Christ," *Theology and Sexuality* 11 (2004): 72–102; Martti Nissinen, "Homosexuality: I. Ancient Near East and the Hebrew Bible/Old Testament," *EBR* 12 (2016): 290–97, at 290.

2. This sentence has been interpreted as a reference to pederasty, which designates sexual activities between two males of unequal status, usually between an adult and an adolescent boy. Such practices were the dominant and socially acknowledged form of same-sex behavior in certain regions of the ancient Hellenistic world, but they were usually rejected in Second Temple Judaism.[21] The concern may be that such activities could often have been nonconsensual and abusive, specifically in the context of prostitution.[22] By ancient standards, the specific problem would have been that the act of penetrating was widely considered as the epitome of masculinity. Hence, a penetrated male was seen as "effeminate" and the act as such as shameful. The question is, however, whether such sexual practices are really intended here. While Paul's earlier statement in 1 Corinthians 6:9 can be understood in this fashion, it does not fit Romans 1:26 with its reference to sexual practices between women.

3. Another interpretive alternative is that at least the statement about "females" is not about same-sex activities. The wording "exchanged natural intercourse for unnatural" (1:26) might instead designate other forms of sexual activities such as oral or anal intercourse, which would avoid pregnancy. Only the argument about "males" is explicitly about same-sex behavior.[23] Such an understanding may, however, be questioned since both parts of this extended sentence are connected with "and in the same way" (ὁμοίως τε), which makes it uncertain that substantially different sexual practices are being envisaged.[24]

21. Several sources in Second Temple Judaism and early Christianity condemn Rome and the gentiles for customs of sexual practices between males, male prostitution of boys, and pederasty (*Sibylline Oracles* 3.185–87, 596–99; 2 Enoch 34:1-2; Philo, *Spec.* 3.37–42; *Abr.* 133-41; Did 2.2). Cf. William Loader, "Homosexuality: IV. Judaism," *EBR* 12 (2016): 301–3; David G. Peterson, *Romans*, EBTC (Bellingham, WA: Lexham Press, 2020), 122–26.

22. In this case, the practices in Romans 1:26-27 would not include homoerotic relationships between consenting adults. Cf. Robin Scroggs, *The New Testament and Homosexuality: Contextual Background for Contemporary Debate* (Philadelphia: Fortress, 1983), 116.

23. James E. Miller, "The Practices of Romans 1:26: Homosexual or Heterosexual?," *NovT* 37 (1995): 1–11, at 10; Roy Bowen Ward, "Why Unnatural? The Tradition behind Romans 1:26–27," *HTR* 90 (1997): 263–84; Jeramy Townsley, "Paul, the Goddess Religions, and Queer Sects: Romans 1:23-28," *JBL* 130 (2011): 707–28, at 710–16.

24. Moore, *Beauty Parlor*, 143.

4. It has also been suggested that the sentence does indeed deal with same-sex practices (or "homosexuality") but that these ancient texts do not need to be read as statements with ultimate moral relevance today and can therefore be set aside.[25] Yet, if this argument in Romans is understood as belonging to the foundations of the subsequent christological and soteriological concepts, then the question is if these are not likewise irrelevant today and for that reason dispensable.[26]

5. A final position suggests that the sentence in Romans 1:26-27 deals with sexual behavior in the context of widespread goddess idol cults, perhaps the Isis cult in Rome, which posed a direct threat to Paul's ministry. It focuses on the observation that the section starts with a reference to idol worship or idolatry, which is being repeated (1:23, 24).[27]

Any commentary on Romans needs to take the statement in 1:26-27 seriously. If feminist biblical interpretation is, among other things, concerned about the oppression of women (and other marginalized social groups such as LGBTQI+ people), then this passage, as it has traditionally been understood, presents a specific problem.[28] Interestingly, the sentence is not only *unique in Paul's letters*. It is even *unique in the entire New Testament* because none of its writings ever mention same-sex relations. What then are we to say about these things?

To tackle the problem, I propose to explore the historical situation of the first readings or "performances" of the entire letter in Rome and the rhetorical function of this passage on behalf of Phoebe, Paul's avatar. This means acknowledging the woman who was physically in Rome

25. William Loader, "Reading Romans 1 on Homosexuality in the Light of Biblical/Jewish and Greco-Roman Perspectives of Its Time," *ZNW* 108 (2017): 119–49.

26. Bernadette J. Brooten, "Paul's Views on the Nature of Women and Female Homoeroticism," in *Immaculate and Powerful: The Female in Sacred Image and Social Reality*, ed. Clarissa W. Atkinson, Constance H. Buchanan, and Margaret R. Miles, Harvard Women's Studies in Religion 1 (Boston: Beacon, 1985).

27. Swancutt, "Stoics," 44; Jack Rogers, *Jesus, the Bible, and Homosexuality: Explode the Myths, Heal the Church*, rev. exp. ed. (Louisville: Westminster John Knox, 2009), 72–74; see also Beverly Roberts Gaventa, *When in Romans: An Invitation to Linger with the Gospel According to Paul* (Grand Rapids: Baker Academic, 2016), 84–85; Robert K. Gnuse, "Seven Gay Texts: Biblical Passages Used to Condemn Homosexuality," *BTB* 45 (2015): 68–87.

28. Castelli, "Romans," 282.

for the scholarly endeavor of reciting and interpreting Romans. It also means challenging traditional *his*-story from the critical perspective of *her*-meneutics and adopting an intersectional approach. In an initial step, therefore, I suggest recognizing Romans 1:18-32 for what it is: an opening section of a letter that leads toward arguments in subsequent chapters about the grace of God and the status of humans, if not the entire world. What difference does that make? The first chapter of Romans clearly condemns many forms of unethical behavior. But the entire passage never addresses anyone in the audiences. Rather, it speaks about an anonymous other group referred to as "they" or "them": "God gave *them* over to an unfit mind" (1:28); therefore they "who practice such things deserve to die" (1:32). When recited to the assemblies in Rome, the passage was likely met with much approval since it lists the standard Hellenistic Jewish criticism of the religion and morality of the gentiles. "We can readily imagine Phoebe reading the letter to a gathering of believers at Rome, at least some of whom would nod their heads in smug agreement with the condemnation of 'those' other people who do such dreadful things."[29]

But listen to the next words in Romans 2:1: "Therefore you are without excuse, O human who judges others, for in passing judgment on another you condemn yourself."[30] Paul and Phoebe now address the audience directly as "you." And later they even warn those who judge: "By your hard and impenitent heart you are storing up wrath for yourself on the day of wrath, when God's righteous judgment will be revealed" (2:5). Clearly, Paul and Phoebe are on a mission to show that there are some who potentially judge the behavior of others. In fact, they expect that many in the assemblies at Rome would have judgmental attitudes. They have *carefully constructed* the section in 1:18-32 as a *rhetorical device*. On the one hand, it includes a comprehensive list of vices so that Paul and Phoebe could demonstrate their actual point, stated later in 3:21-31: all humans are sinners and need the salvation that is offered in Jesus Christ alone. The list of vices and, with it, the entire pericope in Romans 1:18-32 are a "trap" or "trick" or "bait and switch." According to Beverly Roberts Gaventa, "At 2:1, Paul springs the trap on just such a reader, observing that the willingness to condemn others also constitutes a form of denying God. Romans 2:1-16 sharply rebukes the one who judges others, perhaps by way of anticipating chapter 14, with its more extended affirmation of

29. Gaventa, *Mother*, 129.

30. For this translation, which differs from the NRSVue, see comments under "Translation Matters" on Romans 2:1 below, p. 66.

the perils of judging others."[31] Hence, these sentences belong to an *interactive rhetorical strategy*. As such, they resemble the trap that the prophet Nathan used to lead King David to pronounce judgment in a certain situation that was ultimately his own (2 Sam 12:1-15). This is more plausible when considering the final sentence of David's response to Nathan: "the man who has done this deserves to die" (2 Sam 12:5 [LXX]). The similarity to the statement in Romans 1:32 is no coincidence: "that those who practice such things deserve to die." Besides, the switch between the parable with its anonymous characters "in a certain city" (2 Sam 12:1) and Nathan's sudden exclamation, "You are the man!" (12:7) resembles Romans where 2:1 introduces a similar turn toward the audience. But *what* may be the *purpose* of this interactive bait-and-switch strategy here?

With the recitation of the letter to the Romans still in its initial stage, Paul and Phoebe know that they need to do something about prejudices. That becomes evident when resisting the temptation to neglect the participating female agent, namely, Phoebe. As the person who delivered and recited the letter in Rome, she could likely have been met with some degree of bias or prejudice due to the disrepute of Corinth, the city that she and Paul were associated with. Paul knew this because Prisca and Aquila had already had such an experience when they arrived in Rome from Corinth several months earlier. And Phoebe, the minister from Cenchreae in Corinth (Rom 16:1), would have lived to see that as well.

That Phoebe has something to do with the sentence in Romans 1:26-27 can also be deduced from another peculiar observation: Few have taken note of the fact that ancient texts on same-sex practices customarily focus on *males*. In the legal texts of the Torah, Leviticus 18:22 ordains: "You shall not lie with a male as with a woman; it is an abomination." Leviticus 20:13 echoes this regulation. Same-sex relations or activities between *women*, however, are *never mentioned* in these laws. That observation equally applies to other ancient Near Eastern texts.[32] A gendered interpretive

31. Gaventa, *Mother*, 129. Some aspects of the interpretation of Romans 1:18-32 as a rhetorical strategy can also be found in L. William Countryman, *Dirt, Greed, and Sex: Sexual Ethics in the New Testament and Their Implications for Today*, rev. ed. (Minneapolis: Fortress, 2007), 121–22; Gignac, *L'épître*, 119.

32. See the concise comment: "The ANE sources, including the HB, say nothing about female-to-female sexual-erotic activity" (Nissinen, "Homosexuality," 295; cf. also Martti Nissinen, "Are There Homosexuals in Mesopotamian Literature?," *JAOS* 130 [2010]: 73–77). The reason for this is most likely the androcentric nature of most ancient Near Eastern literary sources. It shows that Paul stepped out of this realm to some degree when writing Romans; it may, of course, be debated whether this was for better or worse, depending on the interpretation of the sentence in Romans 1:26-27.

approach needs to take note of the peculiarity that in Romans, same-sex activities between women are not only mentioned; they are *even mentioned first* (Rom 1:26). This surprising aspect has puzzled some scholars.[33] The reason is, in my opinion, that *Phoebe* is the person who recites the text and that this sentence has to do with her own identity as a woman.

What may be, therefore, the reason for the rhetorical trick or bait-and-switch strategy? I suggest that it is because of Phoebe—and perhaps also because of Prisca if the letter was first read in her assembly. It makes sense that in this situation, Paul and Phoebe would have included a statement from the perspective of women, not men. An intersectional reading leads even further; it recognizes triple trouble. It acknowledges that Phoebe comes with another two stigmas, besides being a woman. She is likely not married and, in particular, she may formerly have been enslaved. Let us explore these additional aspects. Because Phoebe is a single woman, some in the audiences in Rome may have secretly wondered about her sexual orientation.[34] As a gentile woman, she also fits those anonymous characters depicted in Romans 1:18-32. Finally, as a freedwoman, she would have had to cope with the social stigma of enslavement that remained even after manumission. Some of that had to do, once more, with the fact that she could not have refused any sexual assault by her former master or masters. This particular aspect was epitomized by the fact that she came from a city known for its temple of Aphrodite, the goddess of love and fertility, where enslaved women were available for sacred prostitution.[35]

The Plight of Enslaved Women in the Greco-Roman World

A gendered exploration of enslavement in the Greco-Roman world exposes that women were more vulnerable than men. Not many sources are specific about this aspect. Yet, the problem is epitomized in classical Greek sources, such as the *Iliad*, which mention primarily enslaved women (e.g., Chryseis, Briseis, Iphis, Hecamede) as war spoils (*Il.* 1.12-13, 29-30, 111-115; 2.688-689; 6.666-668, etc.) while men were either ransomed or

33. For example, Scroggs, *Homosexuality*, 115.

34. For further details on Phoebe, including her marital status, see below on Romans 16:1-2.

35. See Barbette Stanley Spaeth, "Paul, Prostitutes, and the Cult of Aphrodite in Corinth," *BAR* 49 (2023): 65–68.

immediately killed in battle. Sexual intercourse between these women and the male protagonists is explicitly mentioned (Chryseis with Agamemnon, Briseis and Diomede with Achilles, Iphis with Patroclus). This specific predicament of enslaved women corresponds to Greek manumission inscriptions that often convey that an emancipated enslaved woman had previously been the master's sexual partner.[36] By analogy, one may infer that in Roman households, enslaved women were also the victims of their master's desire. According to Marianne Bjelland Kartzow, "A female slave was primarily valued for her reproductive or sexual capital."[37] It is telling to correlate this aspect with the annual Roman festival called *Matralia*, a women's celebration of the goddess Mater Matutua. At this occasion, several free and privileged women would choose an enslaved girl for ceremonial beating at a sanctuary and subsequent expulsion. There was neither any law forbidding such a practice nor public uproar to shun it. This event was probably a manifestation of feelings of jealousy of Roman female citizens toward enslaved girls who had no options of resisting unremitting sexual advances and assaults by their masters.[38] To add to the complexity of the problem, an enslaved woman may have known that, given her helpless and undesirable situation, her situation could be improved by conceiving and giving birth to a child of her master. In fact, enslaved women who were related to their masters by blood had a chance of eventually being freed; furthermore, they had a chance to marry their master (while being prohibited from marrying anyone else without their ex-master's consent).[39]

36. Yvon Garlan, *Slavery in Ancient Greece*, trans. Janet Lloyd, rev. exp. ed. (Ithaca: Cornell University Press, 1988), 29–37; Orlando Patterson, *Freedom in the Making of Western Culture*, Freedom 1 (New York: Basic Books, 1991), 50–55; Jennifer A. Glancy, *Slavery in Early Christianity* (Minneapolis: Fortress, 2006), 53.

37. Marianne Bjelland Kartzow, *The Slave Metaphor and Gendered Enslavement in Early Christian Discourse: Double Trouble Embodied*, Routledge Studies in the Early Christian World (London: Routledge, 2018), 100.

38. Carolyn Osiek and Margaret Y. MacDonald, *A Woman's Place: House Churches in Earliest Christianity* (Minneapolis: Fortress, 2006), 276; Angela N. Parker, "One Womanist's View of Racial Reconciliation in Galatians," *JFSR* 34 (2018): 23–40, at 36.

39. Werner Eck, "Sklaven und Freigelassene von Römern in Iudaea und den angrenzenden Provinzen," *NovT* 55 (2013): 1–21, at 17–18; Peter Hunt, "Manumission: Ancient Rome," in *Macmillan Encyclopedia of World Slavery*, vol. 2, ed. Paul Finkelman and Joseph C. Miller (New York: Macmillan, 1998), 548–49.

Enslaved people who had not become victims of inhumane treatments often inflicted on them could sometimes attain their freedom. This could be their patrons' gesture of appreciation, acknowledgment, and gratitude; it was sometimes ordained by testament. Alternatively, enslaved people who had the right to earn money (and whose masters agreed) could save up to redeem themselves.[40] According to the *lex Aelia Sentia* from 4 CE, emancipation was restricted to enslaved people at or above the age of thirty years (and could be granted only by owners above twenty years of age). Enslaved people were no longer eligible for manumission if they had been punished by torture, branding, or fighting in the arena. When enslaved people were fortunate enough to be freed, a particular tax called *uicesima libertatis* was applied throughout the Roman Empire.[41] The procedure of liberating an enslaved person, usually a public ceremony performed by a judge, was the *manumissio* (literally "sending out from the hand").[42] The enslaved person received the *pileus*, a felt cap, as a symbol of manumission. This procedure reinstated the personhood to the enslaved person and reintegrated him or her into society; he or she was now a *libertus*/*liberta* (in Greek ἀπελεύθερος/ἀπελεύθερα). The change in social rank was particularly manifest through a change in name. The freedperson took on the *nomen gentilicium* (the surname) of the former owner, indicating that he or she was henceforth his or her client. Thus, freedom through *manumissio* meant, for a former enslaved person, being integrated into the Roman society in one of the patron-client networks. Finally, ancient Rome differed from ancient Greece by acknowledging the new status of freedpersons through bestowing citizenship on them, including the right to vote. Ancient literary sources evince the importance of manumission, as enslaved persons are rarely ever mentioned, but manumitted persons are.[43]

There is no doubt that manumission was a coveted

40. Orlando Patterson, *Slavery and Social Death: A Comparative Study* (Cambridge, MA: Harvard University Press, 1982), 223.

41. Keith R. Bradley, *Slaves and Masters in the Roman Empire: A Study in Social Control* (New York: Oxford University Press, 1987), 104–6.

42. Laura S. Nasrallah, *Archaeology and the Letters of Paul* (Oxford: Oxford University Press, 2019), 68–71.

43. O. F. Robinson, "Ancient Rome," in Finkelman and Miller, *Macmillan Encyclopedia of World Slavery*, vol. 1, 71; Hunt, "Manumission," 547; Nasrallah, *Archaeology*, 55–58, 72–73.

goal for enslaved persons. But unfortunately, the social stigma remained. It was largely impossible to remove the taint of enslavement even after emancipation.[44] Adding insult to injury, ancient authors would often ridicule freedpersons in satires.[45] An intersectional exploration of the history of enslavement will, furthermore, need to acknowledge that the situation was even worse for women. If they were freed, it did not improve their options or life circumstances by much due to the additional social stigma of previously having been the victim of their former master's unrestrained sexual assaults. Therefore, a former enslaved women could become "a prostitute, a *mima*, or, if she were lucky, a housewife, doing much the same work as an *ancilla* did but in her own home. If she had caught the fancy of someone of high social status, she would be his *concubina* not his wife: it was not respectable to marry a *libertine*."[46] Enslaved women in ancient Rome knew the hardship of intersectionality, even after *manumissio*.[47] I concur with Orlando Patterson, however, who describes the paradoxical situation that, in the history of early Greece, the notion and ideal of personal freedom developed among enslaved women.[48]

Due to these three factors, people in the city of Rome were likely to have sneered at Phoebe. After all, chastity was considered a prime honorable feature of women. In the eyes of most Roman citizens, the

44. J. Albert Harrill, *Slaves in the New Testament: Literary, Social, and Moral Dimensions* (Minneapolis: Fortress, 2006), 36–52.

45. Larry L. Welborn, "Inequality in Roman Corinth: Evidence from Diverse Sources Evaluated by a Neo-Ricardian Model," in *The First Urban Churches*, vol. 2: *Roman Corinth*, ed. James R. Harrison and Larry L. Welborn, WGRW 8 (Atlanta: SBL Press, 2016), 58–75.

46. Gillian Clark, "Roman Women," *GR* 28 (1981): 198. See also Patterson, *Freedom*, 50–51, who considers women to be enslaved persons par excellence.

47. For studies on the institution of enslavement in the ancient Greco-Roman world, see Orlando Patterson, "Slavery," *Annual Review of Sociology* 3 (1977): 407–49; Patterson, *Freedom*, 48–63; Clark, "Roman Women," 197–98; Walter Scheidel, "The Comparative Economics of Slavery in the Greco-Roman World," in *Slave Systems: Ancient and Modern*, ed. Enrico Dal Lago and Constantina Katsari (Cambridge: Cambridge University Press, 2008); Nasrallah, *Archaeology*, 40–75.

48. Patterson, *Freedom*, 54.

legitimate place of a virtuous woman was her home. She was either married to a husband or under the tutelage of a male father figure. And here comes Phoebe who has nothing to do with any of that, traveling the Mediterranean, from port to port and all the way from Corinth of all places. She embodies the perfect counter role to patriarchal expectations toward women in terms of modesty and chastity. The Romans would probably have scoffed at her. Is she not some "Corinthian maid"? Should one listen to her at all, even if she comes with a letter from the apostle Paul? An intersectional approach to Romans recognizes that *this* is the very problem Paul and Phoebe needed to address preemptively after the opening section of Romans, *not* disembodied and timeless teaching on sexuality. The problem was the potential self-righteousness of the audiences in Rome. For the sake of proclaiming the gospel, it was necessary to ensure that the remainder of the letter would get a fair hearing if it was read by a person like Phoebe who literally spells triple trouble.

The problem that needed to be addressed proactively was, however, not limited to Phoebe's situation. In the opening section of Romans, Paul shares his plans to visit Rome *himself* (Rom 1:10-11). This means he also needs to "clear the way" for his own future visit and anticipate possible reactions. What does an intersectional approach of Paul as the author of the letter yield? First, he was a Jewish believer in Christ. Given the recent edict of Claudius by which Jewish believers in Christ had been expelled, all those who belonged to this specific religious group had become outsiders who needed to hope for their reintegration upon their return to Rome. This was possible but nevertheless required a conscious effort. Second, Paul was not married either. That circumstance, together with his career as a missionary who had long-standing connections with Corinth, where he was also staying when working on Romans (see 16:23), led to potential suspicions toward him as well. Some might even have wondered about his own sexual orientation. His assembly in Corinth was known to have problems in the area of sexual licentiousness, as Paul himself had acknowledged (1 Cor 6:9). The double reference to idolatry in Romans 1:23-24, which can be seen as an implicit allusion to the temple of Aphrodite in Corinth, corresponds to that.

These are the reasons why the section in Romans 1:18-32 was written. It was never intended as a manual of timeless doctrine on sexuality. Regarding Romans 1:26-27, Michael Theobald notes: "It is striking that Paul does not address the topic in the parenetic, moral-exhortatory part of his letter (Rom 12–15:13)."[49] That section of the letter summarizes important issues of practical relevance from previous sections. It does not, however, mention same-sex activities anywhere. Hence, *they are of no moral or practical relevance in the entirety of this letter*.[50] Instead, the sentence in Romans 1:26-27 and the larger pericope in 1:18-32 have been crafted to cope with the anticipated self-righteousness of the audiences in Rome. They were composed as a *canvas* for these audiences *to project a spectrum of potential prejudices* against Phoebe and, by extension, against Paul himself.

Two further comments are in order: First, these potential prejudices converge around sexual licentiousness, hence the focus on this problem in Romans 1:26-27, presented separately for females and males. Human ontology is conceptualized once more in these binary categories, somewhat akin to the binary categories of "Jew" and "Greek" in 1:16. But these binary categories are questioned and effectively deconstructed in 2:1 where prejudice against such presumed "wickedness" is disavowed. Ultimately, the strategy of declaring all humans sinners and proclaiming redemption in Christ for all aims at overcoming traditional religious and cultural metrics for the—typically negative—assessment of human identity.

Second, from this perspective, one may conclude that the precise type of sexual behavior of females in Romans 1:26 was intentionally left ambiguous (contrary to 1:27, which is explicitly about same-sex behavior). The goal was not a definite reference for the purpose of condemnation. Instead, it is consciously left open, providing a psychologically savvy description of sexual behavior that allowed audiences to project whatever they may have considered inappropriate.

This section served cathartic purposes, inserted after the initial *captatio benevolentiae* with the intent to detoxify a potentially poisonous atmosphere. Only after these prejudices had, with Romans 2:1-12, been called on and thus neutralized was it possible to move on with the actual theological program of the letter. As an interactive rhetorical strategy that is guided by the predictability of the toxic imagination of these audiences, however, the section in 1:18-32 or the one sentence in 1:26-27 should not

49. Theobald, "Paul and Same-Sex Sexuality," 55.

50. This is similar to the proclamation of Jesus who also condemned judging others (Matt 7:1-5; Luke 6:37-42; Luke 18:9-14) while never saying a word about same-sex (or homoerotic) practices.

be used as grounds for modern moral instructions or assessments. In the words of Beverly Roberts Gaventa: "To use this passage to justify the exclusion of persons who are homosexual would be the grossest distortion of Romans and its claims about God's radical and universal grace."[51] And Theodore W. Jennings Jr. notes: "The exclusion of persons on the basis of sexual orientation or same-sex practices brings with it the fundamental distortion of the Bible generally and of the traditions concerning Jesus in particular."[52]

A section with such a rhetorical strategy is, in fact, unique in Paul's letters, as are comments on same-sex practices. This explains its atypical vocabulary, although it is a genuine literary section of Romans. It has a unique purpose and can be properly understood only in connection with the next section of the letter.

Judgment and Human Sin (2:1-16)

This section is traditionally categorized as a diatribe (on this rhetorical genre, see above, p. lxvi). It consists of two distinct pericopes. The first (Rom 2:1-11) features an indictment of those who judge others and envisages the "judgment of God" together with such topics as kindness, patience, and forgiveness. This leads to a standard of human accountability according to "deeds" in correlation with God's impartial judgment. The second pericope (2:12-16) problematizes the universality of human sin and stresses the importance of the performance of the law.[53]

51. Beverly Roberts Gaventa, "Romans," in *Women's Bible Commentary*, ed. Carol A. Newsom, Sharon H. Ringe, and Jacqueline E. Lapsley, 3rd ed. (Louisville: Westminster John Knox, 2012), 552.

52. Theodore W. Jennings Jr., *The Man Jesus Loved: Homoerotic Narratives from the New Testament* (Cleveland: Pilgrim, 2003), 3.

53. It is customary to divide the section of Romans 2:1-16 into a total of three separate pericopes (Jewett, *Romans*, 192, 194–95, 204; Wolter, *Römer*, 1:166, 173). Such a division would correspond to the NRSVue or NIV, both of which start a new sentence in 2:6. In the Greek text, however, the sentence of Romans 2:5 extends until verse 8. It does not seem advisable, therefore, to assign sections of a single continuous sentence to two different pericopes. Thus, I consider the impressive chiasm in 2:6-11 an integral but concluding part of the first section and reduce the number of distinct sections in Romans 2:1-16 to two. As will be shown below, however, I consider them to be more distinct in terms of their contents than most other interpreters.

Rom 2:1-16

2:1Therefore you are without excuse, whoever you are, when you judge others, for in passing judgment on another you condemn yourself, because you, the judge, are doing the very same things. 2We know that God's judgment on those who do such things is in accordance with truth. 3Do you imagine, whoever you are, that when you judge those who do such things and yet do them yourself, you will escape the judgment of God? 4Or do you despise the riches of his kindness and forbearance and patience? Do you not realize that God's kindness is meant to lead you to repentance? 5But by your hard and impenitent heart you are storing up wrath for yourself on the day of wrath, when God's righteous judgment will be revealed. 6He will repay according to each one's deeds: 7to those who by patiently doing good seek for glory and honor and immortality, he will give eternal life, 8while for those who are self-

TRANSLATION MATTERS: Romans 2:1

The NRSVue rendering "Therefore you are without excuse, whoever you are, when you judge others" obscures the fact that the words ὦ ἄνθρωπε, literally "O human," are in the vocative. As such, they are a direct address of someone, and this person may have been in the audience. The NIV translates: "You, therefore, have no excuse, you who pass judgment on someone else"; that rendering is barely more successful in conveying such a crucial aspect of Romans 2:1.[54] A better translation is "Therefore you are without excuse, O human who judges others . . ."

The section in Romans 2:1-16 is the immediate continuation of 1:18-32, which should be understood as a canvas provided for the audience in Rome to project a range of prejudices against Phoebe and Paul. The syntactic connection with the preceding argument is manifest through the use of the inferential conjunction διό ("therefore"), which is the first word of the section. Phoebe is now explicit about the problem of prejudices and aims to neutralize them. How can 2:1-16 be understood from this perspective?

54. Richard N. Longenecker mentions the "fairly general fashion as 'whoever you are who passes judgment' " to conclude that it must refer to "some imaginary interlocutor" (Longenecker, *Romans*, 241). All of this is based on the inappropriate NRSVue (or older NRSV) rendering. (In addition, Longenecker both misrepresents the Greek text of Romans 2:1 and mistranslates it in his *Romans*, 241 line 1.)

seeking and who obey not the truth
but injustice, there will be wrath and
fury. 9There will be affliction and distress for everyone who does evil, both
the Jew first and the Greek, 10but glory
and honor and peace for everyone who
does good, both the Jew first and the
Greek. 11For God shows no partiality.

12All who have sinned apart from the
law will also perish apart from the law,
and all who have sinned under the law
will be judged in accordance with the
law. 13For it is not the hearers of the law
who are righteous in God's sight but the
doers of the law who will be justified.
14When gentiles, who do not possess
the law, by nature do what the law requires, these, though not having the law,
are a law to themselves. 15They show
that what the law requires is written on
their hearts, as their own conscience
also bears witness, and their conflicting
thoughts will accuse or perhaps excuse
them 16on the day when, according to
my gospel, God through Christ Jesus
judges the secret thoughts of all.

TRANSLATION MATTERS: Romans 2:15-16

There are two necessary corrections to these two verses. First, the NRSVue renders Romans 2:15: "They [gentiles] show that what the law requires is written on their hearts, as their own conscience also bears witness, and their conflicting thoughts will accuse or perhaps excuse them." A more literal translation of Greek οἵτινες ἐνδείκνυνται τὸ ἔργον τοῦ νόμου, however, is "They show that the deed of the law." This passage picks up the key word ἔργον, "deed," from Romans 2:6 that appeared within a quotation from Jewish Scriptures. The NRSVue rendering obscures this connection and the concern about such a "deed of the law" in 2:15, toward the end of the text section. Second, the NRSVue renders Romans 2:16: "on the day when, according to my gospel, God through Christ Jesus judges the secret thoughts of all." The last words are a translation of the Greek τὰ κρυπτὰ τῶν ἀνθρώπων, literally "the secrets of humans." The entire diatribe in chapter 2, however, deals with human activity, specifically human "judgment" (2:1-5) and later "deeds" (2:6) that will be subject to divine judgment through punishment or reward. Greek τὰ κρυπτά is, as such, not exclusively a reference to "secret thoughts." As a noun that means "secrets," it may imply both human actions and thoughts. Therefore, the conceptual reduction to "secret thoughts" in the NRSVue is unwarranted.[55]

As mentioned above, this section of Romans is characterized by an abrupt rhetorical shift. While the previous pericope referred to an

55. The NIV renders "people's secrets." See also Jewett, *Romans*, 218: "the secrets of humans"; Wolter, *Römer*, 1:165, 188: "das Verborgene der Menschen."

anonymous group that was addressed as "they" or "them," the letter suddenly switches to "you" (second-person singular): "Therefore you are without excuse, O human who judges others,[56] for in passing judgment on another you condemn yourself, because you, the judge, are doing the very same things" (2:1). The last occurrence of pronouns in the second person was in the opening section of the letter in Romans 1:8-15 where they referred to the assembly in Rome. In 2:1, therefore, the "you" means exactly the same; Phoebe turns directly to the audience in the city of Rome. Here, the Greek words ὦ ἄνθρωπε—literally "O human"—are even in the vocative, thus implying such a direct address. Much of the sentence in 2:1 is even being repeated in 2:3 for further emphasis: "O human, when you judge those." It is clear from these words that the problem is "judgment," understood as prejudice—not by an imaginary interlocutor or by a Jew, but by some in the audience in Rome.[57]

The next step is that Paul and Phoebe present the anticipated audiences with the divine perspective: "We know that God's judgment on those who do such things is in accordance with truth" (2:2). Those who judge others will be judged by God. The retributive logic involved in this concept is that of the law of retaliation, also called *lex talionis*; its most famous expression is the maxim "eye for eye, tooth for tooth, hand for hand, foot for foot" in Exodus 21:24 (see also Lev 24:20; Deut 19:21; referenced by Jesus in Matt 5:38). The application of such a legal principle here would result in judgment for judgment. But while Paul and Phoebe had problematized human judgment in the previous sentence, they now turn to God; it is "God's judgment" that will be on those who judge others. They use the epistolary disclosure formula "we know" to connect with the audience (1 Cor 8:1: "we know that 'all of us possess knowledge'"). Here, it constitutes a change from the second-person verbs and includes the audiences of the letter. They and Phoebe know that God will judge those humans who judge others. By way of a rhetorical question, the

56. For this translation, which differs from the NRSVue, see comments under "Translation Matters" on Romans 2:1 above, p. 66.

57. Richard N. Longenecker notes: "But whom is Paul addressing or talking about in 2:1-16? . . . This was an exceedingly difficult matter for such earlier interpreters as Origen, Jerome, Augustine, and Erasmus to determine, and it continues to plague commentators today" (Longenecker, *Romans*, 240). Many scholars attribute these words to an imaginary interlocutor; cf. Jewett, *Romans*, 193, 195–96; Wolter, *Römer*, 1:166. Other scholars have assumed that the one who judges is a "typical Jew." Stanley K. Stowers has refuted this argument as Christian stereotyping; cf. Stanley K. Stowers, *A Rereading of Romans: Justice, Jews, and Gentiles* (New Haven: Yale University Press, 1994), 13.

sentence repeats that those humans do not escape the judgment of God. In the following, this negative human attitude is juxtaposed with the attributes of God, namely, divine kindness, patience, and forgiveness.

Associating a judicial context, the word "judgment" usually has the sense of "condemnation." There is a striking preponderance of vocabulary indicative of judgment in Romans 2:1-11: the verb κρίνω ("to judge, pass judgment on, condemn"; also, "to prefer") occurs four times (Rom 2:1abc, 3); the related compound verb κατακρίνω ("to judge, pass judgment on, condemn") occurs once (2:1). In addition, the noun τὸ κρίμα ("verdict, condemnation, punishment") is attested twice (2:2, 3), together with δικαιοκρισία ("righteous judgment," 2:5). A suggestive parallel to this section in terms of both rhetorical structure and vocabulary can be found in chapter 14, which belongs to the parenetic part of the letter. It features the verb κρίνω or the related compound verb κατακρίνω no fewer than nine times (Rom 14:3, 4, 5[bis], 10, 13[bis], 22, 23; see below).

The section in Romans 2:1-11 focuses on prejudice as human "judgment" to disavow it by pointing to the judgment of God. The words "you are without excuse, O human who judges others, for in passing judgment on another you condemn yourself"[58] (2:1) leave no doubt about the intentions. This was most likely a challenge for some in the audience of Rome, as Paul and Phoebe had been able to predict their attitudes (with helpful input from their friends Prisca and Aquila, who may have had similar problems upon their return to Rome). Is it at all conceivable that Paul would have asked Phoebe to challenge people in Rome in such a fashion? A comparison with his previous letter to the Galatians shows that there too he had surprised his addressees through the use of unconventional methods, namely, by skipping the customary thanksgiving section at the start of his letter only to immediately rebuke the audience (Gal 1:6-10).[59] Paul was definitely capable of such rhetorical moves.

Paul and Phoebe do not, however, dwell on human deficiencies. First, Phoebe abruptly turns toward her audiences in Rome and addresses them as "you" while switching to exposing their prejudice. Then she gently introduces a theological vision centered on God's kindness, forbearance, and patience (Rom 2:4) to lead the way out of the human dilemma. In the Jewish Scriptures, these terms are used to convey God's compassion toward

58. For this translation, which differs from the NRSVue, see comments under "Translation Matters" on Romans 2:1 above, p. 66.

59. Peter Oakes, *Galatians*, Paideia: Commentaries on the New Testament (Grand Rapids: Baker Academic, 2015), 23.

humans (Isa 42:14; 64:12 [LXX]). It is no surprise, therefore, that Paul and Phoebe repeat one of these terms later when articulating the concept of atonement as human redemption (Rom 3:26). In Romans 2, however, they stress that such kindness should lead to repentance (μετάνοια). Otherwise, God's wrath would be poured out over the human hardness of heart. There is no tolerating human judgment. In the Greek text, this important aspect is being explicated in a long sentence that comprises 2:5-8. It thus features a presentation of God's impartial judgment with concomitant standards of human accountability according to "deeds." Most of this lengthy sentence is structured as a three-level chiasm (the repetition in reverse sequence of words or ideas in succeeding sentences or clauses):

A God will judge according to one's deeds (2:6)
    B For those who do good, reward (2:7)
        C For those who do evil, punishment (2:8)
        C′ For evil Jews and Greeks, punishment (2:9)
    B′ For good Jews and Greeks, reward (2:10)
A′ God judges impartially (2:11)[60]

These principles about divine retribution are taken from the Jewish Scriptures. The first line in Romans 2:6, which mentions the correspondence between deed and reward, quotes a passage that appears in both Psalm 61:13b (LXX), where it is presented as a consequence of God's "strength" and "mercy" (Ps 61:13a [LXX]), and Proverbs 24:12 (LXX), where the argument is rather that God knows everything that is in human minds. From here, Paul and Phoebe deduce in Romans that the criterion for the judgment will be "deeds." Romans 2:7 lists three terms firmly embedded in the Greco-Roman honor-shame system: "glory" (δόξα), "honor" (τιμή), and "immortality" (ἀφθαρσία). At least Paul and Phoebe can be certain that their audiences understand this type of argument! It means that no human will be spared; this can be good or bad news.

Such a judgment call is not new in Paul's letters. Not without pathos, he had previously admonished his recipients:

> "[T]he work of each builder will become visible, for the day will disclose it, because it will be revealed with fire, and the fire will test what sort of work each has done. If the work that someone has built on the foundation survives, the builder will receive a wage." (1 Cor 3:13–14)

60. Wolter, *Römer*, 1:166, 173.

> "For all of us must appear before the judgment seat of Christ, so that each may receive due recompense for actions done in the body, whether good or evil." (2 Cor 5:10)
>
> "Do not be deceived; God is not mocked, for you reap whatever you sow." (Gal 6:7)

Hence, Paul was on familiar terrain when marshalling this argument again in Romans 2, now with its conclusion, "God shows no partiality" (v. 11), because of the egalitarian ethos "in Christ."[61] All of these aspects evince that he and Phoebe were very serious about what they wrote—because of the potential problems that Phoebe might just be dismissed on grounds of prejudices for being a woman, from the city of Corinth, and perhaps even a former enslaved person. This had nothing to do with an imaginary interlocutor but with some very real members of the audiences in Rome, which is evident when the parenetic section of this letter is considered (Rom 12:1–15:13). There, only the admonition against judging is reiterated: "Let us therefore no longer pass judgment on one another, but resolve instead never to put a stumbling block or hindrance in the way of a brother or sister" (14:13). It is obvious, therefore, that judgment is the crucial issue in the first chapters of the letter.

Paul and Phoebe were likewise on familiar terrain when stating that the divine punishment is for "the Jew first and the Greek" (Rom 2:9); here, they even repeated it in the next sentence about the corresponding reward (2:10). They had employed the same terminology in 1:16 to indicate the universal reach of his gospel, which they had defined as a dynamic power for salvation. But now, they gradually move from the human predicament of fallenness to the explication of justification and redemption as the main topics of chapter 3.

The key word "deeds" (ἔργα, Rom 2:6) from the Septuagint quotation prompts Paul and Phoebe to continue with a section on parameters of Jewish identity for gentiles in Romans 2:17-29. But once more, they are concerned about the universality of their statements. They preface that section, therefore, with another one about human sin that also addresses the question of how gentiles relate to the law (2:12-16). It is worth noting that, up to this point, the term "law" has not yet appeared in Romans. But now the term has, in the NRSVue, no fewer than four occurrences in 2:12 alone and a total of eleven occurrences in 2:12-16 (in the Greek

61. Esther Kobel, *Paulus als interkultureller Vermittler: Eine Studie zur kulturellen Positionierung des Apostels der Völker*, Studies in Cultural Contexts of the Bible 1 (Paderborn: Brill; Schöningh, 2019), 95.

text of 2:12-16 [twenty-eighth Nestle-Aland edition], that corresponds to nine occurrences of the noun νόμος, "law," plus two occurrences of the adverb ἀνόμως, "lawlessly"). The term "law" clearly is at the center of the argument from here on. And with it, a piece of Septuagint theology enters the discourse since the term νόμος, "law," is imported from there. The problem that the Greek νόμος is not a direct or ideal translation of the Hebrew noun תורה, which rather means "instruction, direction, guidance," cannot be discussed here at length but must nevertheless be kept in mind. Many of the legal overtones of "law" would be absent from the discussion if it was based on the Hebrew instead of the Greek term.[62]

A fundamental premise is that those who fulfill the law will be justified (2:13). Therefore, regardless of whether one cultural or religious group has no law in the sense of the Torah or whether another cultural or religious group does, both will experience God's judgment. One will perish; the other will be judged. Paul deliberately distinguishes the terminology; the verb ἀπόλλυμι means "to perish" in an absolute sense (1 Cor 1:18; 8:11; 2 Cor 2:15, etc.). But it does not refer to a judgment in the strict sense under the Torah, as several Jewish text traditions show (see 2 *Bar*. 48:47: "Their end accuses all of them [the ungodly], and your law, which they have transgressed, punishes them in your day"; similarly, *Jub*. 5:13: "And judgment is decreed upon all and written on the tablets of heaven without unrighteousness, and upon all who turn aside from his way which is ordained them to walk in it").[63] Eventually, the possibility is being entertained that "gentiles, who do not possess the law, by nature do what the law requires [φύσει τὰ τοῦ νόμου ποιῶσιν]" (Rom 2:14). It has been suggested that this line is about the status of converted gentiles.[64] I consider it unlikely, however, that Paul, together with Phoebe, would have applied the term "by nature" to the response of gentiles who have heard the gospel and become believers in Christ. They may rather have assumed that there are righteous gentiles, capable of doing good, after all. In doing so, Paul and Phoebe ultimately destabilize categories

62. On the much-debated relation between Hebrew תורה and Greek νόμος, see Alan F. Segal, "Torah and Nomos in Recent Scholarly Discussion," in *The Other Judaisms of Late Antiquity*, ed. Alan F. Segal, BJS 127 (Atlanta: Scholars Press, 1987), 131–45; Mogens Müller, "Die Bedeutung der Septuaginta für die Entfaltung neutestamentlicher Theologie," in *Die Septuaginta—Geschichte, Wirkung, Relevanz: 6. Internationale Fachtagung veranstaltet von Septuaginta Deutsch (LXX.D), Wuppertal 21.–24. Juli 2016*, ed. Martin Meiser et al., WUNT 405 (Tübingen: Mohr Siebeck, 2018), 733, 751.

63. Schlier, *Römerbrief*, 76.

64. Jewett, *Romans*, 213.

such as "Jews" and "gentiles" here and in subsequent sections. They are "undermining these powerful identifying markers in an attempt to show that all people are in the same boat."[65] This new egalitarian status is conveyed in the fruitful cooperation of Paul and Phoebe.

The conclusion of the diatribe is noteworthy (Rom 2:15-16). It is prompted by the earlier reference to Psalm 61:13b (LXX) and Proverbs 24:12 (LXX) in Romans 2:6. Now, referring back to the key word ἔργον, "deed," Phoebe will tell her audiences in Rome first that gentiles show how the "deed of the law"[66] may be "written on their hearts," which in itself could be another allusion to Scripture traditions (Jer 31 [MT]/38 [LXX]). Thus, she gets to comment on her own situation as a gentile. As "heart" is a reference to the cognitive function of humans in ancient Near Eastern texts, the continuation of Romans 2:15 is a reference to the memory of past actions. Those can lead to "conflicting thoughts" that may "accuse or perhaps excuse them." Phoebe thinks about what one would call "qualms" today, or "pangs of conscience" and reminds the audience in Rome about it. Such a comment would be irrelevant with little traction had there been no actual problem at stake; yet here, in the face of prejudice, it sadly is significant. Phoebe continues that such conflicting thoughts will occur "on the day when, according to my gospel, God through Christ Jesus will judge the secrets of humans."[67] With that, she returns to the verb "to judge" (κρίνω) one last time. But whereas earlier in the diatribe, the judge was always God alone, fully in line with the Scripture reference, now Jesus is included in his eschatological role of ultimate power and authority.

Second, Paul and Phoebe mention "my gospel." Paul has, indeed, previously proclaimed that all humans will appear before the judgment seat of Christ (2 Cor 5:10). This concept has then been adopted in Deutero-Pauline literature (2 Thess 1:7-10; 2 Tim 4:1). Yet the focus of Paul's gospel is not on the aspect of judgment but on the role of Jesus Christ as savior in this eschatological event. This is Paul's own gospel message. Phoebe would have been able to speak about "my gospel" in her own right and from her own perspective. As a member or even leader of the congregation in Corinth that had received Paul's letters in the past, she was familiar with his message and had adopted it. She could, therefore, wholeheartedly support this statement and its christological focus.

65. Gaventa, *When in Romans*, 32.

66. Regarding this translation, which differs from the NRSVue, see the comments under "Translation Matters" above on Romans 2:15.

67. Regarding this translation, which differs from the NRSVue, see the comments under "Translation Matters" above on Romans 2:16.

Third, the object of the divine judgment is literally "the secrets of humans" (Rom 2:16). A comprehensive category, these "secrets" comprise the thoughts and actions of humans. The explicit reference of "humans" marks a return to the start of this diatribe featuring the words "O human" (ὦ ἄνθρωπε) in an abrupt rhetorical shift. This correlation offers a clue as to what Paul and Phoebe have in mind now. The divine judgment, through Jesus Christ, is comprehensive, but it includes human judgment, specifically in the form of prejudice. Such prejudices may only be conflicting thoughts that have the power of self-accusation (2:15), in which case they may remain secret. Yet such prejudices may also have been manifest through biased conversations or other actions. In this case, they may still be hidden from the knowledge of Phoebe but known to the assembly. Either way, this is a conclusion to the diatribe that addresses the problem of prejudices and offers a christological solution.

In sum, the diatribe in Romans 2:1-16 consists of two distinct thematic pericopes. The first, in 2:1-11, is characterized by its preponderance of terminology about human judgment. It starts with an indictment of those in the Roman audiences who judge others in order to disavow prejudice. Through a turn from there to divine judgment, human "deeds" come into view as the object of God's judgment. It is only in the second section, in 2:12-16, that the universality of human sin as such is being discussed. This discussion leads from the realm of gentiles to that of gentiles who seek to adopt a Jewish identity in the next section (2:17-29).

"The Jews and the Law" (2:17-29)

After the diatribe in Romans 2:1-16, the letter returns to a more theoretical style, even though it continues to address the audience as "you" (second-person singular). The topic now is the person who self-references as a "Jew" in relation to obedience to "the law." The first section in 2:17-24 discusses the betrayal of religious privileges in fifteen coordinated elements: five claims of religious identity, followed by five claims of religious privileges, followed by five betrayals of religious admonitions. The second section in 2:25-29 discusses the nonexemption through circumcision or Jewish lineage as circumcision is void in case of transgressions. The NRSVue assigns the heading "The Jews and the Law" to Romans 2:17-29, which it extends to include 3:1-8. This structure will be disputed and an alternate structure and heading will be proposed below.

Rom 2:17-29

17But if you call yourself a Jew and rely
on the law and boast of your relation to
God 18and know his will and determine
what really matters because you are instructed in the law, 19and if you are sure
that you are a guide to the blind, a light
to those who are in darkness, 20a correc-
tor of the foolish, a teacher of children,
having in the law the embodiment of
knowledge and truth, 21you, then, who
teach others, will you not teach yourself? You who preach against stealing,
do you steal? 22You who forbid adultery,
do you commit adultery? You who abhor
idols, do you rob temples? 23You who
boast in the law, do you dishonor God
by your transgression of the law? 24For,
as it is written, "The name of God is blasphemed among the gentiles because
of you."

TRANSLATION MATTERS: Romans 2:25-26

The NRSVue renders the Greek term ἀκροβυστία as "uncircumcision" in Romans 2:25a, 26b and as "the uncircumcised" in verse 26a; the NIV translates "not circumcised." Both the NRSVue and the NIV, therefore, choose the opposite of "circumcision," the dominant topic of these sentences. It is the term for a traditional medical intervention undertaken on male genitals. The Greek term ἀκροβυστία, however, literally means the "foreskin" (or "prepuce," from Latin *praeputium*) that covers the glans and is typically retractable. It is a creation by the translators of the Septuagint; Greek pagan literature customarily uses the words ἀκροπόστιον and ἀκροποσθία instead. On the one hand, the term is used here as a synecdoche (*pars pro toto*) for gentile males whose cultures and religions usually did not require circumcision. On the other hand, as a synecdoche it designates the entire gentile community (Gal 2:7).[68] Therefore, it also includes gentile women, even if the foreskin belongs to a male organ.[69] From the perspective of feminist biblical interpretation, it is nevertheless evident that such physical markers are restricted to men and manifest their privileged cultural and religious status. Such language is, therefore, deeply androcentric and evinces the patriarchic culture of Greco-Roman antiquity.

68. Based on Ephesians 2:11, it has been suggested that the usage of this terminology may have been far from respectful. Both "circumcision" and "foreskin" (the latter perhaps being an equivalent to the modern-day expression "dickhead") may have been lewd epithets for the purpose of challenging, ridiculing, or even insulting the other group. Cf. Joel Marcus, "The Circumcision and the Uncircumcision in Rome," *NTS* 35 (1989): 67–81; Jewett, *Romans*, 232, 301.

69. Judith M. Lieu, "Circumcision, Women and Salvation," *NTS* 40 (1994): 358–70, at 361.

Rom 2:17-29 (cont.)

[25]Circumcision indeed is of value
if you obey the law, but if you are a
transgressor of the law your circumcision has become uncircumcision.
[26]So, if the uncircumcised keep the
requirements of the law, will not their
uncircumcision be regarded as circumcision? [27]Then the physically uncircumcised person who keeps the law
will judge you who, though having the
written code and circumcision, are a
transgressor of the law. [28]For a person
is not a Jew who is one outwardly, nor
is circumcision something external and
physical. [29]Rather, a person is a Jew
who is one inwardly, and circumcision
is a matter of the heart, by the Spirit,
not the written code. Such a person
receives praise not from humans but
from God.

TRANSLATION MATTERS: Romans 2:28-29

The translation of these two verses in the NRSVue is based on numerous additions to the Greek text. The text of the NRSVue is, therefore, no immediate rendition of that of Romans 2:28-29. Robert Jewett presents the translation as follows: "For not the public [Jew] is a Jew, nor is public [circumcision], by flesh, circumcision; rather, the hidden Jew [is a Jew], and circumcision of the heart, in spirit rather than letter, [is circumcision]; [he is a Jew] whose praise is not from people but from God."[70] All words in square brackets are additions, illustrating the degree to which interpretation dictates the translation. An alternate translation that instead emphasizes ostentatious activity has been provided by Matthew V. Novenson: "For it is not the Jew on display, nor the circumcision on display in the flesh, but the Jew in secret, and the circumcision of the heart in *pneuma*, not in letter, whose praise [is] not from people but from God."[71] This translation has the advantage of not inserting words such as "true" (NRSV) or "real" (RSV) to describe the identity of a Jew or the nature of circumcision in Romans.[72] Moreover, "this translation takes into account the final clause of v. 29, (according to which the) central focus of Romans 2:28-29 is the praise of God, not true Jewishness or true circumcision."[73]

70. Jewett, *Romans*, 219. The Greek equivalent of Jewett's English translation is found in Charles E. B. Cranfield, *A Critical and Exegetical Commentary on the Epistle to the Romans*, vol. 1, ICC (Edinburgh: T&T Clark, 1975), 175. For the latter, see also Matthew Thiessen, "Paul's Argument against Gentile Circumcision in Romans 2:17-29," *NovT* 56 (2014): 373–91, at 376; Thiessen, *Paul*, 57.

71. Matthew V. Novenson, "The Self-Styled Jew of Romans 2 and the Actual Jews of Romans 9–11," in *The So-Called Jew in Paul's Letter to the Romans*, ed. Rafael Rodríguez and Matthew Thiessen (Minneapolis: Fortress, 2016), 138–39; see also John M. G. Barclay, "Paul and Philo on Circumcision: Romans 2.25-9 in Social and Cultural Context," *NTS* 44 (1998): 536–56; Thiessen, "Argument," 377.

72. For another similar problem of translation, see comments on Romans 9:6b below.

73. Thiessen, "Argument," 377.

From the first sentence in this passage, the discussion now moves to chief questions about one's religious and cultural identity. Like the start of the diatribe in Romans 2:1, this section switches to the second-person singular "you." One may envision, once more, that what follows is spoken directly to various audiences in Rome—at least to those who would apply the parameters in the discourse to themselves.[74] Who are they?

The answer is given in Romans 2:17: "But if you call yourself a Jew." For centuries, scholars have debated the exact religious or cultural identity of the person in this verse and in the pericope of 2:17-29. And it has mostly been suggested that the person is a Jew or even a Jewish teacher who proudly self-references as such.[75] Therefore, most Bible editions place this section under a heading such as "The Jews and the Law."[76] The problem is that, according to this opinion, the "true" Jew is the "spiritual" Jew. On the other hand, Jewish identity is correlated with hypocritical behavior; the "Jew" here is being condemned as a detestable bigot.[77] In an attempt to negotiate such critical opinions, Daniel and Jonathan Boyarin affirm that "true Jewishness lay, according to Paul, precisely in renunciation of difference and entry into the one body of Christ. Anyone at all can be Jewish, and those who 'call themselves Jews' are not necessarily Jewish at all."[78]

An alternative position, however, views Romans 2:17 differently. The careful reader will notice an important detail in the sentence "if you call yourself a Jew": It is not about Jewish religious and cultural identity as such; rather, it problematizes the desire of somebody else to claim this particular identity. The referent is, therefore, a gentile, not a Jew. Already

74. According to Robert Jewett, the pericope addresses once more an "imaginary interlocutor," although Jewett recognizes the problem that "each rhetorical question is formulated in second person style, so that the audience is forced to condemn itself" (Jewett, *Romans*, 227). Obviously, the easier interpretive approach is to deny the existence of the imaginary interlocutor and read the passage at face value.

75. Fitzmyer, *Romans*, 315 (his heading is "Transgression of the Law by Jews"); Valerie Griffiths, "Romans," in *The IVP Women's Bible Commentary*, ed. Catherine Clark Kroeger and Mary J. Evans (Downers Grove, IL: InterVarsity, 2002), 632; Mark D. Nanos, "Romans," in *The Jewish Annotated New Testament: New Revised Standard Version Bible Translation*, ed. Amy-Jill Levine and Marc Zvi Brettler (Oxford: Oxford University Press, 2011), 258; Longenecker, *Romans*, 290 ("Denunciation of Jews and Jewish Failures"), 292.

76. This is the heading in the NRSV, the NRSVue, and the NIV. The NKJV has: "The Jews Guilty as the Gentiles."

77. Jewett, *Romans*, 227.

78. Daniel Boyarin and Jonathan Boyarin, "Diaspora: Generation and the Ground of Jewish Identity," *Critical Inquiry* 19 (1993): 693–725, at 697. See also Claudia Setzer, "Does Paul Need to Be Saved?," *BibInt* 13 (2005): 289–97, at 291–95.

early interpreters of the text arrived at this insight (Origen, *Commentary on Romans* 2.11.4), and it has been recovered more recently.[79] It can be corroborated by the observation that the cognate verb "to bear a name" (Greek ὀνομάζω) is employed elsewhere to refer to someone who claims a contested identity (1 Cor 5:11). Furthermore, the scriptural quotation that is intended to substantiate the argument in Romans also deals with gentiles (Rom 2:24).[80]

The long sentence comprising Romans 2:17-20 manifests the theoretical style of this new section; it features a carefully structured *enumeratio* of three sets of five aspects of religious identity exploring a variety of key parameters. The first series of five refers to taking comfort in the law, boasting in God, claiming to know God's will, and having the capacity of religious assessment; these four parameters are based on the fifth of being educated in the law (Rom 2:17-18). Here and elsewhere in the letter (3:27; 4:2; 5:2, 3, 11; 15:17), the Greek terminology for boasting "targets the merit-based culture of the Graeco-Roman world."[81] Relating to a person who competes for honor in this culture, the Jewish law is introduced early on as a crucial factor of religious identity. The second series targets five moral and pedagogical privileges, namely, being an ethical guide to "blind" gentiles, a light to them in darkness, a tutor of fools, a teacher of the immature, and a connoisseur of legal truth (2:19-20). The concluding series of five questions enumerates betrayals of religious admonitions. The implied charge is that the hearers teach others but not themselves, that they both preach against stealing and speak against adultery but do it themselves, that they abhor idols but rob temples, and that they boast in the law but dishonor it (2:21-23).[82] The references to the iconic Ten Commandments (Decalogue) are salient (Exod 20:15/ Deut 5:19 about the prohibition of stealing, Exod 20:14/Deut 5:18 about the prohibition of adultery), as is the inversion of the items in Romans

79. Runar M. Thorsteinsson, *Paul's Interlocutor in Romans 2: Function and Identity in the Context of Ancient Epistolography*, ConBNT 40 (Stockholm: Almqvist & Wiksell, 2003), 159; Novenson, "Self-Styled Jew," 133–62.

80. See the discussion of the combined quotation from Isaiah 52:5 (LXX) and Ezekiel 36:20, 22 (LXX) below.

81. James R. Harrison, *Paul's Language of Grace in Its Graeco-Roman Context*, WUNT 2/172 (Tübingen: Mohr Siebeck, 2003), 219; Brigitte Kahl, *Galatians Re-imagined: Reading with the Eyes of the Vanquished*, Paul in Critical Contexts (Minneapolis: Fortress, 2010), 270.

82. Jewett, *Romans*, 220.

2:21-22. The accusation of committing temple robbery was probably a well-known topic in the first century CE Roman world.[83]

Beyond a doubt, these are very important criteria for Jewish identity in the first century CE. The actual charge is reminiscent of the diatribe in Romans 2:1, which is about doing the very thing one rejects in others. The discourse has, therefore, been moved from the categoric disavowal of prejudice to that of gentiles who publicly endorse and enforce Jewish standards only not to follow them. But is such an *enumeratio* with no fewer than fifteen aspects not too harsh and potentially judgmental in its own right? This may be the case, yet Romans 2:24 goes on to feature a combined Scripture quotation from Isaiah 52:5 (LXX) and Ezekiel 36:20, 22 (LXX) only to bolster the argument. It states: "The name of God is blasphemed among the gentiles because of you." *Prima vista*, one may think that this quotation is about Jews whose behavior brings dishonor to their God among gentiles. But the opposite is the case. It bemoans the crisis in foreign lands, such as Egypt and Assyria, where God's people have come to reside, that God's name is despised due to the howls of the gentile rules.[84]

Hence, it is clear that the section in Romans in 2:17-24 addresses gentiles who aspire to adopt a Jewish identity. It does not criticize religious hypocrisy of Jews but the attempts of others to compete for such an identity. The ramifications of this insight have usually been discussed only in theory. Yet two aspects need to be mentioned: First, a gentile who claims Jewish identity is a person with a hybrid identity (or with multiple citizenships). In this case, it is interesting to note that Paul himself, as a Jew who is now living and operating in the Greco-Roman world that he calls "Greek," has a hybrid identity.[85] Therefore, Paul knows what he is talking about; he is aware of the benefits and disadvantages of claiming a different identity.

Second, many in the various assemblies of Christ believers in Rome were gentiles who also had hybrid identities or multiple citizenships. Phoebe, a gentile herself, gets to explicitly refer to her audiences as gentiles (Rom 11:13). Likewise, she greets many people with Greek names in chapter 16 while only one person (Miriam, 16:6) has a generic Jewish

83. According to Josephus (*Ant*. 18.81-84), Tiberius took measures in 19 CE in response to an incident in which a Jew posing as a teacher of the law indeed embezzled a financial donation for a temple. Cf. Jan Dochhorn, "Der Vorwurf des Tempelraubs in Röm 2,22b und seine politischen Hintergründe," *ZNW* 109 (2018): 101–17.

84. Thiessen, *Paul*, 63.

85. See the pertinent comments in the introduction above.

name.[86] Many of them would nevertheless have been members of Jewish synagogues prior to adopting their new faith in Jesus Christ. Thus, many of them knew of the problems that the section in 2:17-24 describes. This was no hypothetical discourse but one that was of immense relevance for those in the assemblies in Rome. More specifically, it is historically plausible that Romans was first being read in the assembly of Prisca and Aquila. This is the reason why they, as a married couple, are the first to be greeted in Romans 16:3-5. Prisca and Aquila are most likely a Roman noblewoman and a Jewish former enslaved person.[87] Hence, both had to negotiate hybrid identities from different perspectives in their own lives and in their couple. This is most likely the reason why Paul and Phoebe venture into this debate early on in the letter. This was no abstract topic of little relevance for a few but a matter of utmost importance to many in the audiences. It was, on the one hand, a topic of religious-cultural significance. On the other hand, hybrid identity could have been a positive feature for a career in Rome. Pertinent discussions of this topic would certainly have included matters such as ethical behavior and observance of rites.

The latter is exemplified in the next section. Here, the focus is on the prominent theme of "circumcision" (περιτομή), which is discussed in relation to "uncircumcision" (ἀκροβυστία, literally "foreskin") as its opposite (Rom 2:25). The term "circumcision" occurs six times in 2:25-29 while "uncircumcision/uncircumcised" occurs four times. In the ancient world, circumcision became so identifiable with Judaism that its adherents were sometimes called simply "the circumcised." Romans 3:1 and 3:30 do the same, but for the moment, a discussion of the topic problematizes Jewish identity and its external attributes. Specifically, 2:26 returns to aspects already dwelt upon in 2:14, namely, whether "the uncircumcised" (called "gentiles" previously) are capable of obeying the law. The climax of the section is this: "For it is not the Jew on display [οὐ γὰρ ὁ ἐν τῷ φανερῷ Ἰουδαῖός ἐστιν], nor the circumcision on display in the flesh, but the Jew in secret, and the circumcision of the heart in *pneuma*, not in letter, whose praise [is] not from people but from God [οὗ ὁ ἔπαινος οὐκ ἐξ ἀνθρώπων ἀλλ' ἐκ τοῦ θεοῦ]" (2:28-29).[88] What is such an identity based on "circumcision of the heart" that is destined for divine acknowledgment? For Paul and

86. For a detailed discussion, see below at 16:6.

87. For details on Prisca and Aquila, see below on Romans 16:3-5.

88. For this translation, which differs from the NRSVue, see comments under "Translation Matters" on Romans 2:28-29 above.

Phoebe, it is no longer inextricably bound to external markers and signs. They thus reduce the value of individual and corporate identity based on rituals and external status symbols. With that, they challenge circumcision as the initiation ritual of Second Temple Judaism. Instead, they envision "the circumcision of the heart"; this phrase is well known in traditional Jewish literature such as the Torah (e.g., "Circumcise, then, the foreskin of your heart, and do not be stubborn any longer," Deut 10:16; similar 30:6; Lev 26:41) and prophetic texts (Jer 4:4; 6:10; 9:25; Ezek 44:7, 9). It often refers to admonitions to obey God's law.[89] The term "heart" (לב/καρδία) in these passages does not allude to emotions but to the seat of human cognitive capacities; "without heart" means "senseless" (Jer 5:21; 13:22). The phrase of a law written on human "hearts" evokes an image of internalization as quasi-instinctive knowledge that is already known from Jewish prophetic scriptures (Jer 31:31-34 [MT]/38:31-34 [LXX]).[90] The related phrase "circumcision of the heart" thus aims at a fundamental transformation of the human being through intimate knowledge of God.

Coaching: Improvement of Behavior or Personal Transformation

In a study on coaching and mentoring in large US corporations, Jane Renton addresses the question of why coaching programs aimed at the improvement of the performance of employees typically do not yield lasting results. She observes that much of the coaching was directed at the improvement of employee behavior. High performers, however, distinguish themselves through their inner attitude and motivation. They specifically share the same beliefs and vision of the corporate management. The crucial aspect is, therefore, that of identification with the company and its leadership, which should be included in coaching strategies.[91] "Train people to change their inner motivations and you start changing their behavior very quickly."[92] This crucial insight in the secular realm corresponds to that of Social Anthropologist

89. Jewett, *Romans*, 236.

90. William L. Holladay, *Jeremiah 1: A Commentary on the Book of the Prophet Jeremiah, Chapters 1–25*, Hermeneia (Minneapolis: Fortress, 1986), 197.

91. Jane Renton, *Coaching and Mentoring: What They Are and How to Make the Most of Them*, Economist Books (New York: Bloomberg, 2009), 121–22.

92. Renton, *Coaching and Mentoring*, 124.

Véronique Altglas who, in her study of neo-Hinduism and modern Kabbala traditions, describes the proposal of new ways to salvation through the development of the self and the deep transformation of one's own life.[93] Both the corporate world and religious groups have thus discovered in somewhat analogous ways the importance of personal transformation, which takes into account body, soul, and spirit as the totality of the human being. To obtain such a holistic change, the domain of spirituality is being combined with coaching, a field that has, until recently, been decidedly secular. Particularly in business coaching, spirituality is now being integrated as a goal to achieve as well as a toolbox to accomplish personal transformation.[94] In a way, this new development in personal coaching and mentoring is akin to the vision of the prophet Jeremiah who proclaimed a time when the law would be written on human hearts.

Véronique A. Pioch-Eberhart

Romans 2:28-29 proposes the idea of the circumcision of the heart in *pneuma*, not in letter. It is about a process of holistic personal transformation of the human being that would result in an intimate connection with God. It juxtaposes this idea of holistic transformation to that of external behavior "on display" that is also paraphrased as "in letter." Such an antithesis is a Pauline innovation and appears for the first time in his description of his own identity as a minister "of a new covenant, not of letter but of spirit" (2 Cor 3:6). The apostle thus conveys a vision that is not limited to the modification of a set of behavior for others to see and approve, but—in line with the ideal of Jewish Scriptures—of a deep personal transformation.

Some historical background helps to illuminate the degree to which circumcision came to epitomize Jewish identity and was contested as such. In the ancient Near East, various other nations practiced circumcision as well; it was not unique to Jews. It was only during the exile in Babylon that it became the characteristic marker of Jewish identity

93. Véronique Altglas, "Exotisme Religieux et Bricolage," *Archives de Sciences Sociales Des Religions* 167 (2014): 315–32, at 324.

94. Donald W. McCormick, "Spirituality and Management," *Journal of Managerial Psychology* 9 (1994): 5–8.

because the Babylonians did not practice it. The Torah conveys this development through, for example, the narrative of the eternal covenant between God and Abraham; the sign of this covenant is circumcision (Gen 17:9-14).[95] During the Hellenistic period, Antiochus IV Epiphanes sought to Hellenize Jews by outlawing circumcision in order to create a homogeneous population. Some Jews, therefore, underwent epispasm (the practice of regrowing the foreskin). This was one of the factors that kindled the Maccabean zeal for the Jewish law. The subsequent Hasmonean state even implemented forced circumcision at times (1 Macc 1:15, 48, 60-61; 2 Macc 2:46; 6:10; Josephus, *Ant.* 13.257-258).[96]

In the New Testament Gospels, circumcision plays a subordinate role (the term does not occur in, for example, Mark or Matthew; only Luke mentions in 1:59; 2:21 that circumcision rites were performed on John the Baptist and Jesus, for each on the eighth day). According to the Gospel of Thomas 53, the disciples asked Jesus: "Is circumcision beneficial or not?" Jesus responded to them: "If it were beneficial, their father would beget them already circumcised from their mother. Rather, the true circumcision in spirit has become completely profitable."[97] That answer seems to indicate that Jesus was, if anything, critical of the rite. Paul's stance toward the practice was also not unambiguous, as selections from his letters make clear. The practice was now obsolete according to his gospel message, as he had already declared in 1 Corinthians 7:19: "Circumcision is nothing, and uncircumcision is nothing, but obeying the commandments of God is everything." In Galatians, Paul had also dwelt on this topic and almost repeated what he had written earlier: "For in Christ Jesus neither circumcision nor uncircumcision counts for anything; the only thing that counts is faith working through love" (Gal 5:6; see also 6:13, 15). He likewise declared emphatically: "Listen! I, Paul, am telling you that if you let yourselves be circumcised, Christ will be

95. Francesca Stavrakopoulou, *God: An Anatomy* (London: Picador, 2022), 129.

96. John J. Collins, "A Symbol of Otherness: Circumcision and Salvation in the First Century," in *Seers, Sibyls and Sages in Hellenistic-Roman Judaism*, JSJSup 54 (Leiden: Brill, 1997), 211–35; Gaventa, "Romans," 552; Kenneth Atkinson, *A History of the Hasmonean State: Josephus and Beyond*, Jewish and Christian Texts in Contexts and Related Studies 23 (New York: Bloomsbury, 2016), 25–28.

97. Translation according to Helmut Koester and Thomas O. Lambdin, "The Gospel of Thomas (II,2)," in *The Nag Hammadi Library in English*, ed. James M. Robinson, 3rd rev. ed. (San Francisco: HarperSanFrancisco, 1990), 124–38.

of no benefit to you" (5:2).[98] Yet, from what is known at least about the audience in Galatia, Paul does not criticize Jews regarding their circumcision. Instead, he objects that gentiles would have to be circumcised, particularly if the rite would be connected with soteriological relevance.[99] In Philippians 3:2-3, Paul goes on to warn: "Beware of the dogs, beware of the evil workers, beware of those who mutilate the flesh! For it is we who are the circumcision." These passages from various Pauline letters show that the rite of circumcision was intrinsically linked to true religious-cultural identity. And such identity can be extended to gentile members through observance of the law, that is, through proper ethics (see also 1 Cor 10:18; Rom 9:6).

Some of Paul's comments related to circumcision sound rather harsh. One may wonder why he did not show more tolerance as he did on the issue of celibacy or the eating of idol meat. Was this simply his rhetoric toward gentiles? But there is another corollary that may explain Paul's stance. The discourse about circumcision puts patriarchy in the ancient world and its associated androcentric literature into vivid display. As Beverly Roberts Gaventa notes: "The use of these categories raises questions for women, since the categories are limited to males and would appear to exclude women from consideration."[100] Hence, Paul's argument in favor of "uncircumcision," which he makes to include gentiles, can *mutatis mutandis* also be read in favor of women.[101] According to Tatha Wiley,

> The law is gender-specific. Formulated from a male perspective, the law marks the rights, prerogatives, and obligations of men. . . . The sign of

98. Bruce Hansen, *All of You Are One: The Social Vision of Galatians 3.28, 1 Corinthians 12.13 and Colossians 3.11*, LNTS 409 (London: T&T Clark, 2010), 105: "Paul had demoted all cultural indices apart from those based on participation in Christ and refuses not their preservation but their use as bases of exclusion and judgement."

99. Pamela Eisenbaum, "Is Paul the Father of Misogyny and Antisemitism?," *CrossCurrents* 50 (2000): 506–24, at 517.

100. Gaventa, "Romans," 552. See also Castelli, "Romans," 290.

101. Griffiths, "Romans," 634. Circumcision as a sign of the covenant can also be problematized yet in a different direction. As Shaye J. D. Cohen notes, "If circumcision is the covenant, then Ishmael, and by extension all circumcised gentiles, should be part of the covenantal people, but they are not" (Shaye J. D. Cohen, *Why Aren't Jewish Women Circumcised? Gender and Covenant in Jerusalem* [Berkeley: University of California Press, 2005], 13).

> the covenant is male circumcision. . . . Males are full members of the covenant community. . . . Gender difference in covenant membership reinforced the inferiority of women in relation to men.[102]

In the end, the argument in Romans 2:17-29 fundamentally challenges the privilege of circumcised men to allow for the inclusion not only of gentiles into the Body of Christ but also of women. The previous discourse had destabilized cultural and religious categories such as "Jews" and "gentiles." Now it implicitly destabilizes those of gender as well to attain the new vision of a radically democratic "*ekklēsia* of wo/men." It is worth reflecting on the urgency of this implied challenge if it is not read to the audiences of this letter by a man but by a woman with a leading position in her own faith community. Phoebe is someone who would have been excluded from full inclusion in the religious-cultural group if circumcision were still the sign of its members, or she would have been included only by proxy (for which she would have needed to be married). Her presence as a gentile woman in the communities of Rome was made possible through the new entry ritual of baptism available to both women and men alike. She is, thus, the embodiment of the new democratic "*ekklēsia* of wo/men."

The Jews and the Law: The Jewish Advantage (3:1-8)

With its vivid question-and-answer style, the section in Romans 3:1-8 returns to the literary genre of the diatribe (see already 2:1-16; on this rhetorical genre, see above, p. lxvi). More broadly, it addresses questions concerning universal sin (3:1-20). The first pericope, however, now turns to questions concerning Jewish identity by refuting objections to impartial judgment in 3:1-8.

The NRSVue assigns the heading "The Jews and the Law" to the sections of Romans 2:17-29 and 3:1-8, thus treating them as one extended discourse about genuine Jewish identity. This understanding, however, has been disputed (see above, pp. 77–79). The following table is intended to clarify the commonly suggested interpretation and the alternative proposed here.

102. Tatha Wiley, *Paul and the Gentile Women: Reframing Galatians* (New York: Continuum, 2005), 81–82.

Rom 3:1-8

3:1 Then what advantage has the Jew?
Or what is the value of circumcision?
2 Much, in every way. For in the first
place, the Jews were entrusted with
the oracles of God. 3 What if some were
unfaithful? Will their faithlessness nul-
lify the faithfulness of God? 4 By no
means! Although every human is a liar,
let God be proved true, as it is written,
"So that you may be justified in
your words
and you will prevail when you
go to trial."
5 But if our injustice serves to confirm
the justice of God, what should we
say? That God is unjust to inflict wrath
on us? (I speak in a human way.) 6 By
no means! For then how could God
judge the world? 7 But if through my
falsehood God's truthfulness abounds
to his glory, why am I still being judged
as a sinner? 8 And why not say (as
some people slander us by saying
that we say), "Let us do evil so that
good may come"? Their judgment is
deserved!

Comparison: Structures of Romans 2:1–3:8

Common Interpretation		*Alternative Interpretation*	
2:1-16	The Righteous Judgment of God	2:1-16	Judgment and Human Sin
2:1-5	The indictment of the imaginary interlocutor	2:1-11	Indictment of those who judge others and the "judgment of God"
2:6-11	Impartial judgment according to works		
2:12-16	The performance of the law	2:12-16	Gentiles and the law
2:17-29	The Jews and the Law (continues in 3:1-8)	2:17-29	Gentiles who "call themselves Jews" (Claim to Jewish identity)
2:17-24	The betrayal of Jewish prerogatives	2:17-24	The hypocrisy of gentiles who preach the law but do not observe it
2:25-29	Nonexemption through circumcision or Jewish lineage	2:25-29	God praises the "secret Jew" (the gentile) who observes the law
3:1-8	The Jews and the Law (continued from 2:17-29)	3:1-8	The Jews and the Law (new thematic section)

Romans 3:1 starts with two nominal sentences that form a beautiful parallelism in Greek. Both sentences showcase the equivalence of the terms "Jew" and "circumcision."[103] With them, the discourse now turns toward Jewish identity. The parallelism reinforces the question about a possible benefit of being an adherent of this religion (or a member of this culture). These questions have been looming large after the section in 2:17-24 about gentiles who had the desire to claim this identity; that must have been a situation of hybrid identity shared by many in the assemblies in Rome. But Jewish identity is Paul's religious and cultural identity. This is manifest in, for instance, 3:5 where Paul speaks about "our injustice" or in 3:7, which is about "my falsehood" and asks: "Why am I still being judged as a sinner?" The first-person singular indicates Paul's original voice as Jew. Furthermore, his questions sound neither polemical nor ironic; they have a pragmatic nature and are objective and respectful. The term ὠφέλεια, deployed only here in Paul's letters, refers to expediency or profitability (similar to its use in *Papyrus Oxy*. 12, No. 1409.11).

The answer is, as befits a diatribe, concise: "Much, in every way" (3:2). This is no surprise as Paul and Phoebe have argued repeatedly for "the Jew first" (Rom 1:16; 2:9, 10). They now explain—by using the very term "first" of that expression—that "the Jews were entrusted with the words[104] of God" (3:2). This is no immediate reference to the Scripture canon of Torah, Prophets, and Writings (*Tanakh*/תנך)[105] but rather to its depiction of the God of Israel and Judah who creates the world and communicates and acts with it through speaking. That is a clever move to avoid offending the traditionally Jewish Christ believers in the audience, even if they are small in numbers. It is, moreover, also about Paul himself as he belongs to this group. Finally, it shows that the connection that he envisages between different cultural and religious groups does not erase the individual identity of each group. It means, rather, that the God of the Jews is acknowledged as the God of all.[106]

103. Eisenbaum, "Father," 517–18.

104. NRSVue translates instead "oracles of God." The broad spectrum of meanings of Greek λόγιον, however, is by and large equivalent to λόγος, ῥῆμα, λόγιον, or ῥῆσις, all of which mean primarily "word, speech." It seems advisable, therefore, to translate the phrase as "words of God."

105. Tanakh is an acronym for the Hebrew Bible consisting of the initial Hebrew letters (T + N + K) of each of the text's three major parts: Torah (Pentateuch), Nevi'im (Prophets), and Ketuvim (Writings).

106. Jewett, *Romans*, 242.

An important question about this diatribe concerns, first, the identity of the dialogue partners. The Q&A in Romans 3:1-2 could be easily imagined as a theological discussion between a Jewish and a gentile Christ believer. It has become customary to read it as involving the hypothetical "interlocutor" once more; the other role would be Paul's.[107] If 3:2 conveys Paul's response—is it possible, then, that the query in 3:1 about that advantage of the Jew was not only one that Phoebe, who is a gentile, might have had but that she had even asked it at some point in time?[108] While this idea about the origins of the dialogue in Romans 3 certainly remains hypothetical, we can use historical imagination to envision how Phoebe may have been a contributor to the letter. Such an embodied interpretation is also necessary to avoid the temptation of visualizing Paul as an isolated genius writing his letter as a monograph. Yet, this is not how Romans was produced in first-century Corinth. Instead, Paul was surrounded by companions, friends, coworkers, and other people who would have participated to a larger or lesser degree in the task of letter writing (see above, pp. liii–lx). An actual discussion between Phoebe and Paul is, therefore, not implausible at all. Second, if this were true, then there would have been less of a challenge for Phoebe to recite and interpret the letter upon her arrival in the assemblies of Rome as she would have been familiar with at least this portion of the argument (and likely others).

Romans 3:3 features an inquiry about the faithlessness of a Jew.[109] Some scholars assign the passage to Paul (in this case as a rhetorical question); some to the interlocutor[110]—whom I continue to see as Phoebe. Both positions amount to the same, as Paul is the one who needs to respond. The question is a wordplay that is prompted by the verb ἐπιστεύθησαν, "they

107. Stanley K. Stowers, "Paul's Dialogue with a Fellow Jew in Romans 3:1-9," *CBQ* 46 (1984): 707–22.

108. For further details on Phoebe, including her ethnic background, see below on Romans 16:1-2.

109. In Romans 3:3, the NRSVue translation "What if some were unfaithful?" assumes a different punctuation from the Greek text in Nestle-Aland, twenty-eighth edition, which is τί γάρ; εἰ ἠπίστησάν τινες, "What then? If some were unfaithful." Robert Jewett explains that the logic of such a question "seems to demand the answer 'Yes,' the use of μή prepares the audience for the negative answer that Paul provides with a vehement denial. I therefore translate the first question as 'What then if some were unfaithful,' which brings it directly into relationship with Paul's answer in v. 2" (Jewett, *Romans*, 244).

110. Longenecker, *Romans*, 343; Jewett, *Romans*, 244.

were entrusted," in 3:2. It deploys an impressive spectrum of terminology built on the πιστ- stem: ἠπίστησαν, "they were unfaithful"; ἀπιστία, "faithlessness"; and τὴν πίστιν τοῦ θεοῦ, "the faithfulness of God." It conveys rhetorically the correlation between both sides: being entrusted with the "words of God" is no assurance of a person's faithfulness to God. But this problem is only on the human side of things; it does not mean that God is also unfaithful, which is Paul's response in 3:4 with an emphatic "by no means," a characteristic stylistic feature of a diatribe.[111]

This question about faithfulness to God is somewhat akin to that of the broken covenant in Jewish traditions; it can be broken only by humans, not by God.[112] The answer is corroborated with a Scripture quotation from Psalm 50:6 (LXX). What is interesting is that this passage is not just any Scripture verse. It belongs to the psalm of David that features his prayer after his adultery with Bathsheba and after he had her husband Uriah the Hittite killed in battle; to be even more precise, after the prophet Nathan had confronted David with a story to lead the king into the bait and switch trap of pronouncing judgment about himself (2 Sam 12:1-15). With this intertext, one may recognize an allusion back to the passage Romans 1:18-32 in connection with 2:1-11 that functioned like just such a trap to confront prejudices in the assemblies of Rome. Indeed, slander will be addressed explicitly in Romans 3:8.

Yet, for the moment, Paul and Phoebe embark on another debate about "the justice of God" (Rom 3:5). It is motivated by the occurrence of equivalent terminology in Psalm 50:6 (LXX). The special twist in the argument here is that divine justice is not made manifest through God's own activity but through the very injustice of humanity.[113] First, the wording "our injustice" showcases, as mentioned above, that Paul answers from the

111. Changwon Song, *Reading Romans as a Diatribe*, StBibLit 59 (New York: Lang, 2004), 32–53, 65–79.

112. Recent scholarship has introduced the phrase "Individualisierung des Bundesbruchs" ("individualization of the breach of covenant") to articulate this characteristic unilateral design of covenantal theology. It is based on the observation that God's covenant is given to all of Israel, but breaking it by, for instance, failing to follow certain covenantal regulations such as circumcision remains an individual problem that cannot endanger the divine commitment to the collective (Walter Groß, "Noch einmal: Individualisierung des Bundesbruchs in der Priesterschrift: Eine Überprüfung," in *Jeremia, Deuteronomismus und Priesterschrift: Beiträge zur Literatur- und Theologiegeschichte des Alten Testaments; Festschrift für Hermann-Josef Stipp*, ed. Andreas Michel and Nicole Katrin Rüttgers, ATSAT 105 [St. Ottilien: EOS–Editions, 2019], 69–86).

113. Wolter, *Römer*, 1:218.

vantage point of his own identity as a Jew (see also Rom 3:7). Second, this is interesting poststructural rhetoric as it undermines the binary concepts of justice, in particular the purported superiority of God as the divine judge (3:6). If human injustice serves to showcase divine justice, then the definition of the latter depends on the definition of the former. In that sense, the mutual dependence exposes and deconstructs the dominant standard of divine justice.[114] In their conversation, Paul and Phoebe have previously destabilized the cultural and religious categories "Jews" and "gentiles," a rhetorical move that would, by extension, also destabilize those of "men and women" with regard to their membership in the cultural and religious community. Here they also deconstruct the categories of "just" and "unjust" as well as "divine" and "human" as such. This leads to the question in Romans 3:7: "But if through my falsehood God's truthfulness abounds to his glory, why am I still being judged as a sinner?" Indeed, after all religious fundamentals have been challenged, would not even the notion of judgment of sin be rendered obsolete?

Such radical deconstruction, however, is not met with unanimous acceptance. In fact, it must have been suspicious to many—or unpleasant to those who had much to lose. Therefore, slander arose, mentioned explicitly in Romans 3:8: "And why not say (as some people slander us by saying that we say), 'Let us do evil so that good may come'? Their judgment is deserved!" In this sentence, I understand the first-person plural of βλασφημούμεθα, literally "we are being slandered," as a reference to both Phoebe and Paul together. (Phoebe, as a congregational leader from Corinth, has previously been among the recipients and audience of at least four of Paul's letters. Hence, she belongs to those who have been influenced by his proclamation.) They both are being maligned for their gospel message that fundamentally challenges the established cultural and religious matrix.[115] The explicit reference to slander in this sentence may be understood as retrospective evidence that this was already the problem throughout Romans 1:18–2:11. In the recent past, Paul had at times complained about facing "insults" (2 Cor 12:10); now Phoebe and he share this predicament together.

114. For a definition of poststructuralism, see Jennifer L. Koosed, *Reading the Bible as a Feminist*, BRP 2/2 (Leiden: Brill, 2017), 32–34.

115. Lukas Borman, "Biographie und Rhetorik: Das Paulusbild der Deuteropaulinen," in *Receptions of Paul in Early Christianity: The Person of Paul and His Writings through the Eyes of His Early Interpreters*, ed. Jens Schröter, Simon Butticaz, and Andreas Dettwiler, BZNW 234 (Boston: de Gruyter, 2018), 171.

None Is Righteous (3:9-20)

From a formal perspective, this section continues the diatribe, even though the bulk of it consists of an extended catena of scriptural quotations demonstrating the universality of sin. Romans 3:9-20 is the logical consequence of the previous diatribe that I have interpreted as a discourse between Paul and Phoebe. After the deconstruction of the established cultural and religious matrix, and with it of traditional hegemonies, what is left for those who previously held the position of dominance and power? Are they even "at a disadvantage?"[116] Yet the answer can only be: "No, not at all" (3:9). This has nothing to do with Paul's personal admission of guilt in Romans 3:5, etc., but reflects on the new situation of those having lost their status from the perspective of the gospel message. Therefore, the religious-cultural binary, "both Jews and Greeks," is repeated once more, but this time only to affirm that all are at the same level. In all preceding instances, the audiences always heard "the Jew first" (Rom 1:16; 2:9, 10, and also indirectly in 3:1). After their discussion, Paul and Phoebe now indicate the end of this idea. "Jews and Greeks" are still distinct groups, but they are at the same level. This is the consequence of acknowledging sin instead of denying it. But sin is no longer a shame factor. In the radically democratic "*ekklēsia* of wo/men," not only people of different cultural or ethnic origins and of different social status and professions and of different genders are all at the same level; the fallen ones are too. In Rome, Phoebe proclaims that all "are under sin"; the NRSVue adds the noun "power," which results in the phrase: "all . . . are under the power of sin."[117] No one is higher; no one is lower; only Christ is the "head." This is the new social order of God's people.

116. The NRSVue translates Greek προεχόμεθα in Romans 3:9 as "Are we any better off?" This rendering, however, is unlikely. The verb is either a middle that has active meaning or a passive form of προέχω, "to stand out, be prominent." The first option would be rendered "Do we have an advantage?" while the second one conveys the opposite, "Are we at a disadvantage?" In this case, it would repeat the analogue question of Romans 3:1 about the advantage of Judaism. Besides the NRSVue, also the NIV, NKJV, NASB 1995, and Reina Valera 1995 prefer the first version; see also Schlier, *Römerbrief*, 97; Thomas Schreiner, *Romans*, 2nd ed., BECNT 6 (Grand Rapids: Baker Academic, 2018), 168–71. It is, however, unlikely since a middle with active voice of προέχω is attested nowhere else. Hence, grammatically the most likely option is the second option: "Are we at a disadvantage?" It explores, therefore, the contrary stance of Romans 3:1 in the sense of being at the bottom of hierarchies (Stowers, *Rereading*, 173; Fitzmyer, *Romans*, 324, 330–31).

117. Gaventa, *Mother*, 129.

Rom 3:9-20

9What then? Are we any better off? No,
not at all, for we have already charged
that all, both Jews and Greeks, are
under the power of sin, 10as it is written:
"There is no one who is righteous,
not even one;
11there is no one who has
understanding;
there is no one who seeks
God.
12All have turned aside; together
they have become
worthless;
there is no one who shows
kindness;
there is not even one."
13"Their throats are opened
graves;
they use their tongues to
deceive."

A catena of Scripture quotations is set out to support the insight that humans are sinful and could not possibly claim to be justified in their own right (Rom 3:10-18). This is the longest scriptural catena in the letter to the Romans (see also 9:25-29; 15:9-12). Paul and Phoebe rely on the authority of Scripture and consciously include the formula "as it is written . . ." (3:10). Taken all from the Septuagint, these quotations are of various origins:

Passage in Romans	*Origin in LXX*	*Equivalent in MT*
3:10-12	Ps 13:1-3 echoing Ps 52:1-3 and Eccl 7:21	Ps 14:1-3 echoing Ps 53:1-3 and Eccl 7:20
3:13	Pss 5:10; 139:4	Pss 5:10[118]; 140:4[119]
3:14	Ps 9:28	Ps 10:7
3:15-17	Isa 59:7-8 abbreviated, echoing Prov 1:16	Isa 59:7-8 abbreviated, echoing Prov 1:16
3:18	Ps 35:2	Ps 36:2[120]

118. Psalm 5:10 (MT) corresponds to Psalm 5:9 (ET).
119. Psalm 140:4 (MT) corresponds to Psalm 140:3 (ET).
120. Psalm 36:2 (MT) corresponds to Psalm 36:1 (ET).

"The venom of vipers is under
their lips."
[14]"Their mouths are full of
cursing and bitterness."
[15]"Their feet are swift to shed
blood;
[16]ruin and misery are in their
paths,
[17]and the way of peace they have
not known."
[18]"There is no fear of God
before their eyes."

[19]Now we know that, whatever the
law says, it speaks to those who are
under the law, so that every mouth may
be silenced and the whole world may
be held accountable to God. [20]For no
human will be justified before him by
deeds prescribed by the law, for through
the law comes the knowledge of sin.

Some of these Greek quotations are taken over literally, some are abbreviated, and some are slightly altered.[121] The combination of these passages has been attributed to a Jewish setting that was similar to that of producing the *Psalms of Solomon*.[122] They explore various areas of human depravity, covering such things as foul speech, which is not surprising in consideration of the recent complaint about slander (Rom 3:8) and the extreme of murder. The root problem is that "there is no one who seeks God" (3:11). This is immediately connected to a lack of understanding; those who do not seek God do not, therefore, have any wisdom. The scriptural catena has the purpose of confirming the claim that every human is under the power of sin: "There is no one who is [just[123]], not even one" (οὐκ ἔστιν δίκαιος οὐδὲ εἷς, 3:10).

In Romans 3:18, the term "fear" (φόβος) is mentioned for the first time in this letter. Its origin is Psalm 35:2 (LXX). It is quoted exactly according to this Greek translation that accurately reflects Psalm 36:2 (MT)[124] where the psalmist contrasts a transgressor of the law and a just Jew who stands

121. See the detailed analysis in Longenecker, *Romans*, 357; Katja Kujanpää, *The Rhetorical Functions of Scriptural Quotations in Romans: Paul's Argumentation by Quotations*, NovTSup 172 (Leiden: Brill, 2010), 38–61.

122. Martin C. Albl, *"And Scripture Cannot Be Broken": The Form and Function of the Early Christian Testimonia Collections*, NovTSup 96 (Leiden: Brill, 1999), 174–77.

123. On this translation of δίκαιος, see comments regarding the rendering of "justification" above (on Rom 1:17).

124. Psalm 36:2 (MT) corresponds to Psalm 36:1 (ET).

in due awe of God. In Romans, the charge that there "is no fear of God before their eyes" summarizes the lack of human obedience and serves as a fitting conclusion to the catena. The picture of humanity that results from these quotations is utterly negative. In Psalm 35:2 (LXX)/36:2 (MT), however, the psalmist contrasts the transgressor of the law with a just Jew who stands in due awe of God to worship at the temple (Ps 35:9-10 [LXX]/36:8-9 [MT]).[125] Thus, the Scripture passage does not share the negative understanding of humanity that emerges from the catena in Romans. Even the book of Ecclesiastes/Qohelet, from which one quotation is included, knows a distinctive connection between fear and joy.[126] This observation evinces the selective use of Scripture in Romans.

Next is another epistolary disclosure formula, "now we know" (οἴδαμεν δέ), to connect with the audience at this crucial moment. The conclusion adopts elements from the previous Scripture catena: "whatever the law says, it speaks to those who are under the law, so that every mouth may be silenced and the whole world may be held accountable to God" (Rom 3:19). This sentence features a chiasm and deploys terminology that is common in Greco-Roman legal practice (Plato, *Leg*. 954).[127] It has a global scope ("every mouth"; "the whole world") and conveys God's judgment. What may be the value of the law for that? Another Scripture reference, now from Psalm 143:2 (LXX), suggests: "For no human will be justified before him by deeds of the law, for through the law comes the knowledge of sin" (Rom 3:20).[128] First, the focus is back on the significance of the "deeds of the law," mentioned already twice in 2:6 and 2:15 (and again later, 3:28). These passages mostly summarize what Paul had written previously in Galatians 2:16: "yet we know that a person is justified not by the works of the law but through the faith of Jesus Christ. And we have come to believe in Christ Jesus, so that we might be justified by the faith of Christ and not by doing the works of the law, because no one will be justified by the works of the law."[129] The question of whether these

125. Fitzmyer, *Romans*, 336.

126. Eunny P. Lee, *The Vitality of Enjoyment in Qohelet's Theological Rhetoric*, BZAW 353 (Berlin: de Gruyter, 2005), 86, 121–22.

127. Jewett, *Romans*, 265.

128. For this translation, which differs from the NRSVue, see comments under "Translation Matters" on Romans 2:15 above.

129. In these passages, Paul may indeed be using the term "deeds of the law" for slightly different referents. Sometimes the emphasis may be more on human activities to fulfill the law and sometimes more on the laws themselves. Cf. Michael Wolter, *Paulus: Ein Grundriss seiner Theologie*, 3rd ed. (Neukirchen-Vluyn: Neukirchener Verlag, 2021), 353–54.

statements discredit the entire law as a way to salvation has been widely discussed. It seems, however, that it does include ethical rules.[130] Romans, however, ultimately contests the idea that the law could be a moral guide leading humans to justification. Such a somewhat pessimistic view was not uncommon in Jewish apocalyptic literature (4 Ezra 7:46).

Second, a positive function is assigned to the Jewish law: It has the function to instruct humans about sin.[131] Yet while this statement is with the Jewish law in mind, its global scope shows that the law is also an identity marker and a measure for human achievement in any culture. With that, all humans are on equal footing (see already Rom 3:9).

This was, then, the opinion of those first-century Jews who believed in Christ. Four positions were being held in Second Temple Judaism at the time: First, Jewish believers in Christ and their gentile converts who insisted on full observance of the Mosaic law, including circumcision for gentiles who believed in Jesus; second, Jewish believers in Christ and their gentile converts who did not insist on circumcision but did require gentiles to keep some purity laws; third, Jewish believers in Christ and their gentile converts who did not insist on circumcision for gentile Christians and did not require their observing purity laws in regard to food; fourth, Jewish Christians and their gentile converts who did not insist on circumcision and Jewish food laws and saw no abiding significance in the cult of the Jerusalem temple.[132]

Justification Through Faith Alone (3:21-31)

This pericope consists of two literary sections: a theoretical description presenting the manifestation of justification in Christ for all (Rom 3:21-26) is followed by a diatribe about the oneness of the God of Jews and gentiles (3:27-31).

130. The question of the precise referent and meaning of the expression "deeds of the law" has seen an intensive debate in the so-called New Perspective on Paul. Cf. James D. G. Dunn, "The New Perspective: Whence, What and Whither?," in *The New Perspective on Paul: Collected Essays*, ed. James D. G. Dunn, WUNT 185 (Tübingen: Mohr Siebeck, 2005), 22–26; Michael Bachmann, "J. D. G. Dunn und die Neue Paulusperspektive," *ThZ* 63 (2007): 25–43.

131. Jan Lambrecht, *The Wretched "I" and Its Liberation: Paul in Romans 7 and 8*, Louvain Theological & Pastoral Monographs 14 (Louvain: Peeters, 1992), 23.

132. William S. Campbell, *Paul's Gospel in an Intercultural Context: Jew and Gentile in the Letter to the Romans*, Studies in the Intercultural History of Christianity 69 (Frankfurt: Lang, 1992), 105.

Rom 3:21-31

21But now, apart from the law, the righteousness of God has been disclosed
and is attested by the Law and the
Prophets, 22the righteousness of God
through the faith of Jesus Christ for all
who believe. For there is no distinction,
23since all have sinned and fall short of
the glory of God; 24they are now justified by his grace as a gift, through
the redemption that is in Christ Jesus,
25whom God put forward as a sacrifice
of atonement by his blood, effective
through faith. He did this to demonstrate his righteousness, because in
his divine forbearance he had passed
over the sins previously committed; 26it
was to demonstrate at the present time
his own righteousness, so that he is

TRANSLATION MATTERS: Romans 3:21, 22

The NRSVue renders the term δικαιοσύνη in Romans 3:21, 22 as "righteousness" (see also NIV). This is an appropriate translation as this English word falls within the semantic range of the term δικαιοσύνη. Yet the problem is that, in 3:24 (and in 5:1), the NRSVue translates the related verb δικαιόω as "to justify." Moreover, in 4:25, even the noun δικαίωσις, which is from the same word stem, is rendered differently: "[Jesus] was handed over to death for our trespasses and was raised for our justification." Even if there is a semantic overlap between the noun "righteousness" and the verb "to justify," such decisions by the editorial board of the NRSVue nevertheless obscure the fact that these words are all from the same Greek stem.[133] To avoid this misperception and subsequent problems for the interpretation, I shall render the noun δικαιοσύνη as "justification" (and the related adjective δίκαιος as "just/justified").[134]

133. These choices of translation are also mentioned in Longenecker, *Romans*, 154, 167–76, 388, 393. By contrast, the Revidierte Lutherübersetzung 2017 translates δικαιοσύνη as "Gerechtigkeit" and δικαιόω as "gerecht werden" while the Traduction œcuménique de la Bible features the noun "justice" and the verb "justifier," thus using one word stem to render the Greek nouns and verbs of the δικ- stem. See also Wolter, *Römer*, 1:242, 246–48; Gignac, *L'épître*, 164, 166–74. The translation problem of the NRSVue and NIV is also manifest in English commentaries. Joseph A. Fitzmyer renders δικαιοσύνη in Romans 3:21, 22, etc. as "uprightness" (and the adjective δίκαιος as "upright") but translates the related verb δικαιόω as "to justify" (Fitzmyer, *Romans*, 253, 257–58, 341–44). Aware of this problem, Robert Jewett consistently renders all the nouns, adjectives, and verbs of the δικ- stem based on the English stem "right" ("righteousness, right, to set right"; Jewett, *Romans*, 135, 268, 272–73).

134. This is also the choice of translation in, for example, Robert M. Calhoun, *Paul's Definitions of the Gospel in Romans 1*, WUNT 2/316 (Tübingen: Mohr Siebeck, 2011), 157–68.

righteous and he justifies the one who has the faith of Jesus.

[27]Then what becomes of boasting? It is excluded. Through what kind of law? That of works? No, rather through the law of faith. [28]For we hold that a person is justified by faith apart from works prescribed by the law. [29]Or is God the God of Jews only? Is he not the God of gentiles also? Yes, of gentiles also, [30]since God is one, and he will justify the circumcised on the ground of faith and the uncircumcised through that same faith. [31]Do we then overthrow the law through this faith? By no means! On the contrary, we uphold the law.

TRANSLATION MATTERS: Romans 3:22

The NRSVue translates the Greek phrase διὰ πίστεως Ἰησοῦ Χριστοῦ in Romans 3:22 as "through the faith *of* Jesus Christ" (italics added). The genitive of Ἰησοῦ Χριστοῦ is thus understood as a subjective genitive; this statement is, therefore, about the faith or trust that Jesus Christ had himself, and most likely his faith or trust in God, or alternatively the trustworthiness of Jesus Christ. The understanding of the NRSVue is grammatically possible; a subjective genitive can have this meaning.[135] Such a rendering nevertheless constitutes a notable change over against NRSV and RSV (see also NIV), all of which translate "through the faith *in* Jesus Christ" (italics added), thus interpreting the genitive of Ἰησοῦ Χριστοῦ as an objective genitive. This understanding is also attested in, for instance, the Revidierte Lutherübersetzung 2017 ("Glauben an Jesus Christus"), the Traduction œcuménique de la Bible ("la foi en Jésus Christ"), and the Reina Valera 1995 ("la fe en Jesucristo").[136] Which interpretive option is preferable? First, some similar phrases in the *Corpus Paulinum* (e.g., Phil 1:27 τῇ πίστει τοῦ εὐαγγελίου "through faith in the gospel") or in the Gospels (Mark 11:22 ἔχετε πίστιν θεοῦ "have faith in God") clearly support the latter choice. Second, in Romans 3:22, the phrase in question continues with "for all who believe," focusing on the faith *of* humans who believe or trust and not on the personal faith of Christ.[137] Hence, the objective genitive that is about human faith or trust *in* Jesus Christ is preferable.

135. See also, for example, Stowers, *Rereading*, 202; Teresa Morgan, *Roman Faith and Christian Faith:* Pistis *and* Fides *in the Early Roman Empire and Early Churches* (Oxford: Oxford University Press, 2015); Nijay K. Gupta, "Paul and *Pistis Christou*," in *The Oxford Handbook of Pauline Studies*, ed. Matthew V. Novenson and R. Barry Matlock (Oxford: Oxford University Press, 2022), 470–87.

136. See also, for example, Schlier, *Römerbrief*, 105; Fitzmyer, *Romans*, 345–46; Arland J. Hultgren, *Paul's Letter to the Romans: A Commentary* (Grand Rapids: Eerdmans, 2011), 154–55, 623–61; Ryan S. Schellenberg, "Οἱ Πιστεύοντες: An Early Christ-Group Self-Designation and Paul's Rhetoric of Faith," *NTS* 65 (2019): 33–42.

137. Jewett, *Romans*, 278.

The exposition of justification in Romans 3:21-31 has sometimes been considered the heart of this letter.[138] Phoebe communicates its emphatic start with the following words: "But now . . . " (Νυνὶ δὲ . . . , 3:21). At the same time, in the drama of salvation that unfolds in front of the audiences in Rome, the "now" ushers in something like a new era after the previous gloomy discourse on sin and all the things humans are not capable of achieving in 2:12–3:20. Read with concerns for gender equality, it is interesting that she explains that all humans are on equal footing. This is so because justification is available not by any religious achievement but through two elements: first, through faith in Jesus, the Jewish messiah (3:21-22), and second, as a gift, through the redemption that is in Christ Jesus (3:24). Both elements actually work together; faith in Christ is the trust that this free redemption is sufficient.

There is nothing for humans to do beyond such faith. Eliminating all claims of honorable superiority, the argument presupposes the Greco-Roman honor-shame system yet introduces a paradigm shift. This interpretation of the gospel invites all marginalized people, including women, to become part of the diverse body of Jesus (Rom 12:4-8). It puts all humans on equal footing, similar to the baptismal formula in Galatians 3:28 that affirmed unity in Christ despite diversity.[139]

Paul's letter to the Galatians features a number of commonalities with this section of Romans, which is specifically manifest in passages on justification by faith.

Juxtaposition of Similar Passages in Romans and Galatians, Topic: "Justification"[140]

Rom 3:21-22	But now, *apart from the law*, the [*justification*] of God has been disclosed and is attested by the Law and the Prophets, the [*justification*] of God *through the faith* [*in*] *Jesus Christ for all who believe.*	Gal 2:16	A person is *justified not by the works of the law* but *through the faith* [*in*] *Jesus Christ.*

138. Fitzmyer, *Romans*, 341–42.

139. Elisabeth Schüssler Fiorenza, *In Memory of Her: A Feminist Theological Reconstruction of Christian Origins* (New York: Crossroad, 1983), 213; Hansen, *All of You Are One*, 103–6, 191–96; Koosed, *Reading*, 21–22.

140. Similar text between both columns is indicated by italics.

Rom 3:22-23	For *there is no distinction, since all have sinned* and fall short of the glory of God . . .	Gal 2:17	. . . in our effort to be justified in Christ, *we ourselves have been found to be sinners,* . . .

These aspects of the gospel have, therefore, been part of Paul's proclamation of justification for quite a while. They may be considered the backbone of his theology. What exactly are the parameters of this gospel message? Justification has been disclosed "apart from the law" (χωρὶς νόμου, Rom 3:21). To avoid the perception that these words are spoken by an antinomian, it should be mentioned that there is no claim that freedom from the law through faith in Christ would be the only way to salvation for Paul's fellow Jewish contemporaries. This gospel is not obligatory to all people, even though it is available to all people. God did not revoke the covenant with Israel (11:2, 25-36). However, God has shown another path toward salvation, a novel one. Similar to 1:2, Paul and Phoebe claim that, despite its novelty, this path has been attested in the Law and the Prophets (3:21). In fact, they go on to explicate its core mostly by drawing on traditional atonement concepts of Second Temple Judaism. This is nothing short of a paradigm shift. These ideas and images of atonement have become a central component of Christian theology. Yet they are also the object of considerable scholarly dispute about their exact meaning and continued relevance.

Some Christian scholars today, including feminists, reject atonement theology. According to the NRSVue rendering of Romans 3:25, God put Jesus forward "as a sacrifice of atonement by his blood" (ἱλαστήριον . . . ἐν τῷ αὐτοῦ αἵματι). This key passage about atonement seems to presuppose a bloodthirsty God who requires death as the precondition of showing divine love. Because it is used to give meaning to the death of Jesus on the cross, atonement theology is also considered to be inherently violent. Finally, the logic of vicarious atonement or penal substitution, by which an innocent victim suffers and dies for the salvation of others, is incomprehensible in the postmodern world.[141] Elsa Tamez warns of parallels between notions of sacrifice and suffering to "the abuse of paternal authority in regard to sons and daughters."[142] Depth psychologist Ingeborg Clarus

141. Christian A. Eberhart, *The Sacrifice of Jesus: Understanding Atonement Biblically*, 2nd ed. (Eugene, OR: Wipf & Stock, 2018), 5–7.

142. Elsa Tamez, "Justification as Good News for Women: A Re-reading of Romans 1–8," trans. Sheila E. McGinn, in *Celebrating Romans: Template for Pauline Theology; Essays in Honor of Robert Jewett*, ed. Sheila E. McGinn (Grand Rapids: Eerdmans,

voices the concerns of modern people that the Father-God demanded the blood and the cruel sacrifice of crucifixion by his human Son. She conveys her concern about the vengeful deity whose anger at the imperfections of his creatures can be appeased only by having his son slaughtered.[143] And Harold Wells asks: "If we preach the grace of God, and derive our personal and social ethic from it, are we thereby implicated in a 'retributive' doctrine about a God who insists on being paid in blood as the price of grace? Does grace, then, cease to be grace?"[144] All of these questions challenge the very heart of how much of Christian proclamation commonly conveys human salvation. In light of such concerns, some advocate for the abandonment of atonement in the Christian Church.[145]

In consideration of this situation, what can be said about the ideas regarding atonement in this section of Romans? The following aspects need to be discussed to arrive at a fair assessment. First, the message about atonement is embedded in a larger discourse about the justification of God and about redemption. The Greek δικ- stem (the stem word is δίκη, "penal justice" or "punishment") has no fewer than seven occurrences in the section of Romans 3:21-26 alone, which features the noun "justification" (δικαιοσύνη, Rom 3:21, 22, 25, 26), the related verb "to justify" (δικαιόω, 3:24, 26), and the adjective "just" (δίκαιος, 3:26). A high concentration of this terminology is manifest in 3:26 (indicated by italics): "it was to demonstrate at the present time his own *justification* so as to be *just* and to *justify* the one who has faith in Jesus."[146] Paul and Phoebe revisit the term in this section after employing it already in the thematic statement of his letter in 1:16-17. There, it was used to announce the "gospel" of "God's saving power for everyone who believes." Thus,

2004), 183. See also Bärbel Mayer-Schärtel, "Erlösung durch Selbsterniedrigung? Feministische Anfragen an die traditionelle Soteriologie," in *Abschied von der Schuld? Zur Anthropologie und Theologie von Schuldbekenntnis, Opfer und Versöhnung*, ed. Richard Riess (Stuttgart: Kohlhammer, 1996), 170–79.

143. Ingeborg Clarus, *Das Opfer: Archaische Riten modern gedeutet* (Düsseldorf: Patmos, 2005), 154.

144. Harold Wells, "Not Moral Heroes: The Grace of God and the Church's Public Voice," in *Doing Ethics in a Pluralistic World: Essays in Honour of Roger C. Hutchinson*, ed. Phyllis D. Airhart, Marilyn J. Legge, and Gary L. Redcliffe, Comparative Ethics Series (Waterloo, ON: Wilfrid Laurier University Press, 2002), 84.

145. Cf. Stephen Finlan, *Problems with Atonement: The Origins of, and Controversy about, the Atonement Doctrine* (Collegeville, MN: Liturgical Press, 2005), 3–5, 117–24.

146. This translation of Romans 3:26 differs from the NRSVue, which reduces the occurrences of the Greek δικ- stem from three to two. For the translation of Greek δικ- stem and the noun δικαιοσύνη, see the comments regarding the rendering of "justification" above ("Translation Matters" on Rom 3:21, 22).

"justification" (δικαιοσύνη) is a central term in this section,[147] and with it in the entire letter. Surprisingly, however, Paul has barely used it in his previous writings. It is missing entirely in 1 Thessalonians. There is only one occurrence in 1 Corinthians, although that is worthy of a reflection. In that letter, Paul proclaims the reversal of the traditional honor-shame system: "God chose what is foolish in the world to shame the wise; God chose what is weak in the world to shame the strong" (1 Cor 1:27). This is to the advantage of all those in the assembly of Corinth who lacked acquired honor in the form of power or ascribed honor in the shape of noble birth (1:26). With the fundamental parameters of the honor-shame system undone, there is no longer any boasting before God about human achievements. Instead, humans can only boast about the Lord Christ Jesus, "who became for us wisdom from God [ὃς ἐγενήθη σοφία ἡμῖν ἀπὸ θεοῦ], and [justification] [δικαιοσύνη][148] and sanctification [ἁγιασμὸς] and redemption [ἀπολύτρωσις]" (1:30). In this dense soteriological statement, Paul celebrates Jesus as God's *Chokmah-Sophia-Sapientia-Wisdom*. As such, Jesus is also the embodiment of divine justification. These various aspects and much of this terminology are being repeated in Romans 3:21-26, with the exception that "justification" (δικαιοσύνη) is now mentioned not one but four times, accompanied by another three occurrences of other words of the Greek δικ- stem. Moreover, the diatribe in Romans 3:27-31 also focuses on the question of boasting (see below, pp. 108–110).

Second, the term "redemption" (ἀπολύτρωσις) is separate from these terms. It points to the sphere of economics. Its origins may be found in two different spheres, the first of which is the release of prisoners or hostages through the payment of a ransom.[149] Due to the ubiquity and importance of the military realm in the Greco-Roman world, audiences knew about prisoners of war and attempts to release them. In addition, the term "redemption" may also refer to money paid for the manumission of enslaved persons. Considering that a large percentage of the population in the ancient Greco-Roman world was enslaved, this soteriological concept was intelligible to many—in a dangerously tangible

147. Wolfgang Kraus, "Der Erweis der Gerechtigkeit Gottes im Tode Jesu nach Röm 3,21-26," in *Judaistik und Neutestamentliche Wissenschaft: Standorte—Grenzen—Beziehungen*, ed. Lutz Doering, Hans-Günther Waubke, and Florian Wilk, FRLANT 226 (Göttingen: Vandenhoeck & Ruprecht, 2008), 194.

148. This translation of 1 Corinthians 1:30 differs from the NRSVue. For the translation of the noun δικαιοσύνη, see the comments regarding the rendering of "justification" above under "Translation Matters" on Rom 3:21, 22.

149. Sophia Niepert-Rumel, *Metaphernkombinationen in der neutestamentlichen Rede vom Tod Jesu*, WUNT 2/563 (Tübingen: Mohr Siebeck, 2021), 630–31.

fashion. Many members of congregations of Jewish believers in Christ were enslaved people, and the sphere of enslavement is, therefore, a frequent source for metaphors in New Testament texts. Furthermore, Israel's foundational salvation narrative in the Hebrew Bible was the exodus from enslavement in Egypt. The taste of freedom was powerfully conveyed through the terminology of "redemption."[150]

Also illuminating is a passage in 2 Corinthians, a letter that features the term "justification" (δικαιοσύνη) seven times.[151] There, Paul describes being "in Christ" (ἐν Χριστῷ) as "a new creation [καινὴ κτίσις]: everything old has passed away; look, new things have come into being" (2 Cor 5:17). This is followed by another soteriological passage (2 Cor 5:18-21) with no fewer than two occurrences of the term "reconciliation" (καταλλαγή) and three of the verb "to reconcile" (καταλλάσσω). Specifically, Paul labels his own activity "ministry of reconciliation" (διακονία τῆς καταλλαγῆς, 5:18). He also explains how God has obtained this reconciliation: "For our sake God made the one who knew no sin to be sin, so that in him we might become the [justification] of God [ἵνα ἡμεῖς γενώμεθα δικαιοσύνη θεοῦ ἐν αὐτῷ]" (5:21). This sentence has the only occurrence of the phrase "[justification] of God" in Paul's letters prior to Romans 1:17; 3:22.

What emerges from these soteriological statements? Justification is *God's activity* on behalf of and in favor of humans. It describes the state of being a new creation "in Christ" because Jesus has taken over human sin. The logic of this statement can be called "interchange" (see also 2 Cor 8:9: "you know the generous act of our Lord Jesus Christ, that though he was rich, yet for your sakes he became poor, so that by his poverty you might become rich").[152] Every person in the assembly, including Paul, is now the "[justification] of God."[153] This spectrum of christological passages illustrates the extreme form of the humility and altruism that

150. Douglas A. Campbell, *The Rhetoric of Righteousness in Romans 3.21-26*, JSNTSup 65 (Sheffield: JSOT, 1992), 119–30.

151. The translation practice of NRSVue in 2 Corinthians regarding δικαιοσύνη is inconsistent. Sometimes, the noun is rendered as "justification" (e.g., 2 Cor 3:9), sometimes it is rendered as "righteousness" (e.g., 2 Cor 5:21; 6:7, 14). To avoid this terminological inconsistency, I am choosing "justification" in 3:9 as well.

152. Morna D. Hooker, "On Becoming the Righteousness of God: Another Look at 2 Cor 5:21," *NovT* 50 (2008): 358–75; Stephen Finlan, *Sacrifice and Atonement: Psychological Motives and Biblical Patterns* (Minneapolis: Fortress, 2016), 87–88.

153. Thomas Söding, "Sühne durch Stellvertretung: Zur zentralen Deutung des Todes Jesu im Römerbrief," in *Deutungen des Todes Jesu im Neuen Testament*, ed. Jörg Frey and Jens Schröter, WUNT 181 (Tübingen: Mohr Siebeck, 2005), 375–96.

was manifest in the proexistence of Jesus and conveyed by it.[154] Romans 3 also describes the elimination of human sin and God's initiative in it. Now the key terminology is that of "justification." The reason may have to do with the location of Phoebe's audiences. Rome regarded itself as the source of justice that flowed to all its conquered nations. "Justice" had already been celebrated as one of the virtues of Caesar Augustus, and a temple to the Roman goddess Justice had been founded in Rome in 13 BCE. These were terms and concepts of national pride for Rome and its inhabitants. Due to that, the choice of terminology in Romans has been called a "political declaration of war" on the Roman Empire.[155] It is clear that Paul and Phoebe reject its internal social system, its politics, and its imperialism.

Surprising as it may be, Paul and Phoebe use vocabulary related to atonement only once in this letter, that is, in Romans 3:25, where they employ the Greek term ἱλαστήριον. Its precise origin, meaning, and appropriate rendering are disputed, and with it the proper understanding of their ideas about atonement. It is clear, however, that it never means "sacrifice of atonement" in any Septuagint texts.[156] Earlier, scholars explored a number of possible backgrounds of this idea. For example, a martyrological background with reference to 4 Maccabees 17:22 has been considered.[157] Yet, the redating of this book to the late first or early second century CE renders such a connection impossible considering the date of composition of Romans.[158] Likewise, the usage of the term ἱλαστήριον in the Greco-Roman culture has been considered. There, the word designates objects given to deities as "votive offering" (or "propitiatory offering") to obtain divine favors or to convey feelings of gratitude; even the Trojan Horse featured an inscription that labeled it as "ἱλαστήριον." It also appears in a few altar inscriptions that read Καίσαρος ἱλαστηρίου,

154. On the concept of "proexistence" and its definition, see below at Rom 8:31-39, pp. 207–211.

155. Neil Elliott, *The Arrogance of Nations: Reading Romans in the Shadow of Empire*, Paul in Critical Contexts (Minneapolis: Fortress, 2010), 62; Nasrallah, *Archaeology*, 184.

156. Cilliers Breytenbach, *Versöhnung: Eine Studie zur paulinischen Soteriologie*, WMANT 60 (Neukirchen-Vluyn: Neukirchener Verlag, 1989), 168. This is, however, the translation of ἱλαστήριον in the NRSVue and the NIV.

157. Ernst Käsemann, *An die Römer*, 3rd ed., HNT 8a (Tübingen: Mohr Siebeck, 1974), 90; Daniel C. Ullucci, *The Christian Rejection of Animal Sacrifice* (Oxford: Oxford University Press, 2012), 75–76.

158. Jan W. van Henten, "Datierung und Herkunft des vierten Makkabäerbuches," in *Tradition and Re-interpretation in Jewish and Early Christian Literature: Essays in Honour of Jürgen C. H. Lebram*, ed. Jan W. van Henten et al., StPB 36 (Leiden: Brill, 1986), 136–49.

"(Altar of) the reconciling Caesar," dating between 31 and 27 BCE.[159] The function of the term "blood," however, remains unclear if ἱλαστήριον is understood as such a votive offering.[160]

In search of an alternative background, Wolfgang Kraus explores the Septuagint equivalents of traditional cult terminology and takes into consideration the so-called mercy seat, which is called ἱλαστήριον in Greek. The ἱλαστήριον is the centerpiece of the Jewish sanctuary, the tabernacle tent.[161] According to the Torah, it is a rectangular gold slab measuring 2.5 cubits (3.67 feet/1.11 meters) by 1.5 cubits (2.20 feet/0.67 meters) on top of the ark of the covenant (Exod 25:17-22; 37:6-9). Its ends feature two cherubim "of hammered work" (Exod 25:18), made of one piece with it. The cherubim stretch out their wings toward each other to embrace the empty space above the center of the mercy seat.

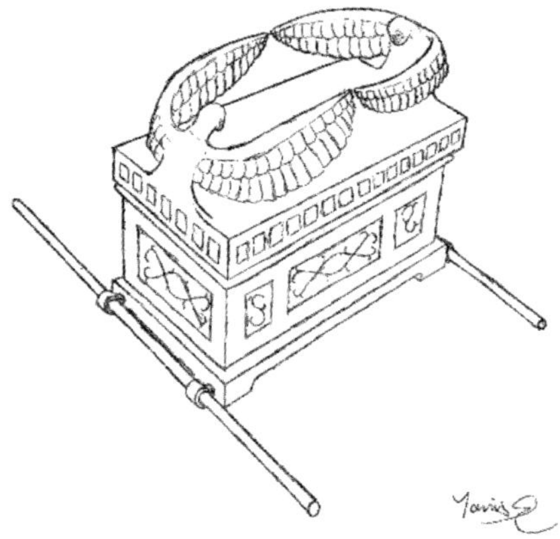

Ark of the Covenant, drawing by Yanis Emmanuel Eberhart. Reproduced by permission of Wipf and Stock Publishers.

159. Stefan Schreiber, "Das Weihegeschenk Gottes: Eine Deutung des Todes Jesu in Röm 3,25," *ZNW* 97 (2006): 88–110; Mark Wilson, "*Hilasterion* and Imperial Ideology: A New Reading of Romans 3:25," *HTS Teologiese Studies/Theological Studies* 73 (2017): 1–9.

160. Kraus, "Erweis," 202.

161. Friedrich Büchsel and Johannes Herrmann, "ἱλαστήριον," *TDNT* 3 (1965): 318–23; Wolfgang Kraus, *Der Tod Jesu als Heiligtumsweihe: Eine Untersuchung zum Umfeld der Sühnevorstellung im Römer 3,25–26a*, WMANT 66 (Neukirchen-Vluyn: Neukirchener Verlag, 1991), 23, 31, 260; Kraus, "Erweis," 205; Hultgren, *Paul's Letter to the Romans*, 156–60, 662–75; S. Tamar Kamionkowski, *Leviticus*, WCS 3 (Collegeville, MN: Liturgical Press, 2018), 154.

According to the priestly theology of the Second Temple period, this cult device is nothing less than the location of God's presence in the sanctuary, as the designation "the ark of the covenant of the Lord of hosts, who is enthroned on the cherubim" (1 Sam 4:4; see also 2 Sam 6:2; 2 Kgs 19:15; 1 Chr 28:2; Pss 80:2; 99:1) indicates.[162] It effectively imagines God as hovering on top of the mercy seat. In light of these reflections, the Greek term ἱλαστήριον in Romans 3:25 should be rendered as "place of atonement." On the Day of Atonement, the high priest would sprinkle the blood of sin offerings against this cultic appurtenance while taking measures for his protection because of God's presence.[163] Effecting atonement for the sanctuary, this blood rite had the purpose of purging sins and impurity (Lev 16:15-16, 33). Thus, atonement is conceptually similar to consecration. Such atoning power was due to the animal's life that was considered to be in its blood (Lev 17:11).[164] These blood application rites were the very center of the priestly atonement theology according to the Torah. New Testament texts from the later decades of the first century CE also make the connection of blood, purification, and forgiveness inherent in these rituals, for example, the christological statement that "the blood of Jesus . . . cleanses us from all sin" (1 John 1:7; see also Heb 9:22). They also align it with the concept of atonement (1 John 2:2; 4:10).

Form-critical scholarship has determined that Romans 3:25-26 most likely features an earlier hymnic fragment consisting of the following shorter text: "whom God put forward as a place of atonement by his blood because in his divine forbearance, he had passed over the sins previously committed."[165] Why would Paul and Phoebe have adopted such a hymn drawing on traditional Jewish rituals and atonement? When Paul had previously communicated his soteriological message (e.g., 1 Cor 1:26-31; 2 Cor 5:16-21), he did so without them. It is possible that now he, with the assistance of Phoebe, was eager to include terminology

162. Büchsel and Herrmann, "ἱλαστήριον," 318.

163. In its only other occurrence in the New Testament in Hebrews 9:5, ἱλαστήριον also refers to this device and has this meaning. The NKJV and NASB 1995 render the term ἱλαστήριον as "propitiation," Revidierte Lutherübersetzung 2017 translates "Sühne," Traduction œcuménique de la Bible "expiation," and Reina Valera 1995 "propiciación." See also Jewett, *Romans*, 268, 284–87: "mercy seat"; Gignac, *L'épître*, 164–65, 169: "instrument de Grand Pardon"; Wolter, *Römer*, 1:242, 256–59: "Gnadenort."

164. Kraus, *Heiligtumsweihe*, 22, 150–57, 168–90, 260–61; Friedhelm Hartenstein, "Zur symbolischen Bedeutung des Blutes im Alten Testament," in Frey and Schröter, *Deutungen des Todes Jesu im Neuen Testament*, 136.

165. Kraus, "Erweis," 195–97; Tamez, "Justification," 184.

and imagery that represented his own religion. In a way, the idea that Christ Jesus was the "place of atonement" was a method of literally filling a void. The ark of the covenant, a key object in Solomon's temple, is never mentioned in connection with the Second Temple. Josephus writes about the holy of holies: "In it there was nothing at all" (Josephus, *B.J.* 5.219; see also Tacitus, *Hist.* 5.9). Literally to fill that void, Second Temple Judaism engaged in a process of abstraction and transformation in the development of its atonement theology.[166] As part of this process, Paul and Phoebe now suggest that God has established an alternative place of atonement in Christ. With its application of priestly images from the Torah, this solution would have appealed to Jewish members in the audience; after all, Paul knew that Phoebe would have read the letter first in the assembly of Prisca and Aquila, who had been former members of a Jewish synagogue in Rome. By contrast, much of the later christological and soteriological arguments in Romans would go on to explore pagan (or secular) backgrounds (Rom 5:6-11; see below).

How, then, is the process of forgiveness of human sins imagined in the imagery of Romans 3:21-26 drawing on atonement? It is not easy to understand what follows; the core of this pericope features one of the most densely packed sentences with no fewer than eight prepositions in the relative clause.[167] But what is clear is that the "place of atonement" is combined with the term "blood." This association evokes priestly atonement rituals through blood application that are central to the annual Day of Atonement ceremonies. Just as these rituals purified the Jewish sanctuary, so "the blood of Jesus his Son cleanses us from all sin" (1 John 1:7). Atonement is, thus, conceptualized as purification and leads to consecration.[168]

What are the implications of these exegetical reflections for feminist biblical scholarship? On the one hand, concerns that the use of atonement terminology necessarily evokes violent images of a cruel or vengeful deity have no foothold in Romans 3. The key term as such does not mean "sacrifice." On the other hand, sacrificial rituals in Second Temple Judaism are misconstrued if the theory of satisfaction by Anselm of Canterbury (1033–1109) would be declared as normative for their interpretation.[169] As has been demonstrated, neither sacrificial rituals nor cultic blood application rites enact a vicarious death but operate through the logic of purification and consecration.

166. Thomas Hieke, *Levitikus 16–27*, HThKAT (Freiburg: Herder, 2014), 608.

167. Finlan, *Problems*, 39.

168. Eberhart, *Sacrifice*, 86, 97–98, 132.

169. This is correctly stated in Tamez, "Justification," 183–84.

Elsa Tamez requests certain attributes that would make a message of salvation adequate and authentic for women. She writes: "Therefore, to speak to them of the grace of God is a liberating message for women. In the first case, grace opposes any laws that require a person to earn human rights or dignity."[170] That is exactly what this passage states about God's reconciliation and justification in Jesus Christ: it is God's initiative and activity alone (Rom 3:22-25; see also Cor 5:18-21) and completely free (Rom 3:24).[171] The soteriological concepts in Romans convey an absolute declaration about the new being of those who are "in Christ." They are not invitations to imitate whatever logic may be perceived to be operative behind this spectrum of different soteriological images. Thus, the proclamation of the humiliation of Jesus for the empowerment of humans does *not* mean that humans need to imitate Jesus or renounce everything "for Christ's sake" to obtain salvation. Humans also do not need to risk their lives or undergo crucifixion for their reconciliation. The new identity as a new being "in Christ" is valid without such proof. It is being grasped through faith, understood as trust in the love of God for all humans. This message has been applied successfully from a postcolonial perspective when reflecting on the project of the Truth and Reconciliation Commission of Canada that invited witness of the oppression of former First Nations and/or Metis students in church-run residential schools. The new identity of justification by grace, of being convicted of sin and nevertheless accepted by God allowed for a more efficacious, truthful, and faithful response and established a basis of healing after centuries of suffering.

One may wonder why the message of reconciliation and atonement in Romans 3 features remarks like: "But now, apart from the law, the [justification] of God has been disclosed" (Rom 3:21) and "they are now justified by his grace as a gift" (3:24). Once more, when Paul had communicated his soteriological message previously (e.g., 1 Cor 1:26-31; 2 Cor 5:16-21), he had not mentioned any of that. The specific aspect that divine justification is now attainable "apart from the law" includes traditional Jewish law. It may be interpreted with respect to the presence of both Phoebe as the reader of the letter in front of the audiences in Rome and their female members such as Prisca, Miriam (Mary), Junia, Tryphaena and Tryphosa, Persis, the mother of Rufus, Julia, and the sister of Nereus (Rom 16:3-5, 6, 7, 12, 13, 15). If these elements are indeed the ingredients of a liberating message for women, as Elsa Tamez states, then Paul and

170. Tamez, "Justification," 185.

171. Niepert-Rumel, *Metaphernkombinationen*, 658.

Phoebe had wisely chosen to include them in their letter. They convey that God shows divine justification by actively justifying humans (3:26), and that includes the liberation of women. Hence in this regard, there is no longer any distinction among humans.

Since all initiative and all activity of this scenario of reconciliation, justification, and atonement are God's, there is nothing for humans to boast about. This is the initial theme of the diatribe (on this rhetorical genre, see above, p. lxvi) in Romans 3:27-31: "Then what becomes of boasting? It is excluded" (Ποῦ οὖν ἡ καύχησις; ἐξεκλείσθη, 3:27). The term "boasting" (καύχησις) had been mentioned in 2:17 ("But if you . . . boast of your relation to God") and 2:23 ("You who boast in the law"). All of this is out of place now. The reason is "the law of faith" (3:27), which is better understood in the generic sense of "principle" or "realm of faith."[172]

If it was just mentioned that the message of reconciliation and atonement in Romans 3 had included new elements, then one may note that Paul had already touched upon the topic of boasting in 1 Corinthians 1:31 through a quotation from Jeremiah 9:22-23 (LXX) that humans can only boast about the Lord Christ Jesus. This sentence concluded his celebration of Jesus Christ as the embodiment of God's *Chokmah-Sophia-Sapientia-Wisdom*. Paul and Phoebe now revisit this important aspect in Romans 3:27-31. Paul's remarks in 1 Corinthians 1:26-29, however, demonstrated that such comments were directed against the traditional honor-shame system of the Greco-Roman world and its concomitant all-pervasive culture of self-advertisement in the competitive arena of the public court of reputation/honor. This was the space where *his*-stories were celebrated; this was the space where patriarchy was maintained and developed. Paul's ban of boasting, therefore, targets Rome's kyriarchal "pyramid of honor" with all of its facets.[173] Honoring a few selected heroes comes at the expense of downgrading and shaming many other humans. Shame can only be eliminated if at the same time honor is uprooted. That

172. There is an extensive discussion regarding the exact meaning of this phrase. The Greek term νόμος can carry the semantic meaning of "principle, rule, realm of influence," which is rather applicable here (Peter von der Osten-Sacken, *Die Heiligkeit der Tora: Studien zum Gesetz bei Paulus* [München: Kaiser, 1989], 23–33; Klaus Haacker, *Der Brief des Paulus an die Römer*, THKNT 6 [Leipzig: Evangelische Verlagsanstalt, 1999], 93; Michael Theobald, "Der Kanon von der Rechtfertigung [Gal 2,16; Röm 3,28]: Eigentum des Paulus oder Gemeingut der Kirche?," in *Studien zum Römerbrief*, ed. Michael Theobald, WUNT 136 [Tübingen: Mohr Siebeck, 2001], 178–82).

173. Kahl, *Galatians*, 270; Elisabeth Schüssler Fiorenza, *Ephesians*, WCS 50 (Collegeville, MN: Liturgical Press, 2017), lxxx.

is what Paul and Phoebe have in mind when they write that "there is no distinction, since all have sinned and fall short of the glory of God" (Rom 3:22-23). The term "glory" (δόξα) is central in honor-and-shame semantics. If it is being eliminated here and elsewhere on an individual and/or corporate level, then the honor-shame system breaks down. Moreover, they write: "For we hold that a person is justified by faith apart from works prescribed by the law" (3:28). The broader program leads not only to the unity of different cultural and religious groups but also to that between women and men. It creates space for *her*-meneutics; it makes it possible to insert the stories of women into the narratives of the Greco-Roman world.[174] Ultimately, it is the precondition of the radically democratic "*ekklēsia* of wo/men."

Along the way, the elimination of the traditional honor-shame system also leads to the affirmation of the oneness of the God of Jews and gentiles. In the words of Régis Burnet: "Paul is outraged that ethnic differences matter more than common salvation."[175] Romans features the emphatic theological conclusion of such a vision of reconciliation, justification, and atonement: "Or is God the God of Jews only? Is he not the God of gentiles also? Yes, of gentiles also, since God is one" (Rom 3:29-30). This type of Q&A theology conveys the idea that, first, it is indeed the God of Judaism who is being shared with the rest of the world. It was already stated earlier in the letter that God's "justification" was revealed to humans "through faith for faith" (Rom 1:17). The point of departure was the faith of the Jews, which was considered as the source of that of the "Greeks," an interpretation that is consistent with Paul's self-understanding as a Jew who is an apostle to the gentiles. It designated a progression of faith and referred to Paul's very own missionary activities—and for the moment to those of Phoebe as his avatar.[176] As the faith of the Jews, it also shows an unwavering commitment to monotheism. "God is one" is a reference to the distinctive faith confession of Second Temple Judaism: "Hear, O Israel: The LORD our God, the LORD is

174. Stephanie Y. Mitchem, "Womanists and (Unfinished) Constructions of Salvation," *JFSR* 17 (2001): 85–100, at 99.

175. Régis Burnet, *Le Nouveau Testament*, 3rd ed. (Paris: Presses Universitaires de France, 2021), 21: "Paul est outré de constater que les différences ethniques comptent davantage que le salut commun."

176. Kobel, *Paulus als interkultureller Vermittler*, 124–25.

one" (Deut 6:4[177]). But while this statement would allow Paul to display his pride in his Jewish tradition, it should be noted that Greeks also had a so-called philosophic monotheism that acknowledged the oneness of a deity, if only in an elative sense; their deity was unique, singular, and without any denial of the existence of other gods. It is already attested by the Greek philosopher Xenophanes (ca. 570–480 BCE).[178] Even if less of a typical feature of Greek religion, this aspect is important. It means that the confession of the oneness of God would also have allowed Phoebe, the gentile, to wholeheartedly join in this specific argument.

Second, Paul and Phoebe also declare that this Jewish God "will justify the circumcised on the ground of faith and the uncircumcised through that same faith" (Rom 3:30). Once again, this terminology refers to Jews and gentiles. While considered as separate groups, the good news is that God justifies both. This is what Romans will show later, including the importance of "faith" as a traditional Jewish parameter (4:1-12).

A final thought concerns the "law" in Romans 3:31. This terminology would have sounded very familiar to Jewish members of the audiences in Rome. It has, however, also a more general meaning. As the word "law" occurs twice in both the question and the answer, but in each case without the article (see already 3:21), it may have been employed with a more generic sense to also appeal to the gentile audience in Rome. But Paul and Phoebe show respect for such a law. "Since it is not the law itself but rather boasting about performance under the law that is excluded by Christ, faith in him is not only affirmed by the Jewish law but also upholds law."[179]

177. The NRSVue translates Deut 6:4 as "Hear, O Israel: The Lord is our God, the Lord alone." Thus, the NRSVue omits the monotheistic implications of this key statement. The Septuagint, however, translates Deut 6:4: "Hear, O Israel: The Lord our God is one (or the only) Lord (Ἄκουε, Ισραηλ, κύριος ὁ θεὸς ἡμῶν κύριος εἷς ἐστιν)." This Greek version is, in turn, quoted in Mark 12:28-34 where a scribe asks Jesus about the most important commandment. "Jesus answered, 'The first is, "Hear, O Israel: the Lord our God, the Lord is one"' " (12:29). The scribe's response in 12:32, therefore, confirms that Deut 6:4 is really about the oneness of God. Hence, its rendition in NRSVue should be corrected.

178. Paula Fredriksen, "The Question of Worship: Gods, Pagans, and the Redemption of Israel," in *Paul within Judaism: Restoring the First-Century Context to the Apostle*, ed. Mark D. Nanos and Magnus Zetterholm (Minneapolis: Fortress, 2015), 196.

179. Jewett, *Romans*, 303.

Romans 4:1–5:21

The Gift of Grace: Including Women

Abraham, an Example of Faith (4:1-12)

In the theological part about the gospel of Jesus Christ, the second section deals with faith, sin, and the gift of grace. It explicates terms and ideas that have been introduced and discussed to some degree in the first section of this part. The pericope in Romans 4:1-12 contains a diatribe and a midrash about Abraham's justification by faith, implicitly moving toward the inclusion of women.[1]

Romans 4 continues with four important topics from chapter 3: "deeds," justification, faith, and circumcision.[2] In fact, one of the last preceding arguments had to do with the justification of both the circumcised and the uncircumcised through faith (3:30). Now it offers the story of Abraham as proof from Jewish Scriptures (chapter 4 features a total of five Scripture quotations, similar to 10:5-13; 11:1-10). The section starts with a question: "What then are we to say was gained by Abraham, our ancestor according to the flesh?" (4:1).[3] With this epistolary disclosure formula, Phoebe

1. On the rhetorical forms of diatribe and midrash, see above, p. lxvi.

2. Michael Wolter, *Der Brief an die Römer*, vol. 1: *Röm 1–8*, EKKNT 6/1 (Neukirchen-Vluyn: Neukirchener Verlag; Ostfildern: Patmos, 2014), 277.

3. A different translation of this notoriously difficult sentence is provided in Richard B. Hays, "'Have We Found Abraham to Be Our Forefather According to the Flesh?' A Reconsideration of Rom 4:1," *NovT* 27 (1985): 76–98.

Rom 4:1-12

4:1What then are we to say was gained by Abraham, our ancestor according to the flesh? 2For if Abraham was justified by works, he has something to boast about, but not before God. 3For what does the scripture say? "Abraham believed God, and it was reckoned to him as righteousness." 4Now to one who works, wages are not reckoned as a gift but as something due. 5But to one who does not work but trusts him who justifies the ungodly, such faith is reckoned as righteousness. 6So also David pronounces a blessing on those to whom God reckons righteousness apart from works:

7"Blessed are those whose
iniquities are forgiven
and whose sins are covered;
8blessed is the one against whom
the Lord will not reckon
sin."

now turns to the audiences in Rome to garner their attention for the following discourse on these topics. Her presentation combines midrashim with elements of the diatribe to ensure the full attention of the audiences and to persuade them (4:1-25). Finally, Phoebe invokes "Abraham, our ancestor."[4] In his letter to the Galatian churches, Paul had already affirmed "those who believe" to be descendants of Abraham (Gal 3:6-7). There can be little doubt that, for Jews, Abraham had the greatest authority in all religious matters. Paul's vision for his assemblies was one of inclusion and unity "in Christ" through mutual respect and loving care.[5] This is, by and large, in alignment with what the name of "Abraham" means, which is interpreted as "ancestor of a multitude of nations" in Genesis 17:4-6 (see the acknowledgment in Rom 4:17).[6] One may add that Abraham's name before the name change was "Abram," which means "exalted father" and implies such an ancestor.

4. Elizabeth A. Castelli, "Romans," in *Searching the Scriptures*, vol. 2: *A Feminist Commentary*, ed. Elisabeth Schüssler Fiorenza (New York: Crossroad, 1994), 287–88.

5. Helmut Koester, *Introduction to the New Testament*, vol. 2: *History and Literature of Early Christianity*, Hermeneia (New York: de Gruyter, 1987), 144; Brigitte Kahl, "Krieg, Maskulinität und der imperiale Gottvater: Das Augustusforum und die messianische Re-Imagination von 'Hagar' im Galaterbrief," in *Doing Gender—Doing Religion: Fallstudien zur Intersektionalität im frühen Judentum, Christentum und Islam*, ed. Ute E. Eisen, Christine Gerber, and Angela Standhartinger, WUNT 302 (Tübingen: Mohr Siebeck, 2013), 278; Laura S. Nasrallah, *Archaeology and the Letters of Paul* (Oxford: Oxford University Press, 2019), 181.

6. Not to be forgotten, Abraham's wife Sarai becomes Sarah, interpreted as "princess of nations" (Gen 17:15-16).

[9]Is this blessing, then, pronounced only on the circumcised or also on the uncircumcised? We say, "Faith was reckoned to Abraham as righteousness." [10]How then was it reckoned to him? Was it before or after he had been circumcised? It was not after but before he was circumcised. [11]He received the sign of circumcision as a seal of the righteousness that he had by faith while he was still uncircumcised. The purpose was to make him the ancestor of all who believe without being circumcised and who thus have righteousness reckoned to them, [12]and likewise the ancestor of the circumcised who are not only circumcised but follow the example of the faith that our ancestor Abraham had before he was circumcised.

In the Torah, Abraham is a pivotal character. He not only received an everlasting covenant from God, of which circumcision is the sign (Gen 17:1-14). He is also the one who opened the concept of covenant for "the other" so as to become an embodiment of the bridge between God's specific covenant with Israel and the universal covenant with all humans and living creatures.[7] Abraham, therefore, appears as one of the first names in the New Testament canon, namely, at the beginning of the genealogy of Jesus (Matt 1:2); one of the best ways of ensuring an authoritative presentation of Jesus was to call him "the son of Abraham" (1:1). Quite simply, Abraham was the epitome of Judaism. And as such, he was being invoked as the ultimate religious authority for Phoebe's discourse in Rome.

The question in Romans 4:1 about the gain of Abraham is aimed at "fleshly capacities." The prepositional phrase "according to the flesh" (κατὰ σάρκα, Rom 4:1) may be correlated with the verb of the sentence to provide a link to the question of whether Abraham performed "deeds of the law" prior to being justified by God.[8] Paul and Phoebe first turn

7. Castelli, "Romans," 287–88; Thomas Hieke, "Abram / Abraham as Prefiguration of the Covenant in the Torah," in *Covenant-Concepts of Berit, Diatheke, and Testamentum: Proceedings of the Conference at the Lanier Theological Library in Houston, Texas, November 2019*, ed. Christian A. Eberhart and Wolfgang Kraus, in collaboration with Richard Bautch, Matthias Henze, and Martin Rösel, WUNT 506 (Tübingen: Mohr Siebeck, 2023), 70.

8. Robert Jewett, *Romans: A Commentary*, Hermeneia (Minneapolis: Fortress, 2007), 308. A different opinion is presented in Joseph A. Fitzmyer, *Romans: A New Translation with Introduction and Commentary*, AB 33 (New York: Doubleday, 1993), 371; Wolter, *Römer*, 1:280; Alain Gignac, *L'épître aux Romains*, Commentaire biblique: Nouveau Testament 6 (Paris: Cerf, 2014), 184, 189, 197.

to "boasting," the characteristic expression accompanying successful activities but also connoting the habit of self-advertisement in the honor-shame culture. The implied statement that Abraham was not justified by "[deeds]" (4:2) targets the merit-based culture of the ancient Roman world.[9] Phoebe then turns to the Jewish Scriptures, which she intentionally notes (4:3). She cites Genesis 15:6 (LXX): "And Abram believed God, and it was reckoned to him as [justification]."[10] This Scripture passage allows her to present Abraham as an example of faith. Based on the narrative chronology, the argument is effective due to its simplicity: Abraham believed in God first (Gen 15) but was circumcised later (Gen 17; yet just to be on the safe side, Phoebe prefers to spell out this insight explicitly in Rom 4:10). Therefore, justification must be a matter of faith rather than circumcision, which is considered a "merit."[11] In Romans 4:7-8, Phoebe doubles up with Scripture quotations by referencing the psalmist David and quoting Psalm 31:1-2 (LXX). The passage is about the "blessedness" of those whose sins are forgiven. Here, too, Phoebe prefers to spell out that God's crediting of justification occurs "apart from [deeds]" (Rom 4:6).[12] Thus, God is presented as the sole actor of justification and forgiveness. In a skillful paraphrase of the Torah narrative, Phoebe now suggests to her audiences that "the sign of circumcision" was only a "seal" of Abraham's justification. In this argument, circumcision becomes the sign of something else, that is, the "[justification] that he had by faith," which was ascribed to Abraham while he was still uncircumcised.[13] The conclusion of the paragraph is stunning: "The purpose was to make him the ancestor of all who believe without being circumcised and who

9. James R. Harrison, *Paul's Language of Grace in Its Graeco-Roman Context*, WUNT 2/172 (Tübingen: Mohr Siebeck, 2003), 219; Brigitte Kahl, *Galatians Re-imagined: Reading with the Eyes of the Vanquished*, Paul in Critical Contexts (Minneapolis: Fortress, 2010), 270. The NRSVue translates the four occurrences of the term ἔργα in Romans 4:2-6 as "works." As mentioned above (see comments on the translation of a similar phrase in Rom 2:15), "deeds" is preferable for the sake of consistency of terminology throughout the letter.

10. This translation differs from the NRSVue. For the translation of the noun δικαιοσύνη, see the comments regarding the rendering of "justification" above under "Translation Matters" on Rom 3:21, 22.

11. Reinhard Feldmeier and Hermann Spieckermann, *Der Gott der Lebendigen: Eine biblische Gotteslehre*, TOBITH 1 (Tübingen: Mohr Siebeck, 2011), 304–5.

12. Richard N. Longenecker, *The Epistle to the Romans: A Commentary on the Greek Text*, NIGTC (Grand Rapids: Eerdmans, 2016), 498–99.

13. Klaus Berger, "Abraham in den paulinischen Hauptbriefen," *MThZ* 17 (1966): 47–89, at 67.

thus have [justification] reckoned to them, and likewise the ancestor of the circumcised who are not only circumcised but who also follow the example of the faith that our ancestor Abraham had before he was circumcised" (Rom 4:11-12). Abraham is, hence, being presented as the prototype of Jewish group identity and the paradigm of the vision of unity for the communities of faith "in Christ."[14]

Phoebe had addressed this topic in 2:25-29 to argue that the "circumcision of the heart" would, rather, be destined for divine acknowledgment. That argument is intended to challenge the significance of the rite for gentiles who may be interested in claiming Jewish identity; it aims at a fundamental transformation of humans. Such transformation is part of the larger "group-making project" to achieve radical unity among the different groups who belong to Christ, specifically Jews and gentiles.[15] By extension, it also aims at the full inclusion of women because the new entry ritual of baptism has replaced circumcision.[16] While in Paul's earlier letter to the Galatians, this may have been more of an implicit upshot, there is a different degree of urgency to this aspect in the letter to the Romans since a woman who holds a leadership position in her own faith community presents the argument. The vision of unity among the different groups is, in its version in Galatians 3:28, envisioned along three parameters, namely, *religious or ethnic identity* ("no longer Jew or Greek"), the *status of personal liberty* ("no longer slave or free"), and *gender* ("no longer male and female"). As will be shown later,[17] it is probably no coincidence that Phoebe likely happens to embody the weaker side of each binary. In this case, she would be the manifestation and personification of this new democratic "*ekklēsia* of wo/men." In addition, enslaved females in the ancient Roman world knew the hardship of intersectionality more than anyone else. This was a lasting memory even years after manumission had made

14. Beverly Roberts Gaventa correctly observes that, while focusing on Abraham's faith, the passage in Romans 4 neglects that the text of Genesis actually puts the emphasis on his obedience. Cf. Beverly Roberts Gaventa, *When in Romans: An Invitation to Linger with the Gospel According to Paul* (Grand Rapids: Baker Academic, 2016), 55–56.

15. Caroline Johnson Hodge, "The Question of Identity: Gentiles as Gentiles—but also Not—in Pauline Communities," in *Paul within Judaism: Restoring the First-Century Context to the Apostle*, ed. Mark D. Nanos and Magnus Zetterholm (Minneapolis: Fortress, 2015), 153–73; Caroline Johnson Hodge, *If Sons, Then Heirs: A Study of Kinship and Ethnicity in the Letters of Paul* (Oxford: Oxford University Press, 2007), 120–31.

16. Tatha Wiley, *Paul and the Gentile Women: Reframing Galatians* (New York: Continuum, 2005), 81–82.

17. See comments on Romans 16:1-2 below.

them freedpersons, painfully refreshed on a regular basis by the not-so-secret disdain of those higher up in the "pyramid of honor," sometimes manifest in blatant mockery. Due to the experience of enslavement, the vision of and desire for personal freedom first developed among enslaved women.[18] If she was indeed a freedperson, then Phoebe may also have been a visionary of and advocate for emancipation and personal liberty.

It is instructive to reflect on the discourse about Abraham as a paradigm of justification through faith and against circumcision from the vantage point of Phoebe, who had the privilege to read some of Paul's letters in the past. The arguments that she presents to her audiences in Rome are by no means abstract or irrelevant theological exercises. Instead, they are intended to legitimize both her personal identity as a full member of her own assembly "in Christ" in Cenchreae and her leadership position there. They are, moreover, intended to justify her current mission as Paul's envoy from Corinth and her very task of reciting their letter. Without the liberating message of the gospel, already her presence in Rome could have been challenged by her audiences there on these several aspects. By extension, such arguments continue to be valid for other women and marginalized people; they should be heard as a message of empowerment and liberation.

Faith Realizes God's Promise (4:13-25)

This section is the second part of the diatribe on Abraham's justification through faith in Romans 4:1-25. It expands the midrash showing that Abraham's promise comes to those who are justified through faith. The emphasis on God's promise toward all humans provides the basis for the argument of the inclusion of women.

TRANSLATION MATTERS: Romans 4:13, 16, 18

The NRSVue translation of Romans 4:13 about the promise that did not come to Abraham or "to his descendants" through the law is an interpretive possibility. The Greek term here (and in 4:16, 18; 9:29) is σπέρμα, which means literally "sperm." The figurative meaning of σπέρμα as "descendant" is attested and within its semantic range. Two comments are, however, in order, particularly in consideration of the parallel text in Galatians 3. First, the NRSVue is inconsistent as the same term σπέρμα occurs three times in a very similar context in

18. Orlando Patterson, *Freedom in the Making of Western Culture*, Freedom 1 (New York: Basic Books, 1991), 54.

Rom 4:13-25

[13]For the promise that he would inherit
the world did not come to Abraham or
to his descendants through the law
but through the righteousness of faith.
[14]For if it is the adherents of the law
who are to be the heirs, faith is null
and the promise is void. [15]For the law
brings wrath, but where there is no
law, neither is there transgression.
[16]For this reason the promise depends on faith, in order that it may rest
on grace, so that it may be guaranteed to all his descendants, not only
to the adherents of the law but also to
those who share the faith of Abraham
(who is the father of all of us, [17]as it is
written, "I have made you the father
of many nations"), in the presence of
the God in whom he believed, who
gives life to the dead and calls into
existence the things that do not exist.
[18]Hoping against hope, he believed
that he would become "the father of
many nations," according to what was
said, "So shall your descendants be."
[19]He did not weaken in faith when he
considered his own body, which was
already as good as dead (for he was

Galatians 3:16 where it is rendered "offspring" (see also 3:19, 29). (A footnote at each instance indicates that the word can also mean "seed," but the meaning of "sperm" remains unmentioned.) This translation practice thus obscures the fact that "descendent" and "offspring" in these two texts are equivalents of the same Greek word.[19] Second, in Romans 4:13, the noun σπέρμα is a collective noun; the NRSVue translation "to his descendants" in the plural is, therefore, correct. Galatians 3:16 makes an explicit point, however, about the fact that the term σπέρμα in its reference text in Genesis 22:18 (LXX), which translates Hebrew זרע ("sperm, seed"), is singular, not plural: "Now the promises were made to Abraham and to his offspring; it does not say, 'And to offsprings,' as of many, but it says, 'And to your offspring,' that is, to one person, who is Christ." This nuance about the "one person" is given up in Romans 4:13, as the continuation in 4:16-18 shows.

The diatribe on Abraham's justification through faith continues with new arguments on other topics. The focus is now on "law" (νόμος). This term, which has not been mentioned so far in chapter 4, is attested five times in Romans 4:13-16 alone. It is juxtaposed with "justification," the overarching theme of the entire diatribe. This is evident in the very first sentence: "For the promise that he would inherit the world did not come to Abraham or to his descendants through [ ] law [διὰ νόμου] but

19. The NIV renders σπέρμα as "offspring" in Romans 4:13, but as "seed" in Galatians 3:16. Hence, the NIV is also inconsistent in its translation practice.

Rom 4:13-25 (cont.)

about a hundred years old), and the
barrenness of Sarah's womb. [20]No
distrust made him waver concerning the promise of God, but he grew strong in his faith as he gave glory to
God, [21]being fully convinced that God was able to do what he had promised.
[22]Therefore "it was reckoned to him as righteousness."
[23]Now the words, "it was reckoned to him," were written not for his sake alone
[24]but for ours also. It will be reckoned to us who believe in him who raised Jesus our Lord from the dead,
[25]who was handed over for our trespasses and was raised for our justification.

through the [justification][20] of faith" (4:13). Although the NRSVue (just like the NIV) renders "through the law," the Greek text of 3:15 repeats the wording of Romans 3:21, 31 where "law" occurs without an article. This means that Paul and Phoebe may have used the word once more in a generic sense to also appeal to the gentiles in the audiences of Rome.[21] They combine it with key terminology from the *propositio* ("main thesis") of the letter about the gospel, which is presented there as "God's saving power" by justification through faith (1:16-17). The new element of the argument is that already Abraham received God's promise in such a way. Abraham's trust was truly paradigmatic; neither his old age nor the barrenness of Sarah's womb were reasons for doubt (4:19).

It has not gone unnoticed that some of the arguments based on Jewish Scriptures have changed over time. Paul had previously affirmed that God's promise had been made to Abraham and "to his descendant" (literally "to his sperm," Gal 3:16), which was a reference only to Christ. Contrary to this constriction, Paul and Phoebe appeal in Romans 4:13 to God's promises to Abraham while using "sperm" (σπέρμα) as a collective noun (hence the NRSVue translation "to his descendants"). It now refers to Abraham as the ancestor of "many nations" (Rom 4:17-18), which are understood as both Jews and gentiles.[22] This will be revisited and further problematized later (9:6-18).

20. This translation of the noun δικαιοσύνη in Romans 4:13 differs from the NRSVue. For the translation chosen here, see the comments regarding the rendering of "justification" above ("Translation Matters" on Rom 3:21, 22).

21. Mark D. Nanos, "Romans," in *The Jewish Annotated New Testament: New Revised Standard Version Bible Translation*, ed. Amy-Jill Levine and Marc Zvi Brettler (Oxford: Oxford University Press, 2011), 262.

22. Thomas H. Tobin, *Paul's Rhetoric in Its Context: The Argument of Romans* (Peabody, MA: Hendrickson, 2004), 2. See also Castelli, "Romans," 288.

Juxtaposition of Similar Passages in Romans and Galatians, Topic: "Abraham"[23]

Rom 4:13	. . . *the promise* that he would inherit the world did not come to Abraham or to his *descendants* [literally *"sperm"*] through [ ] law . . .	Gal 3:16	Now *the promises* were made to Abraham and to his *offspring* [literally *"sperm"*]; it does not say, "And to *offsprings*" [literally *"sperms"*], as of many, but it says, "And to your *offspring*" [literally *"sperm"*], that is, to one person, who is Christ.	Rom 9:7-8	. . . not all of Abraham's children are his *descendants*[24] [literally *"sperm"*], but "it is through Isaac that descendants [literally *"sperm"*] shall be named for you." This means that it is not the children of the flesh who are the children of God, but the children of *the promise* are counted as *descendants* [literally *"sperm"*].
Rom 4:18	Hoping against hope, he believed that he would become "the father of many nations," according to what was said, "So shall your *descendants* be."				

From a feminist perspective, two interesting details need to be pointed out about Romans 4:13-25. First, Abraham is portrayed as a positive example of faith. On the one hand, this faith is neither a doctrinal commitment nor an adoption of a specific theological view. It is, rather, Abraham's deep trust that God will not abandon him, his family, and his descendants. On the other hand, "Abraham's trust is important, but it is God's faithfulness, not Abraham's faith, that creates the possibilities and makes the difference. . . . *God* is the truly important subject."[25] Therefore, humans have nothing to boast about (3:27). Also, this faith is the central element in Paul's and Phoebe's group-making project; it has social ramifications as it involves notions of both trust and fidelity.[26]

23. Similar text in these columns is indicated by italics.

24. For this translation, see comments below under "Translation Matters" on Romans 9:7a.

25. Sigve K. Tonstad, *The Letter to the Romans: Paul among the Ecologists*, Earth Bible Commentary 7 (Sheffield: Sheffield Phoenix, 2016), 151 (italics original).

26. Murray Smith, "God's Righteousness, Christ's Faithfulness, and 'Justification by Faith Alone' (Romans 3:21-26)," in *Romans and the Legacy of St Paul: Historical,*

Second, only Abraham and his descendants are recipients of God's promises. It is characteristic of the androcentrism of the narratives in the Hebrew Bible (and in the Septuagint) and in Romans that Sarah, Abraham's wife, has not been depicted as a recipient of the divine promise despite the fact that the promised descendants were, of course, also hers. In a similar way, her faith would not be considered worthy of consideration. Sarah's name is mentioned in Romans 4:19, but only to illustrate the strength of Abraham's faith who continued to believe notwithstanding his wife's barrenness. Once again, these ancient texts emerge as *his*-stories, not *hers*. This also applies to Galatians, Paul's earlier letter, where Hagar is mentioned by name, but Sarah is not, even if the NRSVue includes her name in the heading of the paragraph (Gal 4:21-31). Although Sarah is equated to "the Jerusalem above" and called "our mother" (μήτηρ ἡμῶν, Gal 4:26), which are both remarkable, she nevertheless remains entirely anonymous. This fact vividly demonstrates the status difference between women and men in ancient patriarchal societies throughout the ages. It is interesting, then, that Sarah's name is finally mentioned in Romans 4:19, if only as an area of concern for Abraham and in order to highlight *his* faith. One may conjecture that Phoebe had pledged to include Sarah's name, even if Sarah had not been advanced to the status of an example of faith. Most likely, that was simply in keeping with the popular tradition of Jewish lists of heroes in sacred texts who are presented as examples of moral and spiritual qualities for readers to emulate—these lists customarily focus on men (see, e.g., Sir 44:1–49:16; Wis 10:1-21; 4 Macc 18:6-24; 4 Ezra 7:106–111). In light of this, it is remarkable that, in a New Testament text authored a few decades after Romans, Sarah is eventually included in such a list (Heb 11:11; this is, however, distorted in NRSVue, which continues to render the passage in an androcentric fashion).[27]

Theological, and Social Perspectives, ed. Peter G. Bolt and James R. Harrison, Occasional Series 1 (Macquarie Park: SCD Press, 2019), 211.

27. According to Mary Ann Beavis and HyeRan Kim-Cragg, the chapter known as "Examples of Faith" in Hebrews 11:1-40 is different from these other Jewish catalogues of heroes because it features several explicit references to women, such as Sarah (Heb 11:11), Rahab (11:31), and women who "received their dead by resurrection" (11:35; cf. Mary Ann Beavis and HyeRan Kim-Cragg, *Hebrews*, WCS 54 [Collegeville, MN: Liturgical Press, 2015], 134). However, the NRSVue depicts only Abraham, not Sarah, as the example of faith in Heb 11:11. Previously, NRSV even had: "By faith he [Abraham] received power of procreation, even though he was too old—and Sarah herself was barren . . ." But this is a rather "awkward" rendition (Beavis and Kim-Cragg, *Hebrews*, 143). Instead, most other Bible translations make Sarah the model

What Phoebe proclaims in Rome about the "law" conveys a critical view: "If it is the adherents of the law who are to be the heirs, faith is null and the promise is void. For the law brings wrath (ὁ γὰρ νόμος ὀργὴν κατεργάζεται), but where there is no law, neither is there transgression (οὗ δὲ οὐκ ἔστιν νόμος οὐδὲ παράβασις)" (Rom 4:14-15). According to these sentences, there is either a regimen of law or a regimen of faith. Both cannot coexist side by side. The law would devalue both faith and God's promise. The well-known narrative of Abraham is used to demonstrate the importance of faith and its precedence over the law.[28] The law only brings "wrath" (ὀργή); earlier usages of the term (1:18; 2:5, 8; 3:5) indicate that this is about divine wrath. But such a statement, not just about law in general, but specifically about *the* Torah—as indicated by the definite article in 4:15—is a challenge to any type of piety that focuses on the law, holds it in high esteem, and proclaims personal devotion to it (see, e.g., Ps 119). Paul and Phoebe joined all those in Second Temple Judaism who had a different opinion, and they had declared it already earlier (Rom 3:20). Why are they of this opinion? There is an ethical dimension to this discourse. If the law is no longer at the center of the religious culture, then the focus shifts away from policing its related rules. "In other words, there is no accountability if there is no responsibility given."[29] Furthermore, as mentioned above, an ongoing concern is that the Torah, due to its emphasis on circumcision, effectively bans women from full inclusion in religious communities. With Phoebe's leadership position in Corinth and her mission to deliver the letter to the Romans at stake, the law could have been invoked to nourish prejudices. Phoebe's mission to proclaim the gospel as the liberating power of God could be successful only under the regimen of faith that establishes the new democratic *ekklēsia* of wo/men.

---

of faith, such as NIV: "And by faith even Sarah, who was past childbearing age, was enabled to bear children because she considered him faithful . . . " (see also NASB 1995; Revidierte Lutherübersetzung 2017; Traduction œcuménique de la Bible; cf. Beavis and Kim-Cragg, *Hebrews*, 145). The inclusion of women in this list may have to do with the possible involvement of a woman, namely Prisca, in the authorship of Hebrews. Centuries later, Jewish literature was gradually getting accustomed to include women in similar catalogues as well (b. Meg. 14a; cf. Shulamit Valler, "Who is *ēšet ḥayil* in Rabbinic Literature?," in *A Feminist Companion to Wisdom Literature*, ed. Athalya Brenner, 85–99, FCB 9 [Sheffield: Sheffield Academic Press, 1995]; Beavis and Kim-Cragg, *Hebrews*, 136–37).

28. Wolter, *Römer*, 1:298–99.

29. Valerie Griffiths, "Romans," in *The IVP Women's Bible Commentary*, ed. Catherine Clark Kroeger and Mary J. Evans (Downers Grove, IL: InterVarsity, 2002), 635.

This new regimen relies on both God's justification and on faith. Already in the case of Abraham, his faith "was reckoned to him as [justification]" (Rom 4:22, repeated from v. 3, again with quotation of Gen 15:6). The same applies in the days of Paul and Phoebe, as they make explicitly clear: "It will be reckoned to us who believe in him who raised Jesus our Lord from the dead, who was handed over for our trespasses and was raised for our justification (ὃς παρεδόθη διὰ τὰ παραπτώματα ἡμῶν καὶ ἠγέρθη διὰ τὴν δικαίωσιν ἡμῶν)" (Rom 4:24-25). Adopting an earlier credal formula, these sentences describe God as the object of human faith. At the same time, this is faith in a God who has taken the initiative to save humanity through the death and resurrection of Jesus. Phoebe revisits some of the christological statements from the opening section of the letter (1:4) and also aspects of the atonement terminology of Romans 3:21-26. She thus makes the decisive move to include her own faith and that of the groups who believe "in Christ," as the switch to the first-person plural pronoun "us" (4:24) shows.[30] This faith centers on Christ as the manifestation of the Jewish *Chokmah-Sophia-Sapientia-Wisdom* concept.

While it is plausible that a credal formula has been implemented in the christological statement of Romans 4:24-25, contemporary scholarship has also reached near-unanimous agreement that the passage "who was handed over for our trespasses and was raised for our justification" in 4:25 evokes the famous suffering servant song in Isaiah 52:13–53:12.[31] Based on this reference, the statement in Romans is often understood to articulate vicarious redemption for the forgiveness of human sins.[32] Recently, however, methodological difficulties have been pointed out in many of the arguments in support of the reference to Isaiah 52:13–53:12. It is true that an emblematic passage like Isaiah 53:10a (MT) features the

30. James W. Thompson, *The Church According to Paul: Rediscovering the Community Conformed to Christ* (Grand Rapids: Baker Academic, 2014), 137; Gaventa, *When in Romans*, 100.

31. Heinrich Schlier, *Der Römerbrief*, HTKNT 6 (Freiburg: Herder, 1977), 136; Fitzmyer, *Romans*, 389; Shiu-Lun Shum, *Paul's Use of Isaiah in Romans: A Comparative Study of Paul's Letter to the Romans and the Sibylline and Qumran Sectarian Texts*, WUNT 2/156 (Tübingen: Mohr Siebeck, 2002), 189–93; Wolter, *Römer*, 1:311–12; Thomas Schreiner, *Romans*, 2nd ed., BECNT 6 (Grand Rapids: Baker Academic, 2018), 251.

32. Jörg Frey, "Die Deutung des Todes Jesu als Stellvertretung: Neutestamentliche Perspektiven," in *Stellvertretung: Theologische, philosophische und kulturelle Aspekte*, vol. 1: *Interdisziplinäres Symposion Tübingen 2004*, ed. Johanna Christine Janowski, Bernd Janowski, and Hans P. Lichtenberger (Neukirchen-Vluyn: Neukirchener Verlag, 2006), 103–4.

idea—unique in the Hebrew Bible—of someone vicariously giving his life for others. Paul and Phoebe would, therefore, have adopted the logic of vicarious redemption from that Hebrew Bible passage. Scholars have recently become attentive, however, to the fact that Paul did not translate the Hebrew text when dictating this letter to Tertius; instead, he would have referred to the Old Greek text (i.e., the LXX). Yet that text differs significantly from the Hebrew text; it reads: "And/Yet the Lord desires to cleanse him from his blow; if you offer a sin offering, your soul shall see a long-lived offspring" (Isa 53:10a [LXX]). Eliminating the unique aspect of vicarious redemption that is characteristic of the Hebrew text, the Greek version endorses instead the rewards of offering a particular type of cultic sacrifice. If the Greek text no longer contains any idea of vicarious redemption, then this specific soteriological aspect cannot have been adopted in Romans 4:25 (or in any other New Testament writing).[33] Rather, Paul and Phoebe imagine the redemptive logic that they had already adopted in their atonement imagery in 3:21-26 and will present anew and in a different version in chapter 5. The particular aspect of the resurrection, however, now points in the direction of victory over death, which was still absent in chapter 3. The death and resurrection of Jesus are soteriologically connected. The latter rehabilitates the former and sets it apart from other execution events or, more broadly, any other human death.[34]

Results of Justification (5:1-11)

From a formal perspective, this passage spells out consequences of justification in a community. The focus is first on peace and boasting (Rom 5:1-5), followed by a christological rationale of justification as current reconciliation and future salvation (5:6-11). All of this has significant ramifications for the status of women in the community.

In the christological-soteriological paragraph Romans 3:21-26, the central term has been "justification" (δικαιοσύνη). The participle of the related

33. Wolfgang Kraus, "Jesaja 53 LXX im frühen Christentum—eine Überprüfung," in *Beiträge zur urchristlichen Theologiegeschichte*, ed. Wolfgang Kraus, BZNW 163 (Berlin: de Gruyter, 2009), 176–77.

34. Arnfríður Guðmundsdóttir, "Crucified—So What? Feminist Rereadings of the Cross-Event," in *T&T Clark Companion to Atonement*, ed. Adam J. Johnson (London: Bloomsbury T&T Clark, 2017), 354.

Rom 5:1-11

5:1Therefore, since we are justified by
faith, we have peace with God through
our Lord Jesus Christ, 2through whom
we have obtained access to this grace
in which we stand, and we boast in
our hope of sharing the glory of God.
3And not only that, but we also boast
in our afflictions, knowing that affliction
produces endurance, 4and endurance
produces character, and character produces hope, 5and hope does not put
us to shame, because God's love has
been poured into our hearts through the
Holy Spirit that has been given to us.
6For while we were still weak, at the
right time Christ died for the ungodly.
7Indeed, rarely will anyone die for a
righteous person—though perhaps for

verb, "justified" (δικαιωθέντες), is the first word of the Greek text of Romans 5. It signals that what follows spells out the ramifications of justification for humans. As such, this passage is a rhetorical *transitio*.[35] That such justification is "by faith" (5:1) is added immediately, but it should have been clear to the audiences after the preceding passages about the paradigmatic faith of Abraham. The question now is how the existence of those who are justified can be described. The verb that depicts the condition and situation of those who are justified is a first-person plural indicative verb, "we have." It continues the usage of language in the preceding chapter that explicitly suggested an immediate application of the referenced text for the present time and situation: "It will be reckoned to us who believe in him" (4:24). It includes, therefore, not only the members of the communities in Rome but also Paul and those around him when the letter was written in Corinth.[36] Phoebe is thus included as a person who was present at that time and as the person who now recites the letter aloud in Rome.

Phoebe proclaims that those who are justified by faith "have peace with God" (Rom 5:1). Thus, the theological and practical ramifications of justification lead humans to a situation "of peace and reconciliation issuing from [God's] grace and mercy and guaranteeing the hope of salvation, for they are no longer under wrath."[37] This terminology refers to an important concept for both Second Temple Judaism and the Greco-Roman world. In text traditions of the former, "peace" is a central idea usually conveyed by the Hebrew term שלום (*shālôm*). It refers specifically

35. Jewett, *Romans*, 347–48; Longenecker, *Romans*, 551.
36. Wolter, *Römer*, 1:318; Thompson, *The Church According to Paul*, 137.
37. Fitzmyer, *Romans*, 395.

a good person someone might actually dare to die. [8]But God proves his love for us in that while we still were sinners Christ died for us. [9]Much more surely, therefore, since we have now been justified by his blood, will we be saved through him from the wrath of God. [10]For if while we were enemies we were reconciled to God through the death of his Son, much more surely, having been reconciled, will we be saved by his life. [11]But more than that, we even boast in God through our Lord Jesus Christ, through whom we have now received reconciliation.

to right individual and corporate relationships with God, as the Aaronite blessing conveys (Num 6:24-26). True peace can only be obtained from and with God (Ps 85). These texts evoke God as a powerful king (Ps 29:10-11), conveying the political dimension of this theological vision. It is also manifest in the notion of the "covenant of peace" (ברית שלום, διαθήκη εἰρήνης, Ezek 34:25; 37:26-27) and associated with an eschatological utopia of undisturbed lives in the wilderness and the rich blessings of abundant harvests (Ezek 34:25-27; similar Hos 2:20 [2:18 (ET)], see also Isa 27:6; 65:17-25; Amos 9:13; Ezek 47:9-12; 4 Ezra 8:52). Sometimes even the political reunification of the divided kingdoms is part of it (Ezek 37:22). Whether or not real peace can be proclaimed is a matter of dispute; Jeremiah criticized the false prophets for declaring: " 'Peace, peace,' when there is no peace" (Jer 6:14). But שלום also has a broader meaning; its root conveys a status of "well-being," "health," "prosperity," and "balance."[38] In the New Testament, much of this semantic spectrum is activated in the Greek noun εἰρήνη, "peace." It implies the absence of enmity and war (Rom 5:10-11). In Romans, this concept is focused on the crucifixion of Jesus Christ. Sometime later, such theological ideas have helped to develop the theologoumenon of "the God of peace" (Phil 4:9). A wish of "peace" with this particular meaning is part of every introduction (*exordium*) of Paul's letters (Rom 1:7; 1 Cor 1:3; 2 Cor 1:2; Gal 1:3; Phil 1:2; 1 Thess 1:1; Phlm 3).

But peace also had a prominent place in the imperial propaganda of the Roman Empire and its imperial cult. It was known as *Pax Romana* ("Roman peace") in Latin. Inaugurated by Emperor Augustus in 27

38. Franz-Josef Stendebach, "שלום," *TDOT* 15 (2006): 13–48; Feldmeier and Spieckermann, *Gott*, 291–92, 453–54, 505–7.

BCE after centuries of intense warfare by the Roman republic, it was also called *Pax Augusta*. It was celebrated as a golden age of successful Roman imperialism accompanied by internal political stability, order, and economic growth. For example, the Roman historian and senator Velleius Paterculus (ca. 19 BCE–ca. 31 CE) offered the following *laudatio*:

> Trust has returned to the Forum; dissension has been removed from the Forum, campaigning from the Campus Martius, discord from the Senate house. Justice, equity, and diligence, long buried and forgotten, have been restored to the state. Magistrates once more have authority; the Senate, honor; the courts, dignity. . . . The *peace of Augustus* has spread into the regions of the rising sun and of the setting sun, to the boundaries of the southernmost and northernmost lands. The peace of Augustus protects every corner of the world from fear of banditry. . . . The provinces have been liberated from the outrageous misconduct of magistrates. Honor lies waiting for those who deserve it; and the wicked do not escape punishment. (Velleius Paterculus, *A History of Rome* 2.126.2-5)

This period lasted for more than two centuries, concluding only with the death of Emperor Marcus Aurelius in 180 CE. The term *Pax Romana* became highly influential in Roman politics in the middle of the first century CE, just prior to the writing of Romans. Although celebrated, it was also known that this peace had a twofold problem: it benefitted only a limited elite at the apex of the social hierarchy, and it came at a cost as it was based on military victory. Even the Roman historian and politician Tacitus (56–117 CE) acknowledged the plight of subjugated nations:

> Among the many British war chiefs was one called Calgacus who was preeminent in valor and in birth. He is reported to have addressed in the following manner the assembled crowd of Britons who were clamoring for battle. . . . "Up until this day, we who live in this last strip of land and last home of liberty have been protected by our very remoteness. . . . But now the farthest limits of Britain have been opened up. . . . Beyond us, there are no tribes, nothing except waves and rocks and, more dangerous than these, the Romans, whose oppression you have in vain tried to escape by obedience and submission. Plunderers of the world they are, and now that there is no more territory left to occupy their hands which have already laid the world waste, they are scouring the seas. If the enemy is rich, they are greedy; if the enemy is poor, they are power-hungry. . . . They rob, they slaughter, they plunder—and they call it 'empire.' Where they make a waste-land, they call it 'peace.'" Nature has planned that each man love his children and family very dearly. Yet these are torn from us by conscription to be slaves elsewhere.

> And our wives and sisters, even if they escape rape by an enemy, are yet defiled by Romans pretending to be friends. (Tacitus, *Agric.* 29-31)

Paul had, in a previous letter, already included a critical reference to the slogan of imperial propaganda about the *Pax Romana*: "When they say, 'There is peace and security' [εἰρήνη καὶ ἀσφάλεια], then sudden destruction will come upon them, as labor pains come upon a pregnant woman, and there will be no escape!" (1 Thess 5:3).[39] The apostle had benefitted from certain achievements of the Roman Empire, such as the efficient infrastructure that facilitated his own travels—and now also those of Phoebe. But he had a different vision of peace, proclaiming instead an empire of justice based on nonviolence and selfless love.[40] Its logic will be explained toward the end of Romans 5:1-11. What was the driving force behind this reconceptualization of peace? The adherents of the communities that believed in Christ barely belonged to those who would have celebrated Rome's peace propaganda. Consisting of enslaved persons, former enslaved and free persons, and many who belonged to those who were denigrated as "barbarians," they would have known the seemingly endless suffering of the subjugated peoples. Consisting also of many women, they would not have been among those to have celebrated the heroism and honor of warfare. Most of them were victims of Roman imperialism, a status permanently inscribed into the existence of some of them through the institution of enslavement. In consideration of scholarly discussions of her identity, Phoebe may have been one of them who, after years of oppression and exploitation as a former enslaved woman, most likely still suffered from trauma.[41] Her intersectional vantage point would have required a different type of salvation to restore her life. For people like her, Stephanie Y. Mitchem proposes a search for wholeness rather than formulaic answers.[42] To overcome her trauma resulting from repeated assaults on her identity and personal value, Phoebe literally embarked on a journey that begins—to apply Mitchem's ideas—with the affirmation of her own identity as a woman, a former enslaved person,

39. See Florence M. Gillman, Mary Ann Beavis, and HyeRan Kim-Cragg, *1–2 Thessalonians*, WCS 52 (Collegeville, MN: Liturgical Press, 2016), 87.

40. Udo Schnelle, *The First One Hundred Years of Christianity: An Introduction to Its History, Literature, and Development*, trans. James W. Thompson (Grand Rapids: Baker Academic, 2020), 266.

41. For further details on Phoebe's identity, see the comments below on Romans 16:1-2.

42. Stephanie Y. Mitchem, "Womanists and (Unfinished) Constructions of Salvation," *JFSR* 17 (2001): 85–100, at 98–99.

and a gentile. The inclusion in the assemblies of believers in Christ was the starting point of her healing process and restored her sense of peace with God. The fact of the restored relationship with God provides peace of mind that then makes a difference within one's social environment.

A different vision of peace is possible "through our Lord Jesus Christ" (Rom 5:1). Paul and Phoebe had just used the title "Lord" in the previous sentence (4:24); both usages should be seen in connection with the initial presentation of "the gospel concerning his [God's] Son, who . . . was declared to be Son of God with power according to the spirit of holiness by resurrection from the dead, Jesus Christ our Lord" (1:3-4). It is the resurrection that functions as the ultimate revelation of Jesus as the embodiment of the Jewish *Chokmah-Sophia-Sapientia-Wisdom* concept. As such, Jesus provides humans with the privilege of "access [προσαγωγή] to this grace in which we stand" (5:2). The noun "access" must be understood against the common practice of limited access to those at the top of social hierarchies and to their reserved spaces. This applied to the religious and the secular realm. Different types of temple cults usually had strictly regulated access just like the seats of political power. Access to the sacred precincts in Jerusalem during the Second Temple period was governed by purity regulations; witnessing sacrificial rituals at the temple itself was the exclusive right of men (a wall separated the forecourt of the women from the forecourt of the men and priests; only the latter had access to the "altar of burnt offerings"). Rules of access could become theological battle grounds; the community in Qumran thought that they deserved exclusive access to God (1QH 12:20-26). In a similar fashion, Herodotus wrote about "processions and approaches" (πομπὰς καὶ προσαγωγάς) to Greek sanctuaries (*Hist.* 2.58). The Athenian soldier and historian Xenophon (ca. 430–357 BCE) mentions that those who wanted an audience with the Persian emperor Cyrus "were to court favor as my friends for access" (*Cyr.* 1.3.8; 7.5.45).[43] The privilege of access to God through Jesus Christ is the source of empowerment for those shunned and relegated to the margins by society.

Paul and Phoebe spell out the consequence of this new privileged status: "we boast in our hope of sharing the glory of God. And not only that, but we also boast in our afflictions, knowing that affliction produces endurance, and endurance produces character, and character produces hope, and hope does not put us to shame, because God's love has been

43. Michael Wolter, *Rechtfertigung und zukünftiges Heil: Untersuchungen zu Röm 5,1–11*, BZNW 43 (Berlin: de Gruyter, 1978), 113–16; Jewett, *Romans*, 349–50.

poured into our hearts through the Holy Spirit that has been given to us" (Rom 5:2-5). The direct references to the Greco-Roman honor-shame system are manifest by her employment of key terminology, such as "to boast" with two occurrences, "glory" and "to put to shame." Paul and Phoebe target, therefore, the backbone of the Greco-Roman culture in which the quest for honor was the supreme purpose in life while being shamed was to be avoided at any cost. This system has been reconfigured in the communities of believers in Christ because of the participation in Christ. It bestows hope of "glory" on members of these communities and allows them to boast about it. Earlier, Phoebe had proclaimed to the audiences in Rome that boasting was excluded (3:27)—if understood in the traditional way as the promoting of one's own achievements. But now, a new type of countercultural boasting is announced that is focused on God. With this new orientation, however, boasting itself is transformed into praise of God. It allows humans to "boast" even about their suffering. It has been noted that the phrasing "our sufferings" appears to hint at specific concerns. Robert Jewett suggests that the difficulties related to the expulsion of assembly leaders under Claudius and their return after 54 CE may be included just like Paul's own sufferings that were known in Rome.[44] Yet, the multifaceted sufferings of Phoebe would have most certainly been part of it as well, including her trauma resulting from continuous sexual assault from the time when she was an enslaved woman. It might include the social stigma thereafter, including the fact that a freedwoman had a hard time finding a husband, and now potential prejudices in the assemblies in the city of Rome where it is likely that not all welcomed her because of who she was. Phoebe's triple trouble as a woman, a gentile, and a former enslaved person leaves a lot of suffering for her to bear. Not to forget that Phoebe's various audiences in the city of Rome lived and met in areas like the notorious Trastevere and the district around Porta Capena (see above, pp. lxxii–lxxx). They had either low-wage jobs or were even worse off as enslaved people. The topic of afflictions was certainly accessible to all.

With a powerful "we," however, Phoebe gets to present her own narrative of salvation to her various audiences in Rome. It is connected with Abraham's faith that she had interpreted as trust in God's ability to offer new life in the face of death (Rom 4:17).[45] Phoebe now invites her listeners to share her perspective. Suffering is typically nothing to boast

44. Jewett, *Romans*, 353.

45. Peter Oakes, *Reading Romans in Pompeii: Paul's Letter at Ground Level* (Minneapolis: Fortress; London: SPCK, 2009), 141.

about, but she gets to announce the paradox that apparent negatives are being transformed into positives. In addition, Paul too had his share of suffering to bear; he had recently written to the Galatians about his own persecution "for the cross of Christ" (Gal 6:12; see also the more detailed description of afflictions in 2 Cor 11:23-31). Valerie Griffiths emphasizes: "Paul will boast in the situations of suffering brought about by his choices to live for God. This is a direct challenge to those who proclaim that an outwardly comfortable life, relatively free of suffering, marks a true, beloved disciple of the Lord."[46]

With a climax, Phoebe now connects human afflictions with three qualities that she links in a chain of causality. Afflictions, she explains, produce endurance, which produces character, which produces hope (Rom 5:3-4). A gendered exploration will note that, in the Greco-Roman culture, "endurance" was generally considered to be primarily a manly virtue that would prevent cowardice and make a person a better soldier, as discussed by philosophers such as Socrates and Plato (*Lach.* 193a; *Theaet.* 177b). It was, indeed, a "virtue"; this term itself is derived from Latin *vir*, "man." It would define "courage," which in Greek is ἀνδρεία, connected to ἀνήρ, "man." Could endurance really have worked for Phoebe and other female members of the assemblies in Rome? It is remarkable, then, that traditional literature of Second Temple Judaism features a number of narratives in which not only men but also women are examples of both courage and endurance (e.g., 4 Macc 1:7-12) while displaying "the nobility of your faith" (τὴν τῆς πίστεως γενναιότητα, 17:2). As Lynn H. Cohick comments about the books of 2 Maccabees, 4 Maccabees, and the Acts of Paul and Thecla: "Devout reason reveals its remarkable power in providing mothers with manly courage."[47] Although these books postdate Romans, their narratives about suffering and dying show that Second Temple Judaism had a firm commitment to respond to oppression with resistance, in which women were just as brave as men.

Parallels to ethical exhortation presented in a chain of causality also exist in Jewish literature. According to the book of Wisdom 6:17-20, the beginning of wisdom (σοφία) is "the most sincere desire for instruction," which leads to "love," which is equivalent to "the keeping of her laws," which is equivalent to "assurance of immortality," which "brings one

46. Griffiths, "Romans," 635.

47. Lynn H. Cohick, "Mothers, Martyrs, and Manly Courage: The Female Martyr in 2 Maccabees, 4 Maccabees, and the Acts of Paul and Thecla," in *A Most Reliable Witness: Essays in Honor of Ross Shepard Kraemer*, ed. Susan Ashbrook Harvey et al., BJS 358 (Providence: Brown University Press, 2015), 132.

near to God." While, here, "love" is but a preliminary element that leads to the ultimate goal of proximity to God, such "love" is itself the ultimate goal in Romans 5:5. As the true ingredient of the new democratic "*ekklēsia* of wo/men," the concept of love is the result of God's own Spirit working in humans. The equivalence of Spirit and Wisdom is often affirmed in biblical texts (e.g., Exod 31:3; 35:31; Deut 34:9; Isa 11:2; Wis 1:6; 7:7; Acts 6:10; Rom 8:6; 1 Cor 12:8, etc.).[48]

A new section in Romans 5:6-11 focuses on a christological rationale of justification, presented here as current reconciliation and future salvation. It elaborates on the topic of justification mentioned in 5:1; the section in 5:2-5 was thus a thematic digression spurred by the term "peace" in 5:1b. The term "love" in this section now prompts Phoebe to explain the topic of reconciliation to her audiences. She adopts an *a minore ad maius* inference (Hebrew: קל וחמר, "light and heavy"), which customarily offers a minor and well-accepted argument only to move on to a similar argument at a larger scale.[49] The paradigm of ultimate love is Jesus Christ; the specific event that demonstrates this love is his death on the cross. Hence, Phoebe first mentions that "Christ died for the ungodly"; she actually starts by saying "while we were still weak" (5:6) and will later call humans "enemies" of God. None of these three terms flattered her audiences; the word "ungodly," for example, has been used in chapters 1 and 3 in descriptions of human depravity.

> Presumably, Jews in the Roman congregations came from within the synagogue. . . . Gentile believers in this early period almost certainly came from the ranks of those who had already been associated with the synagogue. If they were not full proselytes, they at least were associated with God's people and probably made that association with Judaism precisely because of its strong moral teaching. To hear themselves characterized as weak, ungodly sinners who had been God's enemies would be more than a bit puzzling, possibly even offensive. It is all too easy to imagine someone objecting to Phoebe, the bearer and the reader of the letter, "Who you calling 'sinner,' lady?"[50]

These concerns about unflattering attributes are all the more urgent in consideration of the fact that the visitor to the city of Rome came

48. April De Conick, *Holy Misogyny: Why the Sex and Gender Conflicts in the Early Church Still Matter* (New York: Continuum, 2011), 22.

49. Jörg Frey, "Paulus als Pharisäer und Antiochener: Biographische Grundlagen seiner Schriftrezeption," in *Von Jesus zur neutestamentlichen Theologie: Kleine Schriften II*, ed. Benjamin Schliesser, WUNT 368 (Tübingen: Mohr Siebeck, 2016), 329.

50. Gaventa, *When in Romans*, 36.

from Corinth, the detested harbor city out east that was proverbially notorious for its peculiar combination of luxury, sexual immorality, and a population of freedpersons. Given a rather matter-of-fact attitude of citizens of Rome, a more natural instinct was resorting to haughtiness, if not outright prejudices against anyone from this city.

Second, Phoebe also states: "But God proves his love for us in that while we still were sinners Christ died for us. Much more surely, therefore, since we have now been justified by his blood, will we be saved through him from the wrath of God" (Rom 5:8-9). These lines, particularly the terms "justified" and "blood," remind the audiences of the vocabulary of atonement in Romans 3:21-26. But are these the same images? The next sentence is "For if while we were enemies we were reconciled to God [κατηλλάγημεν τῷ θεῷ] through the death of his Son, much more surely, having been reconciled [πολλῷ μᾶλλον καταλλαγέντες], will we be saved by his life" (5:10). The soteriological key term is now "to reconcile."

The possible origins of the concept of reconciliation and its related meaning are much debated among scholars. It clearly refers to a vicarious death.[51] Is it derived from the narratives about the Maccabean martyrs (2 Macc 7:1-42; 8:29),[52] or instead from Deutero-Isaiah's fourth song of the suffering servant (Isa 52:13–53:12) or atoning sin offerings?[53] Or does the imagery originate in the ancient Greco-Roman diplomatic/political sphere of enmity, warfare, and peace?[54] The advantage of the last interpretation is that it succeeds in accounting for and integrating other imagery in the context of these passages. Paul and Phoebe imagine enmity between humanity and God; because of human sin, God's wrath

51. The formula that someone "died/gave himself for" someone else can be found frequently in Paul's writings, where it is also one of the most important christological-soteriological paradigms to convey the gospel message (Rom 4:25; 5:6, 8; 14:15; 1 Cor 8:11, etc.). These kinds of formulas are well known from martyrdom motifs in Greek drama; cf. L. Stephanie Cobb, *Dying to Be Men: Gender and Language in Early Christian Martyr Texts*, GTR (New York: Columbia University Press, 2008).

52. Wolter, *Rechtfertigung*, 44–45.

53. Otfried Hofius, "Erwägungen zur Gestalt und Herkunft des paulinischen Versöhnungsgedankens," in *Paulusstudien*, ed. Otfried Hofius, WUNT 51 (Tübingen: Mohr Siebeck, 1989), 1–14.

54. Cilliers Breytenbach, *Versöhnung: Eine Studie zur paulinischen Soteriologie*, WMANT 60 (Neukirchen-Vluyn: Neukirchener Verlag, 1989); Cilliers Breytenbach, "Versöhnung, Stellvertretung und Sühne: Semantische und traditionsgeschichtliche Bemerkungen am Beispiel der paulinischen Briefe," *NTS* 39 (1993): 59–79; Ferdinand Hahn, *Theologie des Neuen Testaments*, vol. 1: *Die Vielfalt des Neuen Testaments: Theologiegeschichte des Urchristentums*, 2nd ed. (Tübingen: Mohr Siebeck, 2005), 261–65. Some of the problems in this scholarly debate have to do with an incompatible usage of terminology.

needs to be propitiated. In other passages, this terminology signifies that damaged relations have been restored through the mediation of somebody who risked his or her life for this purpose. Christ intercedes; this concept imagines him in a perilous mission in the context of military conflicts. His death is, therefore, vicarious (Rom 5:6-11). Paul included the idea that the death of Christ would attain human salvation already in his very first letter: "For God has destined us not for wrath but for obtaining salvation through our Lord Jesus Christ, so that whether we are awake or asleep we may live with him" (1 Thess 5:9-10). In another previous letter, Paul also employed the idea of reconciliation when proclaiming a "God who reconciled us to himself through Christ." He finally referred to his own activity as "ministry of reconciliation" and his preaching as "the message of reconciliation" (2 Cor 5:18-20). This passage features the Greek verb "to reconcile" (καταλλάσσω) and the noun "reconciliation" (καταλλαγή) no fewer than five times. Thus, in 2 Cor 5:20, Paul makes a comprehensive statement about his own apostolic mission.

Juxtaposition of Similar Passages in Romans and 2 Corinthians, Topic: "Reconciliation"[55]

Rom 5:10	For if while we were enemies *we were reconciled to God* through the death of his Son, much more surely, *having been reconciled*, will we be saved by his life.	2 Cor 5:19-20	. . . in Christ *God was reconciling the world to himself*, not counting their trespasses against them, and entrusting the message of *reconciliation* to us. So we are ambassadors for Christ, since God is making his appeal through us; we entreat you on behalf of Christ, *be reconciled to God*.

The soteriological image of reconciliation was widely accessible in the Greco-Roman world given the importance and appeal of military achievements. Rome even related stories of the triumphal death of a general by the name of Regulus whom the Carthaginians captured, tortured, and—according to some accounts—put to death by crucifixion (Horace, *Saec.* 3.5.40-50; Seneca, *Prov.* 3.69).[56] The topic of a heroic death was, therefore, commonplace. Yet, while standard Hellenistic paradigms of reconciliation

55. Similar text in these columns is indicated by italics.

56. Joseph R. Dodson, "The Convict's Gibbet and the Victor's Car: The Triumphal Death of Marcus Atilius Regulus and the Background of Col 2:15," *HTR* 114 (2021): 182–202, at 191–95.

were based on the identification of the guilty party, an appeal process, and reparations to mitigate the problem, Paul and Phoebe reframe them decisively. For them, God is the author and initiator of reconciliation, not humans (Rom 5:8). Divine compassion is only recognized when one understands that in Jesus, God was willing to be crucified. This new soteriological concept has been called a "paradigm shift."[57] It is a potent image to present Christ's death on the cross as God's saving power.

The imagery of reconciliation in Romans 5:6-11, however, differs from that of atonement in 3:21-26. Both pericopes operate with different parameters at various levels. The former imagines a military battlefield; the latter, worship at a sanctuary. The ultimate goal in the former is peace; in the latter, it is holiness. The following table illustrates these differences:

Comparison: Atonement and Reconciliation Imagery in Romans

	Romans 3:21-26: Atonement	Romans 5:6-11: Reconciliation
Background	Sanctuary/Temple	Battlefield, political/diplomatic offices
Responsible Agents	Priests	Kings, military generals, soldiers/armies
Effective Event	Sacrificial rituals, Atonement rituals	Diplomatic missions, military campaigns, battles
Means/Material Agents	Sacrificial materials (animals, grains, blood),	Soldiers (vicarious death)
Required Qualities	Purity, sanctity	Courage, training, and experience in battle
Original Problem	Impurity, sin	Conflict, enmity
Ultimate Goal	Sanctity ("atonement")	Peace ("reconciliation")
Outcome/Solution for Humans	Approach/enter sanctuary, encounter God, blessing	Encounter the other group/nation, life (by avoiding defeat = death on the battlefield or enslavement)

57. John T. Fitzgerald, "Paul and Paradigm Shifts: Reconciliation and Its Linkage Group," in *Paul Beyond the Judaism/Hellenism Divide*, ed. Troels Engberg-Pedersen (Louisville: Westminster John Knox, 2001), 244–57.

According to the atonement paradigm, the crucifixion of Jesus is the event that is the new place of atonement. The means or material agent is the blood of Jesus; by means of the inherent life, it has the power of purification or consecration. This blood consecrates humans. Thus, their sin or impurity is purged. According to the reconciliation paradigm, the crucifixion of Jesus is the event of reconciliation. The means of reconciliation is his death, which put an end to enmity between humans and God. Humans have, therefore, peace with God. Hence, both paradigms have, as their core event, the death of Jesus. But since the original problem (sin/impurity; conflict) differs in each paradigm, the corresponding goal/solution is different as well (sanctity; peace). Yet, both paradigms convey that, ultimately, humans can meet and relate to God.

The Need to Reinvent Reconciliation

Chemin toujours complexe et nécessairement original, la réconciliation doit être à chaque fois réinventée. Il n'y a pas de modèle à emprunter et, en même temps, comme l'a si fortement souligné Hannah Arendt, après ses travaux sur les trois totalitarismes qui l'on amenée à douter de l'action politique et à réfléchir sur la fragilité du temps humain. C'est ainsi que, pour elle, le *par*don ne peut-être monopolisé par une culture ou un courant d'idée : dans un sens laïc, il peut être mis à disposition de tous.[58]	Always a complex and necessarily original path, reconciliation must be reinvented each time. There is no model to follow and, at the same time, as Hannah Arendt so strongly underlined after her work on the three totalitarianisms that led her to doubt political action and to reflect on the fragility of the human era. This is how, for her, *for*giveness cannot be monopolized by a culture or a set of ideas: in a secular sense, it can be made available to everyone.[59]

Bernard Philippe

58. Excerpt from Bernard Philippe, "Partager sa propre expérience de réconciliation? Réflexion sur l'Europe et la paix," *Bulletin du Centre de recherche français à Jérusalem* 25 (2014): 1–8, at 4 (italics original), http://journals.openedition.org/bcrfj/7350. The text references Hannah Arendt, *Condition de l'homme moderne*, Liberté de l'esprit (Paris: Calmann-Lévy, 2005).

59. ET: CAE.

There must have been some urgency to include a message not only about peace with God (Rom 5:1) but also about reconciliation. Paul and Phoebe had probably received word from their former colleagues and friends, Prisca and Aquila, about internal tensions in the assemblies of Rome. Their origin was the return of those Jewish believers in Christ who had recently been expelled. Prisca and Aquila were among them. Through his avatar Phoebe, Paul now wants to support their reintegration into the assemblies in Rome (see above, pp. lxxxi–lxxxii).

Nevertheless, two further aspects need to be considered. First, some may find the terminology of death troubling. Often overlooked, however, is the fact that Paul and Phoebe attribute salvific value also to the *life* of Christ in Romans 5:10 (this brief comment is later explicated in 5:12-21). And second, the conceptual background of diplomacy and warfare is clearly a domain that celebrates masculinity and the heroism of men.[60] It raises questions of how women would relate to the associated savior figure and whether they find such reconciliation applicable. Arnfríður Guðmundsdóttir proposes that ways to redeem the relevance of the cross are to understand it as a symbol of the *kenosis* ("self-emptying") of patriarchy and to maintain the constitutive connection with incarnation.[61]

Adam and Christ (5:12-21)

This section is characterized by a change after the first-person plural pronouns of the previous one; it is dominated by third-person singular pronouns. Applying the focus on death that dominated the conclusion of the previous paragraph, it describes how the abundant grace in Christ overwhelms the reign of death because of Adam's sin.

TRANSLATION MATTERS: Romans 5:12, 15

The NRSVue renders Romans 5:12: "just as sin came into the world through one *man*, and death came through sin, and so death spread to *all* because *all* have sinned."[62] In the same way, the NRSVue translates a few lines later (5:15): "For if

60. Kahl, "Krieg," 282–87.

61. Guðmundsdóttir, "Crucified," 349, 354. See also Luise Schottroff, "Toward a Feminist Reconstruction of the History of Early Christianity," in *Feminist Interpretation: The Bible in Women's Perspective*, ed. Luise Schottroff, Silvia Schroer, and Marie-Theres Wacker, trans. Martin Rumscheidt and Barbara Rumscheidt (Minneapolis: Fortress, 1998), 177–254.

62. Italics in the biblical references added.

Rom 5:12-21

12Therefore, just as sin came into the
world through one man, and death
came through sin, and so death spread
to all because all have sinned—13for sin
was indeed in the world before the law,
but sin is not reckoned when there is
no law. 14Yet death reigned from Adam
to Moses, even over those who did not
sin in the likeness of Adam, who is a
pattern of the one who was to come.

15But the free gift is not like the trespass. For if the many died through the
one man's trespass, much more surely
have the grace of God and the gift in
the grace of the one man, Jesus Christ,
abounded for the many. 16And the gift is
not like the effect of the one man's sin.
For the judgment following one trespass brought condemnation, but the
gift following many trespasses brings

the many died through the one *man's* trespass, much more surely have the grace of God and the gift in the grace of the one *man*, Jesus Christ, abounded for the many." In both of these passages as well as in 5:18-19 (with another three occurrences), the NRSVue translates the Greek noun ἄνθρωπος as "man."[63] The term ἄνθρωπος, however, is the general Greek term for "human," "human being," or "person"; the term with the gender-specific meaning of "man" is typically ἄρσην, "male" (as opposed to θῆλυ, "female," see Gen 1:27 [LXX]; Rom 1:26-27; Gal 3:28), or ἀνήρ, "man" (as opposed to γυνή, "woman," see 1 Cor 11:3; also Diogenes Laertius, *Lives* 1.33). Hence, Romans 5:12 should rather be rendered: "just as sin came into the world through one *human*." This statement is not about gender but about the human species that Adam as its prototype represents according to the Yahwist's creation narrative (Gen 2:7). This is also clear from the very wording in Romans 5:12 itself, which literally states: "and so death spread to all *humans* because all have sinned." It is obvious that the anthropological reality of death applies to "humans," not just to "men" (as if "women" would live forever).[64] Probably out of concern for consistent translation, however, the NRSVue omits the term "human" here, thus leaving ἄνθρωπος untranslated.

This second half of chapter 5 continues to explain the meaning of the grace of God in Jesus Christ. It may be interpreted as being connected to the brief comment in Romans 5:10 that humans will be "saved by his life," which remains without further explanation there. Romans

63. NASB 1995 reads: "just as through one man sin entered into the world, and death through sin, and so death spread to all men."

64. Beverly Roberts Gaventa, "Romans," in *Women's Bible Commentary*, ed. Carol A. Newsom, Sharon H. Ringe, and Jacqueline E. Lapsley, 3rd ed. (Louisville: Westminster John Knox, 2012), 552.

Rom 5:12-21 (cont.)

justification. [17]If, because of the one
man's trespass, death reigned through
that one, much more surely will those
who receive the abundance of grace
and the gift of righteousness reign in
life through the one man, Jesus Christ.
[18]Therefore just as one man's trespass led to condemnation for all, so
one man's act of righteousness leads
to justification and life for all. [19]For just as
through the one man's disobedience the
many were made sinners, so through
the one man's obedience the many will
be made righteous. [20]But law came in,
so that the trespass might increase, but
where sin increased, grace abounded all
the more, [21]so that, just as sin reigned
in death, so grace might also reign
through justification leading to eternal
life through Jesus Christ our Lord.

5:12-21 is less focused on sin as such but illustrates the abundance of grace in Christ (5:15-17, 20-21) for believers (5:17-19, 21). To convey this important theme, a comparison between the realms of Adam and Christ dominates the pericope.[65] It starts with Adam as the "one [human]" who introduced sin into the world and, with it, death as the natural outcome of sin (5:12). The contrast to this figure of Adam is Christ. Before moving to an exploration of the latter, two aspects need to be discussed. First, the depiction of the human predicament is a lot more generalized according to Romans 5:12-15 than it is according to the Torah/the Pentateuch. There, human wickedness may be a point of complaint, but righteous persons nevertheless do exist and are the center of the narratives (e.g., Noah in Gen 6:9; Abram/Abraham in Gen 12–25). Thus, a statement that "all have sinned" (Rom 5:12; see also 3:23) corresponds, rather, to Paul's anthropological vision. He wrote previously: "But in fact Christ has been raised from the dead, the first fruits of those who have died. For since death came through a human, the resurrection of the dead has also come through a human, for as all die in Adam, so all will be made alive in Christ" (1 Cor 15:20-22). While Paul has pitched Adam against Christ and does so again in Romans 5, traditional Jewish Scripture passages often pitch the sinful masses against a singular righteous character. Victory over death is not envisaged, although there is great emphasis on the exceptional length of the lives of the patriarchs, which may be seen as a functional equivalent (Gen 9:29; 25:7, etc., see also Gen 5:5).

65. Jewett, *Romans*, 370.

Second, the exclusive association of Adam with sin and death appears to be somewhat random. Elsewhere, Paul had attributed the first sin of humanity to Eve (2 Cor 11:3). This was not his idea; blaming bad things on women rather than taking responsibility for it was a rather typical move of patriarchal chauvinism. Thus, literature of the Second Temple period could claim, "From a woman sin had its beginning, and because of her we all die" (Sir 25:24; see also 26:6-9; 42:14). Accordingly, a retelling of the second creation story in 2 Enoch 30:17-18 has: "I imposed sleep upon him, and he fell asleep. And while he was sleeping, I took from him a rib. And I created for him a wife, so that death might come (to him) by his wife." That none of these attributions are benign is clear from Wisdom 2:24, according to which, thematically related, "through an adversary's envy death entered the world."[66] Given that the existence of sin and death has been blamed on Eve, representing women in general, it is surprising that the hamartiological discourse from 2 Corinthians 11:3 is altered in Romans 5:12-14 to assign the blame on Adam.[67] It has been surmised that women "may sense their exclusion from this text."[68] In light of its topic, however, one may just as well assume a sense of relief on the part of women that the tradition of patriarchal chauvinism has been dismissed.

What may have been the reason for such a change? While it is certainly possible that Paul had decided to alter his argument by himself, it is worth considering once more the situation of corporate authorship in the city of Corinth, where he wrote this letter assisted by, and possibly in an ongoing conversation with, Phoebe. It is not difficult to imagine that she would have sneered at such hamartiological-anthropological chauvinism. After all, if one takes the second creation narrative as the basis of the argument, did not God pronounce the commandment not to eat from the tree of the knowledge of good and evil exclusively to Adam (Gen 2:16-17)—if only because at that point in time, Eve had not even been created yet (2:21-22)? Why then blame Eve, who had not even witnessed the prohibition? Fortunately, Paul was easily convinced (but

66. See John R. Levison, *Portraits of Adam in Early Judaism: From Sirach to 2 Baruch*, JSPSup 1 (Sheffield: JSOT Press, 1988), 51–52, 168, 176–78; Teresa Ann Ellis, "Is Eve the 'Woman' in Sirach 25:24?," *CBQ* 73 (2011): 723–42.

67. Pheme Perkins, "Adam and Christ in the Pauline Epistles," in *Celebrating Paul: Festschrift in Honor of Jerome Murphy-O'Connor, OP, and Joseph A. Fitzmyer, SJ*, ed. Peter Spitaler, CBQMS 48 (Washington, DC: Catholic Biblical Association of America, 2011), at 143–46.

68. Gaventa, "Romans," 552.

not so the Deutero-Pauline author who repeated once more: "Adam was not deceived, but the woman was deceived and became a transgressor" [1 Tim 2:14]). Even though Adam had a special place of honor as the "father" of Israel (2 En. 33:10; 58:1-2), he now became the proleptic human who had introduced sin into the world. And Adam is now being contrasted with Jesus in Romans 5:12-21. Both representatively affect the fate of the whole world.

Starting in Romans 5, the discourse about sin in this letter changes. In previous chapters, sin was mentioned as a general problem of humanity. But now and in subsequent chapters, it is depicted as something like a personalized power. Sin (ἁμαρτία) "reigns" (βασιλεύω, Rom 5:21; 6:12), "has dominion" (κυριεύω, 6:14), "enslaves" (δουλεύω, 6:6; 6:14-22; 7:14), "deceives" (ἐξαπατάω, 7:11), and even "kills" (ἀποκτείνω, 7:11). *Mutatis mutandis*, people can "be dead" to sin (6:11) and can be "set free from sin" (6:18). Like a kind of pandemic, sin afflicts all of the descendants of Adam without exception. The sentence in Romans 5:12 mitigates the punch of the previous paragraph that invited everybody in the audiences to admit to their own weaknesses. Now they hear (not for the first time in the letter) that it is not their own fault! Rather, no mortal being can escape from this predicament.

Yet despite the frequency of the term "sin," the focus of Romans 5:12-21 is not on sin.[69] At the center is "grace." In Rome, Phoebe gets to proudly present another comparison, this time between the free divine gift and human trespasses and sins in light of their eschatological consequences: "But the free gift is not like the trespass. For if the many died through the one [person's] trespass, much more surely have the grace of God and the gift in the grace of the one [person], Jesus Christ, abounded for the many" (Rom 5:15). It is repeated in an analogous fashion in 5:16, this time with focus on the final judgment and condemnation; then it is explicitly correlated with the vocabulary of the *propositio* ("main thesis") of this letter in 1:17 about the gospel, namely, justification: "one [person's] act of [justice] leads to justification and life for all" (5:18). There is a happy end to proclaim: "grace might also reign through justification leading to eternal life through Jesus Christ our Lord" (5:21). Since this good news is not contingent on any human contribution or effort, but a free gift, it is

69. The noun "sin" (ἁμαρτία) and related terminology appear eighty-one times in the undisputed Pauline letters; sixty of those instances are in Romans. See the discussion of the topic in Beverly Roberts Gaventa, *Our Mother Saint Paul* (Louisville: Westminster John Knox, 2007), 125–36, 198–200.

available to all, regardless of age, gender, status, or ethnicity. This gospel message empowers Phoebe, who knew the hardship of intersectionality, to stand in front of her audiences in the city of Rome and speak to them as the person she is. She knew what she was talking about because she had tasted the free gift of justification in Jesus Christ that leads to new life.

Romans 5:12-21 is about the fundamentals of human identity. Ontologically speaking, are humans sinners or are they "righteous" or "justified"? And in the wake of existential philosophy, modern interpreters will particularly ask: How can the fundamentals of human identity change by the action of *someone else*? The logic of this passage can only be understood if one considers the logic of corporate identity in the ancient Greco-Roman or Mediterranean world with its relational culture of patron-client networks. The sudden change in status is what clients could experience if their patrons acquired additional honor or inflicted shame on themselves. Such achievements (or lack thereof) would then, by extension, be transmitted and lead to the addition of honor for the clients (or shame if patrons brought dishonor upon themselves). Likewise, a sudden change in status is what clients could experience if they chose a different patron altogether, assuming the client had no patron before or a patron of lower status. In either case, the status of the client is upgraded by the new choice. Phoebe, therefore, does not make any ontological claims about human nature but defines it in a corporate and relational way; these relations are derived from the ancient patron-client system. While this may be somewhat difficult to understand for modern interpreters because they live in individualistic cultures, a similar logic governs the adherence to sport clubs or national sport teams. The success of these teams is likewise transmitted to their fans and supporters who will celebrate as if they had won themselves—or will mourn a loss.

Romans 6:1–8:39

Freedom through the Love of Christ

Dying and Rising with Christ (6:1-14)

In the theological part of Romans, the third section in 6:1–8:39 turns to fundamental themes such as death and life, bondage and freedom, and ultimately the love of Jesus Christ. It picks up key terms of the second section (4:1–5:21) and problematizes them along a number of questions that have been posed by Paul's opponents. This section does not venture on to new themes, but helps to solidify the arguments and address challenges preemptively.

In 6:1–7:13, Phoebe has three questions for her audiences in the city of Rome for this purpose. They all start with: "What then are we to say?" (τί οὖν ἐροῦμεν;), or short: "What then?" As rhetorical questions, they all lead to the emphatic exclamation: "By no means!" (μὴ γένοιτο). This Q&A format indicates that the rhetorical genre is, once again, that of a diatribe (on this rhetorical genre, see above, p. lxvi). The questions are similar as they all deal with sin and law and go on to define human behavior; this section is about ethics. It also connects to the parenetic section in 12:1–15:13 with practical advice.

In 6:1–7:13, the three lead questions are:

1. "Should we continue in sin in order that grace may increase?" (6:1)
2. "Should we sin because we are not under law but under grace?" (6:15)
3. "That the law is sin?" (Or rather: "Is the law sin?") (7:7)

Rom 6:1-14

6:1What then are we to say? Should
we continue in sin in order that grace
may increase? 2By no means! How can
we who died to sin go on living in it?
3Do you not know that all of us who
were baptized into Christ Jesus were
baptized into his death? 4Therefore
we were buried with him by baptism
into death, so that, just as Christ was
raised from the dead by the glory of
the Father, so we also might walk in
newness of life.

5For if we have been united with
him in a death like his, we will certainly
be united with him in a resurrection like
his. 6We know that our old self was crucified with him so that the body of sin
might be destroyed, so we might no
longer be enslaved to sin. 7For whoever has died is freed from sin. 8But
if we died with Christ, we believe that
we will also live with him. 9We know
that Christ, being raised from the dead,
will never die again; death no longer
has dominion over him. 10The death he
died, he died to sin once for all, but the
life he lives, he lives to God. 11So you
also must consider yourselves dead to
sin and alive to God in Christ Jesus.

12Therefore do not let sin reign in
your mortal bodies, so that you obey
their desires. 13No longer present
your members to sin as instruments
of unrighteousness, but present yourselves to God as those who have been
brought from death to life, and present
your members to God as instruments
of righteousness. 14For sin will have no
dominion over you, since you are not
under law but under grace.

Various pericopes related to these themes are interspersed into this main structure, for example, an illustration of freedom from the law (7:1-6).

What the audiences and readers encounter in Romans 6:1–7:13 may sound familiar. Paul had used many of the arguments and addressed several of the themes already earlier in Galatians:

Juxtaposition of Similar Passages in Romans and Galatians, Topics: Baptism and Freedom[1]

Rom 6:4	Therefore we were buried with him by *baptism* into death, so that, just as Christ was raised from the dead by the glory of the Father, so we also might walk in newness of life.	Gal 3:27	As many of you as were *baptized* into Christ have *clothed yourselves with Christ*.

1. Similar text in these columns is indicated by italics.

Rom 6:6 Rom 7:4	We know that *our old self was crucified with him* so that the body of sin might be destroyed, so we might *no longer be enslaved to sin.* [Y]ou have *died to the law* through the body of Christ, so that you may belong to another, *to him who was raised from the dead* in order that we may bear fruit for God.	Gal 2:19	For *through the law I died to the law*, so that I might live to God. *I have been crucified with Christ.*
Rom 6:7 Rom 6:18	For whoever has died is *freed from sin.* [Y]ou, having been *set free from sin*, have become *enslaved to* [*justification*].	Gal 5:1 Gal 5:13	*For freedom* Christ has *set us free*. Stand firm, therefore, and *do not submit again to a yoke of slavery.* For you were *called to freedom.*
Rom 6:12-13	Therefore, *do not let sin reign in your mortal bodies, so that you obey their desires*. No longer present your members to sin as instruments of unrighteousness, but *present yourselves to God as those who have been brought from death to life*, and present your members to God as instruments of [justification].[2]	Gal 5:16-17	Live by the Spirit, I say, and *do not gratify the desires of the flesh*. For *what the flesh desires is opposed to the Spirit, and what the Spirit desires is opposed to the flesh*, for these are opposed to each other, to prevent you from doing what you want.

These various concepts have been part of Paul's gospel message for quite a while. The arguments that Paul, with the active assistance of Phoebe (and potentially others), has now decided to present to the audiences in the city of Rome contain a certain level of recycled materials.

Starting in the first rhetorical question, Romans 6:1-14 features no fewer than ten repetitions of the term "sin." This is an example of a *paronomasia* (a repetition of the same word or word stem in close proximity) and of an *enumeratio* (a coordinated series of terms listed next to

2. The NRSVue renders this term "righteousness." For the alternative translation of the Greek term δικαιοσύνη as "justification," see comments above under "Translation Matters" on Romans 3:21, 22.

each other), here with a series of tens. But the paragraph does not stay there. It is also structured through the contrast of "dead," "death," and "to die" against "life/to live," together with "resurrection" and "raised from the dead." The argument uses verbs in the indicative to take stock of the situation of justification; here, the past tense indicates what was before, and the present tense, the current state. Then an imperative conveys the exhortation to live according to the calling. A typical example is Romans 6:10-11: "The death he died, he died to sin once for all, but the life he lives, he lives to God. So you also must consider yourselves dead to sin and alive to God in Christ Jesus." Phoebe thus presents the contrast with the goal of describing the new identity of the baptized members of the assemblies of Christ believers. In fact, so far the term "baptism" has not yet been mentioned in Romans. It occurs in this chapter for the first time, and it does so no fewer than three times: being "baptized [βαπτίζω] into Christ Jesus" means being "baptized into his death" (Rom 6:3); being "buried with him by baptism (βαπτισμός) into death" means that "we also might walk in newness of life" (6:4). For aesthetic purposes, the sentence in 6:3 is organized as a chiasm:

A ἐβαπτίσθημεν — A we have been baptized

  B εἰς Χριστὸν Ἰησοῦν — B into Christ Jesus

  B′ εἰς τὸν θάνατον αὐτοῦ — B′ into his death

A′ ἐβαπτίσθημεν — A′ we have been baptized

It is clear that the pre-Pauline baptismal formula in Galatians 3:28 about unity "in Christ" despite differences in religious or ethnic identity ("no longer Jew or Greek"), status of personal liberty ("no longer slave or free"), and gender ("no longer male and female") is in the background. All of this is in response to the first rhetorical question: "Should we continue in sin in order that grace may increase?" (6:1). The correct answer is, of course, a resounding: "By no means!" or "No way!"[3] But Phoebe, just like Paul before her, needs to convince opponents in the audience, and that requires patience and the best arguments they can muster as a team. It also shows that the gospel message of justification through faith in Christ has not always been fully understood.

3. Robert Jewett, *Romans: A Commentary*, Hermeneia (Minneapolis: Fortress, 2007), 395.

So what is the best way to effectively convey how grace is available for humans and changes their lives? Phoebe explains what baptism means for believers in Christ through the participationist model of salvation. This model operates with compound verbs containing the prefix συν- that means "with" or the preposition συν (6:8a), resulting in an extended *anaphora* (repetition of subsequent words or syllables):

Rom 6:4	Therefore *we were buried with him* . . .	*συνετάφημεν οὖν αὐτῷ* . . .
Rom 6:5	For if *we have been united with him* . . . . . . *we* will certainly *be united with him in a resurrection like his.*	εἰ γὰρ *σύμφυτοι γεγόναμεν* . . . . . . ἀλλὰ *καὶ τῆς ἀναστάσεως ἐσόμεθα*
Rom 6:6	. . . our old self was *crucified with him* . . .	. . . ὁ παλαιὸς ἡμῶν ἄνθρωπος *συνεσταυρώθη* . . .
Rom 6:8	But if *we died with Christ,* we believe that *we will also live with him.*	εἰ δὲ *ἀπεθάνομεν σὺν Χριστῷ,* πιστεύομεν ὅτι *καὶ συζήσομεν αὐτῷ* . . .

Furthermore, the words "we also" convey the same idea (6:4). These sentences thus repeat various aspects of the same soteriological model of being "in Christ." Such a participatory atonement paradigm is itself reminiscent of avatar representation when Paul and Phoebe attribute crucial events in the life of Jesus to believers: "For if we have been united with him in a death like his, we will certainly be united with him in a resurrection like his" (6:5). Paul's thinking has always been thoroughly corporate, and he was a team player. This was manifest in both his soteriology and his decision to entrust Phoebe with the task of delivering and reciting the present letter.

With that, a new model of aliveness emerges. It consistently incorporates Jesus Christ; the new aliveness is possible only with him. A key phrase is "So you also must consider yourselves dead to sin and alive to God in Christ Jesus" (6:11). According to Morna D. Hooker, it is clear "why Paul finds it easier to speak of dying with Christ as a past event than to describe rising with Christ in the same way. For . . . the 'last enemy', death, is not yet destroyed, and though Christians have died with Christ, it cannot be said of them, as it is of Christ, that they 'will never die again.'"[4] This new state of life "in Christ" is the hallmark

4. Morna D. Hooker, *From Adam to Christ: Essays on Paul* (Eugene, OR: Wipf & Stock, 2008), 44.

of Pauline theology and Christology. The expression is typical of his writings and primarily attested in Pauline texts (with ninety-eight occurrences in authentic letters of Paul and sixty-three in Deutero-Pauline literature).[5] Elsa Tamez writes:

> To pass from death to life is a Pauline theological figure that expresses a radical change in human existence. It deals with two types of opposing life: one with the characteristics of death, and another with the characteristics of resurrection. One opts to abandon the existence that by its mortal characteristics produces death, and one receives a new way to live. In some parts of the Bible this is called conversion, *metanoia*.[6]

Central or not, the participationist concept of human salvation was evidently not easy to understand and challenging for some in Phoebe's audiences. Alternative christological-soteriological models were atonement (Rom 3:21-26) and judicial imagery (8:31-38). Their conceptual backgrounds were the religious temple with its worship and the secular court system. The participationist model evokes notions of a corporate mysticism involving unity with Christ. It is no longer prevalent in our modern culture. To repeat, in this model, sin appears as a cosmic power that is in the world, exercises dominion or reigns with the power to enslave people, who then can die to it. Humans, therefore, need to break free from the bondage of this cosmic force. "[D]o not let sin reign in your mortal bodies, so that you obey their desires" (6:12). This warning is later complemented in the parenetic section of Romans with the exhortation to render one's body to God (12:1, see below). Today, one is inclined to deploy the abstract terminology of "structural sin" to reference roughly the same phenomenon.[7] Human entanglements in society were specifically manifest in ancient patron-client relationships in which the fate of the patron, for better or for worse, was shared by the client. The same could be said about the identity of the patron that is shared by the client.

5. Michael Wolter, *Paulus: Ein Grundriss seiner Theologie*, 3rd ed. (Neukirchen-Vluyn: Neukirchener Verlag, 2021), 235.

6. Elsa Tamez, "The Challenge to Live as Resurrected: Reflections on Romans Six and Eight," trans. Gloria Kinsler, *Spiritus: A Journal of Christian Spirituality* 3 (2003): 86–95, at 88. See also Philip F. Esler, *Conflict and Identity in Romans: The Social Setting of Paul's Letter* (Minneapolis: Fortress, 2003), 202–17.

7. On "structural sin," see Christine Schaumberger, "Subversive Bekehrung, Schulderkenntnis, Schwesterlichkeit, Frauenmacht: Irritierende und inspirierende Grundmotive kritisch-feministischer Befreiungstheologie," in *Schuld und Macht: Studien zu einer feministischen Befreiungstheologie*, ed. Christine Schaumberger and Luise Schottroff (Munich: Kaiser, 1988), 251–88.

In this imagery, Jesus Christ has the crucial role of an aide. In their soteriological key passage, Paul and his avatar Phoebe juxtapose the innocence of Jesus and the sin of humans who cannot free themselves from their existential bondage. Therefore, salvation is existential exchange; the involved parties swap their predicaments. Christ shared the human predicament of sin and death while humans receive the privilege of participating in his holiness, glory, and eternal life. The loss of one party is the gain of the other. It effectively leads to the gift of a new identity for humans. It is an alternative model for ethics that some viewed with suspicion. In the words of Luise Schottroff: "Paul rigorously argued the position that living according to God's will, as written in the Torah, is not possible without faith in Christ. Much to his sorrow, most Jews of his time did not accept this position, if they knew it at all. But holding that position meant not that Paul did no longer regard himself as a Jew [*sic*]."[8] Phoebe is a gentile woman; she arrived in the city of Rome and is now standing in front of its audiences as the embodiment of Paul's vision of faith "in Christ" according to the participationist model. She has been the victim of the horrors of Roman imperialism with its concomitant reliance on free labor by enslaved people. If she was indeed a formerly enslaved person, then she remembers having once been socially dead. She has, however, experienced an era in her life under a new paradigm. Yet, Roman society was a kyriarchy[9] organized and structured through the patronage system; women had little to say and had no real place of influence or authority in society. Phoebe had chosen to question such a society. "The good news for justified men and women who embrace faith as a new way of life, just like the faith of Jesus Christ, is a new awareness of being free women and men, and the realization that in faith it is possible to transform society where sin reigns in the structures opposed to women."[10]

8. Luise Schottroff, "'Law-Free Gentile Christianity'—What about the Women? Feminist Analyses and Alternatives," in *A Feminist Companion to Paul*, ed. Amy-Jill Levine with Marianne Blickenstaff, FCNTECW 6 (London: T&T International, 2004), 192.

9. The term *kyriarchy*, "rule of the masters or lords," was introduced by Elisabeth Schüssler Fiorenza as a better term than patriarchy, "rule of the fathers," for theorizing domination and oppression, in that it facilitates the understanding that power relations are pyramidal and interlocking, rather than simply binary. Those with most power in society are at the top of the pyramid—as masters or lords—and not all men are equally empowered. See Elisabeth Schüssler Fiorenza, *Wisdom Ways: Introducing Feminist Biblical Interpretation* (Maryknoll, NY: Orbis Books, 2001), 102–34.

10. Elsa Tamez, "Justification as Good News for Women: A Re-reading of Romans 1–8," trans. Sheila E. McGinn, in *Celebrating Romans: Template for Pauline Theology; Essays in Honor of Robert Jewett*, ed. Sheila E. McGinn (Grand Rapids: Eerdmans, 2004), 187.

Slaves of Justification[11] (6:15-23)

A new paragraph starts in Romans 6:15 with "What then?"[12] It is followed by the second of the three lead questions about sin and grace. These questions indicate, once more, the genre of the diatribe (see above, p. lxvi). Its theme is being a "slave/enslaved person" of justification, which means living under grace and the lordship of Christ. It starts with a diatribal discussion about the question of remaining in sin (6:15-19a) and moves on to a theological rationale of the exchange of one's rule (6:19b-20), only to conclude with a dialogue about the results of two kinds of freedom (6:21-23).[13] Those topics may be of specific interest for Phoebe. She is not only a gentile; she may also be a freedwoman, that is, a former enslaved person. I suggest that the pericope in Romans 6:15-23 was authored either by Paul specifically for her as his avatar (or jointly by both) or by Phoebe herself because she had potentially appropriated her former identity and predicament as an enslaved woman to articulate her own faith. Such an individual profile is evinced by the fact that this pericope has no clear parallel in earlier letters of Paul. It is either a custom-made pericope for Phoebe or by Phoebe or both.[14]

In this pericope, two terms are central: "sin" (ἁμαρτία), with seven occurrences, and "slave/enslaved person" (δοῦλος), likewise with seven occurrences, plus one attestation of "enslaved to God" (δουλωθέντες δὲ τῷ θεῷ, Rom 6:22). Another key term is "free" or "freed." It relates to both "sin" and "slave" as that state of a person who has abandoned sin for the sake of virtues and/or shaken off the bondage of enslavement.

11. NRSVue has "Slaves of Righteousness." For the alternative term "justification," see comments above under "Translation Matters" on Romans 3:21, 22 (p. 96).

12. This is the text division in, for example, the NRSVue and the NIV. The Greek New Testament (Nestle-Aland 28th ed.), however, inserts the paragraph break between Romans 6:11 and 12 while setting 6:15 as a continuation of v. 14.

13. Frank J. Matera, *Romans*, Paideia: Commentaries on the New Testament (Grand Rapids: Baker Academic, 2010), 145–48; Michael Wolter, *Der Brief an die Römer*, vol. 1: *Röm 1–8*, EKKNT 6/1 (Neukirchen-Vluyn: Neukirchener Verlag; Ostfildern: Patmos, 2014), 386–87 (where the pericope comprises Rom 6:12-23).

14. With these considerations about the origins of Romans 6:15-23, I am entering into a discussion with Elizabeth A. Castelli who suggests that this pericope is neither about women nor about enslaved people (Elizabeth A. Castelli, "Romans," in *Searching the Scriptures*, vol. 2: *A Feminist Commentary*, ed. Elisabeth Schüssler Fiorenza [New York: Crossroad, 1994], 294). I will return to this issue at the end of the discussion of Romans 8:39 (see below) to do so with a more holistic view of who may have been behind this pericope.

Rom 6:15-23

15What then? Should we sin because we are not under law but under grace? By no means! 16Do you not know that, if you present yourselves to anyone as obedient slaves, you are slaves of the one whom you obey, either of sin, which leads to death, or of obedience, which leads to righteousness? 17But thanks be to God that you who were slaves of sin have become obedient from the heart to the form of teaching to which you were entrusted 18and that you, having been set free from sin, have become enslaved to righteousness. 19I am speaking in human terms because of your limitations. For just as you once presented your members as slaves to impurity and lawlessness, leading to even more lawlessness, so now present your members as slaves to righteousness, leading to sanctification.

20When you were slaves of sin, you were free in regard to righteousness. 21So what fruit did you then gain from the things of which you now are ashamed? The end of those things is death. 22But now that you have been freed from sin and enslaved to God, the fruit you have leads to sanctification, and the end is eternal life. 23For the wages of sin is death, but the free gift of God is eternal life in Christ Jesus our Lord.

In this sense, it should be noted that, in Romans 6:18, 20-23, the verb "to free" (ἐλευθερόω) demonstrates that Paul and Phoebe, when using the term δοῦλος (as both the noun "slave/enslaved person" and the adjective with the meaning of "enslaved") or δουλόω ("to enslave") in 6:16-20, etc. (see already Rom 1:1), did have the institution of enslavement in antiquity in mind. Hence the correct translation of δοῦλος in Romans is not "servant" but "slave/enslaved person," as only for such a person, liberation (as emancipation/*manumissio*) is an important goal and ideal. The juxtaposition of imagery of "slave/enslaved person" versus "freedom" with "life" and "death" vehemently demonstrates the fact that the institution of enslavement meant social death for those affected by it and that freedom as the end of enslavement was perceived as a return to life. According to Orlando Patterson, the notion of personal freedom developed specifically among enslaved women.[15] The current passage about being freed from powers proves this assumption as it adopts specifically the perspective of women.

15. Orlando Patterson, *Freedom in the Making of Western Culture*, Freedom 1 (New York: Basic Books, 1991), 54–55.

Enslavement in Rome

The Roman culture was a kyriarchal "pyramid of honor." Acquired honor was obtained through, for example, military achievements and successful business operations. A critical ramification of this principle is that those who came out as the losers in the arena of honor and shame—as captives of wars or debtors with unpayable debt—had such loss permanently inscribed onto their own bodies and into their lives (and sometimes those of their descendants) through the institution of enslavement. This needs to be stated at the outset of any exploration of the topic of enslavement in the world of ancient Rome (or, more broadly, the ancient Mediterranean culture). While their fate was undesirable, enslaved people were not necessarily understood as occupying the lowest status of the societal hierarchy for the simple reason that they were exempt from acquiring public honor altogether.[16] They were not only the property of their respective masters; more than that, their legal status was indeed that of property, which means they were not even accorded personhood, and often they were treated accordingly.[17] Enslaved people, therefore, did not have low status in Rome's kyriarchal "pyramid of honor." Rather, they were without status. For the affected person, enslavement meant social death.[18] Where enslavement was the result of war captivity, this state had even another dimension.

> The slave is violently uprooted from his milieu. He is desocialized and depersonalized. This process of social negation constitutes the first, essentially external, phase of enslavement. The next phase involves the introduction of the slave into the community of his master, but it involves the paradox of introducing him as a nonbeing.[19]

16. Orlando Patterson, "Paul, Slavery and Freedom: Personal and Socio-Historical Reflections," *Semeia* 83/84 (1998): 263–79.

17. O. F. Robinson, "Ancient Rome," in *Macmillan Encyclopedia of World Slavery*, vol. 1, ed. Paul Finkelman and Joseph C. Miller (New York: Macmillan, 1998), 71, 76; Christoph Kähler, "Sklaverei: II. Neues Testament," *TRE* 31 (2000): 373–77, at 374. The status of enslaved people in the Roman world may be called an "ontological blur" (Laura S. Nasrallah, *Archaeology and the Letters of Paul* [Oxford: Oxford University Press, 2019], 40).

18. This is the title of the classic of Orlando Patterson, *Slavery and Social Death: A Comparative Study* (Cambridge, MA: Harvard University Press, 1982). See also Sheila Briggs, "Can an Enslaved God Liberate? Hermeneutical Reflections on Philippians 2:6-11," *Semeia* 47 (1989): 137–53, at 143–44.

19. Patterson, *Slavery*, 38; see also Mary Ann Beavis, *The First Christian Slave: Onesimus in Context* (Eugene, OR: Cascade Books, 2021), 14–29.

But even this statement needs to be differentiated further. Although the place of enslaved persons in the Roman world was clearly defined as nonbeing, it was to some degree ambiguous. Despite social death, their social rank ultimately depended on two factors: the status of their masters and their skills or the type of work they were assigned to (and could) perform. As a typical characteristic of the ancient patronage system, the patron's status determined that of every client much more than a client's absolute status.[20] This aspect highlights the ambiguity of the social rank of enslaved persons. Despite being considered "property" and exempt from the acquisition of honor, which rendered them *de facto* without status, enslaved persons could nevertheless have a social position of respect and authority, all of which *were* accompanied by social rank. Thus, enslaved persons who belonged to the imperial household and had the title "slave of Caesar" may have had a higher social rank than most of the free population of the empire.[21] Enslaved persons associated with Caesar in this way could rise to positions of immense power and wealth; archaeological studies of grave inscriptions have identified thousands of them as such.[22] In addition, some enslaved persons had respectable jobs. While it is a sad reality that many had the tragic fate of being forced to row on galleys, toiling in Egyptian mines (where they usually remained to die), or even being thrown to the beasts for the amusement of crowds in amphitheaters, others were chosen to occupy respected positions as administrators, accountants, secretaries, teachers, physicians, nurses, cooks, hairdressers, handmaids, or seamstresses.[23] And while living conditions varied, domestic enslaved persons who worked in a Roman *domus*

20. This aspect of the patronage system is conveyed by the fact that even ossuary inscriptions would still indicate that a person was a "freedperson," thus implying a former status of having been enslaved, if the name of the patron of high status who liberated him or her could be associated with it. Cf. Werner Eck, "Sklaven und Freigelassene von Römern in Iudaea und den angrenzenden Provinzen," *NovT* 55 (2013): 1–21.

21. Paul R. C. Weaver, "Social Mobility in the Early Roman Empire: The Evidence of the Imperial Freedmen and Slaves," *Past & Present* 37 (1967): 3–20.

22. Jewett, *Romans*, 100.

23. Keith Hopkins, "Novel Evidence for Roman Slavery," *Past & Present* 138 (1993): 3–27, at 6; Peter Temin, "The Labor Market of the Early Roman Empire," *The Journal*

("house") may have enjoyed a situation that was better than that of many free urban poor in Rome. Enslaved persons working as accountants sometimes had the right to earn money. An enslaved person in the *familia Caesaris* ("family of Caesar") may even have actually owned a *servus vicarious* ("substitute slave").[24] For their achievements in these various professions, they could ultimately be freed, which was usually their patrons' gesture of appreciation, acknowledgment, and gratitude. Once more, these aspects highlight the ambiguity of the reality of enslavement in the Roman world. To some degree, enslaved people lived in a parallel society, although they sometimes inhabited the same houses as their patrons. Enslavement could be a destiny for inhuman treatment and rather imminent, brutal death, or it could mean a somewhat respectable career with ultimate liberty, thus preparing people for a form of integration into Roman society.

The lives of enslaved people were precarious. "Slavery was a cruel and repressive institution, enforced by hatred and fear. 'All slaves are enemies,' stated a Roman proverb."[25] According to Orlando Patterson, "Slavery is always a relationship that rests ultimately on force." Therefore, "it is hardly surprising that in every slave society the master has the power to inflict corporal punishment."[26] A harsh overall treatment corresponded to the master's "right of life and death over his slaves (the *jus vitae necisque*)."[27]

There is some speculation that Paul himself may have been the son of former enslaved persons. This would be a natural explanation for his Roman citizenship (Acts 22:27) since it was the practice of Rome to make enslaved persons citizens upon manumission. Paul would, therefore, have inherited Roman citizenship from his parents.[28] In that case,

of Interdisciplinary History 34 (2004): 513–38, at 536: "Skilled slaves were valuable to merchants and wealthy citizens."

24. Patterson, *Slavery*, 300.

25. Hopkins, "Evidence," 5.

26. Patterson, *Slavery*, 190.

27. Patterson, *Slavery*, 190.

28. Valerie Griffiths, "Romans," in *The IVP Women's Bible Commentary*, ed. Catherine Clark Kroeger and Mary J. Evans (Downers Grove, IL: InterVarsity, 2002), 637; Esther Kobel, *Paulus als interkultureller Vermittler: Eine Studie zur kulturellen Positionierung*

he could have related to Phoebe's potential pain regarding her former life to some degree and would have understood her lingering trauma. If Phoebe herself is indeed a former enslaved person, then the problem of identity is clearly more immediate for her.

In Romans 6:16, the argument starts with a rhetorical question: "Do you not know that . . . ?" It is plausible that, in view of the precise point being made about the obedience of enslaved persons, Phoebe references the common knowledge of enslavement among her Roman audiences. This was a smart move. She speaks from her heart, even if it meant tapping into painful memories. Furthermore, many of those in her audiences in Rome were descendants of former enslaved people; after all, the Jewish presence in Rome had its origins in the arrival of Jewish prisoners of war after the conquest of Palestine in 63 BCE.[29] The institution of enslavement was painfully familiar to many of the people gathered when Phoebe recited the letter. She put the emphasis on complete subordination. The verb that the NRSVue renders as "present yourselves" literally means "yield oneself, place oneself at the disposal of" (παριστάνω), implying the voluntary placement at the disposal of another. It specifically means "to stand by the side of someone as a slave" (see the analogous usage in Epictetus, *Diss.* 1.25.23).[30] The choice that Phoebe presents is to serve either "sin" or "obedience" (Rom 6:16). She gets to praise her audiences at this critical point. Her words that "you . . . have become obedient from the heart" (Rom 6:17) allude to the passage in Romans 2:29 about the deep, fundamental transformation of the believer that evoked the image of quasi-instinctive knowledge from Jewish prophetic Scriptures (Jer 31:31-34 [MT]/38:31-34 [LXX]) akin to the "circumcision of the heart." She thus affirms her respect for her audiences and that she accepts

---

des Apostels der Völker, Studies in Cultural Contexts of the Bible 1 (Paderborn: Brill; Schöningh, 2019), 103–4.

29. Raymond E. Brown and John P. Meier, *Antioch and Rome: New Testament Cradles of Catholic Christianity* (New York: Paulist Press, 1983), 93. Of the twenty-six names in the list of greetings in Romans 16, a large percentage indicates people of slave origins. Cf. Peter Lampe, *Die stadtrömischen Christen in den ersten beiden Jahrhunderten: Untersuchungen zur Sozialgeschichte*, 2nd ed., WUNT 2/18 (Tübingen: Mohr Siebeck, 1989), 136–53; Peter Lampe, "Roman Christians under Nero (54–68 CE)," in *The Last Years of Paul: Essays from the Tarragona Conference, June 2013*, ed. Armand Puig i Tàrrech, John M. G. Barclay, and Jörg Frey, with the assistance of Orrey McFarland, WUNT 352 (Tübingen: Mohr Siebeck, 2015), 125.

30. Jewett, *Romans*, 415–16.

them as fellow believers in Christ. Conceptually, this is the key to an ethical life. It is the result of salvation because "the free gift of God is eternal life in Christ Jesus our Lord" (Rom 6:23).

Along the way, however, there is a strong deployment of terminology based on enslavement for the status of the believer. In previous letters, Paul rarely called himself or other members of his assemblies "slave/ enslaved person" or mentioned that they would "serve." He used the metaphors of enslavement primarily to designate the former status of humans under sin. In Galatians 4:7, for instance, Paul writes: "So you are no longer a slave but a child, and if a child then also an heir through God." The new status is, therefore, *not enslavement under God* but *childhood*. The difference in terminology marks an important change of paradigm.[31] This is why the phrase in Romans 6:16 is slightly surprising as it states: "you are slaves of the one whom you obey, either of sin, which leads to death, or of obedience, which leads to [justification]" (repeated in Rom 6:18; see also 7:25b-c). It reverts to the image of enslavement for believers. One may conjecture that Phoebe was herself captured by her past and, therefore, kept drawing on its language when Paul may have preferred to leave it behind to convey the status of freedom of those who hear and believe the gospel message.

The next chapter of Romans continues with an illustration from the vantage point of women, but that has been obscured by the malestream tradition of biblical scholarship.

An Analogy from Marriage: Freedom from the Law (7:1-6)

This section begins with another epistolary disclosure formula: "Do you not know?" (see also Rom 6:3 and 6:16). It introduces a syllogism concerning life in Christ as freedom from the law. It consists of premises from marital law (7:1-3) and then of an application about the concrete experience of freedom from the law (7:4-6). The term "law" (νόμος) occurs no fewer than eight times in these six verses. The argument is about how to obtain freedom from it.[32] It is noteworthy that for this purpose, it specifically adopts the perspective of women.

31. See, however, the exceptions in 1 Corinthians 7:22 (the "free" person is now a "slave belonging to Christ"); 9:19; and 2 Corinthians 4:5 (Paul says: "we proclaim Jesus Christ as Lord and ourselves as your slaves for Jesus's sake"); Galatians 5:13 ("enslaved to one another").

32. Matera, *Romans*, 168; Wolter, *Römer*, 1:409.

Rom 7:1-6

[7:1]Or do you not know, brothers and sisters—for I am speaking to those who know the law—that the law is binding on a person only during that person's lifetime? [2]Thus a married woman is bound by the law to her husband as long as he lives, but if her husband dies, she is discharged from the law concerning the husband. [3]Accordingly, she will be called an adulteress if she belongs to another man while her husband is alive. But if her husband dies, she is free from that law, and if she belongs to another man, she is not an adulteress.

[4]In the same way, my brothers and sisters, you have died to the law through the body of Christ, so that you may belong to another, to him who was raised from the dead in order that we may bear fruit for God. [5]For while we were living in the flesh, our sinful passions, aroused by the law, were at work in our members to bear fruit for death. [6]But now we are discharged from the law, dead to that which held us captive, so that we are enslaved in the newness of the Spirit and not in the oldness of the written code.

TRANSLATION MATTERS: Romans 7:2

The NRSVue rendering "a married woman" of Greek ὕπανδρος γυνή is semantically correct; the adjective ὕπανδρος means "married." But while the English term can be used for both husband and wife, the Greek term applies only to a woman indicating her marriage to a man, not vice versa. Being a composite of ὑπό + ἀνήρ, it literally means "under a man" in the sense of "under the power of a man." The term graphically indicates the status difference between man and woman during their marriage and, as a result thereof, hints at the associated power dynamics. It also indicates that, once married, the woman is solely defined in relation to her husband as "'chattel' who lacks power, rights or duty under the law."[33] A translation that expresses these aspects of unilateral agency and power dynamics to some degree may be: "a woman whom a man has taken as his wife."

In this chapter, Phoebe adopts a new perspective. Previously, she presented arguments or imagery that was more specifically accessible to Jewish and Greco-Roman *men* (Rom 3:21-26; 5:1-11). Now she presents an analogy or an illustration in front of her audiences in Rome to convey

33. Judith Romney Wegner, *Chattel or Person? The Status of Women in the Mishnah* (New York: Oxford University Press, 1988), 13. See also Castelli, "Romans," 283; Pamela Thimmes, "'She Will Be Called an Adulteress . . .': Marriage and Adultery Analogies in Romans 7:1-4," in McGinn, *Celebrating Romans*, 200.

a key aspect of her Christology—which she does from the vantage point of a woman.[34] Her discourse itself features a broad terminological spectrum from chapter 6, continuing ideas of bondage and liberation.[35] In this argument against the validity of the traditional law for believers in Christ, she references Jewish marital law according to which a wife is bound to her husband during his lifetime yet released upon his death (7:1-6). These rules somewhat correspond to the Torah law concerning marriage and divorce in Deuteronomy 24:1-4 (LXX). They describe the situation where a man takes a wife and marries her (literally "lives with her," συνοικέω) but divorces her for a reason and sends her away. It specifies that he may not take her back into his house after she has become another man's wife, even if that man divorces her or dies. Besides being a stark demonstration of ancient Near Eastern patriarchy, this rule does not even mention a state of freedom for the woman. Instead, it concludes with a description of the "abhorrent" situation brought about by the "defilement" of the former wife and warns the man not to "bring guilt on the land" (Deut 24:4). Independent thinking is required to turn this regulation into a syllogism of freedom from the law. Before pursuing the actual argument, it should be stated that Roman civil law differed from Jewish law in this respect; in Rome, either partner had the right to divorce the other. The argument in Romans 7:1-6 in which the escape from marriage is only conceivable under the condition of the husband's death is solely based on Jewish law. It shows that Phoebe has become familiar with these legal standards but problematizes them as a gentile.

The passage addresses the audiences as adept in the law (Rom 7:1), which may probably be understood as a *captatio benevolentiae* ("capture of goodwill"; see already 1:9-10). What the audiences know is the premise that a law is only valid during a person's lifetime. This is now applied to marital law: it is binding only until the death of the husband (7:2). In a second minor premise, adultery is, somewhat similarly, defined as being applicable only during the husband's lifetime (7:3). Hence, after his death, "she is free from that law [ἐλευθέρα ἐστὶν ἀπὸ τοῦ νόμου]." What is interesting about this passage is that Phoebe has already stated in the previous chapter that a person "in Christ" has attained freedom from

34. This is the reason why the pericope in Romans 7:1-6 has been one of the texts of choice for feminist biblical interpreters; cf. Sheila E. McGinn, "Feminist Approaches to Paul's Letter to the Romans," in McGinn, *Celebrating Romans*, 168–69.

35. Andrzej Gieniusz, "Rom 7,1-6: Lack of Imagination? Function of the Passage in the Argumentation of Rom 6,1–7,6," *Bib* 74 (1993): 389–400, at 390.

sin (6:18). Now she moves on to demonstrate that a space of freedom exists for these people.

To comprehend her argument of freedom from the law, however, Phoebe expects her audience to adopt a woman's perspective and to identify with her. Her syllogism does not work from the perspective of a man, as Jewish marital law is unilateral in this regard. Both men and women in her audiences are invited, therefore, to identify with the woman; this includes reflecting on her disadvantaged situation as a divorced person and on the destructive potential of the Torah description that her "defilement" would have caused an "abhorrent" situation. Elizabeth A. Castelli notes: "By using women to think with, Paul (like other authors who use gender and social roles as metaphors and analogies) helps to underwrite the understanding of women's roles on which his argument depends."[36] One may add that his decision to send Phoebe to the city of Rome and entrust her with the task of reciting the letter that likely is the result of a lengthy period of mutual discussions does exactly the same.

It is worth noting that these aspects were employed to advance the vision of a radically democratic *ekklēsia* of wo/men. Paul has used female images and language in earlier letters. For example, he wrote that he fed his congregation with milk (1 Cor 3:2). Similarly he evoked the image of a nurse who nurtures and cares for infants or young children (1 Thess 2:7). Such language shows Paul's appreciation of women in the context of his missionary activity and some level of familiarity with their daily realities. This imagery is also reminiscent of wisdom teachings illustrating God's care for the human offspring (Prov 3:11-12). As a member of Paul's assemblies, Phoebe clearly felt encouraged to continue on this path. She had come to understand that the experience of women was no longer a realm of "defilement" or embarrassment or shame. Her argument counters the shameful accusation of the woman as "adulteress" (Rom 7:3). In three parallel premises, two similar pronouncements are made first about the woman and then as well about the audience:[37]

Rom 7:2	but if her husband dies, *she is discharged from the law* concerning the husband.
Rom 7:3	But if her husband dies, *she is free from that law.*
Rom 7:6	But now *we are discharged from the law,* dead to that which held us captive.

36. Castelli, "Romans," 283.

37. In this table, similar statements are indicated by italics.

These three premises expect the audiences, addressed as "we" in Romans 7:6, to adopt the argument and identity of the woman with the double premise about her in 7:2 and 7:3. Michael Wolter notes that the expressions "discharged from the law" and being "free from that law" (7:2, 3, 6) occur only here in ancient Greek literature; they are unique expressions. They will be repeated in the next chapter (8:2). He also observes similarities to a passage in 1 Corinthians 7:39 about a woman's right to remarry after her husband's death even though that text is not used for further arguments about the law.[38] It should be remembered that one of the recipients of Paul's letter to Corinth may have been Phoebe! Finally, similar ideas about the Spirit have also been presented in Galatians, although they are not identical. According to that letter, the Spirit frees the believers from bondage to the law of Moses (Gal 5:1-21). In Romans, by contrast, the Spirit becomes its own sort of "law," now liberating humans from sin and death.

In addition to these three premises about being "discharged/free" from the law, Phoebe also makes a statement about having died to the law. This one is also similar to passages in previous letters of Paul.

Juxtaposition of Similar Passages in Romans, Galatians, and 2 Corinthians
Topic: "Died to the Law, Raised from the Dead"[39]

Rom 7:4	In the same way, my brothers and sisters, *you have died to the law* through the body of Christ, so that *you may belong to another*, to him *who was raised from the dead* in order that we may bear fruit for God.	Gal 2:19-20	For *through the law I died to the law*, so that *I might live to God*. I have been crucified *with Christ*, and it is no longer I who live, but it is Christ who lives in me. *And the life I now live in the flesh I live by faith in the Son of God*, who *loved me and gave himself for me*.	2 Cor 5:15	And *he died for all*, so that those who live *might live no longer for themselves* but *for the one who for their sake died and was raised.*

38. Wolter, *Römer*, 1:411.
39. Similar phrases in these columns are indicated by italics.

This comparison shows that the updated version of the argument in Romans is shorter than that in Galatians but exceeds the length of that in 2 Corinthians. Common elements are having "died to the law," the result of belonging to someone else, and the connection with death/ crucifixion and life/rising. Phoebe then provides another explanation about how the law aroused "sinful passions" and that freedom is possible for those who are "dead to that which held us captive" (Rom 7:5-6; also 14:7-9). Her conclusion draws once more on the term "slave/enslaved person" that defines her identity even after her emancipation. She states: "we are enslaved in the newness of the Spirit and not in the oldness of the written code" (7:6). As a person who once had potentially been in a situation of social death as an enslaved person, Phoebe now celebrates her new life, along with the dignity and respect she experiences. A new era has started for her, beginning with baptism (even if it is not explicitly mentioned). "If believers die in baptism to the sinful passions by which they were once held, then the law through which these sinful passions were once provoked no longer has a function and so is something from which believers have been released."[40]

Romans 7:1-6 appears to be a very personal pericope that advances a theological argument but does so time and again by drawing on terminology and imagery from Phoebe's traumatic past. While her argument has been presented with the initial description of the woman who is ὕπανδρος, "under (the power of) a man" and thus explicitly refers to marriage, it has somewhat of a proximity to the predicament of an enslaved woman who was forced to serve a male master. As such, she was also "under (the power of) a man"! Sometimes, such enslaved women were released upon the death of their masters. This could be the additional undertone of this pericope. It is conceivable that Phoebe's past as an enslaved person was both too painful and too shameful; she was not comfortable to share details about it or use it as a straightforward illustration for theological arguments. This is why she may have preferred to choose an anonymous woman as the main character of her illustration. But one final observation is still in order. The audiences in Rome—and perhaps also the modern readers—may have noticed that Phoebe's image from marriage evokes the death of the husband twice (Rom 7:2, 3). But there is not a single word about possible grief or sorrow, nor about potential

40. Thomas H. Tobin, *Paul's Rhetoric in Its Contexts: The Argument of Romans* (Peabody, MA: Hendrickson, 2004), 224.

ensuing social problems. May such a narrative of death reflect the trauma of a woman who, when she was "under (the power of) a man" as an enslaved person, was exposed to sexual assaults without any possibility to defend herself? This possibility will be considered later.[41]

Romans 7:1-6 has received rather mixed responses from modern interpreters. Eighty years ago, a scholar showered it with praise.[42] But since then, critical voices have dominated. Certain logical inconsistencies have been observed, such as the argument that uses the death of the husband whereas the person who died was not the one who was set free to belong to another, as 7:4 suggests in the application for the audience. "The illustration, therefore, has gone hopelessly astray. . . . We shall do best to ignore the illustration."[43] While it is true that the arguments remain somewhat incompatible within these lines, their focus appears to be less on the law that is now obsolete than on the new adherence. The woman in the illustration whose husband has died is now free to marry another man (7:3). In the application, the audience likewise is said to "belong to another" (7:4); "we are enslaved in the newness of the Spirit" (7:6). This idea is an apt summary of the previous argumentation in chapter 6.[44] For Phoebe, freedom means to be in a new relationship of true love; this is what this pericope illustrates. It depicts a person who has overcome a painful past and emerges as a new individual who has found new life in freedom.

The Law and Sin (7:7-13)

For a third time, we encounter an opening question: "What then are we to say?" (Rom 7:7). Once more, it indicates the text genre of the diatribe (see above, p. lxvi). The passage consists of two sections. Romans 7:7-13 starts with the third rhetorical question: "Is the law sin?" (7:7).[45] And a

41. See the reflections on Romans 16:1 below.

42. Richard C. H. Lenski, *The Interpretation of St. Paul's Epistle to the Romans 1–7* (Columbus, OH: Wartburg Press, 1945), 743–44.

43. Charles H. Dodd, *The Epistle of Paul to the Romans*, MNTC (London: Hodder & Stoughton, 1932; rev. ed. London: Collins, 1959), 100–101. See also Gieniusz, "Lack," 389–400.

44. Gieniusz, "Lack," 400.

45. This is the translation of the NASB 1995 and NKJV; the Revidierte Lutherübersetzung 2017 ("Ist das Gesetz Sünde?") and Traduction œcuménique de la Bible ("La loi serait-elle péché?") are equivalent. See further, Joseph A. Fitzmyer, *Romans: A New Translation with Introduction and Commentary*, AB 33 (New York: Doubleday, 1993), 462, 466; Arland J. Hultgren, *Paul's Letter to the Romans: A Commentary* (Grand Rapids: Eerdmans, 2011), 274, 682.

Rom 7:7-13

[7]What then are we to say? That the law is sin? By no means! Yet, if it had not been for the law, I would not have known sin. I would not have known what it is to covet if the law had not said, "You shall not covet." [8]But sin, seizing an opportunity through the commandment, produced in me all kinds of covetousness. For apart from the law sin lies dead. [9]I was once alive apart from the law, but when the commandment came, sin revived [10]and I died, and the very commandment that promised life proved to be death to me. [11]For sin, seizing an opportunity in the commandment, deceived me and through it killed me. [12]So the law is holy, and the commandment is holy and just and good.

[13]Did what is good, then, bring death to me? By no means! It was sin that was working death in me through what is good, in order that it might be shown to be sin, so that through the commandment sin might become sinful beyond measure.

third time, the answer is the resounding: "By no means!" or "No way!" After clarifying that believers in Christ do not continue to sin so that grace may increase (6:1) and likewise do not sin because they are not under law but under grace (6:15), the two main subjects of these questions are now combined. Are "sin" and "the law" the same? This may be considered a logical next question. Both terms dominate this section; "sin" has a total of nine occurrences, plus one attestation of "sinful," while "law" appears six times. It is clear from the definite article in 7:7 that "the law" is the Jewish law. Earlier in this letter, Paul and Phoebe had used "law" without the article to refer to law in general (3:21, 31), but this is not the case here.

Scholars have identified a number of problems with this passage. Sigve K. Tonstad, for instance, thinks that the question in 7:7 "seems far beyond the pale"; perhaps an inquiry that the law is now unimportant or powerless would have been warranted, but not this one.[46] Tonstad goes on to state:

> Even from a purely secular point of view it is a challenge to logic to make "the law" complicit in sin. . . . In a Jewish mode of thinking, the affront to the law is worse because the law comes with the prestige of being God-given, and its ennobling powers should be even less in doubt.[47]

46. Sigve K. Tonstad, *The Letter to the Romans: Paul among the Ecologists*, Earth Bible Commentary 7 (Sheffield: Sheffield Phoenix, 2016), 207.

47. Tonstad, *Romans*, 207.

It is true that the Jewish law had an important position for many Jews during the Second Temple period. But one should be cautious not to underestimate the diversity of Jewish groups and their differences in their stance toward the law. As mentioned earlier, a controversial discussion about the Jewish law occurred at the very heart of the Second Temple period; even some of the so-called sectarian texts from Qumran attest to that. This diverse spectrum of Judaism included Paul's groups that questioned the "law" as an obligatory moral norm and obedience to it as the exclusive way of salvation. Paul's ambivalence in this sense is manifest in an earlier letter where he writes: "To the Jews I became as a Jew, in order to gain Jews. To those under the law I became as one under the law (though I myself am not under the law) so that I might gain those under the law. To those outside the law I became as one outside the law (though I am not outside God's law but am within Christ's law) so that I might gain those outside the law" (1 Cor 9:20-21). It demonstrates that for Paul, being "a Jew" is an identity that can be separated from being "under the law." There may be an intersection between these two groups, but they are not identical.

The pericope in Romans 7:7-13 pinpoints the most relevant questions about the Jewish law. For one, the answer is affirmative: "Yet, if it had not been for the law, I would not have known sin" (7:7). This is not a new assertion in the letter but a recapitulation of 3:20. But now the argument moves on to problematize the topic of covetousness together with an explanation of sin's deceptive power by means of the law. With the words "I would not have known what it is to covet if the law had not said, 'You shall not covet' " (7:7), the sentence makes explicit that this topic is another reference (see already 2:21-23) to the Decalogue: "You shall not covet your neighbor's house; you shall not covet your neighbor's wife, male or female slave, ox, donkey, or anything that belongs to your neighbor" (Exod 20:17; see also Deut 5:18 [LXX]/5:21 [MT]). This commandment, however, puts on full display the patriarchal standards of the ancient Near East by addressing only men (and not women) and by listing a wife among a man's possessions (this applies to both versions; worse, however, the wife is even less valuable than the man's house according to Exod 20:17).[48] In the Greco-Roman society of the first

48. Judith Plaskow, *Standing again at Sinai: Judaism from a Feminist Perspective* (San Francisco: HarperSanFrancisco, 1991), 25–26; Athalya Brenner, "An Afterword: The Decalogue—Am I an Addressee?," in *A Feminist Companion to Exodus to Deuteronomy*, ed. Athalya Brenner, FCB 6, 1st ser. (Sheffield: Sheffield Academic, 1994), 255–58.

century CE, it likely captures social dysfunctionality as a form of social Darwinism that typically describes the "competition of the survival of the fittest through the acquisition of status and the accumulation of power over others . . . and doing so in order to appropriate whatever resources they might have, thereby bolstering one's status storehouse."[49] This is the typical mindset that informs competition in the honor-shame system.

One should note, however, that in Romans 7:7 Paul and Phoebe have decided not to quote the full commandment but only the first two words (according to the Greek text). On the one hand, we may assume that many in the ancient audiences know such key traditions from the Torah by heart. They would, therefore, be able to fill in from memory what remained unmentioned. On the other hand, it is also possible that there is a problem of shame and trauma. After all, such androcentric texts painfully remind a woman like Phoebe of her low status in ancient Mediterranean societies, including Second Temple Judaism. Is this the reason why Phoebe is reluctant to recite the commandment in full? After all, it is only the list of the objects of coveting that makes its androcentric nature explicit. Leaving the list out may reduce the problem a woman in antiquity had with this text. That is at least one plausible argument for the brevity of the reference.

The unnamed "I" that appears in verse 7 has prompted scholars to go on a quest for who this may be. So far, the identity and potential situation of the character have remained unresolved, leaving the entire pericope and its meaning somewhat enigmatic. Stanley Stowers interprets this pericope as an example of the classical rhetorical device of speech-in-character (Greek προσωποποιΐα), assuming that its unnamed character is the same as the imaginary interlocutor in Romans 2:1-16.[50] But in the interpretation of that passage, it has been proposed above that the sudden switches to "you" (second-person singular) in 2:1 after another anonymous group in the previous chapter was addressed as "they" or "them" is spoken to the audience of Phoebe in the city of Rome, as the vocative "O human" indicates. In light of that, the applicability of Stowers's hypothesis for 7:7-13 (including as well vv. 14-25) must be

49. Bruce W. Longenecker, "What Did Paul Think Is Wrong in God's World?," in *The New Cambridge Companion to St. Paul*, ed. Bruce W. Longenecker, Cambridge Companions to Religion (Cambridge: Cambridge University Press, 2020), 181.

50. Stanley K. Stowers, "Romans 7.7-25 as a Speech-in-Character (προσωποποιία)," in *Paul in His Hellenistic Context*, ed. Troels Engberg-Pedersen, SNTW (Edinburgh: T&T Clark, 1994); Stanley K. Stowers, *A Rereading of Romans: Justice, Jews, and Gentiles* (New Haven: Yale University Press, 1994), 273.

questioned.[51] Scholars in the past have read the passage as an autobiographical reference to Paul's life prior to his conversion or, alternatively, as a meditation about the postconversion struggle of experiencing justification in the context of continuing sinfulness.[52] Several variations of this view have been proposed as well. For instance, Robert Jewett takes these lines as a reference to Paul's preconversion experience in which sin took the form of the competitive urge to develop zeal for the Pharisaic traditions (Gal 1:14). In the competitive environment of the Greco-Roman and Jewish cultures, the desire to excel in zealous behavior for the sake of honor had invaded the arena of religion and made it a perversion.[53] Will N. Timmins suggests instead that Paul employs a paradigmatic "I" to present his personal apology regarding the law. Paul does not assign the "I" to an imaginary interlocutor with whom he enters into dialogue for argumentative purposes but presents his own voice. In that case, the pericope in Romans 7:7-13 would feature no fictive use of the "I" and no diatribal exchange.[54] Yet, against all of these proposals, it must be stated that the phrase "I was once alive apart from the law" in 7:9 is a questionable fit for Paul. As a traditional Jew with formal training as a Pharisee, he never would have had a period in his life that corresponds to this description. Is Paul, therefore, really the enigmatic "I"?

Alternatively, it has been conjectured that the background is, rather, the primeval history and that the unnamed "I" is the character of Adam, sometimes seen as still entangled with elements of Paul's own experience.[55] Other more recent approaches, incorporating Second Temple Jewish traditions about Eve with tragic Greek laments, see the "I" as Eve (and not Adam) in the role of the tragic, lamenting woman to serve a pedagogi-

51. See also the criticism in Will N. Timmins, *Romans 7 and Christian Identity: A Study of the "I" in Its Literary Context*, SNTSMS 170 (Cambridge: Cambridge University Press, 2017), 12–34.

52. James D. G. Dunn, "Rom 7,14-25 in the Theology of Paul," *ThZ* 31 (1975): 257–73; Mark A. Seifrid, "The Subject of Rom 7:14-25," *NovT* 34 (1992): 313–33; Jan Lambrecht, *The Wretched "I" and Its Liberation: Paul in Romans 7 and 8*, Louvain Theological & Pastoral Monographs 14 (Louvain: Peeters, 1992), 42, 59–91.

53. Jewett, *Romans*, 449–50.

54. Timmins, *Romans 7*, 92–136. See also Brice L. Martin, "Some Reflections on the Identity of the ἐγώ in Rom. 7:14–25," *SJT* 34 (1981): 39–47.

55. Hermann Lichtenberger, *Das Ich Adams und das Ich der Menschheit: Studien zum Menschenbild in Römer 7*, WUNT 164 (Tübingen: Mohr Siebeck, 2004), 107–86; Hultgren, *Romans*, 275–94, 681–91; Joseph A. Marchal, "The Disgusting Apostle and a Queer Affect between Epistles and Audiences," in *Reading with Feeling: Affect Theory and the Bible*, ed. Fiona C. Black and Jennifer L. Koosed, SemeiaSt 95 (Atlanta: SBL Press, 2019), 127–31.

cal function. This may be corroborated by the verbal parallel between Romans 7:11 ("For sin . . . deceived me [ἐξηπάτησέν με] and through it killed me") and Eve's response to God in Genesis 3:13 ("The serpent tricked me [ἠπάτησέν με], and I ate").[56] Indeed, as has already been shown above, there are text traditions that blame Eve for the origin of human sin and death (Sir 25:24; 2 *Bar.* 48:42-43), and they are also included in Deutero-Pauline literature (1 Tim 2:14). What remains questionable about the two variations of this interpretation is the emphasis on and repeated reference to "the law" that makes them less than promising solutions for a scene in the primeval history where this topic is of no relevance.

Once scholars accept the possibility that the unnamed "I" does not have to be male but may be female, however, the elephant in the room is, in my opinion, a woman who is not hidden at all. The "I" is neither some imaginary interlocutor nor Paul nor Adam or Eve; after all, none of them are mentioned in Romans 7. Instead, the "I" is Phoebe who is standing right in front of her audiences while reciting the very lines that modern scholars struggle to assign. Would not the peculiar phrase "I was once alive apart from the law, but when the commandment came, sin revived" in 7:9 fit her, the gentile woman? Could Phoebe be sharing her ambivalent experience of having encountered the law in either first contacts with Judaism in synagogues in Corinth or even in groups of Jewish Christ believers? In retrospect, could the person who wants to be a Jew in 2:17-24 and who has a high appreciation for the law without being able to keep it not also be Phoebe?

Read from this perspective, much of Romans 7:7-13 makes sense. Phoebe associates a revival of sin with the law. It meant death for her although it was a promise of life. "For sin, seizing an opportunity in the commandment, deceived me and through it killed me. So the law is holy, and the commandment is holy and just and good" (7:11-12). This has to do with how Paul had instructed the assemblies in Corinth.

Paul and Enslaved Women in Corinth

Paul had admonished the Corinthians: "Do you not know that wrongdoers will not inherit the kingdom of God? Do not be deceived! The sexually immoral, idolaters, adulterers, male prostitutes, men who engage in illicit sex, thieves, the greedy, drunkards, revilers, swindlers—none of these will inherit the

56. Nicholas Elder, "'Wretch I Am!' Eve's Tragic Speech-in-Character in Romans 7:7-25," *JBL* 137 (2018): 743–63.

kingdom of God. And this is what some of you used to be" (1 Cor 6:9-11a). This is the reason for Paul's stern advice on sexuality in 1 Corinthians 5:1-13; 7:1-16, which includes references and allusions to the Torah (Deut 13:6-8; 17:7, 12; 19:19; 21:21; 22:21, 24). Yet, the social reality of the Corinthian church was that many poor women without formal education and political influence—freeborn and enslaved—made up the majority of the community. Most likely, some of them had no option of refusing prostitution, and many of the men had the practice of going to see these prostitutes. Others may have been enslaved women who did not have the right to refuse continuous sexual assault from their masters. Paul neglects this somber reality in his statement.[57]

Phoebe, and with her perhaps other women, may have been intent on living up to the new standards, which she accepted as sacred and positive. But the daily reality in a city like Corinth with its notorious combination of luxury and sexual decadence did not leave them much choice. What Phoebe describes is a mixture of deep-seated shame about the past, the ongoing trauma that still lingers many years after her *manumissio*, and the inner conflict of a person who knew that moral impeccability was impossible to attain.

This view is particularly manifest in Romans 7:14. Phoebe uses her status as a former enslaved person to conceptualize the human predicament of bondage to sin. One may have objected to this interpretation by pointing to 7:24, which, in the older NRSV and other Bible translations, stated explicitly: "Wretched *man* that I am!" How could this ever apply to a woman? The section must, therefore, be about Paul or Adam. But, as it turns out, "wretched *man*" is, once more, a malestream mistranslation that obscures the presence of women in biblical texts and the reconstruction of the first-century realities of Jewish believers in Christ. This will now be explored through the use of *her*-meneutics.

57. Jennifer A. Glancy, "Obstacles to Slaves' Participation in the Corinthian Church," *JBL* 117 (1998): 481–501, at 494–501. See also Jennifer A. Glancy, "The Sexual Use of Slaves: A Response to Kyle Harper on Jewish and Christian *Porneia*," *JBL* 134 (2015): 215–29; Luise Schottroff, *Der erste Brief an die Gemeinde in Korinth*, ThHK 7 (Stuttgart: Kohlhammer, 2013), 106; Christian Wolff, *Der erste Brief des Paulus an die Korinther*, 3rd ed., THKNT 7 (Leipzig: Evangelische Verlagsanstalt, 2011), 2.

The Inner Conflict (7:14-25)

The new section begins in Romans 7:14 with the disclosure formula "for we know that." The first part (7:14-16) problematizes how the law can be considered spiritual and good while humans are under the paradox of sin. The second part (7:17-20) seeks to explicate how sin is responsible for the human predicament of spiritual schizophrenia. These first two sections are closely related, which is manifest in almost verbatim repetitions of phrases in 7:15, 19, on the one hand, and 7:17, 20, on the other. The third part (7:21-25) offers an explanation of how the law of sin captures the self. Might these sections address the specific predicament of women?

The verbatim repetitions of phrases in Romans 7:15, 19 and in 7:17, 20 are the key to both sections. The first set of repetitions conveys the ethical dilemma of humans as their actions fall short of their well-meant intentions. The outcome is that the "I" does "the very thing I hate" (7:15) or "the evil I do not want" (v. 19). The second set of repetitions assigns the human dilemma to the power of sin. The sentence "but in fact it is no longer I who do it but sin that dwells within me" (7:17) is similar to: "Now if I do what I do not want, it is no longer I who do it but sin that dwells within me" (v. 20).[58] This problem is initially presented as intrinsically human; it is sandwiched between two lines featuring the metaphors of enslavement: "I am of the flesh, sold into slavery under sin" (7:14); "So then, with my mind I am enslaved to the law of God, but with my flesh I am enslaved to the law of sin" (v. 25). This is a reminder that Paul introduces himself as a "slave/enslaved person" at the very beginning of this letter (1:1). Peter Oakes notes:

> A slave would seem likely to view Paul as expressing his (or someone else's) experience in terms of theirs. More specifically, Paul was painting a picture of their present experience, as Christian slaves whose actions were constrained by non-Christian owners. . . . Whatever the subtleties of Romans 7, for sexually exploited Christian slaves this is an expression of the acute tension of their present existence.[59]

While I agree with the general contents of this statement, I would add that it most likely expresses the experience of enslaved persons for the very reason that it represents the voice of one of theirs. Who else

58. Jan Lambrecht, "The Line of Thought in Romans 7,15-20," *Bib* 85 (2004): 393–98, at 393.

59. Peter Oakes, *Reading Romans in Pompeii: Paul's Letter at Ground Level* (Minneapolis: Fortress; London: SPCK, 2009), 147.

Rom 7:14-25

14For we know that the law is spiritual,
but I am of the flesh, sold into slavery under sin. 15I do not understand
my own actions. For I do not do what
I want, but I do the very thing I hate.
16Now if I do what I do not want, I agree
that the law is good. 17But in fact it is
no longer I who do it but sin that dwells
within me. 18For I know that the good
does not dwell within me, that is, in my
flesh. For the desire to do the good lies
close at hand, but not the ability. 19For I
do not do the good I want, but the evil
I do not want is what I do. 20Now if I
do what I do not want, it is no longer I
who do it but sin that dwells within me.
21So I find it to be a law that, when I
want to do what is good, evil lies close
at hand. 22For I delight in the law of
God in my inmost self, 23but I see in
my members another law at war with
the law of my mind, making me captive to the law of sin that dwells in my
members. 24Wretched person that I am!
Who will rescue me from this body of
death? 25Thanks be to God through
Jesus Christ our Lord!

So then, with my mind I am enslaved
to the law of God, but with my flesh I am
enslaved to the law of sin.

could have done a better job at convincingly conveying such a personal passage to the audiences in Rome than Phoebe, who may have been a former enslaved person? In that case, she would have been at least in part the embodiment of this complex passage. While being enslaved, she would, of course, have been used to executing orders of others that neither corresponded to her wishes nor were the result of her inner initiative. Naturally, she would often have done things that she hated or considered evil. Because she conveys this difficult topic, but does so through deeply personal imagery, she invites her audiences to join and admit that they too are sinners who have experienced this human plight. This discourse resembles Greek philosophy to some degree, particularly Platonic concepts.[60] Important differences, however, exist; for example, there are no parallels to the idea that humans are deceived by sin in the Platonic tradition, nor is there any rejection of sin as such.[61] Neverthe-

60. Emma Wasserman, "Paul Among the Philosophers: The Case of Sin in Romans 6–8," *JSNT* 30 (2008): 387–415.

61. Hans Dieter Betz, "The Concept of the 'Inner Human Being' (Ὁ ἔσω ἄνθρωπος) in the Anthropology of Paul," *NTS* 46 (2000): 315–41, at 332–34.

less, this passage could have strongly resonated with the audience due to its existential authenticity.[62]

If Romans 7:14-25 resonates with its audience, then the question may still be asked: Who exactly is that "wretched person" in 7:24?[63] Such a phrase is also attested in classical Greek literature. There, however, this self-referential exclamation is usually placed on the lips of a *female* character. It is known from Medea's cry of despair, "What, wretched woman, have I done?" The reason for her misery is that, despite her will to do the good, she was overpowered by her anger (Seneca, *Med.* 989, and, in a similar way, Euripides, *Med.* 1273-1280).[64] This depiction is paralleled by another cry of despair, this time on the lips of the daughter of King Aeëtes, who also laments her lack of self-mastery (Ovid, *Metam.* 7.17-21).[65] All of these Greek traditions of tragic laments assign the role of

62. Tonstad, *Romans*, 224, with reference to Beverly Roberts Gaventa, "The Shape of the 'I': The Psalter, the Gospel, and the Speaker in Romans 7," in *Apocalyptic Paul: Cosmos and Anthropos in Romans 5–8*, ed. Beverly Roberts Gaventa (Waco, TX: Baylor University Press, 2013), 77–91.

63. The NRSV, like the NASB 1995, KJV, and NKJV, translates: "Wretched man that I am!" The NIV has, in a similar fashion: "What a wretched man I am!" (see also James I. Packer, "The 'Wretched Man' Revisited: Another Look at Romans 7:14-25," in *Romans and the People of God: Essays in Honor of Gordon D. Fee on the Occasion of His 65th Birthday*, ed. Sven K. Soderlund and Nicholas T. Wright [Grand Rapids: Eerdmans, 1999], 70–81; James D. G. Dunn, *The Theology of Paul the Apostle* [Grand Rapids: Eerdmans, 1998], 473–74, 495; David G. Peterson, *Romans*, EBTC [Bellingham, WA: Lexham Press, 2020], 301–2). The Greek phrase is Ταλαίπωρος ἐγὼ ἄνθρωπος. In comments above regarding the correct translation of Romans 5:12, 15, it has already been stated that the Greek term ἄνθρωπος typically does not have the meaning of "man" as opposed to a woman but rather designates a "human," "human being," or "person." Therefore, a more appropriate—and gender-inclusive—rendering of Romans 7:24 would be "What a wretched person/human I am!" See the Revidierte Lutherübersetzung 2017 ("Ich elender Mensch!"); Reina Valera 1995 ("¡Miserable de mí!"); furthermore Joachim Jeremias, "Ἄνθρωπος, Ἀνθρώπινος," *TDNT* 1 (1964): 364–67, at 364; Ernst Käsemann, *An die Römer*, 3rd ed., HNT 8a (Tübingen: Mohr Siebeck, 1974), 189–200; Fitzmyer, *Romans*, 472, 476 ("Wretch that I am"); Reinhard Feldmeier, "Vater und Töpfer? Zur Identität Gottes im Römerbrief," in *Between Gospel and Election: Explorations in the Interpretation of Romans 9–11*, ed. Florian Wilk and J. Ross Wagner with the assistance of Frank Schleritt, WUNT 257 (Tübingen: Mohr Siebeck, 2010), 380; Aaron Sherwood, *Romans: A Structural, Thematic, and Exegetical Commentary* (Bellingham, WA: Lexham Press, 2020), 410.

64. See also the modern opera with the title *Medea: O Wretched Woman!* by the modern Greek composer Mikis Theodorakis (1925–2021).

65. Stowers, *Rereading*, 260–64.

the "wretch" to a *woman*. Medea is also someone who meditates on the inner conflict of knowing what is right but doing evil when planning to murder the new bride and her own children who are still with her unfaithful husband, Jason: "I am being overcome by evils. And I know, indeed, that what I am about to do is evil" (Euripides, *Med.* 1078).

An Ancient Controversy Between Men and Women

The poetry of Euripides reflects on a larger controversy between men and women in ancient Greece; this is also a topic in his *Medea*. On the one hand, Euripides may articulate a misogynistic position, obviously on the lips of men: "Whoever stops slandering women will be called a wretch and not wise" (Euripides, *Fragments* 36 N^2).

On the other hand, there is the reciprocation by Medea about her unfaithful husband, Jason: "He knows full well that my whole life was bound up with him; and he, my husband, has turned out to be the worst of men. For of all things which are living and have judgment we women are the most wretched creatures." (Euripides, *Med.* 228-234)[66]

Who is Medea? She is a former princess of the kingdom of Colchis. Remarkably, the setting of the play is in front of Medea's house, which is in no other location than the city of Corinth. Thus, several of these aspects fit Phoebe, who is also a woman from Corinth. The "wretched *man*" in Romans 7:24 (according to most older Bible translations) who is rather a "wretched *person*" (according to the Greek text of the New Testament) is actually a wretched *woman*.[67] And this woman, Medea, is also a gentile, not a Jew, which is another personal aspect that Phoebe shares with this character. Since, following the 49 CE edict of Claudius, her audiences in Rome consist mostly of gentiles, Phoebe draws on Greek tragedy to ensure the acceptance of her dramatic reflections on the human plight of enslavement to sin and death. Of course, this is not to say that the

66. See also Laura McClure, "'The Worst Husband': Discourses of Praise and Blame in Euripides' Medea," *CP* 94 (1999): 373–94.

67. Elder, "Wretch," 743–44.

passage is *only* for women. "The cry of the 'I' is not a cry inside women and men like Medea and Paul, but it is a cry of all people who have been living under powerful oppression and slavery throughout history and imprisoned in a victimized existence."[68]

The following contribution about the reception history of Romans 7:23-24 shows that, not surprisingly, these sentences about the ambiguities of the human predicament spoke nevertheless very directly to women.

The Stripping of the Flesh: A Reading by Catherine of Siena

Caterina Benincasa, better known as Catherine of Siena (1347–1380 CE), is famous for her spiritual experiences and her involvement in the religious and political crises of her time. A daring laywoman, she is said to have even encouraged the pope to return to Rome. Among her works is the *Dialogue*, Catherine of Siena's conversation with God. There are many references to Scripture in this text, including fifty-seven references to the letters of Paul; twenty of these are to the letter to the Romans, some mentioned two to four times.

Catherine of Siena is particularly interested in the law of the body as opposed to the law of the spirit. Paul's exclamation: "Wretched person that I am! Who will rescue me from this body of death?" (Rom 7:24) is quoted four times, either literally or implicitly.[69] Chapter 45 in the *Dialogue* teaches that the soul detached from the body is no longer subject to it; it has won the struggle against "the perverse law of sensuality"[70] and can therefore see God with bliss "without the burden of this body."[71] "Do you know what is the most special good the blessed have? It is to have their will filled with what they long for. They long for me and they possess and taste me without any resistance, for they have left behind the body's heaviness."[72]

68. Samuel Byrskog, "Adam and Medea—and Eve: Revisiting Romans 7,7-25," in *Paul's Graeco-Roman Context*, ed. Cilliers Breytenbach, BETL 277 (Leuven: Peeters, 2015), 298–99.

69. Catherine of Siena, *The Dialogue*, CWS (New York: Paulist Press, 1980), 91 (chap. 45), 105 (chap. 51), 149 (chap. 79), 153 (chap. 83).

70. "And you have that perverse law that is always fighting against the spirit" (reference to Rom 7:23, chap. 51), in Catherine of Siena, *The Dialogue*, 105.

71. Catherine of Siena, *The Dialogue*, 77.

72. Catherine of Siena, *The Dialogue*, 91.

But this detachment cannot be carried out without discernment guided by charity.[73] Romans 7:24 is still quoted literally in chapters 79 and 83. The first of these occurrences has as its context the (temporary) silence of God for the soul "in eager longing."[74] The Lord momentarily withdraws the union with the soul and makes "the soul return to the vessel that is her body, so that the body's feeling, which had been completely lost because of the soul's emotion, returns."[75] Chapter 83 argues that the apostle Paul desires to be freed from his mortal body because "it seemed to him that his body's weight rebelled against him, blocked him off from great perfection, from the fulfilling of desire that the soul receives after death."[76]

Now, this theme of the body from which one must detach oneself is very important for Catherine, who at the age of fifteen cut her hair to show that she belonged to Christ and voluntarily and progressively deprived herself of food (another desire for detachment from the body) in communion with the distress of the world and the church of her time and in order to show the precedence of divine nourishment. Her body was thus transformed, detached from itself, as reported by her hagiographer Raymond of Capua, who insists on the transformation of this body, through successive renunciations, to become a true "mystical body": "From then on, inhabited and transformed by Christ, she acceded to another nature and assimilated the supernatural powers of the glorious bodies, which allowed her, by a divine investiture, to become the fertile mother of many disciples."[77] Catherine of Siena not only received the letter to the Romans as a spiritual book but also desired to live it in her flesh, or, rather, in the stripping of her flesh.

Florence Draguet

As for Romans, it is now clear that the problem is not the law as such. The real problem is the human condition with its inexorable entanglement under sin and the way in which it responds to the law. The law as such is good and holy, but humanity is under the deceptive power of sin

73. Catherine of Siena, *The Dialogue*, 44.
74. Catherine of Siena, *The Dialogue*, 147.
75. Catherine of Siena, *The Dialogue*, 148.
76. Catherine of Siena, *The Dialogue*, 153.
77. André Vauchez, *Catherine de Sienne: Vie et passions* (Paris: Cerf, 2015), 133.

that leads to death. The law is mainly a tool that makes humans aware of this paradoxical dilemma of the human predicament.

Furthermore, because of the focus on the quest for the identity of the enigmatic "I" and the associated description of the human ethical dilemma, it is easily overlooked that this section provides an answer to the question, "Who will rescue me?" The response is "Thanks be to God through Jesus Christ our Lord!" (Rom 7:24-25a). It is similar to a previous exclamation in this letter (6:17) and other ones in the Corinthian correspondence (1 Cor 15:57; 2 Cor 2:14; 8:16; 9:15). Indeed, the exclamation in Romans 7:25a appears as a shortened version of that in 1 Corinthians 15:57, which had presented resurrection as the solution to the dilemma of physical death (1 Cor 15:35-58). It may also summarize the section in Romans 6 that deals with human enslavement to sin but sees salvation in the new state of being "slaves to [justification]." The salvation of humanity from death is in the free gift of eternal life in Christ. Like these previous exclamations, Romans 7:25a also assigns the role of savior to Jesus Christ in connection with the title "Lord," but it does not yet explain the "how." This will be explicated in Romans 8.

The concluding sentence of chapter 7 attempts to summarize the preceding argument with the following words: "So then, with my mind I am enslaved to the law of God, but with my flesh I am enslaved to the law of sin" (Rom 7:25b-c). It is often considered to be a marginal gloss added either by Paul himself (then perhaps intended to be placed between 7:23 and 24) or by an anonymous later scribe (who did not fully comprehend the argument in the previous chapter where the human being is enslaved either to one *or* the other power but never to the law).[78] Since this chapter featured a syllogism at its beginning (7:1-6) about an analogy from marriage that was likewise characterized by a certain lack of logical coherence in its argument (see above, p. 162), one may wonder whether this was due to the cooperation between Paul and Phoebe and/or even other contributors at the time of writing the letter in the house of Gaius in Corinth. If Paul's letters were already notorious for a certain level of difficulty among later New Testament authors (2 Pet 3:15-16) and thereafter for their exceptional length (see the comment on Romans in the *Canon Muratori*), then it would not be surprising that such problems were perceived even earlier during the very process of original composition. This may perhaps explain the inconsistencies both at the start and at the conclusion of chapter 7.

78. Hermann Lichtenberger, "Der Beginn der Auslegungsgeschichte von Römer 7: Röm 7,25b," *ZNW* 88 (1997): 284–95.

Life in the Spirit (8:1-17)

This section focuses on the Spirit of God, presenting a thesis and rationale regarding its cosmic struggle with "flesh." After presenting the thesis in 8:1, the sentences in 8:2-4 show that Christ frees believers who are then able to fulfill the law through the Spirit. This allows women to be part of God's family.

TRANSLATION MATTERS: Romans 8:14

Romans 8:14 is a central christological statement: "For all who are led by the Spirit of God are children of God (υἱοὶ θεοῦ)." Both the NRSVue and the NIV render Greek υἱοί as "children" for a gender-inclusive text version, although the term literally means "sons."[79] It obscures, however, the specific allusion of the syntagm "sons of God" to the christological title of Christ Jesus as "Son (of God)" that permeates this letter (e.g., Rom 1:4; see also 1:3, 9; 5:10; 8:3). In addition, the adoption laws of the ancient Roman world favored sons over daughters, which is the ultimate point of the image. Therefore, a preferable translation would be: "For all who are led by the Spirit of God are sons of God."

TRANSLATION MATTERS: Romans 8:15b-16

The NRSVue has the following text: "you received a spirit of adoption. When we cry, 'Abba! Father!' it is that very Spirit bearing witness with our spirit that we are children of God." A footnote in the biblical texts of Romans 8:16 indicates an alternate rendering of these two clauses: "Or *a spirit of adoption, by which we cry, 'Abba! Father!' The Spirit itself bears witness*." This translation reflects a different interpretation of ἐν ᾧ, which is understood as a conjunction in the NRSVue where it is rendered as "when." Since, however, the entire pericope is about the new baptismal state of "being in," this interpretation is less likely. A preferable translation of ἐν ᾧ is "by which" or "in whom/in him." It also involves allotting the words "by which we cry, 'Abba! Father!' " to the subsequent sentence. This alternative is featured in, for example, the NIV: "rather, the Spirit you received brought about your adoption to sonship. And by him we cry, '*Abba*, Father.' The Spirit himself testifies with our spirit that we are God's children."[80]

---

79. See also the Revidierte Lutherübersetzung 2017 ("Gottes Kinder"). By contrast, the NASB 1995 and NKJV have "sons of God."

80. See also Alphonse Maillot, *L'épître aux Romains: Epître de l'œcuménisme et théologie de l'histoire* (Paris: Le Centurion; Geneva: Labor et Fides, 1984), 213; Dieter Zeller, *Der Brief an die Römer*, RNT (Regensburg: Friedrich Pustet, 1985), 149; Douglas J. Moo, *The Epistle to the Romans*, NICNT (Grand Rapids: Eerdmans, 1996), 502.

Rom 8:1-17

8:1 Therefore there is now no condemnation for those who are in Christ Jesus.
2 For the law of the Spirit of life in Christ
Jesus has set you free from the law of
sin and of death. 3 For God has done
what the law, weakened by the flesh,
could not do: by sending his own Son
in the likeness of sinful flesh and to deal
with sin, he condemned sin in the flesh,
4 so that the just requirement of the law
might be fulfilled in us, who walk not
according to the flesh but according to
the Spirit. 5 For those who live according to the flesh set their minds on the
things of the flesh, but those who live
according to the Spirit set their minds
on the things of the Spirit. 6 To set the
mind on the flesh is death, but to set
the mind on the Spirit is life and peace.
7 For this reason the mind that is set on
the flesh is hostile to God; it does not
submit to God's law—indeed, it cannot,
8 and those who are in the flesh cannot
please God.

9 But you are not in the flesh; you
are in the Spirit, since the Spirit of
God dwells in you. Anyone who does
not have the Spirit of Christ does not

Romans 8:1-2 presents a response to, or continuation of, a number of earlier christological and soteriological topics and concepts. First, the term "condemnation" appeared as the antithesis to "justification" in Romans 5:16, 18. It is now stated once again that "no condemnation" exists "for those who are in Christ Jesus" (8:1). This pericope combines the variety of preceding images of atonement (3:21-26) and reconciliation (5:6-11). Second, the phrase "in Christ Jesus" also shows that Romans 8 is a key chapter that will now define the christological identity of the Jewish believers that has been referenced earlier (3:24; 6:11, 23; see also 1:5-6). Third, the double premises of the woman in 7:2, 3 that the audience is expected to adopt in 7:6 about being "free" or "discharged" from the law are also repeated here (8:2). In fact, and looking more broadly at the entirety of Romans 8:1-17, this section is characterized by sentences and phrases that mostly start with conjunctions such as "as a result" (ἄρα), "for" (γάρ), "so that" (ἵνα), "as, because" (διότι). It strings together insights that appear, therefore, as logical consequences of previous chapters. At the same time, chapter 8 is closely connected to the next section in Romans 9–11 about God's election of Israel and salvation for all.[81]

In particular, the second sentence features the first occurrence of the term "Spirit" (Rom 8:2) in this section. It is equivalent to the concept of "being in Christ" and introduces the opposition between that term and

81. Tobin, *Rhetoric*, 251–72.

Rom 8:1-17 (cont.)

belong to him. [10]But if Christ is in you,
then the body is dead because of sin,
but the Spirit is life because of righteousness. [11]If the Spirit of him who
raised Jesus from the dead dwells in
you, he who raised Christ Jesus from
the dead will give life to your mortal
bodies also through his Spirit that
dwells in you.

[12]So then, brothers and sisters, we
are obligated, not to the flesh, to live
according to the flesh—[13]for if you live
according to the flesh, you will die, but
if by the Spirit you put to death the
deeds of the body, you will live. [14]For
all who are led by the Spirit of God are
children of God. [15]For you did not receive a spirit of slavery to fall back into
fear, but you received a spirit of adoption. When we cry, "Abba! Father!" [16]it
is that very Spirit bearing witness with
our spirit that we are children of God,
[17]and if children, then heirs: heirs of
God and joint heirs with Christ, if we
in fact suffer with him so that we may
also be glorified with him.

"flesh," which is another typical feature of Romans 8:1-17. Entirely in line with what was said before, "flesh" remains the negative factor in Phoebe's theological concept: It has weakened the law and is "sinful" (it is literally called "the flesh of sin," 8:3). Likewise, the purpose of salvation through the incarnation of Christ Jesus is that "he condemned sin in the flesh" (8:3), together with its corollary, death on earth. As for the sphere of human involvement, "flesh" is to be avoided at any cost. The advice is to "walk not according to the flesh" (8:4) because "to set the mind on the flesh is death" (8:6). Ultimately, it is clear that "those who are in the flesh cannot please God" (8:8). By contrast, the "Spirit" is the positive factor presented as the antithesis to "flesh": By walking "according to the Spirit," humans actually fulfill the law (8:4).[82]

These binary categories reflect a dualistic worldview. Elizabeth A. Castelli notes her concerns about such arguments: "The language of this passage poses numerous difficulties for feminist analysis. . . . When the figure of the feminine is ideologically aligned with the flesh, how are women to understand their position with respect to this worldview?"[83] Castelli's concerns are valid with regard to traditional Platonic dualism. Yet, the assumption presented here, that the sentences and sections in Romans 7–8 are Phoebe's and belong to her discourse from an explicitly

82. Eduard Schweizer, "πνεῦμα: E. III: Paul," *TDNT* 6 (1968): 415–37, at 433.
83. Castelli, "Romans," 285–86.

female vantage point, may change the assessment of this argument. Phoebe refers to the standards of Jewish marital law that are built on patriarchal privileges (Rom 7:1-6). But by inviting the audiences to adopt the perspective of the woman in this image, she exposes the problem and presents a solution, which then becomes the basis of her christological argument. The dualism of "Spirit" versus "flesh" does not categorically assign women or anybody else to the realm of flesh. New life in the Spirit is a relational existence that is not based on any anthropological or ontological dichotomy. Instead, it is determined through adherence to Christ.[84] In the analogy from marriage in Romans 7:1-6, the solution was the possibility that the woman can, after the death of her husband, be related to another man. This is the new existential situation of those who believe in Christ; they now belong to him. Such new life is accessible to women and men alike. Phoebe would be its embodiment and role model when she arrived in Rome to share the gospel message. As a person who knows the triple trouble of being a woman, a gentile, and potentially also a former enslaved person, her message about being set free comes as a personal testimony of life in a new allegiance.

The statement in Romans 8:2 should, therefore, be understood in analogy to 7:6. Both sentences can be considered as an *inclusio*, which is a thematic repetition that frames a section.[85] These two passages shall be juxtaposed with another two prominent occurrences of the term "to free" (ἐλευθερόω) or "free person/freedperson" (ἐλεύθερος) in previous letters (1 Cor 9:19; 2 Cor 3:17; Gal 5:1) and another occurrence in Romans 8:21.

Comparison of Statements about Freedom in Paul's Soteriology[86]

Rom 7:6	But now *we are discharged from the law*, dead to that which held us captive, so that we are enslaved *in the newness of the Spirit* and not in the oldness of the written code.
Rom 8:2	For the law *of the Spirit of life in Christ Jesus has set you free from the law* of sin and of death.
Rom 8:21	. . . that the creation itself *will be set free from its enslavement* to decay and *will obtain the freedom* of the glory of the children of God.

84. Jörg Frey, "Die paulinische Antithese von 'Fleisch' und 'Geist' und die palästinisch-jüdische Weisheitstradition," *ZNW* 90 (1999): 45–77.

85. Lambrecht, *Wretched*, 33.

86. Similar text in the following comparative table is indicated by italics.

1 Cor 9:19	*For though I am free [lit. "a free person"]* with respect to all, *I have made myself a slave* to all, so that I might gain all the more.
2 Cor 3:17	Now *the Lord is the Spirit*, and *where the Spirit of the Lord is, there is freedom*.
Gal 5:1	*For freedom Christ has set us free*. Stand firm, therefore, and *do not submit again to a yoke of slavery*.

As Romans 7:6 is the application of the entire section about the analogy from marriage in 7:1-6 that conveys the freedom from the law, chapter 7 in its entirety is about this crucial argument. According to the theology/soteriology of Phoebe and Paul, humans are, therefore, effectively "freed" from the law. Their identity is that of "freedmen" and "freedwomen." The status of personal freedom has now been explicated in two somewhat analogous ways: by imagery based on marital law (7:1-6) and on the institution of enslavement (6:18, 20; see also 1:1, etc.). In the former conceptual background, the death of the husband would have marked the moment of liberation; in the latter, it is the event of emancipation/*manumissio*.[87] To repeat, the juxtaposition of imagery of "enslaved person" versus "freedom" with "life" and "death" clearly hints at the fact that the institution of enslavement meant social death while the end of enslavement was perceived as a return to life. The notion of personal freedom developed specifically among enslaved women,[88] and the statement of liberation from the "law," understood here as the realm of influence of sin and death, should be seen as the personal testimony of Phoebe, the former enslaved woman. While Phoebe will revisit this key message, with special attention to the term of "glory," and apply it to the entire creation in Romans 8:21, Paul had previously indicated that he was willing to give up his status as a freedman in Christ to advance his mission (1 Cor 9:19). At the same time, this freedom is connected to the presence of the Spirit of "the Lord" (2 Cor 3:17). All of these aspects are presented in a binary opposition to "bondage" and "enslavement." The chart above shows that these aspects have been, and are, consistent elements of Paul's gospel message. This is why Phoebe now gets to proclaim it also in the city of Rome.

87. See comments on enslavement in the ancient Greco-Roman world above.
88. Patterson, *Freedom*, 54–55.

Luther and Liberation

It is part of the reception history of Romans 8:2 (and other related passages) that a certain Martin Luder in the early sixteenth century CE changed his name to "Luther" (or "Elutheros/Eleutherius") in response to this message of liberation epitomized by the Greek terms "to free" (ἐλευθερόω) and "free person/freedperson" (ἐλεύθερος). Luther was baptized in 1483 as Martin Luder (or Ludher). Rife with negative connotations (*Luder* in German means "poor stupid creature" or "licentious woman"), his last name solicited many a sarcastic comment. In 1512 or 1517 (the year of posting the Ninety-Five Theses), Martin Luder therefore decided to change his name to "Luther," which he probably also did to publicly convey his new understanding of the gospel of freedom that subsequently became the driving force behind the Protestant Reformation.[89] A few centuries later, in 1934, a Baptist minister in Atlanta, Georgia, by the name of Mike King Sr. traveled to Berlin, Germany, for a church convention. His visit to the Reformation sites and his admiration of the great Reformer's theology prompted him to change both his own name and that of his five-year-old son, Mike Jr., to Martin Luther King. It may be suggested that the message of freedom from bondage that Paul and Phoebe had proclaimed almost two thousand years earlier was a contributing factor to the Protestant Reformation and to the development and success of the US Civil Rights Movement.

It is, nevertheless, somewhat surprising to hear the expression "the law of the Spirit of life in Christ Jesus" in Romans 8:2. Paul never used such a phrase in previous letters. It is also unusual that the "law" appears as the subject of the verb "has set you free," of which the object is another appearance of the term "law." What could it mean that the law frees from the law? It has been suggested that the precise wording was chosen for the sake of linguistic balance between the two occurrences of "law." But what exactly does the term "law" (νόμος) mean, in particular its first occurrence in this phrase? In the letter thus far, this noun was

89. Lewis W. Spitz, "Luther and Humanism," in *Luther and Learning: The Wittenberg University Luther Symposium*, ed. Marilyn J. Harran (Selinsgrove, PA: Susquehanna University Press, 1985), 71–72; Bernd Moeller and Karl Stackmann, *Luder—Luther—Eleutherius: Erwägungen zu Luthers Namen* (Göttingen: Vandenhoeck & Ruprecht, 1981).

used with three different meanings: first, to refer to the Jewish law, the Torah (e.g., 3:20, 21; 7:22, 25); second, more broadly to law in general (e.g., 3:21, 31); and third, in the common sense of "principle" or "realm of influence" (3:27; 7:21, 23). Attempts have been made to show that the first occurrence of "law" imagines a christologically restored version that now leads to genuine life. In this case, the purpose is "to make clear that the resolution coincides precisely with the portrayed dilemma."[90] But is the interpretation warranted that the *law* frees the "you" from the *law*? This would be a unique claim in Pauline literature. It seems more plausible to understand the first occurrence of "law" once more in the sense of "realm of influence," which refers to the empowerment through the Spirit. As such, it is parallel to the following sentence, which explains that it is indeed God who is the initiator of human salvation (8:3).[91] The incarnation of the Son is what conquered sin on earth. This was one of the first aspects of the gospel mentioned at the start of this letter (1:3). Furthermore, the question of the desperate human in 7:24 was: "*Who* will rescue me from this body of death?" The question was not "What?" Rather, the preliminary response was that the rescue is "through Jesus Christ our Lord" (7:25). For Paul and Phoebe, salvation remains the key focus of the gospel message, and it is always the activity of God through the Son Jesus Christ.

Terminological analogies, specifically the words "peace" (εἰρήνη) in 8:6 and "hostile" (ἔχθρα, literally "enmity") in verse 7, show that this passage is also reminiscent of the earlier section about reconciliation through the death of Jesus in Romans 5:6-11. The focus now is on the fact that "the just requirement of the law" is being fulfilled (8:4). To achieve that, believers in Christ "walk not according to the flesh but according to the Spirit" (8:4). While the verb "to walk" involves human actions, the parallel phrase in 8:5-6 employs the verb "to set one's mind on" (φρονέω). It alludes to Greek literature, for example, Aeschylus's description of the "presumptuous pride and impious thoughts [κἀθέων φρονημάτων]" of invading armies who experience calamity because of their impiety of ravaging temples (Aeschylus, *Pers.* 808). Setting the mind on the Spirit is, by contrast, an admonition for a woman. It is addressed to Electra who

90. Leander E. Keck, "The Law and 'The Law of Sin and Death' (Rom 8:1-4): Reflections on the Spirit and Ethics in Paul," in *The Divine Helmsman: Studies on God's Control of Human Events, Presented to Lou H. Silberman*, ed. James L. Crenshaw and Samuel Sandmel (New York: Ktav, 1980), 49.

91. Matera, *Romans*, 190–91.

has "changed her mind [φρόνημα . . . μεταστάθη]" and is "now thinking holy thoughts [φρονεῖς γὰρ ὅσια νῦν]" (Euripides, *El.* 1201-1204). The careful binary antithesis of both ways of "mindfulness," however, goes back to Paul and Phoebe.[92]

The third section starts with Phoebe directly addressing the assemblies as "you" (Rom 8:9). Her discourse in Romans 8:9-11 continues to focus on the Spirit. Chapter 8 is saturated with references to it. There were already five occurrences of the term in 8:1-8; they are followed by another six in this section and likewise six attestations in the fourth argument in 8:12-17 about how the Spirit turns humans into children of God. In fact, the first verse alone features no fewer than three occurrences of the term over its two sentences: "But you are not in the flesh; you are in the Spirit, since the Spirit of God dwells in you. Anyone who does not have the Spirit of Christ does not belong to him" (8:9). This Spirit has been introduced as the dynamic force of life. It is the force that made Jesus the Son of God through resurrection (1:4, revisited in 8:11) and fills humans with the gift of love (5:5).[93]

In chapter 8, it is specifically the opposition to "flesh" that determines the usage of "Spirit," as is already manifest in 8:9. These concepts are, once more, similar to Galatians, where Paul rebuked his addressees as "foolish" because after a life "with the Spirit," they were "now ending with the flesh" (Gal 3:3). In the parenetic section of that letter, he consequently exhorted them repeatedly to live by the Spirit (Gal 5:16, 25), which is similar to Romans 8:4. In their present letter, Paul and Phoebe also connect these ideas with that of justification[94] (Rom 8:10). Thus, a comprehensive spectrum of terminology drawing on atonement and reconciliation appears. The focus, however, turns toward ethics and practical conduct. The parenetic section in Romans 12:1–15:13 is already in sight: "Thanks to the Spirit which abides in each woman and man, the bodies of women and men are clothed and vivified."[95]

The last aspect to be added to these reflections about life in the Spirit of God is that there is a special status for those who believe in Christ. This

92. Jewett, *Romans*, 487.

93. Carl R. Holladay, *Introduction to the New Testament: Reference Edition* (Waco, TX: Baylor University Press, 2017), 535.

94. The NRSVue renders this term "righteousness." For the alternative translation of the Greek term δικαιοσύνη as "justification," see comments above under "Translation Matters" on Romans 3:21, 22.

95. Tamez, "Justification," 188.

is what the fourth and final argument in Romans 8:12-17 relates about the Spirit that emboldens humans to see themselves as children of God. Phoebe recapitulates that life according to the flesh means death while life by the Spirit means life (8:12-13). Yet, that sounds like a rather traditional moral exhortation. Already Moses advised Israel: "I call heaven and earth to witness against you today that I have set before you life and death, blessings and curses. Choose life so that you and your descendants may live" (Deut 30:19).[96] The new element is introduced in 8:14: "For all who are led by the Spirit of God are [sons] of God."[97] The verb "to lead" (ἄγω), which is distinctively Pauline terminology (Gal 5:18), expresses a movement of being "carried away" by a spiritual force.[98] This sentence conveys the special individual and corporate status of believers but obscures three important aspects: First, the new group members receive a high status relative to the consideration that a daughter would also be a family member but has a lower status. Second, both sons and daughters stand to inherit, but access to large and wealthy estates was preferably given to sons, and it was prohibited to give daughters a large patrimony. This idea will be further explicated soon (Rom 8:17). And third, the specific terminology "sons of God" may even be a reference to the christological title of Christ Jesus that permeates this letter (Rom 1:4; see also 1:3, 9; 5:10; 8:3). It would be difficult to hear this sentence and the term "son" without making that connection. Phoebe shows in 8:16-17 that she has no problem using the gender-inclusive Greek term τέκνα, "children," for the same statement.[99] Therefore, the use of the different term "son" in 8:14 must have been a conscious choice, yet it applies to men and women.

The culture of adoption along these parameters was not only a social reality in the Roman world but also an image used for the visual depiction of the superiority of Rome vis-à-vis the subjugation of "barbarians." For example, certain Roman coins displayed the head of Augustus on the

96. Matera, *Romans*, 196.

97. For this translation of "sons of God," see comments above under "Translation Matters" on Romans 8:14.

98. Hans Dieter Betz, *Galatians: A Commentary on Paul's Letter to the Churches in Galatia*, Hermeneia (Philadelphia: Fortress, 1979), 281.

99. Kathleen E. Corley, "Women's Inheritance Rights in Antiquity and Paul's Metaphor of Adoption," in *A Feminist Companion to Paul*, ed. Amy-Jill Levine with Marianne Blickenstaff, FCNTECW 6 (London: T&T International, 2004), 119–20; Caroline Johnson Hodge, *If Sons, Then Heirs: A Study of Kinship and Ethnicity in the Letters of Paul* (Oxford: Oxford University Press, 2007), 110.

obverse with the inscription: "AVGVSTVS DIVI F," which is the abbreviation of *divi filius* ("son of god"). The reverse depicts a scene of adoption: a barbarian man offering his child to the elevated and enthroned Augustus.[100] That child would then also be the "son" of Augustus and recognize him as "father." Both aspects constitute the child's status change. The adoption mentioned in Romans 8:14-16 works along the same logic.

This means that the new status of believers has two aspects: First, it implies being indeed children of God, the "Father." And second, it means having the right to the title "son" that Christ had as well, making believers effectively brothers and sisters of Christ.[101] This idea is explicated, for instance, in Mark 3:34-35, where Jesus pronounces: "Here are my mother and my brothers! Whoever does the will of God is my brother and sister and mother [οὗτος ἀδελφός μου καὶ ἀδελφὴ καὶ μήτηρ ἐστίν]." With that, the new family of the children of God is established. "Women and men guided by the Spirit are converted into sisters and brothers through divine adoption. . . . Paul here is proclaiming a new kind of interpersonal relations [*sic*] permeated with solidarity. In this new humanity there is no gender which can be considered inferior."[102] The description of this new status for believers as "sons" marks a crucial paradigm shift in the conceptualization of human identity. The status as "sons" replaces that of obedience toward the law. The proclamation of such a paradigm shift was more than teaching. It was part of the theology of baptism, where, as a performative speech act, it creates the social reality of the radically democratic *ekklēsia* of wo/men. Through the repetition here and in Galatians 3:28, this new identity is newly invoked.[103] William S. Campbell sees the topic of sonship as central for these chapters and as determining the argumentative text units:

> Sonship, as it is developed in 8:14-15, builds on the consolidation of themes in 6:12–8:11; this is evident particularly in 8:12-17, where the negative formulations that were applied to the Christian life in 6:1-11

100. Angela N. Parker, "One Womanist's View of Racial Reconciliation in Galatians," *JFSR* 34 (2018): 23–40, at 32–33. These coins are displayed online by the American Numismatic Society at http://numismatics.org/collection/1937.158.433.

101. Holladay, *Introduction*, 535.

102. Tamez, "Justification," 188.

103. James C. Walters, "Paul, Adoption, and Inheritance," rev. Jerry L. Sumney, in *Paul in the Greco-Roman World: A Handbook*, vol. 1, ed. J. Paul Sampley, 2nd ed. (London: Bloomsbury, 2016), 63; James M. Scott, "Cosmopolitanism in Gal 3:28 and the Divine Performative Speech-Act of Paul's Gospel," *ZNW* 112 (2021): 180–200, at 199.

> (death to sin, release from enslavement to sin) are replaced by the positive theme of divine "sonship." The argumentative unit is therefore 6:1–8:13 which is succeeded by a second unit beginning in 8:14 and continuing through to 11:36.[104]

A key constituent in this process is the cry, "Abba! Father!" (Αββα ὁ πατήρ, Rom 8:15). In the letter, it appears as a Greek transliteration of the Aramaic word אבא, which is the emphatic form of אב, "father"; this passage is therefore bilingual. In the days of Paul and Phoebe, this form was commonly used as an address to a father in the vocative as well as the noun "the father" and finally as "my father" in the first-person possessive form.[105] Here in Romans, it appears as the address of God after "(our) father" was mentioned in 1:7 and 6:4. Its meaning and theological ramifications will be further problematized below. For the moment, we should take note of the impressive similarity between 8:14-17a and its *Vorlage* in Galatians 4:5b-7, which shall be illustrated here.

Comparison of Statements about the Spirit of Adoption and the Cry "Abba! Father!" (according to the NRSVue, with revisions)[106]

Rom 8:14-17a	For all who are led by *the Spirit of God* are *[sons] of God*. For *you did not receive a spirit of slavery* to fall back into fear, but *you received a spirit of adoption* [, in whom] *we cry, "Abba! Father!"* . . . [T]hat very *Spirit* bear[s] witness with our spirit that we are *children* of God, and if *children*, then *heirs*: *heirs of God* and *joint heirs with Christ*.
Gal 4:5b-7	so that *we might receive adoption as children*. And because you are children, God has sent *the Spirit* of his Son into our hearts, *crying, "Abba! Father!"* So *you are no longer a slave* but *a [son]*, and if *a [son]* then also *an heir through God*.

This juxtaposition shows that the key passage has grown from Galatians 4:5b-7 to Romans 8:14-17a. It also shows a strong terminological consistency, much of which recapitulates central language and concepts: humans in a state of "slavery/enslavement" will be upgraded to "sons," which implies adoption; this happens through the "Spirit of God/his Son"; the manifestation of the ascendance to the new status is the "Abba" cry.

104. William S. Campbell, "'All God's Beloved in Rome!' Jewish Roots and Christian Identity," in McGinn, *Celebrating Romans*, 69.

105. Betz, *Galatians*, 211.

106. Similar text in the following comparative table is indicated by italics.

New elements in Romans 8:14-17a are, first, an explicit reference to fear that is now overcome (8:15). It is remarkable that, through the immediate connection with the "spirit of slavery/enslavement" in this sentence, this aspect emerges as the existential angst that most enslaved persons would have experienced on an almost daily basis given the precarious predicament of their lives due to the randomness of their treatment, including punishment, sexual exploitation, and the perfect legality of their execution. That enslaved people are expected to serve with "fear" is, for example, mentioned in Ephesians 6:5 ("Slaves, obey your earthly masters with [fear] and trembling") and other Jewish and Greco-Roman sources (e.g., Philo, *Virt.* 124; Plutarch, *Dion.* 40.3; *Mor.* 251a).[107] We may assume that the addition of this element is due to Phoebe's involvement in the production of this letter. How is this existential angst overcome? It is through "adoption" (υἱοθεσία; the Greek term means literally "placing a son").[108] This is a word that occurs more often in Paul's writings (and one other New Testament text attributed to him) than in any other text source from antiquity: apart from Galatians 4:5, it appears two more times in Romans (8:23; 9:4) and once in a Deutero-Pauline text (Eph 1:5).[109] Drawing on the Roman patronage system, the term describes the insertion of a person into a new family network. Its result is a new and indestructible relationship between God and the believer to replace the previous status of existential ambivalence. The believer now has a new "father" (in the sense of the *paterfamilias*).[110] That new status is publicly indicated by a name change; the old name is replaced by the new name of the adopting father.

The second new element in Romans 8:14-17a is the expansion of the idea of inheritance to that of becoming also "joint heirs with Christ" (8:17). Combining several concepts and images from previous chapters and

107. On the circumstances of enslavement in the Roman world, see above. See also Beverly Roberts Gaventa, *When in Romans: An Invitation to Linger with the Gospel According to Paul* (Grand Rapids: Baker Academic, 2016), 104.

108. Johnson Hodge, *If Sons*, 69.

109. The term "adoption" (υἱοθεσία) is not attested in the literature of Second Temple Judaism (neither in the Greek Septuagint nor with a Hebrew equivalent in the Hebrew Bible). It also does not occur in other New Testament texts outside of the *Corpus Paulinum*. It is attested, however, in several inscriptions and papyri from antiquity. Cf. Eduard Schweizer, "υἱοθεσία: D. In the New Testament," *TDNT* 8 (1972): 399; Johnson Hodge, *If Sons*, 69.

110. L. Michael White, "Paul and *Pater Familias*," in *Paul in the Greco-Roman World: A Handbook*, vol. 2, ed. J. Paul Sampley, 2nd ed. (London: Bloomsbury, 2016), 171–203. See also above.

pericopes (6:3, baptized into Christ Jesus means being baptized into his death; 7:4, you belong to another; 8:11, the Spirit who raised Jesus from the dead dwells in you and will give life), Romans 8:14-17 presents the quintessence of the theological and christological foundation of life in the Spirit to attain a state of freedom. The connection with baptism is more immediate in Galatians but still not absent in Romans (see above on 6:3). The sentence in 8:15 implies that the address of God is not only spoken but shouted, probably alluding to a *Sitz im Leben* of baptismal celebrations. Strategically savvy, Phoebe uses the first-person plural form of the verb "we cry." It invites all members of the assemblies in Rome to identify with the contents. They will readily draw on their own baptismal experience and thus accept the gospel message. And it is safe to say that there was an actual audible response from the different audiences in Rome when Phoebe recited these words, fixating the people in front of her with her eyes. A *forte fortissimo* "Abba! Father!" could be heard from the lips of most (but arguably not all) who were present. All of this helped to overcome a potential for rejection of Phoebe because of her gender, her identity as a gentile and potentially as a former enslaved person, and her city of origin.

Moreover, the participationist model of salvation that dominated Romans 6:4-8 is attested once more in 8:16-17 with another four compound verbs containing the prefix συν- (which means "with"), resulting in another extended *anaphora* (repetition of subsequent words or syllables):

To bear witness with	συμμαρτυρέω
being joint heirs with	συγκληρονόμος
to suffer with	συμπάσχω
to glorify with	συνδοξάζω

These two sentences in 8:16-17 also feature a climax or gradation (the key word of a preceding clause is taken up in the next phrase; see Rom 5:3-5). It makes for an easily memorable literary style. The last three elements are all about the connection to Christ. Therefore, this soteriological model demonstrates the equality of status that humans conceptually have with Christ and conveys terminologically the idea that believers are now, as heirs, "in Christ."[111] Conveying once more the idea of a free gift (see already 3:24), this is the rhetorical climax of the pericope. It adopts terminology from 4:13-14 about God's promise to Abraham, the

111. Oda Wischmeyer, "The Letter to the Romans," in *Paul: Life, Setting, Work, Letters*, ed. Oda Wischmeyer, trans. Helen S. Heron (London: T&T Clark, 2012), 245–76.

father of "many nations" (Rom 4:17-18), understood as both Jews and gentiles. "By presenting baptism as new kinship, Paul crafts a myth of collective identity for gentiles; they can trace their beginnings not only to their baptism into Christ but also to their ancestor, Abraham, in whose seed they were blessed. Baptism into Christ creates an aggregative connection between gentiles and Jews."[112] With that, the claim is even broader. The descendants are heirs not just of promises but also of the divine patrimony in its fullest sense.[113] Salvation according to these parameters is, in essence, about new individual and corporate life, and God's Spirit is a spirit of life. Before long, Phoebe will also inject the term "love" to enrich his idea for her audiences in Rome; no doubt, people "in Christ" are beloved children of God. "Paul goes on to speak of 'us' in even more extravagant terms, as those who are adopted by God, who are able to call God 'Father,' who are heirs along with Christ, who are even glorified with Christ as their 'brother.' "[114] A new personal status of glory awaits those who believe. "Adoption through the spirit is one of a variety of ways to conceive of relatedness; the spirit makes that relation both tangible and material."[115] Earlier, Phoebe conveyed similar ideas through the analogy of marriage in Romans 7:1-6, according to which a woman attains a state of freedom to enter a relationship with another man, which also conveys adherence to Christ.

A recurrent central word is "spirit," often as the "Spirit of God." In Romans 8:15, it is the "spirit of adoption" that affirms the new status as sonship and heirs of God. If the idea of "adoption" was little known in Second Temple Jewish literature, the opposite is the case with the concept of "spirit." It is well known that the Hebrew term for "spirit," רוח, is feminine. In Second Temple literature, the term designates the power emanating from God (1 Sam 11:6; Ps 51:11; 139:7; Isa 11:2-3; Ezek 36:26-28; 37:1-14; T. Levi 2:3; 18:11). It is, thus, somewhat equivalent to the notion of the "hand of God," although רוח conveys personhood more strongly. As an assistant to God, רוח is already present during the act of creation (Gen 1:2) and in creation (Prov 8:22-31; Wis 8:6), pervading everything (Wis 7:22-23). She guides and accepts all at her all-inclusive table (Prov 9:1-5). At the same

112. Johnson Hodge, *If Sons*, 67.

113. Jewett, *Romans*, 501.

114. Gaventa, *When in Romans*, 104. This powerful message helps to neglect the fact that these images are, once more, somewhat contradictory. For example, the new ultimate status as "heir" would require the death of the father, which is nowhere being considered and senseless in language applied to God (Johnson Hodge, *If Sons*, 183n18).

115. Johnson Hodge, *If Sons*, 76.

time, רוח is a concept that eschews exact definition and does not allow for a monolithic explanation. This dynamic female force has, however, been transformed to the neuter noun πνεῦμα in the Greek language. The usage in the Septuagint has, therefore, influenced New Testament writings (Acts 2:1-13; 1 Cor 15:45), even if they quote from their Bible (Acts 2:17-19 = Joel 2:28-30 [LXX]/3:1-3 [MT]).[116] In the process, female aspects have been erased from the overall image of God, which has been reduced to male aspects.[117]

This development needs to be seen in connection with the associated imagery of God, the "Father." Its centrality in New Testament Christology and theology is epitomized by the famous Our Father prayer (Matt 6:9-13; Luke 11:2-4) that is still included in liturgical worship of most Christian denominations all over the planet. Likewise, Jesus is depicted as pleading with God during his prayer in the Garden of Gethsemane, shortly before his arrest, with the following words: "'Abba, Father, for you all things are possible [Αββα ὁ πατήρ, πάντα δυνατά σοι]; remove this cup from me, yet not what I want but what you want'" (Mark 14:36).[118] Here, Jesus would have employed the same Aramaic word, "Father" (אבא), and, with it, also the same bilingual address of God as in the Pauline letters (Rom 8:15; Gal 4:6). This scene is featured at a prominent place in the gospel narrative. It shows Jesus in an intimate moment full of doubt and desperation shortly before his passion and death. The prayer and its address of God, however, are a gesture of trust and consolation. A similar address is also known from yet another, even more ancient prayer. It may have been spoken by an orphan: "I have no father, I have no mother. You, O gods, are my father, you are my mother." It is a prayer of a Hittite king and more than three thousand years old.[119] It also conveys a trusting relationship toward the deity. Hence, this element of prayer practice was not unique to ancient Israel or Second Temple Judaism (or Christianity).

116. Friedrich Baumgärtel, "πνεῦμα: B. Spirit in the OT; C. Spirit in Judaism," *TDNT* 6 (1968): 359–68; Hermann Kleinknecht, "πνεῦμα: A. πνεῦμα in the Greek World," *TDNT* 6 (1968): 334–59; Helmut Koester, *Paul and His World: Interpreting the New Testament in Its Context* (Minneapolis: Fortress, 2007), 207; Johnson Hodge, *If Sons*, 72–77.

117. Although, see, e.g., Elizabeth Johnson, *She Who Is: The Mystery of God in Feminist Theological Discourse* (New York: Crossroad, 1992); Virginia Ramey Mollenkott, *The Divine Feminine: The Biblical Imagery of God as Feminine* (New York: Crossroad, 1983).

118. The synoptic parallels have dropped the Aramaic address of God (Matt 26:39: "My Father"; Luke 22:42: "Father").

119. Itamar Singer, *Hittite Prayers*, SBLWAW 11 (Atlanta: SBL, 2002), 24 §2; Harry A. Hoffner Jr., "'The King's Speech': Royal Rhetorical Language," in *Beyond Hatti: A Tribute to Gary Beckman*, ed. Billie Jean Collins and Piotr Michalowski (Atlanta: Lockwood, 2013), 147.

Native American Concepts of "Father," "Spirit," and "Mother Earth"

The Shoshonis . . . include in their belief system *Tam Apö* ("Our Father"), the supreme Creator, represented by the sun and the moon; thunder, lightning, and wind spirits; spirits of nature that give supernatural power to medicine men or warriors and appear often as animals and birds; *Tam mbia* (Mother Earth); other spirits; and the spirits of the dead. That of the Dakotas includes Wakan Tanka, the Supreme Being; divinities of the atmosphere including the four winds; rulers of animal species; guardian spirits; *Maka* (Mother Earth); diverse other spirits; and the spirits of the dead. Native cultures generally believe that divine spirits reside in all things, and such immanent habitation constitutes the sacredness of all.[120]

Khiok-khng Yeo

An interpretation of Romans from a feminist perspective will need to problematize that the address of God as "Father" reduces the image of God to male aspects. Furthermore, it needs to explore what kind of relationship is envisioned with this address. To start with the latter, a prominent proposal took the address of God as "Father" as an indication of a relationship characterized by almost childlike trust.[121] This interpretation was soon challenged. According to Mary Rose D'Angelo, these addresses were directed against patriarchal family structures of the Roman world and its imperial cult, which celebrated the emperor as a *paterfamilias*.[122] While the countercultural potential of passages such as Romans 8:15 and

120. Excerpt from Khiok-khng Yeo, "Christ and the Earth in Pauline and Native American Understandings," in *Cross-Cultural Paul: Journeys to Others, Journeys to Ourselves*, ed. Charles H. Cosgrove, Herold Weiss, and Khiok-khng Yeo (Grand Rapids: Eerdmans, 2005), 196.

121. Gerhard Kittel, "ἀββᾶ," *TDNT* 1 (1932): 5–6; Joachim Jeremias, *Abba: Studien zur neutestamentlichen Theologie und Zeitgeschichte* (Göttingen: Vandenhoeck & Ruprecht, 1966), 15–67; see also the similar position by Robert Hamerton-Kelly, "God the Father in the Bible and in the Experience of Jesus: The State of the Question," in *God as Father?*, ed. Johann Baptist Metz and Edward Schillebeeckx, Eng. ed. Marcus Lefébure, Concilium 143 (Edinburgh: T&T Clark; New York: Seabury, 1981), 101.

122. Mary Rose D'Angelo, "Abba and 'Father': Imperial Theology and the Jesus Traditions," *JBL* 111 (1992): 611–30, at 623; Mary Rose D'Angelo, "Theology in Mark and Q: Abba and 'Father' in Context," *HTR* 85 (1992): 149–74. See also Martina S. Gnadt, "'Abba Isn't Daddy': Aspekte einer feministisch-befreiungstheologischen Revision des 'Abba Jesu,'" in *Von der Wurzel getragen: Christlich-feministische Exegese*

Galatians 4:6 is not necessarily clear, it is obvious that they derive their logic from the patron-client culture of the Greco-Roman world. It made sense to use this background to convey theological ideas. The specific aspect is that a status change is possible through a new patron. According to Romans, God is the higher patron, exceeding all earthly patrons.

This rationale for the usage of the term "father" also addresses the first concern regarding the shift to the male depiction of God and why it is effective for Phoebe's audiences. Because of the patriarchal/kyriarchal "pyramid of honor" in the Roman world, no female image of supreme authority would have been available to Paul or his avatar Phoebe to draw on. For the same reason, the argument in Romans 8:14-15 about adoption under the androcentric Roman law necessitated talking about "sons" due to their preferred situation; speaking of neither "children" nor "daughters" would have had the full weight of the argument. And the next pericope starts with a brief reference to "glory" (8:18) that also had its place in the honor-shame culture. Paul and Phoebe selected the imagery they knew would be understood by the audiences in Rome to convey their idea of a democratic *ekklēsia* of wo/men. In doing so, they were, however, complicit to some degree in perpetuating these political and religious structures. This is unfortunate—previous and subsequent pericopes of Romans demonstrate that Paul and Phoebe were not at all reluctant to use female imagery in their God-talk.

Future Glory (8:18-30)

A new pericope starts in Romans 8:18 with a call to logical reasoning: "I consider . . . " It comprises three text units. First, there is a thesis concerning present suffering in view of future glory (8:18). Second, typically connected with the conjunction "for, therefore" (γάρ, here in postpositive position), there are several sentences that form an explanation of hopeful suffering in the context of a groaning creation (8:19-27). Thus, it employs female imagery to convey its argument. Finally, the passage features a climactic celebration of the glory to be manifested in the elect (8:28-30). With that, this passage provides a message of encouragement for women and marginalized people.

---

in Auseinandersetzung mit Antijudaismus, ed. Luise Schottroff and Marie-Theres Wacker, BibInt 17 (Leiden: Brill, 1996), 115–31.

Rom 8:18-30

18I consider that the sufferings of this
present time are not worth comparing
with the glory about to be revealed to
us. 19For the creation waits with eager
longing for the revealing of the children
of God, 20for the creation was subjected
to futility, not of its own will, but by the
will of the one who subjected it, in hope
21that the creation itself will be set free
from its enslavement to decay and will
obtain the freedom of the glory of the
children of God. 22We know that the
whole creation has been groaning together as it suffers together the pains
of labor, 23and not only the creation, but
we ourselves, who have the first fruits
of the Spirit, groan inwardly while we
wait for adoption, the redemption of our
bodies. 24For in hope we were saved.
Now hope that is seen is not hope, for
who hopes for what one already sees?
25But if we hope for what we do not see,
we wait for it with patience.

26Likewise the Spirit helps us in our
weakness, for we do not know how to
pray as we ought, but that very Spirit
intercedes with groanings too deep for
words. 27And God, who searches hearts,
knows what is the mind of the Spirit, because the Spirit intercedes for the saints
according to the will of God.

28We know that all things work together for good for those who love God,
who are called according to his purpose. 29For those whom he foreknew
he also predestined to be conformed
to the image of his Son, in order that
he might be the firstborn within a large
family. 30And those whom he predestined he also called, and those whom
he called he also justified, and those
whom he justified he also glorified.

TRANSLATION MATTERS: Romans 8:19

The NRSVue renders this sentence as: "For the creation waits with eager longing for the revealing of the children of God." As in 8:14, the NRSVue and the NIV render the Greek noun υἱοί as "children" to obtain a gender-inclusive text version. While the term υἱοί is in the masculine plural, it is intended to include both "sons and daughters" and is best translated inclusively.[123] It obscures the allusion of the syntagm "sons of God" to the parallel syntagm in 8:14 with its connection to Roman adoption practices, on the one hand, and the christological title of Jesus, on the other.

The audiences in Rome have now been listening to Phoebe's recital of the letter that Paul had been writing in conversation with her for almost

123. See also the Revidierte Lutherübersetzung 2017 ("Gottes Kinder"). By contrast, the NASB 1995 and NKJV have "sons of God."

one hour. The attention span of people in antiquity was probably greater than today. But Paul and Phoebe had nevertheless decided to switch the imagery once again to ensure continuity of attention. Doing that abruptly would serve this purpose even better. Therefore, without warning, Phoebe now starts to talk about nature. She does so, however, in a different rhetorical style. After the almost triumphalist lines about adoption and inheritance with a loud cry of a confession (8:15), Phoebe now gets to return to a more theoretical discourse genre. This is already manifest in her first words, "I consider" (8:18); it continues in the explanations of 8:22 and 28 with "We know." These opening phrases indicate that the arguments will be based on strict logical rules.[124] Despite the new topic of nature, however, neither the sustained focus of the recent chapters on the experience and perspective of women nor the theme of "spirit" changes.

The first theme is suffering, cast in contrast to glory. Suffering was first mentioned in Romans 5:3, where it was part of a climax or gradation. Of course, anyone in the assemblies in Rome could relate to that. To repeat, this topic may specifically be related to either the experience of some in the audience following the expulsion of assembly leaders under Claudius or to Paul's own sufferings that had been shared in Rome by Prisca and Aquila or to the multifaceted sufferings of Phoebe, the "triple trouble" woman who knows all about intersectionality. And finally, most people in her Roman audiences lived and met in areas like the notorious Trastevere with its humid lowlands. Inhabiting overcrowded apartment buildings, many of them worked at the port of the Tiber and associated warehouses, if they were not even worse off as enslaved persons. It was not fun to be at the bottom social stratum of the city of Rome—or to live the misery of a firsthand experience of social death. Clearly, wherever Phoebe showed up to recite the text of Romans, everybody could painfully relate to the topic of suffering. The question was rather how bad their individual and corporate predicament was—and how to rationalize it accordingly. The "solution" is to contrast the present suffering with "the glory about to be revealed to us" (8:18). There is, thus, a goal taken from the context of the all-pervasive honor-shame culture, which is why everybody could relate to it as well. Some consider "glory" the key theme of Romans 8:18-30 because the term frames it (8:18, 30).[125] What does this "glory" refer to? The next section in Romans will explain it.

124. Hans-Wolfgang Heidland, "λογίζομαι, λογισμός," *TDNT* 4 (1967): 284–92, at 284.
125. Moo, *Romans*, 508.

Now the topic of creation is introduced surprisingly: "For the creation waits with eager longing for the revealing of the [sons] of God" (8:19).[126] The noun "creation, nature" appears in four consecutive verses, Romans 8:19-22; in the last three of them, even as the subject of the sentence. This demonstrates in impressive fashion the breadth of God's salvation through the associated salvation through Jesus Christ and the agency of the Spirit.[127] After all, Paul always had a broad vision of God's mission. First, he traveled as far as the geographic area of modern Greece to proclaim the gospel message; now, he sends Phoebe even farther West to the city of Rome. Ultimately, he hopes to travel even farther West to Spain (15:22-29). But he is able to think even further outside the box than that. Eventually, all of the earth is implicated in his vision of salvation, which is mentioned explicitly in 8:21.[128]

The identity of the "[sons] of God" is determined through the context of this chapter. The same syntagm is attested in 8:14; there it was determined that the gendered expression referred to a status change through adoption (υἱοθεσία), by which a person entered into a new relationship to the adopting father who becomes his new "father of the family" (*paterfamilias*). At the same time, that person receives the very honorific title of Christ, making believers effectively Christ's brothers and sisters. Their suffering and glory were already mentioned in 8:17, which is now being explicated. As in this sentence, Phoebe can later likewise use the gender-inclusive term "children of God" (8:21). The term "sons" is, therefore, not intended to exclude women. Their revelation refers to the gradual process of the dispersal of the gospel message. It may, furthermore, refer back to the *propositio* (main thesis) in Romans 1:16-17 about the revelation of God's justification through faith. In that case, as Susan Eastman argues, it may include Israel as the people of origin of that faith.[129] The sections in Romans 9–11 may then be understood as conveying Paul's own "groaning and travail on Israel's behalf, and on behalf of the vindication of God's righteousness" (see below, pp. 217–262).[130]

126. For the translation of "sons of God," which differs from the NRSVue, see comments under "Translation Matters" on Romans 8:19 above.

127. Richard N. Longenecker, *The Epistle to the Romans: A Commentary on the Greek Text*, NIGTC (Grand Rapids: Eerdmans, 2016), 719.

128. In this sense, Paul's vision of salvation somewhat approximates Indigenous concepts of "Mother Earth" as outlined above, even if differences remain.

129. Susan Eastman, "Whose Apocalypse? The Identity of the Sons of God in Romans 8:19," *JBL* 121 (2002): 263–77.

130. Eastman, "Whose Apocalypse?," 263–77.

In the next sentences, Paul and Phoebe revert to terminology of enslavement and freedom, applied to their discourse about nature: "the creation itself will be set free from its enslavement to decay and will obtain the freedom of the glory of the children of God" (8:21). The drama of reconciliation and liberation of the world is a cosmic one. It is an ongoing process, which is the very rationale for the persistence of the aforementioned suffering in the world. The idea of extending the message to all of creation is just as noteworthy as that of employing imagery from the experience of enslaved persons for this purpose.[131] Robert Jewett also notes that the enslaved persons and freedpersons who made up the bulk of the assemblies of Christ believers in the city of Rome could not entirely overcome exploitation by their masters and patrons, hence the saliency of the picture.[132] It shows that Paul and Phoebe care about the physical manifestation of this world and not just about some distant or eschatological spiritual world. Psychosomatic unity governs their anthropology; any idea of an immortal soul or a disembodied spirit are excluded.

An indication of the importance of the imagery of the enslaved creation is that it is joined with motifs yet again from the realm of women's experience: "We know that the whole creation has been groaning together as it suffers together the pains of labor, and not only the creation, but we ourselves, who . . . groan inwardly while we wait for adoption, the redemption of our bodies" (Rom 8:22-23).[133] A minor detail in this lengthy sentence is the fact that "adoption" appears as something that has yet to be attained while 8:15 introduces it as a past event. Three other aspects deserve particular attention: First, there is a lot of "making noise" in these soteriological passages of Romans. Taken from the liturgy of baptismal celebrations, the sentence in 8:15 already encouraged the audiences of Phoebe to shout, "Abba! Father!" Now, there is audible groaning of creation, which is the groaning of a woman (8:22);[134] it is followed by a loud cry of believers (8:23). According to Sigve K. Tonstad, "The Spirit is decisively on the side of the groaners with a voice that does nothing to hush the intensity because

131. Oakes, *Romans*, 149.

132. Robert Jewett, *Saint Paul Returns to the Movies: Triumph over Shame* (Grand Rapids: Eerdmans, 1999), 164.

133. This imagery is the reason why the pericope in Romans 8:18-25 has been one of the texts of choice for feminist biblical interpreters; cf. McGinn, "Approaches," 168–69.

134. Luiza Sutter Rehman, "To Turn the Groaning into Labor: Romans 8.22-23," in Levine, *A Feminist Companion to Paul*, 77.

the Spirit joins in with '*inexpressible* groans.'"[135] This is a description of a physical experience of both the natural predicament of creation and the corresponding salvation. Once more Tonstad: "The symphonic complexity is immense because music that is played in major key (8.15, 31-39) blends with musical scores played in minor key (8.22, 23, 26)—but not in the sense that all things are equal."[136] And Luiza Sutter Rehman: "*Not* to sigh quietly and practice patience is precisely the point here; the issue is to cry aloud, to protest, to demand abundant life and justice."[137]

Second, this passage dovetails imagery from two backgrounds: enslavement and women's experience. With the deployment of the term συνωδίνω ("to have birth-pains with"), Paul and Phoebe use imagery drawn from the vantage point of women. Paul has done so before, for example, in Galatians 4:19 to articulate his role as a nurturer of communities: "My little children, for whom I am again in the pain of childbirth until Christ is formed in you." Nancy Calvert-Koyzis suggests: "Paul would certainly have been familiar with the dangers of giving birth. His metaphor of labor would have been poignant in a house-church setting among those who had birthed and nurtured infants, but also for those who had lost infants or wives."[138] His fondness of imagery drawing on this area is also manifest elsewhere when he compares his relationship to his assemblies of believers to that of a nurse who cares for her own children (1 Thess 2:7). He can even complain that the people in Corinthians still need milk (i.e., breast milk) to drink (1 Cor 3:2). Beverly Roberts Gaventa notes about Paul's usage of these images "that one way in which Paul thinks of himself is not only as a father to believers (1 Cor. 4:15) but also as their mother. That maternal role is connected with the gospel itself, which ushers in a new age by means of 'groaning in labor pains.'"[139] Later, in the situation of Romans, it also makes sense to associate the inclusion of a similar passage with the fact that Phoebe, a woman, traveled to Rome to deliver and recite the letter, specifically in Prisca's assembly.

135. Tonstad, *Romans*, 239 (italics original).

136. Tonstad, *Romans*, 240.

137. Sutter Rehman, "Groaning," 75 (italics original).

138. Nancy Calvert-Koyzis, "The Maternity of Paul and the New Community in Christ: A Response to Hilary Elder," in *Strangely Familiar: Protofeminist Interpretations of Patriarchal Biblical Texts*, ed. Nancy Calvert-Koyzis and Heather Weir (Atlanta: SBL, 2009), 228.

139. Beverly Roberts Gaventa, "Romans," in *Women's Bible Commentary*, ed. Carol A. Newsom, Sharon H. Ringe, and Jacqueline E. Lapsley, 3rd ed. (Louisville: Westminster John Knox, 2012), 553.

This kind of imagery was well known and widely used in the ancient Near East, Second Temple literature, and the Greco-Roman culture where it was sometimes juxtaposed with loud exclamations or even vocal music. Thus, Isaiah promises: "Shout for joy, O barren one who has borne no children; burst into song and shout, you who have not been in labor! For the children of the desolate woman will be more than the children of the one who is married" (Isa 54:1; see also 66:7; 1QH 11:1-18). Even older is the deployment of the metaphor of giving birth in the prayer of the Hittite Queen Puduhepa: "Among humans there is a saying: 'To a woman in travail the god yields her wish.' I, Puduhepa, am like a woman in travail . . . , so grant my request" (*CTH* 384).[140] There is a possibility that Puduhepa spoke her prayer while being about to deliver one of King Ḫattušili III's children. Many references can also be found in later Greek literature; in Homer's literature, they are used as metaphors for the violent pain of wounds sustained in battle (Homer, *Il.* 11.269, 271) or the cries of pain of Cyclops (Homer, *Od.* 9.415). In all of these instances, the image is typically used to convey a crisis and suffering.[141] It also appears to be closely related to the character of the "wretched person" in Romans 7:24 who is actually a wretched woman. From this phrase, the question of "who will rescue me from this body of death?" still echoes and will be answered soon. For Paul and now also Phoebe, birth pangs are not the result of punishment but a sign of the arrival of the eschatological new life. Every creative change is the result of some form of suffering.

If the passage in Romans 8:22-23 dovetails imagery from enslavement and women's experience, then it taps into two of the three pairs of binary parameters of the baptismal formula in Galatians 3:28, namely, the status of personal liberty and gender. As will be shown later, Phoebe, the gentile woman who was perhaps also a former enslaved person, embodies all three of them.[142]

Third and finally, the statement in Romans 8:22-23 contains already the third cluster of extended *anaphoras* (repetitions of subsequent words or syllables) in this letter (see also 8:26).

140. Claudia D. Bergmann, *Childbirth as a Metaphor for Crisis: Evidence from the Ancient Near East, the Hebrew Bible, and 1QH XI, 1–18*, BZAW 382 (Berlin: de Gruyter, 2008), 57–58.

141. Sutter Rehman, "Groaning," 76; Bergmann, *Childbirth*, 59.

142. See comments on Romans 16:1-2 below.

Rom 6:4-8:

συνθάπτω	to bury with
σύμφυτος	united with (also: native)
συσταυρόω	to crucify with
συζάω	to live with
(also: ἀπεθάνομεν σὺν Χριστῷ)	we have died with Christ

Rom 8:16-17:

συμμαρτυρέω	bear witness with
συγκληρονόμος	being joint heirs with
συμπάσχω	to suffer with
συνδοξάζω	to glorify with

Rom 8:22-23, 26:

συστενάζω	to groan with
συνωδίνω	to have birth pains with
συναντιλαμβάνομαι	to help with

All of these compound verbs containing the prefix συν- ("together with") show that Paul and Phoebe have a grand vision of the unity of all components of the world and all groups of humanity. These three clusters of terminology all belong to the participationist model of salvation, evincing once more the centrality of the idea of being "in Christ" for the identity of Jewish groups of believers. The corporate exclamation of creation in response to its painful experience, expressed with double emphasis in Romans 8:22, is oriented toward the act of cosmic salvation that was already mentioned in 8:15-17. A similar experience is expressed in the Roman world. The *Eclogues* (or *Bucolics*) by Virgil (70–19 BCE) consist of ten poems on general pastoral topics. In one of them, Virgil predicts that the misery of the present time will come to an end because a regent would restore the world's lost golden age. Nature would produce plentifully as its manifestation and the stain of human impiety would be eliminated from the earth (Virgil, *Ecl.* 4.11.41). Roman priests and citizens soon proclaimed Caesar Augustus as this ruler who fulfilled Virgil's prophecy. The gospel message of Paul and Phoebe was similar and yet different. Jesus Christ is their regent and savior, approved by God through the resurrection. Yet, like in Virgil's poetry, the scope of this salvation is cosmic and also pertains to nature that will be liberated.[143] "The Law is linked with nature. . . .

143. Longenecker, *Romans*, 724–25.

However, God's mercy goes even beyond this initial revelation. The Christ event has opened the creation to a reality beyond nature, the reality of grace where God rules alone, above the Law."[144]

A postcolonial and ecological perspective recognizes this text as divine restoration of the totality of creation, which groans with pain inflicted by various destructive powers. In different cultural contexts around the globe, these powers have been labelled and conceptualized differently, even though core ideas often remain similar. For example, in minjung theology of South Korea, these forces are called *han*, while those threatening the destruction of nature are known as "nature's *han*."[145] Similar views exist in ecotheological hermeneutics born out of Indigenous worldviews.

The Earth's Body: From Painful Sin to Joyful Transcendence

"The whole creation has been groaning together as it suffers together the pains of labor" (Rom 8:22-23) metaphorically describes the punishment for the Christian original sin of the sensual body, projected onto any embodied being, including the earth. Paul the Apostle illustrates what is known as solastalgia in the current climate crisis.[146] The psychological distress at the unrelenting biocultural extinction expressed as sorrowful pangs is a collective experience, ostensibly increasing immediacy, intensity, and scope.The established Christian narrative of an apocalyptic punishment exacerbates the projections of fear, helplessness, and uncertainty. Still, Paul ensures redemption for the natural body, endorsing an eschatological relief awaiting the love of the Christian God, the Father.

Indigenous traditional worldviews—broad in their distinctiveness in expression and context—tell a different story. There is no inherent wrongdoing in the earth's phenomena. Instead, origin stories celebrate the body of creation as a cause of joy, gratitude, awe, and reverence. Everyday spiritual practices make sense of natural cycles to generate identity narratives based on the earth's relationality. The qualities and characteristics of the sky

144. McGinn, "Approaches," 174.

145. In minjung (Korean: "people's") theology, *han* is the compressed feeling of suffering in response to injustice and oppression and articulated as anger, despair, or pain. Cf. Andrew Sung Park, *The Wounded Heart of God: The Asian Concept of Han and the Christian Doctrine of Sin* (Nashville: Abingdon, 1993).

146. Glenn Albrecht et al., "Solastalgia: The Distress Caused by Environmental Change," *Australas Psychiatry* 15/1 (2007): 95–98.

and landscapes offer orientations for migratory seasons, nomadic movement, agricultural cycles, social affairs, and rites of passage. Flourishing depends on the environment's health, which consequently dictates tribal health. The human community's ability to assess and respect these observations will encourage the natural equilibrium.

Indigenous perspectives worldwide share remarkably similar views in conceiving the earth as a Mother. In this sense, origin stories influence spiritual exercises to ascertain the human family line back to the earth. Accordingly, group identity includes all creation as kin, each with part and purpose. This sensible world order generates belonging and responsibility for stewarding the earth and protecting all relations—human and other-than-human—in a shared environment.

Mother Earth is loving, nourishing, and generous, yet also has the power of threatening and destroying life. The labor pangs may be perceived as aiming to conciliate apparent dynamic opposites of life and death. Earth's phenomena are a constant—however elusive—quest for balance that we must aspire to encourage and support. Birth, growth, death, decay, and regeneration are stages that embrace the life cycle as a process of returning to the Mother. It is a manner of reciprocating to the earth as food for others. We become earth by living in service, compassion, benefit, kindness, and love for all creation. Every expression of life—including death—is a cause for courage, admiration, and hope for coming together to care for our first Mother. Service, therefore, becomes the path to happiness. In caring for the earth, there is no groaning, just chants of love.

Canel amo nican tocenchan in tlalticpac
Ca zan achitzin ca
Ca zan cualachic
Ca zan titotonio ca.

Zan ipaltzinco
Titiximatico
In Totecuio.

Canel umpa tocenchan
umpa tocenpopoliuiian
umpa tlatlalpatlaoa
ca oiccen onquiz.

~ * ~

Prayer for the Dead

Truth is our shared home is not here on Earth
we are only merely here
simply a good bit
to warm to the Sun

Only merely in this place
we come to know ourselves
in our Divinity
Truth is, our shared home is where our shared home is, where we are consumed,
where the Earth widens,
where we become related.

—Florentine Codex[147]

Yuria Celidwen

147. Translations of poetry from Nahuatl into English by Yuria Celidwen.

Romans 8:18-25 has become a key passage for discussions of ecotheological hermeneutics and is sometimes considered their mantra.[148] The concept of solastalgia mentioned by Yuria Celidwen can then be read reciprocally alongside Romans 8 as a way of exploring the connection between human and nonhuman creation.

The last extended sentence in Romans 8:24-25 has no fewer than three occurrences of the noun "hope" plus two of the verb "to hope." Paul and Phoebe explain that hope is, by its very nature, something invisible: "But if we hope for what we do not see, we wait for it with patience" (8:25). Similar to the ambiguity over "adoption," which is sometimes presented as a past event and sometimes as something projected into the future (8:15 versus 8:23), Paul has previously presented salvation as eschatological (see 5:9, 10; 1 Thess 2:16; 5:9; 1 Cor 3:15; 5:5; 10:33), but now it appears as a past event: "we were saved" (Rom 8:24). The solution is that salvation is "in hope"; it has not been fully realized yet and requires patience.

The next verses feature another example of the participationist model of salvation when announcing that God's Spirit helps humans in their weakness (Rom 8:26). As in Romans 6:4-8; 8:16-17, 22, they continue the grand vision of the unity of all components of the world, including humanity. Yet with the call for patience, human weakness is now acknowledged. Therefore, 8:26 is about the human inability to find words in prayer. But in this situation, the Spirit intercedes with groans that cannot be heard.[149] Thus, Phoebe adds a last facet to the exploration of the theme of groaning that is allotted a place in the grand vision of the unity of all: "Our own groaning . . . and the groaning . . . of the Spirit are united to the groaning . . . of the creation in a concerted prayer to God for the resurrection of the body."[150] Human weakness is, therefore, no impediment for the grace of God. The initiative of God through the intercession of the Spirit is affirmed another time in 8:27.

Given the length of the discourses of salvation in Romans so far, the spectrum of atonement and reconciliation imagery, and the treasury of terminology, it is surprising that the term "love" has been mentioned only once so far. In 5:8, at the heart of a dense section about reconciliation,

148. David G. Horrell, Cherryl Hunt, and Christopher Southgate, *Greening Paul: Rereading the Apostle in a Time of Ecological Crisis* (Waco, TX: Baylor University Press, 2010), 63.

149. Gaventa, *When in Romans*, 114.

150. Tamez, "Justification," 188.

Phoebe assured the assemblies in Rome: "God proves his love for us in that while we still were sinners Christ died for us." This vicarious death will soon be addressed further. For the moment, Phoebe has the joyful task of announcing a happy end to the drama of humans, the world, and God: "We know that all things work together for good for those who love God" (8:28). This is now the second occurrence of the term "love," and it will be mentioned more often soon (8:35, 37). It may be that Paul and Phoebe had decided to keep one of the most potent theological terms for the latter stages and climax of her proclamation. The presentation of human salvation through the initiative of God would clearly have been impossible without this term.

In the ancient Mediterranean world, the term "love" would have evinced female imagery. Gentiles were certainly familiar with the great goddess Isis who was invoked by the cultic name of "love" (ἀγάπη). Despite origins in the ancient Egyptian religion where she was depicted as a devoted wife and mother, Isis had become one of the most popular deities of the Greco-Roman world where she was venerated as a goddess of rebirth and life after death.[151] Judith Plaskow describes the lasting attractiveness of this goddess until the present day:

> Feminist followers of the Goddess find in her both a rich and life-affirming alternative to the (upstart) male God and the point of intersection of all the themes of new naming feminist spirituality involves. The Goddess is, of course, God-She, but in a clearer and more powerful way. Not simply a feminine reworking of the masculine deity but an ancient power in her own right, she gathers to her all the qualities and prerogatives of the goddesses of many names. She is Asherah, Ishtar, Isis, Afrekete, Oyo, Ezuli, Mary, and Shekhinah. She is lover, creator, warrior, grantor of fertility, lawgiver, maiden, mother, and crone.[152]

The connection of this phrase about love with the next about God's "purpose" (πρόθεσις) of selection is made audible through an anaphoric series of five Greek words in Romans 8:28-30, all starting with προ-: besides πρόθεσις, also προγινώσκω ("to foreknow"), προορίζω ("to predestine," twice), and πρωτότοκος ("firstborn"). These prominent lines proclaim a *pro*-active God who procures salvation according to the protocol of love to produce a large family (v. 29). In this context, the term

151. Sharon K. Heyob, *The Cult of Isis Among Women in the Graeco-Roman World*, EPRO 51 (Brill: Leiden, 1975), 67; Reginald E. Witt, *Isis in the Ancient World* (Baltimore: Johns Hopkins University Press, 1997), 243, 266.

152. Plaskow, *Standing*, 146.

"purpose" does not imply a doctrine of predestination but has been chosen to reassure the vulnerable and troubled audiences in Rome that their lives matter "in the grand plan of God for the restoration of the creation."[153] Questions remain about the background and meaning of the argument. Caroline Johnson Hodge correlates the passage to the imagery of sonship/adoption in 8:15-17 and argues that the point of this passage is rather status change along those lines of thought.[154] This interpretation is corroborated by similar terminology and imagery in Philippians 3:20-21, where Paul celebrates "our citizenship . . . in heaven" that is established by Jesus Christ, the expected "Savior" and "Lord" who will "transform the body of our humiliation that it may be conformed to the body of his glory." It evinces the intrinsic connection between the idea of status change and the imperial cult of Rome (see above, pp. 184–186). "Glory" is also the ultimate goal of the transformational process according to the rhetorical means of a classic climax (the key word of a preceding clause is taken up in the next phrase) in Romans 8:30.

Moreover, "image" terminology harks back to Jewish wisdom theology. The book of Wisdom presents Wisdom (σοφία) not only as "breath of the power of God" and "a pure emanation of the glory of the Almighty" but also as "a spotless mirror of the working of God, and an image of his goodness" (Wis 7:24-26). Wisdom is, therefore, conceptually similar to, or at times even identical with, the divine Spirit and the Logos. Philo, a contemporary of Paul, speaks instead of the cosmogonical "word" as God's "image" and "firstborn" (Philo, *Conf.* 146-147; see also *Opif.* 25; *Leg.* 3.96; *Spec. Laws* 1.81; 3.83, 207). He also knows rational spirits that were "formed according to the archetypal form of the divine image" (Philo, *Spec. Laws* 1.171). Human beings were created in the image of God's "image." This results in three levels: God, the Image, and humans in the image of the Image. All of this imagery resembles that of Romans 8:29, even if it lacks the term "wisdom." Elsewhere, however, Paul had called Jesus the "power of God and the wisdom of God" (1 Cor 1:22-24). Ultimately, Philo describes the believer in Christ with terminology of both God's Spirit and Jesus, the Logos. This is in accordance with the idea in Romans that believers become brothers and sisters of Christ (Rom 8:14).

153. Jewett, *Romans*, 529.
154. Johnson Hodge, *If Sons*, 111.

Romans 8 or the "Victory of Love": A Meditation by Adrienne Von Speyr

Medical doctor and spiritual writer of the twentieth century Adrienne von Speyr wrote an entire book about one chapter in Paul's letter to the Romans: *Sieg der Liebe: Betrachtungen über Römer 8* (*The Victory of Love: Reflections on Romans 8*).[155] Who is this woman and why did she choose to focus on this one chapter?

Adrienne von Speyr was born in 1902 in La Chaux-de-Fonds (Switzerland) and died in 1967 in Basel. Educated in the Protestant Reformed tradition, she became a Catholic after a long spiritual journey and after her encounter with the Jesuit theologian Hans Urs von Balthasar. Passionate about the search for God and his Word, she wrote nearly seventy books. Increasingly ill and blind, she dictated many of her writings to the German theologian with whom she also founded a secular institute of Ignatian inspiration: the Community of St. John (Johannesgemeinschaft). Her literary work reflects her knowledge of human suffering (her own suffering and that of the sick she cared for), of married life (she was married twice), and of the depth of her prayer life. She wrote, above all, commentaries on the Bible (Old and New Testaments), including four volumes on the Gospel of John, and meditations on various themes such as Mary (*Magd des Herrn*, 1948), prayer (*Gebetserfahrung*, 1965), obedience (*Das Buch vom Gehorsam*, 1966). And among this list of works, there is *Sieg der Liebe* dedicated exclusively to Romans 8. Why does von Speyr devote an entire book to one chapter in Romans? Hans Urs von Balthasar provides us with an answer. In his preface to the book, he states: "The eighth chapter of the Letter to the Romans is such a radiant, blasting trumpet-call in the tremendous symphony of the Pauline writings that we may let its message have its effect on us even when taken out of the context of the Letter."[156] This richness justifies the writing of her commentary of almost one hundred pages. To do this, von Speyr comments on the chapter verse by verse, distinguishing four parts:

8:1-11: The Separation
vv. 12-18: The Inheritance
vv. 19-27: The Hope
vv. 28-39: The Certainty

155. Adrienne von Speyr, *Sieg der Liebe: Betrachtungen über Römer 8*, 2nd ed., (Einsiedeln: Johannes Verlag, 2008).

156. Adrienne von Speyr, *The Victory of Love: A Meditation on Romans 8* (San Francisco: Ignatius Press, 1990), Kindle "Foreword."

Her commentary is clearly all about *the Victory of Love*. Believers experience a "separation" for a new life in Christ "today"—von Speyr insists on this word. They recognize their condition as "co-heirs" of the Son, which opens them to a magnificent hope. And, at the end, God appears as the great victor who, in the Holy Spirit, makes them participate in his own victory: "This certainty comes from God and is part of his love; for it would not be enough if God always gave us the victory without granting us, who belong to him, this certainty of being victors. . . . The victory belongs to them, is theirs, a tremendous victory, willed and guaranteed by God: the victory of Love."[157] This work is of very great density. It shines by its depth, by its hope, by its poetic style. I give here only one example, perhaps arousing the desire to discover it further: "This hope is a ray of divine light, a permanent opening in the closing door, a tomorrow in the midst of a today that already seems to belong to yesterday. Hope is hope of liberation, and that means of the possibility of a new choice that would lead men to become children of the glory of God."[158]

Florence Draguet

One may hope that liberating aspects in Romans, such as the adoption of a female perspective in some of the arguments and the respect for women as important collaborators in chapter 16, will serve as empowerment for women and all marginalized people today.

God's Love in Christ Jesus (8:31-39)

This pericope, which concludes the section on freedom through the love of Christ in Romans 6:1–8:39, consists of four subsections, featuring three sets of rhetorical questions and one final section with an *enumeratio* (a coordinated series of terms listed next to each other). It is located at the geographic center of the letter; there are 216 verses before this passage and 218 verses after it. Depending on how one structures the entire letter, this passage could be considered the final statement of what came before or the opening of the following section in 9:1–11:36.

157. von Speyr, *Victory*, Kindle comment on 8:38-39.
158. von Speyr, *Victory*, Kindle comment v. 21.

Rom 8:31-39

[31]What then are we to say about these
things? If God is for us, who is against
us? [32]He who did not withhold his own
Son but gave him up for all of us, how
will he not with him also give us everything else? [33]Who will bring any charge
against God's elect? It is God who justifies. [34]Who is to condemn? It is Christ
who died, or rather, who was raised,
who is also at the right hand of God,
who also intercedes for us. [35]Who will
separate us from the love of Christ?
Will affliction or distress or persecution or famine or nakedness or peril or
sword? [36]As it is written,

"For your sake we are being killed
all day long;
we are accounted as sheep to
be slaughtered."

[37]No, in all these things we are more
than victorious through him who loved
us. [38]For I am convinced that neither
death, nor life, nor angels, nor rulers,
nor things present, nor things to come,
nor powers, [39]nor height, nor depth, nor
anything else in all creation will be able
to separate us from the love of God in
Christ Jesus our Lord.

Paul and Phoebe start this pericope with a comprehensive retrospective question: "What then are we to say about these things?" (8:31a). It announces, on the one hand, that Romans 8:31-39 is yet another diatribe (on this rhetorical genre, see above, p. lxvi). On the other hand, it announces something like a—at least preliminary—summary or a celebratory moment of evaluative reflection, indicating that important aforementioned aspects will be revisited and previous terminology may recur. Among these are the topics of suffering, the death of Christ, election, and love as well as the unquestionable connection with God through the integration into the family of believers through the act of adoption. The analogy to the pericope in Romans 5:1-11 is particularly salient.

	Rom 5:1-11	*Rom 8:31-39*
Justify	5:1, 9	8:33
Suffering/distress	5:3	8:35-37
God's love	5:5, 8	8:35, 39
Death of Christ	5:6, 10	8:34, 39
Saved from wrath	5:9	8:31-34
Resurrection of Christ	5:10	8:34
Rejoicing in God	5:11	8:31-39

The broadest and most important aspect of this retrospective summary, however, is as simple as it is basic: "If God is for us, who is against us?" (8:31b). Such a rhetorical question naturally solicits a negative response.

With God on the side of us, nothing in the entire universe can really ever go wrong. This theological insight transcends and unites the diverse spectrum of previous images and discourses about salvation.

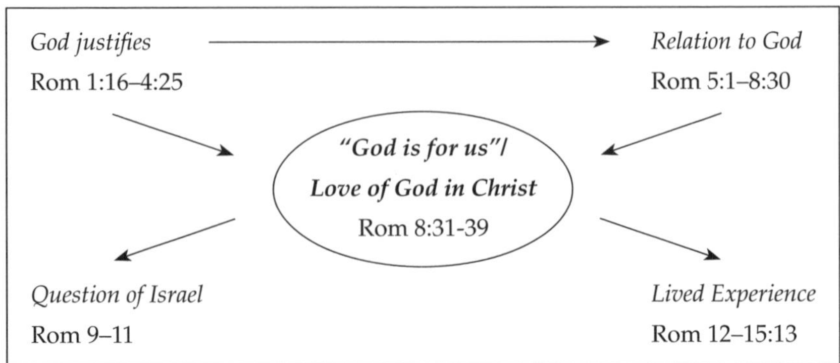

Deep theological or soteriological insights do not need to be complex. Despite a certain notoriety for convoluted theories and far-fetched arguments, Paul has demonstrated that he is also capable of presenting ideas in a simple fashion: "For the Son of God, Jesus Christ, whom we proclaimed among you, Silvanus and Timothy and I, was not 'Yes and No,' but in him it has always been 'Yes.' For in him every one of God's promises is a 'Yes'" (2 Cor 1:19-20). That barely needs any explanation if read in Sunday school. In theological or scholarly jargon, this basic insight about the life of Jesus "for" others is called "proexistence."[159]

In this pericope, all questions are formulated in the future tense, the ensuing phrases—however they may be interpreted—in the present tense so as to convey that they apply immediately. The decision to understand Romans 8:31-39 as a diatribe, however, does not mean that the passage cannot have an almost hymnic quality, considering, for instance, the poetic beauty of the correlative pairs "death/life," "angels/rulers," "things present/things to come," and "height/depth."[160] According to Sigve K. Tonstad, it certainly has a celebratory ring.

159. The term "proexistence" (and its German equivalent *Proexistenz*) broadly describes the life, death, and resurrection of Jesus on behalf of others and "for" them. Cf. Heinz Schürmann, *Gottes Reich—Jesu Geschick: Jesu ureigener Tod im Licht seiner Basileia-Verkündigung* (Freiburg: Herder, 1983); Ferdinand Hahn, *Theologie des Neuen Testaments*, vol. 2: *Die Einheit des Neuen Testaments: Thematische Darstellung*, 2nd ed. (Tübingen: Mohr Siebeck, 2005), 410–12.

160. Edward Adams, *Constructing the World: A Study of Paul's Cosmological Language*, SNTW (Edinburgh: T&T Clark, 2000), 184; Tonstad, *Romans*, 259.

> I will now invite the reader to imagine with me how this passage most likely inspired and electrified vulnerable believers when Paul's letter was first read aloud in house churches in Rome. To get this right, we shall imagine that the letter is read by its likely carrier, Phoebe. We shall further imagine that Paul's message is catching on to the extent that the believers find their hearts "strangely warmed," unable to stay silent when Phoebe reads aloud the most poignant rhetorical questions. Again, raising the stakes still higher, we shall try to get used to the thought that we are reading a letter that resonates like the Gettysburg Address and Martin Luther King, Jr.'s "I have a dream" speech.[161]

This manifesto about God's love would certainly have solicited applause and a vivid response. Its language is powerful, its images graphic. Due to the omnipresence of the cult of the great goddess Isis in the ancient Mediterranean world, its implications were particularly accessible for gentiles in the audiences in the city of Rome. But there is more. A sentence in Romans 8:32 alludes to a key passage from the Torah: "He who did not withhold his own Son but gave him up for all of us, how will he not with him also give us everything else?" This is a reference to the iconic narrative in Genesis 22:1-19 about Abraham's sacrifice, also called "Aqedah" ("binding" of Isaac) in the Jewish rabbinic tradition. According to this narrative, the angel who intervenes just in time to save the life of Abraham's son Isaac praises the father with the following words of God: "By myself I have sworn, says the Lord: Because you have done this, and for my sake have not spared your beloved son, I will indeed bless you" (Gen 22:16-17 [LXX]). This narrative had a rich reception history in literary traditions of Second Temple Judaism. In the book of *Jubilees*, for instance, heaven is imagined as a law court where Mastemah appears as Abraham's adversary and accuser (*Jub.* 17.15–18.16). Thus, the narrative in Genesis 22:1-19 came to epitomize human trial and obedience. Some traditions even extended the rewards of obedience to Isaac who has become aware of the impending threat. Taking initiative, he requests that he be bound on the altar (4Q225 2:4; Tg. Ps.-J.; Tg. Neof. I; Gen. Rab. 56:8). The employment of the narrative of Abraham's sacrifice/ the Aqedah in Romans 8 reflects these stages, not the text of the Torah (Gen 22), as the repeated questions about the adversary in 8:31b and accusations in 8:33 and condemnations in 8:34 show. The setting here is an eschatological law court assuming a judicial authority that brings charges against humans. In light of that, the crucial soteriological aspect

161. Tonstad, *Romans*, 259.

is that the authorities are on the side of humans.[162] Here is, then, another illustration of the powerful "God is for us" in Romans 8:31.

The importance of this soteriological and christological climax is conveyed in two further aspects. First, despite the concise nature of the "God is for us" (or in conscious contradistinction to it), Phoebe now lists a catalogue of seven forms of adversities (likely numerically corresponding to the seven questions in the pericope of Romans 8:31-39) to problematize divine love: "Who will separate us from the love of Christ? Will affliction or distress or persecution or famine or nakedness or peril or sword? As it is written: 'For your sake we are being killed all day long; we are accounted as sheep to be slaughtered' " (8:35-36). Similar lists are attested in various Jewish and Greco-Roman sources.[163] Paul too has used analogous catalogues before (1 Cor 4:10-13; 2 Cor 6:4-5; 11:23-29; 12:10). These lists invite the audiences to find aspects that correspond to their own experiences of antagonism. That would allow them to embrace the proclamation and accept the message. Of note is specifically the last item, "sword," because it is the only one that Paul has not mentioned in previous catalogues. It is a reference to capital punishment, which was carried out with a short sword or dagger (Matt 10:34, 38-39; Acts 12:2; Heb 11:34; Rev 13:10). With this noun, the authority of the Roman Empire and its political hegemony are in view. Rome had demonstrated its authority during the enforcement of the 49 CE edict of Claudius that led to the eviction of Jewish Christ believers from Rome (see below, pp. 338–339).

Second, in Romans 8:36, Phoebe also explicitly indicates the inclusion of a Scripture quotation to ensure positive reception. This is noteworthy because after lengthy Scripture citations in, for example, Romans 3 and extended references to biblical characters in chapter 4, there has been a remarkable absence of such quotations throughout chapters 5–8 (not counting the short allusion in 8:32). But now, a quotation from Psalm 43:23 (LXX)/44:22 (MT) is included, a community lament that targets the injustice that Israel has experienced at the hands of its enemies. Beyond

162. Wendy Zierler, "In Search of a Feminist Reading of the Akedah," *Nashim: A Journal of Jewish Women's Studies & Gender Issues* 9 (2005): 10–26; Christian A. Eberhart, "The Term 'Sacrifice' and the Problem of Theological Abstraction: A Study of the Reception History of Genesis 22:1-19," in *The Multivalence of Biblical Texts and Theological Meanings*, ed. Christine Helmer (Atlanta: SBL, 2006), 47–66.

163. David E. Fredrickson, "Paul, Hardships, and Suffering," in *Paul in the Greco-Roman World: A Handbook*, ed. J. Paul Sampley, 1st ed. (Harrisburg, PA: Trinity Press International, 2003), 178.

the immediate lines cited by Phoebe, it also recognizes God's loyalty that has been manifest in the experience of national salvation.[164]

In the end, Romans 8:31-39 is an epic hymn of victory. The NRSVue renders 8:37 as follows: "in all these things we are more than victorious [ἐν τούτοις πᾶσιν ὑπερνικῶμεν] through him who loved us." Dieter Zeller has coined the much-referenced noun "supervictory" to render the Greek verb in an attempt to express a superlative triumph in the midst of suffering, condemnation, and apparent defeat.[165] Beverly Roberts Gaventa puts it differently but means the same: "We need to recognize this for what it is: trash talk. Paul looks at all the harmful circumstances in which human beings live, he sees behind those the work of God's own enemies, and he confidently declares that God will have the last word. . . . Rendered in the vernacular, what Paul means is: 'You are going down.'"[166] Concluding the section, an impressive series (*enumeratio*) of tens in Romans 8:38-39 provides the explicit response to 8:35 that nothing "will be able to separate us from the love of God in Christ Jesus our Lord." In all of these theological images, the constant connection with God through the agency of Jesus, the Christ, is central. It is through Jesus that God has provided salvation for humans. Such salvation can be articulated as atonement (3:21-26) or as reconciliation (5:6-11). Salvation is only possible through this new connection with God through Jesus (7:3-4). It is imagined as a relationship based on love, mentioned twice (8:37, 39) in these two final sentences. This love is based on the initiative of God, not humans: the "supervictory" is because God has loved us, not vice versa; likewise, the assurance of a continuous relationship with God is because of the love of God. And the fact that this relationship cannot be destroyed is now being celebrated. All of these images convey the ceaseless and unlimited love of God for this world as the geographic center of the letter.

So far so good—but what about women's perspectives and experiences in this epic tale of "supervictory" and trash talk? First, are not the courtroom scenario and the military allusions once more derived from imagery based on male domains? Would first-century women have been able to fully relate to that kind of imagery? Although concerns like these are valid, some scholars have indeed affirmed that Romans

164. Alain Gignac, *L'épître aux Romains*, Commentaire biblique: Nouveau Testament 6 (Paris: Cerf, 2014), 328.

165. Zeller, *Römer*, 167 (German: "Supersieg"). The term has been adopted as "supervictor" in Jewett, *Romans*, 548; Gaventa, *When in Romans*, 104.

166. Gaventa, *When in Romans*, 40.

8:31-39 might address women's concerns.[167] This text follows, however, the extended sequence in 6:1–8:30 that frequently dealt with women's experiences. It is my opinion that, with its similarity to the arguments in 5:1-11, the pericope of 8:31-39 does represent more of a male perspective. This is not surprising in consideration of the fact that, starting in 9:1, the discourse returns clearly to deeply personal reflections of Paul about his own identity and relationship to his religious peers.

Second, what about the imagery of sonship and adoption as the new paradigms of human freedom and status change? Should feminist interpretation not criticize any hierarchical structures in christological imagery that demand the subordination as "sons" to God, the father, or the ecclesiological image of subordinate humans vis-à-vis Jesus as "Lord"? Should it not reject any of these binary categories as inherently oppressive? It may indeed be true that there are limits to the applicability of these christological and soteriological images in modernity. According to Romans, however, salvation could only be conceptualized as status change for humans from a low social position and as freedom from oppression; these images are derived from the matrix of the Roman patronage culture. This is why, for example, the image of God, the "Father," is invoked in Romans 8:15. It is my assumption that these images were accessible to both women and men, as Phoebe and Paul demonstrate. Their success was due precisely to the fact that they drew on ever-pervasive sociocultural standards. As such, these images helped Phoebe and Paul not only to understand the good news and redefine their own personal identities. They also empowered them to travel the world and share the good news elsewhere. At the same time, it is likely that these images were a contributing factor to the perpetuation of systemic patriarchy in the realm of religion and culture. It may be considered collateral damage to the core of the message of freedom and radical democracy, which included the equality of women and men.

In concluding the interpretation of the third section of Romans in 6:1–8:39 from a feminist perspective, it is time for a final overview and summary of all the passages written from the vantage point of Phoebe, a woman and possibly a former enslaved person. The compact conglomeration of arguments and imagery in these three chapters dealing with either enslavement or the situation of women or drawing on these backgrounds is surprising.

167. Oakes, *Romans*, 140.

Romans 6:1–8:30: Arguments and Imagery Based on Enslavement or the Situation of Women

	Enslavement	Situation of Women
Rom 6:6	. . . no longer be enslaved to sin.	
Rom 6:15-23	*Slaves of [Justification]* (you . . . have become enslaved to [justification]; 6:16, 18) (freed from sin and enslaved to God; 6:22)	
Rom 7:1-6		*An Analogy from Marriage* (Thus a married woman is bound by the law to her husband as long as he lives, but if her husband dies, she is discharged from the law concerning the husband; 7:2) (if she belongs to another man, she is not an adulteress; 7:3)
Rom 7:7-13	*The Law and Sin* (I would not have known what it is to covet if the law had not said, "You shall not covet"; 7:7) (Did what is good, then, bring death to me? By no means! It was sin that was working death in me; 7:13)	
Rom 7:14-25a	*The Inner Conflict* (For the desire to do the good lies close at hand, but not the ability. For I do not do the good I want, but the evil I do not want is what I do; 7:18-19) ("Wretched person that I am!" 7:24, with quotation from character of Medea)	
Rom 7:25b-c	So then, with my mind I am enslaved to the law of God, but with my flesh I am enslaved to the law of sin.	
Rom 8:1-17	*Life in the Spirit* (you did not receive a spirit of slavery to fall back into fear; 8:15)	

Rom 8:18-30	*Future Glory* (the creation itself will be set free from its enslavement to decay and will obtain the freedom of the glory of the children of God; 8:21)	*Future Glory* (the whole creation has been groaning together as it suffers together the pains of labor, and not only the creation, but we ourselves, who have the first fruits of the Spirit, groan inwardly while we wait for adoption; 8:22-23)

In light of this overview, one may say that the entirety of Romans 6:1–8:30, that is, almost all of the three central chapters, has Phoebe in mind and is influenced by who she is as a woman and likely as a traumatized former enslaved person. The successive topics and themes of sin and divine justification, freedom from the law and the human predicament, and life in the Spirit of God are all presented with imagery and terminology that belongs either to the realm of enslavement or to the situation of a woman. Their seamless consistency warrants the consideration that certain portions of Romans were authored either by Paul specifically for Phoebe as his avatar or by Phoebe herself, if they were not the result of a dialogue between the two (and potentially others). In the case of Romans 6:15-23, for example, the assumption about the involvement of Phoebe emerged because that pericope has no clear parallel to earlier letters of Paul. Beyond that, Paul and Phoebe knew that, most likely, the first presentation of their joint letter would be in the assembly of Prisca and Aquila who were good friends from Corinth. Both Phoebe and Prisca were leaders of their respective assemblies (see below, pp. 325, 326, 340–342). Hence, between the cities of Corinth and Rome, women were in charge of almost all things pertaining to the original performance of this letter.

With these considerations, I am now entering into a brief discussion with Elizabeth A. Castelli regarding her suggestion that the passage in 6:15-23 is neither about women nor about enslaved persons.[168] I propose that both a specific study of this section and the broad overview of Romans 6:1–8:30 allow a different assessment. While the applicability of the arguments presented in the various chapters and the impact of metaphors drawing on the realm of women's experience and enslavement

168. Castelli, "Romans," 294.

for christological and theological arguments on the audiences may be debated, it must nevertheless be acknowledged that their imagery allows mixed audiences multiple points of reference and identification from their lives. In Rome, a woman who was potentially a former enslaved person was tasked with the first performances, which took place in front of groups of people with a high percentage of former and current enslaved persons, among them again many women. Would a letter written neither about women nor about enslaved persons, as Castelli's challenge goes, have left any immediate or long-term impact? I doubt that.

Yet, while assuming the active involvement of Phoebe and the presence of Prisca in Rome, I am nevertheless resisting the temptation to think that this letter is the ultimate manifesto of freedom and Paul once more the uncontested hero behind it. His cooperation with Phoebe may have been his first co-ed experience of that nature. After all, Paul appears to have traveled without female accompaniment, and his special friendship with Prisca was of limited duration. There were, thus, limits to what can be expected of this letter in terms of insights into women's concerns despite Phoebe's participation. But the letter nevertheless features remarkable aspects that have contributed to its individual profile and importance through the centuries. Among them are images of enslavement that may previously have been successful in helping a former enslaved woman to conceptualize the gospel message and transform her life after the tragedy of her past. I am assuming, therefore, that chapters 6–8 in Romans, including 6:15-23, are also about women and enslaved persons who are privileged to hear the good news of liberation, new membership in the family of God, and ever-transcending love. These are important ingredients of the radically democratic *ekklēsia* of women and men, enslaved or free people, and Jews or gentiles.

Romans 9:1–11:36

The Election of Israel: The Depth of God's Wisdom

God's Election of Israel (9:1-18)

TRANSLATION MATTERS: Romans 9:3

The NRSVue renders Paul's emotional plea for Israel in Romans 9:3 as "for the sake of my own brothers and sisters, my own flesh and blood." The Greek text has "ὑπὲρ τῶν ἀδελφῶν μου τῶν συγγενῶν μου κατὰ σάρκα," so the noun συγγενεῖς remains virtually untranslated, as κατὰ σάρκα alone could be rendered as "flesh and blood."[1] While the translation presented in NRSVue is semantically possible, the words "fellow Israelite(s)" appear later in the letter (Rom 16:7, 11, 21) as equivalent of the same Greek term. The translation practices of NRSVue, therefore, are inconsistent and conceal the fact that the list of greetings in chapter 16 consciously repeats the vocabulary found in chapter 9 to designate Paul's Jewish compatriots. To maintain terminological consistency, a better translation of Romans 9:3 is "for the sake of my own brothers and sisters, my relatives according to the flesh."

The fourth and final section in the theological part of the letter (Rom 1:18–11:36) deals with God's election of Israel and

1. The NRSV translates συγγενεῖς here as "my kindred," which sounds somewhat outdated; the NIV has "my people." The Revidierte Lutherübersetzung 2017 renders "meine Stammverwandten," the Traduction œcuménique de la Bible "ceux de ma race," and the Reina Valera 1995 "los que son mis parientes," all of which are equivalent.

Rom 9:1-18

[9:1]I am speaking the truth in Christ—I
am not lying; my conscience confirms
it by the Holy Spirit—[2]I have great
sorrow and unceasing anguish in my
heart. [3]For I could wish that I myself
were accursed and cut off from Christ
for the sake of my own brothers and
sisters, my own flesh and blood. [4]They
are Israelites, and to them belong the
adoption, the glory, the covenants, the
giving of the law, the worship, and the
promises; [5]to them belong the patriarchs, and from them, according to the
flesh, comes the Christ, who is over all,
God blessed forever. Amen.

[6]It is not as though the word of God
has failed. For not all those descended
from Israel are Israelites, [7]and not all
of Abraham's children are his descendants, but "it is through Isaac that descendants shall be named for you."
[8]This means that it is not the children
of the flesh who are the children of
God, but the children of the promise
are counted as descendants. [9]For the
word of the promise is this: "About this
time I will return, and Sarah shall have a
son." [10]Nor is that all; something similar
happened to Rebecca when she had
conceived children by one husband, our

salvation for all (Rom 9:1–11:36). Its main themes are salvation and the destiny of Israel in connection with God's wrath and mercy. It problematizes whether or not universal salvation requires that God would have rejected Israel in favor of the gentiles, which raises the question of God's very faithfulness. These are matters of fundamental importance for the personal identity of a Jew like Paul and for his ongoing mission to the gentiles.[2]

The function of this fourth section in Romans 9–11 has been described as a scriptural illustration of the preceding third section (Rom 6–8) or as another step in the development of Paul's major theme (1:16-17). Some consider this section as the climax of the doctrinal section.[3] As we shall see, the three chapters of Romans 9–11 artfully combine a proclamation about God (theology) with the proclamation about Christ (Christology).[4]

2. A detailed terminological, syntactic, and rhetorical analysis of this section is presented in Florian Wilk, "Rahmen und Aufbau von Römer 9–11," in *Between Gospel and Election: Explorations in the Interpretation of Romans 9–11*, ed. Florian Wilk and J. Ross Wagner with the assistance of Frank Schleritt, WUNT 257 (Tübingen: Mohr Siebeck, 2010), 228–29.

3. Krister Stendahl, *Paul Among Jews and Gentiles, and Other Essays* (Philadelphia: Fortress, 1976), 3–4, 85; Beverly Roberts Gaventa, "On the Calling-Into-Being of Israel: Romans 9:6-29," in Wilk and Wagner, *Between Gospel and Election*, 255–69.

4. Wolfgang Kraus, "Die Bedeutung von Römer 9–11 im christlich-jüdischen Gespräch," in Wilk and Wagner, *Between Gospel and Election*, 516.

ancestor Isaac: [11]even before they had
been born or had done anything good or
bad (so that God's purpose of election
might continue, [12]not by works but by his
call) she was told, "The elder shall serve
the younger." [13]As it is written,

"I have loved Jacob,
but I have hated Esau."

[14]What then are we to say? Is there
injustice on God's part? By no means!
[15]For he says to Moses,

"I will have mercy on whom I have
mercy,
and I will have compassion
on whom I have
compassion."

[16]So it depends not on human will or
exertion but on God who shows mercy.
[17]For the scripture says to Pharaoh, "I
have raised you up for this very purpose, that I may show my power in
you and that my name may be proclaimed in all the earth." [18]So then he
has mercy on whomever he chooses,
and he hardens the heart of whomever
he chooses.

The opening of this section shows that something different follows after Romans 8:31-39 more specifically or 6:1–8:39 more broadly. Whereas the preceding section mostly featured first-person plural pronouns ("we"), 9:1-5 is dominated by the first-person singular: "I am speaking the truth in Christ—I am not lying" (9:1). For a moment, the identity of this "I" character is unclear, but the words "for the sake of my own brothers and sisters, my [relatives] according to the flesh"[5] in 9:3 disclose that it is Paul who considers himself an "Israelite" (9:4; see also below, 11:1). The following reflections on Judaism are, therefore, rather emic (i.e., from *within* the social group). And with that, there is a "strong personal presence of Paul"[6] in all of Romans 9–11. The difference is also marked by the mood that the sentences convey to the audiences. While the previous chapter was pathos-filled, hymnic, and solicited an enthusiastic response due to its diatribe style, 9:2 now mentions "great sorrow and unceasing anguish." Earlier feelings of confidence and joy are, therefore, replaced by sadness and pain. This is also expressed through, on the one hand, the double assurance of stating "the truth" and repeating the same with "I am not lying" (9:1) and, on the other hand, through Paul's wish to be

5. The NRSVue renders "for the sake of my own brothers and sisters, my own flesh and blood." For the alternative translation presented here, see comments above under "Translation Matters" on Romans 9:3.

6. Philip F. Esler, *Conflict and Identity in Romans: The Social Setting of Paul's Letter* (Minneapolis: Fortress, 2003).

"accursed" (ἀνάθεμα εἶναι, 9:3) for the sake of Israel.[7] After the ecstatic celebration of the epic drama of victory, it is now time to consider the other side. What about Paul's own people? This question appears to have been haunting him for a while.

It is interesting to reflect on the fact that, in the historical situation of the first performances of Romans, the person who spoke these lines was *not* Paul but still Phoebe. It is a gentile woman who now gets to express personal concerns of Paul, the Jewish man. After several paragraphs from the perspective either of Phoebe or of Phoebe and Paul, we now return to reflections that are clearly those of Paul alone, as the words "my own brothers and sisters, my [relatives] according to the flesh" in Romans 9:3 indicate (see also further biographical notes in 10:1 and 11:1). Phoebe is now back in her role of Paul's virtual face and avatar; she no longer speaks on behalf of herself.

Paul's sorrow is described by means of a synonymous parallelism in an artful chiastic pattern:[8]

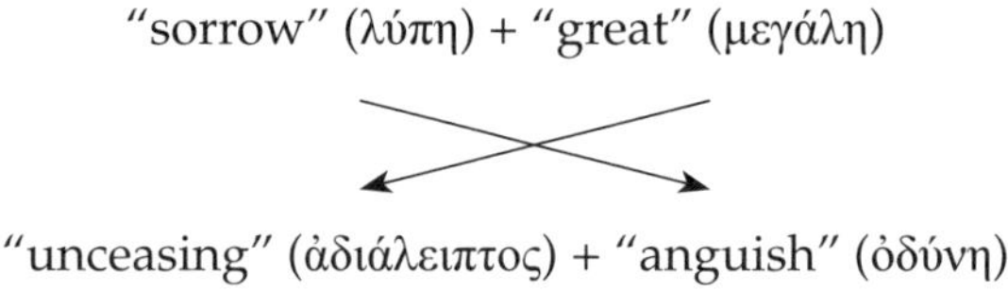

Paul is profoundly troubled; this mood provides the framework for what follows.[9] Paul's distress is about the "Israelites" (9:4). This term is interesting insofar as in this letter, Paul has always used the word "Jew" (1:16; 2:9-10, 17; 9:24; 10:12); elsewhere, his own religion is typically "Judaism" (Gal 1:13-14). He never used "Israel" or "Israelite." Now, however, he does; these terms will occur thirteen times in Romans 9:1–11:36. "Israel" is the sacred older name that had become the temporary designation for the Northern Kingdom but was applied to the Southern Kingdom in postexilic times (Mic 3:1; Isa 5:7; 65:9, 15, 22; Sir 17:17; *Jub.* 33.20).[10] Paul prefers

7. Richard N. Longenecker points out that these words are the strongest of all claims of truthfulness in Paul's New Testament letters. Cf. Richard N. Longenecker, *The Epistle to the Romans: A Commentary on the Greek Text*, NIGTC (Grand Rapids: Eerdmans, 2016), 782.

8. Folker Siegert, *Argumentation bei Paulus, gezeigt an Röm 9–11*, WUNT 34 (Tübingen: Mohr Siebeck, 1985), 122.

9. Sigve K. Tonstad, *The Letter to the Romans: Paul among the Ecologists*, Earth Bible Commentary 7 (Sheffield: Sheffield Phoenix, 2016), 264.

10. Joseph A. Fitzmyer, *Romans: A New Translation with Introduction and Commentary*, AB 33 (New York: Doubleday, 1993), 545.

to use it when talking about his own religious and cultural identity (Rom 11:1; see also 2 Cor 11:22; Phil 3:5). Israel is, however, especially known as the recipient of God's promises in the literature of Second Temple Judaism. And the concern that Paul is setting out to discuss is the possible abandonment of these promises. These chapters are just as much about the destiny of Israel as they are about the trustworthiness of God.

For the remainder of this first section in Romans 9:1-5, Phoebe's task is to remind her audiences of key identifiers of Second Temple Judaism. These establish its privileged position in salvation history. First and foremost, there are "adoption" (υἱοθεσία) and "glory" (δόξα, 9:4). Both terms have been recycled from their recent christological usage in 8:15, 23 (for "adoption") and in 8:18, 21 (for "glory"; see also 8:30).[11] As stated above, both terms have been derived from the honor-shame system of the Roman world. This means that, on the one hand, the audiences in Rome could easily comprehend them because they sounded very familiar. On the other hand, it implies that the socioreligious culture of Second Temple Judaism to which Paul belonged was to some degree also an honor-shame culture. The term "adoption" is, however, used in a somewhat different way in 9:4 because it is said to be the possession of ethnic Israel.[12]

The same applies to the other term. "Glory" also has another meaning since it is a frequent technical term for the divine radiance of the saving presence of God (Exod 15:6, 11; 16:10) and the place of residence of that presence in the temple in Jerusalem (1 Kgs 8:11; see also Exod 40:34 [tabernacle]). It is thus akin to the later rabbinic term *shekhinah* that designates the divine "dwelling."[13] Closely related is the fifth term, "worship" (λατρεία), which references the cult at this sanctuary.[14] Other elements are "the covenants" (αἱ διαθῆκαι) and "the giving of the law" (ἡ νομοθεσία,

11. The close connection of Romans 9–11 with 8:14-39 and 12:1-8 is manifest through, for example, a variety of shared terminology. Cf. Neil Elliott, *The Rhetoric of Romans: Argumentative Constraint and Strategy and Paul's Dialogue with Judaism*, JSNTSup 45 (Sheffield: Sheffield Academic, 1990), 257; William S. Campbell, "'All God's Beloved in Rome!' Jewish Roots and Christian Identity," in *Celebrating Romans: Template for Pauline Theology; Essays in Honor of Robert Jewett*, ed. Sheila E. McGinn (Grand Rapids: Eerdmans, 2004), 71; Wilk, "Rahmen," 232–35.

12. James C. Walters, "Paul, Adoption, and Inheritance," rev. Jerry L. Sumney, in *Paul in the Greco-Roman World: A Handbook*, vol. 1, ed. J. Paul Sampley, 2nd ed. (London: Bloomsbury, 2016), 64.

13. Michael Wolter, *Der Brief an die Römer*, vol. 2: *Röm 9–16*, EKKNT 6/2 (Göttingen: Vandenhoeck & Ruprecht; Ostfildern: Patmos, 2019), 34.

14. Paula Fredriksen, "How Jewish Is God? Divine Ethnicity in Paul's Theology," *JBL* 137 (2018): 193–212, at 197.

Rom 9:4). Both of them are organically connected in the Torah narratives. The Mosaic covenant at Mount Sinai (Exod 24) is related to, and in a way the product of, God's remembrance of the covenant with the patriarchs (Exod 2:23-24). It is the occasion where the two stone tablets of the covenantal law, engraved by the finger of God, are revealed and then proclaimed to Israel (Exod 24:12-18; 31:18; 32:15-16).

Nevertheless, the plural of the term "covenant" is rare in literature of Second Temple Judaism. Paul, however, uses plural forms in Romans 9:4 and Galatians 4:24 ("two covenants").[15] In the latter, he had developed "a rather adventurous and unique interpretation"[16] about the existence of two different covenants representing two women, Hagar and Sarah (the latter remains anonymous but can be identified as Sarah). The first covenant of Hagar signifies the one of Sinai that is degenerated; it represents enslavement and adherence to circumcision. The second "corresponds to the Jerusalem above" and represents freedom (Gal 4:25-26).[17] Paul has abandoned this earlier covenant allegory en route to another plural of the term in Romans 9:4. Now it is a reference to the multitude and diversity of covenants in the Torah and elsewhere. Covenants, even if labeled "eternal" (Gen 9:16; 17:7-8; Exod 31:16; Lev 24:8, etc.), periodically succeeded one another. Covenant theology is not static but dynamic; it is re-actualized in response to new existential and cultural challenges. These are also the reasons for innovative variations such as the "covenant of peace" (Isa 54:10; Ezek 37:26–27) or Jeremiah's "new covenant" (Jer 31:31-34 [MT]/38:31-33 [LXX]). Similar tendencies are manifest in Qumran literature. A "new/renewed covenant" (ברית חדשה) is mentioned in the Cairo Geniza copy of the Damascus Document 6:19; 8:21; 19:33; 20:12. It is different from that of Jeremiah 31:31 in that the sectarian community cherished special divine revelations called "hidden things" about halachic and legal matters. This assembly believed, however, that at least a selected group of its members was capable of fulfilling the divine law. For that purpose, it instituted a community council of twelve men and

15. The term "covenant" occurs eight times in four of Paul's letters (Rom 9:4; 11:27; Gal 3:15, 17; 4:24; 1 Cor 11:25; 2 Cor 3:6, 14). Thus, the theme of covenant is not too prominent for the apostle.

16. Jens Herzer, "The Significance of Covenant Theology in Galatians and Romans," in *Covenant-Concepts of Berit, Diatheke, and Testamentum: Proceedings of the Conference at the Lanier Theological Library in Houston, Texas, November 2019*, ed. Christian A. Eberhart and Wolfgang Kraus, in collaboration with Richard Bautch, Matthias Henze, and Martin Rösel, WUNT 506 (Tübingen: Mohr Siebeck, 2023), 473.

17. Angela Standhartinger, "'Zur Freiheit . . . befreit'? Hagar im Galaterbrief," *EvTh* 62 (2002): 288–303; Herzer, "Significance," 473–78.

three priests who were expected to obtain atonement on behalf of the community through obedience to the laws and the study of Scripture (1QS 8:1-10; 9:4; see also 1QSa 1:2-3; 3:22).[18]

Another entitlement of the people of Israel are "the promises" (αἱ ἐπαγγελία, Rom 9:4). This terminology is again familiar from earlier usage (see 4:1-24) and shows the interconnectedness of the entire section with the rest of the letter. God's "promises" to Abraham according to Genesis 15:5 have already been mentioned four times (Rom 4:13, 14, 16, 20); the plural of the term may have been chosen because of promises given to Abraham (Gen 12:2-3; 13:14-17; 15:4-5, etc.), Isaac (Gen 26:3-5), Jacob (Gen 28:13-15), and even Moses (Deut 18:18-19) and David (2 Sam 7:8-16).[19] After these various elements, Romans describes the climax as follows: "to them belong the patriarchs, and from them, according to the flesh, comes the Christ" (Rom 9:5a). Paul and Phoebe recognize Jesus as the Jewish Messiah; that is indicated by the choice of the honorific title "Christ," the Greek equivalent of Hebrew "Messiah" (both terms mean "anointed" in either language). But whereas the patriarchs are said to firmly belong to them (NIV translates more literal: "theirs are the patriarchs"), Jesus is "from them, according to the flesh." The words "from them" associate the aspect of Jewish origins just as much as they convey a sense of separation, and "according to the flesh" is another limitation of the affiliation—in Romans, the realm of "the Spirit" is the one of the new eon (2:29; see also 1:3-4).[20] This is a first indication, carefully introduced, to the problem that Phoebe now has to present on behalf of Paul.

The pericope of Romans 9:1-5 concludes with a doxology in 9:5b-c. The syntax of these phrases is the subject of a long-standing scholarly debate.[21] While the minor matter of punctuation leads to considerably different syntactic results, the following reading, which differs from the NRSVue, is preferable: "and from them, according to the flesh, comes the Christ. [May] God who is over all [be] blessed forever. Amen."[22]

18. Richard J. Bautch, *Glory and Power, Ritual and Relationship: The Sinai Covenant in the Postexilic Period*, LHBOTS 471 (New York: T&T Clark, 2009), 138–53.

19. Longenecker, *Romans*, 786–87.

20. Wolter, *Römer*, 2:36–37.

21. Robert Jewett, *Romans: A Commentary*, Hermeneia (Minneapolis: Fortress, 2007), 567–68; Longenecker, *Romans*, 787–91.

22. Alphonse Maillot, *L'épître aux Romains: Epître de l'œcuménisme et théologie de l'histoire* (Paris: Le Centurion; Geneva: Labor et Fides, 1984), 238, 240; Brendan Byrne, *Romans*, SP 6 (Collegeville, MN: Liturgical Press, 1996), 288; Beverly Roberts Gaventa, *When in Romans: An Invitation to Linger with the Gospel According to Paul* (Grand Rapids: Baker Academic, 2016), 63.

Folker Siegert has noted that there is a threefold pattern of *homoioteleuton* (similar sounding endings in close proximity) in 9:4, with identical -θεσία, -α, -αι/-θεσία, -α, -αι endings in sequence.[23] In addition, an impressive combination of *homoioteleuton* and a *paronomasia* (repetition of the same word or word stem in close proximity) is manifest in the eightfold repetition of Greek -ῶν/ὧν/ὤν:[24]

Rom 9:3	τῶν ἀδελφῶν (bis) τῶν συγγενῶν (bis)	"of the brothers" "of the relatives"[25]
Rom 9:4b	ὧν	"of whom"
Rom 9:5a Rom 9:5b Rom 9:5c	ὧν ὧν ὤν	"of whom" "of whom" "(who) was"

These repeated rhetorical features are intended to underscore the pathos of the paragraph and solicit a favorable reception of what has already been announced at the outset as an ambiguous section.

In Romans 9:1-5, Paul summarizes important aspects from Jewish history. All of the promises that the assemblies in Rome received and celebrate belong first and foremost to Israel.[26] But this rich spectrum of privileges and prerogatives is commensurate to Paul's sorrow, which will be explicated and correlated with a vision of salvation for Israel in the next paragraphs. Yet, the desperation of Paul about Israel's traditional privileges, conveyed by Phoebe to the audiences in Rome, is echoed in our days by the Jewish scholar Judith Plaskow:

> When, for example, God enters into a covenant with Abraham and says to him, "This is my covenant, which you shall keep, between me and you and your descendants after you: Every male among you shall be circumcised" (Gen. 17:10), women can hear this only as establishing our marginality. Even if circumcision is not itself the covenant but only the sign of the covenant, what role can women have in the covenant community when the primary symbol of the covenant pertains only to men? This important passage seems to presuppose a religious community composed of males only, an impression reinforced by other

23. Siegert, *Argumentation*, 122.

24. English translations are literal and do not necessarily follow the NRSVue.

25. For this alternate translation of the noun "relatives," which differs from "flesh and blood" in the NRSVue, see the comments on Romans 9:3 above.

26. Jewett, *Romans*, 566; Longenecker, *Romans*, 787.

texts. The covenant at Sinai is spoken in male pronouns, for example, and its content assumes male hearers.[27]

Plaskow feels excluded from the covenantal traditions of Judaism because she is a woman. Similar concerns have previously been voiced about the Ten Commandments (Exod 20:2-17/Deut 5:6-21). The larger concern is frustration about the invisibility of women in these constitutive and normative text traditions of Judaism. Such feelings may lead to the abandonment of religions or to creative attempts to renew and reenvision the ancient tradition.[28] The latter is what Paul, Phoebe, and their communities of Jewish believers in Christ did. Their goal was the establishment of inclusive communities across gender and status boundaries, the democratic *ekklēsia* of wo/men. A "triple trouble" person, Phoebe herself is the embodiment of the inclusive ethos of these groups and its successful implementation.

A particular feature of the pericope in Romans 9:1-5 is its point of departure in God's free and generous love that extends justification to all who believe in Christ Jesus. This expression of love leads to the question about God's previous promises to Israel. But at the same time, the point of departure is also the answer to this question since God's covenant and faithfulness have not changed.[29]

Phoebe now offers her audiences in Rome a midrash on Israel and election, seen in light of the free gift of divine mercy (Rom 9:6-18). The connection with the preceding paragraph is established through the terms "Israelites" and "Israel" in 9:4, 6 as well as through "flesh" in 9:3, 8. Phoebe addresses a problem related to the earlier claim that the gospel is "God's saving power" (1:16). Now the urgent question is why many among Israel have not yet accepted the faith in Jesus. The response: "It is not as though the word of God had failed" (9:6a). An extensive review of divine election follows. Returning one more time to Abraham in his capacity as "father of many nations" (see above, 4:17, 18), the letter explores several foundational narratives mostly from the Torah (Gen

27. Judith Plaskow, *Standing Again at Sinai: Judaism from a Feminist Perspective* (San Francisco: HarperSanFrancisco, 1991), 82. See also Judith Plaskow, "Bringing a Daughter into the Covenant," in *WomanSpirit Rising: A Feminist Reader in Religion*, ed. Carol P. Christ and Judith Plaskow (New York: HarperOne, 1992), 179–84.

28. Elizabeth A. Castelli, "Romans," in *Searching the Scriptures*, vol. 2: *A Feminist Commentary*, ed. Elisabeth Schüssler Fiorenza (New York: Crossroad, 1994), 292–93.

29. Valérie Nicolet Anderson, "Une relecture paulinienne de l'histoire d'Israël (Rm 9–11)," in *Ancient and Modern Scriptural Historiography = L'historiographie biblique, ancienne et modern*, ed. George J. Brooke and Thomas Römer, BETL 207 (Leuven: Leuven University Press; Peeters, 2007), 274.

18:10; 21:12; 25:23; Mal 1:2-3; Exod 9:16; 33:19). The lesson is that among Abraham's sons, Isaac was chosen while other descendants, such as Ishmael (Gen 16:15) or the sons of Keturah (25:1-4), were not. The same applies to Isaac's and Rebecca's sons: Jacob was chosen, but not Esau (Rom 9:11-13). The principle of election is, therefore: "it is not the children of the flesh who are the children of God, but the children of the promise are counted as descendants" (9:8).[30]

Paul had previously employed similar ideas about true religious-cultural identity, for example, in 1 Corinthians 10:18: "Consider the people of Israel: Are not those who eat the sacrifices partners in the altar?" Romans now presents a similar argument that "not all those descended from Israel are Israelites" (οὐ γὰρ πάντες οἱ ἐξ Ἰσραὴλ οὗτοι Ἰσραήλ, 9:6). To avoid overinterpretation and specifically misinterpretation, it is important to adopt a literal rendition of this statement, which is not about a "true" or "real" or "eschatological" or "spiritual" Israel.[31] Instead, it simply observes that the Torah narratives trace the history of Israel through Isaac (Gen 17:21) while acknowledging that other sons established their lives and kinship groups elsewhere. Hence, Abraham's firstborn son Ishmael received God's blessing although he remained outside of the covenant. Nonetheless, he became the father of twelve princes and the ancestor of many descendants. Known as the "Ishmaelites," they ultimately became the Arabs (Gen 17:20). And the descendants of Esau settled in Edom to establish the culture of the Edomites (36:1).

In these sample narratives from the Torah, women are mentioned alongside their husbands who are the direct recipients of the divine promises. *Prima vista*, Sarah may not appear as a model of godly conduct as she laughs at the idea of bearing a child at her advanced age (Gen 18:12-15). But Abraham himself was the first to find the divine proposal that he may have a son with his wife funny (17:17). By contrast, Rebecca is the one who takes initiative upon her first encounter with Isaac, who remains passive (24:62-67).[32] Women are, therefore, also noteworthy characters. In Romans 9, Sarah and Rebecca appear next to their husbands. Women are, however, of interest only as wives of husbands; they are support-

30. As in Romans 4:13, 18 above (and earlier in Gal 3:16), the literal translation of the Greek noun σπέρμα in Romans 9:8 is "sperm."

31. See also Wolter, *Römer*, 2:48. Previously, the NRSV had "For not all Israelites truly belong to Israel."

32. Irmtraud Fischer, "Genesis 12–50: Die Ursprungsgeschichte Israels als Frauengeschichte," in *Kompendium feministische Bibelauslegung*, ed. Luise Schottroff and Marie-Theres Wacker, 2nd ed. (Gütersloh: Kaiser; Gütersloher Verlagshaus, 1999), 18.

ing actresses at best. The androcentrism of the constitutive narratives of Second Temple Judaism is, once again, on display and has left its marks. This is surprising since other sections of Romans successfully resist such androcentric tendencies (see Rom 6–8, etc.).

Paul and Phoebe reenvision the principle of election in Jewish tradition. They do not question it as such. But they put the emphasis on God's purpose, not Israel's failure. Thus, they focus on the initiative of God who administers election by stressing that the intention is the salvation of all, not condemnation.[33] Therefore, the verb "to be merciful" is the key term in this chapter. It also pervades the last sample narrative in Romans 9:15-17. Its focus is the resistance of the indocile Pharaoh to Israel's liberation from bondage in Egypt (Exod 3:10–12:36 [LXX]) by relating his conversation with Moses between the plague of boils and the plague of hail (the sixth and seventh plague; Exod 9:16 [LXX]). Historical accuracy aside, this story is another illustration of God's mercy and sovereignty.[34] Pharaoh's resistance and Israel's election are both due to God's initiative (Rom 9:18). "Israel exists not by virtue of its own faithfulness or goodness but by God's creative act."[35] Election happens as an act of God's freedom and mercy.[36]

Universal Salvation in Romans 9–10

Romans 9–10 belongs to the third section of Paul's letter (Rom 9:1–11:36).[37] The importance of this section as the climax of Romans is appreciated by many current interpreters of the letter, compared to earlier interpreters who had considered the three chapters as diverting from the

33. Elsa Tamez, "Der Brief an die Gemeinde in Rom: Eine feministische Lektüre," in Schottroff and Wacker, *Kompendium feministische Bibelauslegung*, 570.

34. Arland J. Hultgren, *Paul's Letter to the Romans: A Commentary* (Grand Rapids: Eerdmans, 2011), 367. See also the observation by Beverly Roberts Gaventa: "The Exodus account affirms both that God hardened Pharaoh's heart *and* that Pharaoh hardened his own heart (Exod 8:28; 9:34; 13:15; see also 1 Sam 6:6), but it is noteworthy that Paul says nothing of Pharaoh's disposition to be stubborn" (Gaventa, "Israel," 264 [italics original]).

35. Gaventa, *When in Romans*, 65.

36. Jewett, *Romans*, 582; Frank J. Matera, *Romans*, Paideia: Commentaries on the New Testament (Grand Rapids: Baker Academic, 2010), 224–26.

37. Thomas H. Tobin, *Paul's Rhetoric in Its Contexts: The Argument of Romans* (Peabody, MA: Hendrickson, 2004), 320, 379.

topic of Romans 1–8.[38] Recent studies attest that the different sections of Romans represent an articulated entity, with the subject of each leading to the next.[39]

In Romans 9–10, righteousness continues as a dominant theme. The two chapters discuss Israel's precarious situation (9:2-3) because of Israel's misconceived pursuit of righteousness on the basis of the law (9:30–10:3). This prevents them from benefitting from the promise of God's saving righteousness. Paul employs extensive Scripture citations (9:25-26, 27-29; 10:5-21) to show that the inclusion of gentiles does not deny God's faithfulness to the promises to Israel (9:6a, 19).[40]

Romans 9–10 gives proof that the righteousness that comes from God fulfills the law, because Christ is the goal of the law (10:4) so that God's righteousness might reach everyone who believes. Romans 10:4 must be related to 8:1-4, which suggests that God, by sending Jesus to die for us, has fulfilled the just requirement of the law in those who walk according to the Spirit. In these chapters, a shift from the law to Christ as the center of the revelation of righteousness depends on the use of the verb of election, "to call" (καλέω), which is used within the context of the distinction between the righteousness from the law and the righteousness from faith (9:31-32; 10:3-21).

Romans 9:6-18 is a detailed exposition of how God's relationship with Israel had never been based on works of the law but on God's sovereign will to show mercy. The potter-clay metaphor (9:20-23) describes God's creative power and sovereign freedom in relation to human beings, who must show creaturely obedience (Gen 2:7, 9, 19; Isa 29:16; 45:9; Jer 18:1-6; Lam 4:2; Wis 15:7; Sir 33:10-13).[41] Two specific terms in Romans 9:22-23 express a basic distinction among human beings in the divine act of creation: "objects of mercy" and "objects of wrath." Both phrases correspond to similar ones in verse 21, which endorses the right of the potter to make out of the same lump "one object for special use" and "another for ordinary use." Since both vessels are shaped

38. Douglas J. Moo, *The Epistle to the Romans*, NICNT (Grand Rapids: Eerdmans, 1996), 547–52; Thomas Schreiner, *Romans*, 2nd ed., BECNT 6 (Grand Rapids: Baker Academic, 2018), 460.

39. See, for instance, Tobin, *Rhetoric*, 84–87; Schreiner, *Romans*, 460.

40. Schreiner, *Romans*, 462.

41. Moo, *Romans*, 603; Schreiner, *Romans*, 504–5.

from the same clay lump (9:21), they share the characteristic fragility of human nature, united by sinfulness and the need for salvation.

The vessels of mercy, however, are distinguished through the verb καλέω. This verb refers specifically to God's creative power in the life of Abraham (Rom 4:17); it determined the naming of descendants in Israel (9:7), unambiguously described as "not by works" (9:12) but by God's mercy (9:15-16). The same divine creative power embraces those who believe, Jews and gentiles (9:24), who are being "prepared" for God's glory (9:22-23). This verb describes the identity of Christians because, having experienced the mercy of God's call (9:24), they are enabled by the Spirit to live by the grace of God's call, since all those who call on the name of the Lord are saved (10:12-13).

MarySylvia Nwachukwu

As MarySylvia Nwachukwu notes, Paul and Phoebe quote extensively from Jewish Scriptures in this discussion of the status of Israel. That section of Romans 9–10 features at least thirty-seven quotations and allusions.[42] And chapter 9 contains more Scripture references than the subsequent two chapters. These quotations are primarily from the Torah, usually for the purpose of anchoring the argument in the foundations of Israel's heritage, and from the prophetic books (with a preference for Isaiah[43]), often for the purpose of christological or soteriological application. Fewer quotations are from the books of Psalms and Samuel–Kings; one concluding quotation is from the book of Job. All of these references draw on the Greek text of the Septuagint.[44] That text can, at times, differ rather substantially from the Hebrew text (MT).[45]

42. Castelli, "Romans," 293; Nicolet Anderson, "Une relecture," 273; Matera, *Romans*, 252–55.

43. Tonstad, *Romans*, 267–85.

44. On the one exception in Romans 9:33 where two amalgamated quotations from Isaiah 28:16 and 8:14 are included that also amalgamate the Hebrew and Greek version, see the comments below, p. 240.

45. Jewett, *Romans*, 719–20.

Scripture Use in Romans 9–11[46]

Rom 9		*Rom 10*		*Rom 11*	
9:7	Gen 21:12	10:5	Lev 18:5	11:2	1 Sam 12:22; Ps 94:14
9:9	Gen 18:10, 14	10:6-8	Deut 9:4; 30:12-14		
9:12	Gen 25:23			11:3	1 Kgs 19:10, 14
9:13	Mal 1:2-3	10:11	Isa 28:16	11:4	1 Kgs 19:18
9:15	Exod 33:19	10:13	Joel 2:32	11:8	Isa 29:10; Deut 29:4
9:17	Exod 9:16	10:15	Isa 52:7		
9:20	Isa 29:16; 45:9	10:16	Isa 53:1	11:9b-10	Ps 69:22-23
9:25	Hos 2:23	10:18	Ps 19:3	11:26-27	Isa 59:20-21; 27:9
9:26	Hos 1:10	10:19	Deut 32:21		
9:27-28	Isa 10:22-23; Hos 1:10	10:20	Isa 65:1	11:34	Isa 40:13
9:29	Isa 1:9	10:21	Isa 65:2	11:35	Job 41:3
9:33	Isa 28:16; 8:14				

Such continuous references to Jewish Scriptures demonstrate that Paul and Phoebe intend these paragraphs to convince those in the audiences of traditional Jewish origins or those who want to adopt this particular identity (on the latter, see Rom 2:17). Any argument based on these Scripture references would have gained in authoritativeness.

God's Wrath and Mercy (9:19-29)

From a formal perspective, the second pericope is another diatribe (on this rhetorical genre, see above, p. lxvi) introducing an objection to the doctrine of God's selective purpose (9:19) and then responding to it (9:20-29). The latter is primarily done by means of Scripture quotations.

TRANSLATION MATTERS: Romans 9:20

The NRSVue translates the response to a question as follows: "But who indeed are you, a human, to argue with God?" (Rom 9:20, the NRSV and NIV are similar). This translation obscures once more[47] the fact that the Greek words ὦ ἄνθρωπε, "O human," are in the vocative and, as such, directly address the dialogue partner (or the audiences in Rome).

46. Matera, *Romans*, 253.

47. See the comments above under "Translation Matters" on Romans 2:1, p. 66.

Rom 9:19-29

[19]You will say to me then, "Why then does he still find fault? For who can resist his will?" [20]But who indeed are you, a human, to argue with God? Will what is molded say to the one who molds it, "Why have you made me like this?" [21]Has the potter no right over the clay, to make out of the same lump one object for special use and another for ordinary use? [22]What if God, desiring to show his wrath and to make known his power, has endured with much patience the objects of wrath that are made for destruction, [23]and what if he has done so in order to make known the riches of his glory for the objects of mercy, which he has prepared beforehand for glory—[24]including us whom he has called, not from the Jews only but also from the gentiles? [25]As he also says in Hosea,

"Those who were not my people
I will call 'my people,'
and her who was not beloved
I will call 'beloved.' "

A question marks the beginning of a new section in Romans 9:19. It indicates another diatribe: "You will say to me then." This is a discussion between a "me" and a "you," addressed in the vocative as "[O human]" (ὦ ἄνθρωπε, v. 20).[48] Is this the imaginary interlocutor, so that this would just be a theoretical dialogue in someone's head? Or is it perhaps based on an actual discussion between Paul and Phoebe (and even other members of the assembly) or Paul and Gaius, Paul's host in the city of Corinth where the letter was written (16:23)? Or are these perhaps even questions—related to him beforehand—that members of the assemblies in Rome have been posing to criticize Paul's proclamation? We do not know.

The question registers an objection to the idea of God's selectiveness: "Why then does he still find fault? For who can resist his will?" (Rom 9:19). Paul and Phoebe now use the well-known image of the potter and the clay for their response. They employ a quotation from Isaiah 29:16 (LXX) and 45:9 (LXX), but due to its wide appeal, this motif also occurs in other Scripture passages (Isa 64:8; Jer 18:1-6; Ps 2:9; Sir 33:13). Once again, therefore, the arguments are, in typical Jewish midrashic fashion, based on the interpretation of biblical texts. The reply to the objection follows the reasoning of theodicy. The image of the potter and the clay is about God as the Creator and humans as creation—after all, God shaped the first human being "from the dust of the ground" (Gen

48. Stanley K. Stowers, *The Diatribe and Paul's Letter to the Romans*, SBLDS 57 (Chico, CA: Scholars Press, 1981), 180–84; Christoph Heilig, *Paulus als Erzähler? Eine narratologische Perspektive auf die Paulusbriefe*, BZNW 237 (Berlin: de Gruyter, 2020), 490.

Rom 9:19-29 (cont.)

[26]"And in the place where it was
said to them, 'You are not
my people,'
there they shall be called
children of the living
God."
[27]And Isaiah cries out concerning
Israel, "Though the number of the
children of Israel were like the sand
of the sea, only a remnant of them will
be saved, [28]for the Lord will execute
his sentence on the earth quickly and
decisively." [29]And as Isaiah predicted,
"If the Lord of hosts had not left
descendants to us,
we would have fared like
Sodom
and been made like Gomorrah."

2:7).[49] How, then, could the latter complain to the former about oneself? Or what room is there for human initiative if God is fully in command? Such questions are typical for wisdom literature, and Phoebe displays a particular affinity to this genre. Famous is the line from Job's response to Eliphaz (Job 9:1-13; cf. 4:17-21) and Bildad (9:14-24; cf. 8:3): "He snatches away; who can stop him? Who will say to him, 'What are you doing?' " (Job 9:12). Similar, but perhaps less familiar are meditations in the book of Wisdom about the power (Wis 11:21–12:2) and sovereignty of God (12:12-18). From the latter section are the following four lines:

> For who will say, "What have you done?"
> or will resist your judgment?
> Who will accuse you for the destruction of nations that you made?
> Or who will come before you to plead as an advocate for the unrighteous?
> (Wis 12:12)

These passages from the wisdom literature of Second Temple Judaism affirm the insignificance of humans who have no business arguing with God, specifically if that would entail allegations of divine injustice, sovereignty, or reign. Phoebe now formulates the consequence for her audiences, which she does once more in analogy to a passage from Wisdom. Its adoption in Romans is illustrated in the following table:

49. Wolter, *Römer*, 2:71.

Rom 9:21-23	Wis 15:7
Has the potter no [authority[50]] over the clay, to make out of the same lump one object for [honor] and another for [dishonor[51]]? What if God, desiring to show his wrath and to make known his power, has endured with much patience the objects of wrath that are made for destruction, and what if he has done so in order to make known the riches of his glory for the objects of mercy, which he has prepared beforehand for glory.	A potter kneads the soft earth and laboriously molds each vessel for our service, fashioning out of the same clay both the vessels that serve clean uses and those for contrary uses, making all alike, but which shall be the use of each of them the worker in clay decides.

The comparison shows that both texts operate with the image of a "potter" (κεραμεύς/πηλουργός) and mention their daily activity of "kneading" (θλίβω, Wis 15:7) or simply "making" (ποιέω, Rom 9:21) "vessels" or "objects" (σκεῦος). Potters are thus in charge of the production of merchandise out of "soft earth" (Wis 15:7) or "clay" (Rom 9:21) according to their intention. The point of the image in both Wisdom and Romans is that the potter has the "authority" (ἐξουσία) or "power" (δυνατός) to decide for the best usage of the vessels or objects, although these are all shaped out of the same material with no difference in quality. This sets up a dualism: According to Wisdom, some vessels "serve clean [καθαρός] uses," but others are "for contrary [ἐναντίος] uses." The term "clean" indicates traditional Jewish purity categories and belongs to the

50. The NRSVue renders the Greek noun ἐξουσία as "right" (similar the RSV, NRSV, NIV). The concern behind the initial question, however, appears to be one of domination and sovereignty rather than of legal prerogative, which makes "authority" a better choice. Cf. Werner Foerster, "ἐξουσία," *TDNT* 2 (1964): 560–75, at 567; Simon Légasse, *L'Épître de Paul aux Romains*, LD 10 (Paris: Cerf, 2002), 605–9.

51. In the NRSVue, the second half of the question of Romans 9:21b is translated as "one object for special use and another for ordinary use?" (similar to the NIV). The NASB 1995, however, renders "for honorable use and another for common use?" The NKJV has "one vessel for honor and another for dishonor?" Joseph A. Fitzmyer's translation is comparable to the NRSVue, but he notes as an alternative, similar to the NKJV: "one vessel for honor, another for dishonor" (Fitzmyer, *Romans*, 564, 569). The latter choices are preferable as the vocabulary "for honor" (εἰς τιμήν) and "for dishonor" (εἰς ἀτιμίαν) is firmly embedded in the Greco-Roman honor-shame culture and should be interpreted from there (see above, pp. 20–25).

sanctuary. The objects "for contrary uses" are actually idols, produced for idol worship, as Wisdom 15:8 makes clear. With its reference to the second commandment (Exod 20:4-6; Deut 5:8-10), the imagery here is concerned with essential religious tenets.

In her adoption for the Roman audiences, Phoebe takes over the gist of this image but modifies and strengthens the antithesis between fine ware and common ware. First, she switches from traditional Jewish purity categories to terminology reflecting the Greco-Roman honor-shame system when she speaks of "one object for [honor] and another for [dishonor]" (Rom 9:21b). The term "honor" (τιμή, see also Rom 2:7, 10; 12:10) is, indeed, the key category of this system and the perpetual goal of all aspiring men; other related terms are "to aspire to honor" (φιλοτιμέομαι), "honored" (ἔνδοξος), "honored/respected" (δόκιμος), "to receive great honor" (συνδοξάζω), and "to regard as exceptionally honored/to exalt" (ὑπερυψόω). The phrase "honor to whom honor is due" will occur later in this letter (13:7) while "dishonor" (ἀτιμία) was attested previously (1:26). Furthermore, another key term equivalent to "honor" is "glory." It features twice in this passage (9:23) and has occurred once before in this chapter (9:4). Phoebe reuses familiar categories to convey her point.

Second, Phoebe intensifies the antithesis of the image by referring to "objects of wrath" (σκεύη ὀργῆς) for destruction and to the others as "objects of mercy" (σκεύη ἐλέους) prepared for glory (Rom 9:22-23). Even if the point is that God's authority allows for the production of both, the contrast is striking.[52] This image, so deeply steeped in Jewish wisdom concepts, carefully juxtaposes the sovereignty of God, the potter, to the inactivity of humans, the objects.

What are the referents of these images? Who are the "objects of wrath," who the "objects of mercy"? Who is in for "destruction," who for "glory"? A famous application of the image of the potter is that in Jeremiah 18:1-6, according to which God asks the prophet: "Come, go down to the potter's house, and there I will let you hear my words" (Jer 18:2). It then mentions a spoiled vessel that the potter swiftly reworks into a better vessel. God then asks: "Can I not do with you, O house of Israel, just as this potter has done?" (18:6). Is the referent in Romans 9:22-23, therefore, also Israel, which would make Israel the "object of wrath"? Some have indeed arrived at such a conclusion.[53] But it does not really fit. In fact, the referent in Romans is different and has already been named. It is *not*

52. Gaventa, "Israel," 266.

53. James D. G. Dunn, *Romans 9–16*, WBC 38a (Dallas: Word, 1988), 567–68.

Israel. Instead, the wording that God "has endured with much patience" and the term "destruction" point back to Romans 9:17. From that context, it is clear that both aspects are about God who did not destroy Pharaoh at the first sign of resistance but kept the story of confrontation and apparent defeat going—almost like a retarding narrative element—until the exodus from Egypt. When it finally happened, it was an even more impressive display of divine power that culminated in the destruction of Pharaoh and his entire army. God had "much patience," to the chagrin of Israel, but the eventual victory and liberation of Israel were the vindication that God's plan had not failed.[54]

In addition, the term "glory" has, aside from its importance in the Greco-Roman honor-shame system, another central meaning as a frequent technical term in the Septuagint. There, it prominently appears, as has been noted above, in the narrative of the exodus of Israel from Egypt as a manifestation of God's saving presence (Exod 15:6, 11; 16:10).[55] This aspect corroborates the interpretation that the referent of the "object of wrath" is no one else but Pharaoh.

Paul and Phoebe continue this line of thought. They transition to "we/us" in Romans 9:24 to solicit full attention, only to immediately claim inclusion with "the riches of his glory for the objects of mercy."[56] Not Jews alone, but also gentiles belong to the covenant people; these soteriological dynamics are consistent with the earlier statement that salvation and faith had been given "for the Jew first and also for the Greek" in 1:16 (see also 3:29; 10:12). What this means will be explicated in another impressive catena of Scripture citations about gentiles in 9:25-26 and about Jews in 9:27-29. It is a composite from Hosea 2:25b-c and 2:1b-c, conveying in moving words the inclusion of someone who was previously an outsider. A key phrase is "And in the place where it was said to them, 'You are not my people,' there they shall be called [sons] of the living God" (Rom 9:26).[57] It harks back to the idea of the adoption that conveys status

54. Gaventa, "Israel," 267; Heilig, *Erzähler*, 667–73.

55. Wolter, *Römer*, 2:77.

56. J. Ross Wagner, "'Not from the Jews Only, But Also from the Gentiles': Mercy to the Nations in Romans 9–11," in Wilk and Wagner, *Between Gospel and Election*, 422.

57. In the quotation from Hosea 2:1 in Rom 9:26 both the NRSVue and the NIV render Greek υἱοί as "children" to obtain a gender-inclusive text version, although the term literally means "sons" (see also Reina Valera 1995: "hijos del Dios viviente"; by contrast, the RSV, NASB 1995, and NKJV have "sons of the living God"). As mentioned above, the translation as "children" obscures the specific allusion of the syntagm "sons of God" to the christological title of Christ Jesus that permeates this

change and recognition of God as Father (Rom 8:14-15).[58] Earlier in her life, Phoebe, the gentile woman who had potentially been enslaved, had been such an outsider. But she experienced that salvation by adoption is for all, and she is the living testimony of the transformative power of the Jewish gospel message that is also available for gentiles.

The next two quotations in Romans 9:27-29 are from Isaiah 10:22 and 1:9. Both shorten their *Vorlage* in the Septuagint. They deal with similar topics: "remnant" and "descendants, offspring, seed" (literally "sperm").[59] Paul and Phoebe use promises of old from the time of Israel's Assyrian captivity to interpret their own situation. The specific choice of the passage may be due to the fact that it contains this term that Paul and Phoebe have used in earlier arguments (Rom 4:13, 16, 18; 9:7-8). Sometimes, these two quotations are read as examples of Israel's destruction because they invoke familiar topics from history such as Sodom and Gomorrah (v. 29).[60] But the purpose for the selection of these two quotations was most likely the same as that for the previous quotations from Hosea. As these are about salvation and inclusion, so are both quotations from Isaiah. The gist is that, amid a scenario of seemingly utter destruction, the story of God and Israel nevertheless continues. A group of "descendants" or a "remnant" survives and continues to exist through God's active support. Therefore, the word of God has not failed—which has been the whole point of the passage. Paul and Phoebe will address the problem of what happens with Israel later (Rom 11:1-6). For the moment, the question of Romans 9:6 is answered affirmatively.[61]

---

letter (Rom 1:4; see also 1:3, 9; 5:10; 8:3). A preferable translation is "there they shall be called sons of the living God."

58. Campbell, "Beloved," 69. See also Matthew Thiessen, *Paul and the Gentile Problem* (New York: Oxford University Press, 2016), 97.

59. The quotation from Isaiah 1:9 in Romans 9:29 demonstrates once more that New Testament authors mostly relied on the Septuagint as their scriptural basis, not on the Hebrew Bible. In the latter, Isaiah 1:9a reads: "If the Lord of hosts had not left us a few survivors (שריד)." In the Septuagint, the sentence is slightly different: "If the Lord of hosts had not left us sperm/descendants (σπέρμα)." The difference between the Hebrew and Greek text of Isaiah 1:9 is that the noun "sperm/descendants" (σπέρμα) replaces "survivor" (שריד). Whatever the reasons for this change, Romans 9:29 adopts the Greek text. (On the meaning of the Greek term σπέρμα, see the comments above under "Translation Matters" on Romans 4:13, 16, 18.) See also Fitzmyer, *Romans*, 572; Klaus Haacker, *Der Brief des Paulus an die Römer*, THKNT 6 (Leipzig: Evangelische Verlagsanstalt, 1999), 189.

60. Gaventa, "Israel," 268; Wolter, *Römer*, 2:91.

61. Matera, *Romans*, 229–30.

Israel's Unbelief (9:30–10:4)

The opposition between gentiles and Israel in Romans 9:30-31 is picked up and mirrored in 10:19-21. Furthermore, the usage of terminology such as "justification" and "faith" or "to believe" characterizes the arguments throughout 10:21. Therefore, Romans 9:30–10:4 and 10:5-21 may be considered as a continuous passage presented in two subsections.[62]

The colloquial question at the start of the section indicates the genre of a diatribe (on this rhetorical genre, see above, p. lxvi), an angry speech or piece of writing that severely criticizes something or someone (Rom 9:30). This is a change after the lengthy Scripture catena. Yet from a formal perspective, the preceding paragraph was likewise a diatribe. The focus of the current pericope is on justification (δικαιοσύνη).[63] The term occurs no fewer than eight times in these few lines, which is particularly noteworthy since Paul barely used it in his previous writings.[64] The deployment of the term here is the immediate result of the portrayal of the sovereignty and authority of Israel's God in Romans 9:19-29. If God is in charge of the destiny of Israel and keeps saving it because it is the "object of mercy" (9:23), then that is proof of God's active agency of justifying humans. This agency is in the background of a long sentence in Greek in 9:30-31 with a two-pronged statement. The first is the following: "Gentiles, who did not strive for [justification], have attained it, that is, [justification] through faith" (9:30). Since the gentiles never endeavored to attain justification, their justification can only demonstrate the free attribution and gift of justification by God, as was first indicated in Romans 3:21-26 (see above, pp. 95–108).

A difficult and much debated sentence follows in Romans 9:31. It is crucial for the exact understanding of the dilemma of Israel's justification according to Paul and Phoebe: "but Israel, who did strive for the law of [justification] [νόμον δικαιοσύνης], did not attain that law [εἰς νόμον οὐκ ἔφθασεν]."[65] The immediate repetition of the term "law" in the Greek text shows that this term is the focus of the sentence.

62. Jewett, *Romans*, 607–8; Matera, *Romans*, 239; Wilk, "Rahmen," 228–29, 253.

63. For this translation of the Greek term δικαιοσύνη as "justification," which differs from the NRSVue, see the comments above on "Translation Matters" about Romans 3:21, 22.

64. Frank Schleritt, "Das Gesetz der Gerechtigkeit: Zur Auslegung von Römer 9,30-33," in Wilk and Wagner, *Between Gospel and Election*, 271–97.

65. The older NRSV rendering "the righteousness that is based on the law" was grounded in interpretive liberties. The Greek syntagm νόμος δικαιοσύνης literally

Rom 9:30–10:4

[30]What then are we to say? Gentiles, who did not strive for righteousness, have attained it, that is, righteousness through faith, [31]but Israel, who did strive for the law of righteousness, did not attain that law. [32]Why not? Because they did not strive for it on the basis of faith but as if it were based on works. They have stumbled over the stumbling stone, [33]as it is written,

"See, I am laying in Zion a stone
that will make people
stumble, a rock that will
make them fall,
and whoever trusts in him will
not be put to shame."

[10:1]Brothers and sisters, my heart's desire and prayer to God for them is that they may be saved. [2]For I can testify that they have a zeal for God, but it is not based on knowledge. [3]Not knowing the righteousness of God and seeking to establish their own, they have not submitted to God's righteousness. [4]For Christ is the culmination of the law so that there may be righteousness for everyone who believes.

The "law" is what Israel did not manage to attain. As the law is what leads to justification in a broader sense, the latter has not been fulfilled. Human efforts have proven futile to achieve justification before God. "While Israel has been running a race that it did not win, the gentiles have won a race they never entered."[66] Elsewhere in the New Testament gospel tradition, the adage "the last will be first, and the first will be last" (Matt 20:16) conveys the idea that human efforts will not be the factor to determine ranks in God's kingdom; the accompanying parable (Matt 20:1-15) portrays this kingdom as an egalitarian society and affirms in its own way God's sovereignty. Paul and Phoebe, however, appear to go further in Romans 9:31. Their insistence that "Israel . . . did not attain that law" is a fundamental challenge to the efficiency of traditional religion and constitutes nothing short of a paradigm shift. As mentioned

means "law of justification" as the object of Israel's striving (see also Jewett, *Romans*, 606–7, 609–10). It has been proposed, however, that one would have expected "the righteousness/justification of the law' " to be that object; cf. Heikki Räisänen, *Paul and the Law*, WUNT 29 (Tübingen: Mohr Siebeck, 1983), 53. The continuation of the sentence shows, however, that the intended object is indeed the word "law" (νόμος), which is repeated immediately as that which Israel was unable to attain. Therefore, the preferable translation is "the law of justification"; cf. Siegert, *Argumentation*, 142.

66. Gaventa, *When in Romans*, 66. See also Schleritt, "Gesetz," 272–81, 296; Michael Wolter, *Paulus: Ein Grundriss seiner Theologie*, 3rd ed. (Neukirchen-Vluyn: Neukirchener Verlag, 2021), 359.

above, in the Second Temple period, there were controversial discussions about the Jewish law. Paul's assemblies have participated in this discussion. Their argument is that God's justification is available apart from the law, which is also manifest in the observation that, according to the Torah, the faith of Abraham preceded the law (Rom 4:1-12). Galatians and Romans, therefore, present similar ideas:

Gal 2:16: "A person is justified not by the [deeds][67] of the law but through the faith [in] Christ Jesus."[68]

Gal 3:13: "Christ redeemed us from the curse of the law by becoming a curse for us."

Gal 5:6: "For in Christ Jesus neither circumcision nor uncircumcision counts for anything; the only thing that counts is faith."

Rom 3:21: "But now, apart from the law, the [justification] of God has been disclosed and is attested by the Law and the Prophets"

Rom 7:4: "You have died to the law through the body of Christ."

Rom 8:2: "The law of the Spirit of life in Christ Jesus has set you free from the law of sin and of death."

The claim is that divine justification is no longer available through the traditional path. Romans 9:32 explains that this is because Israel's efforts were "based on [deeds]" and not "based on faith." This emphasis on faith is not new in Pauline writings, as we have seen. What appears to be new is the unambiguous statement that Israel "did not attain that law" (9:31). But it is similar to the one in Romans 9:6 that the Torah narratives trace the history of Israel through Isaac while acknowledging that other sons (Ishmael, the sons of Keturah) established their lives and kinship groups elsewhere. The current context provides the additional detail that "zeal for God" (10:2) is a contributing factor for the loss of justification. These attempts to attain justification through one's own efforts have been misguided because Israel did not submit to *divine* justification. The common theme behind these

67. On the translation of the Greek noun ἔργον as "deed," which differs from the NRSVue, see comments above under "Translation Matters" on Romans 2:15, 16.

68. For the translation "faith in Christ Jesus," which differs from the NRSVue, see comments above under "Translation Matters" on Romans 3:22.

reflections, therefore, is the sovereignty and authority of the God of Israel that humans are expected to acknowledge (see also Rom 9:19-29).

Another Scripture quotation, this time from Isaiah, is announced ("as it is written," Rom 9:33) to corroborate this claim. What follows are two amalgamated quotations from Isaiah 28:16 and 8:14. The former passage is about Zion, the place of eschatological hope and salvation. It imagines the activity of God who places "a foundation stone" and "a precious cornerstone" as a stable foundation. In this image, the stone exemplifies safety. In the latter passage, however, the prophet announces that God "will become a sanctuary, a stone one strikes against; for both houses of Israel he will become a rock one stumbles over, a trap and a snare for the inhabitants of Jerusalem" (Isa 8:14 [MT]). That is primarily a call of judgment. The object of judgment is the stone itself, which is identified with God.

Yet, the Greek version in the Septuagint provides a substantially different text with an addition: "And if you put your trust in him, he [i.e., God] will become your sanctuary, and you will not meet him like a stumbling stone or a rock that makes you trip. But the house of Jacob (sits) in a trap, and in a pit (lie) who reside in Jerusalem" (Isa 8:14 [LXX]). In this version, the stone is no longer an object of judgment under the condition that humans trust. The aspects of judgment are added, but they are not associated with the stone. Romans 9:33 mentions "a stone that will make people stumble" and "a rock that will make them fall." This quotation takes over the aspect of judgment found in Isaiah 8:14 (MT), and it is the stone that epitomizes it. But the continuation shows that this stone is, at the same time, an object of salvation: "and whoever trusts in him will not be put to shame." Hence, the quotation in Romans 9:33 not only *amalgamates two passages from Isaiah 28:16 and 8:14*; it *also amalgamates the Hebrew and Greek version of the latter*.[69] It does not propose an application of the object of trust. For the moment, this leaves open the question of whether faith in Christ or the gospel message is imagined. Only when this quotation is revisited later (Rom 10:11) is it made clear that faith in Christ is intended.

Christ is mentioned immediately, however, with regard to the law and [justification]. Romans 10:4 features the much-quoted sentence: "For Christ is the culmination of the law [τέλος γὰρ νόμου] so that there may

69. Klaus Baltzer, Jürgen Kabiersch, Klaus Koenen, Arie van der Kooij, and Florian Wilk, "Esaias: Isaias/Das Buch Jesaja," in *Septuaginta Deutsch: Erläuterungen und Kommentare zum griechischen Alten Testament*, vol. 2: *Psalmen bis Daniel*, ed. Martin Karrer and Wolfgang Kraus (Stuttgart: Stuttgarter Bibelgesellschaft, 2011), 2525.

be [justification] for everyone who believes." The correct translation and interpretation of the Greek noun τέλος, however, is much disputed. While NRSVue renders it as "culmination," the NRSV had "end," which is different. Indeed, Joseph A. Fitzmyer maintains that the sense of the Greek noun τέλος cannot be both "end" and "goal" (and, by extension, "culmination") because one denies the other.[70] Yet in Romans 10:4, both aspects appear to be intended. To be sure, Paul has argued that the era of the law has come to an end, as mentioned above (Gal 2:16; 3:13; 5:6; Rom 3:21; 7:4; 8:2). And in Romans 6:22, the critical noun τέλος is clearly employed in the sense of "end."[71] But this is complemented by statements that the law is *not* to be overthrown:[72]

> *Rom 3:31:*
> Do we then overthrow the law through this faith? By no means! On the contrary, *we uphold the law.*
>
> *Rom 8:3-4:*
> For God has done what the law, weakened by the flesh, could not do: by sending his own Son in the likeness of sinful flesh and to deal with sin, he condemned sin in the flesh, so that *the just requirement of the law might be fulfilled in us*, who walk not according to the flesh but according to the Spirit.
>
> *Rom 13:8:*
> Owe no one anything, except to love one another, for *the one who loves another has fulfilled the law.*

In Christ, therefore, the law is fulfilled, and Christ is simultaneously its culmination or goal.[73] Its function as an ethical directive is over. Instead, its role is restricted to knowledge of sin, as has been asserted earlier

70. Fitzmyer, *Romans*, 584.

71. Esler, *Conflict*, 285.

72. In the following, statements about the law are indicated by italics.

73. See also the NIV ("culmination of the law"), New Living Translation; furthermore, the contribution in this volume by MarySylvia Nwachukwu, pp. 227–229. Cf. Maillot, *L'épître*, 264–68; Steven R. Bechtler, "Christ, the Τέλος of the Law: The Goal of Romans 10:4," *CBQ* 56 (1994): 288–308; Byrne, *Romans*, 309, 312 ("Christ is the [true] goal of the law"); Jean-Noël Aletti, *Israël et la loi dans la lettre aux Romains*, LD 173 (Paris: Cerf, 1998), 214–26; Friedrich Avemarie, "Israels rätselhafter Ungehorsam: Römer 10 als Anatomie eines von Gott provozierten Unglaubens," in Wilk and Wagner, *Between Gospel and Election*, 306–15; Wolter, *Römer*, 2:95, 107–14; Paula Fredriksen, "What Does It Mean to See Paul 'within Judaism'?," *JBL* 141 (2022): 359–80, at 377–78.

(Rom 3:20; 7:7). From now on, the crucial factor for the fulfillment of the law is the power of love (8:31-39; 13:8-10; see also 15:1-6). In that specific sense, Christ is indeed the "end" of the law—because it is being fulfilled in a different way.[74] But either option makes the fundamental question regarding the faithfulness of God toward the chosen people of Israel behind Romans 9–11 even more urgent.[75] The next paragraphs will provide Paul's and Phoebe's answer.

Salvation Is for All (10:5-21)

The section in Romans 10:5-21 may be considered the continuation of 9:30–10:4, in which case it would be its second subsection. It consists of a *pesher* (scriptural interpretation) confirming justification through faith (10:5-13) and a syllogism with scriptural proof about the gospel (10:14-21). The first section (*pesher*) starts with a unit on the contrast between justification through the law and through faith (10:5-7). Its second unit deals with oral confessions of faith in Christ (10:8-10). In the third unit, a Scripture quotation prompts a reflection about the inclusiveness of faith (10:11-13). The second section (syllogism) first outlines, in inverse chronological order, the events leading to conversion (10:14-15), followed by the concession that not all have accepted the gospel message (10:16). This leads to the inference that faith is the result of hearing (10:17). The conclusion is that gentiles responded to the gospel while some Jews did not (10:18-21).[76]

Romans 10:5-13 starts where the previous section left off: with the sovereignty and authority of God. Moreover, it moves from one Scripture quotation or reference to the next. The first is from Leviticus 18:5 and affirms the nature of justification according to the law, even though all it says is "the person who does these things will live by them" (Rom 10:5). This position is now contrasted in a *pesher* (scriptural interpretation) with a statement regarding justification through faith (10:6-7). It is *prima vista* an enigmatic passage: "But the [justification] that comes from

74. See also Dieter Zeller, *Der Brief an die Römer*, RNT (Regensburg: Friedrich Pustet, 1985), 182, 185–86; Fitzmyer, *Romans*, 581, 584–85; Légasse, *L'Épître de Paul aux Romains*, 639, 642–44; Jan Lambrecht, "No Longer a Distinction Between Jew and Greek: A Critical Reflection on Romans 9,30–10,13," in *Paul's Graeco-Roman Context*, ed. Cilliers Breytenbach, BETL 277 (Leuven: Peeters, 2015), 489, 493–94.

75. Kraus, "Bedeutung," 507.

76. Wilk, "Rahmen," 228–29, 253.

Rom 10:5-21

[5]Moses writes concerning the righteousness that comes from the law, that "the person who does these things will live by them." [6]But the righteousness that comes from faith says, "Do not say in your heart, 'Who will ascend into heaven?' " (that is, to bring Christ down) [7]"or 'Who will descend into the abyss?' " (that is, to bring Christ up from the dead). [8]But what does it say?

"The word is near you,
in your mouth and in your
heart"

(that is, the word of faith that we proclaim), [9]because if you confess with your mouth that Jesus is Lord and believe in your heart that God raised him from the dead, you will be saved. [10]For one believes with the heart, leading to righteousness, and one confesses with the mouth, leading to salvation. [11]The scripture says, "No one who believes in him will be put to shame." [12]For there is no distinction between Jew and Greek; the same Lord is Lord of all and is generous to all who call on him. [13]For "everyone who calls on the name of the Lord shall be saved."

[14]But how are they to call on one in whom they have not believed? And

faith says, 'Do not say in your heart, "Who will ascend into heaven?" ' (that is, to bring Christ down) 'or "Who will descend into the abyss?" ' (that is, to bring Christ up from the dead)." First, this *pesher* presents justification like a character that speaks. Such embodied "speech-in-character" discourses are typical features of both ancient rhetoric and wisdom literature. They were used to render certain sections of a more complex argument easier to follow.

Second, whereas the preceding quotation from Leviticus was properly announced and cited, the sentence in 10:6-7 does neither one nor the other. It does not make explicit that it is a paraphrase of Deuteronomy 30:11-14 (LXX), which is about "this commandment that I am commanding you today." And it is that commandment that is not far away but near to the listener. The aspect of proximity is also the point of Romans 10:8. It is noteworthy how easily Paul and Phoebe swap aspects of the law for the gospel of Christ that is evoked in the following sentences. Pauline theology replaces the core of the law with Christ, understood as a wisdom figure. This is only possible if Christ, as the end of the law, is also its goal, as was mentioned in 10:4.[77] Furthermore, one should take note of the conclusion of the passage in Deuteronomy 30:11-14 (LXX):

77. Avemarie, "Ungehorsam," 309.

Rom 10:5-21 (cont.)

how are they to believe in one of whom
they have never heard? And how are
they to hear without someone to proclaim him? 15And how are they to proclaim him unless they are sent? As it is
written, "How beautiful are the feet of
those who bring good news!" 16But not
all have obeyed the good news, for Isaiah says, "Lord, who has believed our
message?" 17So faith comes from what
is heard, and what is heard comes
through the word of Christ.
18But I ask, have they not heard?
Indeed they have:

"Their voice has gone out to all
the earth
and their words to the ends of
the world."

19Again I ask, did Israel not understand?
First Moses says,

"I will use those who are not a
nation to make you jealous;
with a foolish nation I will
provoke you."

20Then Isaiah is so bold as to say,

"I have been found by those who
did not seek me;
I have shown myself to those
who did not ask for me."

21But of Israel he says, "All day long I
have held out my hands to a disobedient and contrary people."

"No, the word is very near to you; it is in your mouth and in your heart *for you to observe.*"[78] It is telling that the last words about obedience are dropped in the adaptation in Romans 10:8-9 and replaced by a call to oral confession and belief in one's heart.[79] In that sense, Christ is the end of the law, or, more specifically, Christ is the *end* of *obedience* to the law. The salvation (10:9) that Phoebe has been charged to proclaim in the city of Rome is based on justification that is no longer grounded in human efforts (such as going to the heavens or to the abyss) but in faith in Jesus as the Christ, which was manifest in the resurrection. Once more, such faith acknowledges and celebrates the sovereignty of the God who raised Jesus.

In Romans 10:11-13, another Scripture quotation, this time from Isaiah 28:16, affirms that those who believe will not be put to shame. It then combines two ideas mentioned previously, namely, that of the oneness of God (see Rom 3:29-30) leading to the inclusion of Jew and gentile/Greek (1:16; 3:29).[80] Yet another quotation from Joel 2:32 (LXX)/3:5 (MT)

78. Italics not in the original.

79. Aletti, *Israël*, 221.

80. Esler, *Conflict*, 287.

concludes the section; it conveys that those who call on the name of the Lord will be saved (Rom 10:13). These reflections prompt the need for the preaching of the gospel message, which is the topic of the next passage.

The second section (Rom 10:14-21) features a syllogism about conversion. It moves in inverse chronological sequence, starting with the moment of calling on the name of the Lord that follows conversion and going back to the proclamation of the gospel message and, at the very start, the dispatch of messengers (v. 15). It is carefully composed of four rhetorical questions, all starting with the interrogative particle "how" (πῶς). They invite a crescendo of negative responses from the audiences in the city of Rome: "It is impossible!"[81] The desired effect is, nevertheless, an important achievement for Phoebe. The syllogism is, after all, about the very mission that she had embarked on and is currently fulfilling. At the same time, it is also about Paul's mission. Paul and Phoebe are messengers of the gospel. Faith is the result of what is heard, and what is heard comes through the gospel of Christ. Phoebe asks her audiences to celebrate this moment. She attaches another quotation from Isaiah 52:7 when she says: "As it is written, 'How beautiful are the feet of those who bring good news!'" (Rom 10:15). This Scripture quotation can likewise be understood as a self-reference![82] In the book of Isaiah, the feet of the messenger are said to be "on the mountains"; but for good reasons, this phrase is left out in Romans—after all, Phoebe had arrived by ship. Furthermore, the Hebrew *Vorlage* reads "how beautiful" (מה־נאוו), but two different Greek text versions of the Septuagint both have "how time" (or "how timely," ὡς ὥρα). The Lucianic family of Septuagint texts restores the meaning of the Hebrew text, however, to "how beautiful" (ὡς ὡραῖοι).[83] This is the version that Paul and Phoebe have chosen against the mainstream of Septuagint versions for their citation (Rom 10:15). It is possible that the term "beautiful" is intended as a more or less concealed reference to the name of Phoebe that has—with its meaning of "radiant"—a similar semantic spectrum.[84] As the preacher of the good news, Phoebe is beautiful!

Yet, the celebration is interrupted by the concession that not all have heeded the gospel message (Rom 10:16), followed in 10:17 by a recapitulation of the gist of 10:14 that faith is the result of hearing. The subsequent

81. Avemarie, "Ungehorsam," 316–17.

82. Wolter, *Römer*, 2:132.

83. Jewett, *Romans*, 639; Wolter, *Römer*, 2:130–31.

84. On the person of Phoebe and the meaning of her name, see below (Rom 16:1).

questions are all presented in a first-person singular style, "but I ask" (v. 18). They are similar to 9:1-3 and 10:2-3, where Paul expressed his personal anguish about his compatriots who have not attained God's justification. In Romans 10:18, a double negative question follows that solicits a positive response from the audiences: "Have they not heard?" Robert Jewett notes about the communicative situation: "The audience must answer, 'Yes, they have heard!' In this shrewd rhetorical move, Paul places his audience in the position of responding immediately to close out the possibility of an excuse that he himself has suggested."[85]

To corroborate these reflections, Phoebe includes a medley of four Scripture citations (10:18-21). She first quotes Psalm 18:5 (LXX)/19:4 (MT) about the voice of messengers who have gone out into the world. Next is Deuteronomy 32:21: "I will use those who are not a nation to make you jealous; with a foolish nation I will provoke you" (Rom 10:19). That one is from the famous Song of Moses (Deut 32:1-43). The verb "to provoke to jealousy" (παραζηλόω) assumes a key function for the way Paul and Phoebe view and proclaim matters of salvation.[86] Despite their distress about the fate of Israel, they perceive a grand design behind it. For them, believing gentiles will be the catalysts for the faith in Christ Jesus among Israel. The words "those who are not a nation" refer, for example, to the gentiles in Deuteronomy 32:21 and in the quotation in Romans 10:19. In the next chapter, this terminology is repeated. There, "salvation" is said to have come to the gentiles "so as to make Israel jealous" (Rom 11:11). The conclusion is that gentiles responded to the gospel while some in Israel did not.

The logic of this explanation is difficult to comprehend for most modern interpreters. How could jealousy be a catalyst for faith among Israel? Philip F. Esler explores the meaning of this rationale in the matrix of the ancient honor-shame system.[87] The result for the argument in Romans 10 is that Israel may see others who are vicariously enjoying the benefits of God's favor. In 10:20-21, the final two citations from Isaiah 65:1 and 65:2 confirm this interpretation as they describe a state of being "found" of those who did not seek. Israel is, however, labeled "a disobedient and contrary people" (Rom 10:21).[88]

85. Jewett, *Romans*, 643.

86. Fitzmyer, *Romans*, 599; Wolter, *Römer*, 2:132, 136–38.

87. Esler, *Conflict*, 288–99.

88. Jewett, *Romans*, 647–49; Wolter, *Paulus*, 428–29.

Israel's Rejection Is Not Final (11:1-10)

The previous challenge of the status of Israel prompts an immediate response. Paul and Phoebe are ready to provide it. From a formal perspective, it comes as a diatribe and midrash (on these rhetorical genres, see above, p. lxvi). All arguments are heavily interspersed with Scripture citations and references.[89]

In Romans 11:1, a question looming large over the previous discourse is finally posed explicitly: "I ask, then, has God rejected his people?" (Even this question is an allusion to Scripture, in this case to Ps 94:14.) Ever since Romans 10:18 used Psalm 18:5 (LXX)/19:4 (MT) about the message of the gospel that has gone out into the world, ever since Romans 10:19 used Deuteronomy 32:21 to speak about the jealousy of Israel and call it a "foolish nation," and, worse, ever since Romans 10:21 employed Isaiah 65:1-2 to call Israel a "disobedient and contrary people" and, on top of that, mention another people that God chose instead, the pressing question is what happened to God's chosen people. Given these previous sentences, one would expect a positive answer—God *has* rejected Israel. Instead, Phoebe proclaims another "By no means!" The question and its short response are, one more time, formal aspects of a diatribe. They signal: This will be easy to understand. But is "by no means" really the expected response? Why do all of the previous arguments not amount to a rejection of Israel?

As in Romans 9:1-5, the first-person singular is now combined with another affirmation of Paul's Jewish identity. Paul invokes that he is "an Israelite, a descendant of Abraham, a member of the tribe of Benjamin" (11:1). He emphasizes the fact that he wants the comments on Judaism to be understood not as etic (from *outside* the social group or from the *external* perspective of an observer) but as emic (from someone *within* the social group).[90] Paul has done that repeatedly (2 Cor 11:22; Phil 3:5). He then explicates the "by no means" by turning the initial question into a statement: "God has not rejected his people whom he foreknew" (Rom 11:2a). So far, so good. The audiences await with much anticipation.

But, to answer the grand underlying question, the audiences will still continue to be disappointed for a while. It is only in Romans 11:26 that they will finally hear, for the first time: "And in this way all Israel will

89. Wilk, "Rahmen," 228–29, 253.

90. Alan F. Segal, *Paul the Convert: The Apostolate and Apostasy of Saul the Pharisee* (New Haven: Yale University Press, 1990), 48; Caroline Johnson Hodge, "Apostle to the Gentiles: Construction of Paul's Identity," *BibInt* 13 (2005): 270–88, at 271.

Rom 11:1-10

[11:1]I ask, then, has God rejected his
people? By no means! I myself am an
Israelite, a descendant of Abraham, a
member of the tribe of Benjamin. [2]God
has not rejected his people whom he
foreknew. Do you not know what the
scripture says of Elijah, how he pleads
with God against Israel? [3]"Lord, they
have killed your prophets, they have
demolished your altars; I alone am left,
and they are seeking my life." [4]But what
is the divine reply to him? "I have kept
for myself seven thousand who have
not bowed the knee to Baal." [5]So, too, at
the present time there is a remnant chosen by grace. [6]But if it is by grace, it is
no longer on the basis of works, otherwise grace would no longer be grace.

[7]What then? Israel has not achieved
what it was pursuing. The elect have
achieved it, but the rest were hardened, [8]as it is written,

"God gave them a sluggish
spirit,
eyes that would not see
and ears that would not hear,
down to this very day."

[9]And David says,

"Let their table become a snare
and a trap,
a stumbling block and a
retribution for them;
[10]let their eyes be darkened so
that they cannot see,
and keep their backs forever
bent."

be saved." But for now, all that Phoebe gets to do is reiterate accusations of ever different episodes of Israel's *his*-story full of antagonism and disobedience. This time, the audiences are invited to excerpts of the narrative in 1 Kings 19:1-18 about the prophet Elijah who complains about being persecuted. Although Phoebe relates the response of God that seven thousand men who have not bowed the knee to Baal are retained (1 Kgs 19:18/Rom 11:4), the application only yields that a "remnant" has been chosen (Rom 11:5). This is, once again, the group of believers in Christ. With that, Paul and Phoebe still maintain that the rest of Israel has stumbled (11:11). Despite the emphatic "By no means!" the audiences are still waiting for the response for why Israel, and this means not just a remnant but *all of Israel*, has not been rejected.

For the moment, the focus returns to the topic of grace. The Greek noun χάρις occurs no fewer than four times in Romans 11:5-6, which is only one sentence in the Greek text. With that focus, the discussion continues to be about the refutation of "[deeds]" (ἔργα)[91] while maintaining

91. For this translation, which differs from the NRSVue, see comments above under "Translation Matters" on Romans 2:15-16.

the sovereignty of God. Two further Scripture citations from Isaiah 29:10 (LXX) and Psalm 68:23-24 (LXX) corroborate the arguments that, apart from the small group of the elect, Israel has been rejected.[92] This is also stated explicitly in the next sentence in Romans 11:11 (see below). Yes, Israel has "stumbled." The question is only whether this was *by God's initiative* and if there was, therefore, a *deeper purpose* behind it. That is what Paul and Phoebe explore with their audiences in the following section.[93]

The Salvation of the Gentiles (11:11-24)

A diatribe and allegorical enthymeme dealing with the missional purpose of Israel's stumbling provide a partial response to the previous questions about Israel's rejection. It amounts to good news for gentiles such as Phoebe as it attempts to correlate rejection and acceptance, proposing an interdependent vision of God's saving power for all.

The Q&A of Romans 11:11 shows that the diatribe style of the previous paragraph continues. More than that, this paragraph starts with the same words as 11:1, "So I ask."[94] The rhetorical question whether Israel has stumbled so as to fall solicits a negative reply from the audiences in Rome. It is parallel to 11:1: "I ask, then, has God rejected his people?"[95] The aspects of "stumbling" (πταίω) and "falling" (πίπτω) in 11:11 are

92. The text of Psalm 68:23-24 (LXX) corresponds to Psalm 69:23-24 (MT) (ET: Ps 69:22-23). Both are significantly different from each other, and the citation in Romans 11:9 is again different from Psalm 68:23-24 (LXX). The NRSVue translation of Psalm 69:23-24 (MT) is the following: "Let their table [שלחן] be a trap for them, a snare for their allies. Let their eyes be darkened so that they cannot see, and make their loins tremble continually" (Ps 69:22-23 [ET]). The equivalent of Psalm 68:23-24 (LXX) is (differences in italics): "Let their table before them become a snare [εἰς παγίδα], and *for retribution and for* a stumbling block [εἰς σκάνδαλον]. Let their eyes be darkened so they cannot see, and *bend their backs* continually." The citation in Romans adds "and a trap" (καὶ εἰς θήραν) in 11:9a and "for them" (αὐτοῖς) in v. 9b, changes that emphasize elements of the Septuagint *Vorlage*. In all three versions, however, "the table" is the crucial element. The citation may have been employed in Romans 11 because dining customs were a major bone of contention among the audiences in Rome, as will be discussed in 14:1–15:6 (Esler, *Conflict*, 295–96).

93. Alain Gignac, *Juifs et Chrétiens à l'École de Paul de Tarse: Enjeux identitaires et éthiques d'une lecture de Romains 9–11*, ColSB 9 (Montreal: Médiaspaul, 1999), 227; Jewett, *Romans*, 658–64; Wolter, *Römer*, 2:142–58.

94. The words are the same in the Greek text. The NRSVue renders the Greek phrase λέγω οὖν differently in either instance: "I ask, then" in Romans 11:1, "so I ask" in 11:11.

95. Tonstad, *Romans*, 283.

Rom 11:11-24

11So I ask, have they stumbled so as
to fall? By no means! But through their
stumbling salvation has come to the
gentiles, so as to make Israel jealous.
12Now if their stumbling means riches
for the world and if their loss means
riches for gentiles, how much more will
their full inclusion mean!

13Now I am speaking to you gentiles. Inasmuch as I am an apostle to
the gentiles, I celebrate my ministry 14in
order to make my own people jealous
and thus save some of them. 15For if
their rejection is the reconciliation of
the world, what will their acceptance
be but life from the dead? 16If the part
of the dough offered as first fruits is
holy, then the whole batch is holy; and
if the root is holy, then the branches
also are holy.

17But if some of the branches were
broken off, and you, a wild olive shoot,
were grafted among the others to share
the rich root of the olive tree, 18do not

reminiscent of the "stumbling stone" of Christ in 9:32-33 and 11:9 (see also later in 11:22 and 14:4).[96] It is somewhat clear that the audiences are still awaiting the same answer as earlier in 11:1.

The proof of Paul and Phoebe takes up the rest of the pericope (11:12-24). After the preceding passages, it is noteworthy that the present one features no more Scripture citation. In this regard, Romans 11:11-24 is almost unique in this fourth and final section of the theological part of the letter (Rom 9–11).

A brief comment is now inserted that Paul is "an apostle to the gentiles" (ἐθνῶν ἀπόστολος, Rom 11:13). It is, for the moment, only addressed to these gentiles. This happens after a moment ago, Paul insisted on his identity as an "Israelite" (11:1). He is, thus, displaying his multiple citizenships; he has a complex identity. The question is how one relates to the other. In Rome, Phoebe presents these reflections about Paul as a gentile woman. She delivers them yet belongs to the same group of people that is being addressed.

In Romans 11:11 and 13, the idea first presented in 10:19 is picked up again that God's plan of salvation is to make the people of Israel "jealous." And finally, the thought is brought to its conclusion: "Now if their

96. Jewett, *Romans*, 672–73; Mark D. Nanos, "'Broken Branches': A Pauline Metaphor Gone Awry? (Romans 11:11-24)," in Wilk and Wagner, *Between Gospel and Election*, 342–47.

boast over the branches. If you do boast, remember: you do not support the root, but the root supports you. [19]You will say, "Branches were broken off so that I might be grafted in." [20]That is true. They were broken off on account of unbelief, but you stand on account of belief. So do not become arrogant, but be afraid. [21]For if God did not spare the natural branches, neither will he spare you. [22]Note then the kindness and the severity of God: severity toward those who have fallen but God's kindness toward you, if you continue in his kindness; otherwise you also will be cut off. [23]And even those of Israel, if they do not continue in unbelief, will be grafted in, for God has the power to graft them in again. [24]For if you have been cut from what is by nature a wild olive tree and grafted, contrary to nature, into a cultivated olive tree, how much more will these natural branches be grafted back into their own olive tree.

stumbling [τὸ παράπτωμα αὐτῶν[97]] means riches for the world and if their loss means riches for gentiles, how much more will their full inclusion mean!" (11:12). Negative scenes from Israel's *his*-story have been referenced so often that it comes as a relief to hear that "their full inclusion" is now finally being considered. It is presented in the *a minore ad maius* (from the lesser to the greater) rationale. Furthermore, it appears as the first and last element in a four-piece chiastic argument:

11:12 A. Israel's stumbling and inclusion helps gentiles

 11:13 B. Paul's apostleship to the gentiles

 11:14 B′. Paul's apostleship to Israel

11:15 A′. Israel's rejection and inclusion helps gentiles.[98]

With that, this section explains how "reconciliation" (καταλλαγή) has been made available to the world (11:15). The term "reconciliation" harks back to the christological-soteriological section in Romans 5:6-11 that also presented its argument in an *a minore ad maius* structure. But more than that, it goes also back to the *propositio* (main thesis) of the letter (1:16), which suggested that faith came from the Jew first to the

97. The Greek noun παράπτωμα could also be rendered as "trespass"; cf. Fitzmyer, *Romans*, 608, 611.

98. Jewett, *Romans*, 670.

Greek. Hence, the letter has been presupposing all along that Israel had faith and was the source of God's salvation for the gentiles. There, a quotation from the prophet Habakkuk substantiated the argument that "the one who is [just][99] will live by faith" (Hab 2:4 [LXX], cited in Rom 1:17). The same emphasis on faith emerged from Romans 4:1-12 about Abraham's faith (see also Gal 3:29). All of this indicates that Israel's later rejection is understood as a change of direction, and as such it is partial and temporary—and instigated by God.[100]

An important question is why these argumentative maneuvers in Romans 11:11-24 about Israel's rejection were necessary. Mark N. Nanos thinks that they were "calculated to be insulting."[101] And Matthew V. Novenson comments:

> In the Letter to the Romans, Paul attributes this noetic hardening to the agency of God himself. . . . Why would God do such a thing? Well, Paul reasons, it is an eschatological necessity that God should have mercy on all people. Gentiles had always been disobedient ("by nature", Gal 2:15), so now, quite straightforwardly, God can have mercy on them. Jews, however, had always been mostly obedient; hence God has *made* them temporarily disobedient now so that he can very soon have mercy on them, too (Rom 11:30-32). This explanation may seem strange, but then, the phenomenon Paul was trying to explain was itself strange: the Jewish messiah had appeared, but only gentiles, not Jews (for the most part), were bowing the knee to him. Desperate times call for desperate explanatory measures. None of this, however, amounts to abandoning Judaism.[102]

Desperate or not, Paul and Phoebe do resort to novel explanations and images; their success in conveying the desired contents remains to be seen. These explanations and images are similar to, or perhaps even based on, apocalyptic sources of Second Temple Judaism about the impending end of time and the conviction that Israel's impurity and sin are factors that delay the arrival of the promised Messiah.

99. For this translation, which differs from the NRSVue, see the comments above on Romans 1:17 (p. 44) and on Romans 3:21 (p. 96).

100. Alain Gignac, *L'épître aux Romains*, Commentaire biblique: Nouveau Testament 6 (Paris: Cerf, 2014), 410–17; Gaventa, *When in Romans*, 68–71.

101. Nanos, "Broken Branches," 349.

102. Matthew V. Novenson, "Did Paul Abandon either Judaism or Monotheism?," in *The New Cambridge Companion to St. Paul*, ed. Bruce W. Longenecker, Cambridge Companions to Religion (Cambridge: Cambridge University Press, 2020), 246 (italics original).

The next two images both explore sanctity. First, there is a brief allegory in Romans 11:16a about "a first fruit" (ἡ ἀπαρχή)[103] and "the whole batch." It draws on sacrificial regulations from the Second Temple period. The underlying logic is found in Leviticus 2:1-3 and Numbers 15:17-21. According to Leviticus 2:1-3, a grain offering (θυσία, also translated in English as "cereal offering") consists of choice flour, oil, and frankincense; it is for the priests except for a small token portion that is burned on the main altar. It is considered "holy" (Lev 2:3) because it has been brought to the sanctuary. Numbers 15:17-21 (LXX) further specifies that a donation of a loaf of dough is to be presented as "a first fruit" (ἀπαρχή). A token portion, therefore, that remains at the sanctuary determines the status of the remaining offering.[104] In chronological perspective, that "first fruit" is also the very first part of a larger entity that precedes the rest. In Romans, the term has previously been used in this sense for those who have already received the Spirit while still waiting for adoption (Rom 8:23). It will be employed again in Romans 16:5b to designate the first person in a province to have adopted the new faith in Christ (see also 1 Cor 16:15). The meaning for the context of Romans 11 is that the holiness of the "first fruit" that was there at the start will be transferred to the rest. Yet, it is Israel that has this special quality of holiness. That image is a call to humility as it suggests that the new, precious quality of the rest has been adopted from elsewhere. In essence, however, it only repeats the statement about the dynamics of faith from Jew to "Greek" in Romans 1:16.[105]

Second, a further image about the expansion of sanctity is added in the same sentence. Romans 11:16b states: "and if the root is holy, then the branches also are holy." It operates by the same logic as the first half of the sentence. The image of the holy root sets the stage for the famous allegory of the olive tree.[106] In 11:17-24, gentile believers in Christ are compared to a wild olive shoot. It is grafted into a cultivated olive tree "to share the rich root of the olive tree." According to this image, "the church of the Gentiles is an extension of the promises of God to Israel and not Israel's

103. This is the literal translation of the Greek noun, which is in the singular. The NRSVue renders it in the plural: "first fruits."

104. Thomas Hieke, *Levitikus 1–15*, HThKAT (Freiburg: Herder, 2014), 200–205. See also Wolfgang Kraus, *Das Volk Gottes: Zur Grundlegung der Ekklesiologie bei Paulus*, WUNT 85 (Tübingen: Mohr Siebeck, 1996), 314.

105. Kraus, *Das Volk Gottes*, 315; Benjamin D. Gordon, "On the Sanctity of Mixtures and Branches: Two Halakic Sayings in Romans 11:16-24," *JBL* 135 (2016): 355–68.

106. On the question regarding the genre of Romans 11:17-24, see Siegert, *Argumentation*, 167–71; Byrne, *Romans*, 341.

displacement."[107] In ancient as well as in modern horticulture, however, it was customary to graft a cultivated branch into a wild tree stem. Philip F. Esler explains that young wild olive bushes or saplings are dug up and transplanted into agricultural groves and gardens. After initial trimming, shoots or branches from cultivated olives are later grafted onto them. "The rationale for this practice is that branches from cultivated olive trees produce the best fruit, whereas wild olive trees have extensive root systems (needed for taking in as much water as possible) and often also have greater disease resistance."[108] Therefore, Paul and Phoebe have inversed basic parameters of their image, according to which the wild branches (representing the gentiles) are grafted into the cultivated stem. Were they ignorant of the prevailing practices of olive cultivators? That is unlikely; in this case, the peculiar inversion must have been intended. "In opting for the wild olive, . . . Paul was consciously crafting an image most unflattering to the non-Judeans."[109] This is already the first move in the direction of the next sentences; there, Paul and Phoebe issue a stern warning against boasting aimed at a "blatantly arrogant Gentile Christian."[110] Throughout the development of the image of Israel's temporary rejection, the danger is evident that an undifferentiated response would view the temporary rejection as permanent. If boasting about their status was what Gentiles had resorted to, then that was not the intended outcome. This could be an implicit reference to the quarreling parties in the assemblies of Rome. On the other hand, the inversion of the image of the grafting practices may also be understood as hinting at the common reversal of cultural standards prevailing in the assemblies of believers in Christ. In the context of the patriarchy/kyriarchy of the Roman Empire, the radically democratic *ekklēsia* of wo/men was intrinsically characterized by a reversal of standards. In light of this, the inversion of the image of the grafting practices may almost have a tongue-in-cheek quality. Whatever the reasons for the inversion, the image of grafting

107. Johan Christiaan Beker, *Paul the Apostle: The Triumph of God in Life and Thought* (Philadelphia: Fortress, 1980), 332.

108. Esler, *Conflict*, 302. See also Philip F. Esler, "Ancient Oleiculture and Ethnic Differentiation: The Meaning of the Olive-Tree Image in Romans 11," *JSNT* 26 (2003): 103–24.

109. Esler, "Ancient Oleiculture and Ethnic Differentiation," 122. It is noteworthy that this is not the only inversion in these chapters in Romans. Mark Reasoner also describes "redemptive inversions" of Jeremiah's language regarding Israel. Cf. Mark Reasoner, "The Redemptive Inversions of Jeremiah in Romans 9–11," *Bib* 95 (2014): 388–404.

110. Jewett, *Romans*, 669.

that Paul and Phoebe chose powerfully conveys that the combination of two independent components leads to a united product that is of higher quality. It motivates the assemblies in Rome to embrace the "others" and view them as a valuable addition, rather than rejecting them as foreign intruders. It is better to be together than apart!

By contrast, boasting was a typical behavior in the competitive arena of the honor-shame culture of the Roman world. It was both an instinctive comportment in response to individual success and a calculated activity to advertise one's achievements with the goal of proper attribution of acquired honor. As such, it was also a violation of the egalitarian ethos of the radically democratic *ekklēsia* of wo/men. Sure enough, those in "Israel" were not members of these communities of faith yet, but even outsiders were included in that egalitarian ethos and protected under it. Boasting in all of its forms was, therefore, simply "excluded" (Rom 3:27; see also 2:17, 23; in previous letters, 1 Cor 13:4). To set the record straight and clearly convey her argument, Phoebe now literally issues a threat. On the one hand, she admonishes the group of gentile believers not to be proud (Rom 11:20); after all, "the root supports you" (v. 18). On the other hand, she states: "For if God did not spare the natural branches, neither will he spare you" (v. 21). Such an unambiguous argument was probably permissible since it came directly from Phoebe, a fellow gentile. She comments on their shared status as believers in Christ who, according to this view, have been privileged to receive the spot of Israel. She concludes with the urge to be constantly cognizant of both God's "kindness" and "severity": God can be kind to those who have responded with kindness but can also respond with severity toward those who have decided to reject the divine provisions of grace (Rom 11:22-24).[111]

The allegory of the olive tree in Romans 11 has been much debated in scholarship and beyond. It was developed to illustrate both the intimate connection between gentiles and Israel as well as the oneness of God's people in correspondence to God's oneness (3:29-30). It shows that a better fruit can be obtained only when both, the cultivated stock and the new branches, are combined and share a new existence together. Nevertheless, the image "does not erase the distinctiveness of the two subgroups."[112] It also demonstrates that an inferior fruit will result if anyone continues alone or resists the new union.

111. Tobin, *Rhetoric*, 364–65; Peter Oakes, *Reading Romans in Pompeii: Paul's Letter at Ground Level* (Minneapolis: Fortress; London: SPCK, 2009), 160; Gaventa, *When in Romans*, 73.

112. Esler, *Conflict*, 300.

We may assume that much of what Paul and Phoebe decided to communicate through this specific allegory and, more broadly, Romans 9–11 was designated to facilitate the reintegration of Jewish Christ believers into the assemblies in Rome. As mentioned above, after the expulsion of these believers following the edict of Claudius in 49 CE, gentile believers found themselves in charge of these assemblies. When members with traditional Jewish origins started to return to Rome after 54 CE, they were outnumbered by gentiles. The latter were also not inclined to yield leadership positions. For that and other reasons, tensions had developed. Phoebe's message in Rome was supposed to contribute to the appreciation of the traditions of Second Temple Judaism to which some in the assemblies had previously belonged. It was supposed to foster an atmosphere of respect and interdependence of the ethnic groups despite differences. Likewise, the purpose would also have been the reconciliation between the assemblies of those who believed in Christ with the synagogue communities in Rome. Recent tensions that were epitomized by the expulsion of many would now appear as having been part of the grand design of God.[113]

Has the message of the allegory of the olive tree and the larger section of Romans 9–11 been successful and properly understood? While this question is difficult to answer, the success of the argument in light of the historical situation may be assumed. Nonetheless, there are problems with the allegory. First, Mark D. Nanos points out that subsuming all gentiles, regardless of their ethnic differences, under the one image of the wild olive shoot denies any variety in their social identity. "Paul arguably expresses the stereotyping perspective of an insider toward the outsider, one who lumps together the out-group (non-Israelites) but recognizes among his own in-group (Israelites) rich diversity."[114] This goes to show that Paul (and Phoebe) had developed the argument in support of Jewish groups. Second, concerns have been voiced about what may be called "replacement ecclesiology" in this allegory. Terence L. Donaldson thinks that it became a prominent image to deny Israel its status as God's people.

> Romans 11 contains statements that have been taken as supportive of what might be termed "replacement ecclesiology," that is, the idea that the (Gentile) church owes its existence to the rejection of Israel, God having rejected the one and put the other in its place. Such ideas

113. Oakes, *Romans*, 160–61.

114. Nanos, "Broken Branches," 353–54.

> formed a central strand of the *adversus Judaeos* tradition of early Gentile Christianity and thus contributed in no small measure to the legacy of Christian anti-Semitism. Much of Romans 11 could be referred to in this connection.[115]

There is no doubt that what may be labeled "replacement ecclesiology" could have its roots in Romans 11:17-24. The goal of this image was to convey the proximity of Israel and gentiles and their mutual dependence in the epic drama of global salvation. But just as the apocalyptic expectations of Second Temple Judaism that Paul shared about the imminent end of time did not become reality, so his desire remained unfulfilled that the image of the olive tree would promote the unity of Israel and gentiles. An expression of the attainable harmony between both groups was, most likely, the collection for Jerusalem that Paul was overseeing. But the success of this project was also questionable. So what of the allegories and images in Romans? Elizabeth Castelli admonishes: "The task for a progressive feminist reading of Paul, one attentive to the embeddedness of anti-Semitism in the history of Christianity, is to pose the question of how texts are put to use in various contexts to rationalize certain claims of power."[116] With that in mind, one needs to be critical of any attempt to usurp the place of divine election. As two millennia of Jewish-Christian relations as well as recent *his*-story have shown, the ancient vision of mutual respect and understanding has frequently remained unfulfilled. Too often and in too many places, Christians of most denominations have been involved in the disenfranchisement and violent persecution of their Jewish parent generation.[117] With that, they have disregarded Israel's holiness that Paul and Phoebe have evoked in Romans 11:16. The threat of Romans 11:22 that God may cut the wild olive shoots and reverse the grafting process has not always been taken seriously.[118]

All Israel Will Be Saved (11:25-36)

The concluding section in Romans 9–11 consists of five subsections dealing with and celebrating the mystery of global salvation. It has taken

115. Terence L. Donaldson, " 'Riches for the Gentiles' (Rom 11:12): Israel's Rejection and Paul's Gentile Mission," *JBL* 112 (1993): 81–98, at 82.

116. Castelli, "Romans," 293.

117. Kraus, "Bedeutung," 521.

118. Tamez, "Brief," 572.

Rom 11:25-36

25 I want you to understand this mystery,
brothers and sisters, so that you may
not claim to be wiser than you are: a
hardening has come upon part of Israel
until the full number of the gentiles has
come in. 26 And in this way all Israel will
be saved, as it is written,
"Out of Zion will come the
Deliverer;
he will banish ungodliness
from Jacob."
27 "And this is my covenant with
them,
when I take away their sins."
28 As regards the gospel they are enemies for your sake, but as regards election they are beloved for the sake of
their ancestors, 29 for the gifts and the
calling of God are irrevocable. 30 Just as
you were once disobedient to God but
have now received mercy because of
their disobedience, 31 so also they have

Paul and Phoebe a while to arrive at this point, but in Romans 11:25-27, they finally lift the veil.[119] This section connects directly to the preceding illustration of the olive tree (11:17-24), as the preposition "so" (γάρ, 11:25) indicates,[120] and its contents are, in fact, similar. Its structure, moreover, corresponds to the opening section of Romans 9–11 in 9:1-5.[121] Thus, the "mystery" (11:25) would correspond to the expression of "great sorrow and unceasing anguish" (9:2) because of the situation of Israel. Furthermore, the desire of Paul to be "accursed" and separated from Christ for the sake of his own people (9:3) can now be understood as mirroring the logic of salvation in the context of replacement ecclesiology. If Israel was cut off to allow the inclusion of others, perhaps Paul's exclusion would have allowed their inclusion?

The term "mystery" is supposed to indicate the perspective of a mystic whose ideas and experiences may often be beyond analysis. Even if publicly disclosed, its origin and content remain partially incomprehensible.[122] The term "hardening" that is employed for the main problem in the salvation history was already mentioned earlier (as a verb in Rom 11:7) and alluded to in the reference to Pharaoh (9:17). It is clear, then, that God is seen as working behind the scenes. The replacement logic is

119. Gaventa, *When in Romans*, 68.

120. The NRSVue, NRSV, and NIV leave this preposition untranslated.

121. Wilk, "Rahmen," 239. Alternatively, the section in Romans 11:25-32 has been interpreted as a summary of the entirety of Romans 9–11; cf. Mary Ann Getty, "Paul and the Salvation of Israel: A Perspective on Romans 9–11," *CBQ* 50 (1988): 456–69.

122. Florian Wilk, *Die Bedeutung des Jesajabuches für Paulus*, FRLANT 179 (Göttingen: Vandenhoeck & Ruprecht, 1998), 66.

now been disobedient in order that, by
the mercy shown to you, they also may
now receive mercy. 32For God has imprisoned all in disobedience so that he
may be merciful to all.

33O the depth of the riches and wisdom and knowledge of God! How unsearchable are his judgments and how
inscrutable his ways!

34"For who has known the mind of
the Lord?
Or who has been his
counselor?"
35"Or who has given a gift to him,
to receive a gift in return?"
36For from him and through him and to
him are all things. To him be the glory
forever. Amen.

a temporary measure, only in place until "the full number" of gentiles will have been saved.

To put an end to all ambiguity, Paul and Phoebe now state that, in the end, "all Israel will be saved [πᾶς Ἰσραὴλ σωθήσεται]" (Rom 11:26). But even this statement has led to an ongoing scholarly debate regarding its exact meaning; some claim that salvation can only be intended to apply to those of "faith."[123] An amalgamated Scripture quotation from Isaiah 59:20 and Jeremiah 31:33 corroborates the important claim of Israel's salvation. It rests once more on God's initiative and activity: On the one hand, "the Deliverer" will come from Zion to save Israel (Rom 11:26). This is, finally, an unambiguous reference to Jesus Christ in what is otherwise a chapter without a plethora of christological allusions or statements. On the other hand, divine forgiveness of sins is offered along with "my covenant with them" (11:27). The latter is a reference to the new covenant in Jeremiah 31 (MT)/38 (LXX) that envisions God as the sole guarantor of the covenant while humans will be capable of fulfilling it because it is now internalized. It references the Deuteronomic-Deuteronomistic stage in the development of covenantal theology that stresses unilateral divine initiative and ownership of the covenant.[124]

Next is an enthymeme on the theological significance of the mystery in terms of the gospel's global mission (Rom 11:28-32). It uses harsh terminology such as "enemies." This sounds dramatic, but in sharp

123. Christopher Zoccali, "'And So All Israel Will Be Saved': Competing Interpretations of Romans 11:26 in Pauline Scholarship," *JSNT* 30 (2008): 289–318.

124. Karin Finsterbusch, "'Ich habe meine Tora in ihre Mitte gegeben': Bemerkungen zu Jer 31,33," *BZ* 49 (2005): 86–92.

contrast, Phoebe gets to call Israel "beloved" (v. 28). This term here and later (16:5, etc.) signifies divine election just as well as communal love.[125] God's faithfulness is now put on display; "ancestors" and "gifts" match the aspects of Israel's privileges listed in Romans 9:4. The argument then moves toward divine "mercy," mentioned four times in two sentences (11:30-32). This development mirrors the four references to "grace" earlier in 11:5-6 and thus reminds the audiences of the divine authority behind the grand epic of human salvation. Both terms have an implicit connection to "love." As mentioned above, that term is strongly connected to the cult of the great goddess Isis who was invoked by the name of "love" and who was venerated as a goddess of rebirth and life after death in the Greco-Roman world.

The concluding paragraph of this fourth and final section in the theological part of the letter (Rom 9–11) contains three components. It first features a praise of God's mysterious majesty. "O the depth of the riches and wisdom and knowledge of God! How unsearchable are his judgments and how inscrutable his ways!" (11:33). Consisting of three attributes of God (riches, wisdom, knowledge, 11:33), this section continues with three questions (11:34-35) and concludes with a final praise of God that uses three prepositional phrases ("from him," "through him," and "to him," 11:36). Central in the three attributes is, once again, *Chokmah-Sophia-Sapientia-Wisdom*. It is firmly connected with traditions of Second Temple Judaism, as has been noted above (see also Job 11:6; 12:13; Dan 2:20). At the same time, it remains an implicit allusion to Christ, even if Christology is rather absent from Romans 9–11. It is hoped that God's "knowledge" helps to solve the "mystery" of divine salvation history—in that case, it would also help to alleviate the internal tensions in the assemblies of Christ believers in Rome.

The three questions in Romans 11:34-35 explicate the three divine attributes of verse 33. They consist of Scripture quotations: the citation from Isaiah 40:13 comes with two questions; that from Job 41:3 has one. All three questions point to the limits of human comprehension; nobody can compete with God's mind, which is why humans would make poor counselors to God and have, in the end, nothing to bargain with God (see previously 1 Cor 2:16).[126] Once more, the lesson is that humans have, across the board, nothing to boast. *All* glory belongs to God alone—*soli deo gloria*.

125. Oda Wischmeyer, "Das Adjektiv ΑΓΑΠΗΤΟΣ in den paulinischen Briefen: Eine traditionsgeschichtliche Miszelle," *NTS* 32 (1986): 476–80, at 478–79.

126. Gaventa, *When in Romans*, 73.

From a feminist perspective, the soteriological principle of replacement that undergird some of the fourth section of Romans (chaps. 9–11) may be scrutinized. First, such logic operates on rigorous binary soteriological categories. It seems that Paul (and with him, Phoebe) has adopted the understanding of the Torah, and here specifically of the book of Genesis, that divine selection can only be available for one single descendant but not for two or even a multitude of them. Thus, either Isaac or Ishmael was the recipient of God's full blessing, not both of them. And in order to say, "I have loved Jacob," it was necessary to pronounce as well, "but I have hated Esau." Are there not more rooms in God's house? Why would God be so selective when it comes to who is elected? Romans 9–11 then tries to present the argument that the dualism of divine election is a preliminary phenomenon. Although the "remnant" of Christ believers are saved now by God's grace and the rest of Israel is not, this situation will be overturned eventually because God is sovereign and will not be found unfaithful. Under this assumption—*and* by calling on divine "mystery"—Israel will also be saved, so the theological problem is solved. One may ask, however, whether such a replacement ecclesiology is not prompted by an analysis of the local problems in the assemblies in Rome where tensions between believers of gentile and Jewish origins needed to be mitigated. Outside of this context, the applicability and usefulness of this soteriological model may be questioned. The rather disastrous continuation of Paul's missionary career after his departure from the city of Corinth indicates that at least his vision of reconciliation between gentile assemblies and Jewish communities in and around Jerusalem remained unfulfilled. Whether or not that was due to the ambiguities of these theological concepts or even these images and allegories is difficult to ascertain, but it can be problematized.

Second, from the perspective of intersectionality, one may ask whether the emphasis on ethnic-religious binaries permeating Romans 9–11 does not amount to a certain disregard of other urgent difficulties and challenges in the assemblies (for instance, pertaining to gender or the status of free people versus unfree). Would any of these arguments be useful to end the oppression and marginalization of women? To help enslaved females? A comparison with the rich coverage of these topics in the third section of Romans (chaps. 6–8)[127] shows that the present, fourth section is rather devoid of any concerns around gender aspects and personal

127. See also the table "Romans 6:1–8:30: Arguments and Imagery Based on Enslavement or the Situation of Women" above, pp. 213–214.

status. Paul's letter to Philemon demonstrates that the apostle was capable of venturing into areas like these, but that would have required his attentiveness to social and other problems and less to abstract theological reasoning. Romans, however, was also intended to prepare a base for Paul's future missionary work in Spain (Rom 15:24-28) and position him as a competent and trustworthy leadership personality. The result is, hence, a document that brims with scriptural references and restricts the discourse largely to the religious-ethnic realm. Its practical relevance is spelled out in detail in the next section on parenetic matters.

Romans 12:1–15:13

Living as God's Loving People

The New Life in Christ (12:1-8)

Romans 12:1 is the start of a new section of the letter, namely, the parenetic (or ethical/hortatory) section (12:1–15:13). After sometimes dense and highly complex theological, christological, soteriological, and/or ecclesiological discourses about gentiles and Jews/Israel, women and men, enslaved and free people, etc., what follows is a lot more hands-on in nature and easier to comprehend. If in previous chapters there was ever the concern whether the intricate theorizing has any practical ramifications at all, then the letter now spells out at least some of it. The audiences in the city of Rome could see for themselves: The gospel message that Paul had tasked Phoebe to deliver and recite to them was not just a "pie in the sky, by and by." It made a difference in lived reality, providing clear practical instructions for all in the community and Roman society, including women and marginalized ("weak") people.[1]

1. Beverly Roberts Gaventa, *When in Romans: An Invitation to Linger with the Gospel According to Paul* (Grand Rapids: Baker Academic, 2016), 76.

Rom 12:1-8

12:1 I appeal to you therefore, brothers and sisters, on the basis of God's
mercy, to present your bodies as a living sacrifice, holy and acceptable to
God, which is your reasonable act of
worship. 2 Do not be conformed to this
age, but be transformed by the renewing of the mind, so that you may dis-
cern what is the will of God—what is
good and acceptable and perfect.
3 For by the grace given to me I say
to everyone among you not to think of
yourself more highly than you ought
to think but to think with sober judg-

TRANSLATION MATTERS: Romans 12:1

The NRSVue rendering "to present your bodies as a living sacrifice, holy and acceptable to God" (παραστῆσαι τὰ σώματα ὑμῶν θυσίαν ζῶσαν ἁγίαν εὐάρεστον τῷ θεῷ) is grammatically possible. An alternative translation, which recognizes the three attributes as a triadic figure, is "to present your bodies as a sacrifice, living, holy and acceptable to God."[2] Scholars have not yet discussed a third option, namely, the translation "to present your bodies as a living and holy sacrifice, acceptable to God." It takes note of the threefold *homoioteleuton* (similar sounding endings in close proximity) of the Greek terms θυσίαν ζῶσαν ἁγίαν, which suggests that, among the three attributes, "living" and "holy" belong together and should be connected with "sacrifice" of which they designate ontological qualities. By contrast, the third attribute, "acceptable," describes the intended effect of this sacrifice on God.

Another translation matter in this sentence is that the presentation of "bodies" in the plural is correlated here to a "sacrifice" in the singular (so also the NRSVue). Bible translations and commentators have sometimes rendered the singular as a plural ("sacrifices").[3] Yet in his deployment of cultic metaphors, Paul and Phoebe instead envisage the presentation of many bodies as one collective sacrificial offering, not as many sacrifices.[4] The exact translation epitomizes their vision for collective salvation constituting a community of believers. Many "bodies" together are one sacrifice in one corporate "spiritual worship."[5]

2. Robert Jewett, *Romans: A Commentary*, Hermeneia (Minneapolis: Fortress, 2007), 724–25.

3. See the NIV (1984); Joseph A. Fitzmyer, *Romans: A New Translation with Introduction and Commentary*, AB 33 (New York: Doubleday, 1993), 637–39.

4. Angelika Reichert, *Der Römerbrief als Gratwanderung: Eine Untersuchung zur Abfassungsproblematik*, FRLANT 194 (Göttingen: Vandenhoeck & Ruprecht, 2001), 233; Peter Oakes, *Reading Romans in Pompeii: Paul's Letter at Ground Level* (Minneapolis: Fortress; London: SPCK, 2009), 99–100.

5. Alternatively, the NIV translates "true and proper worship" (Reina Valera 1995: "vuestro verdadero culto"); the KJV, NKJV, NET have "reasonable service." Yet, the

ment, each according to the measure of faith that God has assigned. 4For as in one body we have many members and not all the members have the same function, 5so we, who are many, are one body in Christ, and individually we are members one of another. 6We have gifts that differ according to the grace given to us: prophecy, in proportion to faith; 7ministry, in ministering; the teacher, in teaching; 8the encourager, in encouragement; the giver, in sincerity; the leader, in diligence; the compassionate, in cheerfulness.

Before beginning the detailed interpretation of the ideas, ethical advice, and so forth in Romans 12:1–15:13, it is worth reflecting on two aspects: First, there is the simple observation that Paul and Phoebe needed to give ethical advice as such. It is the direct consequence of their earlier insistence that humans are, in their opinion, discharged from the law (Rom 7:1-6) and that Christ is, as the "culmination" or "goal," also the "end" of the law (10:4; see also 3:21-31; 8:2; Gal 2:16). Paul and Phoebe could, therefore, not just point to the law (particularly to its ethical portions) and recommend it for observance. If the law had come to an end (besides being useful for the definition of "sin," as claimed in Rom 3:20), then they still owed the answer of what members of the assemblies in Rome were to do practically. That is the purpose of the parenetic section.

And second, the parenetic section of the letter is in Romans 12:1–15:13. This section is *not* a second installment after a first such section in Romans 1:18-32 or its continuation. The paragraph in 1:18-32 had a different purpose; it was written to detoxify a potentially poisonous atmosphere in various assemblies in Rome. This means that it was *not* intended as a first paragraph of ethical directives. It served rather as a canvas to project a spectrum of potential prejudices against Phoebe and possibly also against Paul (see above, pp. 63–64). The anticipated prejudice was, therefore, immediately problematized and dispelled (2:1-11). Judgment is, however, a topic that will be addressed in its own right in the current

reference to presenting "your bodies" in Romans 12:1 makes clear that the point of true worship is not only a matter of inner attitude or rational reflections. It is about an embodied form of worship. At the same time, the reference to "the renewing of the mind" that occurs still in the same sentence (Rom 12:2) as well as further appeals to the realm of thoughts shows that the semantic spectrum of the term nonetheless includes intellectual pursuits. Cf. Douglas J. Moo, *The Epistle to the Romans*, NICNT (Grand Rapids: Eerdmans, 1996), 748, 751–53.

parenetic section (14:1-13). Yet, for the reasons outlined above, the topic of same-sex activities is no longer addressed here. This can only mean that it is of no real ethical concern for Paul and Phoebe.

The section in Romans 12:1–15:13 is closely correlated with the preceding ones. This is immediately evident when "God's mercy" (Rom 12:1a) is invoked with terminology reminiscent of divine mercy/grace and the forgiveness of sins in Romans 9:15-23; 11:30-32; and elsewhere. And in fact, everything in this first paragraph is presented as the outflowing of divine mercy or compassion, actualized in relationships.[6] Also the sacrificial terminology (12:1b) is similar to that in the christological paragraph of 3:21-26. In addition, the word "bodies" occurred in 6:12-19 in combination with "grace." Thus, the exhortation to render one's body to God in Romans 12:1 can be understood as the positive complement in response to the negative warning in 6:12.[7] This implies, however, that one needs to be aware that the contents of the chapters on ethics are not necessarily timeless moral lessons applicable for all places on earth. They are as preliminary as the associated theological or christological arguments. One depends on the other. If we question some of the dogmatic arguments or consider them obsolete, then this will *mutatis mutandis* also call into question the ethical consequences.

The new structural unit is immediately indicated by the usage of "I appeal to you" (Rom 12:1). Paul uses this verb once more in his letter to Philemon 8-9, where he mentions that he could very well "order" or "command you to do your duty"; here he employs the Greek verb ἐπιτάσσω. He states, however: "yet I would rather appeal to you on the basis of love," this time using the verb παρακαλῶ. It is, thus, a term that does not rest on a mandate of power or authority but hopes for understanding and actions based on agreement to what has been conveyed previously. Such semantic implications of the term may be understood as equivalent to the announcement in the opening section of the letter: "For I long to see you so that I may share with you some spiritual gift so that you may be strengthened—or rather so that we may be mutually encouraged by each other's faith, both yours and mine" (Rom 1:11-

6. Sigve K. Tonstad, *The Letter to the Romans: Paul among the Ecologists*, Earth Bible Commentary 7 (Sheffield: Sheffield Phoenix, 2016), 292–94.

7. Heinrich Schlier, *Der Römerbrief*, HTKNT 6 (Freiburg: Herder, 1977), 351; Arland J. Hultgren, *Paul's Letter to the Romans: A Commentary* (Grand Rapids: Eerdmans, 2011), 438; Richard N. Longenecker, *The Epistle to the Romans: A Commentary on the Greek Text*, NIGTC (Grand Rapids: Eerdmans, 2016), 918.

12). Paul never managed to travel to Rome under these terms. Instead, Phoebe went on his behalf, and her mission was, if anything, to provide such mutual encouragement. One may speculate that a parenetic appeal from a woman would have had less of an authoritative character given the status of women in the ancient patronage system.

The appeal or urging is "to present your bodies as a living [and holy] sacrifice, acceptable to God [παραστῆσαι τὰ σώματα ὑμῶν θυσίαν ζῶσαν ἁγίαν εὐάρεστον τῷ θεῷ]" (Rom 12:1).[8] This sentence employs the term "body" that occurred in Romans 6:12; 8:11; it indicates the realm of practical activities with a focus on actions. The essence of the encouragement is conveyed through terminology drawn from the Second Temple in Jerusalem and its related worship. This terminology is used metaphorically.[9] Its interpretation has, for several reasons, caused problems. One needs, however, to be conscious of the fact that the temple and its liturgies were important for Judaism during the Second Temple period. At the time of composition of Romans, that temple was still standing and fully operational.[10] Its imagery was, therefore, a preferred source for metaphors or allusions. Paul has used similar language previously; sometimes the sanctuary is mentioned explicitly: "For God's temple is holy, and you are that temple" (1 Cor 3:17; see also 6:18-19). Likewise, the address of the audiences in Rome as "saints" (Rom 1:7) is related to the sanctuary and similar to calling the sacrifice in 12:1 "holy." The quality of holiness here appears as a trust placed in the care of the believers.[11] This makes the task of deciphering such terminology all the more urgent.

Unfortunately, after its destruction, the temple fell into oblivion, and with it not only details of its rituals and worship liturgies but also the insider knowledge of their meanings. In addition, modern scholarship has rather neglected these areas of inquiry. As a consequence, sacrificial metaphors not only in Romans 12:1 but elsewhere in the New Testament have often been misinterpreted. Some of these problems have to do with the characteristic misconception that sacrificial rituals exclusively involve animals and are in essence mainly about slaughter, connected with ideas

8. For this translation, which differs from the NRSVue, see the comments above under "Translation Matters" on Romans 12:1 (p. 264).

9. Michael Wolter, *Der Brief an die Römer*, vol. 2: *Röm 9–16*, EKKNT 6/2 (Göttingen: Vandenhoeck & Ruprecht; Ostfildern: Patmos, 2019), 251.

10. Hultgren, *Romans*, 439.

11. J. Paul Sampley, *Walking between the Times: Paul's Moral Reasoning* (Minneapolis: Fortress, 1991), 76.

that blood rites and suffering are intrinsic to sacrifice.[12] Related metaphors, therefore, are habitually interpreted in negative ways. In parenetic contexts, they appear to promote nothing but self-denial and submission. Therefore, "many women have seen themselves as 'living sacrifices' and have experienced that as profoundly destructive."[13]

If the point of a sacrificial ritual was indeed slaughter or killing, then the metaphor of a "living sacrifice" in Romans 12:1 would, however, be an oxymoron.[14] Instead, the Greek noun θυσία conveys an act of giving and transformation. In the Septuagint, this term is, among other things, the main equivalent of the Hebrew term מנחה, the technical word for the grain offering according to Leviticus 2 (briefly alluded to in Rom 11:16a). It occurs with a similar meaning in the *leges sacrae*, Greek offering tariffs dating from the first century BCE to the third century CE. These tariffs contain detailed instructions for sacrifices at local temples and employ the term θυσία for both animal sacrifice *and* vegetal offerings.[15] Plants, however, cannot be slaughtered. Therefore, this technical term for sacrifice has nothing to do with killing or violence.

Paul employs the term "sacrifice" with the same semantic spectrum to express his gratitude for material support (or a contribution to his collection for Jerusalem) from the congregation in Philippi: "a pleasing sacrifice, acceptable for God"[16] (θυσίαν δεκτήν, εὐάρεστον τῷ θεῷ, Phil

12. See, for example, the statement in the recent study of Benjamin J. Ribbens, *Levitical Sacrifice and Heavenly Cult in Hebrews*, BZNW 222 (Berlin: de Gruyter, 2016), 135: "The levitical laws . . . described what kind of animal and what characteristics it must have for a sacrifice to be efficacious. Sacrifice was a holistic process beginning with slaughter and culminating with blood manipulation." All elements of this brief summary statement are incorrect. First, sacrificial rituals involve not only animals but also vegetal materials, including details about their type and quality (Lev 2). Second, not a single sacrificial ritual begins with slaughter; they all start with the selection of the sacrificial material, which is followed by the approach of the offerer to the sanctuary. Third, not a single sacrificial ritual culminates with blood manipulation. They all culminate with the burning rite on the altar of burnt offerings in front of the sanctuary. It is unfortunate that exegetical studies focusing on sacrifice misconstrue essential aspects of sacrifice so significantly.

13. Beverly Roberts Gaventa, "Romans," in *Women's Bible Commentary*, ed. Carol A. Newsom, Sharon H. Ringe, and Jacqueline E. Lapsley, 3rd ed. (Louisville: Westminster John Knox, 2012), 554.

14. Edgar Krentz, "The Sense of Senseless Oxymora," *CurTM* 28 (2001): 577–84, esp. 581–82.

15. Fred S. Naiden, *Smoke Signals for the Gods: Ancient Greek Sacrifice from the Archaic through Roman Periods* (Oxford: Oxford University Press, 2013), 280–82.

16. This translation of Phil 4:18 is my own. In the rendition of NRSVue ("a fragrant offering, a sacrifice acceptable and pleasing to God"), the parallels to the sacrificial cult of Second Temple Judaism and the terminology of Leviticus (LXX) are lost.

4:18). Clearly, then, Paul had neither blood rites nor killing nor other negative aspects in mind when using such terminology. Instead, he wanted to express the idea that the referent is transformed during the experience of human worship. The aspect of transformation is, after all, explicitly conveyed by the Greek verb μεταμορφόω ("to transform") in Romans 12:2. What was previously profane is now, after a process of metamorphosis, sacred and acceptable to God. Such consecration has its origin and goal in God.[17] Here and in Romans 12:1, sacrificial metaphors also comprise the gratitude of the recipients of the gifts. Paul, the agent in charge of this process of sacred transformation, is therefore called "a minister [λειτουργός] of Christ Jesus" and performs a "priestly service [ἱερουργέω] of the gospel of God" (15:16).[18]

Aside from their familiarity with the topic from religious texts and traditions, the members of the assemblies in Rome would have actually witnessed sacrificial rituals in their city in two forms: as small-scale token sacrifices of domestic cults and as large-scale sacrifices paid for by wealthy patrons (and the state) on the occasion of festivals and games. This would be the dominant template for some to understand the language in Romans 12:1. The noun "sacrifice," θυσία, is in the singular while "bodies," σώματα, is plural, conveying the idea that many people engage in a unified act.[19] Even at this stage in the parenetic discourse, the vision of Paul and Phoebe is to transform different individuals with diverse gifts into a unified whole that, as the "body of Christ," is sacred. This is the topic of 12:4-8, which relies to a large degree on previous imagery of 1 Corinthians 12. The purpose is to recognize unity among members of assemblies with different gifts: "For as in one body we have many members and not all the members have the same function, so we, who are many, are one body in Christ, and individually we are members one of another" (Rom 12:4-5). For obvious reasons, such a body metaphor was very commonsensical to any audience. Not surprising, it is widely attested in Greco-Roman literature.[20] In that sense, one may read

17. Gaventa, "Romans," 554.

18. On Romans 15:16, see below.

19. Reichert, *Gratwanderung*, 233.

20. See, for example, Plutarch, *Phil.* 8 where the same expression, ἓν σῶμά, "one body," as in Romans 12:4 is employed. In fables by Aesop and Menenius Agrippa, the state is described as a "body." The point is that some members revolt against the stomach only to face starvation; in this way, they rediscover their organic unity (Aesop *Fab.* 132; Dio Chrysostom *Orat.* 33.16; Livy *Hist.* 2.32; Epictetus *Diss.* 2.10.4-5). According to Seneca, humans are part of the world body (Seneca *Ep.* 95.52). Cf. Beverly Roberts Gaventa, *Our Mother Saint Paul* (Louisville: Westminster John Knox, 2007), 144.

portions of Romans as examples of the progressive Roman orientation of the authors.

The comparison shows that 1 Corinthians 12:13 attributes the unity of all to baptism "into one body—Jews or Greeks, slaves or free." This element has now been appropriated in Romans 12, where the entire section is summarized and shortened. The paragraphs also appear in inverse order, now moving from the theme of unity in Christ to the actual gifts. Second, in 1 Corinthians 12, the Spirit is central; it is not mentioned in Romans 12 but replaced by the term "grace." Third, both lists of gifts are similar in their detailed presentation of the variety of gifts among the members of the assemblies. The gifts mentioned in Romans 12:6-8 are, however, rather different from those in 1 Corinthians 12:8-11. Not a single item appears in both lists.[21] Finally, it lists four tasks belonging to the office of proclamation: prophecy, ministry, teacher, and encourager (Rom 12:6-8). Among these, the term "ministry" (διακονία) is used elsewhere for Paul's apostleship (11:13; 15:25, 31) and notably even for the office of government rulers (13:3-4). It sheds light on the meaning of the term διάκονος as one of Phoebe's titles (16:1).

Another cultic metaphor in Romans 12:1b is "your reasonable act of worship." In consideration of similar terminology in 1:9, it envisages an embodied form of worship that includes the human mind and is based on its renewal (12:2). The accumulation of cultic metaphors in the opening sentences of the parenetic section of Romans is surprising (see also 15:16). A reason for this is that the assemblies of believers in Christ had discontinued actual sacrificial rituals, which were part and parcel of the worship of other religious communities. The discontinuation facilitated the idea that the members of these communities themselves were sacrificial offerings to God. They would engage with their lives to realize God's love and justice in the world.[22]

In Romans 12:3, Phoebe presents her audiences in Rome with an appeal to humility and charity. It continues the new perspective that those in Christ are all members of the body of Christ. All of the various gifts are for the good of all—and not for one's own self-promotion. The related directive has been rendered by Robert Jewett in a way that respects the fourfold variation on the stem φρον- in the Greek text (*paronomasia*): "do not be superminded above what you ought to be minded but set your mind on

21. Gaventa, *When in Romans*, 80.

22. Elsa Tamez, "Der Brief an die Gemeinde in Rom: Eine feministische Lektüre," in *Kompendium feministische Bibelauslegung*, ed. Luise Schottroff and Marie-Theres Wacker, 2nd ed. (Gütersloh: Kaiser; Gütersloher Verlagshaus, 1999), 573.

being soberminded" (μὴ ὑπερφρονεῖν παρ' ὃ δεῖ φρονεῖν ἀλλὰ φρονεῖν εἰς τὸ σωφρονεῖν).[23] This is particularly elegant language for something Phoebe had said before in concise diatribe jargon: "Then what becomes of boasting? It is excluded" (3:27). Warnings against boasting have also occurred elsewhere in the letter (2:17, 23; 5:1-3, 11; 11:18-19). Related is the warning in 11:20 not to become proud but to rather stand in awe.[24] With a spiritual perspective, all members of the assemblies were to be content with their function or position in the community. Against the backdrop of the Greco-Roman honor-shame system, it is clear that this appeal envisages a different type of society. Sentences like these, therefore, undermine that system, both in terms of ascribed honor and acquired honor. The gospel message shows its countercultural depth-dimension. With regard to the various offices in the assemblies, there is no longer any basis for seeing oneself as superior.[25] If everything is due to faith and faith is God's free gift, then "superminded" is out and "soberminded" is trending. This is exactly what the call not to be "conformed to this age" (12:2) is all about.

But this vision of a new civil order goes even further. It also undermines the entire status system as such, as Peter Oakes argues. He exemplifies the impact in the case of an imagined assembly of Christ believers in Rome.

> The 30 people in the model house church stood in a status order that would be broadly agreed by them and by society as a whole. There were subtleties and scope for limited differences of opinion, but there was a fairly clear scale running down from the wealthiest free-born male householders (unless someone else in the house church was particularly well born) to the lowest-level slave. Free-born was above freed, which was above slave. Male was above female. Adult was above child. Wealthy was above poor. Wealth could cut across some other factors. If the church included a relatively well-off widow householder, she would probably have had higher status than poorer male householders. Her status would also be affected by the number of children she had raised. Paul's call does away with the relevance of all this in assessing one's position. All is faith, a gift.[26]

It may be added that, by the terminology of Romans, there was likewise a status order based on ethnicity. On the one hand, being Roman was

23. Jewett, *Romans*, 31.

24. Philip F. Esler, *Conflict and Identity in Romans: The Social Setting of Paul's Letter* (Minneapolis: Fortress, 2003), 312–13.

25. Oakes, *Romans*, 101.

26. Oakes, *Romans*, 101–2. See also Esler, *Conflict*, 313.

above being "barbarian." On the other hand, Jewish was above Greek. The new vision for society does away with every type of status based on ethnic distinctions as well. The people of God is one body that includes both Jews and gentiles. This principle was threatened wherever either gentiles were pressured to become Jews or Jewish believers in Christ were excluded. In the letters to Galatia, Philippi, and in 2 Corinthians, Paul argues against those who envision an exclusively Jewish church. In Romans, the situation is reversed; Paul and Phoebe argue against those who wish to maintain an exclusively gentile church.[27] The common denominator of these letters is the vision of the radically democratic *ekklēsia* of wo/men "in Christ" (Rom 12:5), which is a concept of being vertically connected to Jesus as spiritual Lord of all and horizontally associated with the other members in the assembly of believers. Relationships at that horizontal level are symmetrical. All of this is epitomized by and grounded in the baptismal formula in Galatians 3:28 (see above, pp. lxxxiv–lxxxv). That formula, according to Elisabeth Schüssler Fiorenza, "proclaims that in the Christian community all distinctions of religion, race, class, nationality, and gender are insignificant. All the baptized are equal, they are one in Christ."[28] Such a vision had the power of undermining the honor-shame system *and* the status system of the ancient Roman world.

From the perspective of marginalized members of ancient Greco-Roman societies, including women, the ethos of the Jewish groups of believers in Christ must have been acknowledged because it amounted to an improvement for those of inferior status. The involvement of women at many levels, including that of leadership of assemblies, shows that they were respected and fully integrated. It constitutes an implicit criticism of the dominant society where women and other marginalized groups are considered inferior socially, intellectually, morally, or spiritually. Not only Phoebe, the gentile woman who may formerly have been enslaved, but also Prisca, leader of one assembly in Rome (Rom 16:3-5), and Junia (v. 7) as well as other women embody the ethos of this new era. Their meeting in the Eternal City was only possible because of the very ethos that they proclaimed in their gospel messages. That such a message was not welcome everywhere is part of the next section, specifically Romans 12:14-20.

27. Peter J. Tomson, *Presumed Guilty: How the Jews Were Blamed for the Death of Jesus*, trans. Janet Dyk (Minneapolis: Fortress, 2005), 114.

28. Elisabeth Schüssler Fiorenza, *In Memory of Her: A Feminist Theological Reconstruction of Christian Origins* (New York: Crossroad, 1983), 213. See also Jennifer L. Koosed, *Reading the Bible as a Feminist*, BRP 2/2 (Leiden: Brill, 2017), 21–22.

Marks of the True Christian (12:9-21)

This pericope spells out pragmatic guidelines for genuine love. It starts without any prepositional connection to the preceding units but simply consists of a concise nominal sentence: "Let love be genuine [Ἡ ἀγάπη ἀνυπόκριτος]" (Rom 12:9). As such, it states the theme for a section that elaborates and problematizes it. This short sentence is not about the concept of love in general, as the use of the definite article in Greek indicates.[29] The social context of the early celebration of the Eucharist or Communion, also called "love feast," was the primary frame of reference for the audiences, even if the later discourse extends beyond the immediate communities (12:13-14).[30] This periodic celebration was a manifestation of the message of mutual love, respect for all, and equality. Bread and a chalice of wine representing a new covenant conveyed the continuous relationship of Jesus with those who had accepted a new identity in baptism, available as a free gift.

The section of Romans 12:9-13 is artfully constructed to maximize rhetorical impact, consisting of ten neatly balanced phrases and additional chiastic structures in verses 10-13. Furthermore, 12:14-20 features advice in topical series of fours and twos, besides several wordplays (for instance, "extend" [διώκοντες] and "persecute" [διώκοντας], 12:13-14).[31] This leads to admonitions that elaborate on those in 12:3 to be soberminded rather than superminded. Romans 12:16b, therefore, states: "do not be arrogant, but associate with the lowly." It spells out some consequences of true compassion in 12:15-16a: "Rejoice with those who rejoice; weep with those who weep. [Be intent on having the same mind toward] one another."[32] Various elements of 12:9-21 have appeared in earlier letters of

29. The article is missing in some Bible versions and secondary literature: NRSVue, NIV ("Love must be sincere"), and NKJV, furthermore Esler, *Conflict*, 317. It is included in the Revidierte Lutherübersetzung 2017 ("Die Liebe sei ohne Falsch") and the Reina Valera 1995 ("El amor sea sin fingimiento").

30. Robert Jewett, "Are There Allusions to the Love Feast in Rom 13:8-10?," in *Common Life in the Early Church: Essays Honoring Graydon F. Snyder*, ed. Julian V. Hills et al. (Harrisburg, PA: Trinity Press International, 1998); Jewett, *Romans*, 814; Lallene J. Rector, "Shame and Honor Systems in the Book of Romans: A Psychological Analysis of the Struggle for Superiority within and between the Roman Tenement and House Churches," in *Scripture, Cultures, and Criticism: Interpretive Steps and Critical Issues Raised by Robert Jewett*, ed. Khiok-khng Yeo, Contrapuntal Readings of the Bible in World Christianity 9 (Eugene, OR: Pickwick, 2022), 117–29.

31. David A. Black, "The Pauline Love Command: Structure, Style, and Ethics in Romans 12:9-21," *FilN* 2 (1989): 3–22, at 5–9; Jewett, *Romans*, 756–57.

32. In the NRSVue and NIV, Romans 12:16 is translated as "Live in harmony with one another." The Greek text, however, has τὸ αὐτὸ εἰς ἀλλήλους φρονοῦντες. The verb

Rom 12:9-21

[9]Let love be genuine; hate what is evil;
hold fast to what is good; [10]love one
another with mutual affection; outdo
one another in showing honor. [11]Do not
lag in zeal; be ardent in spirit; serve the
Lord. [12]Rejoice in hope; be patient in affliction; persevere in prayer. [13]Contrib-
ute to the needs of the saints; pursue
hospitality to strangers.

[14]Bless those who persecute you;
bless and do not curse them. [15]Re-
joice with those who rejoice; weep with
those who weep. [16]Live in harmony
with one another; do not be arrogant,
but associate with the lowly; do not
claim to be wiser than you are. [17]Do
not repay anyone evil for evil, but take
thought for what is noble in the sight
of all. [18]If it is possible, so far as it depends on you, live peaceably with all.
[19]Beloved, never avenge yourselves,
but leave room for the wrath of God,
for it is written, "Vengeance is mine; I
will repay, says the Lord." [20]Instead, "if
your enemies are hungry, feed them;
if they are thirsty, give them something
to drink, for by doing this you will heap
burning coals on their heads." [21]Do not
be overcome by evil, but overcome evil
with good.

Paul. He had, for example, commended his own mission "with genuine love [ἐν ἀγάπῃ ἀνυποκρίτῳ]" (2 Cor 6:6) against the "superapostles" who, in Paul's opinion, had abused gifts like love for the sake of power and status (see also 2 Cor 12:9).[33] In addition, the parenetic advice in 1 Thessalonians 5:12-22 contains a number of parallels to Romans 12:9-21, suggesting that it has been a rather stable element in Paul's proclamation.[34] It is, however, not necessarily a highly original component of his gospel message. The warning against retaliation is attested in various forms in ancient literary traditions.[35] The stipulations of Romans 12:17 and 1 Thessalonians 5:15 are almost a quotation of *Joseph and Aseneth* 28.14: "do not pay back evil for evil to any person."

φρονέω, here as a present participle, typically means "to think," denoting an inner attitude (Bertram, "φρήν," 221). It is not necessarily identical with the broader meaning of living one's life, for which often the verb "to walk" (περιπατέω) is employed (see Rom 6:4; 8:4; 13:13). Indeed, the entire verse of 12:16 is about mental disposition and maintains this meaning until the final clause: "do not claim to be wiser than you are [μὴ γίνεσθε φρόνιμοι παρ᾽ ἑαυτοῖς]." In this regard, it is similar to 12:3. Therefore, a translation that better conveys the fact that 12:16 is about individual and corporate thoughts and respects the semantic coherence would be "Be intent on having the same mind toward one another" (Hultgren, *Romans*, 458; see also the NASB 1995, NKJV, Reina Valera 1995).

33. Jewett, *Romans*, 352–55, 758–59.

34. Alain Gignac, *L'épître aux Romains*, Commentaire biblique: Nouveau Testament 6 (Paris: Cerf, 2014), 470–71.

35. See the sources listed in Jewett, *Romans*, 771.

With the admonition to "live peaceably with all" (Rom 12:18), the scope of the discourse is broadened. Appeals have so far been given with a focus on social relationships within the assemblies of Christ believers. The term "all" indicates, however, that now relationships beyond this intimate circle are also considered. The advice given here could be categorized as a strategy of de-escalation with an interest in the good of the larger civic community. In Romans 12:19-21, these maxims are validated by passages from Jewish Scriptures. Here, Deuteronomy 32:35 stresses God's authority in matters of revenge while Proverbs 25:21-22 lauds generosity toward one's enemies as a way to exact revenge without doing evil.

It was widely known that refraining from doing evil in return for having suffered evil was a key maxim for breaking the vicious circle of evil and hatred. The idea is to start a virtuous circle of love and doing good instead. Of course, such advice is also famously included in the Sermon on the Mount (Matt 5:38-42, 43-48). Much later, it belonged to the basic principles of Mohandas Karamchand Gandhi in his quest to end colonialism in India and of Martin Luther King Jr.'s Civil Rights Movement that fought for the end of racial segregation in the Southern United States of America. These rules and appeals in Romans 12:1–15:13 may, therefore, not be the exclusive property of Paul (and to some degree of Phoebe), but its theological basis in Romans 1–11 is.

The countercultural potential of the ethical appeal in chapter 12 is manifest in a rather inconspicuous exhortation: "outdo one another in showing honor" (v. 10). With the noun τιμή, "honor," Paul and Phoebe employ the key term of the honor-shame system, but this advice is to be followed by *all* members of the assemblies in Rome.[36] Everyone is asked to outdo others in showing honor. The revolutionary dimension of this request is immediately evident when one recalls that a significant percentage of the members of these assemblies were enslaved persons. Those enslaved, however, had no social status in Roman society, and there was no provision that they would ever receive honor. The request in 12:10 implies nothing less than that enslaved persons would suddenly be considered worthy of honor; in certain cases, their masters would even have been expected to show them gestures of honor. Peter Oakes comments: "In first-century terms this is outrageous."[37] But one can imagine how this experience would have given a boost to the lowest in society who may have felt that they were "brought from death to life" (6:13) and who would have recognized that Christ gives such life (8:11).

36. The showing of honor outside of the assemblies of believers in Christ will be discussed in Romans 13:7 (see below).

37. Oakes, *Romans*, 110.

The appeal to "outdo one another in showing honor" would, finally, have had a special meaning for Phoebe. She was no longer an enslaved person, but by all implicit and explicit standards of traditional Roman patriarchy, she was not the first in line to receive honor. The role of bringing the letter to Rome and reciting it made her the representative or avatar of Paul. But it is clear that Paul would, as a Jewish male born as a free person, have had a rather different position within the matrix of the traditional honor-shame culture. The success of Phoebe's mission to proclaim the gospel on behalf of Paul was in no small measure dependent on the acceptance of the very egalitarian ethos in the communities that she visited.

The ethical discourse in this paragraph sounds beautiful and depicts an ideal utopian society. It is formulated in a chiastic relationship to the upcoming section about being subject to authorities in 13:1-7, which is exclusively concerned with out-groups.

The world is not always a place where all of these ideas and directives are lived out or have been implemented. More often than not, the opposite is the case. This only means that such an ethical appeal is even more urgent—and still timely today. Two such aspects shall be further discussed in detail.

First, Sigve K. Tonstad applies the ethos presented in Romans 12 to the cause of ecology and suggests that no chapter in Romans would be more applicable for this purpose. The reason is the focus of chapter 12 on compassion, "the sentiment that is most needed and most lacking with respect to critical ecological concerns."[38] Taking all of the planet with all of its forms of life seriously is just another application of the countercultural gospel message. Tonstad argues that previous passages also invite such an interpretation. Examples include the image of the groaning of nonhuman creation that occurs in the same language that humans speak and is perceived by God (Rom 8:22-23). Likewise, a passage that Tonstad reads as cast from the perspective of Eve but that has been understood here as Phoebe's personal statement (see above, pp. 167–168) about deception, desire, and death (7:7-13) also invites such an interpretation. The countercultural message of Romans is, therefore, all the more applicable in our days. Tonstad sees the necessity of a divine economy of seeds that conveys God's generosity, of a divine economy of land that conveys concepts of sustainability, and of a divine economy of mercy that ends the suffering specifically of animals by instilling love for the nonhuman creation.[39]

38. Tonstad, *Romans*, 293.

39. Tonstad, *Romans*, 295–308.

The second aspect is not an application of the ethos of Romans 12 but a call to caution and a warning in light of the change of sociocultural parameters in our modern (or postmodern) world. The ideal of love that does not repay evil for evil but only seeks to do good (12:9), or of love that is always patient and kind without insisting in its own ways (the latter according to 1 Cor 13:4-5) may contribute to an oppressive environment for the identity formation of women in modern (or postmodern) societies. Elisabeth Schüssler Fiorenza problematizes that, because of its centrality, the "Christian principle of love can serve to sustain wo/men's internalized oppression today although the text in its original context may not have done so at all."[40] Schüssler Fiorenza then describes the oppression of women through a genderized development of the term "love" in modern society with different role assignments for women and men. This has led to, among other things, ideals of romantic love and self-sacrificing motherhood for girls and women. In this way, a "conflation of traditional notions of submission and headship with modern notions of romantic heterosexual love is at the heart of patriarchal-kyriarchal relations of oppression today."[41] Tragic consequences are not only unrealistic physical standards of beauty but also domestic violence against women, sexual abuse and harassment, battering, rape, and so on.[42] These negative and harmful global developments—often even promoted in the name of Christianity—clearly run counter to the ethos of love as proclaimed by Paul and Phoebe, which is interested in real equality and mutual care and not a new form of misogyny. Paul's cooperation with Phoebe in the production of Romans and his willingness to entrust her with its transport to Rome and the delivery in front of the audiences there are a demonstration of a very different view of women, including their competencies and reliability.

Being Subject to Authorities (13:1-7)

A diatribe concerning obligations to the governing authorities starts abruptly; no conjunction connects it to the preceding text. But it nevertheless continues the ideas of chapter 12. After the admonitions to have the same mind toward one another (Rom 12:16)[43] and to live peacefully

40. Elisabeth Schüssler Fiorenza, *Sharing Her Word: Feminist Biblical Interpretation in Context* (Boston: Beacon, 1998), 139.

41. Schüssler Fiorenza, *Sharing*, 140.

42. Schüssler Fiorenza, *Sharing*, 140–47.

43. For this translation, which differs from the NRSVue, see the comments above on Romans 12:16 (pp. 273–274).

Rom 13:1-7

[13:1]Let every person be subject to the governing authorities, for there is no authority except from God, and those authorities that exist have been instituted by God. [2]Therefore whoever resists authority resists what God has appointed, and those who resist will incur judgment. [3]For rulers are not a terror to good conduct but to bad. Do you wish to have no fear of the authority? Then do what is good, and you will receive its approval, [4]for it is God's agent for your good. But if you do what is wrong, you should be afraid, for the authority does not bear the sword in vain! It is the agent of God to execute wrath on the wrongdoer. [5]Therefore one must be subject, not only because of wrath but also because of conscience. [6]For the same reason you also pay taxes, for the authorities are God's agents, busy with this very thing. [7]Pay to all what is due them: taxes to whom taxes are due, revenue to whom revenue is due, respect to whom respect is due, honor to whom honor is due.

"with all" (v. 18), the circle is gradually broadened to include the wider civil society. Even though the appeals in Romans 13:1-7 are unique in Pauline writings, they still display some of the same ethos of compassion and de-escalation that characterizes chapter 12. Surprising, however, is the general opinion about the divine institution of civil authorities and the call to obey them. These authorities are most likely those of the city of Rome.[44] In that case, this statement appears to contradict the recent declaration in Romans 12:2 not to be conformed to this world as well as several other countercultural statements in that chapter. While the appeal in Romans 12 is directed at the members of the assembly, the text of 13:1-7, however, has the whole society in mind (Πᾶσα ψυχὴ, "every person," v. 1). The structure of chapters 12 and 13 can be understood as chiastic in the following way:

Chiastic Structure in Romans 12 and 13[45]

Rom 12		*Rom 13*
12:1-2 – A	Living a transformed life	13:11-14 – A[1]
12:3-13 – B	Relationships within in-group	13:8-10 – B[1]
12:14-21 – C	Relationships with out-group	13:1-7 – C[1]

44. Romano Penna, "Évangile et politique à Rome selon Paul et son Épître aux Romains," in *Talking God in Society: Multidisciplinary (Re)constructions of Ancient (Con)texts; Festschrift for Peter Lampe*, vol. 1: *Theories and Applications*, ed. Ute E. Eisen and Heidrun E. Mader, NTOA 120/1 (Göttingen: Vandenhoeck & Ruprecht, 2020), 287.

45. Tarcisius Mukuka, "Reading/Hearing Romans 13:1-7 under an African Tree: Towards a *Lectio Postcolonica Contexta Africana*," *Neot* 46 (2012): 105–38, at 109.

This table illustrates that the parenetic section of the letter is carefully organized. Its paragraphs correspond to select arguments of the previous theological section and apply them. In addition, certain pericopes within the parenetic section feature symmetrical structures.

In general, Romans 13 could be considered an appendix to or an application of chapter 12 to the situation of life in the capital of the Roman Empire. Certain recent local developments (such as the edict of Claudius in 49 CE and corruption of tax farming) may have necessitated a passage like this. Therefore, it is not advisable to consider these directives as Paul's doctrine of the civil state or even its christological grounding, as is sometimes done,[46] since Christ is not mentioned anywhere in these appeals.[47] Rather, the rationale of the directive to subject oneself to authorities (13:1b-c) is firmly anchored in the Jewish wisdom tradition where God is considered to be the source of political authority. For instance, Proverbs 8:14-16 declares about the Jewish God: "I have good advice and sound wisdom; I have insight; I have strength. By me kings reign, and rulers decree what is just; by me rulers rule, and nobles, all who govern rightly." Such advice is also found in Daniel, the only apocalyptic book of the Hebrew Bible: "He [God] changes times and seasons, deposes kings and sets up kings; he gives wisdom to the wise and knowledge to those who have understanding" (Dan 2:21; see also 2:36-38; 4:17; Wis 6:3-4; Sir 10:14; 17:17). These are traditional topics of old.

The further treatment of the topic in Romans is also in line with Paul's and Phoebe's previous arguments. If resistance to authorities appointed by God incurs God's judgment, then the strong theological vision of reality shines through once again. On the other hand, the following statement is kept in rather general terms: "For rulers are not a terror to good conduct but to bad. Do you wish to have no fear of the authority? Then do what is good, and you will receive its approval, for it is God's agent for your good" (Rom 13:3-4). This statement is consistent with other sources from Greco-Roman antiquity (Appian, *Bell. civ.* 3.4.27, 20-22). If anything, it displays a certain level of naiveté.[48] Neither the political-philosophical dilemma of illegitimate authority nor the frequent abuse of power is considered. In

46. Charles E. B. Cranfield, *A Critical and Exegetical Commentary on the Epistle to the Romans*, vol. 1, ICC (Edinburgh: T&T Clark, 1975), 654; James D. G. Dunn, *Romans 9–16*, WBC 38b (Dallas: Word, 1988), 768, 771, 773.

47. Hultgren, *Romans*, 467.

48. Beverly Roberts Gaventa, "Reading Romans 13 with Simone Weil: Toward a More Generous Hermeneutic," *JBL* 136 (2017): 3–22, at 9.

particular, the problem that political systems may be supported only by some constituents but not by others and the fact that the imperial government authorities have been the guarantor of the very patriarchy/kyriarchy that Paul has been opposing through the establishment of countercultural assemblies appears absent from this advice. Only a few years later, Paul himself would be facing the government authorities in Rome, and if legend can be trusted, the outcome was fatal for him. It is probably questionable that he subscribed to the conviction that "rulers are not a terror to good conduct but to bad" until the bitter end.[49]

The encouragement to support the God-given government authority translates into the third argument of this section, namely, the rather mundane call to pay tributes and custom taxes (Rom 13:6-7). It is characterized by concise expression and artful rhetorical style; for instance, the repetition of the four nouns "taxes," "customs," "fear," and "honor," with rhymes, parallelism, and alliteration between "tribute/fear" (φόρος/φόβος) and "custom tax/honor" (τέλος/τιμή) provides a memorable conclusion to the passage despite the mundane topic. Whereas it resembles the pericope in the Synoptic Gospels about paying taxes (Mark 12:13-17 parr.), anything like the cheeky response of Jesus ("Give to Caesar the things that are Caesar's and to God the things that are God's," Mark 12:17) is missing in Romans 13. The term "honor" is another reference to the Greco-Roman honor-shame system; just like before (Rom 2:7; 9:23), any critical distance is missing.

Why then would such a paragraph be included in this letter in the first place? Some scholars have speculated that, during the mid-50s CE, problems due to dishonest tax collecting practices had sparked considerable concern among the city's inhabitants with political authorities. The consequence was widespread resentment, repulsion, and thoughts of revolt. This may have reminded some of the recent intervention of the authorities in response to unrest in the Jewish synagogues leading to the expulsion of Christ believers. The impetus behind the advice, therefore, was preemptive de-escalation.

For many modern scholars, the pericope of Romans 13:1-7 has been a problem and a puzzle. It has been a problem because it has often been understood as a text that legitimizes any form of political government for all times and places. As such, it has been used not only to condone but actively support totalitarian forms of government and/or colonialism

49. Elizabeth A. Castelli, "Romans," in *Searching the Scriptures*, vol. 2: *A Feminist Commentary*, ed. Elisabeth Schüssler Fiorenza (New York: Crossroad, 1994), 296.

with their associated praxis of oppression, racism, and so forth. This is cause for concern from a postcolonial as well as from any human rights perspective. Therefore, Ron Cassidy notes: "These words have caused more unhappiness and misery in the Christian East and West than any other 7 verses in the New Testament by the license they have given to tyrants."[50] Neither the general advice to "be subject to the governing authorities" nor the claim that "those authorities that exist have been instituted by God" in Romans 13:1 nor that to pay taxes in full fits that image.[51] How, then, should these lines be understood?

The entire pericope is unique in Pauline writings. This is one of the reasons why it has sometimes been considered an interpolation,[52] but that proposal has not gained wide approval. Rather, we see here authors—this term is deliberately put in the plural—behind the letter to the Romans who are indeed carefully optimistic about the political government and who have multiple citizenships. This certainly applies to Paul but also to several other collaborators of his in Corinth, including Phoebe, who would have shared this personal predicament. As mentioned above, writing Romans between 56 and 58 CE, not long after Nero's ascension, Paul was probably still optimistic about the new emperor. It was not necessarily clear that his reign would later turn out the way it did. Because of the hybrid identity of Paul, John W. Marshall cautions against expecting too much coherence between different statements of the apostle:

> The temptation to find a confluence of essences, origins and ideals in the person of Paul is a compromising distraction to a historical-critical understanding of Paul informed by the insights of postcolonialism. Employing the concept of hybridity makes it possible to see Paul's thought in a coherent frame, without imputing to it a false coherence. Paul is both "in and of" that world, working in relation to its centre from its margins, gathering and deploying its resources in the interest of his own programme, whether that means swimming with or against the current of imperial power in any particular moment. Though ambivalence is often a terror to dogmatics, it is the condition of colonial existence and thus Paul's.[53]

50. Ron Cassidy, "The Politicization of Paul: Romans 13.1-7 in Recent Discussion," *ExpTim* 121 (2010): 383–89, at 383.

51. Elisabeth Schüssler Fiorenza, *The Power of the Word: Scripture and the Rhetoric of Empire* (Minneapolis: Fortress, 2007), 5.

52. Winsome Munro, "Romans 13:1-7: Apartheid's Last Biblical Refuge," *BTB* 20 (1990): 161–68.

53. John W. Marshall, "Hybridity and Reading Romans 13," *JSNT* 31 (2008): 157–78, at 174.

This statement about Paul would also apply to several of those in Corinth who participated in or assisted with the collective effort of authoring Romans in a winter between 56 and 58 CE over the period of several weeks or months. Furthermore, we see here authors who—taking seriously the very appeal of Romans 12 for compassion and mutual love—care about the various recipients in Rome. Among those recipients were Prisca and Aquila, who had already been evicted from their home a few years earlier and, upon their return to Rome, still struggled to get fully settled. That included assuming the leadership of their assembly in Rome. In light of this situation, it is not unlikely that there was some concern about the growing unrest in the city regarding the tax situation, which may have caused another actual backlash by the municipal administrations. Alternatively, some (either members of the assemblies or of the Jewish synagogues) may have used this situation as a pretext to report new conflict to municipal authorities. The purpose may even have been to solicit another edict to achieve more expulsions. (Not everybody heeded the advice of Romans 12:18 to "live peaceably with all.")

Regarding his own cause, Paul's experience in the Roman Empire was somewhat ambivalent, but as a Roman citizen, he generally enjoyed some level of protection by its government. The *Pax Romana* was also an achievement that did not benefit everyone (as noted above), but it facilitated Paul's missionary journeys and thus helped him to spread his gospel message. These considerations make it likely that he was not necessarily having exclusively antagonistic sentiments toward the government authorities in Rome.

Paul's Counsel on Paying Taxes in Romans 13:1-7

The passage in Romans 13:1-7 seems a "purple patch" of political commentary within Paul's theological reflection. What is its rhetorical logic? Paul greets a whole host of women and men at the end of his letter in Romans 16:3-16. Presumably what he says here about the governing authorities is congenial to them. So who in the community is being warned, "But if you do what is wrong, you should be afraid, for the authority does not bear the sword in vain" (13:4). And who needs to be directed, "Therefore one must be subject, not only because of wrath but also because of conscience. For the same reason you also pay taxes" (13:5-6).

The counsel makes sense if Paul is addressing the same contentious debate among nationalist Jews about whether to pay Roman taxes as the dispute recorded in the Synoptics. There, Jesus resolves the tension: "Give to Caesar the things that are Caesar's and to God the things that are God's" (Mark 12:17 // Matt 22:21 // Luke 20:25). Here, Paul's warning is likely aimed at members of the Roman assemblies who are Jewish-born loyalists to the temple, or émigrés from the Levant to Rome. There's a tragedy looming. The message of this passage acknowledges the concerns of an anxious majority in the assemblies at Rome—native-born residents and citizens. Paul attempts to calm the members of the assemblies who are discomfited by the insurrectionists and those who foment resistance to paying taxes to the Roman government. The message is an attempt to unify the community despite its internal political divisions.

We know what Emperor Vespasian, followed by his son Titus, did within a decade to crush the rebellion of Jews against Roman occupation in the province of Syria. The Tenth Legion laid siege to the city for four years (68–72 CE), razing its neighborhoods with fire, dismantling the walls and buildings of the temple, driving out the residents in terror, and laying waste to surrounding fields and farmland.

What accounts for Romans 13:1-7 was a realistic fear of what could happen if a climate of civil disobedience were not tamped down. While many forms of taxes were imposed by Rome on the provinces and on noncitizens, citizens of Rome were exempt from residence taxes. This means that some members of the assemblies at Rome were required to pay taxes, and others were exempt.[54]

Paul could resolve ethnic, linguistic, class, and gender diversity by their baptism into Christ (Gal 3:28). But he had no power to eliminate Roman tax law or its financial consequences on members of the assemblies depending on their secular status. They could be one body by their baptism into Christ and spiritually equal as Abraham's offspring. Despite their unity in Christ, they fell into different Roman tax brackets.

Paul's warning makes sense rhetorically if the majority in the Roman assemblies were freeborn citizens and native residents or registered residents who felt distressed by the anger toward Rome by a group of fellow believers who refused to pay taxes as an act of civil disobedience. The minority would be Jews angry at Rome before their conversion. They could have believed in Jesus

54. Sven Günther, "Taxation in the Greco-Roman World: The Roman Principate," *Oxford Handbook Topics in Classical Studies* (April 2016), https://doi.org/10.1093/oxfordhb/9780199935390.013.38.

but still hated Rome as an idolatrous, polytheistic, corrupt culture.

Paul's greetings in Romans 16:3-16 to various members of the assemblies could have been political, not merely ministerial. The names could be representatives of the various demographic subgroups who would assure other residents of the assemblies at Rome that Paul is not a political rabble-rouser or a dangerous insurrectionist from Judea. And supportive of members paying their taxes. Is this passage evidence of Paul's own disposition as a Roman citizen?

Eloise M. Rosenblatt

Love for One Another (13:8-10)

A short pericope about the fulfillment of the law through love consists of an admonition (13:8), supported by the rationale that the Ten Commandments are summed up in the commandment about love of the neighbor from the book of Leviticus. It is a circular composition with the commandment of love at its center.[55]

Two terms are key in this short pericope: "love" because of the frequency of its occurrence and πλησίον, "neighbor," because of its quintessential position and importance in the quotation from Leviticus 19:18 (LXX). The reference to love is manifest in no fewer than three occurrences of the verb ἀγαπάω, "to love," and two of the noun ἀγάπη, "love," within these three verses. The focus on the topic of love has been prepared ever since the first mention of the term in the paragraph about the results of justification (Rom 5:1-11), where peace with God has been depicted as the result of atonement through Christ. There, Phoebe spells out the ramifications of the new status of humans in front of God, which has to do with boasting in suffering. This is countercultural behavior, made possible through hope, which is the result of endurance. The claim in Romans 5 is that love is the final consequence. The entire process was considered to happen under the influence of the Holy Spirit. A similar passage is found in Galatians 5:14: "For the whole law is summed up in a single commandment, 'You shall love your neighbor as yourself.'"[56]

55. Wolter, *Römer*, 2:330.

56. Peter Oakes, "Galatians and Romans," in *The New Cambridge Companion to St. Paul*, ed. Bruce W. Longenecker, Cambridge Companions to Religion (Cambridge: Cambridge University Press, 2020), 92.

Rom 13:8-10

[8]Owe no one anything, except to love one another, for the one who loves another has fulfilled the law. [9]The commandments, "You shall not commit adultery; you shall not murder; you shall not steal; you shall not covet," and any other commandment, are summed up in this word, "You shall love your neighbor as yourself." [10]Love does no wrong to a neighbor; therefore, love is the fulfilling of the law.

Both passages, therefore, belong to the larger discussion about the Jewish law within the Second Temple period. It sometimes resulted in proposals to reduce the number of laws that Jewish males were required to observe or made proposals about alternatives. In Romans, previous pertinent passages were, for example, that about Abraham's exemplary faith preceding circumcision as a key expression of the law (4:1-12), and that about Christ, understood as a wisdom figure, being the culmination and the end of obedience to the law (10:4). In previous letters as well as in Romans, therefore, Paul—now in collaboration with Phoebe and potentially other members of the assemblies in Corinth—has been explicit about his stance toward the law. According to Helmut Koester,

> The commandment of love is also the end of the law. It cannot be replaced by moral and lawful actions. When Paul calls the commandment of love the fulfillment of the entire law (Rom 13:8) he does not say that all the prescriptions of law have now gained a new validity. On the contrary, wherever the law erects boundaries in the relationships of human beings to each other these boundaries are abolished by the commandment of love. To be sure, such things as murder, theft, and adultery remain outlawed. But legal boundaries as those between Jews and Gentiles or those that demand subordinate positions for slaves and for women have no longer any validity.[57]

In the New Testament Gospels, the passage in Mark 12:29-31 about the question of which commandment is the first of all parallels Romans 13:8-10 as it also references Leviticus 19:18 (there in connection with Deut 6:4-5). Moreover, the narrative of the Good Samaritan (Luke 10:25-37)

57. Helmut Koester, *Paul and His World: Interpreting the New Testament in Its Context* (Minneapolis: Fortress, 2007), 205.

epitomizes the combination of both terms as neighborly love. It illustrates how real love crosses religious and cultural boundaries. Yet, it also contains implicit criticism of authoritative representatives of one's own religion (a priest and a Levite, Luke 10:31-32) who ignore the precarious situation of the assault victim of the robbers. In recent political discourse, this narrative has been referenced to justify attempts to reject immigration, although this parable is precisely about altruism and love for foreigners.[58] It demonstrates the sad reality that the love ethos of the early assemblies of Jewish believers in Christ is easily neglected or perverted.

There is not necessarily a dichotomy between the love commandment and the Jewish law. Paradoxically, the outcome of the Spirit's work is the fulfillment of the Jewish law—at least regarding its ethical components since its key idea is love. That is explicitly stated twice in this short pericope, namely, in Romans 13:8b and 10. The paradox is conveyed in remarkable fashion in the very quotation from Leviticus 19:18 because this commandment is taken from the Torah, which means it belongs to the Jewish law. If the commandment to love one's neighbor sums up the law but is itself part of the law, then it is clear that love can be the end of the law *and* its fulfillment at the same time. This is most likely the reason for the reference to Leviticus 19:18 in this paragraph. As the focus on love also evokes more broadly the worship of the great goddess Isis whose cultic name was "love" (ἀγάπη), this term would have ensured broad consent within the audiences in the city of Rome.[59] Such associations would have been more immediate than those in modern Western society that have led to a considerable oppression of women through a genderized development of the term "love" with different role assignments for women and men.[60]

In the communal life of the earliest communities of Christ believers, the love that is mentioned in Romans 13:10 had one of its manifestations in shared meals, specifically in the celebration of the Eucharist or Communion. Also called a "love feast," Eucharist was a primary frame of reference for the audiences (see also 12:9).[61]

58. Marianne Bjelland Kartzow and Karin B. Neutel, "Neighbours Near and Far: How a Biblical Figure Is Used in Recent European Anti-Migration Politics," *BibInt* 29 (2021): 358–80.

59. Sharon K. Heyob, *The Cult of Isis Among Women in the Graeco-Roman World*, EPRO 51 (Brill: Leiden, 1975), 67.

60. See the comments above on Romans 12:9-21.

61. Jewett, "Allusions," 265–78; Rector, "Shame," 117–29.

Romans 13:9 lists only four out of ten commandments. Why were some of the commandments chosen and others omitted? Some of the latter category may have been less relevant in the context of the assemblies in Rome. For example, the practice of sabbath observance according to Exodus 20:8-11; Deuteronomy 5:12-15 was controversial there.[62] The law to honor one's father and mother (Exod 20:12 // Deut 5:16) was most likely no longer actionable in light of frequent separations of assembly members from their nuclear families (while the new paradigm of family through adoption became dominant). Finally, the prohibition against bearing false witness (Exod 20:16 // Deut 5:20) would have been inapplicable for most as their low social status or lack thereof did not allow any recourse to the Roman legal system.[63] By contrast, Romans 13:9 mentions those commandments that affect human relationships: adultery, murder, stealing, and covetousness. The last one effectively merges the two commandments concerning coveting a wife and coveting property (Exod 20:17; see also Deut 5:18 [LXX]/5:21 [MT]) through the abbreviated reference "you shall not covet." As mentioned above (see the comments on Rom 7:7), this commandment exposes the patriarchal standards of the ancient Near East by addressing only men (and not women) and by listing a wife among a man's possessions.[64] One can imagine the reaction that such an androcentric text would have triggered in a woman like Phoebe. Structured through the patronage system, Roman society was also a kyriarchy. Phoebe would have been grateful for experiencing a new era in her life due to the egalitarian ethos in the radically democratic *ekklēsia* of wo/men based on Galatians 3:28 and the love ethos in Romans 13:8-10.

An Urgent Appeal (13:11-14)

This admonition to moral alertness contains a reference to an agape/baptismal hymn with references to an eschatological time period. Its first section in Romans 13:11-12a is dominated by terminology about time: the term "time" (καιρός) itself, "hour" (ὥρα), "now, already" (ἤδη),

62. Robert Goldenberg, "The Jewish Sabbath in the Roman World up to the Time of Constantine the Great," *ANRW* 2.19.1 (1979): 414–47.

63. Wayne A. Meeks, *The First Urban Christians: The Social World of the Apostle Paul* (New Haven: Yale University Press, 1983), 84–96; Jewett, *Romans*, 810.

64. Judith Plaskow, *Standing Again at Sinai: Judaism from a Feminist Perspective* (San Francisco: HarperSanFrancisco, 1991), 25–26.

Rom 13:11-14

[11]Besides this, you know what time it is,
how it is already the moment for you
to wake from sleep. For salvation is
nearer to us now than when we became believers; [12]the night is far gone;
the day is near. Let us then throw off
the works of darkness and put on the
armor of light; [13]let us walk decently as
in the day, not in reveling and drunkenness, not in illicit sex and licentiousness, not in quarreling and jealousy.
[14]Instead, put on the Lord Jesus Christ,
and make no provision for the flesh, to
gratify its desires.

"now" (νῦν), "night" (νύξ), and "day" (ἡμέρα). The three finite verbs in this section ("when we became believers" [ἐπιστεύσαμεν], "is far gone" [προέκοψεν], "is near" [ἤγγικεν]) are in the indicative. The appeal is structured through a series of three antitheses that start with a negative aspect followed by the positive one: asleep/awake, night/day, and darkness/light.[65] These sentences are intended to convey the urgency of the ethical behavior as stipulated in the broader context. It is disputed whether or not the "now" is a reference to an eschatological time or simply points to the present. But it is clear that such terminology is aimed at "deeper convulsions in time"[66] and describes the new era that has started with the gospel of Christ. It may correspond to the exhortation in Romans 12:2 to "be transformed by the renewing of the mind."

In the second section, verbs are now in the cohortative to encourage the audiences to adopt concrete actions. The first exhortation is to "throw off the works of darkness and put on the armor of light" (Rom 13:12b). It is similar to previous ethical appeals in Paul's letters (1 Thess 5:8), both of which refer to similar images in Isaiah 59:17. Earlier, Paul had also associated light with Christ when writing that God "has shone in our hearts to give the light of the knowledge of the glory of God in the face of Christ" (2 Cor 4:6). Another key phrase for the ethical appeal is "let us walk decently as in the day," which literally reads "let us walk honorably" (Rom 13:13). Such terminology is again characteristic of other similar hortatory paragraphs in Paul's letters (1 Thess 2:12; 4:1, 12).[67] Therefore, believers in Christ "walk in newness of life" (Rom 6:4); they "walk not according to the flesh but according to the Spirit" (8:4; Gal 5:16).

65. Hultgren, *Romans*, 488–89.
66. Dunn, *Romans 9–16*, 786; see also Tonstad, *Romans*, 326.
67. Esler, *Conflict*, 338.

What exactly are the audiences *not* to do? Romans 13:13 goes on to specify the following behavior: "not in reveling and drunkenness, not in illicit sex and licentiousness, not in quarreling and jealousy." These are three pairs of two vices each. The first pair is about eating or banqueting (see also 14:17), the second has to do with sexual misconduct, and the third with discourse and arguing. Robert Jewett suggests that the entire section of Romans 13:11-14 is not only concerned with the agape meal practice but based on an actual hymn that was sung at these occasions.[68] He renders the second pair as follows: "Not in bouts of sex and indecencies." The Greek term κοίτη that is employed here means literally "bed" but implies by extension also engagement in sexual relations and sexual excesses in the form of adultery. These were commonly associated with the drunken dining pleasures of Greco-Roman symposia.[69] Paul has used the second term previously; it is a frequent noun in catalogues of vices (Gal 5:19-21; see also 2 Cor 12:21; elsewhere Mark 7:22; 1 Pet 4:3; Wis 14:26). A *Sitz im Leben* of eucharistic practices is, therefore, likely for this appeal, as such meetings would have occurred in the evening or occasionally at night. Of interest is the observation that, here, the audiences are confronted with Paul's and Phoebe's stance regarding sexual ethics. This stance promotes a monogamous ideal; other than that, its provisions are aimed at avoiding excesses. There is, however, no specific provision against same-sex activities such as those mentioned in Romans 1:24-27. The behavior listed there is not part of the ethical appeal in this letter toward Jewish believers in Christ.

The inclusion of such a parenetic paragraph about eating or banqueting, sexual misconduct, and arguing had its particular value for the audiences of Christ believers of Rome and their standing and social recognition within the city. First, since many of the members of these assemblies were enslaved persons who were regularly subject to sexual encroachment, such provisions were important to establish an environment of respect and personal safety for all. Enslaved persons had no legal recourse in case of assaults of any nature. Hence, the only provision that would have made a difference for them was a call to prohibit these types of behavior in the first place.

Second, it is possible that these lines may also have been included for the particular purpose of protecting a woman like Phoebe. If she was a

68. Jewett, *Romans*, 817–18.

69. Wolter, *Römer*, 2:342.

single woman who traveled alone, she would have had to live with the fear of unwanted sexual advances or outright assaults during her stay in Rome. As a woman from Corinth of all places, the city with the questionable reputation of commercialized sex, Phoebe did not want to be seen or treated as "a Corinthian maid."[70] Paul was certainly aware of the problem when the plan was made to have the letter to Rome delivered through her. An appeal to the assemblies there to moderate behavior would have been helpful to guarantee her safety. A further request later in the letter to "welcome her in the Lord, as is fitting for the saints" (Rom 16:2) further served this purpose. If it is a goal of feminist biblical interpretation (in conjunction with intersectionality and postcolonial hermeneutics) to contribute to the termination of oppression and marginalization of women, then the inconspicuous plea in 13:13 may be identified as having served those purposes in the past; it will have a similar effect in comparable constellations in the modern world.

The concluding positive appeal in Romans 13:14 is surprisingly unspecific: "Instead, put on the Lord Jesus Christ, and make no provision for the flesh, to gratify its desires." The close parallel in Galatians 3:27 ("As many of you as were baptized into Christ have clothed yourselves with Christ") shows that this language is related to baptism, but it should be understood as a reminder of baptismal confessions. It is dominated by the mystical experience of the Holy Spirit and by the juxtaposition of Christ to "the flesh."[71] The point is to adopt a lifestyle consistent with the spiritual identity of those "in Christ." This lifestyle is the actualization of one's personal baptismal confession.

Do Not Judge Others (14:1-12)

Romans 14:1–15:13 is the last and longest thematic unit within the parenetic section of the letter. It features concrete advice for the members of the audiences aiming at reconciliation of the quarreling groups despite different opinions.[72] The NRSVue considers Romans 14:1-12 one section about exemplary guidelines for the weak and the strong,[73] although one can also restrict the unit to 14:1-9 and consider 14:10–15:4 as the subse-

70. On these details about Phoebe, see further comments below on Romans 16:1-2.

71. Jewett, *Romans*, 827.

72. Bernhard Oestreich, *Performanzkritik der Paulusbriefe*, WUNT 296 (Tübingen: Mohr Siebeck, 2012), 137.

73. See also the same division in Jewett, *Romans*, 833.

Rom 14:1-12

14:1Welcome those who are weak in
faith but not for the purpose of quarreling over opinions. 2Some believe in
eating anything, while the weak eat only
vegetables. 3Those who eat must not
despise those who abstain, and those
who abstain must not pass judgment on
those who eat, for God has welcomed
them. 4Who are you to pass judgment
on slaves of another? It is before their
own lord that they stand or fall. And they
will be upheld, for the Lord is able to
make them stand.

5Some judge one day to be better
than another, while others judge all days
to be alike. Let all be fully convinced in
their own minds. 6Those who observe
the day, observe it for the Lord. Also
those who eat, eat for the Lord, since
they give thanks to God, while those
who abstain, abstain for the Lord and
give thanks to God.

7For we do not live to ourselves,
and we do not die to ourselves. 8If we
live, we live to the Lord, and if we die,
we die to the Lord; so then, whether
we live or whether we die, we are the
Lord's. 9For to this end Christ died and
lived again, so that he might be Lord of
both the dead and the living.

10Why do you pass judgment on
your brother or sister? Or you, why do
you despise your brother or sister? For
we will all stand before the judgment
seat of God. 11For it is written,

"As I live, says the Lord, every
knee shall bow to me,
and every tongue shall give
praise to God."

12So then, each one of us will be held
accountable.

quent unit.[74] The scriptural proof from the combined passages in Isaiah 49:18 (LXX) and 45:23 (LXX) in Romans 14:11 including its introduction and conclusion can, therefore, be drawn either to the preceding or to the subsequent text blocks.

Romans 14:1-12 consists of four pericopes. The first starts with a general appeal to accept the "weak in faith" (14:1). Next is a first exemplification regarding two different types of dietary customs (14:2-4), which is followed by a second exemplification regarding the observance of sacred days (14:5-9). The conclusion is a repetition of the admonition not to judge, which is corroborated by Scripture citations and a reminder of everybody's individual accountability vis-à-vis God (14:10-12).[75]

Romans 14:1-12 starts with the instruction to welcome (προσλαμβάνεσθε, a second plural imperative) the weak. In the Greek text, the passage starts with the words Τὸν δὲ ἀσθενοῦντα, "the weak," which is the object of the

74. Oestreich, *Performanzkritik*, 138–39.

75. Jewett, *Romans*, 833; Gignac, *L'épître*, 504–10.

sentence. The verb προσλαμβάνω, "to welcome," conveys one of the key ideas of this parenetic appeal consisting of openness toward others and their acceptance. It implies "to seek actively to know and to understand another's reasoning and another's judgments, based on the theological assumption that all people belong to God and that God may be served in a variety of ways."[76] The verb occurs four times within 14:1–15:13 (14:1, 3; 15:7 [2x]). As in previous arguments in Romans, its basis is theological and made explicit in the fourth occurrence of the verb: Christ has already welcomed humans (15:7). This is clearly a reference to the atonement and reconciliation of humans through Christ, as put forth in Romans 3:21-26 and 5:6-11, or to God's love made manifest in the adoption of humans according to 8:15-17, 31-39. Interestingly, the verb προσλαμβάνω has not appeared previously in Romans. It will, however, be featured one more time in 16:2 as the recommended action toward Phoebe.

In Romans 14:1-12, the verb "to welcome" is juxtaposed to the admonition not to judge others. Therefore, this passage can be understood as an application of the earlier paragraph on judgment and human sin in Romans 2:1-16. Specifically, 2:1-11 features a preponderance of terminology conveying judgment. The similarity of both sections is illustrated in the following table.

Comparison: Judgment According to Romans 2:1-11 and 14:1-12[77]

2:1-16	Judgment and Human Sin[78]	14:1-16	Do Not Judge Others
2:1	Therefore you are without excuse, [O human who judges others[79]], for in *passing judgment on another you condemn yourself*, because *you, the judge, are doing the very same things.*	14:3	Those who eat *must not despise those who abstain*, and those who abstain *must not pass judgment on those who eat.*
2:3	Do you imagine, whoever you are, that *when you judge those who do such things and yet do them yourself, you will escape the judgment of God?*	14:4	*Who are you to pass judgment* on slaves of another?
		14:10	*Why do you pass judgment on your brother or sister?* Or you, *why do you despise your brother or sister?*

76. Gaventa, "Romans," 555.

77. Similar statements in this table are indicated by italics.

78. For this heading, see comments on Romans 2:1-16 above.

79. For this translation, see comments above under "Translation Matters" on Romans 2:1, p. 66.

2:4	Or do you *despise the riches of his kindness and forbearance and patience?*	14:4	And they will be upheld, *for the Lord is able to make them stand.*

In Romans 14:1-12 alone, the verb κρίνω ("to judge, pass judgment on, condemn"; also: "to prefer") occurs five times (14:3, 4, 5 [2x], 10; see also another three attestations in 14:13 [2x], 22 and the compound verb κατακρίνω, "to judge, pass judgment on, condemn" in v. 23). Furthermore, the noun "quarreling, differentiation" (διάκρισις) in 14:1 is also derived from the same stem. The message not to judge but to welcome others is, therefore, clearly conveyed in this section of the letter and overall in Romans. It echoes the message of Jesus in his famous Sermon on the Mount: "Do not judge, so that you may not be judged. For the judgment you give will be the judgment you get, and the measure you give will be the measure you get. Why do you see the speck in your neighbor's eye but do not notice the log in your own eye?" (Matt 7:1-3; see also Luke 6:37-38). The terminological and conceptual parallels between these passages require almost no further comment regarding the topic. Any behavior described by these words, whether judgment or condemnation or quarreling, is not permitted among those who believe in Christ. The reason is clear and simple: Such behavior demonstrates the failure to acknowledge divine grace, which Christ literally embodies (Rom 14:3, 10).

In Romans 14, Paul and Phoebe zero in on conflicts between different groups in Rome, based on information that Prisca and Aquila had provided. They do not deny the existing differences within the audiences. Instead, they explicitly acknowledge and address the differences among the groups constituting the audience, labeled here the "weak" and the "strong" (this term occurs only later in 15:1). The goal is to establish unity in the assemblies and to propose conflict resolution.[80] But in order to get there, Paul and Phoebe speak in very certain terms about the differences within the group.[81] The passage in 14:7-9 addresses both groups; it pertains to the entirety of human existence. Differences between the lives of people exist, but they are overcome through unity in Christ as "Lord." Romans 14:7-9 is like a hymn and very poetic, featuring parallelisms and word repetitions. It is supposed to encourage the audiences to applaud the statement: Phoebe, "spurred by the poetic form of the preceding lines, expresses the truth of the sentence with great emphasis

80. Esler, *Conflict*, 349.

81. Gaventa, "Romans," 554.

and then pauses. The audiences understand this indirect call for reaction and applauds."[82]

Who are the "weak"? Paul has used this term previously. In 1 Thessalonians 5:14, he writes: "And we urge you, brothers and sisters, to admonish the idlers, encourage the fainthearted, help the weak, be patient with all of them." The association of "weak" with terminology such as "fainthearted" shows that people are envisioned who require affirmation and encouragement. In 1 Corinthians 8:7-12, the term "weak" refers to those who lack "knowledge" about the one God of Israel and therefore consider the consumption of food from offerings to an idol as idolatry.[83] Hence, there is considerable vagueness regarding the meaning of the term "weak" itself. The latter usage, however, shows the connection with dietary customs, as in Romans 14. Here, the "weak" are described as those who "eat only vegetables [λάχανα]" while other groups "believe in eating anything" (14:2).[84] Either group is asked not to judge the other (v. 3).

The reference to eating habits may have been prompted by long-standing problems in various assemblies in Rome, but it may also have to do with the very occasion of Phoebe's visits there. It is likely that each of these visits was organized around a shared meal. At these occasions, the "weak in faith" appear to have insisted on table fellowship only with those who observed certain food laws.[85] The reduced daily menu of "only [leafy] vegetables" (Rom 14:2) does not match any known Jewish kosher regulation.[86] Most likely a metonym for a meatless diet, this term can be understood as a reference to either pagan neo-Pythagorean or diaspora Jewish ideals.[87]

A second exemplification of the problem is added in Romans 14:5-9 regarding the problem of obeying sacred days. Phoebe starts once again with a concise description of the different practices: "Some judge [κρίνω]

82. Oestreich, *Performanzkritik*, 157 (ET: CAE).

83. Wolter, *Römer*, 2:351–52.

84. Esler, *Conflict*, 350. See also Kathy Ehrensperger, *That We May Be Mutually Encouraged: Feminism and the New Perspective in Pauline Studies* (New York: T&T Clark, 2004), 181–83.

85. Gaventa, *When in Romans*, 108–9.

86. In modern times, Jews living in areas where a reliable source of kosher food is not available may opt for vegetarianism.

87. Mark Reasoner, *The Strong and the Weak: Romans 14.1–15.13 in Context*, SNTSMS 103 (Cambridge: Cambridge University Press, 1999), 6–16, 130–38.

one day to be better than another, while others judge [κρίνω] all days to be alike" (v. 5). All of these aspects describe several social groups in Rome. As mentioned above, their differences may only have become relevant upon the invitation to some of them to meet and listen to the letter sent from Corinth. The conflict regarding the days may have been occasioned by the question of which day of the week may have been suitable for assembly meetings for the reading of the letter. In the end, two aspects are crucial: First, the call to accept the other group is mutual and goes in either direction (14:3, 6). And second, for this very reason, Paul and Phoebe use only the term "weak" in chapter 14 and not its opposite, "strong." According to Faith K. Hawkins, their discourse "does not oppose the two groups in dichotomous, hierarchy-producing fashion."[88] Instead, Paul and Phoebe place the discussion of group difference within the matrix of group sameness so that "neither group can or should claim superiority over the other."[89] That Jesus Christ is the example of such behavior is apparent, but it will be mentioned explicitly later (15:3, 5).

In connection with the earlier pericope in Romans 2:1-12, the invitation to welcome others would also have applied to Phoebe. A gentile woman and possibly a former enslaved person, she may have been considered weak by some in the assemblies in Rome according to the traditional standards of the Greco-Roman patriarchal culture. In that case, the appeal in chapter 14 is to accept her nevertheless. Strategically savvy, Phoebe has kept her opinion about herself a secret for the time being. But in Romans 15:1, the "we" reveals that she and Paul consider themselves as "strong." Their strength may be their knowledge of, and faith in, the risen Christ, as the related passage in 1 Corinthians 8:7-12 already suggests. Christ is the dominant theme, specifically in Romans 14:5-9 where the title "Lord" (κύριος) occurs six times.

A combined Scripture quotation from Isaiah 49:18 (LXX) and 45:23 (LXX) confirms that the task of humans is to praise God in worship (Rom 14:11; Paul will quote the same passages from Isaiah again in Phil 2:10-11).[90] All humans are expected to lead a life permeated by, and

88. Faith K. Hawkins, "Does Paul Make a Difference?," in *A Feminist Companion to Paul*, ed. Amy-Jill Levine with Marianne Blickenstaff, FCNTECW 6 (London: T&T International, 2004), 181.

89. Hawkins, "Difference," 181.

90. Wolter, *Römer*, 2:367.

accountable to, the Lord (Rom 14:8-9).[91] In the end, God alone is the judge of humans (v. 10). Due to its impact on the local assemblies in Rome and its christological arguments, Romans 14:1-12 may be considered the climax of the entire letter to the Romans.[92]

Do Not Make Another Stumble (14:13-23)

This paragraph continues the theme of the previous one and is characterized by argumentative coherence regarding its parenetic appeal. Its admonition to avoid negative behavior revisits the problem of judgment one more time: "Let us therefore no longer pass judgment on one another, but resolve instead never to put a stumbling block or hindrance in the way of a brother or sister" (14:13). The verb κρίνω ("to judge, pass judgment on, condemn") is repeated, as the phrase "resolve instead" is also constructed with this verb. This sentence demonstrates the strong emphasis Paul and Phoebe place on the avoidance of judgment. Unfortunately, still today there is necessity for such insistence in most religious communities of most Christian denominations.

The noun σκάνδαλον, "stumbling block," indicates an occasion to take offense. It was twice employed earlier in the letter; in a quotation from Isaiah 8:14 (LXX) in Romans 9:32-33, the audiences in Rome heard about "a stone that will make people stumble" and "a rock that will make them fall." The "stumbling block" is now associated with the noun πρόσκομμα, "hindrance," which can also signify temptation.[93] This term appeared already in 11:9 in a citation from Psalm 68:23-24 (LXX); 69:22-23 (ET) that contains a reference to "their table" that has "become a snare and a trap." That passage features a discourse about Israel's rejection but suggests that it is not final. It is likely that these passages have been employed there to prepare the current discussion of problems regarding dietary customs. Furthermore, this terminology has surfaced in a previous letter of Paul. Those parallels are illustrated in the following table.

91. Gaventa, *When in Romans*, 109; Michael Wolter, *Paulus: Ein Grundriss seiner Theologie*, 3rd ed. (Neukirchen-Vluyn: Neukirchener Verlag, 2021), 243, 253.

92. Peter Wick, *Die urchristlichen Gottesdienste: Entstehung und Entwicklung im Rahmen der frühjüdischen Tempel-, Synagogen- und Hausfrömmigkeit*, BWANT 150 (Stuttgart: Kohlhammer, 2002), 194.

93. Longenecker, *Romans*, 1006.

Rom 14:13-23

[13]Let us therefore no longer pass judgment on one another, but resolve instead never to put a stumbling block or hindrance in the way of a brother or sister. [14]I know and am persuaded in the Lord Jesus that nothing is unclean in itself, but it is unclean for anyone who considers it unclean. [15]If your brother or sister is distressed by what you eat, you are no longer walking in love. Do not let what you eat cause the ruin of one for whom Christ died. [16]So do not let your good be slandered. [17]For the kingdom of God is not food and drink but righteousness and peace and joy in the Holy Spirit. [18]The one who serves Christ in this way is acceptable to God and has human approval. [19]Let us then pursue what makes for peace and for mutual upbuilding. [20]Do not, for the sake of food, destroy the work of God. Everything is indeed clean, but it is wrong to make someone stumble by what you eat; [21]it is good not to eat meat or drink wine or do anything that makes your brother or sister stumble. [22]Hold the conviction that you have as your own before God. Blessed are those who do not condemn themselves because of what they approve. [23]But those who have doubts are condemned if they eat because they do not act from faith, for whatever does not proceed from faith is sin.

Comparison: Stumbling Blocks and Food According to 1 Corinthians 8:8-13 and Romans 14:13-23[94]

1 Cor 8:8-13	*Knowledge about Food for Idols*	14:13-23	*Do Not Cause Another to Stumble*
8:8	"Food will not bring us close to God." We are no worse off if we do not eat and no better off if we do.	14:17	For the kingdom of God is not food and drink.
8:9	But take care that this liberty of yours does not somehow become a stumbling block to the weak.	14:13	Resolve instead never to put a stumbling block or hindrance in the way of a brother or sister.

94. Wolter, *Römer*, 2:371.

8:11	So by your knowledge those weak believers for whom Christ died are destroyed.	14:15	If your brother or sister is distressed by what you eat, you are no longer walking in love. Do not let what you eat cause the ruin of one for whom Christ died.
8:13	Therefore, if food is a cause of their falling, I will never again eat meat, so that I may not cause one of them to fall.	14:20-21	Do not, for the sake of food, destroy the work of God. Everything is indeed clean, but it is wrong to make someone stumble by what you eat; it is good not to eat meat or drink wine or do anything that makes your brother or sister stumble.

These paragraphs in 1 Corinthians 8 and Romans 14 share the concern that the open display of one's personal maturity in religious matters, which is manifest in a degree of freedom from certain dietary restrictions, may become a challenge for others who still observe such customs and cherish them in their own piety. The description of the potential negative effect on these people is graphic and dramatic: they "are destroyed" (1 Cor 8:11) or "distressed" (Rom 14:15) and "stumble" (v. 20). According to both passages, the special problem is that human salvation through the death of Christ may be rejected by some and that, ultimately, freedom from the law through Christ may be lived out with an attitude of superiority, not love. In that case, God's work of salvation may indeed be destroyed (14:20); the proclamation of the gospel message is then sabotaged. This is not the goal of building up an assembly of people who believe in Christ because it contradicts the love ethos and the ideal of care for everyone.

Bernhard Oestreich notes that the appeal to those who "eat anything" is much longer than that to the group labeled "weak." In the end, they are the addressees of the appeal, and it would be their task to ensure the implementation of the love ethics in the assembly. But eventually, both groups find their positions met with approval; Phoebe is, therefore, intent on finding a compromise.[95]

This concern introduces another cultic theme in Romans 14:14, namely, purity. Phoebe proclaims a sentence that is nothing short of revolu-

95. Oestreich, *Performanzkritik*, 161.

tionary: "I know and am persuaded in the Lord Jesus that nothing is unclean in itself [οὐδὲν κοινὸν δι' ἑαυτοῦ], but it is unclean for anyone who considers it unclean [εἰ μὴ τῷ λογιζομένῳ τι κοινὸν εἶναι, ἐκείνῳ κοινόν]." Its positive summary is offered toward the end of the paragraph: "Everything is indeed clean" (πάντα μὲν καθαρά, 14:20).

A diametric contradiction of the purity laws of the Torah, this statement is groundbreaking. In the Torah, the question of which food is clean and which is not is regulated in detail. Leviticus 11 specifies, for example, that particular types of animals (such as camel, hare, pig) are unclean (ἀκάθαρτος). The Israelites are not supposed to eat or touch them lest they become unclean themselves. The Torah, therefore, maps out dualistic categories of clean and unclean for dietary purposes. These categories have had a most enduring influence on Judaism for more than two millennia, where they are the basis of the laws of *kashrut*.[96] Paul had previously challenged these laws when arguing that dietary concerns are of limited religious relevance (1 Cor 8:8). The argument in Romans, however, has attained a new level of reflection, which may well be attributed to Paul's consultations with Phoebe (and potentially even other coworkers) in Corinth between 56 and 58 CE. As a result, Romans 14:14 states that purity is no longer a matter of objective ontological quality of the food item but a matter of human opinions, which are subjective.[97] Such a change in perspective can be explained not only in light of Paul's own multiple citizenships and complex identity. It is also the result of the cultural diversity of his entourage in Corinth and the related concept of hybridity. In different cultural groups, people encountered ever different dietary standards. A process of reflecting on these differences led to the insight in 14:14, which is similar to stoic ideas.[98] It is comparable to the saying of Jesus about purity in Mark 7:18-20 that, however, dissociates ritual purity entirely from dietary categories: " 'Do you not see that whatever goes into a person from outside cannot defile, since it enters not the heart but the stomach and goes out into the sewer?' (Thus he declared all foods clean.)

96. S. Tamar Kamionkowski, *Leviticus*, WCS 3 (Collegeville, MN: Liturgical Press, 2018), 81–82.

97. Gudrun Holtz, "Zwischen Halacha und Stoa: Der subjektive Faktor in Römer 14:14 und seine soziale Funktion," in Eisen and Mader, *Talking God in Society*, 387.

98. Troels Engberg-Pedersen, " 'Everything Is Clean,' and 'Everything That Is Not of Faith Is Sin': The Logic of Pauline Casuistry in Romans 14.1–15.13," in *Paul, Grace and Freedom: Essays in Honour of John K. Riches*, ed. Paul Middleton, Angus Paddison, and Karen Wenell, T&T Clark Biblical Studies (London: T&T Clark, 2009), 22–38.

And he said, 'It is what comes out of a person that defiles [κοινόω].'" This statement challenges the dietary laws in the Torah in its own right. Rabbinic Judaism also knows similar reflections, for instance: "What difference does it make to the Holy One whether one slaughters from the throat or from the nape? Or what difference does it make to Him whether one eats unclean or clean substances?" (Tanhuma, *Parashat Shemini*).[99]

By extension, these voices are important steps on the road toward stopping the exclusion of women, for instance, because of menstruation and after childbirth. The Torah stipulates: "If a woman conceives and bears a male child, she shall be unclean seven days; as at the time of her menstruation, she shall be unclean" (Lev 12:2). If a woman bears a female child, then her uncleanness is twice as long (12:5). This law and its context (12:1-8) about the impurity of Jewish women were even used in Christian churches to exclude women from the eucharistic assembly.[100] Yet, if purity in dietary laws is challenged, then it can also be challenged elsewhere in the Torah. Here too the principle can be applied "that nothing is unclean in itself, but it is unclean for anyone who considers it unclean." Why would the blood of menstruation have to be considered unclean if even the blood of sacrificial animals could, upon physical contact, consecrate both objects (Exod 29:36-37; Lev 16:18-19) and humans (Lev 8:30) to effect atonement (Lev 17:11; see above, p. 105)? A positive understanding of the power of blood can also be found in other cultures, for example, among Native Americans, some of whom consider the blood of menstruation a "very powerful medicine."[101]

The statement in Romans 14 that, as a general rule, all food is clean conceptually corroborates the position of those who have the habit of eating "anything" (14:2). The point of the argument here, however, is not to replace one objectively true dietary law with another new one. The point is, instead, the deep and loving concern for the community of believers: "it is wrong to make someone stumble by what you eat" (v. 20b). In Christ, the law has been fulfilled and has come to an end. Not even a new law should be established.

The fact that Paul advocated for the culmination and end of the law in Christ does not mean that he was no longer a Jew. As mentioned previ-

99. Kamionkowski, *Leviticus*, 94.

100. Kamionkowski, *Leviticus*, 105 ("The Churching of Women" by Susan K. Roll).

101. Gertrude D. Buck, "Healing Story: A Bold Woman in the Crowd," *Consensus* 27 (2001): 11–25, at 13–14. See also Stuart L. Love, "Jesus Heals the Hemorrhaging Woman," in *The Social Setting of Jesus and the Gospels*, ed. Wolfgang Stegemann, Bruce J. Malina, and Gerd Theissen (Minneapolis: Fortress, 2002), 91.

ously, a controversial discussion about the law existed within Judaism, and Paul had participated in it just like Jesus of Nazareth before him. Scholars sometimes claim that Paul was faithful to the Jewish law.[102] Yet, the challenge of purity laws in Romans 14 suggests otherwise.

The following phrase provides a conceptual framework: "the kingdom of God is not food and drink but [justification[103]] and peace and joy in the Holy Spirit" (v. 17). These three key terms refer specifically back to Romans 3:21-31 (for justification); 5:1-5 (for peace); and 8:31-39 (for joy in the Holy Spirit). They are arranged in 14:17 in an antithetical parallelism and also feature a *parechesis* (assonance of different words in close proximity). The terminology about God forms the external frame of the sentence while the elements about human practice are placed in the center. Paul and Phoebe have constructed these sentences carefully. Such proverbial phrases are important elements in oral discourse. They have not only a high degree of persuasive power for the audiences but are also intended to be memorized by them.[104]

In concluding these reflections, it needs to be repeated that the parenetic section of Romans contains no further reference to the topic of same-sex activities (or homosexuality).[105] If no new law should be established, then that insight pertains also to this topic. The parenetic section of Romans demonstrates that Paul and Phoebe have nothing against such practices. Here too the principle of Romans 14:20b applies: "it is wrong to make someone stumble." And also of 14:10: "Why do you pass judgment on your brother or sister?"

Please Others, Not Yourselves (15:1-6)

Romans 15:1-6 consists of three sections. First, it features admonitions concerning proper "pleasing" (Rom 15:1-2); second, it provides a theological rationale in the example of Christ (15:3-4). It concludes with a homiletical benediction (15:5-6).[106]

102. Esther Kobel, *Paulus als interkultureller Vermittler: Eine Studie zur kulturellen Positionierung des Apostels der Völker*, Studies in Cultural Contexts of the Bible 1 (Paderborn: Brill; Schöningh, 2019), 163–64.

103. For the alternate translation "justification," which differs from that of the NRSVue, see comments above under "Translation Matters" on Romans 3:21, 22.

104. Oestreich, *Performanzkritik*, 162–63.

105. Michael Theobald, "Paul and Same-Sex Sexuality: A Plea for a Sensible Approach to Scripture," in *"Who Am I to Judge?" Homosexuality and the Catholic Church*, ed. Stephan Goertz, trans. Alissa Jones Nelson (Berlin: de Gruyter, 2022), 55.

106. Jewett, *Romans*, 875; Gignac, *L'épître*, 522–25.

Rom 15:1-6

[15:1]We who are strong ought to put up with the failings of the weak and not to please ourselves. [2]Each of us must please our neighbor for the good purpose of building up the neighbor. [3]For Christ did not please himself, but, as it is written, "The insults of those who insult you have fallen on me." [4]For whatever was written in former days was written for our instruction, so that by steadfastness and by the encouragement of the scriptures we might have hope. [5]May the God of steadfastness and encouragement grant you to live in harmony with one another, in accordance with Christ Jesus, [6]so that together you may with one voice glorify the God and Father of our Lord Jesus Christ.

Romans 15 and 16

The question of the originality of Romans 15 and 16 was once considered the most difficult problem of New Testament text criticism.[107] Peter Lampe proposed in his text-critical examination of Romans that Paul's original letter consisted of 1:1–16:23 + 16:24.[108] According to Origen, the early Christian theologian Marcion of Sinope (ca. 100–160 CE) had deleted all of chapters 15 and 16 because he wanted the letter to conclude with 14:23, a verse he considered representative of his theology (Origen, *Com. Rom.* 10.43).[109] The theological program of Marcion was characterized by a denial of the continuity between Judaism and Christianity. Therefore, Marcion created the first canon of Christian writings, consisting of ten letters of Paul (Gal, 1 and 2 Cor, Rom, 1 and 2 Thess, Eph [under the title "Laodiceans"], Col, Phil, and Phlm) followed by an edited version of the Gospel according to Luke (starting at 4:31). The purpose was chiefly to set these texts apart from the traditional Jewish Scriptures. It is interesting that, in his editorial work on Romans, Marcion intentionally separated chapters 15 and 16 that, in recent decades, have been of

107. Kurt Aland, "Der Schluss und die ursprüngliche Gestalt des Römerbriefes," in *Neutestamentliche Entwürfe*, TB 63 (München: Kaiser, 1979), 284.

108. Peter Lampe, "Zur Textgeschichte des Römerbriefes," *NovT* 27 (1985): 273–77, at 273–75.

109. Karl P. Donfried, "A Short Note on Romans 16," in *The Romans Debate*, ed. Karl P. Donfried, rev. exp. ed. (Peabody, MA: Hendrickson, 1991), 50; Karl P. Donfried, "False Presuppositions in the Study of Romans," in *The Romans Debate*, 104. See also further comments on Romans 16 below.

utmost interest for the feminist interpretation of Romans. In a similar fashion, a study of textual variants reveals the emphasis that ancient scribes put on Romans 14–16.

Marcion's truncated version of Romans concluded with the following sentence in 14:23: "But those who have doubts are condemned if they eat because they do not act from faith, for whatever does not proceed from faith is sin." As this is no conclusion to a letter in antiquity, a new doxology was needed, leading to the addition of the doxology in 16:25-27.

The tide turned, however, when Harry Gamble compared this passage to stylistic elements of epistolary conclusions in Hellenistic Greek letters, thus producing support for the thesis that Romans 16 was original.[110] Karl P. Donfried proposed two methodological principles for the interpretation of Romans. First, "every other authentic Pauline writing, without exception, is addressed to the specific situations of the churches or persons involved. To argue that Romans is an exception to this Pauline pattern is certainly possible, but the burden of proof rests with those exegetes who wish to demonstrate that it is impossible, or at least not likely, that Romans addresses a concrete set of problems in the life of Christians in Rome."[111] And second: "Any study of Romans should proceed on the assumption that Rom. 16 is an integral part of the original letter. The burden of proof rests with those who would wish to argue the contrary."[112] Donfried's two methodological principles have generally been accepted and followed.[113]

Romans 15:1 finally provides the term "the strong" (οἱ δυνατοί) that complements the mention of "the weak" in chapter 14. It is already known that "the strong" eat "anything" (14:2) and that they are expected to refrain from despising the weak for their obedience of dietary restrictions (14:3) and observance of special sacred days (vv. 5-6). The first-person plural ("we") probably implies, on the one hand, that there

110. Harry Y. Gamble Jr., *The Textual History of the Letter to the Romans: A Study in Textual and Literary Criticism*, SD 42 (Grand Rapids: Eerdmans, 1977), 57–95.

111. Karl P. Donfried, "False Presuppositions in the Study of Romans," in Donfried, *The Romans Debate*, 103–4 (italics original).

112. Donfried, "False," 104.

113. Lampe, *Die stadtrömischen Christen*, 131–35; Beverly Roberts Gaventa, "Paul and the Roman Believers," in *The Blackwell Companion to Paul*, ed. Stephen Westerholm, Blackwell Companions to Religion (Malden: Wiley-Blackwell, 2011), 95.

are members in the assemblies in Rome who can also be counted among the strong. On the other hand, the "we" also includes both Paul and Phoebe as the collective authors of the letter (and potentially even other coworkers in Corinth). Neither Paul nor Phoebe would have followed dietary restrictions based on the Torah or gentile food regulations. Moreover, Paul as a somewhat successful missionary and Phoebe as leader of the church at Cenchreae (Rom 16:1) could, of course, count themselves among "the strong." Finally, their strength may also be their knowledge of (and faith in) the risen Christ (1 Cor 8:7-12; see above, p. 295).

The group of the strong has the exemplary task of putting up "with the failings of the weak and not to please ourselves. Each of us must please our neighbor for the good purpose of building up the neighbor" (15:1-2). Acting on such an appeal would have been considered an honorable task. This ethic of reciprocity was considered compulsory in the Roman world: "For no duty is more imperative than that of proving one's gratitude [*nullum enim officium referenda gratia magia necessarium est*]" (Cicero, *Off.* 1.47).[114] The "neighbor" was an important rhetorical character in Romans 13:8-10 about love for one another. That section featured a citation from Leviticus 19:18 about loving one's neighbor, presented as the fulfillment of the law. The same was, in essence, also stated in Romans 14:15 in the remarks that "walking" in love was incompatible with causing one's neighbor grief.[115]

According to Susan Mathew, the key to understanding the reciprocal principle in the ethical section of Romans is the insight that "the well-being of a person potentially leads to the well-being of the community. . . . The believers form a close-knit family, who are committed to solidarity and mutual care, and mutuality is rooted in their belonging to Christ."[116] Mathew calls this model "Pauline love-mutualism."[117] It is possible that the idea of mutual upbuilding of communities has its origins in the Pauline movement because no precedents have been found elsewhere. This principle is already attested in an appeal in 1 Thessalonians 5:11 where Paul admonishes the congregation to "build up each other." Paul's parenetic appeals have been a somewhat stable element of his proclamation.[118]

Attempts have been made to identify the "weak" and the "strong" with different categories of assemblies in Rome, namely, tenement as-

114. Oestreich, *Performanzkritik*, 165.

115. Esler, *Conflict*, 352–53.

116. Susan Mathew, *Women in the Greetings of Romans 16.1-16: A Study of Mutuality and Women's Ministry in the Letter to the Romans*, LNTS 471 (London: T&T Clark, 2013), 166.

117. Mathew, *Women*, 166.

118. Jewett, *Romans*, 879.

semblies and wealthier house churches. Only the latter could have afforded to obtain food to bring to and share at love feasts, as they had the necessary means for it.[119] Members of the tenement groups would have boasted about keeping the law, food constraints, and observing holy days; members of the house churches would have boasted about freedom from those regulations. In the end, both sides needed to understand that God's grace was given freely to all, including the others.[120]

The theological rationale for this behavior is the example of Christ (Rom 15:3-4, see also v. 7). Here, another Scripture citation from Psalm 68:10 (LXX); 69:9 (ET) is inserted, suggesting the importance of this element for Paul and Phoebe. The citation is about the willing acceptance of insults that others were exposed to. It is employed in Romans so as to describe an aspect of the vicarious dimension of the proexistence of Jesus.[121] It suggests that self-serving pleasure is not what the life and death of Jesus were about, and neither would that be the recipe for healthy loving communities.[122]

An interesting hermeneutical reflection is inserted in Romans 15:4. That Scripture "was written for our instruction" repeats to some degree a statement in 4:23-24 (see also 1 Cor 9:10; 10:11). It shows that the parenetic section of the letter is consciously composed as such and references scriptural traditions according to their presumed purpose. If this is a reflection on the Scripture citation from Psalm 68:10 (LXX); 69:9 (ET), then a dramatic shift has nevertheless occurred because the Psalm verse is about an insult of God, who is addressed in verse 2 (v. 1 [ET]). In the quotation in Romans 15:3, this insult is now that of the audience.[123]

The third element of the pericope in Romans 15:1-6 is a homiletical benediction. It features characteristic Pauline parenetic terminology and ideas: "May the God of steadfastness and encouragement give you the same attitude of mind toward each other" (15:5).[124] This appeal goes all the way back to the start of the parenetic section. In Romans 12:2, Phoebe challenged

119. Rector, "Shame," 120–22.

120. Rector, "Shame," 120–22.

121. On the concept of "proexistence" and its definition, see above at Rom 8:31-39, pp. 207–211.

122. Frank J. Matera, *God's Saving Grace: A Pauline Theology* (Grand Rapids: Eerdmans, 2012), 60.

123. Jewett, *Romans*, 881.

124. The NRSVue translates: "May the God of steadfastness and encouragement grant you to live in harmony with one another" (Rom 15:5). The Greek text, however, describes having the same thoughts and has, thus, a more narrow focus; cf. Georg Bertram, "φρήν, ἄφρων, κτλ," *TDNT* 9 (1974): 220–35, at 221. The NIV offers a more

her audiences to "not be conformed to this age, but be transformed by the renewing of the mind." At the close of the parenetic section, it is now revealed that mutuality in the thoughts of the people is the key. Michael Wolter highlights that a recurring term in this and other similar passages is "one another" (Greek ἀλλήλων, ἀλλήλοις, ἀλλήλους). Here and elsewhere, this pronoun is used to articulate the ideal of a reciprocal egalitarian community, the radically democratic *ekklēsia* of wo/men "in Christ."[125]

Rom 12:10	Love *one another* [εἰς ἀλλήλους] with mutual affection; outdo *one another* in showing honor [τῇ τιμῇ ἀλλήλους προηγούμενοι].
Rom 12:16	Be intent on having the same mind toward *one another* [τὸ αὐτὸ εἰς ἀλλήλους φρονοῦντες].[126]
Rom 13:8	Owe no one anything, except to love *one another* [Μηδενὶ μηδὲν ὀφείλετε εἰ μὴ τὸ ἀλλήλους ἀγαπᾶν].
Rom 14:19	Let us then pursue what makes for peace and for *mutual* upbuilding [τὰ τῆς οἰκοδομῆς τῆς εἰς ἀλλήλους].
Rom 15:7	Welcome *one another* [προσλαμβάνεσθε ἀλλήλους].
Rom 15:14	you yourselves are full of goodness, filled with all knowledge, and able to instruct *one another* [δυνάμενοι καὶ ἀλλήλους νουθετεῖν].
Rom 16:16	Greet *one another* with a holy kiss [ἀσπάσασθε ἀλλήλους ἐν φιλήματι ἁγίῳ].

This principle of mutual love has nothing of an abstract philosophy; it is not just a recommendation for others to implement. Paul and Phoebe are applying this principle themselves and implementing it in their ministries. In fact, the very letter to the Romans is an example of such communal work. As a joint-venture product, this letter is the result of Paul's cooperation with Phoebe and others in the city of Corinth, specifically in the assembly of Cenchreae. They all have worked on this letter ἀλλήλοις, "with one another."

This means nothing else than the full incorporation of women in the ministry of proclaiming the gospel of Jesus Christ. Besides Phoebe, who has been entrusted to deliver the letter to Rome and recite it, Prisca (Rom 16:3-5) and Junia (16:7) are other examples of female leaders in the earliest communities of believers in Christ. The principle of reciprocal love-

literal translation: "May the God who gives endurance and encouragement give you the same attitude of mind toward each other."

125. Wolter, *Paulus*, 323.

126. For this translation, which differs from the NRSVue, see the comments above on Romans 12:16 (pp. 273–274).

mutualism has empowered women and other marginalized members of society to participate in the communities where their humanity and full status in front of God were celebrated. And this celebration was, once more, to happen together and "with one voice" (ἐν ἑνὶ στόματι) to the glory of "the God and Father of our Lord Jesus Christ" (15:6). It was another strategy of ensuring the acceptance of the broader appeal.[127]

The Gospel for Jews and Gentiles Alike (15:7-13)

Romans 15:7-13 starts by revisiting the appeal about welcoming, based on the example of Christ. Now the welcome is to be extended to all.[128] On the one hand, the terminology is reminiscent of that in 14:1 to welcome the "weak in faith." On the other hand, it parallels 15:1-2. Alain Gignac sees the following symmetry between Romans 15:1-6 and 15:7-13:[129]

Symmetry Between Romans 15:1-6 and 15:7-13

15:1-6		15:7-13
15:1-2: We who are strong ought to put up with the failings of the weak and not to please ourselves. Each of us must please our neighbor.	*Appeal*	15:7a: Welcome one another.
15:3a: Christ did not please himself.	*Paradigm of Christ*	15:7b: as Christ has welcomed you.
	(Commentary)	15:8-9a: For I tell you.
15:3b: Ps 68:10 (LXX)	*Scripture Quotation*	15:9b-12: Ps 17:50 (LXX) (= 2 Sam 22:50) + Deut 32:43 + Ps 116:1 (LXX) + Isa 11:10
15:4: For whatever was written in former days was written for our instruction.	*(Commentary)*	
15:5: May the God of steadfastness and encouragement grant you to live in harmony with one another.	*Prayer*	15:13: May the God of hope fill you with all joy and peace in believing.

127. Oestreich, *Performanzkritik*, 166.
128. Hultgren, *Romans*, 529.
129. Gignac, *L'épître*, 531.

Rom 15:7-13

[7]Welcome one another, therefore, just as
Christ has welcomed you, for the glory
of God. [8]For I tell you that Christ has
become a servant of the circumcised on
behalf of the truth of God in order that he
might confirm the promises given to the
ancestors [9]and that the gentiles might
glorify God for his mercy. As it is written,
"Therefore I will confess you
among the gentiles
and sing praises to your name";
[10]and again he says,
"Rejoice, O gentiles, with his
people";
[11]and again,
"Praise the Lord, all you gentiles,
and let all the peoples praise
him";
[12]and again Isaiah says,
"The root of Jesse shall come,
the one who rises to rule the
gentiles;
in him the gentiles shall hope."
[13]May the God of hope fill you with all
joy and peace in believing, so that you
may abound in hope by the power of
the Holy Spirit.

This symmetry demonstrates that Romans 15:7-13 mainly summarizes the previous section about mutual love and, in a way, the rest of the parenetic section of the letter. It also shows that these appeals are for both Jews and gentiles and corroborate such encouragement through Scripture citations.

The first statement about welcoming one another (προσλαμβάνεσθε ἀλλήλους) is substantiated by a reference to Christ who "became a servant of the circumcised [διάκονον γεγενῆσθαι περιτομῆς]." Besides being a repetition of Romans 14:1, it also reflects previous statements such as Romans 3:30 and 4:12, where "circumcision" was a reference to the Jewish people as a whole. It is conceivable that this offensive language goes back to the internal conflict between the assemblies in Rome, where it may have been used in a hostile fashion (see above, p. 75).[130] The status of Christ as "servant" is the actual example for the strong to welcome the weak. More specifically, the antithesis of "circumcision – gentile" corresponds to the antithesis of "weak – strong" in the previous three pericopes.[131]

130. Joel Marcus, "The Circumcision and the Uncircumcision in Rome," *NTS* 35 (1989): 67–81; John Goldingay, "The Significance of Circumcision," *JSOT* 88 (2000): 3–18.

131. Jewett, *Romans*, 893.

The phrases that promises to the ancestors are confirmed and that gentiles should glorify God (Rom 15:8-9) are summary references of the extended discourse in Romans 9–11 on how Israel's election was part of the divine plan to allow for the incorporation of the gentiles into the people of God. As such, they are a unique element of this letter. As its argumentative weight may perhaps have been questionable, it is not surprising that a catena of Scripture quotations is now launched to substantiate it. Phoebe uses the customary introductory formula (15:9; see already 3:10; 11:8) to announce the sequence of no fewer than four quotations in 15:9-12: Psalm 17:50 (LXX) (= 2 Sam 22:50);[132] Deuteronomy 32:43; Psalm 116:1 (LXX); Isaiah 11:10. In the fourth and last quotation in Romans 15:12, the "root of Jesse" is a metaphor for the messiah as ruler of the nations. At the same time, this is a reference to the very first sentence of Romans that introduced Jesus as "descended from David according to the flesh" (Rom 1:3). These subtle allusions finally come to fruition.[133]

All four quotations have been chosen because of their references to the gentiles; these are envisioned to praise God together with the Jews.[134] Taken from the Torah, the Psalms, and the prophets, the quotations are intended to demonstrate that the view of salvation history as presented in the letter is based on, and consistent with, the entirety of the Scripture traditions of Second Temple Judaism.[135] The incorporation of the gentiles into the covenant relationship with God is the paradigm that allows, by extension, also for the idea of the inclusion of all other marginalized groups. With that, the goal of the radically democratic *ekklēsia* of wo/men and all others has been achieved where "there is no longer Jew or Greek; there is no longer slave or free; there is no longer male and female, for all of you are one in Christ Jesus" (Gal 3:28). The very presence of Phoebe, the gentile woman formerly enslaved, is the perfect embodiment not only of this message but also of its success in implementation. Both Paul and

132. Psalm 17:50 (LXX) corresponds to 18:50 (MT) and 18:49 (ET).

133. Matthew Thiessen, *Paul and the Gentile Problem* (New York: Oxford University Press, 2016), 126.

134. Oestreich, *Performanzkritik*, 169.

135. The second quotation from Deuteronomy 32:43 (LXX) features a text that is more than twice as long as that of the Hebrew MT (and English versions). The argument in Romans 15:10 only works based on the Greek Septuagint text, not on the Hebrew text of MT. Also the third quotation from Psalm 116:1 (LXX) (Rom 15:11) is rather different from the Hebrew MT. Cf. Hultgren, *Romans*, 532–33; Wolter, *Römer*, 2:410–13.

Phoebe were aware of this, which made them hopeful that the gospel message of their letter would be met with acceptance.

The final homiletical benediction in Romans 15:13 draws once more on key elements of the gospel. Hope, joy, and peace should fill the hearts of the believers in Christ, not despair and fear. Such a transformation is what the Holy Spirit as agent of God's saving power accomplishes.[136]

136. Gaventa, *Mother*, 132.

Romans 15:14–16:27

Letter Closing: About Phoebe and Other Important Women and Men

Paul's Reason for Writing So Boldly (15:14-21)

Romans 15:14 is the start of the final section (or the epilogue) of the letter (15:14–16:27). Even if the final verses (16:25-27) are recognized as secondary, the remainder is still a surprisingly long finale. Beyond the standard epistolary elements of antiquity, it is a valuable source of information about the earliest assemblies of Jewish believers in Christ and about Paul's practice of ministry.[1]

The first section in 15:14-21 consists of two pericopes: a review of the reasons for writing to the Roman assemblies (15:14-16), featuring a *captatio benevolentiae* ("capture of goodwill"; 15:14) and the actual rationale (15:15-16); and, second, a description of the strategy for the gentile mission and its success (15:17-21), featuring sections about reliance on Christ (15:17-19) and comments on missional selection, which include Scripture citations (15:20-21).[2]

1. Michael Theobald, *Römerbrief*, vol. 2, SKKNT 6/2 (Stuttgart: Katholisches Bibelwerk, 1993), 199.

2. Robert Jewett, *Romans: A Commentary*, Hermeneia (Minneapolis: Fortress, 2007), 903; Alain Gignac, *L'épître aux Romains*, Commentaire biblique: Nouveau Testament 6 (Paris: Cerf, 2014), 544–47.

Rom 15:14-21

14 I myself feel confident about you,
my brothers and sisters, that you yourselves are full of goodness, filled with
all knowledge, and able to instruct one
another. 15 Nevertheless, on some points
I have written to you rather boldly by
way of reminder, because of the grace
given me by God 16 to be a minister
of Christ Jesus to the gentiles in the
priestly service of the gospel of God,
so that the offering of the gentiles may
be acceptable, sanctified by the Holy
Spirit. 17 In Christ Jesus, then, I have
reason to boast of my work for God.
18 For I will not be so bold as to speak of
anything except what Christ has accomplished through me to win obedience
from the gentiles, by word and deed,
19 by the power of signs and wonders,
by the power of the Spirit, so that from
Jerusalem and as far around as Illyricum I have fully proclaimed the gospel
of Christ. 20 Thus I make it my ambition
to proclaim the gospel, not where Christ
has already been named, so that I do
not build on someone else's foundation,
21 but as it is written,

> "Those who have never been told
> of him shall see,
> and those who have never
> heard of him shall
> understand."

The preceding section features many second-person plural pronouns ("you") and states its Scripture citations in the third-person singular. By contrast, Romans 15:14-21 is dominated by the first-person singular, for example: "I myself feel confident [πέπεισμαι] about you" (15:14); "Nevertheless, on some points I have written to you rather boldly [τολμηρότερον δὲ ἔγραψα ὑμῖν]" (15:15). This is an indication that the letter has moved from its parenetic section to concluding remarks of personal relevance. Of course, these lines are still recited aloud by Phoebe. But there are several indicators that show how she is now more, if not entirely, in the role of Paul's avatar. For instance, the phrase about having written boldly evokes the situation of Paul's sojourn in Corinth and its distance both in time and space from the assemblies in Rome, the letter's addresses. In a similar way, 15:17-19 describes the ministry among the gentiles "from Jerusalem and as far around as Illyricum" (v. 19), which obviously has Paul's earlier travels in mind. This pericope is concerned with the apostle's past ministry and its success. In that regard, to the degree that this task is portrayed as winning "obedience from the gentiles, by word and deed" (15:18), the presence of Phoebe, the gentile, is itself the perfect proof of success.

Romans 15:14 begins: "I myself feel confident about you," repeating the verb πέπεισμαι that occurred already in 14:14.[3] The choice of vocabulary here in 15:14 shows that Paul and Phoebe, when writing the letter, were not absolutely certain how the people in Rome were doing because they have not personally met them yet.[4] But based on reports that they have received, they acknowledge that they are doing fine. With this *captatio benevolentiae* ("capture of goodwill"; see 1:9-10), Phoebe gets to flatter the audiences and ensure the sympathetic reception of the letter and its main arguments.

The style of this entire section of the letter is less elaborate than the previous sections. Parallelisms or other rhetorical devices are infrequent and there is a lack in rhythmic style. The exception is the quotation of Isaiah 52:15 in Romans 15:21, but this is because of the synthetic parallelism of Hebrew poetry that did not get lost in the Greek rendering of the Septuagint.[5]

Romans 15:15-16 provides some reflections on the rationale for writing to the Roman assemblies. Here, Phoebe speaks about writing "rather boldly by way of reminder" (v. 15). This is an apologetic comment in light of earlier remarks in the introduction (*exordium*) of the letter (1:1-7) and its prayer of thanksgiving (1:8-15). The latter articulates Paul's hope that he and people in Rome would be "mutually encouraged by each other's faith" (1:12). Such mutual encouragement is what Phoebe and her audiences have hopefully enjoyed. Among these audiences are their dear friends Prisca and Aquila; they will be acknowledged soon (16:3-5). Because of their spiritual maturity and successful leadership of an assembly in Rome, Paul and Phoebe are careful to avoid any appearance of wanting to patronize them. They have nevertheless presented a long and complex theological argument, including its practical application. This was bold, but now the argument is that all of it was already known to the recipients.[6] That is a way of ensuring that nobody objects to it.

3. Different Bible editions all convey approximately the same meaning of the verb while employing different terminology. The NIV has "I myself am convinced . . . that you"; the NKJV has "Now I myself am confident concerning you."

4. Beverly Roberts Gaventa, *Our Mother Saint Paul* (Louisville: Westminster John Knox, 2007), 139.

5. Josef Martin, *Antike Rhetorik: Technik und Methode* (Munich: Beck, 1974), 150.

6. Arland J. Hultgren, *Paul's Letter to the Romans: A Commentary* (Grand Rapids: Eerdmans, 2011), 538–39.

Paul then refers to his calling as "a minister of Christ Jesus to the gentiles in the priestly service of the gospel of God, so that the offering of the gentiles may be acceptable, sanctified by the Holy Spirit" (Rom 15:16). Just as at the start of the parenetic section in 12:1, this phrase employs cultic terminology metaphorically. First, Paul present himself as "a minister [λειτουργός]."[7] That term conveys the inclusion of the gentiles into the people of God, which is understood as a form of worship. As was made clear, the final purpose of Paul's mission to the gentiles is that they join in the praise of God together with the Jews (15:9-11).

Second, his ministry is a "priestly service of the gospel of God [ἱερουργοῦντα τὸ εὐαγγέλιον τοῦ θεοῦ]" (Rom 15:16). This participial clause belongs to the same imagery of priestly service as the previous noun "minister," as the noun ἱερουργία in 4 Maccabees 3:20 shows. It demonstrates the comfort that many Jews of the Second Temple period had with that cultic center of their religion.

Third, also "the offering [προσφορά] of the gentiles" draws on the background of the temple and its rituals. As Robert Jewett points out: "Rather than bringing a sacrifice to the altar as would have been typical for Jewish as well as Greco-Roman worship, Paul's evangelistic proclamation results in a transformation of the Gentiles into 'an acceptable offering' in the fulfillment of an end-time scheme announced in 11:11, 25 and derived from Isa 66:20."[8] The Greek noun προσφορά ("offering") conveys the idea of an approach from the profane space to the sanctuary. It is, however, not attested in the Torah where the sacrificial regulations are found. Instead, it is a frequent term for sacrifices in the Septuagint (especially in the so-called Apocrypha: Dan 3:38 [= Odes 7:38]; 4:37; Sir 14:11; 34:18-19; 35:1; 1 Esdr 5:51) and then in the New Testament (Acts 21:26; 24:17; Eph 5:2; Heb 10:5, 8, 10, 14, 18). It is a late cultic term.

7. Cf. the NRSV, NIV, NASB 1995, NKJV; see also the Traduction œcuménique de la Bible and Reina Valera 1995; furthermore, Joseph A. Fitzmyer, *Romans: A New Translation with Introduction and Commentary*, AB 33 (New York: Doubleday, 1993), 711; Jewett, *Romans*, 906; Richard N. Longenecker, *The Epistle to the Romans: A Commentary on the Greek Text*, NIGTC (Grand Rapids: Eerdmans, 2016), 1023, 1038. This term is sometimes translated as "servant"; cf. the Revidierte Lutherübersetzung 2017 ("Diener"); furthermore, Michael Wolter, *Paulus: Ein Grundriss seiner Theologie*, 3rd ed. (Neukirchen-Vluyn: Neukirchener Verlag, 2021), 156: "Gehilfe." But the term "minister" is preferable as it belongs to the cultic realm of worship and, as such, is somewhat necessitated by the addition of "priestly service."

8. Jewett, *Romans*, 907.

Fourth, the offering of the gentiles should be "acceptable" (the Greek adjective εὐπρόσδεκτος literally means "well-pleasing") and "sanctified by the Holy Spirit." Both terms refer back to and parallel the elaborate exposition of the "living and holy sacrifice, acceptable to God"[9] in Romans 12:1 and evoke the transformation mentioned in 12:2.

It is interesting to reflect on the cultic terminology here in 15:16 and in 12:1 and recognize these metaphors not only as references to Paul's ministry, as has been done frequently, but also to Phoebe's, which has not been done yet. While it is apparent that Paul refers to himself in these sentences as the priest whose ministry transforms and sanctifies gentiles, the side of the gentile offering is represented by Phoebe, the gentile woman who has come to Rome. The abstract metaphors about sacrificial offerings are supported by an embodiment that, to repeat, demonstrates the success of Paul's ministry. But there is more. The fact that Paul trusted her to deliver the letter and that she, therefore, traveled the Mediterranean on her own was further proof of a different form of culture in which women could have a status that was rather elevated compared to that of other traditional societies. It also implies that the title of "minister" that Paul claims is actually deserved by Phoebe; in the service of the gospel, she is a priestess. So when a long sentence in Romans 15:17-19 celebrates Paul's priestly ministry and its power of transformation, then one may acknowledge that, for once, Paul dares to break his own commitment to refrain from boasting (v. 17). But the person who merits this celebration is really Phoebe. This special situation would have motivated the assemblies in Rome to accept the message and to emulate the result, which implies the cooperation between Jews and gentiles and the empowerment of women. That is more than just one step toward the reconciliation of the quarreling parties in the assemblies of Rome.

The end of the sentence in 15:17-19 indicates the geographic scope of Paul's ministry: "so that from Jerusalem and as far around as Illyricum I have fully proclaimed the gospel of Christ" (v. 19). Both locations mentioned in this statement, however, pose problems. First, Jerusalem was the place where Paul received instructions (Gal 1:17) and where his ministry to the gentiles was approved (Gal 2:2). But we do not know of any missionary work of Paul in this city.[10] Second, there is likewise no

9. For this translation, which differs from the NRSVue, see comments above under "Translation Matters" on Romans 12:1.

10. Jerome Murphy-O'Connor, *Paul: His Story* (Oxford: Oxford University Press, 2004), 101–6.

mention in the Acts of the Apostles that Paul would ever have visited the Roman province of Illyricum (or Dalmatia), which was located on the seacoast north of Macedonia and west of Thrace (roughly equivalent to modern Albania). While scholars have proposed several theories as to what Paul may have wanted to convey with this geographic reference,[11] it may simply be seen as a way of designating the territory of Jews and Greeks/gentiles. After all, the goal throughout the letter to the Romans has been to align these two religious-cultural groups, starting with the *propositio* (main thesis) in 1:16-17. Paul and Phoebe now suggest that they have accomplished this goal.

As for the remoteness of these territories, Paul has Phoebe declare that he did not want to tread on someone else's mission grounds (15:20). This statement is once more supported by a Scripture citation (Isa 52:15, in Rom 15:21). It is clearly an allusion to the earlier syllogism about conversion in Romans 10:13-15, according to which faith is the result of listening to the proclamation of the gospel. Paul and Phoebe now add that he is looking for ever new geographic areas to proclaim that message. Thus, two things are made clear. On the one hand, Paul has no plan to carry out his ministry in Rome, as the gospel has already been proclaimed there and assemblies have been established. On the other hand, he implicitly hints at Spain as the territory of his next visit, thus preparing explicit references in 15:24, 28. That sets up the following paragraph.

From the perspective of feminist biblical interpretation, it should be stated that, as may be clear by now, Paul's travels did not just serve the proclamation of a disembodied gospel. An important collateral benefit was that his gospel made a difference for marginalized groups of people, among which were first and foremost women. Through a process of transformation, a new type of society came alive wherever Paul was successful in establishing assemblies of believers in Christ. These groups were the embodiment of the new democratic *ekklēsia* of wo/men. This means that he was an agent who, in the name of Jesus Christ, actively ended the oppression of women wherever he could. As was the case with Phoebe, some of these women would then go on to embark on their own mission to not only proclaim but to be and live that very change. This is what the sacrificial metaphors in Romans 12:1, properly understood, convey; this is the "living sacrifice."

11. Hultgren, *Romans*, 540; Michael Wolter, *Der Brief an die Römer*, vol. 2: *Röm 9–16*, EKKNT 6/2 (Göttingen: Vandenhoeck & Ruprecht; Ostfildern: Patmos, 2019), 432.

Paul's Plan to Visit Rome (15:22-33)

Chapter 15 finishes with Paul's long-standing plan to visit Rome after delivering the collection to Jerusalem. The first words in 15:22 correspond to those of 1:13: "I do not want you to be unaware, brothers and sisters, that I have often intended to come to you (but thus far have been prevented)." What is Paul referring to? He leaves out any graphic details here in Romans, but he had eagerly shared them before. According to 2 Corinthians 11:23-29, he had suffered imprisonments, injuries from stoning and other types of beating, and shipwrecks during the two or three years immediately preceding the writing of Romans. The precariousness of human life in the ancient world was fully on display in his career. In addition, he experienced travel delays for various reasons (weather and danger) and needed to do manual labor to provide food and shelter for himself.[12] Now, however, he is optimistic that things would line up more favorably in the future and announces his apostolic *parousia* in Rome. Not without pathos, Paul has Phoebe declare on his behalf: "I know that when I come to you I will come in the fullness of the blessing of Christ" (Rom 15:29). As we know today, it was not to happen the way Paul had anticipated.

In Romans 15:23-24, Paul expresses his intentions to visit Rome on his way to Spain and to solicit Rome's support for his travels (see also 1:10; 15:28). He would, however, not have traveled in the footsteps of Phoebe, despite the fact that she preceded him. Paul's travels should have brought him first to Palestine at the Eastern fringes of the Roman Empire, then to Rome at the center of Roman power, and from there to Spain at the utmost Western periphery. This would have been a veritable tour across the known world of antiquity. Paul was indeed preparing to shift the geographical focus of his mission from the Greek East to the Latin West.

One specific problem accompanied the intended continuation of his missionary activities in Spain: Paul spoke neither Latin nor any of the local languages of Spain (which were not Spanish, a language that developed much later out of Latin; instead, various Punic dialects were spoken in first-century CE Spain). And the "barbarians" there did not speak Latin or refused to do so.[13] So he needed either a translator or a travel companion who spoke those foreign languages; alternatively, he could

12. Jewett, *Romans*, 922.

13. Edgar C. Polomé, "The Linguistic Situation in the Western Provinces of the Roman Empire," *ANRW* 2.29.2 (1983): 509–53, at 523–25.

Rom 15:22-33

[22]This is the reason that I have so often
been hindered from coming to you.
[23]But now, with no further place for me
in these regions, I desire, as I have for
many years, to come to you [24]when I go
to Spain. For I do hope to see you on
my journey and to be sent on by you,
once I have enjoyed your company for
a little while. [25]At present, however, I
am going to Jerusalem in a ministry to
the saints, [26]for Macedonia and Achaia
were pleased to share their resources
with the poor among the saints at Jerusalem. [27]They were pleased to do this,
and indeed they owe it to them, for if
the gentiles have come to share in their
spiritual blessings, they ought also to
be of service to them in material things.
[28]So, when I have completed this and
have delivered to them what has been
collected, I will set out by way of you to
Spain, [29]and I know that when I come
to you I will come in the fullness of the
blessing of Christ.

[30]I appeal to you, brothers and sisters, by our Lord Jesus Christ and by
the love of the Spirit, to join me in earnest prayer to God on my behalf, [31]that
I may be rescued from the unbelievers
in Judea and that my ministry to Jerusalem may be acceptable to the saints,
[32]so that by God's will I may come to
you with joy and be refreshed in your
company. [33]The God of peace be with
all of you. Amen.

have stayed long enough in Rome to acquire either language himself. But both of these options required a residence in Rome of significant length.

Paul was a real cosmopolitan, and he became more multicultural with each new sojourn. His hope was that corporate multiculturalism would become the hallmark of the new identity of Christ believers' assemblies in Rome. If successful, they would embrace others rather than reject them. It would also be to his own benefit. Paul was a Jew. A Jewish-gentile divide in Rome would, therefore, affect him and his own plans for the near future; overcoming it would be crucial for the success of his further missionary projects. And finally, there was the additional concern that someone writing from Corinth would be facing particular prejudices. All of these matters had to be solved before Paul could have relied on the support of Rome for his future mission projects. Corporate multiculturalism would have been the solution.

According to Romans 15:25-28, Paul brings a collection (κοινωνία) for the "poor" in Jerusalem (v. 26). The reason for this collection is the acknowledgment that the starting point of the gospel message was Jerusalem and that the gentiles received it from there. This progression of faith has already been indicated in the phrase "for the Jew first and also for the Greek" (1:16) in the *propositio* (main thesis) of Romans. Another theological rationale for this endeavor was the allegory of the olive tree that was to convey, with its own peculiarities, the dependence of the gentiles on Judaism (11:17-24).

The ambivalence regarding Paul's standing in Jerusalem and his collection project emerges from the prayer request in Romans 15:30-32. Paul had previously mentioned his own prayers of thanksgiving for the faith of the people in Rome (1:8). Now, he asks for prayerful support for his own upcoming endeavors. But the way he presents this request is telling: "I appeal to you, brothers and sisters . . . to [struggle together with me in prayers] to God on my behalf" (15:30).[14] These words convey some serious foreboding.[15] Paul has a suspicion that trouble may await him and is not reluctant to share his apprehensions with his addressees. Such an open display of personal concerns is unique in Pauline letters. The fateful continuation of Paul's life shows that his suspicion was warranted.[16]

The appeal continues: "that I may be rescued from the [disobedient ones] in Judea [ἵνα ῥυσθῶ ἀπὸ τῶν ἀπειθούντων ἐν τῇ Ἰουδαίᾳ[17]] and that my ministry to Jerusalem may be acceptable to the saints" (Rom 15:31). The participle οἱ ἀπειθοῦντες literally means "the disobedient ones" (NASB 1995) or "the unconvinced" and either refers to those who have not yet adopted the faith in Jesus Christ or designates those with a different opinion from Paul's interpretation, which may specifically have to do with the understanding of the law. The verb "to rescue" (ῥύομαι) conveys the seriousness of the anticipated problems. Its passive form indicates the hope that God may be the one who saves. Paul knew the danger was real; he admits in one of his earlier letters that he had once participated in the violent persecution of "the church of God" in Judea (Gal 1:13, 22-23).[18]

14. The NRSVue rendering "to join me in earnest prayer" is rather weak (previously, the RSV had "to strive together with me in your prayers"). The Greek συναγωνίσασθαί μοι implies a struggle; the NIV translates more appropriately "to join me in my struggle by praying."

15. Hultgren, *Romans*, 562.

16. It is possible that Romans is Paul's attempt to prepare for the potential situation of the failure of his future mission project; cf. Angelika Reichert, *Der Römerbrief als Gratwanderung: Eine Untersuchung zur Abfassungsproblematik*, FRLANT 194 (Göttingen: Vandenhoeck & Ruprecht, 2001).

17. The NRSVue renders this Greek phrase as "that I may be rescued from the unbelievers in Judea" (see also the NRSV, RSV, NIV, NKJV). For the translation chosen here, see the Revidierte Lutherübersetzung 2017 ("den Ungehorsamen"); furthermore, Gignac, *L'épître*, 540.

18. Arland J. Hultgren, "Paul's Pre-Christian Persecutions of the Church: Their Purpose, Locale, and Nature," *JBL* 95 (1976): 97–111.

Another concern has to do with Paul's collection for the poor in Jerusalem. It is uncertain whether it was ever received (see the brief reference in Acts 24:17). One purpose of this collection was to demonstrate the attainable harmony between gentiles and Israel; a second purpose was to mend Paul's tricky relations with those in Jerusalem.[19] But it did more than that. Paul's willingness to put so much on the line for the sake of the "ministry to the saints" (Rom 15:25) shows once again his passion for the support of the marginalized. Such a financial contribution may appear to be a small token in a campaign for an egalitarian society and as an expression of his personal care for the poor. Soon, however, the audiences in Rome would learn that Paul himself had received support by someone else, whom he introduces as his own "benefactor" (16:2, see below). This person is no one else but Phoebe who has now been standing in front of these audiences for hours.

The section in Romans 15:22-33 about Paul's travel plans closes with a benediction: "The God of peace be with all of you. Amen" (15:33). The final word invites the audiences in Rome to reply with an "amen" of their own. The term means "so be it" and unites Phoebe not only with these audiences but also with the absent Paul in affirming God's peace. This peace is the result of the faith in Christ according to Paul's gospel that was proclaimed by Phoebe (see 2:10; 5:1; 12:18; 14:17, 19).[20]

Recommendation of Phoebe (16:1-2)

The first two verses of Romans 16 contain a short letter of recommendation.[21] Such a recommendation typically consists of three formal elements: an explicit recommendation, the identification or naming of the commended person, and a request on behalf of him or her, to be fulfilled by the recipient. A recommendation of representatives "along with our beloved Barnabas and Paul" is featured in Acts 15:25-26. In that particular case, Paul is among the group of people who deliver the letter commissioned by the apostles' council.[22]

19. Gignac, *L'épître*, 548–50.

20. Jewett, *Romans*, 940.

21. The NRSVue has different section assignments in Romans 16, featuring a large section in 16:1-16 with the title "Personal Greetings." While most of this section consists indeed of such greetings, the first extended sentence in 16:1-2 is different, as it is a recommendation of Phoebe. Personal greetings start in v. 3.

22. Bonnie Thurston, *Women in the New Testament: Questions and Commentary*, Companions to the New Testament (New York: Crossroad, 1998), 54; Susan Mathew, *Women in the Greetings of Romans 16.1-16: A Study of Mutuality and Women's Ministry in the Letter to the Romans*, LNTS 471 (London: T&T Clark, 2013), 35–36.

Rom 16:1-2

[16:1]I commend to you our sister Phoebe, a deacon of the church at Cenchreae, [2]so that you may welcome her in the Lord, as is fitting for the saints, and help her in whatever she may require from you, for she has been a benefactor of many and of myself as well.

TRANSLATION MATTERS: Romans 16:1

The recommendation of Phoebe features, as a second credential after "our sister," the title "deacon" according to the NRSVue. The Greek language knows only the form διάκονος for both masculine and feminine.[23] The title "deacon" still exists today but usually refers to a lower rank in the clergy.[24] Therefore, it is important to mention that, in first-century CE communities of Jewish Christ believers, it could have designated an official or even the leader of an organization (see also Phil 1:1).[25] Phoebe is being presented to the Roman assemblies as a person in an

23. Elizabeth A. McCabe, "A Reevaluation of Phoebe in Romans 16:1-2 as a *Diakonos* and *Prostasis*: Exposing the Inaccuracies of English Translations," in *Women in the Biblical World: A Survey of Old and New Testament Perspectives*, ed. Elizabeth A. McCabe (Lanham, MD: University Press of America, 2009), 100.

24. Many English Bible translations render the term διάκονος in Romans 16:1 in a way that obscures Phoebe's status and limits it to a serving function (e.g., "servant," KJV, NASB; "helper," NCV; "who serves," GNT). Cf. Elisabeth Schüssler Fiorenza, "Women in the Early Christian Movement," in *WomanSpirit Rising: A Feminist Reader in Religion*, ed. Carol P. Christ and Judith Plaskow (New York: HarperOne, 1992), 92; Annette Merz, "Phöbe, Diakon(in) der Gemeinde von Kenchreä—Eine wichtige Mitstreiterin des Paulus neu entdeckt," in *Frauen gestalten Diakonie*, vol. 1: *Von der biblischen Zeit bis zum Pietismus*, ed. Adelheid M. van Hauff (Stuttgart: Kohlhammer, 2007), 130–31.

25. According to Luke (who wrote a few decades after Paul), the ministries that a διάκονος carried out were varied: leadership (Luke 22:25-27 [including the "ministry" of Jesus]); apostolic ministry (Acts 1:25); ministry of the table (6:2); ministry of the word (6:4); financial ministry (Luke 8:3; Acts 11:29; 12:25). By contrast, in other passages in Romans, the term "minister/ministry" designates exclusively leadership positions (Rom 11:13; 15:25, 31: refers to Paul's own apostleship; 12:7: leadership tasks involving proclamation; 13:3-4: government rulers). Hence, Phoebe's ministry was most likely that of a congregational leader with focus on proclamation (a "pastor" in modern terminology). See also Elisabeth Schüssler Fiorenza, "Missionaries, Apostles, Coworkers: Romans 16 and the Reconstruction of Women's Early Christian History," *WW* 6 (1986): 420–33, at 426; Ray R. Schulz, "A Case for 'President' Phoebe in Romans 16:2," *Lutheran Theological Journal* 24 (1990): 124–27; Jewett, *Romans*, 944–45; Lynn Japinga, *From Daughters to Disciples: Women's Stories from the New Testament* (Louisville: Westminster John Knox, 2021), 115.

authoritative and influential leadership position of the church at Cenchreae.[26] Hence, a better translation of διάκονος is "minister" (see, e.g., the footnote after "deacon" in the NRSV and NRSVue). Such an understanding is corroborated by the different versions of the subscriptions that several biblical manuscripts add at the end of the text of Romans (see above, p. lvii). They provide insights into the early reception history of Romans. One of the recurring features is the presentation of Phoebe as "minister" or "minister of the church at Cenchreae." In these lines, the term "minister" is beyond a doubt the designation of a significant position, otherwise it would not have been included.

Before starting the interpretation of this final chapter of Romans, it should be noted that a certain sparseness of feminist studies on the preceding fifteen chapters (with just a few exceptions) stands in stark contrast to an abundance of feminist studies on Romans 16. This last chapter has been a focus of feminist interest for roughly the past fifty years mainly because it features a variety of women's names.[27] These studies have resulted in an important correction of the scholarly perception of Paul's ministry and of the development of the earliest assemblies of believers in Christ.

Chapter 16 of the letter begins with a short recommendation (συστατικὴ ἐπιστολή; see also 2 Cor 3:1) of Paul on behalf of Phoebe (Rom 16:1-2). Different from its usage in 3:5 and 5:8, the Greek verb συνίστημι here has the meaning of "to commend, recommend" or "to introduce."[28] It is remarkable, first, that the apostle starts this chapter of personal notes with the name of a woman—he will subsequently mention another seventeen men and nine women by name.[29]

Second, only a woman is recommended as someone who will personally visit Rome (for further ramifications of this aspect, see below). The name Phoebe, attested in the New Testament only in Romans 16:1, means "radiant" in Greek and is a surname of the goddess Artemis (Phoebus

26. It is unfortunate but telling about the problem of the andro-/kyriocentric orientation of biblical scholarship that this simple insight already constitutes "a tremendous advance over the previous consensus, of hardly more than a quarter-century ago, that there simply were no women leaders in the early Christian congregation" (Sheila E. McGinn, "Feminist Approaches to Paul's Letter to the Romans," in *Celebrating Romans: Template for Pauline Theology; Essays in Honor of Robert Jewett*, ed. Sheila E. McGinn [Grand Rapids: Eerdmans, 2004], 169).

27. See McGinn, "Approaches," 166–67.

28. Heinrich Schlier, *Der Römerbrief*, HThKNT 6 (Freiburg: Herder, 1977), 440–41.

29. Elizabeth A. Castelli, "Romans," in *Searching the Scriptures*, vol. 2: *A Feminist Commentary*, ed. Elisabeth Schüssler Fiorenza (New York: Crossroad, 1994), 276; Chantal Reynier, *Les femmes de saint Paul: Collaboratrices de l'apôtre des nations* (Paris: Cerf, 2020), 195.

being the solar epithet of Artemis's brother Apollo).[30] The citation from Isaiah 52:7 in Romans 10:15 may be a more or less hidden allusion to her name with its reference to the beauty of the "feet" of the gospel messenger, thus celebrating her ministry (see above, p. 245). But there are reasons to believe that the life of the woman whom Paul recommends has not always been "radiant." Some have identified the Phoebe of Romans not only as a pagan/gentile but also as a freed enslaved person.[31] If accurate, this means that earlier in her life, she would have experienced what it means to exist as a piece of her master's property, without any status, socially dead, subject not only to injustice, cruelty, and humiliation but potentially also to periodic sexual abuse without even the right to protect herself. While eventually, she would have been fortunate enough to obtain manumission, which would have given her Roman citizenship and facilitated her social integration, the latter would have been limited because of the social stigma that former enslaved women bore (regardless of whether they had been sexually abused or not). While we can only speculate, this may have been the reason why Phoebe may not have been married at the time of her travels to Rome; no Roman citizen other than another freedperson would have considered her as a potential bride, fearing the certain loss of honor among peers for himself and his family. Phoebe's social situation is complex: if her former status was that of an enslaved person, then she has now come to enjoy a certain prestige in the community of Christ believers as minister of the church at Cenchreae and emissary of Paul. It is notable that unlike many biblical women, Phoebe is not introduced in relation to a male figure such as her husband, father, brother, or some other guardian.[32] She appears as an independent agent. According to Romans 16:1-2, her relations to men are, instead, vis-à-vis Paul and the entire church. Needless to say, an earlier experience of enslavement would have left her with a lingering trauma due to the injustice and cruelty she would have suffered. It would have implanted in her a fervent yearning for freedom.

At this point, it is worth revisiting Romans 7:1-6 with its analogy from marriage, presented explicitly to illustrate the idea of freedom from the law.

30. Joan C. Campbell, *Phoebe: Patron and Emissary*, Paul's Social Network: Brothers and Sisters in Faith (Collegeville, MN: Liturgical Press, 2009), 10.

31. Hans-Josef Klauck, *Hausgemeinde und Hauskirche im frühen Christentum*, SBS 103 (Stuttgart: Katholisches Bibelwerk, 1981), 30; Beverly Roberts Gaventa, *When in Romans: An Invitation to Linger with the Gospel According to Paul* (Grand Rapids: Baker Academic, 2016), 9; Reynier, *Les femmes*, 96–98.

32. Castelli, "Romans," 278–79; see also Tatha Wiley, *Paul and the Gentile Women: Reframing Galatians* (New York: Continuum, 2005), 93–94.

Phoebe had invited her audiences to imagine a woman who is ὕπανδρος, "under (the power of) a man" (7:2). With that, she proposed a thought experiment that was consciously gendered. Its key term, "under (the power of) a man," referred to marriage, but at the same time, it would capture the situation of an enslaved woman who had to serve a male master. It is interesting to note that Phoebe's narrative in Romans 7:1-6 evoked the death of the husband twice (7:2, 3) without any hint at emotional trouble on the part of the woman. After his death, Phoebe explained, the woman is finally free. From an intersectional perspective, these aspects may point to a complex yet typical quandary specifically of enslaved women. In general, enslaved persons were "available bodies for their owners."[33] An enslaved woman, however, was "primarily valued for her reproductive or sexual capital."[34] The problem was that, on the one hand, an enslaved woman who was related to her master by blood could improve her undesirable personal situation and had a higher chance of eventually being manumitted. On the other hand, an enslaved woman was often given the opportunity of emancipation under the condition that she would marry her master.[35] Finally, manumission was sometimes granted to both enslaved men and women upon the death of their masters.

In light of this complex situation, is the imagery in Romans 7:1-6 perhaps based on Phoebe's own experience as an enslaved person? Does it potentially reflect the fact that she had suffered from injustice and humiliation at the hands of her former master, including sexual abuse? Is it maybe even a hidden narrative of retribution against the man from whom she had no chance or right to withhold her own body? While such considerations remain necessarily speculative, they would satisfy the feminist maxim to "use women to think with" if, in this particular case, one uses an enslaved woman to think with. That perspective would explain why, on the one hand, the wider context in Romans 6–8 frequently deploys terminology and images from the realm of enslavement. On the other hand, the context also problematizes inner existential conflicts, and agony combined with a yearning for freedom appears to confirm such an understanding. Either

33. Marianne Bjelland Kartzow, *The Slave Metaphor and Gendered Enslavement in Early Christian Discourse: Double Trouble Embodied*, Routledge Studies in the Early Christian World (London: Routledge, 2018), 100.

34. Bjelland Kartzow, *Metaphor*, 101. See also Rebecca Flemming, "*Quae Corpore Quaestum Facit*: The Sexual Economy of Female Prostitution in the Roman Empire," *JRS* 89 (1999): 38–61, at 42.

35. Peter Hunt, "Manumission: Ancient Rome," in *Macmillan Encyclopedia of World Slavery*, vol. 2, ed. Paul Finkelman and Joseph C. Miller (New York: Macmillan, 1998), 548–49.

aspect could suggest that the trauma of enslavement was deeply seated within Phoebe and that the past still occupied her mind. Exegetical studies of modern scholars are, of course, limited because of the lack of knowledge of the lives of ancient authors and other assistants and coworkers who assisted in the process of text production. As Zoltán Kövecses points out, however, "The story of one's life may be a key factor in explaining individual variation in metaphorical conceptualizing."[36]

The climax of it all is a reference to the cry of despair of another woman from Corinth, depicted in Euripedes's fifth-century BC tragedy, *Medea*: "Wretched person that I am!" (Rom 7:24). And Medea, the main character of this well-known ancient tragedy, resorts to killing her husband and her own children because of the injustice that he had inflicted on her (Euripides, *Med.* 228-234). The endless agony of finding consolation and relief to embrace a new life is likewise inscribed into the presentation of Phoebe's gospel of freedom and future glory that she proclaims in Rome. Phoebe may be the personification of the success of the gospel, but she will always carry the scars of past tragedy. In light of this, it is not farfetched that the analogy from marriage in Romans 7:1-6, despite its explicit purpose of illustrating freedom from the law, serves yet another, implicit agenda, namely, that of articulating her personal trauma, perhaps including secret wishes of retribution against a past perpetrator.

In the letter of recommendation of Romans 16:1-2, explicit attributes of Phoebe are "our sister," "[minister]," and "benefactor." First, as "our sister," Phoebe may be introduced as a close associate of Paul and those in his house assembly or, more likely, as a fellow believer in Jesus Christ.[37] Second, as "a [minister] of the church at Cenchreae," Phoebe is specifically presented as an official and/or influential leader of her congregation.[38] Cenchreae was the eastern port for Corinth where Paul dictated his letter to the Romans.[39] It is interesting to note that the letter refers to

36. Zoltán Kövecses, *Metaphor in Culture: Universality and Variation* (Cambridge: Cambridge University Press, 2005), 243.

37. Jewett, *Romans*, 944; Campbell, *Phoebe*, 21–32. Chantal Reynier argues that both aspects, associate and fellow believer, are connected; cf. Reynier, *Les femmes*, 101.

38. Beverly Roberts Gaventa, "Romans," in *Women's Bible Commentary*, ed. Carol A. Newsom, Sharon H. Ringe, and Jacqueline E. Lapsley, 3rd ed. (Louisville: Westminster John Knox, 2012), 555.

39. Archaeological expeditions have been conducted at Cenchreae/Kenchreia (Κεγχρεαί); see the extensive documentation in Robert Scranton et al., *Kenchreai, Eastern Port of Corinth; Results of Investigations by the University of Chicago and Indiana University for the American School of Classical Studies at Athens* (Leiden: Brill, 1978–1981), 5 vols.; esp. 1:37–90.

the name of the seaport to introduce Phoebe but avoids the name of the larger city to which it belongs.

Paul was among those who had been enjoying Phoebe's patronage, as he is eager to indicate in his concluding remarks by presenting her as his "benefactor" (προστάτις, Rom 16:2). The Greek term is the feminine form of προστάτης. In various Bible translations, it has, because of traditional gender expectations and in efforts to downplay Phoebe's influential position, often been translated as "succourer" (KJV) or "helper" (NKJV, RSV; NLT: "she has been helpful"). Yet, in the Greco-Roman world, the term προστάτις signifies a person of prominence with considerable status and wealth. Therefore, "benefactor" is a more suitable rendering.[40] This support may have included the secretarial services of Tertius (16:22), since in antiquity scribes were expensive. Hence, Paul asks that Phoebe be met with special hospitality. Phoebe had "business" to do in Rome; perhaps her trade in Cenchreae was in shipping, which may have seen her travel back and forth to the capital. Therefore, Paul requests that the assemblies in Rome would provide her with the necessary means to support her business endeavors (Rom 16:2). Her next business trip provided Paul with the opportunity to write to the Romans.[41] That would

40. Marie-Françoise Baslez, *Saint Paul* (Paris: Fayard, 1991), 160; Richard B. Hays, "Paul on the Relation between Men and Women," in *A Feminist Companion to Paul*, ed. Amy-Jill Levine with Marianne Blickenstaff, FCNTECW 6 (London: T&T International, 2004), 144; McCabe, "Reevaluation," 104–8; Mathew, *Women*, 5; Kar Yong Lim, " 'For All of You Are One in Christ Jesus' (Gal 3:28): Paul's Social Vision Beyond Inclusivity and Diversity," in *From Malaysia to the Ends of the Earth: Southeast Asian and Diasporic Contributions to Biblical and Theological Studies*, ed. Elaine Wei-Fun Goh et al. (Claremont, CA: Claremont Press, 2021), 83–116, at 104–6; Japinga, *Daughters*, 115–16. See also Erlend D. MacGillivray, "Romans 16:2, προστάτις/προστάτης, and the Application of Reciprocal Relationships to New Testament Texts," *NovT* 53 (2011): 183–99, who sees Phoebe's and Paul's relationship within the dynamic reciprocity of benefaction. Olivette Genest understands the term in the sense of "protector" ("protectrice"; cf. Olivette Genest, "Femmes et ministères dans le Nouveau Testament," *SR* 16 [1987]: 7–20, at 15). Sojung Yoon ("Phoebe, a Minister in the Early Christian Church," in *Distant Voices Drawing Near: Essays in Honor of Antoinette Clark Wire*, ed. Holly E. Hearon [Collegeville, MN: Liturgical Press, 2004], 19–31) notes that in secular Greek literature *prostatis* is used for "leader," or "ruler," in a political sense. In the Roman period, it was used for patrons, those who provided funds and protection, and used their political influence for the benefit of those under their patronage.

41. Michael Wolter, *Der Brief an die Römer*, vol. 1: *Röm 1–8*, EKKNT 6/1 (Neukirchen-Vluyn: Neukirchener Verlag; Ostfildern: Patmos, 2014), 56; Wolter, *Römer*, 2:458; Jan Rüggemeier, "Ein Streifzug durch Roms Gassen und Viertel: Subjektorientierte Perspektiven auf die stadtrömischen Christinnen und Christen im ersten Jahrhundert,"

explain why Paul composed the letter during winter months; ship travels on the Mediterranean would only resume in spring when the weather became more favorable. All of this also indicates why Phoebe was the "benefactor"; due to a certain level of success in her business, she had some financial means at her disposal and was ready to apply them for the support of others.[42]

After this exploration of the three explicit attributes for Phoebe as "sister," "[minister]," and Paul's "benefactor," which are impressive each in their own right, we also need to turn to further ramifications of the three implicit attributes of Phoebe as a woman, as a gentile/pagan, and potentially as a freedwoman (a formerly enslaved person). By coincidence or not, these three additional attributes intersect with all three binary parameters that Paul had evoked to articulate his vision of the new democratic *ekklēsia* of wo/men. According to Galatians 3:28, his group-making project to achieve radical unity among the diverse social groups of his congregation was structured along the three attributes of religious or ethnic identity ("no longer Jew or Greek"), the status of personal liberty ("no longer slave or free"), and gender ("no longer male and female"). As a woman, gentile, and potentially formerly enslaved person, Phoebe emerges as the personification of all of them. Furthermore, she represents the weaker side of each of these three attributes, if (at least in religious matters) gentiles get to adopt Judaism and believe in a Jewish messiah and enslaved persons clearly have a lower status than free people and, in the patriarchy of Greco-Roman antiquity, women had certainly a lower status than men. Connecting all three of these attributes, Phoebe was the embodiment of intersectionality. She still would have had a lasting memory of the cruelty, humiliation, and abuse that she would have suffered as an enslaved woman even if later she became a freedwoman. This experience would have fostered a vision of, and desire for, personal freedom that historically first developed among enslaved women.[43] That vision was strictly countercultural in the context of the predominantly patriarchal/malestream Roman world with its propensity

in *Talking God in Society: Multidisciplinary (Re)constructions of Ancient (Con)texts; Festschrift for Peter Lampe*, vol. 1: *Theories and Applications*, ed. Ute E. Eisen and Heidrun E. Mader, NTOA 120/1 (Göttingen: Vandenhoeck & Ruprecht, 2020), 307–38, at 327.

42. Ute E. Eisen, *Amtsträgerinnen im frühen Christentum: Epigraphische und literarische Studien*, FKDG 61 (Göttingen: Vandenhoeck & Ruprecht, 1996), 156.

43. Orlando Patterson, *Freedom in the Making of Western Culture*, Freedom 1 (New York: Basic Books, 1991), 54.

to glorify the male self at the expense of the other. Hence, Phoebe was the embodiment of Paul's gospel message of inclusion, justification, and new creation. Her very presence may already have conveyed a sense of healing for those affected by marginalization and oppression.

In antiquity, it was customary to mention and recommend the carrier of a letter. In light of Paul's recommendation in Romans 16:1-2, Phoebe was most likely the person who delivered the letter to the congregations in Rome. As mentioned above, this is confirmed in the subscriptions of several biblical manuscripts that add lines like the following after the end of the text: "Letter to the Romans, written through Phoebe, minister (of the church at Cenchreae)"; "written through Tertius, but sent by Phoebe, minister." Since she was on her business trip to Rome, Paul seized the opportunity to give her the letter.[44] The apostle had used private carriers for his letters on other occasions (e.g., Epaphroditus; cf. Phil 2:25-30).[45] Among the various options known in Greco-Roman antiquity for transporting private letters, the choice of Phoebe came with the benefit that she could also perform additional tasks on behalf of Paul. Specifically, Phoebe would have been able to provide the recipients in Rome with further information, for instance, on the complex theological contents of the letter.[46] In antiquity, the recipients commonly expected the letter carrier to convey additional news or information.[47] This has occasionally been mentioned in such letters.[48] Phoebe would then have been in the position of negotiating the complex issues advanced by the letter in a manner typical for the

44. Philip F. Esler, *Conflict and Identity in Romans: The Social Setting of Paul's Letter* (Minneapolis: Fortress, 2003), 117; Elsa Tamez, "Der Brief an die Gemeinde in Rom: Eine feministische Lektüre," in *Kompendium feministische Bibelauslegung*, ed. Luise Schottroff and Marie-Theres Wacker, 2nd ed. (Gütersloh: Kaiser; Gütersloher Verlagshaus, 1999), 558–59; Jewett, *Romans*, 942; Gignac, *L'épître*, 563; Gaventa, *Mother*, 3; Gaventa, *When in Romans*, 12; Angela N. Parker, "One Womanist's View of Racial Reconciliation in Galatians," *JFSR* 34 (2018): 23–40, at 39; Japinga, *Daughters*, 112–16.

45. Whether Timothy may be considered the carrier of 1 Corinthians is unclear (1 Cor 4:17 appears to suggest so, but 16:10 indicates otherwise). Cf. Matthew S. Harmon, "Letter Carriers and Paul's Use of Scripture," *Journal for the Study of Paul and His Letters* 4 (2014): 129–48, at 138–40.

46. Tamez, "Brief," 559.

47. E. Randolph Richards, *Paul and First-Century Letter Writing: Secretaries, Composition and Collection* (Downers Grove, IL: InterVarsity, 2004), 183.

48. See, for instance, the following lines in an ancient papyrus: "The rest please learn from the man who brings you this letter. He is no stranger to us" (*P.Col.* 3.1. Nr. 6.15). Cf. Eldon Jay Epp, "New Testament Papyrus Manuscripts and Letter Carrying in Greco-Roman Times," in *The Future of Early Christianity: Essays in Honor of Helmut Koester*, ed. Birger A. Pearson et al. (Minneapolis: Fortress, 1991), 46.

ancient world. She would have answered questions in case something remained unclear; she would have added her own Midrashic comments to passages if they were too lengthy or too concise or too complicated.

Even more important, however, it was also sometimes expected that the letter carrier read the letter to the recipients. Beverly Roberts Gaventa explains:

> She [i.e., Phoebe] may well have been the one who read the letter aloud among the various house churches in Rome, as no other candidate for that task is named, and it would be most beneficial for Paul to have a reader with whom he could have discussed the letter's content in advance. It is not at all far-fetched, then, to identify Phoebe as the first interpreter of Romans, both in her informal comments to gathered believers at Rome and in her actual reading of the letter (reading any text aloud invariably interprets it, depending on the pace, stance, tone of voice, and many other factors).[49]

While Paul's authorship of Romans is undisputed, Phoebe may be considered his avatar, the person who actually traveled to Rome to deliver and recite the letter in front of several assemblies.

Phoebe as Paul's Avatar

What is the relationship between the letter and the messenger?[50] Avatar is a metaphor for Phoebe who acts in Romans as the "higher self" of Paul. *Avatar*, written and directed by James Cameron, was a science fiction film (2009) in which the humanoid woman Neytiri, played by Zoe Saldana, represents preservation of nature as sacred.[51] The male hero, Jake Sully, played by Sam Worthington, is a paraplegic former Marine. As humans cannot survive in the atmosphere of the moon Pandora, Na'vi-human hybrids called "avatars" have been developed to act in their place and engage with the humanoids. His bonding with Neytiri, in another dimension, gradually defines his new mission to defend fragile nature on a far-off planet. Neytiri teaches Jake how to fly a dragon-bird. She represents the desire of the man-explorer to go where he cannot fly on his own. She embodies his yearning to commit himself to a

49. Gaventa, "Romans," 555. See also Harmon, "Letter Carriers," 139–40; Chantal Reynier, *Vie et mort de Paul à Rome* (Paris: Cerf, 2016), 91.

50. Martin Hengel and Anna Maria Schwemer, *Paul between Damascus and Antioch: The Unknown Years*, trans. John Bowden (Louisville: Westminster John Knox, 1997), 449n1125.

51. See https://en.wikipedia.org/wiki/Avatar_(2009film).

higher, nobler task. "I see you" is her greeting to him and becomes his to her. In this virtual-reality world, an ordinary man projects himself as an environmental hero, taking the side of the primal woman and her tribe, marshalling all the natural forces that are "theirs" to save a sacred environment from exploitation and destruction. In a broader understanding of the term, perhaps Neytiri can be seen as "avatar" of Jake to accomplish his mission.

There are several ways in which Phoebe serves as Paul's avatar—Paul's "other self," the accepted spokesperson, the legitimator and presenter of Paul's letter. First, Paul struggles throughout his letters to defend his legitimacy as an apostle of Jesus Christ, with authority from God. He insists that he was commissioned by Christ. He devotes long passages of his letters to an explanation and historicization of his role as visionary, apostle, and preacher (2 Cor 10–13; Gal 1:11–2:14). Second, Paul struggles against accusations that he is a fraud, a maverick, or self-appointed. His opponents say that he has invented his own gospel, that he may have depended on Jerusalem leaders, but that he is unfaithful and preaching his own ideas. Third, Paul acknowledges that he knows he's not been accepted. He recites a litany of rejection and his stalwart endurance (2 Cor 11:23-27).

Paul is generally on the defensive, having to assert repeatedly that his authority comes from God. His autobiographical accounts of his conversion do not merely provide an introduction of himself to his readers. They serve as a rebuttal to accusations that, since he was not an eyewitness of Jesus's earthly ministry, he does not speak the same message as the "superapostles" (2 Cor 11:5). Even in Romans, Paul refers to his competitors, "those who create dissensions and hindrances, in opposition to the teaching that you have learned" (Rom 16:17). As Martin Hengel and Anna Maria Schwemer note, "The letter presupposes that Paul was accurately informed about conditions in Rome and about the reservations people had about him there."[52]

So what is Paul's relation to Phoebe? The standard interpretation is that Paul authorizes Phoebe, deacon at Cenchreae, a suburb of Corinth in Greece, to personally deliver the letter, explain it to the believers in the assemblies at Rome, and engage them in dialogue about what Paul means. His commendation includes a recognition that she is a benefactor or patroness to many.[53]

52. Hengel and Schwemer, *Paul*, 287.
53. Ed P. Sanders, *Paul* (Oxford: Oxford University Press, 1991), 11.

But is he the one authorizing her, or, rather, is he recognizing that she already enjoys respect by the assemblies at Rome? Is he pressing an advantage by associating himself with her—a woman highly regarded for her learning and leadership, even though she is a Greek, living a considerable distance from Rome?

Phoebe's status as deacon at Cenchreae demonstrates that she was not operating within a social pattern defined by the household code with its patriarchally defined, female-subordinate role. Rather, she represented the *ekklēsia*—the horizontal pattern of discipleship in which disciples, whether women or men, have a relationship of equality with each other because they are one in Christ.[54]

Phoebe must have been a cosmopolitan woman with a sophisticated secular and religious education, a theologian, linguist, rhetorician, teacher, and administrator, knowledgeable about Hebrew Scripture and Jewish law, familiar with Paul's Pharisaic style of argument and his interpretation of the Torah. She could converse coherently about the same thorny issues Paul treats in his letter—to a combined Jewish and gentile audience. She could articulate missionary theology about the resurrection of Jesus and explain the meaning of covenant, justification, sin, and sanctification. She was able to speak Greek to gentile converts of the congregation at Cenchreae; she was fluent in Latin to speak to residents of Rome. It is possible that Paul worked out some ideas in his letter by talking them through with Phoebe.

When Paul commends Phoebe to the assemblies at Rome, he is admitting that many in the audiences there have no direct knowledge of him. Other missionaries preceded Paul, like Priscilla and Aquila. He is confident the Romans know who Phoebe is. The deacon of Cenchreae, by delivering his letter, is vouching for him, serving as his recommender so he will be trusted and his teaching accepted. Ultimately, it is Phoebe herself who is Paul's avatar, his messenger and spokesperson, his alter ego. Paul had male companions—Barnabas, John Mark, Silas, Timothy, and Titus. But it is this extraordinarily learned woman who is Paul's stand-in, an imagined self, a virtual presence for Paul as he entrusts to her the momentous task of explaining his theologically complex letter to the assemblies at Rome

Eloise M. Rosenblatt

54. Adriana Destro and Mauro Pesce, "In and Out of the House: Changes in Women's Role from Jesus's Movement to the Early Churches," in *Gospels: Narrative and History*, ed. Mercedes Navarro Puerto, Marinella Perroni, and Amy-Jill Levine, BW 2.1 (Atlanta: SBL Press, 2015), 311–12.

The ramifications of this historical insight have not always been appropriately considered. One implication is that Phoebe must have been educated enough for this task; she could read. Yet, for Paul to entrust her with the task of commenting on his letter goes far beyond that; it *eo ipso* demonstrates her level of theological competence and conversancy with the ideas of the apostle. And more than that, Paul would have discussed the letter with her in Corinth, probably asking for her opinion on certain passages and integrating ideas from her perspective. This would explain the frequent passages from a female vantage point just as much as the employment of terminology drawing on the background of enslavement.[55] Phoebe was, thus, likely an active contributor to the letter. The participation of a woman as such was not unusual in antiquity. Although formal school education was the privilege of men in the first-century Greco-Roman world, evidence exists that women were involved in the production of ancient private letters as calligraphers, record keepers, and scribes. This adds plausibility to Phoebe's involvement in the process of the production of the letter to the Romans.[56]

We need to add, however, two further significant historical aspects to these insights. First, the statement in Romans 10:17 that "faith comes from what is heard" directly hints at the fact that the gospel was to be received by ear. Hence, the gospel was proclaimed orally. Naturally, Paul's letters were intrinsically connected to the act of oral delivery. According to Werner Kelber, "Paul the rhetor favored a fundamentally oral disposition toward language. . . . Hearing, not sight, was accorded a place of pride in his economy of the sensorium. It was the supersense that facilitated interiorization of sounded words and faith."[57] This is why it came with such a rich spectrum of rhetorical features that were intended to impress the audiences at the moment of oral delivery. Yet, when Romans was heard for the first several times in the assemblies in Rome, it was heard through the voice of a woman, not that of Paul.

55. Gaventa, *When in Romans*, 12–14.

56. William V. Harris, *Ancient Literacy* (Cambridge, MA: Harvard University Press, 1989), 48, 67, 96, 103, 108, 140, 173, 252–63, 271, 328; Kim Haines-Eitzen, *Guardians of Letters: Literacy, Power, and the Transmitters of Early Christian Literature* (Oxford: Oxford University Press, 2000), 41–52; Roger S. Bagnall and Raffaella Cribiore, *Women's Letters from Ancient Egypt, 300 BC–AD 800* (Ann Arbor: University of Michigan Press, 2006).

57. Werner H. Kelber, "Language, Memory, and Sense Perception in the Religious and Technological Culture of Antiquity and the Middle Ages," *Oral Tradition* 10 (1995): 409–50, at 421–22. See also Reynier, *Vie*, 91; Campbell, *Phoebe*, 5.

And second, when speaking of reading, a modern audience naturally assumes that a text is being recited from a book, manuscript, or written notes. But the standard mode of text delivery before an audience in antiquity was different. Greco-Roman antiquity favored oral delivery without notes. Students of rhetoric learned to memorize even longer speeches for the purpose of reciting them freely.[58] This means that Phoebe did not actually read out the sixteen chapters of Romans. She would have recited them by heart, which would have taken at least sixty to eighty minutes without interruption.[59] Hence the rhetorical features of the letter also need to be seen in connection with its oral performance. If the text is a medium for the performer, then it is clear that Phoebe presented much of Romans as her own. In light of recent studies that advocate decentering Paul, it appears as if this is what Paul himself has done through his partnership with Phoebe (and others) to share the gospel with those in Rome.

Phoebe's important role has occasionally been acknowledged in later Christian church traditions. One example is medieval Christian iconography that has captured her central role for all things pertaining to Romans in a Bible manuscript. Created in 1164 CE at the Benedictine monastery Saint-Pierre at Corbie, the manuscript features, in a historiated initial "P" as the first letter of Romans, the apostle Paul with his hand raised to speak. A scroll representing the letter to the Romans itself emanates from him and is received by Phoebe who is identified by name. She also raises her hand to speak, apparently to instruct the assembly of Christ believers in Rome. The image graphically expresses that the person who conveys the letter in an act of oral performance, starting with its first two Latin words *Paulus servus* ("Paul, an enslaved person") and continuing with all its complex christological contents and ethical advice, is Phoebe. She is the person on the ground in Rome.[60]

Paul presents the assemblies in Rome with some tasks regarding Phoebe: They are to "welcome her in the Lord, as is fitting for the saints, and help her in whatever she may require from you" (Rom 16:2). The

58. Martin, *Rhetorik*, 347–56. The ancient culture was not literary but oral. Literature prepared an anticipated act of oral communication, and all reading was done aloud. Cf. Bernhard Oestreich, *Performanzkritik der Paulusbriefe*, WUNT 296 (Tübingen: Mohr Siebeck, 2012), 249.

59. Reynier, *Vie*, 91.

60. Anne L. Clark, "Remembering Phoebe in the Twelfth Century: The Forgotten Deacon in Paul's Letter to Romans," *Journal of Medieval Religious Cultures* 45 (2019): 1–28, at 10–12. (The illustration with the historiated initial "P" is shown at the front of this commentary volume.)

assemblies were expected to host Phoebe. This was, on the one hand, in keeping with the principle in Romans 12:13 to "pursue hospitality to strangers." On the other hand, even if a different Greek verb is employed here, they are also expected to welcome Phoebe (14:1; 15:7). Against all human propensity for judgment, the mercy and love of Christ were supposed to prevail; Phoebe should have been welcomed "just as Christ has welcomed you" (15:7).

Beloved Woman

Mvskoke women of the Muscogee (Creek) Nation have always been honored for their sacred power to conceive, bring forth, and nurture life. The tribe embraces a harmonious female balance to the male energy of its people.[61] Mvskoke tradition also honors their Beloved Women, seasoned wisdom keepers, medicine bearers, educators, and storytellers in their autumnal years. Female voices hold authority throughout our tribe.[62]

In contemplating Phoebe as a life-giving energy in the creation of the letter to the Romans and as a trusted deliverer of the letter to Rome, I imagine her at ease among an intimate gathering of tribal Beloved Women. Within the circle, Phoebe speaks of her community as the "tribe" of Cenchrea and how her own authority grew by servanthood to her people. In storyteller fashion, she describes the creation of the letter.

> Our days were beautiful, like a dance. The Spirit burned like fire within us, and words flowed like water out of us.[63]

It was holy—like ceremony—sacred moments for Paul and Tertius and me as the message to Rome was birthed.

The Beloved Women nod as she continues. "I carried the letter to Rome like a mother shielding her own child." Their thoughts turn to Mother Earth, the many-breasted one, nurturing and sustaining the life of their clans.

In time, the Jews in Rome would also hear her story and be reminded of another

61. Jean Chaudhuri and Joyotpaul Chaudhuri, *A Sacred Path: The Way of the Muscogee Creeks* (Los Angeles: UCLA American Indian Studies Center, 2001), 50. Women in Mvskoke matrilineal society held authority as clan mothers while men carried physical power as warriors, serving in complementary roles.

62. Chaudhuri, *Path*, 49.

63. Chaudhuri, *Path*, 44. Phoebe speaks to the understanding of Mvskoke cosmology, in which fire is a masculine spirit and water is a feminine spirit.

nurturer—El Shaddai—literally, the Almighty Breast, which is a name of God according to Genesis 17:1.[64] The gentiles, too, would recognize Phoebe, the Beloved Woman honored by Paul, who shares in this life-giving message and proclaims it to all who would hear its wisdom, its freedom, its hope.

Laura Marshall Clark
(Mvskoke Nation)

Personal Greetings (16:3-16)

The actual list of greetings to leaders and other individuals in the assemblies in Rome is contained in 16:3-16. It is a long list of sentences with similar syntax, typically starting with the appeal to "greet," then naming the intended recipient, and finally featuring selected bits of further essential information. The short appeal in 16:16a diverges from this pattern as it urges the addressees to greet each other.[65]

After the recommendation of Phoebe, Romans features a list of greetings intended for people in Rome. The high number of names is unparalleled in ancient literature.[66] It is likely that they are mentioned one after another, together with individualized appreciation, to ensure the positive reception of the letter. In this list, two observations regarding women are remarkable. First, only three of the women—the mother of Rufus (16:13), Julia, and the sister of Nereus (16:15)—lack a specific role assignment. This shows that, in the early assemblies of believers in Christ, both men and women had various active roles and leadership positions. And second, the range of roles for women is, in fact, greater than that for men. In particular, two of the highest positions, those of minister and apostle, are correlated to women in Romans 16.[67]

64. Jeff A. Benner, *His Name Is One: An Ancient Hebrew Perspective of the Names of God* (College Station: VBW Publishing, 2003), excerpt on https://www.ancient-hebrew.org/studies-words/meaning-of-el-shaddai.htm. Benner posits that the Hebrew שדי (teat) is often combined with אל (mighty, strong) to create אל שדי (*el shaddai*) as found in Gen 17:1. He interprets its meaning as the "mighty teat" and implies a reluctance in Western culture to attribute breasts to a male God. This has resulted in a "more sanitized" translation of the same term as "God Almighty."

65. Wolter, *Römer*, 2:465.

66. Mathew, *Women*, 35.

67. Thurston, *Women*, 52–53.

Rom 16:3-16

[3]Greet Prisca and Aquila, my coworkers in Christ Jesus, [4]who risked their necks for my life, to whom not only I give thanks but also all the churches of the gentiles. [5]Greet also the church in their house. Greet my beloved Epaenetus, who was the first convert in Asia for Christ. [6]Greet Mary, who has worked very hard for you. [7]Greet Andronicus and Junia, my fellow Israelites who were in prison with me; they are prominent among the apostles, and they were in Christ before I was. [8]Greet Ampliatus, my beloved in the Lord. [9]Greet Urbanus, our coworker in Christ, and my beloved Stachys. [10]Greet Apelles, who is approved in Christ. Greet those who belong to the

The first greetings are addressed to Prisca and Aquila, a married couple of particular importance for the development of the early faith assemblies in Christ (Rom 16:3). The Greek form "Prisca" of a Latin name means "the venerable one." As the names of the couple appear in this particular order, one may note that, after Phoebe in 16:1-2, another woman is the next person to be mentioned. Also, the particular order of the names of this couple "suggests that she was of higher status (possibly she is a freeborn woman married to a former slave) or perhaps that she was the more prominent Christian leader."[68]

There is some discussion as to whether Prisca is a gentile, which several scholars affirm.[69] I support that opinion for two reasons. On the one hand, her name is Latin, which would be unlikely for a person of traditional Jewish background. On the other hand, in the list of Romans 16, Paul has a tendency to call a person of Jewish origin "relative"

68. Gaventa, "Romans," 555. In a similar vein, Margaret Aymer remarks about Prisca/Priscilla: "In the New Testament, she is usually named before her husband, and it is possible that she outranks him" (Margaret Aymer, "Acts of the Apostles," in Newsom, Ringe, and Lapsley, *Women's Bible Commentary*, 544). Cf. also Wendy Cotter, "Women's Authority Roles in Paul's Churches: Countercultural or Conventional?," *NovT* 36 (1994): 350–72, at 352–53.

69. Jerome Murphy-O'Connor identifies both Prisca and Aquila as "freed slaves of Jewish origin" (Murphy-O'Connor, *Paul*, 83). Uncertainty about the Jewish background of Prisca is indicated in Wolter, *Römer*, 2:467–68 (even though her Jewish identity is eventually affirmed); and Linda M. Maloney, *Acts of the Apostles*, WCS 45 (Collegeville, MN: Liturgical Press, 2022), 256. She is considered a gentile in Peter Lampe, "Prisca/Priscilla," *ABD* 5 (1992): 467–68, at 467; Gignac, *L'épître*, 563, 568.

family of Aristobulus. [11]Greet my fellow Israelite Herodion. Greet those in the Lord who belong to the family of Narcissus. [12]Greet those workers in the Lord, Tryphaena and Tryphosa. Greet the beloved Persis, who has worked hard in the Lord. [13]Greet Rufus, chosen in the Lord, and greet his mother—a mother to me also. [14]Greet Asyncritus, Phlegon, Hermes, Patrobas, Hermas, and the brothers and sisters who are with them. [15]Greet Philologus, Julia, Nereus and his sister, and Olympas, and all the saints who are with them. [16]Greet one another with a holy kiss. All the churches of Christ greet you.

(συγγενής, 16:11, 21). He does so in particular in 16:7 where he refers to Andronicus and Junia as "my [relatives]" (τοὺς συγγενεῖς μου).[70] Such a designation is, however, not applied to Prisca and Aquila, although there is no doubt that Aquila himself is of Jewish origin (Acts 18:2). In light of these observations, the only option is that Prisca herself is not of Jewish origin. She is a gentile. Prisca and Aquila are a mixed couple: a gentile noblewoman and a Jewish freedman. As such, they share many aspects that describe the partnership of Paul, the Jewish free man, and Phoebe, the gentile freedwoman. Both Prisca and Aquila and Paul and Phoebe exemplified the harmony between Jewish and gentile believers that was an important topic in the parenetic section of Romans (14:1–15:13).[71]

Aquila's home congregation would have been one of the fourteen Jewish synagogues of the first century in Rome known today.[72] Aquila is mentioned only once in Romans, and no information about his origins is given there. One could assume that his ancestors had been living in Italy for a little more than a century. They could have been among the prisoners of war, brought to Rome or its vicinity after the conquest of Palestine by Pompey in 63 BCE. Luke will later introduce Aquila as "from Pontus" (Acts 18:2). According to that *gentilic* name, he would have come from the

70. On this translation, which differs from the NRSVue, see the comments above on Romans 9:3 (p. 217).

71. Jewett, *Romans*, 955–58.

72. Harry J. Leon, *The Jews of Ancient Rome*, Morris Loeb (Philadelphia: Jewish Publication Society, 1960/5721), 135–66; Peter Lampe, *Die stadtrömischen Christen in den ersten beiden Jahrhunderten: Untersuchungen zur Sozialgeschichte*, 2nd ed., WUNT 2/18 (Tübingen: Mohr Siebeck, 1989), 367–68.

Jewish diaspora in the coastal areas of the Black Sea (roughly the north of modern-day Turkey). That would make him a first-generation inhabitant of Rome. According to a common bias in Greco-Roman antiquity, people from Pontus were thought to be uneducated and dimwitted barbarians. In light of that, Luke's information about Aquila's origin may have been a rhetorical device.

The other known aspect about Aquila is his trade, which is tentmaking. It means that he—and Prisca with him—were independent crafts persons.[73] The income from such a profession would have been meager, and the craft as such would not have given them much of a reputation.[74] Aquila had married Prisca. If she was a woman of higher status than Aquila, then it would offer proof of the egalitarian ethos among the groups of believers in Christ (or already in the traditional synagogue congregations?) and of the possibility of "upward mobility" in the Roman society.

In a previous letter to Corinth written between 53 and 54 CE during his stay in Ephesus, Paul had conveyed greetings from Prisca and Aquila, together with the church in their house (1 Cor 16:19). One may assume that Prisca was its leader. Luke recounts how Paul first met the couple in Corinth (Acts 18:1-3, 18). According to this passage, Aquila and Priscilla (Luke twice uses this order of their names and the diminutive form of Prisca's name) had been residents of Rome but were expelled under the edict of Claudius in 49 CE that banned Jews from Rome.

73. Regarding the trade of tentmaking in antiquity, see Murphy-O'Connor, *Paul*, 28–31. The introduction of "Aquila . . . who had recently come from Italy with his wife Priscilla" in Acts 18:2 remains ambiguous about who is "tentmaker" (σκηνοποιοί, or "leather worker" according to patristic interpreters) in 18:3. Does the plural σκηνοποιοί refer to Aquila and Paul or to Aquila and Priscilla? Or to all three? To what degree is it conceivable that Priscilla/Prisca exercised the same métier so that, as a couple, they were both tentmakers? It has been noted that nothing indicates that Paul's professional collaboration was restricted to Aquila; cf. Ivoni Richter Reimer, *Women in the Acts of the Apostles: A Feminist Liberation Perspective*, trans. Linda M. Maloney (Minneapolis: Fortress, 1995), 196; Christoph Stenschke, "Married Women and the Spread of Early Christianity," *Neot* 43 (2009): 145–94, at 161.

74. Marie Noël Keller, *Priscilla and Aquila: Paul's Coworkers in Christ Jesus*, Paul's Social Network: Brothers and Sisters in Faith (Collegeville, MN: Liturgical Press, 2010). On the poverty scale developed by Steven J. Friesen for the ancient Roman world, Prisca and Aquila still belonged to the lower half, indicating that they led a stable life "with moderate surplus resources" but nevertheless "near subsistence level" (Steven J. Friesen, "Poverty in Pauline Studies: Beyond the So-Called New Consensus," *JSNT* 26 [2004]: 337–57).

The Edict of Emperor Claudius

The Roman historian Suetonius writes in the early second century CE in *Divus Claudius* 25: "He [Emperor Claudius] expelled from Rome the Jews constantly causing disturbances at the instigation of Chrestus" (*Iudaios impulsore Chresto adsidue tumultuantes Roma expulit*). It sounds as if Suetonius mistakes "Chrestus," most likely a reference to "Christ," for a local Jewish leader.[75] The question is, however, what exactly the edict of Claudius stipulated. Luke wrote that "Claudius had ordered all Jews to leave Rome" (Acts 18:2). But according to estimates, the Jewish population of Rome in the middle of the first century CE comprised between twenty thousand and sixty thousand people (see above, p. lxxvii). It is difficult to imagine that such a large population would have been forced to leave in its entirety, as Acts 18:2 implies. It is historically more likely that the imperatorial decree targeted only those among the Jewish synagogue assemblies who had adopted the novel faith in Jesus as the Christ, as appears to be the literal meaning of the comment in *Divus Claudius* 25. In that case, Prisca and Aquila already shared the faith in Christ during their time in Rome; they did not adopt it through their contact with Paul in Corinth.[76]

As members of one of the synagogues in Rome, Prisca and Aquila had adopted the new faith in Christ, and then trouble ensued. After their expulsion, they arrived in Corinth, another large Mediterranean city and important economic center. There, they had to adjust to certain different cultural standards. For example, among the ancient Greeks, women were usually excluded from dinner invitations whereas they were allowed to join men in Rome.[77] It is also possible that the status of Aquila as a

75. Raymond E. Brown and John P. Meier, *Antioch and Rome: New Testament Cradles of Catholic Christianity* (New York: Paulist Press, 1983), 100; Rudolf Brändle and Ekkehard W. Stegemann, "Die Entstehung der ersten 'christlichen Gemeinde' Roms im Kontext der jüdischen Gemeinden," *NTS* 42 (1996): 1–11, at 1–2.

76. Klauck, *Hausgemeinde*, 22; Romano Penna, "Les Juifs à Rome au temps de l'apôtre Paul," *NTS* 28 (1982): 321–47, at 331; Andrie B. du Toit, "Paul's Chronology," in *Guide to the New Testament*, vol. 5: *The Pauline Letters: Introduction and Theology*, ed. Andrie B. du Toit (Pretoria: Kerkboekhandel, 1985), 32–34; Gaventa, "Romans," 549.

77. Dacre Balsdon, "Der Alltag der Frau im antiken Rom," *AW* 10 (1979): 40–56, at 52; Cotter, "Authority," 362–63 (with reference to Cornelius Nepos, *Lives of Famous Men*, preface 6–7).

freedman was different in Corinth as only the Romans, not the Greeks, bestowed citizenship on enslaved persons. Hence, there may have been less acceptance for this mixed couple in Corinth. Perhaps this is one of the reasons why they did not spend much time there.[78]

Paul met the couple upon his arrival in Corinth because they shared the same trade of tentmaking (Acts 18:3). It is quite conceivable that Paul was hired by Prisca and Aquila, who had already established their business. According to Luke, the couple left Corinth with Paul to travel to Ephesus, from where he continued alone to Syria. It is no surprise, therefore, that Paul addresses them in Romans as "my coworkers in Christ Jesus" (Rom 16:3).[79] This phrase features the syntagm "in Christ" as the crucial designation of Paul's ministry (see also 16:7, 9, 10; likewise Gal 3:28, etc.).[80]

These greetings suggest that Prisca and Aquila had returned to Rome prior to 56 or 57 CE. It is possible that Paul himself had sent them to Rome as a "vanguard" to prepare the local assemblies of Christ believers for his arrival.[81] Their return was not, however, celebrated by all. First, Prisca and Aquila returned from Corinth. As mentioned above, this city with its two harbors (Lechaion and Cenchreae) had always had a negative reputation among Romans since it was associated with luxury, sexual immorality, and a population of former enslaved people. Prejudices against former or current inhabitants of Corinth prevailed.

And second, since all believers in Christ of Jewish background had been expelled from Rome, they were now, upon their return, a minority, outnumbered by their gentile sisters and brothers. Prisca and Aquila wondered what to do. They were, however, leading an assembly in their own home; that is acknowledged in Romans 16:5a.[82] Like Phoebe, Prisca

78. Ellen Battelle Dietrick, "The Book of Acts," in *The Woman's Bible: Part 2, Comments on the Old and New Testaments from Joshua to Revelation*, ed. Elizabeth Cady Stanton (New York: European Publishing Company, 1898), 151.

79. Elisabeth Schüssler Fiorenza, *In Memory of Her: A Feminist Theological Reconstruction of Christian Origins* (New York: Crossroad, 1983), 178–79; Genest, "Femmes," 15.

80. Jens Herzer, *Petrus oder Paulus? Studien über das Verhältnis des Ersten Petrusbriefes zur paulinischen Tradition*, WUNT 103 (Tübingen: Mohr Siebeck, 1998), 90–99; Michael J. Lakey, *The Ritual World of Paul the Apostle: Metaphysics, Community and Symbol in 1 Corinthians 10–11*, LNTS 602 (London: T&T Clark, 2019), 16–18.

81. Peter Lampe, "The Roman Christians of Romans 16," in *The Romans Debate*, ed. Karl P. Donfried, 216–30, rev. exp. ed. (Peabody, MA: Hendrickson, 1991), 220; Merz, "Phöbe," 140.

82. On Romans 16:5a, see below.

was another leader of the first Christ believers who had collaborated with Paul in his mission. It has been proposed that the Roman Catholic Church as such, one of the largest religious denominations in the world today, developed from this house church.[83]

As Prisca was a trusted former ally of Paul, one may conjecture that the letter to the Romans was first brought to and recited in her house church. It may have been Prisca and Aquila who had the task of first "welcoming" Phoebe and helping her in other matters according to the request in Romans 16:1-2. This also means that, after Phoebe recited the letter in one of their church meetings, they may have retained their own copy. And it may have been in their church that the controversial discussions over dietary choices (14:1-12) had caused problems rooted in the haughtiness of some. Paul and Phoebe, who both knew Prisca and Aquila well from their days together in Corinth, were eager to help by reminding the quarreling parties that the enactment of the gospel implies mutual love (14:15).

The greetings to Prisca and Aquila also mention that they had "risked their necks for my life" (16:4). These words describe the couple as intimate and important friends. A few decades later, Luke writes about a letter commissioned by the apostles' council that praises Paul himself and Barnabas as people who "have risked their lives for the sake of our Lord Jesus Christ" (Acts 15:26). The Gospel according to John would describe the essence of love in similar terms: "No one has greater love than this, to lay down one's life for one's friends" (John 15:13). These phrases echo ideals of true friendship as endorsed in earlier Hellenistic philosophy.[84] The graphic and drastic words in Romans 16:4 imply, furthermore, that Prisca and Aquila had been willing to face decapitation as part of their cooperation with Paul. As such, these words not only convey the extent of Prisca's and Aquila's altruistic support but also implicitly indicate a somewhat elevated social status of the couple.[85] The fact that this note refers to Prisca as well shows once more the degree to which women were active and implicated in the earliest church work. In Rome, Phoebe gets to express her deep gratitude

83. Suggested by Ellen Battelle Dietrick, "Epistle to the Romans," in Stanton, *The Woman's Bible*, 153.

84. Aristotle, for instance, praised the readiness to give up one's life for the sake of friends (*Eth. nic.* 1169a 19–20).

85. Robert Jewett points out that decapitation as a "form of quick execution was normally the privilege of Roman citizens" and that this precise wording "provides additional confirmation of the high social status of Prisca and Aquila" (Jewett, *Romans*, 958).

to both Prisca and Aquila, together with "all the churches of the gentiles" (16:4). The latter comment is a reminder of the successful ministry that the couple has had in Rome, Corinth, and Ephesus (and perhaps also in other unknown locations). It may furthermore show that Paul not only shared his own life story when proclaiming the gospel of Christ but related at the same time what they had done for him and others.[86]

The development of the earliest churches and assemblies took place mostly in private homes. Early Jewish congregations in Rome were traditionally organized in synagogues; yet, the situation of internal quarrels over the faith in Jesus Christ led to a development that those who shared the faith would henceforth meet in private homes. Such house assemblies were known in both Corinth, where Paul resided when dictating the letter, and in Rome, to where it is addressed. One of these assemblies gathers in the house of Prisca and Aquila; Phoebe gets to greet "the church in their house" (Rom 16:5a).[87] The term "church" (ἐκκλησία) is used here for an assembly in Rome while it is avoided in the letter opening, where Paul addresses "all God's beloved in Rome" (Rom 1:7). This is astonishing because Paul had frequently employed the term in earlier letters (1 Cor 1:2; 10:32; 15:9; 2 Cor 1:1; Gal 1:13; 1 Thess 2:14). He may have used the term only for assemblies that convened in private homes, not for those based in apartment or tenement houses.[88] Overall, one may assume the existence of as many as seven assemblies in Rome, associated with the following people or their households: Prisca and Aquila (Rom 16:3-5); Asyncritus, Phlegon, Hermes, Patrobas, and Hermas (16:14); Philologus, Julia, Olympas, Nereus and his sister (16:15); Aristobulus (16:10); Narcissus (16:11). In addition, other individuals may also have been connected with two more churches (16:5-10, 11, 12-13).

The assemblies in Rome were situated particularly in the crowded tenement buildings of Trastevere and Porta Capena.[89] Still today, a church in the name of "Santa Prisca," built on the foundation of a Roman house, is known in Rome. Owing to her status as one of the first Christ believers, Prisca is also considered a saint in the Roman Catholic Church.[90] Robert Jewett notes that the "Catacomb of Priscilla was located in the

86. Jewett, *Romans*, 958.

87. Lampe, "Christians," 229–30.

88. Carolyn Osiek, "Romans 'Down the Pike': Glimpses from Later Years," in McGinn, *Celebrating Romans*, 159–60.

89. Jewett, *Romans*, 62–63, 65, 69. Thus, the term "house" (οἶκος) does not always refer to a residential house (villa). Moreover, it does not have the figurative meaning of "family" (Gen 7:1; 1 Sam 1:21; PsSal 3:8; Acts 18:8; cf. Klauck, *Hausgemeinde*, 53–56).

90. Gignac, *L'épître*, 568.

country estate of the Acilian family, which further confirms her noble origin."[91] Her extraordinary skills are manifest in the fact that she is known as the teacher of the eloquent Apollos (Acts 18:24-28) who may have adopted his Sophia and Spirit theology from her.[92] Moreover, some modern scholars consider her as a potential author of the otherwise anonymous, but likewise particularly sophisticated, letter to the Hebrews.[93]

At this point, we need to revisit an aspect that has, so far, often been neglected in scholarship. The recommendation of Phoebe in Romans 16:1-2 and the greetings to Prisca and Aquila in 16:3-5 follow Paul's own invocation of his anticipated arrival and presence in Rome in 15:22-33. There was a period in the history of critical exegesis when studies of Romans treated chapter 16 as separate from the previous text.[94] There are, to be sure, some text-critical reasons to do so, despite the fact that only one extant manuscript lacks any of the final two chapters. All of this has to do with Marcion's edition of the first canon of Christian writings that omitted Romans 2:3-11, chapter 4, and all of chapters 9–11 and 15–16.[95] However, arguments in favor of the authenticity of Romans 15 and 16 and against their exclusion prevail.

Assuming the integrity of the text, the neglected aspect is that a series of four people from Corinth are mentioned in Romans 16:3-16: Paul, who dictates his letter in the house of Gaius; Phoebe, the "[minister] of the church at Cenchreae"; and finally Prisca and Aquila, who had withdrawn to Corinth temporarily because of the edict of Claudius. This is a peculiar phenomenon. The letter rallies people in the assemblies of Rome to provide these individuals with strong support and leaves no doubt about their moral integrity and achievements on behalf of the gospel message. Paul and Phoebe probably did this to counter potential prejudices that people either with origins in Corinth or who had been staying there were facing elsewhere in the Roman

91. Jewett, *Romans*, 955.

92. Schüssler Fiorenza, *Memory*, 179.

93. Ruth Hoppin, *Priscilla's Letter: Finding the Author of the Epistle to the Hebrews* (Fort Bragg, CA: Lost Coast Press, 1997); Mary Ann Beavis and HyeRan Kim-Cragg, *Hebrews*, WCS 54 (Collegeville, MN: Liturgical Press, 2015), lix.

94. According to some of these studies, Romans 16 was not only separate but also intended for audiences at a different destination, that is, in Ephesus (see, e.g., Campbell, *Phoebe*, 14–18; a comprehensive discussion and refutation of the argument is presented in Jewett, *Romans*, 8–9).

95. See also above. Cf. Ulrich Schmid, "Marcion and the Textual History of Romans: Editorial Activity and Early Editions of the New Testament," in *Studia Patristica*, vol. 54/2: *Biblical Quotations in Patristic Texts*, ed. Laurence Mellerin and Hugh A. G. Houghton (Leuven: Peeters, 2013), 104, 106; Dieter T. Roth, "Marcion," *EBR* 17 (2019): 880–83, at 881–82.

Empire. This may be the reason why, in his reference letter on behalf of Phoebe, Paul uses the name of the seaport Cenchreae while avoiding the name of Corinth (Rom 16:1). In the entire letter of Paul to the Romans, there is not a single occurrence of the term "Corinth." It is even avoided at the end of the list of greetings where greetings are commissioned from "all the churches of Christ" (16:16b), which may be those in Corinth, and then by a number of individuals in that city (16:21-23). (Only one of the subscriptions mentions that city's name; see above, p. lvii.) Little wonder, perhaps, since the city name was associated with a wide spectrum of sexual immorality.[96]

What would meetings of a "church in their house" (Rom 16:5a) in Rome have looked like, and who was meeting there? The concise phrase does not yield much information, except that these meetings occurred in peoples' private homes. As Prisca and Aquila were the leadership team, one may call their assembly "a craftworker-led house church." In addition, the following can be said:

1. In general, assemblies in Rome belonged to two categories. Some groups enjoyed the patronage of upper- or middle-class members and gathered in their somewhat larger houses. They were probably called "church." Other groups belonged exclusively to the cities' low and lowest classes, with mostly enslaved people and poor freedmen and freedwomen. They met in the crowded locations of their tenement apartments.[97] Occasionally, semiprivate settings (shops, workshops, studios, taverns, etc.), marketplaces, and watersides were also chosen for meetings to accommodate larger gatherings.[98]

2. In either category, however, most members were poor. With few exceptions, they would have lived at or below subsistence level. In light of this, the appeals in Romans to welcome one another (14:1; 15:7) and to

96. On the ambiguous reputation of Corinth, see above, pp. lx–lxiii.

97. Jewett, *Romans*, 64–66. See also Peter Wick, *Die urchristlichen Gottesdienste: Entstehung und Entwicklung im Rahmen der frühjüdischen Tempel-, Synagogen- und Hausfrömmigkeit*, BWANT 150 (Stuttgart: Kohlhammer, 2002), 220–23; Roger Gehring, *House Church and Mission: The Importance of Household Structures in Early Christianity* (Peabody, MA: Hendrickson, 2004), 1–2, etc.; Peter Oakes, *Reading Romans in Pompeii: Paul's Letter at Ground Level* (Minneapolis: Fortress; London: SPCK, 2009), 56–68; Dennis E. Smith, "The House Church as Social Environment," in *Text, Image, and Christians in the Graeco-Roman World: A Festschrift in Honor of David Lee Balch*, ed. Aliou Cissé Niang and Carolyn Osiek, Princeton Theological Monograph Series 176 (Eugene, OR: Pickwick, 2012), 3–21.

98. David L. Balch, "Rich Pompeiian Houses, Shops for Rent, and the Huge Apartment Building in Herculaneum as Typical Spaces for Pauline House Churches," *JSNT* 27 (2004): 27–46; Edward Adams, *The Earliest Christian Meeting Places: Almost Exclusively Houses?*, LNTS 450 (London: T&T Clark, 2013).

"pursue hospitality to strangers" are of particular interest. Such advice would have been important for the destitute who often went hungry. Also the remarks on problems around joint meals (14:1-2, 6) deserve to be considered in this context. Joint meals imply that the poor would be fed. Food allotments are not discussed in the letter to the Romans, so there does not appear to have been a problem around them. While it is true that "the kingdom of God is not food and drink but [justification[99]] and peace and joy in the Holy Spirit" (14:17), the former greatly helps with the latter. A good meal will have been a much appreciated gesture before the proclamation and enactment of God's peace.

3. These groups were, however, relatively small. Some would have had a membership of forty to fifty members; others even less. Certain groups may have just consisted of one extended family with a few friends and acquaintances.[100]

4. The list of greetings in Romans 16 features the names of many women. Some had leading positions (Prisca, Julia, the sister of Nereus); others were attendees.[101] Their presence was not only appreciated but also required since these women were, according to the traditional division of labor, most likely in charge of shared meals that had become characteristic of the assembly meetings. The latter should not be misconstrued, however, as an exclusive assignment of women to the kitchen. As mentioned above, Prisca also appears to have been active in the trade of tentmaking alongside her husband. Neither task precluded leadership functions in the assemblies.

5. The list of greetings also features the names of many enslaved persons or those who descended from such circles. People with Greek names in first-century CE Rome were mostly enslaved persons or their descendants. According to Peter Lampe, two-thirds of the twenty-four names in the list of greetings indicate people who had been enslaved.[102] In addition, there is evidence that assemblies of

99. For this translation, which differs from the NRSVue, see comments above under "Translation Matters" on Romans 3:21, 22.

100. Richard S. Ascough, "What Kind of World Did Paul's Communities Live In?," in *The New Cambridge Companion to St. Paul*, ed. Bruce W. Longenecker, Cambridge Companions to Religion (Cambridge: Cambridge University Press, 2020), 57.

101. Jill E. Marshall, "The Recovery of Paul's Female Colleagues in Nineteenth-Century Feminist Biblical Interpretation," *JFSR* 33 (2017): 21–36, at 34.

102. Lampe, *Die stadtrömischen Christen*, 141–53; Peter Lampe, "Roman Christians under Nero (54–68 CE)," in *The Last Years of Paul: Essays from the Tarragona Conference,*

enslaved people existed in some households (Rom 16:10b, 11b; see below, pp. 352–353).[103]

6. The high number of women and enslaved persons among assembly members implies that most assembly members belonged to the low or lowest socioeconomic strata of the urban society of Rome. Indeed, as mentioned above, enslaved people had no social status at all because they did not count as humans in the Roman society but as property.[104] Most members of these assemblies, therefore, were used to living precarious lives and being in positions of subordination. Even after emancipation, they would have had to cope with social stigmatization, which affected freedwomen more negatively than freedmen. These people would, therefore, have been grateful for hospitality, gestures of respect and love, and the hope of or actual opportunities for upward mobility.[105]

7. In general, these groups considered themselves to be Jewish. Yet, this does not mean that all members had ancestry belonging to Second Temple Judaism. Rather, most members were gentiles who were fascinated by Jewish customs and eager to adopt them (Rom 2:17). There was, however, a vivid discussion about the validity of the Jewish law for gentile Christ believers. Phoebe's message to them was that, for Christ believers, the law had lost its validity as the basis of ethics. Centered around the celebration of the Lord's Supper, mutual love was the characteristic hallmark of eucharistic communities.

In light of this profile of faith assemblies in the Eternal City, Paul's self-introduction as "servant/enslaved person" in the opening of the letter (Rom 1:1) needs to be revisited and problematized, together with the frequent christological and ecclesiological usage of the metaphor of enslavement in other New Testament texts. From an intersectional perspective, Marianne Bjelland Kartzow challenges the common usefulness of this metaphor by pointing to substantial differences in how its

---

June 2013, ed. Armand Puig i Tàrrech, John M. G. Barclay, and Jörg Frey with the assistance of Orrey McFarland, WUNT 352 (Tübingen: Mohr Siebeck, 2015), 125.

103. Lampe, "Christians," 222.

104. Orlando Patterson, *Slavery and Social Death: A Comparative Study* (Cambridge, MA: Harvard University Press, 1982).

105. Stanley K. Stowers, *A Rereading of Romans: Justice, Jews, and Gentiles* (New Haven: Yale University Press, 1994), 75; Oakes, *Romans*, 78–79.

cognitive potential would be perceived among actual enslaved people in antiquity.

> The metaphor of God as a slave owner was not necessarily a liberating one for those who heard these texts. To be a "slave of the Lord" may have worked as a comfort for real enslaved persons, since this relationship may have trumped the relationship between them and their owner. Or it may have simply added to the pain and suffering, and given *a double burden of slavery*. Alternatively, the metaphor may have blended into the slave reality in very complex ways, making it hard to grasp what was real slavery and what was metaphorical slavery.[106]

It is possible that Paul was not aware that the metaphors he employed both for his own ministry and in the context of christological concepts were only of limited usefulness for some in the audience. As a free man in a position of authority and power, he may not have reflected on the ambiguities inherent in this terminology for those who suffered the tragic fate of real enslavement.

Phoebe next conveys greetings to "my beloved Epaenetus" (Rom 16:5b). This is a Greek name that probably designates a freedman. Mentioned immediately after the church in the house of Prisca and Aquila in Rome, Epaenetus was most likely associated with it. The attribute "beloved" (ἀγαπητός) may indicate specific affection for him or that he was a "dear friend,"[107] although it also appears in 1:7 (see also 12:19) as a corporate designation "to all God's beloved in Rome." But with the exception of Prisca and Aquila, Paul and Phoebe have not met Epaenetus and the other people yet, so how can they use such affectionate terminology? The answer is that love is a central term designating the atmosphere of the assemblies of believers in Christ. Earlier in Romans 5:5, Paul and Phoebe write: "God's love has been poured into our hearts through the Holy Spirit that has been given to us." This love is the result of the receipt of the divine spirit that may be conceptualized as Wisdom. Love was also popularized through the cult to the great goddess Isis who was invoked by the name ἀγάπη. It has been made visible and bestowed on humans through the reconciliation in the death of Jesus (Rom 5:8). At the same time, the term "beloved" here and earlier (11:28) signifies divine election just as well as communal love.[108]

106. Bjelland Kartzow, *Metaphor*, 101 (italics original). See also the Contributing Voice "The Slave Metaphor" by Marianne Bjelland Kartzow above, pp. 7–8.

107. Fitzmyer, *Romans*, 733, 736.

108. Oda Wischmeyer, "Das Adjektiv ΑΓΑΠΗΤΟΣ in den paulinischen Briefen: Eine traditionsgeschichtliche Miszelle," *NTS* 32 (1986): 476–80, at 478–79.

Similar to the description of Stephanas and his household in a previous letter (1 Cor 16:15), Epaenetus is "the first convert in Asia for Christ" (literally the "first fruit"). That incident had a special meaning for Paul as it "sparked the conversion of many others in the province,"[109] which was the western portion of Asia Minor. Since the greetings in this chapter are mostly addressed to people who were already believers in Christ before Paul wrote to them, Epaenetus may be considered the only Pauline convert.

According to Romans 16:6, Phoebe told her audiences: "Greet Mary [Μαριάμ], who has worked very hard for you." The name "Mary," featured in the NRSVue, is contested on text-critical grounds and should be replaced. It would, as the Latin name "Maria" (in Greek transcription), most likely refer to a pagan-Latin woman whose name was derived from the Marius family. By contrast, the preferred Semitic variant "Miriam" would refer to a woman of Jewish background. As such, she would likely be from a family of former enslaved people, like Aquila (Rom 16:3-4).[110]

An important question is what the specific wording "who has worked very hard for you" here and in connection with the names of Tryphaena, Tryphosa, and "the beloved Persis" (Rom 16:12) implies. On the basis of parallels in earlier Pauline writings (1 Cor 16:15-18; 1 Thess 5:12-13a), it has been shown that this terminology not only refers to the intensity of work and the associated personal commitment but also implies a charismatic leadership position held by each of these individuals.[111]

The list of greetings continues with another pair of names: "Greet Andronicus and Junia, my [relatives] who were in prison with me; they are prominent among the apostles, and they were in Christ before I was" (Rom 16:7).[112] Anyone who thinks that such a straightforward sentence, cited here in its NRSVue version, could not be the source of controversy will glean from exegetical scholarship of past decades that the opposite

109. Fitzmyer, *Romans*, 736.

110. Lampe, *Die stadtrömischen Christen*, 146–47; Karl-Wilhelm Niebuhr, "Juden in Rom unter Nero: Intellektuelle Netzwerke, religiöse Praxis, geistige Horizonte," in *Tempel, Lehrhaus, Synagoge: Orte jüdischen Lernens und Lebens; Festschrift für Wolfgang Kraus*, ed. Christian Eberhart et al. (Paderborn: Brill; Schöningh, 2020), 292. Despite these text-critical observations, the more recent editions of Nestle-Aland (26th, 27th, 28th eds.) and *GNT* (3rd and 4th eds.) exclusively feature the Latin variant Μαρίαν ("Mary").

111. Schüssler Fiorenza, "Women," 91; Stefan Schreiber, "Arbeit mit der Gemeinde (Röm 16.6, 12): Zur versunkenen Möglichkeit der Gemeindeleitung durch Frauen," *NTS* 46 (2000): 204–26.

112. For the alternate translation of "relatives," which differs from "fellow Israelites" in the NRSVue, see the comments above under "Translation Matters" on Romans 9:3.

is true. Until recently, Bible editions rendered Romans 16:7 in quite a variety of ways, as the following table shows:

Romans 16:7 in Different Bible Editions and Translations

RSV	NIV 1984	NASB 1995	Lutherübersetzung 1984	Traduction œcuménique	Reina Valera 1995
Greet Andronicus and Junias, my kinsmen and my fellow prisoners; they are men of note among the apostles.	Greet Andronicus and Junias, my relatives who have been in prison with me. They are outstanding among the apostles.	Greet Andronicus and Junias, my kinsmen and my fellow prisoners, who are outstanding among the apostles.	Grüßt den Andronikus und den Junias, meine Stammverwandten und Mitgefangenen, welche berühmte Apostel sind.	Saluez Andronicus et Junias, mes parents et mes compagnons de captivité. Ce sont des apôtres éminents.	Saludad a Andrónico y a Junias, mis parientes y compañeros de prisiones. Ellos son muy estimados entre los apóstoles.

These different Bible translations and editions of past decades are based on the Greek New Testament that still featured the Greek word Ἰουνιᾶν in, for instance, the twenty-seventh Nestle-Aland edition (likewise in the fourth edition by Metzger[113]). It is the accusative singular of the masculine form of the name that translates as "Junias." Hence, the case was clear: Paul sends greetings to two men whom he even calls "kinsmen" and "men of note among the apostles," according to RSV.[114] As we know today, several of these aspects of *his*-story need to be, and indeed have been, corrected.

113. See also the accompanying work: Bruce M. Metzger, *A Textual Commentary on the Greek New Testament: A Companion Volume to the United Bible Societies' Greek New Testament*, 3rd ed. (New York: United Bible Societies, 1975), 539.

114. References to "Junias," the male form of the name, can also be found in, for instance, Ernst Käsemann, *An die Römer*, 3rd ed., HNT 8a (Tübingen: Mohr Siebeck, 1974), 392, 394; Genest, "Femmes," 15, 17; Schlier, *Römerbrief*, 442, 444; Jean-Pierre Lémonon, *Les épîtres de Paul: II Romains, Galates*, Commentaires (Paris: Bayard, 1996), 163–65. In 1977, Bernadette J. Brooten noted that virtually all modern Bible translations feature Junias (masc.) rather than Junia (fem.). Her research began the conversation about Junia for modern scholarship and initiated the change. Cf. Bernadette J. Brooten, "'Junia . . . Outstanding among the Apostles' (Romans 16:7)," in *Women Priests: A Catholic Commentary on the Vatican Declaration*, ed. Leonard Swidler and Arlene Swidler (New York: Paulist Press, 1977), 141–44.

Junia: Prominent among the Apostles

Paul ends his letter to the Romans by greeting individuals of the community, which provides an intriguing glimpse of his personal relationships as well as some social and community roles in the Roman *ekklēsia*. Paul includes ten women in this list of greetings, indicating that women were active and significant members of the community—and that Paul thought it socially and theologically important to greet and praise them openly in his letter.

Paul greets Junia in Romans 16:7 and provides several details of her identity. Her name is paired with Andronicus, which most likely means they were married or that they were siblings. Paul names Junia a "relative," which may mean that she was a part of Paul's family. This word may also be translated as "compatriot," however, meaning not that Junia was part of Paul's birth family but that she was a Jew and part of Paul's "kindred" (in Rom 9:3, Paul uses the same word to denote the Jewish people). Junia also endured imprisonment alongside Paul, which means she most likely taught or preached or led communities so as to result in her arrest, just like Paul. This matches his description of her as a prominent apostle. And since Paul mentions that Junia was "in Christ before me," i.e., a follower of Jesus before he was, this may indicate that Junia was part of the first generation of community leaders, possibly a native of Palestine before she lived in Rome.

Junia's identity as a woman apostle has become a source of debate for scholars—but only in the last century, when some have objected to a woman's right or ability to have such a position or have questioned the possibility of this in the ancient world. Early Christian writers, however, clearly accepted and understood Junia as a woman apostle. In the fourth century, John Chrysostom wrote: "Oh how great is the devotion of this woman, that she should be even counted worthy of the appellation of apostle!" (*Homilies on Romans* 31). Only in the twentieth century did debate begin around Junia's identity, and it started in earnest when certain scholars changed her name to the masculine Junias in some Greek editions of the New Testament. There was no historical basis for this name change since there are hundreds of occurrences of the feminine Junia in the first-century Greco-Roman world—and zero occurrences of the masculine Junias or the longer Junianus (of which some have said Junias was a shortening).

Junia is the only woman named an apostle in the New Testament and early Christian texts, but this does not mean that she was an anomaly. The word "apostle" means different things depending on context and when, in the development of the Jesus movement, it is being used. Paul seems to use the word rather fluidly, sometimes meaning a person who has encountered the resurrected Jesus (1 Cor 15:7), sometimes one who was a part of the leadership in Jerusalem (Gal 1:17-19), and sometimes a traveling missionary (1 Cor 9:1-18) or a messenger of a church (2 Cor 8:23; Phil 2:25) or even a combination of these. The author of Luke and Acts, who writes several decades later, seems to narrow the definition of the term by focusing on the twelve apostles. Ironically, the women followers of Jesus in the Luke and Acts narratives would qualify as apostles in Paul's usage of the term: they were there for Jesus's ministry, crucifixion, and post-resurrection appearances (even more than the male disciples); they were part of the core community in Jerusalem (Acts 1:14); and at least one of them—Priscilla—traveled as a missionary. So while Junia may be the only woman *named* an apostle in early Christianity, many others were apostolic women.

Yii-Jan Lin

As Yii-Jan Lin explains, scholars in recent decades have discussed whether the name Junia in Romans 16:7 belongs to a woman or a man. In a peculiar way, one could almost use the term "transgender" to describe the interpretive debate of this name's gender because, originally, there was Junia, the female apostle who was simply part of the early reality of Jewish Christ believers; then there was a Junias, the male apostle who was now made to fit later patriarchal expectations for such a title. Eventually, there was again the original Junia, with her name restored to the one attested female form (since there is a complete lack of attestation of the masculine Junias). Today, there is a broad scholarly consensus that the greetings in 16:7 are, in part, intended for a female recipient and apostle of Jesus Christ.[115] And while the twenty-seventh Nestle-Aland edition still reads Ἰουνιᾶν, the twenty-eighth edition now features the female form Ἰουνίαν.[116]

115. Klauck, *Hausgemeinde*, 30; Ray R. Schulz, "Romans 16:7: Junia or Junias?," *ExpTim* 98 (1987): 108–10; Lampe, *Die stadtrömischen Christen*, 147; Schüssler Fiorenza, "Women," 90; Luise Schottroff, "Toward a Feminist Reconstruction of the History of Early Christianity," in *Feminist Interpretation: The Bible in Women's Perspective*, ed. Luise Schottroff, Silvia Schroer, and Marie-Theres Wacker, trans. Martin Rumscheidt and Barbara Rumscheidt (Minneapolis: Fortress, 1998), 230–31; Eldon Jay Epp, *Junia: The First Woman Apostle* (Minneapolis: Fortress, 2005), 40–68; Jewett, *Romans*, 962 ("the name 'Junias' is a figment of chauvinistic imagination"); Hope Stephenson, "Junia: Woman and Apostle," in McCabe, *Women in the Biblical World*, 117–34; Yii-Jan Lin, "Junia: An Apostle before Paul," *JBL* 139 (2020): 191–209, at 192; Andrea Hartmann, "Junia—A Woman Lost in Translation: The Name IOYNIAN in Romans 16:7 and Its History of Interpretation," *Open Theology* 6 (2020): 646–60.

116. The original Greek manuscripts had no accents; those were only added by later text editors. Hence, both forms are possible. However, a male form of the name remains unattested.

As there is little doubt that Andronicus is a male name, all that remains to be added is that this is a prestigious Greek name frequently given to enslaved persons or freedmen in the Roman world. The Greek term ἐπίσημος ("outstanding") refers to distinct features that characterize a person, not just to the fact that a person is well known to someone else. Thus, Andronicus and Junia had earned considerable recognition through their ministry and were both acknowledged as "apostles."[117] Women were clearly strongly engaged in the ministry of the earliest groups of Jewish Christ believers, which includes the leadership level, as Yii-Jan Lin mentions in her contribution above.

Further names in the list of greetings include Ampliatus, who is "my beloved in the Lord" (Rom 16:8), similar to Stachys (v. 9b). Here too this terminology references love due to the receipt of the divine spirit as a characteristic existential state of Christ believers. There are also Urbanus, "our coworker" (v. 9a); Apelles, "who is approved in Christ" (v. 10); and "my [relative] Herodion" (v. 11a).[118] Potentially a freedman of Roman origin, Urbanus may, as the word "coworker" suggests, have also been a former missionary colleague of Paul. He may also have had to leave Rome in 49 CE due to the conflicts in the Jewish synagogues. Did Urbanus, like Prisca and Aquila, also settle in Corinth for a time? It is possible that Paul met him there, in which case Phoebe may have known him too. Urbanus has now returned to Rome, however, like Prisca and Aquila. Stachys and Apelles both have Greek names, which makes it somewhat likely that they were also enslaved or from families of enslaved people. It has been conjectured that Stachys was part of the gentile majority of the assemblies in Rome; on the other hand, Apelles was a common Jewish name. If both had met Paul previously, then they may have been exiled together to Corinth.[119]

Greetings are, however, also addressed to assemblies of enslaved persons that existed in some households. In Romans 16:10b, Paul greets "those who belong to the family of Aristobulus"; in verse 11b, he greets "those . . . who belong to the family of Narcissus." In both cases, the greetings are addressed only to people in these families, not to Aristobulus or Narcissus themselves. This suggests, on the one hand, that neither of these patrons had been a believer; however, groups among

117. Thomas Schreiner, *Romans*, 2nd ed., BECNT (Grand Rapids: Baker Academic, 2018), 770.

118. For the alternate translation of "relative," which differs from "fellow Israelite" in the NRSVue, see the comments above under "Translation Matters" on Romans 9:3.

119. Jewett, *Romans*, 967.

the enslaved persons of their households had formed faith assemblies. Based on inscriptional evidence, Aristobulus can perhaps be identified as the brother of Herod Agrippa and the grandson of Herod the Great; he had died just before 50 CE.[120] In a similar way, Narcissus may have been an influential administrator who had attained immense political and economic power under Emperor Claudius but was executed in 54 CE.[121] Owing to the fame of Aristobulus and Narcissus, their names had become lasting references for their households, which is why they were still used years after their deaths. Herodion is introduced in Romans 16:11 as Paul's "[relative],"[122] which means that he was of Jewish background (see already in 9:3; 16:7). Herodion may well have belonged to the assembly of enslaved people of Aristobulus. His name indicates that he was likely an enslaved person or a freedman of the Herodian family. As one of the fourteen Jewish synagogue congregations in Rome was that of the "(He)Rodians," he may formerly have belonged to it. In that case, he was probably also forced to leave the Eternal City in 49 CE, like so many other believers in Christ.[123]

According to Romans 16:12a, greetings were also to be conveyed to "those workers in the Lord, Tryphaena and Tryphosa." Both names belong to women, and both are Greek names of enslaved persons. Therefore, they were probably enslaved gentiles or freedwomen. The similarity of their names has given rise to speculations that they were not only sisters but even twin sisters. In 16:12b, "the beloved Persis, who has worked hard in the Lord" is also a woman. Known from epigraphic and literary sources, her name is characteristic of a female enslaved person who had been captured in Persia. Her attribute as "beloved" is the same as that of Epaenetus, Ampliatus, and Stachys; like Miriam (or Mary, 16:6), she is said to be hardworking.[124]

120. In that case, this Aristobulus would have made an appeal against Caligula's placement of a statue of the emperor in the Jerusalem temple, as Josephus mentions (*Ant.* 18.273–76). Cf. Miriam Pucci Ben Zeev, "New Perspectives on Jewish-Greek Hostilities in Alexandria during the Reign of Emperor Caligula," *JSJ* 21 (1990): 227–35; Nicholas H. Taylor, "Popular Opposition to Caligula in Jewish Palestine," *JSJ* 32 (2001): 54–70.

121. Lampe, *Die stadtrömischen Christen*, 136.

122. For the alternate translation of "relative," which differs from the NRSVue, see the comments above under "Translation Matters" on Romans 9:3.

123. Niebuhr, "Juden," 293–94.

124. Schüssler Fiorenza, "Women," 91.

Paul and Phoebe deliver greetings to another ten people by name, plus two anonymous women—the mother of Rufus and the sister of Nereus (16:13-15). Finally, they greet two anonymous groups of people, namely, "the brothers and sisters who are with them" (v. 14b) and "all the saints who are with them" (v. 15b). Overall, these lists of names demonstrate their respect and care for individuals in Rome, although it is apparent that some female members of the assemblies remain anonymous while the names of their brothers or sons are included.

These various names in the list of greetings can be systematized according to several aspects:[125]

1. *Ten (or twelve?) people personally known to Paul:*
   Prisca and Aquila, Epaenetus, Andronicus and Junia, Ampliatus, Urbanus, Stachys, Rufus, and his mother (Apelles? Persis?)

2. *Five people of Jewish background:*
   Aquila, Miriam (Mary), Andronicus and Junia, Herodion

3. *Twelve leaders of five different assemblies:*
   Prisca and Aquila, Asyncritus, Phlegon, Hermes, Patrobas, Hermas, Philologus, Julia, Nereus and his sister, Olympas (plus the groups of Aristobulus and of Narcissus)

4. *Nine women:*
   Prisca, Miriam (Mary), Junia, the mother of Rufus, Tryphaena and Tryphosa, Persis, Julia, the sister of Nereus

5. *Seventeen men:*
   Aquila, Epaenetus, Andronicus, Ampliatus, Urbanus, Stachys, Apelles, Herodion, Rufus, Asyncritus, Phlegon, Hermes, Patrobas, Hermas, Philologus, Nereus, and Olympas

This overview demonstrates that women played a significant role in the development of the early faith communities.[126] Paul knew women and has Phoebe greet an impressive number of them, along with referencing their important positions in the assemblies of early Christ believers. Thus, Paul and Phoebe reject the prevailing patriarchal culture with its androcentric texts and *his*-stories. Oda Wischmeyer observes, however, that this countercultural trend was short-lived. The impressive presence

125. Castelli, "Romans," 276.
126. Hays, "Paul," 144.

of women in Paul's congregations had no equivalent in the second and third generations of the faith communities.[127]

The concluding words of this section in Romans 16 are: "Greet one another with a holy kiss. All the churches of Christ greet you" (Rom 16:16). The prompt for a "kiss" was standard at the end of letters from antiquity. It was a friendly gesture of personal greeting, common in ancient Near Eastern and Mediterranean cultures (it still is today). The prompt for the "*holy* kiss" has been a typical feature at the end of Paul's letters (see 1 Thess 5:26; 1 Cor 16:20; 2 Cor 13:12). As such, it may have referred to or been adopted from a liturgical gesture at either the start or end of assembly meetings or during the celebration of the Eucharist (attested later in Justin, *Apology* 1.65.2). Elsewhere called "kiss of love" (1 Pet 5:14), the "holy kiss" was an indication of the love ethos that permeated the assemblies of Jewish believers in Christ.[128] A token of personal proximity, this practice suggested that the meetings of the earliest groups of believers were about the real encounter of people and the establishment of mutual relations, less about doctrinal discussions or religious theories.

The ensuing expression "All the churches of Christ" (Rom 16:16b) refers, first, to the churches in Corinth, specifically Cenchreae, where Paul was staying when he worked on Romans. Phoebe, who was just reaching the end of her extended recital of this letter, was the minister of this church (16:1). But even here, in 16:16, the actual name of the city is avoided. Only one of the subscriptions would mention it much later: "To the Romans, written from Corinth."[129] This may be seen as an indication of the poor reputation that Corinth had in antiquity (see above, pp. lx–lxiii). Even if Paul had founded the churches in that city and interacted with them for a period of seven years, the preference was to omit the name of the city itself.

Second, the expression in 16:16b also refers to churches elsewhere in the eastern Mediterranean. Paul the networker was, in the end, not tied to one single congregation or city but to many others, for example, Ephesus.[130] He would have wanted these other connections to be remembered as he prepared to visit the capital of the Roman Empire in the near future.

127. Oda Wischmeyer, "Frau," *RGG* 3 (2000): 260–61, at 260.

128. Theobald, *Römerbrief*, 2:234.

129. On the six subscriptions found in several biblical manuscripts of Romans, see above, p. lvii.

130. Wolter, *Römer*, 2:482–83.

Even if he had only introduced himself by his *cognomen* "Paul" at the start of the letter (Rom 1:1), thus relinquishing a key aspect of honor within the traditional honor-shame system of the Roman world, he was nevertheless eager to hint at his wealth of connections that made him the cosmopolitan that he was.

Final Instructions (16:17-23)

This section features two separate pericopes. First, it issues a warning about heretics that concludes with an eschatological wish and a blessing formula (16:17-20). Second, it lists greetings from various people in Corinth (16:21-23).

TRANSLATION MATTERS: Romans 16:22

The NRSVue renders this sentence as follows: "I Tertius, the writer of this letter, greet you in the Lord."[131] A footnote provides the alternative: "Or *I Tertius, writing this letter in the Lord, greet you*." Among these two, the latter is preferable as it renders the syntax of the Greek sentence (ἀσπάζομαι ὑμᾶς ἐγὼ Τέρτιος ὁ γράψας τὴν ἐπιστολὴν ἐν κυρίῳ) more closely—"in the Lord" belongs indeed to "this letter."[132]

The NRSVue presents the text of Romans 16:17-23 as one continuous section. Scholars debate, however, whether it may contain an interpolation in 16:17-20. While some reject such a hypothesis,[133] others defend it.[134] What are some of the main reasons for such an assessment? First, all scholars agree that the warning against heretics in this passage comes as a surprise after the preceding list of warm greetings that conveyed an atmosphere of collegiality and inclusiveness. These greetings and wishes abruptly resume in 16:20b. Thus, the section in 16:17-20a is considerably

131. See also the NRSV, RSV, NIV, NASB 1995, NKJV, Reina Valera 1995; furthermore, Brendan Byrne, *Romans*, SP 6 (Collegeville, MN: Liturgical Press, 1996), 460; Hultgren, *Romans*, 596, 598.

132. Jewett, *Romans*, 978–79; Wolter, *Römer*, 2:495.

133. Gamble, *History*, 42, 52–53, 94; Mathew, *Women*, 37; Wolter, *Römer*, 1:26–27; Wolter, *Römer*, 2:485–86.

134. Wolf-Henning Ollrog, *Paulus und seine Mitarbeiter: Untersuchungen zu Theorie und Praxis der paulinischen Mission*, WMANT 50 (Neukirchen-Vluyn: Neukirchener Verlag, 1979), 226–34.

Rom 16:17-23

[17]I urge you, brothers and sisters, to keep an eye on those who create dissensions and hindrances, in opposition to the teaching that you have learned; avoid them. [18]For such people do not serve our Lord Christ but their own appetites, and by smooth talk and flattery they deceive the hearts of the simple-minded. [19]For your obedience is known to all; therefore, I rejoice over you, but I want you to be wise in what is good and guileless in what is evil. [20]The God of peace will shortly crush Satan under your feet. The grace of our Lord Jesus Christ be with you.

[21]Timothy, my coworker, greets you; so do Lucius and Jason and Sosipater, my fellow Israelites.

[22]I Tertius, the writer of this letter, greet you in the Lord.

[23]Gaius, who is host to me and to the whole church, greets you. Erastus, the city treasurer, and our brother Quartus greet you.

different in tone and mood; the warning against dissensions and offenses suggests an angry author.[135] Second, the appeal not to judge one another in chapter 14 asks for a broad welcome of others (v. 1), recognizes that those who have different opinions may nevertheless serve Christ (v. 18), and values the unity of the assembly above everything else (v. 19). In contrast, 16:17 now urges avoidance of such people without much of an explanation. These are, therefore, considerable thematic contradictions. Third, seven Pauline *hapax legomena* have been identified in this short section while other words are recognized for their atypical definitions.[136] Fourth, the praise of "your obedience [that] is known to all" (16:19) is inconsistent with the praise of "your faith [that] is proclaimed throughout the world" according to the letter opening (1:8). And fifth, the advice "to be wise in what is good and guileless in what is evil" (16:19b) and the promise that God "will shortly crush Satan under your feet" (v. 20a) display, once again, a thoroughly different tone and mood from, for example, the exceedingly cautious phrases in the letter opening. There, in full acknowledgment of the spiritual maturity and previous success of congregational leaders such as Prisca and Aquila, the letter avoids anything that could have been construed as an attempt to patronize the addressees. The desire there to "be mutually encouraged by each other's faith" (1:12) has little in common with the present statement that Satan

135. Schlier, *Römerbrief*, 447.
136. Ollrog, *Paulus*, 230; Jewett, *Romans*, 986–87.

might be crushed under their feet (16:20a). In light of these arguments, the section in Romans 16:17-20 should indeed be considered an interpolation. The resemblance with certain passages in the Pastoral Epistles suggests a date for the insertion toward the end of the first century CE.

Nevertheless, the passage in question has been part of Romans for most of its existence, and its contents have been taken into consideration by many. For instance, the exhortation "I want you to be wise [σοφοὺς εἶναι] in what is good and guileless in what is evil" (16:19) and its inherent dualism have been adopted and developed in Valentinianism, a major Gnostic movement founded in the second century CE. Sophia as a representation of the supreme female principle is at the center of its theological system. Furthermore, the statement that God may "crush Satan under your feet" (v. 20) in a discussion of different ideas could more easily have been the basis of the later misuse of Romans in support of violent expressions of religious nationalistic fervor.

The blessing with the phrase the "grace of our Lord Jesus Christ" in Romans 16:20b would originally have concluded the interpolation in 16:17-20a. It is fashioned according to the similar blessing in 16:24 (see below, pp. 362–364). But in its shorter version, it refers exclusively to those who conform to the antiheretical stance—the grace of Christ is, thus, only for some in the assemblies.[137]

Next is a shorter list of people who have been present in Corinth where the letter was written (16:21-23). Here too that city's name is avoided. Only the names of individual people are mentioned together with the stereotypical "he greets" and additional commending phrases. Hence, Phoebe gets to mention the names of those she would have known rather well, even if they were Paul's longtime colleagues. Among them is Timothy, presented as "my coworker" (v. 21a). This is enough of an epithet to introduce one of Paul's most trusted and long-standing companions; the apostle had a particularly deep relationship with him. Timothy is probably the person who is named as coauthor in a number of Pauline letters (1 Thess 1:1; 2 Cor 1:1; Phil 1:1; Phlm 1). That he is not mentioned as the coauthor at the beginning of Romans might be due to his late arrival in Corinth. As such, it is also an implicit indication of how long it took to produce this letter of sixteen chapters.[138] Lucius, Jason, and Sosipater are "my [relatives]" (Rom 16:21b).[139] Both terms have been employed in the

137. Jewett, *Romans*, 1012–14.

138. Murphy-O'Connor, *Paul*, 55.

139. For the alternate translation of "relatives," which differs from the NRSVue, see the comments above under "Translation Matters" on Romans 9:3.

list of greetings to those in Rome, where Urbanus was also a "coworker" (16:9) and Andronicus and Junia as well as Herodion were "[relatives]" (16:7, 11), that is, likewise of Jewish origins (see 9:3).

The sentence in Romans 16:22 features greetings that are different from the preceding ones: "I Tertius, writing this letter in the Lord, greet you."[140] This note is remarkable for two reasons. First, scribes in antiquity were usually invisible. Here, the scribe leaves that obscurity and becomes visible, if only for a short moment. As scribe (*amanuensis*), it was the task of Tertius to use a metal stylus and wax tablets to write down the text of the letter. Dictation was possible in three different modes: *syllabatim* dictation ("syllable by syllable"), shorthand dictation, or formulation of rough ideas. Then came the period of revisions of the first draft, followed potentially by a time of feedback and input by others. During the production of such a letter, therefore, scribes took on a number of essential functions, such as recorders/transcribers, contributors, and composers.[141]

Second, it is remarkable that Paul allowed Tertius to convey personal greetings. In other letters, it had been Paul's habit to add greetings in his own hand at the end of the text (1 Cor 16:21; Gal 6:11; Phlm 19).[142] No such note appears in Romans. Instead, the scribe was permitted to mention his own name. That is clearly a generous gesture acknowledging his work and celebrating his commitment and contribution. Thus, it showcases the ethos of care and support that characterized Paul's faith communities.[143] The name of Tertius was, therefore, even featured in one of the later subscription lines that reads: "Letter to the Romans, written through Tertius, but sent by Phoebe, minister."[144] For some, the name of this scribe is connected with the letter to the Romans and its message of mutual love and care for the marginalized.

What else is known about Tertius? Only little can be said as he is mentioned nowhere else in the New Testament. His name as such is Latin, occurring here in Greek transcription, and means "the third." It was a

140. For this translation, which differs from the NRSVue, see comments above under "Translation Matters" on Romans 16:22.

141. E. Randolph Richards, *The Secretary in the Letters of Paul*, WUNT 2/42 (Tübingen: Mohr Siebeck, 1991), 23–53; Richards, *Paul*, 64–79.

142. Such notes of personal greeting appear even in Deutero-Pauline texts (see Col 4:18; 2 Thess 3:17).

143. Jewett, *Romans*, 980.

144. MS 337 (see above, p. lvii). The different versions of subscriptions were included in older editions of the Greek New Testament text in Nestle-Aland and in, for example, Jacobus Wettstein, *Novum Testamentum Graecum*, 2 vols. (Graz: Akademische Druck- und Verlagsanstalt, 1962), but have been omitted from Nestle-Aland's twenty-eighth edition.

customary name for enslaved persons; whether this means that he was in fact enslaved is not certain but possible. The addition of the characteristic phrase "in the Lord" implies that Tertius was also a believer in Christ. The syntactic connection of the phrase with "this letter" conveys, however, his own understanding that the service he rendered was to the Lord Jesus Christ.[145]

The next person who sends greetings from Corinth is "Gaius, who is host to me and to the whole church" (16:23). This person may be the Gaius in Corinth who was baptized by Paul (1 Cor 1:14) and the Gaius Titius[146] Justus whose house was next door to the synagogue (Acts 18:7). It is possible that he may have hosted Paul free of charge or for only modest pay. Alternatively, the apostle may, in his capacity as tentmaker, have reciprocated some of the kindness by repairing awnings around the house or installing new ones.[147] The phrase about Gaius being Paul's host means that, in some winter months between 56 and 58 CE, the apostle would have dictated Romans in his house. One can imagine not only his keen interest in what Paul was doing but also some level of active participation.

The additional phrase that Gaius was also host "to the whole church" has caused some discussion among modern scholars. There were as many as five or six congregations in Corinth that met in the private homes of the following people: Aquila and Priscilla; Titius Justus; Crispus (Acts 18:1-8); Chloe (1 Cor 1:11); Stephanas (1 Cor 1:16); and Gaius (Rom 16:23).[148] They were, therefore, not all associated with the house of Gaius. A scholarly consensus has developed that Gaius had instead extended his hospitality to travelers from all over the world.[149] Another possible meaning of this phrase is, however, that Gaius hosted occasional urban or regional conferences (synods) of the congregations in or around Corinth at his home. Most likely, Phoebe would have visited on a regular basis, perhaps accompanied by other members of the church that she led. And when the letter was in its final draft stage and required feedback from an interested, competent, and supportive audience, Gaius and his family, friends, and perhaps even work colleagues may have been ready for something like a "prescreening event," patiently listening to the argu-

145. Richards, *Secretary*, 170–71.

146. Or "Titus" (Τιτου) according to some ancient variants.

147. Murphy-O'Connor, *Paul*, 28–31.

148. Titius Justus (Acts 18:7) and Gaius (Rom 16:23) are probably the same person. Cf. Lampe, "Christians," 229–30; Wolter, *Römer*, 2:470.

149. Jewett, *Romans*, 980–81.

ments and providing positive and negative feedback. As an addressee of several previous Pauline letters to the congregations in Corinth, Gaius (and other church members) could even have advised the apostle on whether certain passages in the new letter were still within the range of his earlier theology. Or might they even have encouraged new theories and practical advice based on their own experiences? In the end, either option is possible.

In any case, Gaius would have been a person of some considerable wealth, which prompts the question what kind of house he might have had. Scholars have, in past decades, made numerous suggestions informed by data about the first-century CE housing situation. Most of these are guided by the intention of obtaining clarity about the situation of eucharistic celebrations in Corinth and their problems (1 Cor 11:17-34). These studies provide, at the same time, insights about the domestic space of the church assemblies and Paul's host.[150]

Erastus in Romans 16:23b is "the city treasurer" of Corinth. He has a Latin name and held a civic office in that city, which aligns with the fact that, after being refounded by Julius Caesar as a Roman colony, Corinth was mostly settled by Roman freedpersons. A Latin inscription was discovered in 1929 between the north market and the theater of Corinth. It features the text: "Erastus in return for his aedileship paved [this area] at his own expense [*ERASTVS. PRO. AED. S. P. STRAVIT*]." On the one hand, this inscription does not include the name of the father of Erastus; therefore he himself must have been a former enslaved person.[151] On the other hand, Erastus had a promising administrative position. An *aedilis* was a Roman magistrate who supervised public affairs. Perhaps Erastus had been promoted from a position as city treasurer in Paul's day to the higher one of *aedilis*, which is when he commissioned the inscription.[152] With such administrative positions in a major Roman city, Erastus may have been a well-to-do person. In that case, Paul's congregations in

150. Jerome Murphy-O'Connor, *St. Paul's Corinth: Texts and Archeology*, GNS 6 (Wilmington, DE: Glazier, 1983), 178–80 (consideration of the villa at Anaploga). On Friesen's poverty scale, Gaius is the only individual ranked in the exact middle, indicating that he led a life "with moderate surplus resources" (a level for those "who employ others"); cf. Friesen, "Poverty," 337–57.

151. Murphy-O'Connor, *Paul*, 86.

152. Steven J. Friesen, "The Wrong Erastus: Ideology, Archaeology, and Exegesis," in *Corinth in Context: Comparative Studies on Religion and Society*, ed. Steven J. Friesen, Daniel N. Schowalter, and James C. Walters, NovTSup 134 (Leiden: Brill, 2010), 231–56.

Corinth, the city known for wealth and luxury (among other things), would have enjoyed the patronage of some of their affluent members.[153]

Finally, the otherwise unknown Quartus, "our brother," also conveys greetings (Rom 16:23). Quartus is another Latin name; it means "the fourth." Perhaps he was the younger brother of Tertius, the scribe. If this is correct and if Tertius was an enslaved person (which is not certain), then Quartus would have been enslaved too. In that case, his epithet as "brother" is remarkable as it appears only here in the list of Romans 16. Since the other individuals who send greetings were also believers in Christ, singling out Quartus as "brother" indicates that Paul wanted to honor him with this special title, as he also does with the enslaved Onesimus in Philemon 16. If Quartus is indeed enslaved, then he is more than that for Paul.[154]

A gendered exploration of the paragraph in 16:21-23 will note that the greetings from these eight people in Corinth are exclusively commissioned by men. Not a single female name is featured. Gaius, Paul's host, most likely had a family; his greetings may have been sent also on behalf of the other family members, which would necessarily have included women. The same could be said about Erastus. Nevertheless, this observation may be an indication of the difference of gender roles between the ancient Greek and Roman cultures.

To be added to the eight names of men from Corinth, however, is the name of Phoebe, the leader of the congregation in Cenchreae. She does not send greetings on her own but is the one who is personally present in Rome to recite all of these greetings on behalf of others.

In the NRSVue, the section in Romans 16:25-27 follows immediately after the list of greetings in 16:21-23. There is, thus, a "hole" in the text; verse 24 is missing (likewise NRSV, RSV, NIV, and Traduction œcuménique de la Bible). Footnotes typically mention the lack of this verse. For instance, the NRSVue has the following footnote: "Other ancient authorities add verse 24, *The grace of our Lord Jesus Christ be with all of you. Amen.*" By contrast, the NASB 1995 and NKJV include the blessing in 16:24 in their main text (placed in square brackets in the NASB 1995). The omission of the verse in some of these Bible versions is based on the Greek text in Nestle-Aland, twenty-eighth edition, which relegates it to the critical apparatus. This edition favors those ancient manuscripts

153. Murphy-O'Connor, *Paul*, 85–86.

154. Wolter, *Römer*, 2:501–2.

that lack the verse against those featuring it. A convincing case has been made, however, that the benediction in 16:24 was deleted only because of the later addition of the doxology in 16:25-27.[155] Hence, the latter is secondary, and the former is original.[156]

The text of the blessing in Romans 16:24 is similar to the one in 16:20b but slightly longer: "The grace of our Lord Jesus Christ be with all of you. Amen." According to Robert Jewett, this version "has the strongest claim to be the original ending of Paul's letter."[157] Its word "all" addresses the broader community of believers in Christ. With that, this blessing conveys a sense of inclusiveness, comprising Jews and gentiles, Greeks and barbarians, "weak" and "strong," educated and uneducated, and women and men. With that, it is a blessing for the democratic *ekklēsia* of wo/men. Actualizing the baptismal confession (Gal 3:28), it epitomizes essential doctrinal and parenetic aspects of Romans.

> All of the competitive antitheses that Paul seeks to overcome in the argument of Romans are hereby encompassed: God's grace is extended to each, without reservation or discrimination. God's impartial love, demonstrated on the cross for all of the human race . . . , is maintained through to the final words of the letter as the proper embodiment of the impartial righteousness of God.[158]

As mentioned above, Paul and Phoebe and the couple Prisca and Aquila are personifications of this ethos of inclusivity and egalitarianism. If indeed Paul, the apostle, and Phoebe, the church leader from Corinth and successful businesswoman, were a Jewish free man and a gentile woman who was formerly enslaved, and if Prisca and Aquila, business owners and leaders of a church in Rome, are a gentile noblewoman and a Jewish former enslaved person, they embody the gospel message of egalitarianism that is possible through mutual love. This implies the possibility for harmony between Jewish and gentile believers that was developed in Romans 14:1–15:13. For all those who may consider their theology too complex or long-winded, the parenetic (or ethical/hortatory) section of the letter already provided a more hands-on guide for practical application. Paul and Phoebe as well as Prisca and Aquila were

155. Gamble, *History*, 130.

156. Accordingly, Romans concludes with 16:24 (Благодать Господа нашего Иисуса Христа со всеми вами. Аминь.) in Russian Orthodox Bible editions such as the Русский Синодальный Перевод (1876/1956).

157. Jewett, *Romans*, 1013.

158. Jewett, *Romans*, 1013.

the living reality of the transformative power of the gospel of inclusivity, presented in two distinct sections. These people epitomized the successful application of the baptismal formula in Galatians 3:28 and the reality of the democratic *ekklēsia* of wo/men "in Christ."

The reason for such a broad and inclusive atmosphere is God's "grace." Those Jews who believe in Christ "stand" in grace (Rom 5:2) and are "in Christ" (6:11, 23; 8:1; 16:3, 7, etc.). As "one body" (12:4-5), they are connected with each other through the bond of love.

The blessing in Romans 16:24 is also similar to other final blessings in Paul's authentic letters, some of which finish with sentences like these:[159]

1 Cor 16:23-24	51–53 CE	*The grace* of the *Lord Jesus* be with you. My love be with all of you in *Christ Jesus*.
Phil 4:23	52–55 CE (or 57–59 CE)	*The grace* of the *Lord Jesus Christ* be with your spirit.
Gal 6:18	54–55 CE (or 50–51 CE)	May *the grace* of our *Lord Jesus Christ* be with your spirit, brothers and sisters. Amen.

This overview reveals the stereotypical form of Paul's final sentences: his benedictions usually feature the word "grace" in connection with "Lord Jesus (Christ)." The one in 1 Corinthians 16:23-24 also features the word "all." These concluding formulas have been very consistent over the years of Paul's ministry.

Final Doxology (16:25-27)

This doxology consists of one long sentence, covering three verses in modern Bible editions. It features summary statements about the nature of the gospel and its proclamation to the gentiles and ends with an expression of praise of God.

As mentioned above, the Greek text of Nestle-Aland, twenty-eighth edition, indicates uncertainty regarding the originality of the sentence in Romans 16:25-27 by setting it in square brackets. Most Bible editions, however, do not distinguish the passage from the remaining main text of Romans, thus featuring it as the conclusion of the letter.[160] It can, nevertheless, hardly be its real ending, judging by a comparison with

159. In the following comparative table, similar phrases are indicated by italics.
160. See the NRSVue, NIV, NASB 1995.

Rom 16:25-27

[25]Now to God who is able to strengthen you according to my gospel and the proclamation of Jesus Christ, according to the revelation of the mystery that was kept secret for long ages [26]but is now disclosed and through the prophetic writings is made known to all the gentiles, according to the command of the eternal God, to bring about the obedience of faith—[27]to the only wise God, through Jesus Christ, to whom be the glory forever! Amen.

similar passages in Paul's other authentic letters (1 Cor 16:23-24; Gal 6:18; Phil 4:23; see above). Many of the stereotypical elements are absent from Romans 16:25-27. Especially to be noted is that Paul never concludes his letters with a doxology. Robert Jewett suggests, therefore, that this passage was added to the version of Romans that Marcion had truncated to fourteen chapters to provide a fitting ending.[161]

Some of the contents of the doxology pick up aspects of the phrase in Romans 11:33: "O the depth of the riches and wisdom and knowledge of God!" Its designation of the gospel as "mystery" that had to be revealed after having been "kept secret," however, has little in common with the actual message of the rest of Romans (despite 11:25). In particular, the idea that all the gentiles may now come to the "obedience of faith" (16:26) is a poor adaptation of a similar statement in 1:5 about the "obedience of faith among all the gentiles" that presents faith as the means of access to grace for both Jews and gentiles. Hence, with its focus on gentiles at the expense of Jews, the doxology in 16:25-27 has a supersessionist impulse. In light of this assessment, it is particularly disconcerting that this concluding benediction is the only passage from chapter 16 of Romans that the *Revised Common Lectionary* includes for worship readings.[162]

161. Jewett, *Romans*, 998; see also Peter Lampe, "Zur Textgeschichte des Römerbriefs," *NovT* 27 (1985): 273–77, at 273–75.

162. Gaventa, *When in Romans*, 6.

Conclusion

Several insights in this exploration of the letter to the Romans from a feminist perspective stand out and should be repeated here. The letter features an impressive message of human empowerment through concepts of [justification],[1] reconciliation, and liberation. Its constitutive elements are God's active engagement for the salvation of humans that leads to personal and global transformation. Thus, the relation between humans and God is being redefined. Most importantly, justification, far from being an ultimate divine attribute or a punitive category that humans would have to fear, is inclusive and restorative (Rom 1:16). Such justification is freely available for all humans through Jesus Christ who is God's place of atonement (3:21-26). Because humans have the privilege of becoming God's children, nothing can possibly separate them from God's love for them (8:31-39). They are no longer enslaved under sin but experience new life. As a consequence, the standards and logic of the ancient honor-shame cultures are eliminated. There is, then, no achievement that humans can boast about; all that remains is celebrating God's grace. Consequently, any judgment, condemnation, or prejudice among humans is out of place (2:1-11; 14:1-16). The result is peace with God (5:1) and mutual love among humans (12:9; 13:8-10); the "weak" are to be welcome and accepted (14:1-2; 15:1). Furthermore, this God has not forgotten the covenant with Israel; all of Israel will be

1. This translation of the Greek noun δικαιοσύνη, which differs from that of NRSVue, is discussed in more detail in the comments above under "Translation Matters" on Romans 3:21, 22 (p. 96).

saved (11:26). This theological program will facilitate the reintegration of Jewish members of the assemblies in the city of Rome into a mostly gentile group. The key to all of the theology, Christology, and soteriology of Romans is a vision of a strong and loving God. Tongue in cheek, one could say that, with these parameters, Romans 1:16 about God's saving power is the John 3:16 passage for the audiences in Rome.

In the prevailing matrix of ancient patriarchal/kyriarchal cultures, these were important operative elements that amounted to a paradigm change in the conceptualization of human identity and for the formation of a radically democratic *ekklēsia* of wo/men. At the same time, some ambiguity remains. The idea of salvation was sometimes presented as a status change toward a position of honor vis-à-vis God. Yet, these very images largely drew on the prevailing patriarchy/kyriarchy and may have contributed to its perpetuation in the realm of religion and culture.

Second, while Paul's authorship of the letter is not disputed among scholars, the acknowledgment of corporate authorship within the epistolary culture of antiquity is important. It leads to the recognition of a number of people in Paul's environment who were instrumental in the production of the letter. It means, for example, that the scribal secretary Tertius, who is allowed to greet the assemblies in Rome in Romans 16:22, is not forgotten as a skilled assistant who was involved in the process of producing the letter. In particular, it means that the contribution of one woman for the proclamation of the early gospel is recognized: Phoebe, who would later be mentioned in subscriptions of several ancient manuscripts. Introduced in Romans 16:1-2 not only as Paul's "sister" and "benefactor" but also as leader of one of the church congregations in Corinth, Phoebe was the person who brought the letter to Rome, where she would have recited it aloud and by heart in front of various audiences. This means that, when Romans was heard for the first several times in Rome, it was heard through the voice of a woman. Despite the fact that she was a gentile woman and possibly a former enslaved person, Paul entrusted her with such an important task; she became his "avatar." Furthermore, several passages of the letter, especially chapters 6–8, suggest that she also contributed directly to the letter. This would explain the unique female vantage point just as much as the employment of terminology drawing on the background of enslavement. Passages about creation groaning in labor pains (Rom 8:22) or the freedom from the law that is explained in analogy to the freedom from marriage following the death of a husband (7:1-6) adopt the vantage point of women. Specifically, the discourse in Romans 7:14-25a about the inner conflict of a human may be understood as articulating the former dilemma of Phoebe herself, once it is clear that the "wretched person" in Romans 7:24 refers in particular to a woman. Inserting Phoebe into the history, including the earliest reception history, of Romans thus helps to solve the riddle of the enigmatic identity of the "I" in chapter 7. Overlooked for millennia, Phoebe is the elephant in the room.

The engagement of a woman for such a task was rather unusual in Greco-Roman antiquity. Why did Paul take the gamble of sending Phoebe? He may have agreed because he recognized that she was the embodiment of his gospel message. Both her leadership position as "[minister]"[2] of the church in Corinth and her mission on behalf of Paul's gospel would have been manifestations of its counter-cultural power and of inclusion and gender equality that were trademarks of the ethos that set apart assemblies of early believers in Christ. It is possible through the celebration of Jesus Christ who is himself the embodiment of God's *Wisdom-Chokmah-Sophia-Sapientia*. While recent scholarship into ancient communities of faith advocates decentering Paul, it appears as if this is what Paul himself has done through his cooperation with Phoebe and in partnering with her to share the gospel with those in Rome. The result is a vision of human society that allows for the full participation of women and men, Jews and gentiles, weak and strong, and free and slave, celebrating God's ever-transcending love for all humans and all of creation. God's grace as divine saving power is wide enough to overcome divisions and antagonisms that people not only in the city of Rome have a proclivity to create. Hence, all are welcome to join in the praise of "the depth of the riches and wisdom and knowledge of God" (Rom 11:33).

2. For this translation, which differs from that of NRSVue, see the comments above under "Translation Matters" on Romans 16:1 (pp. 321–322).

Works Cited

Abraham, Susan B. "Critical Perspectives on Postcolonial Theory." In *The Colonized Apostle: Paul through Postcolonial Eyes*, edited by Christopher D. Stanley, 24–33. Paul in Critical Contexts. Minneapolis: Fortress, 2011.

Adams, Edward. *Constructing the World: A Study of Paul's Cosmological Language*. SNTW. Edinburgh: T&T Clark, 2000.

Adams, Edward. *The Earliest Christian Meeting Places: Almost Exclusively Houses?* LNTS 450. London: T&T Clark, 2013.

Agamben, Giorgio. *The Time That Remains: A Commentary on the Letter to the Romans*. Translated by Patricia Dailey. Meridian: Crossing Aesthetics. Stanford, CA: Stanford University Press, 2005.

Aguilar, Grace. *The Women of Israel*. London: R. Groombridge, 1845; New York: D. Appleton, 1872.

Aland, Kurt. "Der Schluß und die ursprüngliche Gestalt des Römerbriefes." In *Neutestamentliche Entwürfe*, 284–301. TB 63. München: Kaiser, 1979.

Albl, Martin C. *"And Scripture Cannot Be Broken": The Form and Function of the Early Christian Testimonia Collections*. NovTSup 96. Leiden: Brill, 1999.

Albrecht, Glenn, Gina-Maree Sartore, Linda Connor, Nick Higginbotham, Sonia Freeman, Brian Kelly, Helen Stain, Anne Tonna, and Georgia Pollard. "Solastalgia: The Distress Caused by Environmental Change." *Australas Psychiatry* 15/1 (2007): 95–98.

Aletti, Jean-Noël. *Israël et la loi dans la lettre aux Romains*. LD 173. Paris: Cerf, 1998.

Alikin, Valeriy A. *The Earliest History of the Christian Gathering: Origin, Development and Content of the Christian Gathering in the First to Third Centuries*. VCSup 102. Leiden: Brill, 2010.

Altglas, Véronique. "Exotisme Religieux et Bricolage." *Archives de Sciences Sociales Des Religions* 167 (2014): 315–32.

Anderson, Janice Capel, and Stephen D. Moore, eds. *Mark and Method: New Approaches in Biblical Studies*. 2nd ed. Minneapolis: Fortress, 2008.

Aquino, María Pilar, Daisy L. Machado, and Jeanette Rodríguez, eds. *A Reader in Latina Feminist Theology: Religion and Justice*. Austin: University of Texas Press, 2002.

Aquino, María Pilar, and María José Rosado-Nunes, eds. *Feminist Intercultural Theology: Latina Explorations for a Just World*. Studies in Latino/a Catholicism. Maryknoll, NY: Orbis Books, 2007.

Arendt, Hannah. *Condition de l'homme moderne*. Liberté de l'esprit. Paris: Calmann-Lévy, 2005.

Ascough, Richard S. "What Kind of World Did Paul's Communities Live In?" In *The New Cambridge Companion to St. Paul*, edited by Bruce W. Longenecker, 48–66. Cambridge Companions to Religion. Cambridge: Cambridge University Press, 2020.

Astell, Mary. *Some Reflections upon Marriage*. New York: Source Book Press, 1970. Reprint of 1730 ed.; earliest ed. 1700.

Atkinson, Kenneth. *A History of the Hasmonean State: Josephus and Beyond*. Jewish and Christian Texts in Contexts and Related Studies 23. New York: Bloomsbury, 2016.

Avemarie, Friedrich. "Israels rätselhafter Ungehorsam: Römer 10 als Anatomie eines von Gott provozierten Unglaubens." In *Between Gospel and Election: Explorations in the Interpretation of Romans 9–11*, edited by Florian Wilk and J. Ross Wagner with the assistance of Frank Schleritt, 299–320. WUNT 257. Tübingen: Mohr Siebeck, 2010.

Aymer, Margaret. "Acts of the Apostles." In *Women's Bible Commentary*, edited by Carol A. Newsom, Sharon H. Ringe, and Jacqueline E. Lapsley, 536–46. Rev. ed. Louisville: Westminster John Knox, 2012.

Bach, Alice, ed. *Women in the Hebrew Bible: A Reader*. New York: Routledge, 1999.

Bachmann, Michael. "J. D. G. Dunn und die Neue Paulusperspektive." *ThZ* 63 (2007): 25–43.

Bagnall, Roger S., and Raffaella Cribiore. *Women's Letters from Ancient Egypt, 300 BC–AD 800*. Ann Arbor: University of Michigan Press, 2006.

Bahr, Gordon J. "The Subscriptions in the Pauline Letters." *JBL* 87 (1968): 27–41.

Bakhos, Carol, and Gerhard Langer, eds. *The Jewish Middle Ages*. BW 4.2. Atlanta: SBL Press, 2023.

Bal, Mieke. *Lethal Love: Feminist Literary Readings of Biblical Love Stories*. Bloomington: Indiana University Press, 1987.

Balch, David L. "Rich Pompeiian Houses, Shops for Rent, and the Huge Apartment Building in Herculaneum as Typical Spaces for Pauline House Churches." *JSNT* 27 (2004): 27–46.

Balsdon, Dacre. "Der Alltag der Frau im antiken Rom." *AW* 10 (1979): 40–56.

Baltzer, Klaus, Jürgen Kabiersch, Klaus Koenen, Arie van der Kooij, and Florian Wilk. "Esaias: Isaias/Das Buch Jesaja." In *Septuaginta Deutsch: Erläuterungen und Kommentare zum griechischen Alten Testament*. Vol. 2: *Psalmen bis Daniel*, edited by Martin Karrer and Wolfgang Kraus, 2484–2695. Stuttgart: Stuttgarter Bibelgesellschaft, 2011.

Barclay, John M. G. "Paul and Philo on Circumcision: Romans 2.25-9 in Social and Cultural Context." *NTS* 44 (1998): 536–56.

Barraclough, Ray. "Philo's Politics, Roman Rule, and Hellenistic Judaism." *ANRW* 2.21.1 (1984): 417–553.

Bartoloni, Gilda. *La Cultura Villanoviana: All'inizio della storia etrusca*. Rome: Carocci Editore, 2002.

Baskin, Judith R. "Women and Post-Biblical Commentary." In *The Torah: A Women's Commentary*, edited by Tamara Cohn Eskenazi and Andrea L. Weiss, xlix–lv. New York: URJ Press and Women of Reform Judaism, The Federation of Temple Sisterhoods, 2008.

Baslez, Marie-Françoise. "Paul et l'émergence d'un monde 'gréco-romain': Réflexions sur la romanité de l'apôtre." In *Paul's Graeco-Roman Context*, edited by Cilliers Breytenbach, 29–46. BETL 277. Leuven: Peeters, 2015.

Baslez, Marie-Françoise. *Saint Paul*. Paris: Fayard, 1991.

Bauman, Richard A. *Women and Politics in Ancient Rome*. London: Routledge, 1992.

Baumgärtel, Friedrich. "πνεῦμα: B. Spirit in the OT; C. Spirit in Judaism." *TDNT* 6 (1968): 359–68.

Bautch, Richard J. *Glory and Power, Ritual and Relationship: The Sinai Covenant in the Postexilic Period*. LHBOTS 471. London: T&T Clark, 2009.

Beavis, Mary Ann. "Christian Origins, Egalitarianism, and Utopia." *JFSR* 23 (2007): 27–49.

Beavis, Mary Ann. *The First Christian Slave: Onesimus in Context*. Eugene, OR: Cascade Books, 2021.

Beavis, Mary Ann, and HyeRan Kim-Cragg. *Hebrews*. WCS 54. Collegeville, MN: Liturgical Press, 2015.

Bechtler, Steven R. "Christ, the Τέλος of the Law: The Goal of Romans 10:4." *CBQ* 56 (1994): 288–308.

Beker, Johan Christiaan. *Paul the Apostle: The Triumph of God in Life and Thought*. Philadelphia: Fortress, 1980.

Ben Zeev, Miriam Pucci. "New Perspectives on Jewish-Greek Hostilities in Alexandria during the Reign of Emperor Caligula." *JSJ* 21 (1990): 227–35.

Benner, Jeff A. *His Name Is One: An Ancient Hebrew Perspective of the Names of God*. College Station: VBW Publishing, 2003. https://www.ancient-hebrew.org/studies-words/meaning-of-el-shaddai.htm.

Berger, Klaus. "Abraham in den paulinischen Hauptbriefen." *MThZ* 17 (1966): 47–89.

Bergmann, Claudia D. *Childbirth as a Metaphor for Crisis: Evidence from the Ancient Near East, the Hebrew Bible, and 1QH XI, 1–18*. BZAW 382. Berlin: de Gruyter, 2008.

Bertram, Georg. "ἔθνος, ἐθνικός: People and Peoples in the LXX." *TDNT* 2 (1964): 364–69.

Bertram, Georg. "φρήν, ἄφρων, κτλ." *TDNT* 9 (1974): 220–35.

Betz, Hans Dieter. "The Concept of the 'Inner Human Being' (Ὁ ἔσω ἄνθρωπος) in the Anthropology of Paul." *NTS* 46 (2000): 315–41.

Betz, Hans Dieter. *Galatians: A Commentary on Paul's Letter to the Churches in Galatia*. Hermeneia. Philadelphia: Fortress, 1979.

Bhabha, Homi K. *The Location of Culture*. Routledge Classics. London: Routledge: 2004.

Bird, Phyllis A. *Missing Persons and Mistaken Identities: Women and Gender in Ancient Israel*. Minneapolis: Fortress, 1997.

Bjelland Kartzow, Marianne. *The Slave Metaphor and Gendered Enslavement in Early Christian Discourse: Double Trouble Embodied*. Routledge Studies in the Early Christian World. London: Routledge, 2018.

Bjelland Kartzow, Marianne, and Karin B. Neutel. "Neighbours Near and Far: How a Biblical Figure Is Used in Recent European Anti-Migration Politics." *BibInt* 29 (2021): 358–80.

Black, David A. "The Pauline Love Command: Structure, Style, and Ethics in Romans 12:9-21." *FilN* 2 (1989): 3–22.

Blumenfeld, Bruno. *The Political Paul: Justice, Democracy and Kingship in a Hellenistic Framework*. JSNTSup 210. Sheffield: T&T Clark, 2003.

Borman, Lukas. "Biographie und Rhetorik: Das Paulusbild der Deuteropaulinen." In *Receptions of Paul in Early Christianity: The Person of Paul and His Writings through the Eyes of His Early Interpreters*, edited by Jens Schröter, Simon Butticaz, and Andreas Dettwiler, 143–74. BZNW 234. Boston: de Gruyter, 2018.

Børresen, Kari Elisabeth, and Adriana Valerio, eds. *The High Middle Ages*. BW 9.1. Atlanta: SBL Press, 2015.

Boyarin, Daniel. "Paul and the Genealogy of Gender." In *A Feminist Companion to Paul*, edited by Amy-Jill Levine with Marianne Blickenstaff, 13–41. FCNTECW 6. London; New York: T&T International, 2004. (First published in *Representations* 41 [1993]: 1–33.)

Boyarin, Daniel. "Semantic Differences; or, 'Judaism'/'Christianity.'" In *The Ways That Never Parted: Jews and Christians in Late Antiquity and the Early Middle Ages*, edited by Adam H. Becker and Annette Yoshiko Reed, 65–85. TSAJ 95. Tübingen: Mohr Siebeck, 2003.

Boyarin, Daniel, and Jonathan Boyarin. "Diaspora: Generation and the Ground of Jewish Identity." *Critical Inquiry* 19 (1993): 693–725.

Bradley, Keith R. *Slaves and Masters in the Roman Empire: A Study in Social Control*. New York: Oxford University Press, 1987.

Brändle, Rudolf, and Ekkehard W. Stegemann. "Die Entstehung der ersten 'christlichen Gemeinde' Roms im Kontext der jüdischen Gemeinden." *NTS* 42 (1996): 1–11.

Brenner, Athalya. "An Afterword: The Decalogue—Am I an Addressee?" In *A Feminist Companion to Exodus to Deuteronomy*, edited by Athalya Brenner, 255–58. FCB 6, 1st ser. Sheffield: Sheffield Academic, 1994.

Breytenbach, Cilliers. *Versöhnung: Eine Studie zur paulinischen Soteriologie*. WMANT 60. Neukirchen-Vluyn: Neukirchener Verlag, 1989.

Breytenbach, Cilliers. "Versöhnung, Stellvertretung und Sühne: Semantische und traditionsgeschichtliche Bemerkungen am Beispiel der paulinischen Briefe." *NTS* 39 (1993): 59–79.

Briggs, Sheila. "Can an Enslaved God Liberate? Hermeneutical Reflections on Philippians 2:6-11." *Semeia* 47 (1989): 137–53.

Briggs, Sheila. "Galatians." In *Searching the Scriptures*. Vol. 2: *A Feminist Commentary*, edited by Elisabeth Schüssler Fiorenza, 218–36. New York: Crossroad: 1994.

Briggs, Sheila. "What Is Feminist Theology?" In *The Oxford Handbook of Feminist Theology*, edited by Mary McClintock Fulkerson and Sheila Briggs, 73–106. Oxford Handbooks. Oxford: Oxford University Press, 2012.

Brooten, Bernadette J. " 'Junia . . . Outstanding among the Apostles' (Romans 16:7)." In *Women Priests: A Catholic Commentary on the Vatican Declaration*, edited by Leonard Swidler and Arlene Swidler, 141–44. New York: Paulist Press, 1977.

Brooten, Bernadette J. *Love Between Women: Early Christian Responses to Female Homoeroticism*. Chicago Series on Sexuality, History, and Society. Chicago: University of Chicago Press, 1996.

Brooten, Bernadette J. "Paul's Views on the Nature of Women and Female Homoeroticism." In *Immaculate and Powerful: The Female in Sacred Image and Social Reality*, edited by Clarissa W. Atkinson, Constance H. Buchanan, and Margaret R. Miles, 61–87. Harvard Women's Studies in Religion 1. Boston: Beacon, 1985.

Brooten, Bernadette J. "Slavery." In *Encyclopedia of Jewish-Christian Relations Online*, edited by Walter Homolka, Rainer Kampling, Amy-Jill Levine, Christoph Markschies, Peter Schäfer, and Martin Thurner. Berlin; Boston: de Gruyter, 2019. https://www.degruyter.com/database/EJCRO/entry/ejcro.12360416/html.

Brown, Michael J. "Paul's Use of ΔΟΥΛΟΣ ΧΡΙΣΤΟΥ ΙΗΣΟΥ in Romans 1:1." *JBL* 120 (2001): 723–37.

Brown, Raymond E., and John P. Meier. *Antioch and Rome: New Testament Cradles of Catholic Christianity*. New York: Paulist Press, 1983.

Büchsel, Friedrich, and Johannes Herrmann. "ἱλαστήριον." *TDNT* 3 (1965): 318–23.

Buck, Gertrude D. "Healing Story: A Bold Woman in the Crowd." *Consensus* 27 (2001): 11–25.

Burnet, Régis. *Le Nouveau Testament*. 3rd ed. Paris: Presses Universitaires de France, 2021.

Butler, Judith. *Gender Trouble: Feminism and the Subversion of Identity*. Thinking Gender. New York: Routledge, 1990.

Byrne, Brendan. *Romans*. SP 6. Collegeville, MN: Liturgical Press, 1996.

Byrskog, Samuel. "Adam and Medea—and Eve: Revisiting Romans 7,7-25." In *Paul's Graeco-Roman Context*, edited by Cilliers Breytenbach, 273–300. BETL 277. Leuven: Peeters, 2015.

Byrskog, Samuel. "Co-Senders, Co-Authors and Paul's Use of the First Person Plural." *ZNW* 87 (1996): 230–50.

Calhoun, Robert M. *Paul's Definitions of the Gospel in Romans 1*. WUNT 2/316. Tübingen: Mohr Siebeck, 2011.

Calhoun, Robert M. "Same-Sex Relations." In *The Oxford Encyclopedia of the Bible and Law*, edited by Brent A. Strawn, 2:265–71. 2 vols. Oxford: Oxford University Press, 2015.

Calvert-Koyzis, Nancy. "The Maternity of Paul and the New Community in Christ: A Response to Hilary Elder." In *Strangely Familiar: Protofeminist Interpretations of Patriarchal Biblical Texts*, edited by Nancy Calvert-Koyzis and Heather Weir, 227–32. Atlanta: SBL, 2009.

Campbell, Douglas A. *The Rhetoric of Righteousness in Romans 3.21-26*. JSNTSup 65. Sheffield: JSOT, 1992.

Campbell, Joan C. *Phoebe: Patron and Emissary*. Paul's Social Network: Brothers and Sisters in Faith. Collegeville, MN: Liturgical Press, 2009.

Campbell, William S. "'All God's Beloved in Rome!' Jewish Roots and Christian Identity." In *Celebrating Romans: Template for Pauline Theology; Essays in Honor of Robert Jewett*, edited by Sheila E. McGinn, 67–82. Grand Rapids: Eerdmans, 2004.

Campbell, William S. *Paul's Gospel in an Intercultural Context: Jew and Gentile in the Letter to the Romans*. Studies in the Intercultural History of Christianity 69. Frankfurt: Lang, 1992.

Cannon, Katie Geneva. "The Emergence of Black Feminist Consciousness." In *Feminist Interpretation of the Bible*, edited by Letty M. Russell, 30–40. Philadelphia: Westminster, 1985.

Cantarella, Eva. *Bisexuality in the Ancient World*. Translated by Cormac Ô Cuilleanâin. New Haven: Yale University Press, 1992.

Carter, Warren. "Matthaean Christology in Roman Imperial Key: Matthew 1.1." In *The Gospel of Matthew in Its Roman Imperial Context*, edited by John Riches and David C. Sim. London: T&T Clark, 2005.

Carter, Warren. *The Roman Empire and the New Testament: An Essential Guide*. Nashville: Abingdon, 2006.

Cassidy, Ron. "The Politicization of Paul: Romans 13.1-7 in Recent Discussion." *ExpTim* 121 (2010): 383–89.

Castelli, Elizabeth. "*Les Belles Infidèles*/Fidelity or Feminism? The Meanings of Feminist Biblical Translation." In *Searching the Scriptures: A Feminist Introduction*, vol. 1, edited by Elisabeth Schüssler Fiorenza with the assistance of Shelly Matthews, 189–204. New York: Crossroad, 1993.

Castelli, Elizabeth A. "Romans." In *Searching the Scriptures*. Vol. 2: *A Feminist Commentary*, edited by Elisabeth Schüssler Fiorenza, 272–300. New York: Crossroad, 1994.

Catherine of Siena. *The Dialogue*. CWS. New York: Paulist Press, 1980.

Ceulemans, Reinhart. "The Septuagint and Other Translations." In *The Oxford Handbook of Early Christian Biblical Interpretation*, edited by Paul M. Blowers and Peter W. Martens, 33–54. Oxford: Oxford University Press, 2019.

Charmé, Stuart. "The Political Transformation of Gender Traditions at the Western Wall in Jerusalem." *JFSR* 21 (2005): 5–34.

Chaudhuri, Jean, and Joyotpaul Chaudhuri. *A Sacred Path: The Way of the Muscogee Creeks*. Los Angeles: UCLA American Indian Studies Center, 2001.

Claassens, L. Juliana, and Irmtraud Fischer, eds. *Prophecy and Gender in the Hebrew Bible*. BW 1.2. Atlanta: SBL Press, 2021.

Claassens, L. Juliana, and Carolyn J. Sharp, eds. *Feminist Frameworks and the Bible: Power, Ambiguity, and Intersectionality*. LHBOTS 630. London: Bloomsbury T&T Clark, 2017.

Clark, Anne L. "Remembering Phoebe in the Twelfth Century: The Forgotten Deacon in Paul's Letter to Romans." *Journal of Medieval Religious Cultures* 45 (2019): 1–28.

Clark, Gillian. "Roman Women." *GR* 28 (1981): 193–212.

Clarus, Ingeborg. *Das Opfer: Archaische Riten modern gedeutet*. Düsseldorf: Patmos, 2005.

Cobb, L. Stephanie. *Dying to Be Men: Gender and Language in Early Christian Martyr Texts*. GTR. New York: Columbia University Press, 2008.

Cohee, Peter. "Temple Slaves in Ancient Greece and Rome." In *Macmillan Encyclopedia of World Slavery*, edited by Paul Finkelman and Joseph C. Miller, 2:888–89. New York: Macmillan, 1998.

Cohen, Shaye J. D. *Why Aren't Jewish Women Circumcised? Gender and Covenant in Judaism*. Berkeley: University of California Press, 2005.

Cohick, Lynn H. "Mothers, Martyrs, and Manly Courage: The Female Martyr in 2 Maccabees, 4 Maccabees, and the Acts of Paul and Thecla." In *A Most Reliable Witness: Essays in Honor of Ross Shepard Kraemer*, edited by Susan Ashbrook Harvey et al., 123–32. BJS 358. Providence: Brown University Press, 2015.

Collins, Adela Yarbro. "No Longer 'Male and Female' (Gal 3:28): Ethics and an Early Christian Baptismal Formula." *Journal of Ethics in Antiquity and Christianity* 1 (2019): 27–39.

Collins, John J. "A Symbol of Otherness: Circumcision and Salvation in the First Century." In *Seers, Sibyls and Sages in Hellenistic-Roman Judaism*, 211–35. JSJSup 54. Leiden: Brill, 1997.

Cone, James H. *God of the Oppressed*. New York: Seabury, 1975.

Consolino, Franca Ela, and Judith Herrin, eds. *The Early Middle Ages*. BW 6.1. Atlanta: SBL Press, 2020.

Corley, Kathleen E. "Women's Inheritance Rights in Antiquity and Paul's Metaphor of Adoption." In *A Feminist Companion to Paul*, edited by Amy-Jill Levine with Marianne Blickenstaff, 98–121. FCNTECW 6. London: T&T International, 2004.

Cotter, Wendy. "Women's Authority Roles in Paul's Churches: Countercultural or Conventional?" *NovT* 36 (1994): 350–72.

Countryman, L. William. *Dirt, Greed, and Sex: Sexual Ethics in the New Testament and Their Implications for Today*. Rev. ed. Minneapolis: Fortress, 2007.

Cranfield, Charles E. B. *A Critical and Exegetical Commentary on the Epistle to the Romans*. Vol. 1. ICC. Edinburgh: T&T Clark, 1975.

Crenshaw, Kimberlé Williams. "Demarginalizing the Intersection of Race and Sex: A Black Feminist Critique of Antidiscrimination Doctrine, Feminist Theory and Antiracist Politics." *University of Chicago Legal Forum* 1989 (1989): 139–67.

Croasmun, Matthew. "'Real Participation': The Body of Christ and the Body of Sin in Evolutionary Perspective." In *"In Christ" in Paul: Explorations in Paul's Theology of Union and Participation*, edited by Kevin J. Vanhoozer, Constantine R. Campbell, and Michael J. Thate, 127–56. WUNT 2/384. Tübingen: Mohr Siebeck, 2014.

Crook, Zeba. "Honor, Shame, and Social Status Revisited." *JBL* 128 (2009): 591–611.

Daly, Mary. *Beyond God the Father: A Philosophy of Women's Liberation*. Boston: Beacon, 1985.

D'Angelo, Mary Rose. "Abba and 'Father': Imperial Theology and the Jesus Traditions." *JBL* 111 (1992): 611–30.

D'Angelo, Mary Rose. "Theology in Mark and Q: Abba and 'Father' in Context." *HTR* 85 (1992): 149–74.

D'Angelo, Mary Rose. "Women Partners in the New Testament." *JFSR* 6 (1990): 65–86.

de Conick, April. *Holy Misogyny: Why the Sex and Gender Conflicts in the Early Church Still Matter*. New York: Continuum, 2011.

deSilva, David A. *Despising Shame: Honor Discourse and Community Maintenance in the Epistle to the Hebrews*. SBLDS 152. Atlanta: Scholars Press, 1995.

deSilva, David A. "Paul, Honor, and Shame." In *Paul in the Greco-Roman World: A Handbook*, edited by J. Paul Sampley, 2:26–47. 2nd ed. London: Bloomsbury, 2016.

Destro, Adriana, and Mauro Pesce. "In and Out of the House: Changes in Women's Role from Jesus's Movement to the Early Churches." In *Gospels: Narrative and History*, edited by Mercedes Navarro Puerto, Marinella Perroni, and Amy-Jill Levine, 299–320. BW 2.1. Atlanta: SBL Press, 2015.

Dietrick, Ellen Battelle. "The Book of Acts." In *The Woman's Bible: Part 2; Comments on the Old and New Testaments from Joshua to Revelation*, edited by Elizabeth Cady Stanton, 145–51. New York: European Publishing Company, 1898.

Dietrick, Ellen Battelle. "Epistle to the Romans." In *The Woman's Bible: Part 2; Comments on the Old and New Testaments from Joshua to Revelation*, edited by Elizabeth Cady Stanton, 152–54. New York: European Publishing Company, 1898.

Dinkler, Michal Beth. *Literary Theory and the New Testament*. AYBRL. New Haven: Yale University Press, 2019.

Dochhorn, Jan. "Der Vorwurf des Tempelraubs in Röm 2,22b und seine politischen Hintergründe." *ZNW* 109 (2018): 101–17.

Dodd, Charles H. *The Epistle of Paul to the Romans*. MNTC. London: Hodder & Stoughton, 1932. Rev. ed. London: Collins, 1959.

Dodson, Joseph R. "The Convict's Gibbet and the Victor's Car: The Triumphal Death of Marcus Atilius Regulus and the Background of Col 2:15." *HTR* 114 (2021): 182–202.

Donaldson, Terence L. "'Riches for the Gentiles' (Rom 11:12): Israel's Rejection and Paul's Gentile Mission." *JBL* 112 (1993): 81–98.

Donfried, Karl P. "False Presuppositions in the Study of Romans." In *The Romans Debate*, edited by Karl P. Donfried, 102–27. Rev. exp. ed. Peabody, MA: Hendrickson, 1991.

Donfried, Karl P. "A Short Note on Romans 16." In *The Romans Debate*, edited by Karl P. Donfried, 44–52. Rev. exp. ed. Peabody, MA: Hendrickson, 1991.

Dube, Musa W., ed. *Postcolonial Feminist Interpretation of the Bible*. St. Louis: Chalice, 2000.

Dunn, James D. G. "The New Perspective: Whence, What and Whither?" In *The New Perspective on Paul: Collected Essays*, edited by James D. G. Dunn, 1–88. WUNT 185. Tübingen: Mohr Siebeck, 2005.

Dunn, James D. G. *The Partings of the Ways: Between Christianity and Judaism and Their Significance for the Character of Christianity*. London: SCM Press, 1991.

Dunn, James D. G. "Paul's Epistle to the Romans: An Analysis of Structure and Argument." *ANRW* 2.25.4 (1987): 2842–90.

Dunn, James D. G. "Rom 7,14-25 in the Theology of Paul." *ThZ* 31 (1975): 257–73.

Dunn, James D. G. *Romans 1–8*. WBC 38a. Dallas: Word, 1988.

Dunn, James D. G. *Romans 9–16*. WBC 38b. Dallas: Word, 1988.

Dunn, James D. G. *The Theology of Paul the Apostle*. Grand Rapids: Eerdmans, 1998.

Eagleton, Terry. *Ideology: An Introduction*. London: Verso, 2007.

Eagleton, Terry. *Literary Theory: An Introduction*. Anniversary ed. Minneapolis: University of Minnesota Press, 2008.

Eastman, Susan. "Whose Apocalypse? The Identity of the Sons of God in Romans 8:19." *JBL* 121 (2002): 263–77.

Eberhart, Christian A. "Beobachtungen zu Kommunikationsstrategien im frühen Christentum: Zu Insider-Informationen in Mk 5:1-20." In *Talking God in Society: Multidisciplinary (Re)constructions of Ancient (Con)texts; Festschrift for Peter Lampe*. Vol. 1: *Theories and Applications*, edited by Ute E. Eisen and Heidrun E. Mader, 405–24. NTOA 120/1. Göttingen: Vandenhoeck & Ruprecht, 2020.

Eberhart, Christian A. "Kult und die Begegnung mit dem einen Gott in der Septuaginta." In *Handbuch zur Septuaginta—Handbook of the Septuagint*. Vol. 5: *Die Theologie der Septuaginta—The Theology of the Septuagint* (LXX.H 5), edited by Hans Ausloos and Bénédicte Lemmelijn, 165–242. Gütersloh: Gütersloher Verlagshaus, 2020.

Eberhart, Christian A. *The Sacrifice of Jesus: Understanding Atonement Biblically*. 2nd ed. Eugene, OR: Wipf & Stock, 2018.

Eberhart, Christian A. "The Term 'Sacrifice' and the Problem of Theological Abstraction: A Study of the Reception History of Genesis 22:1-19." In *The Multivalence of Biblical Texts and Theological Meanings*, edited by Christine Helmer, 47–66. SymS 37. Atlanta: SBL, 2006.

Eck, Werner. "Sklaven und Freigelassene von Römern in Iudaea und den angrenzenden Provinzen." *NovT* 55 (2013): 1–21.

Ehrensperger, Kathy. *That We May Be Mutually Encouraged: Feminism and the New Perspective in Pauline Studies*. New York: T&T Clark, 2004.

Eisen, Ute E. *Amtsträgerinnen im frühen Christentum: Epigraphische und literarische Studien*. FKDG 61. Göttingen: Vandenhoeck & Ruprecht, 1996.

Eisenbaum, Pamela. "Is Paul the Father of Misogyny and Antisemitism?" *CrossCurrents* 50 (2000): 506–24.

Elder, Nicholas. "'Wretch I Am!' Eve's Tragic Speech-in-Character in Romans 7:7-25." *JBL* 137 (2018): 743–63.

Elliott, Neil. *The Arrogance of Nations: Reading Romans in the Shadow of Empire*. Paul in Critical Contexts. Minneapolis: Fortress, 2010.

Elliott, Neil. *The Rhetoric of Romans: Argumentative Constraint and Strategy and Paul's Dialogue with Judaism*. JSNTSup 45. Sheffield: Sheffield Academic, 1990.

Ellis, Teresa Ann. "Is Eve the 'Woman' in Sirach 25:24?" *CBQ* 73 (2011): 723–42.

Engberg-Pedersen, Troels. "'Everything Is Clean,' and 'Everything That Is Not of Faith Is Sin': The Logic of Pauline Casuistry in Romans 14.1–15.13." In *Paul, Grace and Freedom: Essays in Honour of John K. Riches*, edited by Paul Middleton, Angus Paddison, and Karen Wenell, 22–38. T&T Clark Biblical Studies. London: T&T Clark, 2009.

Epp, Eldon Jay. *Junia: The First Woman Apostle*. Minneapolis: Fortress, 2005.

Epp, Eldon Jay. "New Testament Papyrus Manuscripts and Letter Carrying in Greco-Roman Times." In *The Future of Early Christianity: Essays in Honor of Helmut Koester*, edited by Birger A. Pearson et al., 35–56. Minneapolis: Fortress, 1991.

Eskenazi, Tamara Cohn, and Andrea L. Weiss, eds. *The Torah: A Women's Commentary*. New York: URJ Press and Women of Reform Judaism, The Federation of Temple Sisterhoods, 2008.

Esler, Philip F. "Ancient Oleiculture and Ethnic Differentiation: The Meaning of the Olive-Tree Image in Romans 11." *JSNT* 26 (2003): 103–24.

Esler, Philip F. *Conflict and Identity in Romans: The Social Setting of Paul's Letter*. Minneapolis: Fortress, 2003.

Exum, J. Cheryl. "Second Thoughts about Secondary Characters: Women in Exodus 1.8–2.10." In *A Feminist Companion to Exodus to Deuteronomy*, edited by Athalya Brenner, 75–87. FCB 6. Sheffield: Sheffield Academic, 1994.

Exum, J. Cheryl, and David J. A. Clines, eds. *The New Literary Criticism and the Hebrew Bible*. Valley Forge, PA: Trinity Press International, 1993.

Feldmeier, Reinhard. "Vater und Töpfer? Zur Identität Gottes im Römerbrief." In *Between Gospel and Election: Explorations in the Interpretation of Romans*

9–11, edited by Florian Wilk and J. Ross Wagner with the assistance of Frank Schleritt, 377–90. WUNT 257. Tübingen: Mohr Siebeck, 2010.

Feldmeier, Reinhard, and Hermann Spieckermann. *Der Gott der Lebendigen: Eine biblische Gotteslehre*. TOBITH 1. Tübingen: Mohr Siebeck, 2011.

Fell, Margaret. *Women's Speaking Justified, Proved and Allowed by the Scriptures*. London, 1666.

Feminist Biblical Interpretation: A Compendium of Critical Commentary on the Books of the Bible and Related Literature. Edited by Luise Schottroff and Marie-Theres Wacker. Translated by Lisa E. Dahill, Everett R. Kalin, Nancy Lukens, Linda M. Maloney, Barbara Rumscheidt, Martin Rumscheidt, and Tina Steiner. Grand Rapids: Eerdmans, 2012.

Ferguson, Everett. *Backgrounds of Early Christianity*. 3rd ed. Grand Rapids: Eerdmans, 2003.

Fewell, Danna Nolan, and David M. Gunn. *Gender, Power, and Promise: The Subject of the Bible's First Story*. Nashville: Abingdon, 1993.

Filtvedt, Ole Jakob. "A 'Non-Ethnic' People?" *Bib* 97 (2016): 101–20.

Finger, Reta Halteman. "Getting Along When We Don't Agree: Using Simulation and Controversy to Help Students and Lay Persons Interpret Romans." In *Celebrating Romans: Template for Pauline Theology; Essays in Honor of Robert Jewett*, edited by Sheila E. McGinn, 222–39. Grand Rapids: Eerdmans, 2004.

Finlan, Stephen. *Problems with Atonement: The Origins of, and Controversy about, the Atonement Doctrine*. Collegeville, MN: Liturgical Press, 2005.

Finlan, Stephen. *Sacrifice and Atonement: Psychological Motives and Biblical Patterns*. Minneapolis: Fortress, 2016.

Finsterbusch, Karin. "'Ich habe meine Tora in ihre Mitte gegeben': Bemerkungen zu Jer 31,33." *BZ* 49 (2005): 86–92.

Fischer, Irmtraud. "Genesis 12–50: Die Ursprungsgeschichte Israels als Frauengeschichte." In *Kompendium feministische Bibelauslegung*, edited by Luise Schottroff and Marie-Theres Wacker, 12–25. 2nd ed. Gütersloh: Kaiser; Gütersloher Verlagshaus, 1999.

Fischer, Irmtraud, and Mercedes Navarro Puerto, with Andrea Taschl-Erber, eds. *Torah*. BW 1.1. Atlanta: SBL, 2011.

Fitzgerald, John T. "Paul and Paradigm Shifts: Reconciliation and Its Linkage Group." In *Paul Beyond the Judaism/Hellenism Divide*, edited by Troels Engberg-Pedersen, 241–62. Louisville: Westminster John Knox, 2001.

Fitzmyer, Joseph A. *Romans: A New Translation with Introduction and Commentary*. AB 33. New York: Doubleday, 1993.

Flemming, Rebecca. "*Quae Corpore Quaestum Facit*: The Sexual Economy of Female Prostitution in the Roman Empire." *JRS* 89 (1999): 38–61.

Fletcher, Richard. "Corinth: I. Archaeology." *EBR* 5 (2012): 769–70.

Foerster, Werner. "ἐξουσία." *TDNT* 2 (1964): 560–575.

Foster, Robert L. "The Justice of the Gentiles: Revisiting the Purpose of Romans." *CBQ* 76 (2014): 684–703.

Fredrickson, David E. "Paul, Hardships, and Suffering." In *Paul in the Greco-Roman World: A Handbook*, edited by J. Paul Sampley, 172–97. 1st ed. Harrisburg, PA: Trinity Press International, 2003.

Fredriksen, Paula. "How Jewish Is God? Divine Ethnicity in Paul's Theology." *JBL* 137 (2018): 193–212.

Fredriksen, Paula. "Paul's Letter to the Romans, the Ten Commandments, and Pagan 'Justification by Faith.'" *JBL* 133 (2014): 801–8.

Fredriksen, Paula. "The Question of Worship: Gods, Pagans, and the Redemption of Israel." In *Paul within Judaism: Restoring the First-Century Context to the Apostle*, edited by Mark D. Nanos and Magnus Zetterholm, 175–201. Minneapolis: Fortress, 2015.

Fredriksen, Paula. "What Does It Mean to See Paul 'within Judaism'?" *JBL* 141 (2022): 359–80.

Frey, Jörg. "Die Deutung des Todes Jesu als Stellvertretung: Neutestamentliche Perspektiven." In *Stellvertretung: Theologische, philosophische und kulturelle Aspekte*. Vol. 1: *Interdisziplinäres Symposion Tübingen 2004*, edited by Johanna Christine Janowski, Bernd Janowski, and Hans P. Lichtenberger, 87–121. Neukirchen-Vluyn: Neukirchener Verlag, 2006.

Frey, Jörg. "Die paulinische Antithese von 'Fleisch' und 'Geist' und die palästinisch-jüdische Weisheitstradition." *ZNW* 90 (1999): 45–77.

Frey, Jörg. "Paulus als Pharisäer und Antiochener: Biographische Grundlagen seiner Schriftrezeption." In *Von Jesus zur neutestamentlichen Theologie: Kleine Schriften II*, edited by Benjamin Schliesser, 301–33. WUNT 368. Tübingen: Mohr Siebeck, 2016.

Friesen, Steven J. "Poverty in Pauline Studies: Beyond the So-Called New Consensus." *JSNT* 26 (2004): 323–61.

Friesen, Steven J. "The Wrong Erastus: Ideology, Archaeology, and Exegesis." In *Corinth in Context: Comparative Studies on Religion and Society*, edited by Steven J. Friesen, Daniel N. Schowalter, and James C. Walters, 231–56. NovTSup 134. Leiden: Brill, 2010.

Frymer-Kensky, Tikva. *Reading the Women of the Bible: A New Interpretation of Their Stories.* New York: Schocken Books, 2002.

Gamble, Harry Y., Jr. "The Formation of the Pauline Corpus." In *The Oxford Handbook of Pauline Studies*, edited by Matthew V. Novenson and R. Barry Matlock, 338–54. Oxford: Oxford University Press, 2022.

Gamble, Harry Y., Jr. *The Textual History of the Letter to the Romans: A Study in Textual and Literary Criticism*. SD 42. Grand Rapids: Eerdmans, 1977.

Gandhi, Leela. *Postcolonial Theory: A Critical Introduction*. New York: Columbia University Press, 1998.

Garlan, Yvon. *Slavery in Ancient Greece*. Translated by Janet Lloyd. Rev. exp. ed. Ithaca: Cornell University Press, 1988.

Gaventa, Beverly Roberts. "On the Calling-Into-Being of Israel: Romans 9:6-29." In *Between Gospel and Election: Explorations in the Interpretation of Romans*

9–11, edited by Florian Wilk and J. Ross Wagner with the assistance of Frank Schleritt, 255–69. WUNT 257. Tübingen: Mohr Siebeck, 2010.

Gaventa, Beverly Roberts. *Our Mother Saint Paul*. Louisville: Westminster John Knox, 2007.

Gaventa, Beverly Roberts. "Our Mother St. Paul: Toward the Recovery of a Neglected Theme." In *A Feminist Companion to Paul*, edited by Amy-Jill Levine with Marianne Blickenstaff, 85–97. FCNTECW 6. London: T&T International, 2004.

Gaventa, Beverly Roberts. "Paul and the Roman Believers." In *The Blackwell Companion to Paul*, edited by Stephen Westerholm, 93–107. Blackwell Companions to Religion. Malden: Wiley-Blackwell, 2011.

Gaventa, Beverly Roberts. "Reading Romans 13 with Simone Weil: Toward a More Generous Hermeneutic." *JBL* 136 (2017): 3–22.

Gaventa, Beverly Roberts. "Romans." In *Women's Bible Commentary*, edited by Carol A. Newsom, Sharon H. Ringe, and Jacqueline E. Lapsley, 547–56. 3rd ed. Louisville: Westminster John Knox, 2012.

Gaventa, Beverly Roberts. "The Shape of the 'I': The Psalter, the Gospel, and the Speaker in Romans 7." In *Apocalyptic Paul: Cosmos and Anthropos in Romans 5–8*, edited by Beverly Roberts Gaventa, 77–91. Waco: Baylor University Press, 2013.

Gaventa, Beverly Roberts. *When in Romans: An Invitation to Linger with the Gospel According to Paul*. Grand Rapids: Baker Academic, 2016.

Gehring, Roger. *House Church and Mission: The Importance of Household Structures in Early Christianity*. Peabody, MA : Hendrickson, 2004.

Genest, Olivette. "Faut-il que Paul se taise dans la discussion sur la situation des femmes en christianisme?" *Lumen Vitae* 52 (1997): 297–314.

Genest, Olivette. "Femmes et ministères dans le Nouveau Testament." *SR* 16 (1987): 7–20.

George, Michele. "Slave Disguise in Ancient Rome." In *Representing the Body of the Slave*, edited by Thomas Wiedemann and Jane Gardner, 41–54. Studies in Slave and Post-Slave Societies and Cultures. London: Frank Cass, 2002.

Getty, Mary Ann. "Paul and the Salvation of Israel: A Perspective on Romans 9–11." *CBQ* 50 (1988): 456–69.

Getty-Sullivan, Mary Ann. *Women in the New Testament*. Collegeville, MN: Liturgical Press, 2001.

Gieniusz, Andrzej. "Rom 7,1-6: Lack of Imagination? Function of the Passage in the Argumentation of Rom 6,1–7,6." *Bib* 74 (1993): 389–400.

Gignac, Alain. *Juifs et Chrétiens à l'École de Paul de Tarse: Enjeux identitaires et éthiques d'une lecture de Romains 9–11*. ColSB 9. Montreal: Médiaspaul, 1999.

Gignac, Alain. *L'épître aux Romains*. Commentaire biblique: Nouveau Testament 6. Paris: Cerf, 2014.

Gillman, Florence M., Mary Ann Beavis, and HyeRan Kim-Cragg. *1–2 Thessalonians*. WCS 52. Collegeville, MN: Liturgical Press, 2016.

Glancy, Jennifer A. "Obstacles to Slaves' Participation in the Corinthian Church." *JBL* 117 (1998): 481–501.

Glancy, Jennifer A. "The Sexual Use of Slaves: A Response to Kyle Harper on Jewish and Christian *Porneia*." *JBL* 134 (2015): 215–29.

Glancy, Jennifer A. *Slavery in Early Christianity*. Minneapolis: Fortress, 2006.

Gnadt, Martina S. "'Abba Isn't Daddy': Aspekte einer feministisch-befreiungstheologischen Revision des 'Abba Jesu.'" In *Von der Wurzel getragen: Christlich-feministische Exegese in Auseinandersetzung mit Antijudaismus*, edited by Luise Schottroff and Marie-Theres Wacker, 115–31. BibInt 17. Leiden: Brill, 1996.

Gnuse, Robert K. "Seven Gay Texts: Biblical Passages Used to Condemn Homosexuality." *BTB* 45 (2015): 68–87.

Goertz, Stephan. "'Who Am I to Judge?' An Overview of the Context and the Themes of the Contributions." In *"Who Am I to Judge?" Homosexuality and the Catholic Church*, edited by Stephan Goertz, translated by Alissa Jones Nelson, 1–8. Berlin: de Gruyter, 2022.

Goldenberg, Robert. "The Jewish Sabbath in the Roman World up to the Time of Constantine the Great." *ANRW* 2.19.1 (1979): 414–47.

Goldingay, John. "The Significance of Circumcision." *JSOT* 88 (2000): 3–18.

Goldsworthy, Adrian. *Caesar: Life of a Colossus*. New Haven: Yale University Press, 2006.

Gonzalez, Michelle A. "Latina Feminist Theology: Past, Present, and Future." *JFSR* 25 (2009): 150–55.

Good, Deirdre J. "Reading Strategies for Biblical Passages on Same-Sex Relations." *Theology and Sexuality* 7 (1997): 70–82.

Gordon, Benjamin D. "On the Sanctity of Mixtures and Branches: Two Halakic Sayings in Romans 11:16-24." *JBL* 135 (2016): 355–68.

Griffiths, Valerie. "Romans." In *The IVP Women's Bible Commentary*, edited by Catherine Clark Kroeger and Mary J. Evans, 628–43. Downers Grove, IL: InterVarsity, 2002.

Grimké, Sarah. *Letters on the Equality of the Sexes and the Condition of Woman*. Boston: Isaac Knapp, 1838.

Groß, Walter. "Noch einmal: Individualisierung des Bundesbruchs in der Priesterschrift: Eine Überprüfung." In *Jeremia, Deuteronomismus und Priesterschrift: Beiträge zur Literatur- und Theologiegeschichte des Alten Testaments; Festschrift für Hermann-Josef Stipp*, edited by Andreas Michel and Nicole Katrin Rüttgers, 69–86. ATSAT 105. St. Ottilien: EOS–Editions, 2019.

Gruen, Erich S. *The Construct of Identity in Hellenistic Judaism: Essays on Early Jewish Literature and History*. DCLS 29. Berlin: de Gruyter, 2016.

Gruen, Erich S. *Diaspora: Jews amidst Greeks and Romans*. Cambridge, MA: Harvard University Press, 2002.

Guðmundsdóttir, Arnfríður. "Crucified—So What? Feminist Rereadings of the Cross-Event." In *T&T Clark Companion to Atonement*, edited by Adam J. Johnson, 335–56. London: Bloomsbury T&T Clark, 2017.

Guest, Deryn. *When Deborah Met Jael: Lesbian Biblical Hermeneutics.* London: SCM, 2005.

Günther, Sven. "Taxation in the Greco-Roman World: The Roman Principate." *Oxford Handbook Topics in Classical Studies*. April 2016. https://doi.org/10.1093/oxfordhb/9780199935390.013.38.

Gupta, Nijay K. "Paul and *Pistis Christou*." In *The Oxford Handbook of Pauline Studies*, edited by Matthew V. Novenson and R. Barry Matlock, 470–87. Oxford: Oxford University Press, 2022.

Gwyn, William B. "Cruel Nero: The Concept of the Tyrant and the Image of Nero in Western Political Thought." *History of Political Thought* 12 (1991): 421–55.

Haacker, Klaus. *Der Brief des Paulus an die Römer*. THKNT 6. Leipzig: Evangelische Verlagsanstalt, 1999.

Habel, Norman C., and Peter Trudinger. *Exploring Ecological Hermeneutics*. SymS 46. Atlanta: SBL, 2008.

Hahn, Ferdinand. *Theologie des Neuen Testaments*. Vol. 1: *Die Vielfalt des Neuen Testaments: Theologiegeschichte des Urchristentums*. 2nd ed. Tübingen: Mohr Siebeck, 2005.

Hahn, Ferdinand. *Theologie des Neuen Testaments*. Vol. 2: *Die Einheit des Neuen Testaments: Thematische Darstellung*. 2nd ed. Tübingen: Mohr Siebeck, 2005.

Haines-Eitzen, Kim. *Guardians of Letters: Literacy, Power, and the Transmitters of Early Christian Literature*. Oxford: Oxford University Press, 2000.

Hamerton-Kelly, Robert. "God the Father in the Bible and in the Experience of Jesus: The State of the Question." In *God as Father?*, edited by Johann Baptist Metz and Edward Schillebeeckx, English ed. edited by Marcus Lefébure, 95–102. Concilium 143. Edinburgh: T&T Clark, 1981.

Hansen, Bruce. *'All of You Are One': The Social Vision of Galatians 3.28, 1 Corinthians 12.13 and Colossians 3.11*. LNTS 409. London: T&T Clark, 2010.

Harland, Philip A. "Imperial Cults within Local Cultural Life: Associations in Roman Asia." *AHB* 17 (2003): 85–107.

Harmon, Matthew S. "Letter Carriers and Paul's Use of Scripture." *Journal for the Study of Paul and His Letters* 4 (2014): 129–48.

Harrill, J. Albert. "Paul and Slavery." In *Paul in the Greco-Roman World: A Handbook*, edited by J. Paul Sampley, 2:301–45. 2nd ed. London: Bloomsbury, 2016.

Harrill, J. Albert. *Slaves in the New Testament: Literary, Social, and Moral Dimensions.* Minneapolis: Fortress, 2006.

Harris, William V. *Ancient Literacy*. Cambridge, MA: Harvard University Press, 1989.

Harrison, James R. "Augustan Rome and the Body of Christ: A Comparison of the Social Vision of the *Res Gestae* and Paul's Letter to the Romans." *HTR* 106 (2013): 1–36.

Harrison, James R. *Paul's Language of Grace in Its Graeco-Roman Context*. WUNT 2/172. Tübingen: Mohr Siebeck, 2003.

Harrison, James R. *Reading Romans with Roman Eyes: Studies on the Social Perspective of Paul*. Paul in Critical Contexts. Lanham: Lexington; Fortress, 2020.

Hartenstein, Friedhelm. "Zur symbolischen Bedeutung des Blutes im Alten Testament." In *Deutungen des Todes Jesu im Neuen Testament*, edited by Jörg Frey and Jens Schröter, 119–38. WUNT 181. Tübingen: Mohr Siebeck, 2005.

Hartmann, Andrea. "Junia—A Woman Lost in Translation: The Name IOYNIAN in Romans 16:7 and Its History of Interpretation." *Open Theology* 6 (2020): 646–60.

Harvey, John D. *Listening to the Text: Oral Patterning in Paul's Letters*. ETS 1. Grand Rapids: Baker Academic, 1998.

Hawkins, Faith K. "Does Paul Make a Difference?" In *A Feminist Companion to Paul*, edited by Amy-Jill Levine with Marianne Blickenstaff, 169–82. FCNTECW 6. London: T&T International, 2004.

Hays, Richard B. "'Have We Found Abraham to Be Our Forefather According to the Flesh?' A Reconsideration of Rom 4:1." *NovT* 27 (1985): 76–98.

Hays, Richard B. "Paul on the Relation between Men and Women." In *A Feminist Companion to Paul*, edited by Amy-Jill Levine with Marianne Blickenstaff, 137–47. FCNTECW 6. London: T&T International, 2004.

Hearon, Holly E., and Philip Ruge-Jones, eds. *The Bible in Ancient and Modern Media: Story and Performance*. Eugene, OR: Cascade Books, 2009.

Heidland, Hans-Wolfgang. "λογίζομαι, λογισμός." *TDNT* 4 (1967): 284–92.

Heilig, Christoph. *Paulus als Erzähler? Eine narratologische Perspektive auf die Paulusbriefe*. BZNW 237. Berlin: de Gruyter, 2020.

Heller, Anna. "Stratégies de carrière et stratégies de distinction: La double citoyenneté dans le Péloponnèse d'époque impériale." In *Patrie d'origine et patries électives: Les citoyennetés multiples dans le monde grec d'époque romaine: Actes du colloque international de Tours, 6–7 novembre 2009*, edited by Anna Heller and Anne-Valérie Pont, 127–151. Scripta Antiqua 40. Paris: Ausonius Éditions, 2012.

Helminiak, Daniel A. *What the Bible Really Says about Homosexuality*. Millennium ed. Tajique, NM: Alamo Square Press, 2000.

Hengel, Martin, and Anna Maria Schwemer. *Paul between Damascus and Antioch: The Unknown Years*. Translated by John Bowden. Louisville: Westminster John Knox, 1997.

Henige, David. "He Came, He Saw, We Counted: The Historiography and Demography of Caesar's Gallic Numbers." *Annales de Démographie Historique* 1 (1998): 215–42.

Hens-Piazza, Gina. *The New Historicism*. GBS, Old Testament Series. Minneapolis: Fortress, 2002.

Henten, Jan W. van. "Datierung und Herkunft des vierten Makkabäerbuches." In *Tradition and Re-interpretation in Jewish and Early Christian Literature; Essays in Honour of Jürgen C. H. Lebram*, edited by Jan W. van Henten et al., 136–49. StPB 36. Leiden: Brill, 1986.

Herbert-Brown, Geraldine. "Caesar or Augustus? The Game of the Name in Ovid's 'Fasti.'" *Acta Classica* 54 (2011): 43–77.

Herzer, Jens. *Petrus oder Paulus? Studien über das Verhältnis des Ersten Petrusbriefes zur paulinischen Tradition*. WUNT 103. Tübingen: Mohr Siebeck, 1998.

Herzer, Jens. "The Significance of Covenant Theology in Galatians and Romans." In *Covenant-Concepts of Berit, Diatheke, and Testamentum: Proceedings of the Conference at the Lanier Theological Library in Houston, Texas, November 2019*, edited by Christian A. Eberhart and Wolfgang Kraus, in collaboration with Richard Bautch, Matthias Henze, and Martin Rösel, 457–94. WUNT 506. Tübingen: Mohr Siebeck, 2023.

Herzfeld, Hans. *Geschichte in Gestalten*. Vol. 1. Das Fischer Lexikon. Frankfurt: Fischer, 1963.

Hesberg, Henner von. "Archäologische Denkmäler zum römischen Kaiserkult." *ANRW* 2.16.2 (1978): 911–95.

Heyob, Sharon K. *The Cult of Isis Among Women in the Graeco-Roman World*. EPRO 51. Brill: Leiden, 1975.

Hieke, Thomas. "Abram/Abraham as Prefiguration of the Covenant in the Torah." In *Covenant-Concepts of Berit, Diatheke, and Testamentum: Proceedings of the Conference at the Lanier Theological Library in Houston, Texas, November 2019*, edited by Christian A. Eberhart and Wolfgang Kraus, in collaboration with Richard Bautch, Matthias Henze, and Martin Rösel, 69–88. WUNT 506. Tübingen: Mohr Siebeck, 2023.

Hieke, Thomas. *Levitikus 1–15*. HThKAT. Freiburg: Herder, 2014.

Hieke, Thomas. *Levitikus 16–27*. HThKAT. Freiburg: Herder, 2014.

Hoffner, Harry A., Jr. "'The King's Speech': Royal Rhetorical Language." In *Beyond Hatti: A Tribute to Gary Beckman*, edited by Billie Jean Collins and Piotr Michalowski, 137–54. Atlanta: Lockwood, 2013.

Hofius, Otfried. "Erwägungen zur Gestalt und Herkunft des paulinischen Versöhnungsgedankens." In *Paulusstudien*, edited by Otfried Hofius, 1–14. WUNT 51. Tübingen: Mohr Siebeck, 1989.

Holladay, Carl R. *A Critical Introduction to the New Testament: Interpreting the Message and Meaning of Jesus Christ*. Nashville: Abingdon, 2005.

Holladay, Carl R. *Introduction to the New Testament: Reference Edition*. Waco, TX: Baylor University Press, 2017.

Holladay, William L. *Jeremiah 1: A Commentary on the Book of the Prophet Jeremiah, Chapters 1–25*. Hermeneia. Minneapolis: Fortress, 1986.

Holtz, Gudrun. "Zwischen Halacha und Stoa: Der subjektive Faktor in Römer 14:14 und seine soziale Funktion." In *Talking God in Society: Multidisciplinary (Re)constructions of Ancient (Con)texts; Festschrift for Peter Lampe*. Vol. 1: *Theories and Applications*, edited by Ute E. Eisen and Heidrun E. Mader, 387–404. NTOA 120/1. Göttingen: Vandenhoeck & Ruprecht, 2020.

Hooker, Morna D. *From Adam to Christ: Essays on Paul*. Eugene, OR: Wipf & Stock, 2008.

Hooker, Morna D. "On Becoming the Righteousness of God: Another Look at 2 Cor 5:21." *NovT* 50 (2008): 358–75.

hooks, bell. *Feminism Is for Everybody: Passionate Politics*. Cambridge: South End, 2000.

hooks, bell. "The Oppositional Gaze: Black Female Spectators." In *Feminist Postcolonial Theory: A Reader*, edited by Reina Lewis and Sara Mills, 207–21. New York: Routledge, 2003.

Hopkins, Keith. "Novel Evidence for Roman Slavery." *Past & Present* 138 (1993): 3–27.

Hoppin, Ruth. *Priscilla's Letter: Finding the Author of the Epistle to the Hebrews*. Fort Bragg, CA: Lost Coast Press, 1997.

Hornsby, Teresa J., and Ken Stone, eds. *Bible Trouble: Queer Reading at the Boundaries of Biblical Scholarship*. SemeiaSt 67. Atlanta: SBL, 2011.

Horrell, David G. "Domestic Space and Christian Meetings at Corinth: Imagining New Contexts and the Buildings East of the Theatre." *NTS* 50 (2004): 349–69.

Horrell, David G., Cherryl Hunt, and Christopher Southgate. *Greening Paul: Rereading the Apostle in a Time of Ecological Crisis*. Waco, TX: Baylor University Press, 2010.

Hultgren, Arland J. *Paul's Letter to the Romans: A Commentary*. Grand Rapids: Eerdmans, 2011.

Hultgren, Arland J. "Paul's Pre-Christian Persecutions of the Church: Their Purpose, Locale, and Nature." *JBL* 95 (1976): 97–111.

Hunt, Peter. "Manumission: Ancient Rome." In *Macmillan Encyclopedia of World Slavery*, edited by Paul Finkelman and Joseph C. Miller, 2:547–50. New York: Macmillan, 1998.

Ilan, Tal, Lorena Miralles-Maciá, and Ronit Nikolsky, eds. *Rabbinic Literature*. BW 4.1. Atlanta: SBL Press, 2022.

Irshai, Ronit. "Toward a Gender Critical Approach to the Philosophy of Jewish Law (Halakhah)." *JFSR* 26 (2010): 55–77.

Isasi-Díaz, Ada María. *Mujerista Theology: A Theology for the Twenty-First Century*. Maryknoll, NY: Orbis Books, 1996.

Japinga, Lynn. *From Daughters to Disciples: Women's Stories from the New Testament*. Louisville: Westminster John Knox, 2021.

Jennings, Theodore W., Jr. *The Man Jesus Loved: Homoerotic Narratives From the New Testament*. Cleveland: Pilgrim, 2003.

Jeremias, Joachim. *Abba: Studien zur neutestamentlichen Theologie und Zeitgeschichte*. Göttingen: Vandenhoeck & Ruprecht, 1966.

Jeremias, Joachim. "Ἄνθρωπος, Ἀνθρώπινος." *TDNT* 1 (1964): 364–67.

Jewett, Robert. "Are There Allusions to the Love Feast in Rom 13:8-10?" In *Common Life in the Early Church: Essays Honoring Graydon F. Snyder*, edited by Julian V. Hills et al., 265–78. Harrisburg, PA: Trinity Press International, 1998.

Jewett, Robert. *Romans: A Commentary*. Hermeneia. Minneapolis: Fortress, 2007.

Jewett, Robert. "Romans as an Ambassadorial Letter." *Int* 36 (1982): 5–20.

Jewett, Robert. *Saint Paul Returns to the Movies: Triumph over Shame*. Grand Rapids: Eerdmans, 1999.

Jobling, David. *The Sense of Biblical Narrative: Three Structural Analyses in the Old Testament*. JSOTSup 7. Sheffield: University of Sheffield Press, 1978.

Jobling, David, and Tina Pippin, eds. *Ideological Criticism of Biblical Texts*. SemeiaSt 59. Atlanta: Scholars Press, 1992.

Johnson, Elizabeth A. "God." In *Dictionary of Feminist Theologies*, edited by Letty M. Russell and J. Shannon Clarkson, 128–30. Louisville: Westminster John Knox, 1996.

Johnson, Elizabeth. *She Who Is: The Mystery of God in Feminist Theological Discourse*. New York: Crossroad, 1992.

Johnson-DeBaufre, Melanie, and Laura S. Nasrallah. "Beyond the Heroic Paul: Toward a Feminist and Decolonizing Approach to the Letters of Paul." In *The Colonized Apostle: Paul through Postcolonial Eyes*, edited by Christopher D. Stanley, 161–74. Paul in Critical Contexts. Minneapolis: Fortress, 2011.

Johnson Hodge, Caroline. "Apostle to the Gentiles: Construction of Paul's Identity." *BibInt* 13 (2005): 270–88.

Johnson Hodge, Caroline. *If Sons, Then Heirs: A Study of Kinship and Ethnicity in the Letters of Paul*. Oxford: Oxford University Press, 2007.

Johnson Hodge, Caroline. "The Question of Identity: Gentiles as Gentiles—but also Not—in Pauline Communities." In *Paul within Judaism: Restoring the First-Century Context to the Apostle*, edited by Mark D. Nanos and Magnus Zetterholm, 153–73. Minneapolis: Fortress, 2015.

Jones, Donald L. "Christianity and the Roman Imperial Cult." *ANRW* 2.23.2 (1980): 1023–54.

Junior, Nyasha. *An Introduction to Womanist Biblical Interpretation*. Louisville: Westminster John Knox, 2015.

Kahl, Brigitte. *Galatians Re-imagined: Reading with the Eyes of the Vanquished*. Paul in Critical Contexts. Minneapolis: Fortress, 2010.

Kahl, Brigitte. "Krieg, Maskulinität und der imperiale Gottvater: Das Augustusforum und die messianische Re-Imagination von 'Hagar' im Galaterbrief." In *Doing Gender—Doing Religion: Fallstudien zur Intersektionalität im frühen Judentum, Christentum und Islam*, edited by Ute E. Eisen, Christine Gerber, and Angela Standhartinger, 273–300. WUNT 302. Tübingen: Mohr Siebeck, 2013.

Kähler, Christoph. "Sklaverei: II. Neues Testament." *TRE* 31 (2000): 373–77.

Kamionkowski, S. Tamar. *Leviticus*. WCS 3. Collegeville, MN: Liturgical Press, 2018.

Käsemann, Ernst. *An die Römer*. 3rd ed. HNT 8a. Tübingen: Mohr Siebeck, 1974.

Keck, Leander E. "The Law and 'The Law of Sin and Death' (Rom 8:1-4): Reflections on the Spirit and Ethics in Paul." In *The Divine Helmsman: Studies on God's Control of Human Events, Presented to Lou H. Silberman*, edited by James L. Crenshaw and Samuel Sandmel, 41–57. New York: Ktav, 1980.

Kelber, Werner H. "Language, Memory, and Sense Perception in the Religious and Technological Culture of Antiquity and the Middle Ages." *Oral Tradition* 10 (1995): 409–50.

Kellenbach, Katharina von. *Anti-Judaism in Feminist Religious Writings*. AAR Cultural Criticism 1. Atlanta: Scholars Press, 1994.

Keller, Marie Noël. *Priscilla and Aquila: Paul's Coworkers in Christ Jesus*. Paul's Social Network: Brothers and Sisters in Faith. Collegeville, MN: Liturgical Press, 2010.

Kinukawa, Hisako. "Roundtable Discussion: Anti-Judaism and Postcolonial Biblical Interpretation; Response." *JFSR* 20 (2004): 115–18.

Kittel, Gerhard. "ἀββᾶ." *TDNT* 1 (1932): 5–6.

Kitzberger, Ingrid Rosa, ed. *Autobiographical Biblical Criticism: Between Text and Self*. Leiden: Deo, 2002.

Klauck, Hans-Josef. *Die antike Briefliteratur und das Neue Testament: Ein Lehr- und Arbeitsbuch*. UTB 2022. Paderborn: Schöningh, 1998.

Klauck, Hans-Josef. *Hausgemeinde und Hauskirche im frühen Christentum*. SBS 103. Stuttgart: Katholisches Bibelwerk, 1981.

Kleinknecht, Hermann. "πνεῦμα: A. πνεῦμα in the Greek World." *TDNT* 6 (1968): 334–59.

Kloppenborg, John S. "Associations, Christ Groups, and Their Place in the *Polis*." *ZNW* 108 (2017): 1–56.

Kobel, Esther. *Paulus als interkultureller Vermittler: Eine Studie zur kulturellen Positionierung des Apostels der Völker*. Studies in Cultural Contexts of the Bible 1. Paderborn: Brill; Schöningh, 2019.

Koester, Craig R. " 'The Savior of the World' (John 4:42)." *JBL* 109 (1990): 665–80.

Koester, Helmut. *Introduction to the New Testament*. Vol. 1: *History, Culture, and Religion of the Hellenistic Age*. Hermeneia. New York: de Gruyter, 1987.

Koester, Helmut. *Introduction to the New Testament*. Vol. 2: *History and Literature of Early Christianity*. Hermeneia. New York: de Gruyter, 1987.

Koester, Helmut. *Paul and His World: Interpreting the New Testament in Its Context*. Minneapolis: Fortress, 2007.

Koester, Helmut, and Thomas O. Lambdin. "The Gospel of Thomas (II,2)." In *The Nag Hammadi Library in English*, edited by James M. Robinson, 124–38. 3rd rev. ed. San Francisco: HarperSanFrancisco, 1990.

Koosed, Jennifer L. *Reading the Bible as a Feminist*. BRP 2/2. Leiden: Brill, 2017.

Kövecses, Zoltán. *Metaphor in Culture: Universality and Variation*. Cambridge: Cambridge University Press, 2005.

Kraemer, Ross Shepard, and Mary Rose D'Angelo, eds. *Women and Christian Origins*. New York: Oxford University Press, 1999.

Kraus, Wolfgang. *Das Volk Gottes: Zur Grundlegung der Ekklesiologie bei Paulus*. WUNT 85. Tübingen: Mohr Siebeck, 1996.

Kraus, Wolfgang. "Der Erweis der Gerechtigkeit Gottes im Tode Jesu nach Röm 3,21-26." In *Judaistik und Neutestamentliche Wissenschaft: Standorte—Grenzen*

—*Beziehungen*, edited by Lutz Doering, Hans-Günther Waubke, and Florian Wilk, 192–216. FRLANT 226. Göttingen: Vandenhoeck & Ruprecht, 2008.

Kraus, Wolfgang. *Der Tod Jesu als Heiligtumsweihe: Eine Untersuchung zum Umfeld der Sühnevorstellung im Römer 3,25-26a*. WMANT 66. Neukirchen-Vluyn: Neukirchener Verlag, 1991.

Kraus, Wolfgang. "Die Bedeutung von Römer 9–11 im christlich-jüdischen Gespräch." In *Between Gospel and Election: Explorations in the Interpretation of Romans 9–11*, edited by Florian Wilk and J. Ross Wagner with the assistance of Frank Schleritt, 505–23. WUNT 257. Tübingen: Mohr Siebeck, 2010.

Kraus, Wolfgang. "Jesaja 53 LXX im frühen Christentum—eine Überprüfung." In *Beiträge zur urchristlichen Theologiegeschichte*, edited by Wolfgang Kraus, 149–82. BZNW 163. Berlin: de Gruyter, 2009.

Krauter, Stefan. "Mercy and Monarchy: Seneca's *De clementia* and Paul's Letter to the Romans." *NovT* 63 (2021): 477–88.

Krentz, Edgar. "The Sense of Senseless Oxymora." *CurTM* 28 (2001): 577–84.

Kujanpää, Katja. *The Rhetorical Functions of Scriptural Quotations in Romans: Paul's Argumentation by Quotations*. NovTSup 172. Leiden; Boston: Brill, 2010.

LaCugna, Catherine Mowry. *God for Us: The Trinity and Christian Life*. San Francisco: HarperCollins, 1991.

Lakey, Michael J. *The Ritual World of Paul the Apostle: Metaphysics, Community and Symbol in 1 Corinthians 10–11*. LNTS 602. London: T&T Clark, 2019.

Lambrecht, Jan. "The Line of Thought in Romans 7,15-20." *Bib* 85 (2004): 393–98.

Lambrecht, Jan. "No Longer a Distinction Between Jew and Greek: A Critical Reflection on Romans 9,30–10,13." In *Paul's Graeco-Roman Context*, edited by Cilliers Breytenbach, 487–96. BETL 277. Leuven: Peeters, 2015.

Lambrecht, Jan. *The Wretched "I" and Its Liberation: Paul in Romans 7 and 8*. Louvain Theological & Pastoral Monographs 14. Louvain: Peeters, 1992.

Lampe, Peter. "Aquila." *ABD* 1 (1992): 319–20.

Lampe, Peter. *Die stadtrömischen Christen in den ersten beiden Jahrhunderten: Untersuchungen zur Sozialgeschichte*. 2nd ed. WUNT 2/18. Tübingen: Mohr Siebeck, 1989.

Lampe, Peter. "Paul, Patrons, and Clients." In *Paul in the Greco-Roman World: A Handbook*, edited by J. Paul Sampley, 2:204–38. 2nd ed. London: Bloomsbury, 2016.

Lampe, Peter. "Prisca/Priscilla." *ABD* 5 (1992): 467–68.

Lampe, Peter. "Roman Christians under Nero (54–68 CE)." In *The Last Years of Paul: Essays from the Tarragona Conference, June 2013*, edited by Armand Puig i Tàrrech, John M. G. Barclay, and Jörg Frey with the assistance of Orrey McFarland, 111–29. WUNT 352. Tübingen: Mohr Siebeck, 2015.

Lampe, Peter. "The Roman Christians of Romans 16." In *The Romans Debate*, edited by Karl P. Donfried, 216–30. Rev. exp. ed. Peabody, MA: Hendrickson, 1991.

Lampe, Peter. "Zur Textgeschichte des Römerbriefes." *NovT* 27 (1985): 273–77.

Lee, Eunny P. *The Vitality of Enjoyment in Qohelet's Theological Rhetoric*. BZAW 353. Berlin: de Gruyter, 2005.

Légasse, Simon. *L'Épître de Paul aux Romains*. LD 10. Paris: Cerf, 2002.

Lehtipuu, Outi, and Silke Petersen, eds. *Ancient Christian Apocrypha*. BW 3.2. Atlanta: SBL Press, 2022.

Lémonon, Jean-Pierre. *Les épîtres de Paul: II Romains, Galates*. Commentaires. Paris: Bayard, 1996.

Lenski, Richard C. H. *The Interpretation of St. Paul's Epistle to the Romans 1–7*. Columbus, OH: Wartburg Press, 1945.

Leon, Harry J. *The Jews of Ancient Rome*. Morris Loeb. Philadelphia: Jewish Publication Society, 1960/5721.

Lerner, Gerda. *The Creation of Feminist Consciousness: From the Middle Ages to Eighteen-Seventy*. Women and History 2. New York: Oxford University Press, 1993.

Levine, Amy-Jill. "The Disease of Postcolonial New Testament Studies and the Hermeneutics of Healing." *JFSR* 20 (2004): 91–99.

Levine, Amy-Jill. *The Misunderstood Jew: The Church and the Scandal of the Jewish Jesus*. San Francisco, CA: HarperSanFrancisco, 2006.

Levison, John R. *Portraits of Adam in Early Judaism: From Sirach to 2 Baruch*. JSPSup 1. Sheffield: JSOT Press, 1988.

Lichtenberger, Hermann. *Das Ich Adams und das Ich der Menschheit: Studien zum Menschenbild in Römer 7*. WUNT 164. Tübingen: Mohr Siebeck, 2004.

Lichtenberger, Hermann. "Der Beginn der Auslegungsgeschichte von Römer 7: Röm 7,25b." *ZNW* 88 (1997): 284–95.

Lichtenberger, Hermann. "Jews and Christians in Rome in the Time of Nero: Josephus and Paul in Rome." *ANRW* 2.26.3 (1996): 2142–76.

Liebert, Donald H. "The 'Apostolic Form of Writing': Group Letters Before and After 1 Corinthians." In *The Corinthian Correspondence*, edited by Reimund Bieringer, 433–40. BETL 125. Leuven: Leuven University Press, 1996.

Lieu, Judith M. "Circumcision, Women and Salvation." *NTS* 40 (1994): 358–70.

Lim, Kar Yong. " 'For All of You Are One in Christ Jesus' (Gal 3:28): Paul's Social Vision Beyond Inclusivity and Diversity." In *From Malaysia to the Ends of the Earth: Southeast Asian and Diasporic Contributions to Biblical and Theological Studies*, edited by Elaine Wei-Fun Goh, Kah-Jin Jeffrey Kuan, Jonathan Yun-Ka Tan, and Amos Wai-Ming Yong, 83–116. Claremont, CA: Claremont Press, 2021.

Lin, Yii-Jan. "Junia: An Apostle before Paul." *JBL* 139 (2020): 191–209.

Loader, William. "Homosexuality: IV. Judaism." *EBR* 12 (2016): 301–3.

Loader, William. "Reading Romans 1 on Homosexuality in the Light of Biblical/Jewish and Greco-Roman Perspectives of Its Time." *ZNW* 108 (2017): 119–49.

Longenecker, Bruce W. "What Did Paul Think Is Wrong in God's World?" In *The New Cambridge Companion to St. Paul*, edited by Bruce W. Longenecker, 171–86. Cambridge Companions to Religion. Cambridge: Cambridge University Press, 2020.

Longenecker, Richard N. *The Epistle to the Romans: A Commentary on the Greek Text*. NIGTC. Grand Rapids: Eerdmans, 2016.

Lopez, Davina. "Before Your Very Eyes: Roman Imperial Ideology, Gender Constructs, and Paul's Inter-Nationalism." In *Mapping Gender in Ancient Religious Discourses*, edited by Todd Penner and Caroline Vander Stichele, 115–62. BibInt 84. Leiden: Brill, 2006.

Loubser, Johannes A. "Media Criticism and the Myth of Paul, the Creative Genius, and His Forgotten Co-workers." *Neot* 34 (2000): 329–45.

Loughlin, Gerard. "Pauline Conversations: Rereading Romans 1 in Christ." *Theology and Sexuality* 11 (2004): 72–102.

Love, Stuart L. "Jesus Heals the Hemorrhaging Woman." In *The Social Setting of Jesus and the Gospels*, edited by Wolfgang Stegemann, Bruce J. Malina, and Gerd Theissen, 85–102. Minneapolis: Fortress, 2002.

Luz, Ulrich. *Matthew 1–7: A Commentary*. Translated by James E. Crouch. Hermeneia. Rev. ed. Minneapolis: Fortress, 2007.

MacDonald, Margaret Y. "Paul and Family Life." In *Paul in the Greco-Roman World: A Handbook*, edited by J. Paul Sampley, 1:254–81. 2nd ed. London: Bloomsbury, 2016.

MacGillivray, Erlend D. "Romans 16:2, προστάτις/προστάτης, and the Application of Reciprocal Relationships to New Testament Texts." *NovT* 53 (2011): 183–99.

Maier, Christl M., and Nuria Calduch-Benages, eds. *The Writings and Later Wisdom Books*. BW 1.3. Atlanta: SBL Press, 2014.

Maier, Christl M., and Carolyn J. Sharp. *Prophecy and Power: Jeremiah in Feminist and Postcolonial Perspective*. London: Bloomsbury, 2013.

Maier, Harry O. "Barbarians, Scythians and Imperial Iconography in the Epistle to the Colossians." In *Picturing the New Testament: Studies in Ancient Visual Images*, edited by Annette Weissenrieder, Friederike Wendt, and Petra von Gemünden, 385–406. WUNT 2/193. Tübingen: Mohr Siebeck, 2005.

Maillot, Alphonse. *L'épître aux Romains: Epître de l'œcuménisme et théologie de l'histoire*. Paris: Le Centurion; Geneva: Labor et Fides, 1984.

Malbon, Elizabeth Struthers, and Edgar V. McKnight, eds. *The New Literary Criticism and the New Testament*. JSNTSup 109. Sheffield: JSOT Press, 1994.

Malina, Bruce J., and John J. Pilch. *Social-Science Commentary on the Letters of Paul*. Minneapolis: Fortress, 2006.

Maloney, Linda M. *Acts of the Apostles*. WCS 45. Collegeville, MN: Liturgical Press, 2022.

Marchal, Joseph A. "The Disgusting Apostle and a Queer Affect between Epistles and Audiences." In *Reading with Feeling: Affect Theory and the Bible*, edited by Fiona C. Black and Jennifer L. Koosed, 113–40. SemeiaSt 95. Atlanta: SBL Press, 2019.

Marchal, Joseph A. "Queer Studies and Critical Masculinity Studies in Feminist Biblical Studies." In *Feminist Biblical Studies in the Twentieth Century: Scholar-*

ship and Movement, edited by Elisabeth Schüssler Fiorenza, 261–80. BW 9.1. Atlanta: SBL Press, 2014.

Marcus, Joel. "The Circumcision and the Uncircumcision in Rome." *NTS* 35 (1989): 67–81.

Marshall, Jill E. "The Recovery of Paul's Female Colleagues in Nineteenth-Century Feminist Biblical Interpretation." *JFSR* 33 (2017): 21–36.

Marshall, John W. "Hybridity and Reading Romans 13." *JSNT* 31 (2008): 157–78.

Martin, Brice L. "Some Reflections on the Identity of the ἐγώ in Rom. 7:14-25." *SJT* 34 (1981): 39–47.

Martin, Clarice J. "Womanist Interpretations of the New Testament: The Quest for Holistic and Inclusive Translation and Interpretation." *JFSR* 6 (1990): 41–61.

Martin, Josef. *Antike Rhetorik: Technik und Methode*. Munich: Beck, 1974.

Mason, Steve. *Josephus, Judea, and Christian Origins: Methods and Categories*. Peabody, MA: Hendrickson, 2009.

Matera, Frank J. *God's Saving Grace: A Pauline Theology*. Grand Rapids: Eerdmans, 2012.

Matera, Frank J. *Romans*. Paideia: Commentaries on the New Testament. Grand Rapids: Baker Academic, 2010.

Mathew, Susan. *Women in the Greetings of Romans 16.1-16: A Study of Mutuality and Women's Ministry in the Letter to the Romans*. LNTS 471. London: T&T Clark, 2013.

Matta, Yara. *À cause du Christ: Le retournement de Paul le Juif*. Lectio Divina 56. Paris: Cerf, 2013.

Mayer, Günter. "Midrasch/Midraschim." *TRE* 22 (1992): 734–44.

Mayer-Schärtel, Bärbel. "Erlösung durch Selbsterniedrigung? Feministische Anfragen an die traditionelle Soteriologie." In *Abschied von der Schuld? Zur Anthropologie und Theologie von Schuldbekenntnis, Opfer und Versöhnung*, edited by Richard Riess, 170–79. Stuttgart: Kohlhammer, 1996.

McCabe, Elizabeth A. "A Reevaluation of Phoebe in Romans 16:1-2 as a *Diakonos* and *Prostasis*: Exposing the Inaccuracies of English Translations." In *Women in the Biblical World: A Survey of Old and New Testament Perspectives*, edited by Elizabeth A. McCabe, 99–116. Lanham, MD: University Press of America, 2009.

McClure, Laura. " 'The Worst Husband': Discourses of Praise and Blame in Euripides' Medea." *CP* 94 (1999): 373–94.

McCormick, Donald W. "Spirituality and Management." *Journal of Managerial Psychology* 9 (1994): 5–8.

McFague, Sallie. *Models of God: Theology for an Ecological, Nuclear Age*. Philadelphia: Fortress, 1987.

McGinn, Sheila E. "Feminist Approaches to Paul's Letter to the Romans." In *Celebrating Romans: Template for Pauline Theology; Essays in Honor of Robert Jewett*, edited by Sheila E. McGinn, 165–76. Grand Rapids: Eerdmans, 2004.

McKinlay, Judith E. *Reframing Her: Biblical Women in Postcolonial Focus.* Sheffield: Sheffield Phoenix, 2004.

Meeks, Wayne A. *The First Urban Christians: The Social World of the Apostle Paul.* New Haven: Yale University Press, 1983.

Merz, Annette. "Phöbe, Diakon(in) der Gemeinde von Kenchreä—Eine wichtige Mitstreiterin des Paulus neu entdeckt." In *Frauen gestalten Diakonie.* Vol. 1: *Von der biblischen Zeit bis zum Pietismus*, edited by Adelheid M. van Hauff, 125–40. Stuttgart: Kohlhammer, 2007.

Methuen, Charlotte, Irmtraud Fischer, Mercedes Navarro Puerto, and Adriana Valerio, eds. The Bible and Women: An Encyclopaedia of Exegesis and Cultural History (BW). https://www.bibleandwomen.org.

Metzger, Bruce M. *A Textual Commentary on the Greek New Testament: A Companion Volume to the United Bible Societies' Greek New Testament*. 3rd ed. New York: United Bible Societies, 1975.

Meyers, Carol. *Rediscovering Eve: Ancient Israelite Women in Context.* New York: Oxford University Press, 2013.

Meyers, Carol, Toni Craven, and Ross S. Kraemer, eds. *Women in Scripture: A Dictionary of Named and Unnamed Women in the Hebrew Bible, the Apocryphal/ Deuterocanonical Books, and the New Testament.* Boston: Houghton Mifflin, 2000/Grand Rapids: Eerdmans, 2001.

Miller, David M. "Ioudaios, Ioudaioi." *EBR* 13 (2016): 234–35.

Miller, James E. "The Practices of Romans 1:26: Homosexual or Heterosexual?" *NovT* 37 (1995): 1–11.

Millis, Benjamin W. "The Social and Ethnic Origins of the Colonists in Early Roman Corinth." In *Corinth in Context: Comparative Studies on Religion and Society*, edited by Steven J. Friesen, Daniel N. Schowalter, and James C. Walters, 13–35. NovTSup 134. Leiden: Brill, 2010.

Mitchem, Stephanie Y. "Thinking about Feminist Leadership." *JFSR* 25 (2009): 197–201.

Mitchem, Stephanie Y. "Womanists and (Unfinished) Constructions of Salvation." *JFSR* 17 (2001): 85–100.

Mittmann, Ulrike. *Die Weisheit und der Gottessohn: Studien zur hermeneutischen Grundlegung einer Theologie des Neuen Testaments*. WUNT 462. Tübingen: Mohr Siebeck, 2021.

Moeller, Bernd, and Karl Stackmann. *Luder—Luther—Eleutherius: Erwägungen zu Luthers Namen*. Göttingen: Vandenhoeck & Ruprecht, 1981.

Mollenkott, Virginia Ramey. *The Divine Feminine: The Biblical Imagery of God as Feminine*. New York: Crossroad, 1983.

Moo, Douglas J. *The Epistle to the Romans*. NICNT. Grand Rapids: Eerdmans, 1996.

Moore, Stephen D. *The Bible in Theory: Critical and Postcritical Essays.* Atlanta: SBL, 2010.

Moore, Stephen D. *God's Beauty Parlor: And Other Queer Spaces in and around the Bible*. Contraversions. Stanford: Stanford University Press, 2001.

Moore, Stephen D. *Poststructuralism and the New Testament: Derrida and Foucault at the Foot of the Cross.* Minneapolis: Fortress, 1994.

Morgan, Teresa. *Roman Faith and Christian Faith:* Pistis *and* Fides *in the Early Roman Empire and Early Churches*. Oxford: Oxford University Press, 2015.

Moxnes, Halvor. "Honor and Shame." In *The Social Sciences and New Testament Interpretation*, edited by Richard L. Rohrbaugh, 19–40. Peabody, MA: Hendrickson, 1996.

Mtata, Kenneth. "The 'Gospel' as the Hermeneutic of Emancipation in Paul's Letters: Contemporary Implications." In *Pauline Hermeneutics: Exploring the "Power of the Gospel,"* edited by Eve-Marie Becker and Kenneth Mtata, 13–24. LWF Studies 2016/3. Leipzig: Evangelische Verlagsanstalt, 2017.

Mukuka, Tarcisius. "Reading/Hearing Romans 13:1-7 under an African Tree: Towards a *Lectio Postcolonica Contexta Africana*." *Neot* 46 (2012): 105–38.

Müller, Mogens. "Die Bedeutung der Septuaginta für die Entfaltung neutestamentlicher Theologie." In *Die Septuaginta—Geschichte, Wirkung, Relevanz: 6. Internationale Fachtagung veranstaltet von Septuaginta Deutsch (LXX.D), Wuppertal 21.–24. Juli 2016*, edited by Martin Meiser et al., 730–56. WUNT 405. Tübingen: Mohr Siebeck, 2018.

Munro, Ealasaid. "Feminism: A Fourth Wave?" *Political Insight* (September 2013): 22–25. https://journals.sagepub.com/doi/pdf/10.1111/2041-9066.12021.

Munro, Winsome. "Romans 13:1–7: Apartheid's Last Biblical Refuge." *BTB* 20 (1990): 161–68.

Murphy-O'Connor, Jerome. *Paul: His Story*. Oxford: Oxford University Press, 2004.

Murphy-O'Connor, Jerome. "Review of *Paul and First-Century Letter Writing: Secretaries, Composition and Collection* by E. Randolph Richards." *RB* 112 (2005): 628–33.

Murphy-O'Connor, Jerome. *St. Paul's Corinth: Texts and Archeology*. GNS 6. Wilmington, DE: Glazier, 1983.

Myers, William H. "The Hermeneutical Dilemma of the African American Biblical Student." In *Stony the Road We Trod: African American Biblical Interpretation*, edited by Cain Hope Felder, 40–56. Minneapolis: Fortress, 1991.

Naiden, Fred S. *Smoke Signals for the Gods: Ancient Greek Sacrifice from the Archaic through Roman Periods*. Oxford: Oxford University Press, 2013.

Nanos, Mark D. "'Broken Branches': A Pauline Metaphor Gone Awry? (Romans 11:11-24)." In *Between Gospel and Election: Explorations in the Interpretation of Romans 9–11*, edited by Florian Wilk and J. Ross Wagner with the assistance of Frank Schleritt, 339–76. WUNT 257. Tübingen: Mohr Siebeck, 2010.

Nanos, Mark D. "Romans." In *The Jewish Annotated New Testament: New Revised Standard Version Bible Translation*, edited by Amy-Jill Levine and Marc Zvi Brettler, 253–86. Oxford: Oxford University Press, 2011.

Nash, Jennifer C. "Re-Thinking Intersectionality." *Feminist Review* 89 (2008): 1–15.

Nasrallah, Laura S. *Archaeology and the Letters of Paul*. Oxford: Oxford University Press, 2019.

Navarro Puerto, Mercedes, and Marinella Perroni, eds.; Amy-Jill Levine, English ed. *Gospels: Narrative and History*. BW 2.1. Atlanta: SBL Press, 2015.

Neumeister, Christoff. "Urban Culture in Ancient Rome." *Anthropological Journal on European Cultures* 2 (1993): 21–37.

Neutel, Karin B. *A Cosmopolitan Ideal: Paul's Declaration "Neither Jew Nor Greek, Neither Slave Nor Free, Nor Male and Female" in the Context of First-Century Thought*. LNTS 513. London: T&T Clark, 2015.

Newman, Barbara. *Sister of Wisdom: St. Hildegard's Theology of the Feminine*. Berkeley: University of California Press, 1987.

Nicolet Anderson, Valérie. "Une relecture paulinienne de l'histoire d'Israël (Rm 9–11)." In *Ancient and Modern Scriptural Historiography = L'historiographie biblique, ancienne et modern*, edited by George J. Brooke and Thomas Römer, 269–81. BETL 207. Leuven: Leuven University Press; Peeters, 2007.

Niditch, Susan. *"My Brother Esau Is a Hairy Man": Hair and Identity in Ancient Israel*. New York: Oxford University Press, 2008.

Niebuhr, Karl-Wilhelm. "Juden in Rom unter Nero: Intellektuelle Netzwerke, religiöse Praxis, geistige Horizonte." In *Tempel, Lehrhaus, Synagoge: Orte jüdischen Lernens und Lebens; Festschrift für Wolfgang Kraus*, edited by Christian Eberhart et al., 289–321. Paderborn: Brill; Schöningh, 2020.

Niehoff, Maren R. "A Roman Portrait of Abraham in Paul's and Philo's Later Exegesis." *NovT* 63 (2021): 452–76.

Niepert-Rumel, Sophia. *Metaphernkombinationen in der neutestamentlichen Rede vom Tod Jesu*. WUNT 2/563. Tübingen: Mohr Siebeck, 2021.

Nissinen, Martti. "Are There Homosexuals in Mesopotamian Literature?" *JAOS* 130 (2010): 73–77.

Nissinen, Martti. "Homosexuality: I. Ancient Near East and the Hebrew Bible/Old Testament." *EBR* 12 (2016): 290–97.

Novenson, Matthew V. "Did Paul Abandon either Judaism or Monotheism?" In *The New Cambridge Companion to St. Paul*, edited by Bruce W. Longenecker, 239–59. Cambridge Companions to Religion. Cambridge: Cambridge University Press, 2020.

Novenson, Matthew V. "The Self-Styled Jew of Romans 2 and the Actual Jews of Romans 9–11." In *The So-Called Jew in Paul's Letter to the Romans*, edited by Rafael Rodríguez and Matthew Thiessen, 133–62. Minneapolis: Fortress, 2016.

Nowell, Irene. *Women in the Old Testament*. Collegeville, MN: Liturgical Press, 1997.

Noy, David. "'A Sight Unfit to See': Jewish Reactions to the Roman Imperial Cult." *Classics Ireland* 8 (2001): 68–83.

Oakes, Peter. "Constructing Poverty Scales for Graeco-Roman Society: A Response to Steven Friesen's 'Poverty in Pauline Studies.'" *JSNT* 26 (2004): 367–71.

Oakes, Peter. *Galatians*. Paideia: Commentaries on the New Testament. Grand Rapids: Baker Academic, 2015.

Oakes, Peter. "Galatians and Romans." In *The New Cambridge Companion to St. Paul*, edited by Bruce W. Longenecker, 92–118. Cambridge Companions to Religion. Cambridge: Cambridge University Press, 2020.

Oakes, Peter. *Reading Romans in Pompeii: Paul's Letter at Ground Level*. Minneapolis: Fortress; London: SPCK, 2009.

Oestreich, Bernhard. *Performanzkritik der Paulusbriefe*. WUNT 296. Tübingen: Mohr Siebeck, 2012.

Ollrog, Wolf-Henning. *Paulus und seine Mitarbeiter: Untersuchungen zu Theorie und Praxis der paulinischen Mission*. WMANT 50. Neukirchen-Vluyn: Neukirchener Verlag, 1979.

O'Neill, John C. *Paul's Letter to the Romans*. PNTC. Harmondsworth: Penguin, 1975.

Osiek, Carolyn. "Romans 'Down the Pike': Glimpses from Later Years." In *Celebrating Romans: Template for Pauline Theology; Essays in Honor of Robert Jewett*, edited by Sheila E. McGinn, 149–61. Grand Rapids: Eerdmans, 2004.

Osiek, Carolyn, and Margaret Y. MacDonald. *A Woman's Place: House Churches in Earliest Christianity*. Minneapolis: Fortress, 2006.

Osten-Sacken, Peter von der. *Die Heiligkeit der Tora: Studien zum Gesetz bei Paulus*. München: Kaiser, 1989.

Packer, James I. "The 'Wretched Man' Revisited: Another Look at Romans 7:14-25." In *Romans and the People of God: Essays in Honor of Gordon D. Fee on the Occasion of His 65th Birthday*, edited by Sven K. Soderlund and Nicholas T. Wright, 70–81. Grand Rapids: Eerdmans, 1999.

Paiva Bondioli, Nelson de. "Roman Religion in the Time of Augustus." *Numen* 64 (2017): 49–63.

Park, Andrew Sung. *The Wounded Heart of God: The Asian Concept of Han and the Christian Doctrine of Sin*. Nashville: Abingdon, 1993.

Parker, Angela N. "One Womanist's View of Racial Reconciliation in Galatians." *JFSR* 34 (2018): 23–40.

Parmentier, Élisabeth. *Les filles prodigues: Défis des théologies féministes*. Lieux théologiques 32. Geneva: Labor et Fides, 1998.

Patterson, Orlando. *Freedom in the Making of Western Culture*. Freedom 1. New York: Basic Books, 1991.

Patterson, Orlando. "Paul, Slavery and Freedom: Personal and Socio-Historical Reflections." *Semeia* 83/84 (1998): 263–79.

Patterson, Orlando. "Slavery." *Annual Review of Sociology* 3 (1977): 407–49.

Patterson, Orlando. *Slavery and Social Death: A Comparative Study*. Cambridge, MA: Harvard University Press, 1982.

Pavón, Pilar. "La femme: Objet et sujet de la justice romaine." In *The Impact of Justice on the Roman Empire: Proceedings of the Thirteenth Workshop of the International Network Impact of Empire (Gent, June 21–24, 2017)*, edited by Olivier

Hekster and Koenraad Verboven, 196–211. Impact of Empire 34. Leiden; Boston: Brill, 2019.

Penchansky, David. "Deconstruction." In *The Oxford Encyclopedia of Biblical Interpretation*, edited by Steven McKenzie, 196–205. New York: Oxford University Press, 2013.

Penna, Romano. "Évangile et politique à Rome selon Paul et son Épître aux Romains." In *Talking God in Society: Multidisciplinary (Re)constructions of Ancient (Con)texts; Festschrift for Peter Lampe*. Vol. 1: *Theories and Applications*, edited by Ute E. Eisen and Heidrun E. Mader, 281–306. NTOA 120/1. Göttingen: Vandenhoeck & Ruprecht, 2020.

Penna, Romano. "Les Juifs à Rome au temps de l'apôtre Paul." *NTS* 28 (1982): 321–47.

Perkins, Pheme. "Adam and Christ in the Pauline Epistles." In *Celebrating Paul: Festschrift in Honor of Jerome Murphy-O'Connor, OP, and Joseph A. Fitzmyer, SJ*, edited by Peter Spitaler, 128–51. CBQMS 48. Washington, DC: Catholic Biblical Association of America, 2011.

Peterson, David G. *Romans*. EBTC. Bellingham, WA: Lexham Press, 2020.

Phelps, Mark A. "Nero, the Emperor." *Dictionary of the Bible and Western Culture*, edited by Mary Ann Beavis and Michael J. Gilmour, 363–64. Sheffield: Sheffield Phoenix, 2012.

Philippe, Bernard. "Partager sa propre expérience de réconciliation? Réflexion sur l'Europe et la paix." *Bulletin du Centre de recherche français à Jérusalem* 25 (2014): 1–8. https://journals.openedition.org/bcrfj/7350.

Plaskow, Judith. "Anti-Judaism in Feminist Christian Interpretation." In *Searching the Scriptures: A Feminist Introduction*, vol. 1, edited by Elisabeth Schüssler Fiorenza with the assistance of Shelly Matthews, 117–29. New York: Crossroad, 1993.

Plaskow, Judith. "Bringing a Daughter into the Covenant." In *WomanSpirit Rising: A Feminist Reader in Religion*, edited by Carol P. Christ and Judith Plaskow, 179–84. New York: HarperOne, 1992.

Plaskow, Judith. *Standing Again at Sinai: Judaism from a Feminist Perspective*. San Francisco: HarperSanFrancisco, 1991.

Polomé, Edgar C. "The Linguistic Situation in the Western Provinces of the Roman Empire." *ANRW* 2.29.2 (1983): 509–53.

Porton, Gary G. "Defining Midrash." In *The Study of Ancient Israel: I Mishnah, Midrash, Siddur*, edited by Jacob Neusner, 55–92. New York: KTAV, 1981.

Pui-lan, Kwok. *Postcolonial Imagination and Feminist Theology*. Louisville: Westminster John Knox, 2005.

Pui-lan, Kwok. "Roundtable Discussion: Anti-Judaism and Postcolonial Biblical Interpretation; Response." *JFSR* 20 (2004): 99–106.

Quesnel, Michel. *La première épître aux Corinthiens*. Commentaire biblique. Nouveau Testament 7. Paris: Cerf, 2018.

Räisänen, Heikki. *Paul and the Law*. WUNT 29. Tübingen: Mohr Siebeck, 1983.

Rampton, Martha. "Four Waves of Feminism." October 25, 2015. https://www.pacificu.edu/magazine/four-waves-feminism.

Reasoner, Mark. "The Redemptive Inversions of Jeremiah in Romans 9–11." *Bib* 95 (2014): 388–404.

Reasoner, Mark. *The Strong and the Weak: Romans 14.1–15.13 in Context*. SNTSMS 103. Cambridge: Cambridge University Press, 1999.

Reay, Lewis. "Towards a Transgender Theology: Que(e)rying the Eunuchs." In *Trans/Formations*, edited by Marcella Althaus-Reid and Lisa Isherwood, 148–67. London: SCM Press, 2009.

Rector, Lallene J. "Shame and Honor Systems in the Book of Romans: A Psychological Analysis of the Struggle for Superiority within and between the Roman Tenement and House Churches." In *Scripture, Cultures, and Criticism: Interpretive Steps and Critical Issues Raised by Robert Jewett*, edited by Khiok-khng Yeo, 117–29. Contrapuntal Readings of the Bible in World Christianity 9. Eugene, OR: Pickwick, 2022.

Reichert, Angelika. *Der Römerbrief als Gratwanderung: Eine Untersuchung zur Abfassungsproblematik*. FRLANT 194. Göttingen: Vandenhoeck & Ruprecht, 2001.

Reid, Barbara E., and Shelly Matthews. *Luke 1–9*. WCS 43A. Collegeville, MN: Liturgical Press, 2021.

Renton, Jane. *Coaching and Mentoring: What They Are and How to Make the Most of Them*. Economist Books. New York: Bloomberg, 2009.

Ress, Mary Judith. *Ecofeminism in Latin America*. Women from the Margins. Maryknoll, NY: Orbis Books, 2006.

Reynier, Chantal. *Les femmes de saint Paul: Collaboratrices de l'apôtre des nations*. Paris: Cerf, 2020.

Reynier, Chantal. *Vie et mort de Paul à Rome*. Paris: Cerf, 2016.

Rhoads, David. "Performance Criticism: An Emerging Methodology in Second Testament Studies." *BTB* 36 (2006): 118–33, 164–84.

Ribbens, Benjamin J. *Levitical Sacrifice and Heavenly Cult in Hebrews*. BZNW 222. Berlin: de Gruyter, 2016.

Richards, E. Randolph. *Paul and First-Century Letter Writing: Secretaries, Composition and Collection*. Downers Grove, IL: InterVarsity, 2004.

Richards, E. Randolph. *The Secretary in the Letters of Paul*. WUNT 2/42. Tübingen: Mohr Siebeck, 1991.

Richardson, Peter. *Building Jewish in the Roman East*. JSJSup 92. Waco, TX: Baylor University Press, 2004.

Richter Reimer, Ivoni. *Women in the Acts of the Apostles: A Feminist Liberation Perspective*. Translated by Linda M. Maloney. Minneapolis: Fortress, 1995.

Ringe, Sharon H. "When Women Interpret the Bible." In *Women's Bible Commentary,* edited by Carol A. Newsom, Sharon H. Ringe, and Jacqueline E. Lapsley, 1–9. 3rd ed. Louisville: Westminster John Knox, 2012.

Robinson, O. F. "Ancient Rome." In *Macmillan Encyclopedia of World Slavery*, edited by Paul Finkelman and Joseph C. Miller, 1:70–77. New York: Macmillan, 1998.

Rogers, Jack. *Jesus, the Bible, and Homosexuality: Explode the Myths, Heal the Church*. Rev. exp. ed. Louisville: Westminster John Knox, 2009.

Romney Wegner, Judith. *Chattel or Person? The Status of Women in the Mishnah*. New York: Oxford University Press, 1988.

Ronan, Marian. "Ethical Challenges Confronting the Roman Catholic Women's Ordination Movement in the Twenty-First Century." *JFSR* 23 (2007): 149–69.

Rösel, Martin. *Adonaj—warum Gott 'Herr' genannt wird*. FAT 29. Tübingen: Mohr Siebeck, 2000.

Rosen-Zvi, Ishay, and Adi Ophir. "Paul and the Invention of the Gentiles." *JQR* 105 (2015): 1–41.

Roth, Dieter T. "Marcion." *EBR* 17 (2019): 880–83.

Ruether, Rosemary Radford. *Sexism and God-Talk: Toward a Feminist Theology*. Boston: Beacon, 1993.

Rüggemeier, Jan. "Ein Streifzug durch Roms Gassen und Viertel: Subjektorientierte Perspektiven auf die stadtrömischen Christinnen und Christen im ersten Jahrhundert." In *Talking God in Society: Multidisciplinary (Re)constructions of Ancient (Con)texts; Festschrift for Peter Lampe*. Vol. 1: *Theories and Applications*, edited by Ute E. Eisen and Heidrun E. Mader, 307–38. NTOA 120/1. Göttingen: Vandenhoeck & Ruprecht, 2020.

Rutledge, David. *Reading Marginally: Feminism, Deconstruction and the Bible*. BibInt 21. Leiden: Brill, 1996.

Sakenfeld, Katharine Doob. *Just Wives? Stories of Power and Survival in the Old Testament and Today*. Louisville: Westminster John Knox, 2003.

Saller, Richard P. "Poverty, Honor and Obligation in Imperial Rome." *Criterion* 37 (1998): 12–20.

Sampley, J. Paul. "Living in an Evil Aeon: Paul's Ambiguous Relation to Culture (Toward a Taxonomy)." In *Paul in the Greco-Roman World: A Handbook*, edited by J. Paul Sampley, 2:391–432. 2nd ed. London: Bloomsbury, 2016.

Sampley, J. Paul, ed. *Paul in the Greco-Roman World: A Handbook*. 2 vols. 2nd ed. London: Bloomsbury, 2016.

Sampley, J. Paul. *Walking between the Times: Paul's Moral Reasoning*. Minneapolis: Fortress, 1991.

Sanders, Ed P. *Paul*. Oxford: Oxford University Press, 1991.

Schaumberger, Christine. "Subversive Bekehrung, Schulderkenntnis, Schwesterlichkeit, Frauenmacht: Irritierende und inspirierende Grundmotive kritisch-feministischer Befreiungstheologie." In *Schuld und Macht: Studien zu einer feministischen Befreiungstheologie*, edited by Christine Schaumberger and Luise Schottroff, 153–288. München: Kaiser, 1988.

Scheid, John. "Augustus and Roman Religion: Continuity, Conservatism, and Innovation." In *The Cambridge Companion to the Age of Augustus*, edited by

Karl Galinsky, 175–94. Cambridge Companion to the Classics. Cambridge: Cambridge University Press, 2005.

Scheidel, Walter. "The Comparative Economics of Slavery in the Greco-Roman World." In *Slave Systems: Ancient and Modern*, edited by Enrico Dal Lago and Constantina Katsari, 105–26. Cambridge: Cambridge University Press, 2008.

Schellenberg, Ryan S. "Οἱ Πιστεύοντες: An Early Christ-Group Self-Designation and Paul's Rhetoric of Faith." *NTS* 65 (2019): 33–42.

Schleritt, Frank. "Das Gesetz der Gerechtigkeit: Zur Auslegung von Römer 9,30-33." In *Between Gospel and Election: Explorations in the Interpretation of Romans 9–11*, edited by Florian Wilk and J. Ross Wagner with the assistance of Frank Schleritt, 271–97. WUNT 257. Tübingen: Mohr Siebeck, 2010.

Schlier, Heinrich. *Der Römerbrief*. HTKNT 6. Freiburg: Herder, 1977.

Schmid, Ulrich. "Marcion and the Textual History of Romans: Editorial Activity and Early Editions of the New Testament." In *Studia Patristica*. Vol. 54/2: *Biblical Quotations in Patristic Texts*, edited by Laurence Mellerin and Hugh A. G. Houghton, 99–113. Leuven: Peeters, 2013.

Schneiders, Sandra M. *The Revelatory Text: Interpreting the New Testament as Sacred Scripture*. Rev. ed. Collegeville, MN: Liturgical Press, 1999.

Schnelle, Udo. *The First One Hundred Years of Christianity: An Introduction to Its History, Literature, and Development*. Translated by James W. Thompson. Grand Rapids: Baker Academic, 2020.

Scholz, Susanne. "The Complexities of 'His' Liberation Talk: A Literary Feminist Reading of the Book of Exodus." In *A Feminist Companion to the Bible: Exodus to Deuteronomy*, edited by Athalya Brenner, 20–40. FCB 5. 2nd ser. Sheffield: Sheffield Academic, 2000.

Scholz, Susanne, ed. *Feminist Interpretation of the Hebrew Bible in Retrospect*. Recent Research in Biblical Studies 5, 8, 9. 3 vols. Sheffield: Sheffield Phoenix, 2013, 2014, 2016.

Scholz, Susanne. "From the 'Woman's Bible' to the 'Women's Bible,' The History of Feminist Approaches to the Hebrew Bible." In *Introducing the Women's Hebrew Bible*, 12–32. IFT 13. New York: T&T Clark, 2007.

Scholz, Susanne. "'Tandoori Reindeer' and the Limitations of Historical Criticism." In *Her Master's Tools? Feminist and Postcolonial Engagements of Historical-Critical Discourse*, edited by Caroline Vander Stichele and Todd Penner, 47–69. Global Perspectives on Biblical Scholarship 9. Atlanta: SBL, 2005.

Schottroff, Luise. *Der erste Brief an die Gemeinde in Korinth*. ThHK 7. Stuttgart: Kohlhammer, 2013.

Schottroff, Luise. "'Law-Free Gentile Christianity'—What about the Women? Feminist Analyses and Alternatives." In *A Feminist Companion to Paul*, edited by Amy-Jill Levine with Marianne Blickenstaff, 183–94. FCNTECW 6. London: T&T International, 2004.

Schottroff, Luise. *Lydia's Impatient Sisters: A Feminist Social History of Early Christianity*. Translated by Barbara and Martin Rumscheidt. Louisville: Westminster John Knox, 1995.

Schottroff, Luise. "Toward a Feminist Reconstruction of the History of Early Christianity." In *Feminist Interpretation: The Bible in Women's Perspective*, edited by Luise Schottroff, Silvia Schroer, and Marie-Theres Wacker, translated by Martin Rumscheidt and Barbara Rumscheidt, 177–254. Minneapolis: Fortress, 1998.

Schreiber, Stefan. "Arbeit mit der Gemeinde (Röm 16.6, 12): Zur versunkenen Möglichkeit der Gemeindeleitung durch Frauen." *NTS* 46 (2000): 204–26.

Schreiber, Stefan. "Das Weihegeschenk Gottes: Eine Deutung des Todes Jesu in Röm 3,25." *ZNW* 97 (2006): 88–110.

Schreiner, Thomas. *Romans*. 2nd ed. BECNT 6. Grand Rapids: Baker Academic, 2018.

Schroer, Silvia. "Das Buch der Weisheit." In *Einleitung in das Alte Testament*, edited by Erich Zenger, Christian Frevel, et al., 484–96. 8th ed. Kohlhammer Studienbücher Theologie 1.1. Stuttgart: Kohlhammer, 2012.

Schuller, Eileen, and Marie-Theres Wacker, eds. *Early Jewish Writings*. BW 3.1. Atlanta: SBL Press, 2017.

Schulz, Ray R. "A Case for 'President' Phoebe in Romans 16:2." *Lutheran Theological Journal* 24 (1990): 124–27.

Schulz, Ray R. "Romans 16:7: Junia or Junias?" *ExpTim* 98 (1987): 108–10.

Schürmann, Heinz. *Gottes Reich—Jesu Geschick: Jesu ureigener Tod im Licht seiner Basileia-Verkündigung*. Freiburg: Herder, 1983.

Schüssler Fiorenza, Elisabeth. *Bread Not Stone: The Challenge of Feminist Biblical Interpretation*. Ann. ed. Boston: Beacon, 1995.

Schüssler Fiorenza, Elisabeth. *But She Said: Feminist Practices of Biblical Interpretation*. Boston: Beacon, 1992.

Schüssler Fiorenza, Elisabeth. *Ephesians*. WCS 50. Collegeville, MN: Liturgical Press, 2017.

Schüssler Fiorenza, Elisabeth, ed. *Feminist Biblical Studies in the Twentieth Century: Scholarship and Movement*. BW 9.1. Atlanta: SBL Press, 2014.

Schüssler Fiorenza, Elisabeth. *In Memory of Her: A Feminist Theological Reconstruction of Christian Origins*. New York: Crossroad, 1983/1994.

Schüssler Fiorenza, Elisabeth. "Introduction: Exploring the Intersection of Race, Gender, Status, and Ethnicity in Early Christian Studies." In *Prejudice and Christian Beginnings: Investigating Race, Gender, and Ethnicity in Early Christian Studies*, edited by Laura Nasrallah and Elisabeth Schüssler Fiorenza, 1–23. Minneapolis: Fortress, 2009.

Schüssler Fiorenza, Elisabeth. *Jesus: Miriam's Child, Sophia's Prophet; Critical Issues in Feminist Christology*. 2nd ed. Cornerstones. London: Bloomsbury T&T Clark, 2015; New York: Continuum, 1994.

Schüssler Fiorenza, Elisabeth. "Missionaries, Apostles, Coworkers: Romans 16 and the Reconstruction of Women's Early Christian History." *WW* 6 (1986): 420–33.

Schüssler Fiorenza, Elisabeth. *The Power of the Word: Scripture and the Rhetoric of Empire*. Minneapolis: Fortress, 2007.

Schüssler Fiorenza, Elisabeth. *Revelation: Vision of a Just World*. Proclamation Commentaries. Minneapolis: Fortress, 1991.

Schüssler Fiorenza, Elisabeth. *Sharing Her Word: Feminist Biblical Interpretation in Context*. Boston: Beacon, 1998.

Schüssler Fiorenza, Elisabeth. *Wisdom Ways: Introducing Feminist Biblical Interpretation*. Maryknoll, NY: Orbis Books, 2001.

Schüssler Fiorenza, Elisabeth. "Women in the Early Christian Movement." In *WomanSpirit Rising: A Feminist Reader in Religion*, edited by Carol P. Christ and Judith Plaskow, 84–92. New York: HarperOne, 1992.

Schutte, P. J. W. "When *They*, *We*, and the *Passive* Become *I*—Introducing Autobiographical Biblical Criticism." *HTS Teologiese Studies / Theological Studies* 61 (2005): 401–16.

Schweizer, Eduard. "πνεῦμα: E. III: Paul." *TDNT* 6 (1968): 415–37.

Schweizer, Eduard. "υἱός, υἱοθεσία: D. New Testament." *TDNT* 8 (1972): 363–92.

Scott, James M. "Cosmopolitanism in Gal 3:28 and the Divine Performative Speech-Act of Paul's Gospel." *ZNW* 112 (2021): 180–200.

Scranton, Robert et al. *Kenchreai, Eastern Port of Corinth; Results of Investigations by the University of Chicago and Indiana University for the American School of Classical Studies at Athens*. 5 vols. Leiden: Brill, 1978–1981.

Scroggs, Robin. *The New Testament and Homosexuality: Contextual Background for Contemporary Debate*. Philadelphia: Fortress, 1983.

Sechrest, Love L. *A Former Jew: Paul and the Dialectics of Race*. LNTS 410. London: T&T Clark, 2009.

Segal, Alan F. *Paul the Convert: The Apostolate and Apostasy of Saul the Pharisee*. New Haven: Yale University Press, 1990.

Segal, Alan F. "Torah and Nomos in Recent Scholarly Discussion." In *The Other Judaisms of Late Antiquity*, edited by Alan F. Segal, 131–45. BJS 127. Atlanta: Scholars Press, 1987.

Segovia, Fernando. "Biblical Criticism and Postcolonial Studies: Toward a Postcolonial Optic." In *The Postcolonial Bible*, edited by R. S. Sugirtharajah, 49–65. Sheffield: Sheffield Academic, 1998.

Seifrid, Mark A. "The Subject of Rom 7:14-25." *NovT* 34 (1992): 313–33.

Setzer, Claudia. "Does Paul Need to Be Saved?" *BibInt* 13 (2005): 289–97.

Sherwood, Aaron. *Romans: A Structural, Thematic, and Exegetical Commentary*. Bellingham, WA: Lexham Press, 2020.

Sherwood, Yvonne. *A Biblical Text and Its Afterlives: The Survival of Jonah in Western Culture*. Cambridge: Cambridge University Press, 2000.

Sherwood, Yvonne. "Introduction." In *The Bible and Feminism: Remapping the Field*, edited by Yvonne Sherwood with the assistance of Anna Fisk. New York: Oxford University Press, 2017.

Shum, Shiu-Lun. *Paul's Use of Isaiah in Romans: A Comparative Study of Paul's Letter to the Romans and the Sibylline and Qumran Sectarian Texts*. WUNT 2/156. Tübingen: Mohr Siebeck, 2002.

Siegert, Folker. *Argumentation bei Paulus, gezeigt an Röm 9–11*. WUNT 34. Tübingen: Mohr Siebeck, 1985.

Singer, Itamar. *Hittite Prayers*. SBLWAW 11. Atlanta: SBL, 2002.

Sinnott, Alice M. *The Personification of Wisdom*. SOTSMS. Aldershot: Ashgate, 2005.

Smith, Dennis E. "The House Church as Social Environment." In *Text, Image, and Christians in the Graeco-Roman World: A Festschrift in Honor of David Lee Balch*, edited by Aliou Cissé Niang and Carolyn Osiek, 3–21. Princeton Theological Monograph Series 176. Eugene, OR: Pickwick, 2012.

Smith, Murray. "God's Righteousness, Christ's Faithfulness, and 'Justification by Faith Alone' (Romans 3:21-26)." In *Romans and the Legacy of St Paul: Historical, Theological, and Social Perspectives*, edited by Peter G. Bolt and James R. Harrison, 181–254. Occasional Series 1. Macquarie Park: SCD Press, 2019.

Söding, Thomas. "Sühne durch Stellvertretung: Zur zentralen Deutung des Todes Jesu im Römerbrief." In *Deutungen des Todes Jesu im Neuen Testament*, edited by Jörg Frey and Jens Schröter, 375–96. WUNT 181. Tübingen: Mohr Siebeck, 2005.

Sohn-Kronthaler, Michaela, and Ruth Albrecht, eds. *Faith and Feminism in Nineteenth-Century Religious Communities.* BW 8.2. Atlanta: SBL Press, 2019.

Sojourner Truth. "Ain't I a Woman?" Modern History Sourcebook. https://sourcebooks.fordham.edu/mod/sojtruth-woman.asp.

Song, Changwon. *Reading Romans as a Diatribe*. StBibLit 59. New York: Lang, 2004.

Spaeth, Barbette Stanley. "Paul, Prostitutes, and the Cult of Aphrodite in Corinth." *BAR* 49 (2023): 65–68.

Spencer Miller, Althea. "Feminism, Feminist Hermeneutics: II. New Testament." *EBR* 8 (2014): 1128–30.

Speyr, Adrienne von. *Sieg der Liebe: Betrachtungen über Römer 8*. 2nd ed. Einsiedeln: Johannes Verlag, 2008 (1st ed. 1953).

Speyr, Adrienne von. *The Victory of Love: A Meditation on Romans 8*. San Francisco: Ignatius Press, 1990.

Spitz, Lewis W. "Luther and Humanism." In *Luther and Learning: The Wittenberg University Luther Symposium*, edited by Marilyn J. Harran, 69–94. Selinsgrove, PA: Susquehanna University Press, 1985.

Sprinkle, Preston. "Paul and Homosexual Behavior: A Critical Evaluation of the Excessive-Lust Interpretation of Romans 1:26-27." *BBR* 25 (2015): 497–517.

Standhartinger, Angela. "'Zur Freiheit . . . befreit'? Hagar im Galaterbrief." *EvTh* 62 (2002): 288–303.

Starhawk. "Witchcraft and Women's Culture." In *WomanSpirit Rising: A Feminist Reader in Religion*, edited by Carol P. Christ and Judith Plaskow, 259–68. New York: HarperOne, 1992.

Staubli, Thomas. "Alttestamentliche Konstellationen der Rechtfertigung des Menschen vor Gott." In *Biblische Anthropologie: Neue Einsichten aus dem Alten Testament*, edited by Christian Frevel, 88–133. QD 237. Freiburg: Herder, 2010.

Stavrakopoulou, Francesca. *God: An Anatomy*. London: Picador, 2022.

Stehle, Eva. *Performance and Gender in Ancient Greece: Nondramatic Poetry in Its Setting*. Princeton: Princeton University Press, 1997.

Stendahl, Krister. *Paul among Jews and Gentiles, and Other Essays*. Philadelphia: Fortress, 1976.

Stendebach, Franz-Josef. "שלום." *TDOT* 15 (2006): 13–48.

Stenschke, Christoph. "Married Women and the Spread of Early Christianity." *Neot* 43 (2009): 145–94.

Stephenson, Hope. "Junia: Woman and Apostle." In *Women in the Biblical World: A Survey of Old and New Testament Perspectives*, edited by Elizabeth A. McCabe, 117–34. Lanham, MD: University Press of America, 2009.

Stowers, Stanley K. *The Diatribe and Paul's Letter to the Romans*. SBLDS 57. Chico, CA: Scholars Press, 1981.

Stowers, Stanley K. "Paul's Dialogue with a Fellow Jew in Romans 3:1-9." *CBQ* 46 (1984): 707–22.

Stowers, Stanley K. *A Rereading of Romans: Justice, Jews, and Gentiles*. New Haven: Yale University Press, 1994.

Stowers, Stanley K. "Romans 7.7-25 as a Speech-in-Character (προσωποποιία)." In *Paul in His Hellenistic Context*, edited by Troels Engberg-Pedersen, 180–202. SNTW. Edinburgh: T&T Clark, 1994.

Sutter Rehman, Luiza. "To Turn the Groaning into Labor: Romans 8.22-23." In *A Feminist Companion to Paul*, edited by Amy-Jill Levine with Marianne Blickenstaff, 74–84. FCNTECW 6. London: T&T International, 2004.

Swancutt, Diana M. "Sexy Stoics and the Rereading of Romans 1.18–2.16." In *A Feminist Companion to Paul*, edited by Amy-Jill Levine with Marianne Blickenstaff, 42–73. FCNTECW 6. London: T&T International, 2004.

Taitz, Emily, Sondra Henry, and Cheryl Tallan. *The JPS Guide to Jewish Women 600 B.C.E.–1900 C.E.* Philadelphia: JPS, 2003.

Tamez, Elsa. "Der Brief an die Gemeinde in Rom: Eine feministische Lektüre." In *Kompendium feministische Bibelauslegung*, edited by Luise Schottroff and Marie-Theres Wacker, 557–73. 2nd ed. Gütersloh: Kaiser; Gütersloher Verlagshaus, 1999.

Tamez, Elsa. "The Challenge to Live as Resurrected: Reflections on Romans Six and Eight." Translated by Gloria Kinsler. *Spiritus: A Journal of Christian Spirituality* 3 (2003): 86–95.

Tamez, Elsa. "Justification as Good News for Women: A Re-reading of Romans 1–8." Translated by Sheila E. McGinn. In *Celebrating Romans: Template for Pauline Theology; Essays in Honor of Robert Jewett*, edited by Sheila E. McGinn, 177–89. Grand Rapids: Eerdmans, 2004.

Tamez, Elsa, Cynthia Briggs Kittredge, Claire Miller Colombo, and Alicia J. Batten. *Philippians, Colossians, and Philemon*. WCS 51. Collegeville, MN: Liturgical Press, 2016.

Tatum, Gregory. " 'To the Jew First' (Romans 1:16): Paul's Defense of Jewish Privilege in Romans." In *Celebrating Paul: Festschrift in Honor of Jerome Murphy-O'Connor, OP, and Joseph A. Fitzmyer, SJ*, edited by Peter Spitaler,

275–86. CBQMS 48. Washington, DC: Catholic Biblical Association of America, 2011.

Taylor, Marion Ann, and Agnes Choi, eds. *Handbook of Women Biblical Interpreters: A Historical and Biographical Guide.* Grand Rapids: Baker Academic, 2012.

Taylor, Nicholas H. "Popular Opposition to Caligula in Jewish Palestine." *JSJ* 32 (2001): 54–70.

Temin, Peter. "The Labor Market of the Early Roman Empire." *The Journal of Interdisciplinary History* 34 (2004): 513–38.

Theobald, Michael. "Der Kanon von der Rechtfertigung (Gal 2,16; Röm 3,28): Eigentum des Paulus oder Gemeingut der Kirche?" In *Studien zum Römerbrief*, edited by Michael Theobald, 164–225. WUNT 136. Tübingen: Mohr Siebeck, 2001.

Theobald, Michael. " 'Geboren aus dem Samen Davids . . .' (Röm 1,3): Wandlungen im paulinischen Christus-Bild?" *ZNW* 102 (2011): 235–60.

Theobald, Michael. "Paul and Same-Sex Sexuality: A Plea for a Sensible Approach to Scripture." In *"Who Am I to Judge?" Homosexuality and the Catholic Church*, edited by Stephan Goertz, translated by Alissa Jones Nelson, 43–72. Berlin: de Gruyter, 2022.

Theobald, Michael. *Römerbrief.* 2 vols. SKKNT 6/1–2. Stuttgart: Katholisches Bibelwerk, 1992–1993.

Thiessen, Matthew. *Paul and the Gentile Problem.* New York: Oxford University Press, 2016.

Thiessen, Matthew. "Paul's Argument against Gentile Circumcision in Romans 2:17-29." *NovT* 56 (2014): 373–91.

Thimmes, Pamela. " 'She Will Be Called an Adulteress . . .': Marriage and Adultery Analogies in Romans 7:1-4." In *Celebrating Romans: Template for Pauline Theology; Essays in Honor of Robert Jewett*, edited by Sheila E. McGinn, 190–203. Grand Rapids: Eerdmans, 2004.

Thompson, James W. *The Church According to Paul: Rediscovering the Community Conformed to Christ*. Grand Rapids: Baker Academic, 2014.

Thorsteinsson, Runar M. *Paul's Interlocutor in Romans 2: Function and Identity in the Context of Ancient Epistolography*. ConBNT 40. Stockholm: Almqvist & Wiksell, 2003.

Thurston, Bonnie. *Women in the New Testament: Questions and Commentary*. Companions to the New Testament. New York: Crossroad, 1998.

Timmins, Will N. *Romans 7 and Christian Identity: A Study of the "I" in Its Literary Context*. SNTSMS 170. Cambridge: Cambridge University Press, 2017.

Tinker, Tink, and Mark Freeland. "Thief, Slave Trader, Murderer: Christopher Columbus and Caribbean Population Decline." *Wicazo Sa Review* 23 (2008): 25–50.

Tobin, Thomas H. *Paul's Rhetoric in Its Contexts: The Argument of Romans*. Peabody, MA: Hendrickson, 2004.

Toit, Andrie B. du. "Paul's Chronology." In *Guide to the New Testament*, vol. 5: *The Pauline Letters: Introduction and Theology*, edited by Andrie B. du Toit, 22–35. Pretoria: Kerkboekhandel, 1985.

Tolbert, Mary Ann. "Social, Sociological, and Anthropological Methods." In *Searching the Scriptures: A Feminist Introduction*, vol. 1, edited by Elisabeth Schüssler Fiorenza with the assistance of Shelly Matthews, 255–71. New York: Crossroad, 1993.

Tomson, Peter J. *Presumed Guilty: How the Jews Were Blamed for the Death of Jesus*. Translated by Janet Dyk. Minneapolis: Fortress, 2005.

Tomson, Peter J. *Studies on Jews and Christians in the First and Second Centuries*. WUNT 418. Tübingen: Mohr Siebeck, 2019.

Tonstad, Sigve K. *The Letter to the Romans: Paul among the Ecologists*. Earth Bible Commentary 7. Sheffield: Sheffield Phoenix, 2016.

Torjesen, Karen. "The Early Controversies over Female Leadership." *Christian History* 17 (1988): 20–24.

Townsley, Jeramy. "Paul, the Goddess Religions, and Queer Sects: Romans 1:23-28." *JBL* 130 (2011): 707–28.

Trible, Phyllis. *God and the Rhetoric of Sexuality*. OBT. Philadelphia: Fortress, 1978.

Trible, Phyllis. *Texts of Terror: Literary-Feminist Readings of Biblical Narratives*. OBT 13. Philadelphia: Fortress, 1984.

Ullucci, Daniel C. *The Christian Rejection of Animal Sacrifice*. Oxford: Oxford University Press, 2012.

Valler, Shulamit. "Who is *ēšet ḥayil* in Rabbinic Literature?" In *A Feminist Companion to Wisdom Literature*, edited by Athalya Brenner, 85–99. FCB 9. Sheffield: Sheffield Academic Press, 1995.

Vander Stichele, Caroline, and Todd Penner, eds. *Her Master's Tools? Feminist and Postcolonial Engagements of Historical-Critical Discourse.* Atlanta: SBL, 2005.

Várhelyi, Zsuzsanna. "Statuary and Ritualization in Imperial Italy." *MAAR. Supplementary Volumes* 13 (2017): 87–98.

Vauchez, André. *Catherine de Sienne: Vie et passions*. Paris: Cerf, 2015.

Vouga, François. "L'Épître aux Romains." In *Introduction au Nouveau Testament: Son histoire, son écriture, sa théologie*, edited by Daniel Marguerat, 159–78. Geneva: Labor et Fides, 2000.

Wagner, J. Ross. " 'Not from the Jews Only, But Also from the Gentiles': Mercy to the Nations in Romans 9–11." In *Between Gospel and Election: Explorations in the Interpretation of Romans 9–11*, edited by Florian Wilk and J. Ross Wagner with the assistance of Frank Schleritt, 417–31. WUNT 257. Tübingen: Mohr Siebeck, 2010.

Walker, Alice. *In Search of Our Mothers' Gardens: Womanist Prose.* New York: Harcourt Brace Jovanovich, 1967, 1983.

Walker, William O., Jr. "Romans 1.18–2.29: A Non-Pauline Interpolation?" *NTS* 45 (1999): 533–52.

Walsh, Robyn Faith. *The Origins of Early Christian Literature: Contextualizing the New Testament within Greco-Roman Literary Culture*. Cambridge: Cambridge University Press, 2021.

Walters, James C. "Paul, Adoption, and Inheritance." Revised by Jerry L. Sumney. In *Paul in the Greco-Roman World: A Handbook*, edited by J. Paul Sampley, 1:33–67. 2nd ed. London: Bloomsbury, 2016.

Ward, Roy Bowen. "Why Unnatural? The Tradition behind Romans 1:26-27." *HTR* 90 (1997): 263–84.

Wasserman, Emma. "Paul Among the Philosophers: The Case of Sin in Romans 6–8." *JSNT* 30 (2008): 387–415.

Weaver, Paul R. C. "Social Mobility in the Early Roman Empire: The Evidence of the Imperial Freedmen and Slaves." *Past & Present* 37 (1967): 3–20.

Weems, Renita J. *Battered Love: Marriage, Sex, and Violence in the Hebrew Prophets*. OBT. Minneapolis: Fortress, 1995.

Weems, Renita J. *Just a Sister Away: A Womanist Vision of Women's Relationships in the Bible*. San Diego: Lura Media, 1988.

Welborn, Larry L. "Inequality in Roman Corinth: Evidence from Diverse Sources Evaluated by a Neo-Ricardian Model." In *The First Urban Churches*, vol 2: *Roman Corinth*, edited by James R. Harrison and Larry L. Welborn, 47–84. WGRW 8. Atlanta: SBL Press, 2016.

Wells, Harold. "Not Moral Heroes: The Grace of God and the Church's Public Voice." In *Doing Ethics in a Pluralistic World: Essays in Honour of Roger C. Hutchinson*, edited by Phyllis D. Airhart, Marilyn J. Legge, and Gary L. Redcliffe, 77–98. Comparative Ethics Series. Waterloo, ON: Wilfrid Laurier University Press, 2002.

Wengst, Klaus. *Christologische Formeln und Lieder des Urchristentums*. SNT 7. Gütersloh: Gütersloher Verlagshaus, 1972.

Westfall, Cynthia L. *Paul and Gender: Reclaiming the Apostle's Vision for Men and Women in Christ*. Grand Rapids: Baker Academic, 2016.

Wettstein, Jacobus. *Novum Testamentum Graecum*. 2 vols. Graz: Akademische Druck- und Verlagsanstalt, 1962.

White, L. Michael. "Herod and the Jewish Experience of Augustan Rule." In *The Cambridge Companion to the Age of Augustus*, edited by Karl Galinsky, 361–87. Cambridge Companion to the Classics. Cambridge: Cambridge University Press, 2005.

White, L. Michael. "Paul and *Pater Familias*." In *Paul in the Greco-Roman World: A Handbook*, edited by J. Paul Sampley, 2:171–203. 2nd ed. London: Bloomsbury, 2016.

Wick, Peter. *Die urchristlichen Gottesdienste: Entstehung und Entwicklung im Rahmen der frühjüdischen Tempel-, Synagogen- und Hausfrömmigkeit*. BWANT 150. Stuttgart: Kohlhammer, 2002.

Wilckens, Ulrich, and Georg Fohrer. "σοφία, σοφός, σοφίζω." *TDNT* 7 (1971): 465–528.

Wiley, Tatha. *Paul and the Gentile Women: Reframing Galatians*. New York: Continuum, 2005.

Wilk, Florian. *Die Bedeutung des Jesajabuches für Paulus*. FRLANT 179. Göttingen: Vandenhoeck & Ruprecht, 1998.

Wilk, Florian. "Rahmen und Aufbau von Römer 9–11." In *Between Gospel and Election: Explorations in the Interpretation of Romans 9–11*, edited by Florian Wilk and J. Ross Wagner with the assistance of Frank Schleritt, 227–53. WUNT 257. Tübingen: Mohr Siebeck, 2010.

Wilson, Mark. "*Hilasterion* and Imperial Ideology: A New Reading of Romans 3:25." *HTS Teologiese Studies/Theological Studies* 73 (2017): 1–9.

Wire, Antoinette. "1 Corinthians." In *Searching the Scriptures*, vol. 2: *A Feminist Commentary*, edited by Elisabeth Schüssler Fiorenza, 153–95. New York: Crossroad, 1994.

Wischmeyer, Oda. "Das Adjektiv ΑΓΑΠΗΤΟΣ in den paulinischen Briefen: Eine traditionsgeschichtliche Miszelle." *NTS* 32 (1986): 476–80.

Wischmeyer, Oda. "Frau." *RGG* 3 (2000): 260–61.

Wischmeyer, Oda. "The Letter to the Romans." In *Paul: Life, Setting, Work, Letters*, edited by Oda Wischmeyer, translated by Helen S. Heron, 245–76. London: T&T Clark, 2012.

Wischmeyer, Oda. "Paul's Religion: A Review of the Problem." In *Paul, Luke and the Graeco-Roman World: Essays in Honour of Alexander J.M. Wedderburn*, edited by Alf Christophersen et al., 74–93. JSNTSup 217. London: Sheffield Academic, 2002.

Wiseman, James. "Corinth and Rome I: 228 B.C.–A.D. 267." *ANRW* 2.7.1 (1979): 438–548.

Witt, Reginald E. *Isis in the Ancient World*. Baltimore: Johns Hopkins University Press, 1997.

Wolff, Christian. *Der erste Brief des Paulus an die Korinther*. 3rd ed. THKNT 7. Leipzig: Evangelische Verlagsanstalt, 2011.

Wolter, Michael. *Der Brief an die Römer*. Vol. 1: *Röm 1–8*. EKKNT 6/1. Neukirchen-Vluyn: Neukirchener Verlag; Ostfildern: Patmos, 2014.

Wolter, Michael. *Der Brief an die Römer*. Vol. 2: *Röm 9–16*. EKKNT 6/2. Göttingen: Vandenhoeck & Ruprecht; Ostfildern: Patmos, 2019.

Wolter, Michael. *Paulus: Ein Grundriss seiner Theologie*. 3rd ed. Neukirchen-Vluyn: Neukirchener Verlag, 2021.

Wolter, Michael. *Rechtfertigung und zukünftiges Heil: Untersuchungen zu Röm 5,1–11*. BZNW 43. Berlin: de Gruyter, 1978.

Yee, Gale, ed. *Judges and Method: New Approaches in Biblical Studies*. Minneapolis: Fortress, 1995.

Yeo, Khiok-khng. "Christ and the Earth in Pauline and Native American Understandings." In *Cross-Cultural Paul: Journeys to Others, Journeys to Ourselves*, edited by Charles H. Cosgrove, Herold Weiss, and Khiok-khng Yeo, 179–218. Grand Rapids: Eerdmans, 2005.

Yonge, Charles Duke. *The Works of Philo: Complete and Unabridged*. 3rd. ed. Peabody, MA: Hendrickson, 1995.

Yoon, Sojung. "Phoebe, a Minister in the Early Christian Church." In *Distant Voices Drawing Near: Essays in Honor of Antoinette Clark Wire*, edited by Holly E. Hearon, 19–31. Collegeville, MN: Liturgical Press, 2004.

Zeller, Dieter. *Der Brief an die Römer*. RNT. Regensburg: Friedrich Pustet, 1985.

Zierler, Wendy. "In Search of a Feminist Reading of the Akedah." *Nashim: A Journal of Jewish Women's Studies & Gender Issues* 9 (2005): 10–26.

Zoccali, Christopher. "'And So All Israel Will Be Saved': Competing Interpretations of Romans 11:26 in Pauline Scholarship." *JSNT* 30 (2008): 289–318.

Index of Scripture References and Other Ancient Writings

Index of Subjects